FIRST-CLASS CRICKET MATCHES

1939/40 - 1945

Published by the Association of Cricket Statisticians and Historians, Cardiff CF11 9XR
2012
Typeset by Limlow Books
Printed by City Press, Leeds
ISBN: 978 1 908165 23 7

The Association acknowledges with grateful thanks the assistance of the following for their research:
Charlie Wat and Ray Webster (Australia), Evan Watkin (New Zealand), Kit Bartlett.

Philip Bailey

1939/40

BOMBAY v NAWANAGAR

Played at Brabourne Stadium, Bombay, November 3, 4, 5, 1939.

Match drawn.

NAWANAGAR

1	M.S.Ranvirsinhji	c Hindlekar b Tarapore	22
2	M.H.Mankad	b Tarapore	58
3	S.N.Banerjee	c Khot b Tarapore	106
4	L.Amar Singh	c sub b Khot	67
5	Mubarak Ali	c Havewala b Godambe	23
6	*R.K.Indravijaysinhji	b Tarapore	30
7	R.K.Yadvendrasinhji	st Hindlekar b Tarapore	45
8	S.H.M.Colah	lbw b Tarapore	0
9	R.K.Jayendrasinhji	c U.M.Merchant b Tarapore	3
10	A.F.Wensley	lbw b Tarapore	15
11	†M.Ellum	not out	3
	Extras	b 6, lb 7, nb 2	15
			387

FoW (1): 1-56 (1), 2-108 (2), 3-231 (4), 4-285 (3), 5-286 (5), 6-336 (6), 7-340 (8), 8-350 (9), 9-376 (10), 10-387 (7)

BOMBAY

1	S.M.Kadri	b Mankad	26
2	†D.D.Hindlekar	b Mubarak Ali	11
3	F.K.Nariman	lbw b Banerjee	15
4	*V.M.Merchant	lbw b Mankad	140
5	U.M.Merchant	c Ellum b Banerjee	94
6	R.F.Moss	run out	7
7	J.B.Khot	c Indravijaysinhji b Amar Singh	52
8	D.R.Havewala	c Ellum b Mankad	0
9	K.K.Tarapore	c Banerjee b Mankad	1
10	S.R.Godambe	not out	0
11	M.S.Patel	b Amar Singh	0
	Extras	b 5	5
			351

FoW (1): 1-23 (2), 2-49 (1), 3-64 (3), 4-207 (5), 5-222 (6), 6-341 (4), 7-341 (8), 8-351 (9), 9-351 (7), 10-351 (11)

Bombay Bowling

	O	M	R	W
Patel	14	2	49	0
Godambe	37	5	113	1
V.M.Merchant	12	2	35	0
Tarapore	45.2	9	91	8
Havewala	17	1	54	0
Khot	7	0	20	1
Nariman	2	0	10	0

Nawanagar Bowling

	O	M	R	W
Amar Singh	35.2	5	86	2
Banerjee	21	1	101	2
Mubarak Ali	11	1	29	1
Mankad	31	5	87	4
Wensley	17	4	35	0
Ranvirsinhji	1	0	8	0

Umpires: N.D.Marshall and D.K.Naik. Toss: Bombay

Close of Play: 1st day: Nawanagar (1) 256-3 (Banerjee 94*, Mubarak Ali 6*); 2nd day: Bombay (1) 142-3 (V.M.Merchant 39*, U.M.Merchant 46*).

S.N.Banerjee's 106 took 223 minutes and included 7 fours. V.M.Merchant's 140 took 267 minutes and included 3 fours.

MADRAS v MYSORE

Played at Madras Cricket Club Ground, Chepauk, Madras, November 4, 5, 6, 1939.

Madras won by two wickets.

MYSORE					
1	M.B.Krishna Rao	b Gopalan	0	(2) b Parankusam	8
2	B.R.Nagaraja Rao	c and b Ram Singh	11	(1) b Gopalan	2
3	B.V.Ramakrishnappa	c Rangachari b Ram Singh	7	b Ram Singh	99
4	C.J.Ramdev	b Rangachari	6	lbw b Parthasarathi	10
5	†F.K.Irani	lbw b Ram Singh	14	b Parankusam	32
6	M.G.Vijayasarathi	c Parthasarathi b Rangachari	29	c Narayanaswami Rao b Ram Singh	56
7	*S.Darashah	b Rangachari	21	c Stansfeld b Ram Singh	14
8	K.S.Prabhakar	lbw b Ram Singh	2	b Ram Singh	14
9	G.Pires	c Parankusam b Ram Singh	8	b Parankusam	4
10	A.L.Lingiah	b Rangachari	6	not out	2
11	M.V.Subba Rao	not out	1	b Ram Singh	0
	Extras		3		22
			108		263

FoW (1): 1-0 (1), 2-18 (2), 3-21 (3), 4-36 (4), 5-44 (5), 6-89 (7), 7-92 (8), 8-94 (6), 9-104 (10), 10-108 (9)
FoW (2): 1-3 (1), 2-38 (2), 3-66 (4), 4-120 (5), 5-222 (6), 6-242 (3), 7-251 (7), 8-261 (9), 9-263 (8), 10-263 (11)

MADRAS					
1	A.V.Krishnaswami	b Darashah	2	b Darashah	14
2	A.W.Stansfeld	c Ramakrishnappa b Vijayasarathi	23	b Darashah	2
3	K.Mohanakrishnan	c Darashah b Nagaraja Rao	21	lbw b Darashah	0
4	T.D.Narayanaswami Rao	lbw b Vijayasarathi	8	c Irani b Nagaraja Rao	12
5	A.G.Ram Singh	lbw b Pires	55	c Prabhakar b Vijayasarathi	91
6	G.Parthasarathi	c Prabhakar b Vijayasarathi	40	(7) b Darashah	14
7	*M.J.Gopalan	lbw b Darashah	0	(8) not out	22
8	N.J.Venkatesan	b Darashah	0	(6) b Darashah	36
9	†S.V.T.Chari	lbw b Pires	1	(10) not out	0
10	C.R.Rangachari	not out	4		
11	T.S.Parankusam	lbw b Vijayasarathi	0	(9) run out	0
	Extras		18		9
			172	(8 wickets)	200

FoW (1): 1-4 (1), 2-43 (2), 3-49 (3), 4-62 (4), 5-124 (6), 6- (7), 7- (8), 8-164 (9), 9-171 (5), 10-172 (11)
FoW (2): 1-4 (2), 2-4 (3), 3-29 (1), 4-37 (4), 5-112 (6), 6-146 (7), 7-198 (5), 8-199 (9)

Madras Bowling

	O	M	R	W		O	M	R	W
Gopalan	7	4	9	1	(2)	15	3	43	1
Rangachari	14	1	38	4	(3)	20	2	54	0
Ram Singh	15	3	35	5	(1)	29.2	16	45	5
Parthasarathi	4	0	8	0	(5)	16	3	38	1
Venkatesan	3	0	15	0	(6)	1	0	13	0
Parankusam					(4)	19	1	48	3

Mysore Bowling

	O	M	R	W		O	M	R	W
Nagaraja Rao	18	1	49	1		12	1	26	1
Darashah	23	12	24	3		33	5	78	5
Pires	8	1	29	2	(4)	4	0	10	0
Vijayasarathi	20.4	4	41	4	(3)	21.3	2	47	1
Subba Rao	5	4	2	0	(6)	6	0	22	0
Lingiah	3	0	9	0	(5)	1	0	8	0

Umpires: Toss: Mysore

Close of Play: 1st day: Madras (1) 133-7 (Ram Singh 30*, Chari 0*); 2nd day: Mysore (2) 261-8 (Prabhakar 14*).

EUROPEANS v HINDUS

Played at Brabourne Stadium, Bombay, November 15, 16, 17, 1939.

Hindus won by an innings and 317 runs.

EUROPEANS					
1	S.W.E.Behrend	b Banerjee	5	(2) b Amar Singh	2
2	B.R.T.Greer	c Mankad b Banerjee	4	(1) b C.S.Nayudu	27
3	G.R.R.Brown	b Amar Singh	15	c U.M.Merchant b C.S.Nayudu	22
4	R.F.Moss	b Banerjee	54	b C.S.Nayudu	7
5	D.J.Rimmer	c and b C.S.Nayudu	9	b C.S.Nayudu	17
6	A.F.Wensley	c U.M.Merchant b Banerjee	36	c Jai b Mankad	1
7	J.E.Tew	c C.K.Nayudu b C.S.Nayudu	8	b C.S.Nayudu	4
8	A.N.Brewer	lbw b C.S.Nayudu	10	b Mankad	4
9	*R.Ashley	c U.M.Merchant b C.S.Nayudu	8	c U.M.Merchant b C.S.Nayudu	10
10	R.C.Mushet	not out	0	not out	6
11	†J.N.Compton	st Hindlekar b C.S.Nayudu	0	c sub (M.M.Jagdale) b C.S.Nayudu	1
	Extras	b 9, lb 7, nb 3	19	b 2, lb 1, nb 2	5
			168		106

FoW (1): 1-8 (2), 2-14 (1), 3-43 (3), 4-60 (5), 5-131 (4), 6-139 (6), 7-158 (7), 8-165 (8), 9-168 (9), 10-168 (11)
FoW (2): 1-10 (2), 2-51 (3), 3-60 (1), 4-63 (4), 5-64 (6), 6-68 (7), 7-75 (8), 8-97 (5), 9-104 (9), 10-106 (11)

HINDUS			
1	†D.D.Hindlekar	lbw b Ashley	4
2	M.H.Mankad	lbw b Brown	133
3	L.Amarnath	c Greer b Wensley	57
4	L.Amar Singh	b Ashley	1
5	*C.K.Nayudu	c Tew b Wensley	45
6	V.M.Merchant	b Wensley	192
7	L.P.Jai	lbw b Brown	64
8	C.S.Nayudu	st Compton b Brown	17
9	U.M.Merchant	b Ashley	29
10	K.M.Rangnekar	not out	25
11	S.N.Banerjee	b Wensley	11
	Extras	b 7, lb 5, nb 1	13
			591

FoW (1): 1-16 (1), 2-118 (3), 3-122 (4), 4-194 (5), 5-302 (2), 6-451 (7), 7-522 (8), 8-534 (6), 9-578 (9), 10-591 (11)

Hindus Bowling	O	M	R	W		O	M	R	W
Banerjee	15	2	41	4		5	0	32	0
Amar Singh	27	9	49	1		8	1	16	1
Amarnath	5	0	7	0					
C.S.Nayudu	12.4	1	31	5	(3)	13.2	2	33	7
Mankad	3	0	14	0	(4)	10	2	20	2
C.K.Nayudu	2	0	7	0					

Europeans Bowling	O	M	R	W
Ashley	30	7	135	3
Behrend	15	1	74	0
Wensley	54	5	200	4
Mushet	7	0	41	0
Brown	35	2	121	3
Brewer	2	0	7	0

Umpires: D.K.Kapadia and Vali Ahmed. Toss:

Close of Play: 1st day: Hindus (1) 118-2 (Mankad 56*, Amar Singh 0*); 2nd day: Hindus (1) 548-8 (U.M.Merchant 14*, Rangnekar 8*).

M.H.Mankad's 133 took 240 minutes and included 8 fours. V.M.Merchant's 192 took 253 minutes and included 24 fours.

QUEENSLAND v NEW SOUTH WALES

Played at Brisbane Cricket Ground, Woolloongabba, Brisbane, November 17, 18, 20, 21, 1939.

New South Wales won by three wickets. (Points: Queensland 0, New South Wales 5)

	QUEENSLAND				
1	*W.A.Brown	c and b Pepper	87	c Sismey b Pepper	137
2	G.G.Cook	c Sismey b Cheetham	9	b Cheetham	7
3	T.Allen	c Gilmore b Pepper	77	c Sismey b Pepper	5
4	†D.Tallon	st Sismey b Barnes	12	(6) b Gilmore	24
5	R.E.Rogers	c Sismey b Cheetham	45	(4) c McCabe b Barnes	45
6	G.G.Baker	c Pepper b Cheetham	32	(5) c Sismey b O'Reilly	5
7	C.G.R.Stibe	lbw b O'Reilly	1	b O'Reilly	5
8	L.W.T.Tallon	c and b O'Reilly	1	b O'Reilly	1
9	P.L.Dixon	b Cheetham	13	c Solomon b Pepper	7
10	C.P.Christ	not out	0	not out	6
11	J.A.Ellis	b O'Reilly	0	absent hurt	0
	Extras	b 3, lb 4, nb 6	13	b 9, lb 8, nb 4	21
			290		263

FoW (1): 1-34 (2), 2-170 (1), 3-189 (4), 4-197 (3), 5-274 (5), 6-275 (7), 7-276 (8), 8-290 (6), 9-290 (9), 10-290 (11)
FoW (2): 1-17 (2), 2-38 (3), 3-132 (4), 4-156 (5), 5-214 (6), 6-238 (7), 7-246 (8), 8-252 (1), 9-263 (9)

	NEW SOUTH WALES				
1	*S.J.McCabe	c D.Tallon b Ellis	0	c Christ b Dixon	98
2	J.H.W.Fingleton	c D.Tallon b Cook	0	c D.Tallon b Dixon	5
3	S.G.Barnes	c Dixon b Christ	10	c Christ b Baker	8
4	C.M.Solomon	lbw b L.W.T.Tallon	39	c D.Tallon b Dixon	89
5	D.K.Carmody	b Dixon	0	c L.W.T.Tallon b Dixon	30
6	R.H.Robinson	c Allen b Christ	30	lbw b Cook	4
7	A.G.Cheetham	c Rogers b L.W.T.Tallon	85	b Cook	13
8	C.G.Pepper	lbw b Dixon	81	not out	7
9	W.J.O'Reilly	b Dixon	0	not out	9
10	F.P.J.Gilmore	not out	21		
11	†S.G.Sismey	lbw b Cook	15		
	Extras	b 3, nb 3	6	lb 5	5
			287	(7 wickets)	268

FoW (1): 1-0 (1), 2-2 (2), 3-33 (3), 4-34 (5), 5-57 (4), 6-97 (6), 7-203 (8), 8-203 (9), 9-268 (7), 10-287 (11)
FoW (2): 1-19 (2), 2-35 (3), 3-182 (1), 4-233 (4), 5-236 (5), 6-241 (6), 7-258 (7)

New South Wales Bowling	O	M	R	W			O	M	R	W	
Gilmore	13	0	83	0	1nb		12	1	56	1	1nb
Cheetham	14	1	75	4	2nb		8	0	33	1	1nb
O'Reilly	14.2	6	27	3	3nb		21	5	53	3	2nb
Pepper	15	1	86	2			18.5	2	75	3	
Robinson	1	1	0	0							
Barnes	3	0	6	1		(5)	6	0	25	1	

Queensland Bowling	O	M	R	W			O	M	R	W
Ellis	3	0	4	1						
Cook	16.5	1	57	2			12.2	0	59	2
Dixon	19	2	44	3	3nb	(1)	17	1	67	4
Christ	18	7	62	2			13	1	80	0
L.W.T.Tallon	17	1	104	2			2	0	26	0
Baker	4	0	10	0		(3)	7	1	31	1

Umpires: K.E.S.Fagg and J.A.S.Scott. Toss: Queensland

Close of Play: 1st day: New South Wales (1) 66-5 (Robinson 9*, Cheetham 5*); 2nd day: Queensland (2) 156-4 (Brown 90*); 3rd day: New South Wales (2) 258-7 (Pepper 6*, O'Reilly 0*).

W.A.Brown's 137 took 230 minutes and included 14 fours. 12th Men: M.S.Guttormsen (Qld) and R.V.James (NSW).

SOUTH AUSTRALIA v VICTORIA

Played at Adelaide Oval, November 17, 18, 20, 21, 1939.

South Australia won by three wickets. (Points: South Australia 5, Victoria 0)

VICTORIA					
1	I.S.Lee	c Walker b Cotton	0	c sub (J.Tregoning) b Grimmett	68
2	G.E.Tamblyn	b Grimmett	67	b Grimmett	29
3	A.L.Hassett	c Grimmett b Waite	5	c Walker b Cotton	89
4	K.R.Miller	c Whitington b Cotton	4	b Grimmett	7
5	I.W.G.Johnson	lbw b Grimmett	33	c Bradman b Grimmett	41
6	D.H.Fothergill	c Walker b Grimmett	1	lbw b Waite	10
7	*†B.A.Barnett	lbw b Waite	51	run out	2
8	M.W.Sievers	st Walker b Ward	23	c Klose b Grimmett	56
9	D.T.Ring	c Whitington b Cotton	19	lbw b Waite	31
10	R.B.Scott	b Ward	0	c and b Waite	14
11	L.O.Fleetwood-Smith	not out	0	not out	4
	Extras	b 2, lb 1, nb 1	4	b 3, lb 7, nb 2	12
			207		363

FoW (1): 1-0 (1), 2-5 (3), 3-18 (4), 4-66 (5), 5-72 (6), 6-151 (2), 7-167 (7), 8-192 (8), 9-192 (10), 10-207 (9)
FoW (2): 1-50 (2), 2-120 (1), 3-138 (4), 4-221 (3), 5-253 (5), 6-253 (7), 7-260 (6), 8-320 (9), 9-353 (10), 10-363 (8)

SOUTH AUSTRALIA					
1	R.S.Whitington	c Fleetwood-Smith b Scott	0	b Fleetwood-Smith	27
2	K.L.Ridings	c Sievers b Scott	6	c Ring b Sievers	1
3	*D.G.Bradman	run out (Miller/Sievers)	76	(4) lbw b Ring	64
4	R.A.Hamence	lbw b Scott	6	(5) c Sievers b Ring	99
5	C.L.Badcock	lbw b Fleetwood-Smith	3	(6) c Barnett b Scott	30
6	T.E.Klose	c Hassett b Ring	80	(8) lbw b Ring	0
7	F.A.Ward	lbw b Fleetwood-Smith	1	(9) not out	1
8	M.G.Waite	c Miller b Sievers	67	(7) not out	42
9	†C.W.Walker	c and b Ring	4	(3) b Ring	20
10	C.V.Grimmett	c Sievers b Ring	9		
11	H.N.J.Cotton	not out	1		
	Extras	b 1, lb 1, nb 6	8	b 17, lb 6, w 2, nb 1	26
			261	(7 wickets)	310

FoW (1): 1-0 (1), 2-16 (2), 3-28 (4), 4-35 (5), 5-137 (3), 6-142 (7), 7-220 (6), 8-226 (9), 9-260 (8), 10-261 (10)
FoW (2): 1-10 (2), 2-44 (1), 3-70 (3), 4-182 (4), 5-243 (6), 6-284 (5), 7-290 (8)

South Australia Bowling	O	M	R	W			O	M	R	W	
Cotton	12.2	1	78	3	1nb		23	1	74	1	1nb
Waite	13	1	48	2			35	8	76	3	1nb
Grimmett	19	4	67	3			34.4	7	118	5	
Ward	6	0	10	2			16	0	75	0	
Klose						(5)	8	3	8	0	

Victoria Bowling	O	M	R	W			O	M	R	W	
Scott	11	0	55	3	5nb		14	0	50	1	2w
Sievers	17	4	63	1			14	3	40	1	
Fleetwood-Smith	14	0	59	2		(4)	16	0	78	1	
Ring	18.4	1	76	3	1nb	(3)	26	2	104	4	1nb
Johnson						(5)	4.7	0	12	0	

Umpires: A.G.Jenkins and J.D.Scott. Toss: Victoria

Close of Play: 1st day: South Australia (1) 142-6 (Klose 47*); 2nd day: Victoria (2) 104-1 (Lee 61*, Hassett 13*); 3rd day: South Australia (2) 11-1 (Whitington 9*, Walker 1*).

12th Men: J.Tregoning (SA) and R.A.Dempster (Vic).

BARODA v GUJARAT

Played at Police Gymkhana Ground, Baroda, November 18, 19, 20, 1939.

Baroda won by 52 runs.

BARODA

1	Y.E.Sheikh	lbw b Baloch	1	c Sheikh b Baloch	20
2	S.G.Powar	c and b Baloch	38	b Chippa	29
3	H.R.Adhikari	c Parmar b Baloch	5	(4) st Sahana b Chippa	2
4	†R.B.Nimbalkar	c R.M.Patel b Chippa	15	(5) c J.A.Patel b Baloch	32
5	*W.N.Ghorpade	c Sahana b Chippa	21	(3) lbw b Baloch	8
6	M.M.Naidu	c Parmar b Chippa	3	b Chippa	0
7	S.M.Ambegaokar	c Sahana b Chippa	24	(8) b Baloch	7
8	B.B.Nimbalkar	lbw b Baloch	6	(7) c Sahana b Baloch	27
9	A.G.Gupte	c Pathan b Chippa	0	b Baloch	6
10	E.B.Gai	c Pathan b Chippa	4	c R.M.Patel b Baloch	1
11	J.G.Dhumal	not out	0	not out	10
	Extras		10		24
			127		166

FoW (1): 1- , 2- , 3- , 4- , 5- , 6- , 7- , 8- , 9- , 10-127
FoW (2): 1- , 2- , 3- , 4- , 5- , 6- , 7- , 8- , 9- , 10-166

GUJARAT

1	R.M.Patel	c Ghorpade b Dhumal	9	(2) b Gai	6
2	†J.M.Sahana	c Naidu b Adhikari	5	(1) b Gai	0
3	M.K.Pathan	c Sheikh b Adhikari	43	(4) b Gai	22
4	J.A.Patel	c and b Adhikari	1	(8) lbw b Gai	11
5	C.F.Parmar	b B.B.Nimbalkar	12	(6) lbw b Gai	10
6	B.Mehra	b Sheikh	0	(7) not out	50
7	B.M.Patel	c Dhumal b B.B.Nimbalkar	8	(3) b B.B.Nimbalkar	0
8	U.R.Chippa	b Gai	1	(9) b Adhikari	17
9	P.N.Cambhatta	lbw b B.B.Nimbalkar	4	(5) c R.B.Nimbalkar b Gai	5
10	K.A.Sheikh	not out	0	b Gai	3
11	*M.S.Baloch	b Gai	2	c and b Adhikari	4
	Extras		15		13
			100		141

FoW (1): 1- , 2- , 3- , 4- , 5- , 6- , 7- , 8- , 9- , 10-100
FoW (2): 1- , 2- , 3-21, 4- , 5- , 6- , 7- , 8- , 9- , 10-141

Gujarat Bowling

	O	M	R	W		O	M	R	W
Baloch	23	2	54	4		28.3	6	56	7
Sheikh	10	4	18	0	(3)	8	0	21	0
Chippa	21.2	2	45	6	(4)	26	4	48	3
R.M.Patel					(2)	4	1	7	0
Pathan					(5)	3	0	10	0

Baroda Bowling

	O	M	R	W		O	M	R	W
Gai	18.2	7	38	2		21	5	43	7
B.B.Nimbalkar	12	6	16	3		10	4	36	1
Dhumal	9	3	16	1		5	1	15	0
Ambegaokar	4	0	11	0					
Adhikari	5	4	2	3		5	0	22	2
Sheikh	3	1	2	1	(4)	2	0	12	0

Umpires: Toss:

Close of Play: 1st day: Gujarat (1) 73-5 (Parmar 3*, B.M.Patel 1*); 2nd day: Gujarat (2) 21-3 (Pathan 10*).

MUSLIMS v THE REST

Played at Brabourne Stadium, Bombay, November 18, 19, 20, 1939.

Muslims won by an innings and 11 runs.

THE REST

1	A.C.Pereira	st Dilawar Hussain b Amir Elahi	17	(4) b Nissar	4
2	J.O.Gonsalves	b Saeed Ahmed	3	c Abbas Khan b Jahangir Khan	0
3	†M.B.Cohen	b Nissar	2	(1) run out	5
4	E.Shaw	b Jahangir Khan	15	(7) b Nissar	4
5	V.S.Hazare	c Abbas Khan b Nazir Ali	21	not out	57
6	J.G.Harris	c Saeed Ahmed b Jahangir Khan	9	absent hurt	0
7	G.S.Richards	c and b Jahangir Khan	43	(6) c Wazir Ali b Jahangir Khan	29
8	S.S.Manoharan	c Saeed Ahmed b Amir Elahi	18	(3) b Jahangir Khan	0
9	*A.S.de Mello	c Amir Elahi b Jahangir Khan	5	(10) b Nissar	0
10	E.Alexander	not out	3	(8) c Saeed Ahmed b Nissar	8
11	L.D'Souza	c Ibrahim b Amir Elahi	0	(9) b Nissar	1
	Extras	b 11, lb 6	17	b 9, lb 7, nb 2	18
			153		126

FoW (1): 1-15 (2), 2-19 (3), 3-34 (4), 4-53 (1), 5-68 (5), 6-119 (6), 7-130 (7), 8-143 (9), 9-153 (8), 10-153 (11)
FoW (2): 1-5 (2), 2-5 (3), 3-5 (1), 4-20 (4), 5-75 (6), 6-92 (7), 7-118 (8), 8-122 (9), 9-126 (10)

MUSLIMS

1	S.Mushtaq Ali	b Harris	61
2	S.M.Kadri	lbw b Harris	22
3	K.C.Ibrahim	lbw b Alexander	6
4	*S.Wazir Ali	b Harris	33
5	S.Nazir Ali	c Hazare b D'Souza	34
6	†Dilawar Hussain	b Alexander	38
7	M.Jahangir Khan	b Richards	6
8	Saeed Ahmed	b Alexander	0
9	Abbas Khan	not out	21
10	Amir Elahi	lbw b Hazare	22
11	M.Nissar	b Alexander	22
	Extras	b 13, lb 8, nb 4	25
			290

FoW (1): 1-49 (2), 2-61 (3), 3-126 (1), 4-143 (4), 5-207 (5), 6-214 (6), 7-218 (7), 8-218 (8), 9-261 (10), 10-290 (11)

Muslims Bowling

	O	M	R	W		O	M	R	W
Nissar	13	4	23	1	(3)	14.1	5	29	5
Nazir Ali	9	3	14	1	(5)	4	0	6	0
Amir Elahi	13.2	6	22	3	(4)	14	1	34	0
Jahangir Khan	13	1	52	4	(1)	13	1	29	3
Saeed Ahmed	18	8	25	1	(2)	11	6	10	0

The Rest Bowling

	O	M	R	W
Richards	22	1	89	1
de Mello	1	0	18	0
Alexander	21.5	6	45	4
Harris	21	8	30	3
Hazare	24	4	63	1
Manoharan	4	0	12	0
D'Souza	2	0	8	1

Umpires: N.A.Dubash and D.K.Naik. Toss: The Rest

Close of Play: 1st day: Muslims (1) 104-2 (Mushtaq Ali 51*, Wazir Ali 13*); 2nd day: The Rest (2) 92-5 (Hazare 35*, Shaw 4*).

HINDUS v PARSEES

Played at Brabourne Stadium, Bombay, November 21, 22, 23, 1939.

Match drawn.

PARSEES

1	F.K.Nariman	lbw b Banerjee	6	(2) st Bhandarkar b C.K.Nayudu	29
2	N.F.Canteenwala	lbw b C.S.Nayudu	23	(1) c V.M.Merchant b C.S.Nayudu	39
3	E.B.Aibara	c C.K.Nayudu b Amarnath	22	c U.M.Merchant b C.S.Nayudu	21
4	P.E.Palia	run out	25	(7) c Bhandarkar b Amar Singh	11
5	J.B.Khot	c Bhandarkar b Amar Singh	16	(4) st Bhandarkar b C.S.Nayudu	49
6	*S.H.M.Colah	run out	10	b C.S.Nayudu	13
7	J.N.Bhaya	not out	82	(5) c U.M.Merchant b Banerjee	84
8	M.J.Mobed	c Bhandarkar b C.S.Nayudu	1	(9) not out	18
9	K.K.Tarapore	b C.S.Nayudu	20	(8) st Bhandarkar b C.S.Nayudu	0
10	†M.P.Engineer	c Mankad b Banerjee	8	not out	5
11	S.Darashah	c and b Banerjee	0		
	Extras	b 4, lb 2, nb 1	7	b 9, lb 2, nb 3	14
			220	(8 wickets, declared)	283

FoW (1): 1-6 (1), 2-53 (3), 3-53 (2), 4-92 (4), 5-106 (6), 6-108 (5), 7-109 (8), 8-195 (9), 9-220 (10), 10-220 (11)
FoW (2): 1-57 (2), 2-95 (1), 3-104 (3), 4-179 (4), 5-199 (6), 6-218 (7), 7-219 (8), 8-270 (5)

HINDUS

1	M.H.Mankad	b Khot	9	lbw b Tarapore	24
2	†K.V.Bhandarkar	c Mobed b Tarapore	11	hit wkt b Mobed	60
3	L.Amarnath	c Aibara b Mobed	37	not out	41
4	*C.K.Nayudu	b Tarapore	47	not out	5
5	V.M.Merchant	b Tarapore	4		
6	M.M.Jagdale	lbw b Tarapore	3		
7	C.S.Nayudu	c Aibara b Colah	126		
8	L.Amar Singh	c Aibara b Mobed	11		
9	S.N.Banerjee	c Canteenwala b Palia	56		
10	U.M.Merchant	lbw b Palia	2		
11	K.M.Rangnekar	not out	1		
	Extras	b 5, lb 6, nb 2	13	lb 1	1
			320	(2 wickets)	131

FoW (1): 1-12 (1), 2-46 (2), 3-80 (3), 4-95 (5), 5-113 (6), 6-122 (4), 7-153 (8), 8-305 (7), 9-319 (10), 10-320 (9)
FoW (2): 1-62 (1), 2-126 (2)

Hindus Bowling

	O	M	R	W		O	M	R	W
Banerjee	9.3	1	37	3	(3)	7	1	19	1
Amar Singh	24	3	63	1	(1)	33	9	74	1
Amarnath	12	1	27	1	(2)	3	0	7	0
C.S.Nayudu	27	5	60	3		41	3	127	5
C.K.Nayudu	6	2	12	0		6	2	13	1
Mankad	4	0	14	0		9	1	29	0

Parsees Bowling

	O	M	R	W		O	M	R	W
Darashah	17	3	41	0		5	0	11	0
Khot	12	3	36	1		5	0	10	0
Palia	8	0	33	2					
Tarapore	28	7	77	4	(3)	17	4	39	1
Mobed	34	2	106	2	(4)	15	1	61	1
Colah	2	0	14	1	(5)	4	0	9	0

Umpires: J.Pinto and Vali Ahmed. Toss: Parsees

Close of Play: 1st day: Hindus (1) 62-2 (Amarnath 30*, C.K.Nayudu 8*); 2nd day: Parsees (2) 73-1 (Canteenwala 32*, Aibara 4*).

C.S.Nayudu's 126 took 173 minutes and included 12 fours.

HINDUS v MUSLIMS

Played at Brabourne Stadium, Bombay, November 25, 26, 27, 1939.

Hindus won by five wickets.

MUSLIMS					
1	S.M.Kadri	b Amar Singh	26	b Amar Singh	33
2	S.Mushtaq Ali	c Mankad b C.S.Nayudu	34	b Banerjee	3
3	†Dilawar Hussain	c and b C.S.Nayudu	45	(6) c Rangnekar b C.S.Nayudu	45
4	*S.Wazir Ali	b C.K.Nayudu	33	run out	52
5	S.Nazir Ali	c Banerjee b C.S.Nayudu	18	b C.S.Nayudu	3
6	M.Jahangir Khan	c Hindlekar b C.K.Nayudu	13	(8) b Banerjee	0
7	Saeed Ahmed	c Amarnath b C.S.Nayudu	0	lbw b Banerjee	0
8	Abbas Khan	not out	19	(3) c V.M.Merchant b Banerjee	10
9	Amir Elahi	lbw b C.S.Nayudu	2	c and b C.S.Nayudu	19
10	M.Nissar	c Amarnath b C.S.Nayudu	2	b C.S.Nayudu	1
11	M.Mazhar Mahmood	b C.S.Nayudu	1	not out	4
	Extras	b 4, lb 2	6	b 6, lb 3, nb 1	10
			199		180

FoW (1): 1-54 (2), 2-69 (1), 3-141 (4), 4-141 (3), 5-158 (6), 6-159 (7), 7-188 (5), 8-192 (9), 9-196 (10), 10-199 (11)
FoW (2): 1-16 (2), 2-32 (3), 3-80 (1), 4-93 (5), 5-136 (7), 6-136 (8), 7-138 (4), 8-141 (10), 9-174 (9), 10-180 (6)

HINDUS					
1	†D.D.Hindlekar	b Nissar	4	c Saeed Ahmed b Nissar	13
2	M.H.Mankad	b Amir Elahi	19	b Amir Elahi	73
3	L.Amarnath	c Jahangir Khan b Nissar	28	lbw b Saeed Ahmed	5
4	*C.K.Nayudu	b Amir Elahi	0	(5) b Amir Elahi	18
5	S.N.Banerjee	c Jahangir Khan b Nissar	17	(7) not out	2
6	V.M.Merchant	lbw b Nissar	32	(4) not out	88
7	C.S.Nayudu	c Mushtaq Ali b Nissar	0	(6) lbw b Nazir Ali	14
8	M.M.Jagdale	c Wazir Ali b Amir Elahi	17		
9	L.Amar Singh	lbw b Saeed Ahmed	22		
10	K.M.Rangnekar	lbw b Nissar	14		
11	U.M.Merchant	not out	0		
	Extras	b 2, lb 1, nb 3	6	b 4, lb 4	8
			159	(5 wickets)	221

FoW (1): 1-16 (1), 2-43 (2), 3-43 (4), 4-57 (3), 5-80 (5), 6-80 (7), 7-117 (8), 8-123 (6), 9-155 (10), 10-159 (9)
FoW (2): 1-20 (1), 2-29 (3), 3-150 (2), 4-190 (5), 5-207 (6)

Hindus Bowling	O	M	R	W		O	M	R	W
Banerjee	9	0	37	0		14	2	57	4
Amar Singh	31	14	50	1		25	7	28	1
Amarnath	6	3	7	0	(6)	2	0	9	0
V.M.Merchant	4	1	3	0					
Jagdale	3	0	5	0					
C.S.Nayudu	31.1	4	78	7	(3)	25.1	3	64	4
C.K.Nayudu	9	2	13	2	(4)	5	2	7	0
Mankad					(5)	4	2	5	0

Muslims Bowling	O	M	R	W		O	M	R	W
Nissar	20	3	52	6		9	0	38	1
Mazhar Mahmood	5	1	19	0	(5)	3	0	20	0
Saeed Ahmed	17.3	7	37	1		15	5	25	1
Jahangir Khan	2	0	9	0	(2)	12	2	24	0
Amir Elahi	11	6	36	3	(6)	19	2	80	2
Nazir Ali					(4)	7	1	20	1
Mushtaq Ali					(7)	1	0	6	0

Umpires: N.A.Dubash and D.K.Kapadia. Toss: Muslims

Close of Play: 1st day: Hindus (1) 47-3 (Amarnath 20*, Banerjee 1*); 2nd day: Muslims (2) 141-8 (Amir Elahi 2*).
The match was scheduled for four days but completed in three. Dilawar Hussain retired hurt in the Muslims second innings having scored 29 (team score 136-4) - he returned when the score was 141-8. Abbas Khan kept wicket after lunch on the third day.

HYDERABAD v MADRAS

Played at Gymkhana Ground, Secunderabad, December 1, 2, 3, 1939.

Hyderabad won by an innings and 2 runs.

HYDERABAD			
1	S.R.Mehta	c Chari b Parthasarathi	17
2	†Isa Khan	lbw b Ram Singh	0
3	Asadullah Qureshi	c Chari b Ram Singh	89
4	E.B.Aibara	c Stansfeld b Ram Singh	0
5	*S.M.Hussain	c Parankusam b Rangachari	54
6	B.R.Patel	lbw b Ram Singh	50
7	Ushaq Ahmed	c Chari b Parankusam	66
8	S.M.Hadi	b Gopalan	106
9	S.Ali Abbas	b Parankusam	9
10	Ibrahim Khan	b Ram Singh	36
11	Ghulam Ahmed	not out	4
	Extras		12
			443

FoW (1): 1-2 (2), 2-34 (1), 3-37 (4), 4-140 (5), 5-209 (3), 6-231 (6), 7-331 (7), 8-363 (9), 9-438 (10), 10-443 (8)

MADRAS					
1	A.V.Krishnaswami	b Ghulam Ahmed	6	b Mehta	22
2	A.W.Stansfeld	b Patel	0	b Mehta	13
3	A.G.Ram Singh	b Mehta	44	b Ghulam Ahmed	1
4	B.S.R.Bhadradri	run out	18	not out	62
5	*C.Ramaswami	b Ghulam Ahmed	41	(6) b Mehta	0
6	G.Parthasarathi	lbw b Ghulam Ahmed	62	(7) c Asadullah Qureshi b Mehta	32
7	M.J.Gopalan	c Ghulam Ahmed b Asadullah Qureshi	11	(8) b Mehta	1
8	N.J.Venkatesan	not out	50	(5) b Mehta	5
9	†S.V.T.Chari	lbw b Ghulam Ahmed	4	c Ali Abbas b Ghulam Ahmed	16
10	T.S.Parankusam	c Patel b Ghulam Ahmed	0	b Ghulam Ahmed	0
11	C.R.Rangachari	c Ghulam Ahmed b Ibrahim Khan	17	b Ghulam Ahmed	18
	Extras		9		9
			262		179

FoW (1): 1-2 (2), 2-35 (1), 3-65 (3), 4-80 (4), 5-176 (5), 6-183 (6), 7-195 (7), 8- (9), 9- (10), 10-262 (11)
FoW (2): 1-23 (2), 2-24 (3), 3-45 (1), 4- (5), 5- (6), 6-105 (7), 7-109 (8), 8- (9), 9-147 (10), 10-179 (11)

Madras Bowling	O	M	R	W
Gopalan	20.5	1	54	1
Ram Singh	45	7	136	5
Rangachari	29	1	88	1
Parthasarathi	17	3	68	1
Venkatesan	14	2	34	0
Parankusam	13	2	51	2

Hyderabad Bowling	O	M	R	W	O	M	R	W
Ibrahim Khan	15	2	39	1	13	6	24	0
Patel	3	0	8	1	3	0	10	0
Ghulam Ahmed	40	6	95	5	25.4	5	62	4
Mehta	29	5	54	1	28	9	49	6
Asadullah Qureshi	10	1	51	1	4	1	18	0
Ushaq Ahmed	4	2	6	0	3	1	7	0

Umpires: Toss: Hyderabad

Close of Play: 1st day: Hyderabad (1) 332-7 (Hadi 43*, Ali Abbas 1*); 2nd day: Madras (1) 212-9 (Venkatesan 12*, Rangachari 6*).

BIHAR v BENGAL

Played at Keenan Stadium, Jamshedpur, December 2, 3, 4, 1939.

Bengal won by an innings and 51 runs.

BIHAR

1	S.Banerjee	c Hammond b Dutt	48	(3) st Roy b Chatterjee	26
2	A.Balsora	lbw b Banerjee	0	b Mitra	8
3	B.Sen	c Sadhu b Dutt	30	(1) c Roy b Sadhu	17
4	S.K.Roy	b Dutt	3	c Mitra b Hammond	24
5	M.Dastoor	st Roy b Chatterjee	12	c Hammond b Dutt	10
6	*K.A.D.Naoroji	c Ganguli b Dutt	2	(7) b Banerjee	1
7	S.Chakravorty	b Dutt	11	(9) c Hammond b Chatterjee	4
8	D.King	c Kamal b Dutt	11	(6) lbw b Dutt	6
9	F.Brierley	b Mitra	7	(8) b Chatterjee	1
10	D.S.Khambatta	b Chatterjee	0	(11) not out	0
11	J.Alam	not out	2	(10) c S.Bose b Banerjee	3
	Extras		9		11
			135		111

FoW (1): 1-3 (2), 2-80 (1), 3-84 (3), 4-87 (4), 5-89 (6), 6-102 (7), 7-119 (8), 8-132 (5), 9-132 (10), 10-135 (9)
FoW (2): 1-25 (2), 2-27 (1), 3-70 (4), 4- (5), 5-89 (6), 6-90 (7), 7-102 (3), 8-106 (9), 9- (8), 10-111 (10)

BENGAL

1	S.K.Ganguli	b Khambatta	1
2	†K.R.Roy	c Roy b Khambatta	40
3	S.Bose	c King b Khambatta	33
4	*N.M.Bose	c Khambatta b Chakravorty	67
5	N.C.Chatterjee	c and b Khambatta	42
6	A.N.Hammond	c Alam b Banerjee	72
7	A.Kamal	lbw b Khambatta	0
8	J.N.Banerjee	not out	16
9	S.Mitra	c Brierley b Banerjee	4
10	H.Sadhu	b Banerjee	0
11	S.Dutt	c Khambatta b Brierley	2
	Extras		20
			297

FoW (1): 1-8 (1), 2-53 (2), 3-94 (3), 4-175 (5), 5-235 (4), 6-246 (7), 7-280 (6), 8-291 (9), 9-291 (10), 10-297 (11)

Bengal Bowling

	O	M	R	W	O	M	R	W
Banerjee	7	0	25	1	5.2	2	9	2
Sadhu	14	1	30	0	6	0	31	1
Hammond	5	0	17	0	3	0	10	1
Mitra	6.2	0	20	1	6	1	15	1
Dutt	13	4	32	6	6	0	29	2
Chatterjee	3	1	2	2	2	0	6	3

Bihar Bowling

	O	M	R	W
Khambatta	30	1	109	5
Chakravorty	19	1	68	1
Alam	9	2	31	0
Banerjee	10	0	33	3
Brierley	5	0	28	1
King	3	0	8	0

Umpires: M.K.Banerjee and M.Dutta Roy. Toss: Bihar

Close of Play: 1st day: Bengal (1) 88-2 (S.Bose 29*, N.M.Bose 12*); 2nd day: Bihar (2) 90-6 (Banerjee 14*).

SIND v WESTERN INDIA

Played at Karachi Gymkhana Ground, December 2, 3, 4, 1939.

Match drawn.

WESTERN INDIA					
1	Gatoor	b M.J.Mobed	21	c Qamaruddin Sheikh b Gopaldas	0
2	†Faiz Ahmed	c and b Qamaruddin Sheikh	3	b M.J.Mobed	17
3	Umar Khan	lbw b M.J.Mobed	15	c Hakim Lanewalla b Naoomal Jaoomal	1
4	*K.S.Abdul Khaliq	c Abbas Khan b Gopaldas	0		
5	Nawab of Manavadar	st D.J.Mobed b Lakda	21	(4) not out	88
6	Sukhvantrai	lbw b M.J.Mobed	3		
7	Saeed Ahmed	c and b Naoomal Jaoomal	101		
8	S.B.Gandhi	c Abbas Khan b Naoomal Jaoomal	7		
9	Akbar Khan	c Qamaruddin Sheikh b Naoomal Jaoomal	2		
10	R.P.Rathod	b M.J.Mobed	71	(5) not out	91
11	S.Nyalchand	not out	2		
	Extras		20		13
			266	(3 wickets, declared)	210

FoW (1): 1-7 (2), 2-39 (1), 3-39 (4), 4- (3), 5-61 (6), 6-83 (5), 7- (8), 8-99 (9), 9-258 (7), 10-266 (10)
FoW (2): 1-0 (1), 2-20 (2), 3-22 (3)

SIND					
1	J.W.Anson	b Gandhi	6	c Sukhvantrai b Umar Khan	14
2	A.Dipchand	b Akbar Khan	5	c Nyalchand b Rathod	49
3	Qamaruddin Sheikh	lbw b Gandhi	14	c Gatoor b Rathod	20
4	Abbas Khan	lbw b Saeed Ahmed	13		
5	Naoomal Jaoomal	c Gandhi b Nyalchand	24		
6	Daud Khan	c Faiz Ahmed b Akbar Khan	21	(4) not out	6
7	M.A.Gopaldas	lbw b Saeed Ahmed	26		
8	*M.J.Mobed	b Saeed Ahmed	0		
9	F.G.Lakda	c Faiz Ahmed b Saeed Ahmed	0		
10	Hakim Lanewalla	not out	14		
11	†D.J.Mobed	b Saeed Ahmed	0		
	Extras		4		3
			127	(3 wickets)	92

FoW (1): 1- (1), 2- (2), 3-28 (3), 4-55 (4), 5-70 (5), 6- (6), 7- (8), 8- (9), 9-127 (7), 10-127 (11)
FoW (2): 1- , 2- , 3-92

Sind Bowling	O	M	R	W		O	M	R	W
Qamaruddin Sheikh	14	2	41	1	(6)	7	0	27	0
Hakim Lanewalla	10	3	18	0		6	2	16	0
Gopaldas	20	4	46	1	(1)	10	2	28	1
M.J.Mobed	39.4	8	65	4		16	3	29	1
Naoomal Jaoomal	27	6	45	3	(3)	19	2	52	1
Lakda	16	5	24	1	(5)	15	5	26	0
Daud Khan	3	0	7	0		4	0	12	0
Dipchand	1	1	0	0					
Anson					(8)	3	0	7	0

Western India Bowling	O	M	R	W		O	M	R	W
Saeed Ahmed	31.5	18	23	5					
Gandhi	22	4	47	2					
Akbar Khan	32	15	35	2					
Nyalchand	16	9	18	1	(5)	6	2	9	0
Manavadar					(1)	4	0	17	0
Faiz Ahmed					(2)	7	0	23	0
Umar Khan					(3)	5	0	17	1
Rathod					(4)	7.5	2	23	2

Umpires: Toss: Western India
Close of Play: 1st day: Western India (1) 227-8 (Saeed Ahmed 81*, Rathod 57*); 2nd day: Sind (1) 119-8 (Gopaldas 26*, Hakim Lanewalla 6*).
Saeed Ahmed's 101 took 240 minutes and included 4 fours.

DELHI v RAJPUTANA

Played at Feroz Shah Kotla, Delhi, December 9, 10, 11, 1939.

Rajputana won by seven wickets.

DELHI					
1	G.M.Din	b Bradshaw	0	(4) c Raghbir Singh b Azim Khan	6
2	Fateh Mahomed	run out	0	(1) lbw b Azim Khan	26
3	Musa Khan	b Azim Khan	14	(6) not out	31
4	Ishwar Lal	run out	42	(5) c Naidoo b Azim Khan	2
5	K.Bahadur	b Azim Khan	0	(11) b Abbas	12
6	*Tajammul Hussain	c Naidoo b Azim Khan	6	(8) b Abbas	0
7	Anwar Khan	lbw b Azim Khan	4	lbw b Azim Khan	1
8	S.Mohammad Khan	lbw b Bradshaw	0	(10) b Azim Khan	6
9	S.M.Shafi	b Azim Khan	4	(3) lbw b Abbas	42
10	Shujauddin	not out	5	(2) lbw b Azim Khan	5
11	Riazul Hussain	lbw b Azim Khan	4	(9) b Abbas	1
	Extras		6		6
			85		138

FoW (1): 1-0 (1), 2-3 (2), 3-23 (3), 4-23 (5), 5-35 (6), 6-47 (7), 7-50 (8), 8- (9), 9- (4), 10-85 (11)
FoW (2): 1-16 (2), 2-60 (1), 3-68 (4), 4-70 (5), 5-100 (3), 6-109 (7), 7-110 (8), 8-112 (9), 9-119 (10), 10-138 (11)

RAJPUTANA					
1	A.Wahab	b Fateh Mahomed	0	c Shujauddin b Tajammul Hussain	11
2	†Raghbir Singh	lbw b Fateh Mahomed	5	b Tajammul Hussain	0
3	H.Vohra	b Fateh Mahomed	2		
4	Hansraj	c Anwar Khan b Musa Khan	96	(5) not out	1
5	N.P.Kesari	c Din b Shafi	2	(3) c Din b Tajammul Hussain	0
6	Attique Hussain	b Shujauddin	14		
7	G.R.Naidoo	lbw b Fateh Mahomed	60		
8	*W.H.Bradshaw	b Fateh Mahomed	0		
9	S.Abbas	c Musa Khan b Fateh Mahomed	16		
10	Azim Khan	b Fateh Mahomed	0		
11	Firasat Hussain	not out	1	(4) not out	5
	Extras		11		
			207	(3 wickets)	17

FoW (1): 1-0 (1), 2-2 (3), 3-7 (2), 4-12 (5), 5-51 (6), 6-187 (4), 7-187 (8), 8-202 (7), 9-206 (10), 10-207 (9)
FoW (2): 1-0 (2), 2-2 (3), 3-11 (1)

Rajputana Bowling	O	M	R	W		O	M	R	W
Bradshaw	11	3	19	2		7	2	16	0
Kesari	11	5	24	0		5	1	6	0
Azim Khan	14.4	4	30	6		17	1	55	6
Firasat Hussain	2	0	5	0		6	1	18	0
Abbas	3	2	1	0		13.2	5	26	4
Naidoo	1	1	0	0		3	1	11	0

Delhi Bowling	O	M	R	W		O	M	R	W
Fateh Mahomed	19.3	3	32	7		5.2	2	14	0
Shafi	8	1	25	1					
Riazul Hussain	4	1	12	0					
Shujauddin	27	5	53	1					
Din	7	2	14	0					
Musa Khan	15	4	45	1					
Bahadur	3	0	12	0					
Tajammul Hussain	3	2	3	0	(2)	5	2	3	3

Umpires: Toss: Delhi

Close of Play: 1st day: Rajputana (1) 129-5 (Hansraj 78*, Naidoo 20*); 2nd day: Delhi (2) 119-9 (Musa Khan 24*).

BARODA v NAWANAGAR

Played at Central College Ground, Baroda, December 15, 16, 17, 1939.

Baroda won by ten wickets.

NAWANAGAR					
1	O.Chimanlal	b B.B.Nimbalkar	9	b Nayudu	26
2	I.Oza	st R.B.Nimbalkar b Nayudu	15	c Powar b B.B.Nimbalkar	8
3	S.N.Banerjee	c Sheikh b Gaekwar	1	b Nayudu	9
4	*R.K.Indravijaysinhji	lbw b Gai	11	b Nayudu	30
5	R.K.Yadvendrasinhji	lbw b Gai	16	(6) c Sheikh b Nayudu	7
6	S.H.M.Colah	b Nayudu	1	(7) b Nayudu	39
7	L.Amar Singh	not out	113	(5) lbw b Nayudu	36
8	A.F.Wensley	c Gai b Gaekwar	22	c Nayudu b Gai	22
9	Mubarak Ali	st Powar b Nayudu	2	c R.B.Nimbalkar b Nayudu	2
10	J.R.Oza	b Nayudu	5	b Nayudu	4
11	†M.Ellum	b Nayudu	0	not out	0
	Extras		38		6
			233		189

FoW (1): 1-11 (1), 2-16 (3), 3-40 (4), 4-70 (5), 5-70 (2), 6-91 (6), 7-174 (8), 8-207 (9), 9-227 (10), 10-233 (11)
FoW (2): 1-18 (2), 2-30 (3), 3-49 (1), 4-105 (5), 5-110 (4), 6-125 (6), 7-175 (8), 8-177 (9), 9-188 (7), 10-189 (10)

BARODA					
1	Y.E.Sheikh	c J.R.Oza b Banerjee	1	not out	15
2	V.M.Pandit	run out	10	not out	5
3	†R.B.Nimbalkar	c Amar Singh b Banerjee	9		
4	H.R.Adhikari	c I.Oza b Banerjee	160		
5	C.S.Nayudu	lbw b Amar Singh	55		
6	*W.N.Ghorpade	st Ellum b Wensley	47		
7	M.M.Naidu	lbw b Amar Singh	12		
8	B.B.Nimbalkar	b Amar Singh	85		
9	K.S.Gaekwar	b Banerjee	3		
10	S.G.Powar	lbw b Banerjee	0		
11	E.B.Gai	not out	0		
	Extras		17		4
			399	(no wicket)	24

FoW (1): 1-4 (1), 2-16 (3), 3-28 (2), 4-122 (5), 5-230 (6), 6-249 (7), 7-362 (4), 8-385 (9), 9-385 (10), 10-399 (8)

Baroda Bowling	O	M	R	W		O	M	R	W
Gaekwar	21	4	67	2		19	3	54	0
B.B.Nimbalkar	7	3	20	1		3	0	21	1
Nayudu	21.2	3	83	5		22	1	93	8
Gai	10	5	25	2	(5)	6	1	8	1
Adhikari					(4)	1	0	7	0

Nawanagar Bowling	O	M	R	W		O	M	R	W
Banerjee	31	5	122	5	(2)	4	0	14	0
Amar Singh	32.5	2	120	3	(1)	4	2	6	0
Mubarak Ali	16	5	44	0					
J.R.Oza	11	0	40	0					
Wensley	8	0	56	1					

Umpires: N.D.Marshall and G.D.Shirke. Toss: Nawanagar

Close of Play: 1st day: Baroda (1) 66-3 (Adhikari 18*, Nayudu 23*); 2nd day: Nawanagar (2) 75-3 (Indravijaysinhji 15*, Amar Singh 14*).

L.Amar Singh's 113 took 100 minutes and included 17 fours and 1 six. H.R.Adhikari's 160 took 282 minutes and included 17 fours. S.G.Powar took over as wicket-keeper near the end of the Nawanagar first innings and for the second innings.

SOUTH AUSTRALIA v NEW SOUTH WALES

Played at Adelaide Oval, December 15, 16, 18, 1939.

South Australia won by seven wickets. (Points: South Australia 5, New South Wales 0)

NEW SOUTH WALES					
1	*S.J.McCabe	lbw b Grimmett	40	lbw b Grimmett	47
2	J.H.W.Fingleton	c Bradman b Grimmett	29	b Klose	2
3	S.G.Barnes	b Waite	2	(6) c Walker b Ward	33
4	C.M.Solomon	c Tregoning b Klose	131	(3) c Tregoning b Grimmett	46
5	A.G.Chipperfield	b Cotton	32	(4) lbw b Grimmett	57
6	A.G.Cheetham	c Bradman b Tregoning	32	(7) b Grimmett	2
7	C.G.Pepper	lbw b Klose	22	(8) c Grimmett b Klose	47
8	A.W.Roper	c Ridings b Grimmett	15	(5) c and b Ward	0
9	W.J.O'Reilly	c Walker b Klose	16	c Tregoning b Grimmett	5
10	†S.G.Sismey	not out	5	c Tregoning b Grimmett	3
11	J.E.Walsh	b Klose	1	not out	0
	Extras	b 2, lb 8, w 1	11	b 1, lb 5	6
			336		248

FoW (1): 1-63 (1), 2-70 (3), 3-74 (2), 4-130 (5), 5-225 (6), 6-283 (4), 7-298 (7), 8-322 (8), 9-330 (9), 10-336 (11)
FoW (2): 1-16 (2), 2-60 (1), 3-122 (3), 4-139 (5), 5-171 (4), 6-179 (7), 7-238 (8), 8-244 (9), 9-248 (6), 10-248 (10)

SOUTH AUSTRALIA					
1	R.S.Whitington	c Sismey b Roper	6		
2	K.L.Ridings	c Sismey b Walsh	29	(1) b Cheetham	20
3	*D.G.Bradman	not out	251	not out	90
4	R.A.Hamence	lbw b Pepper	41	lbw b Pepper	12
5	M.G.Waite	b Cheetham	46	not out	28
6	T.E.Klose	c and b O'Reilly	4	(2) b Roper	2
7	J.Tregoning	b O'Reilly	0		
8	†C.W.Walker	b O'Reilly	1		
9	F.A.Ward	b O'Reilly	4		
10	C.V.Grimmett	b O'Reilly	17		
11	H.N.J.Cotton	absent hurt	0		
	Extras	b 21, lb 4, nb 6	31	b 1, lb 3	4
			430	(3 wickets)	156

FoW (1): 1-17 (1), 2-69 (2), 3-161 (4), 4-308 (5), 5-313 (6), 6-313 (7), 7-317 (8), 8-349 (9), 9-430 (10)
FoW (2): 1-9 (2), 2-57 (1), 3-87 (4)

South Australia Bowling	O	M	R	W			O	M	R	W
Cotton	12	0	51	1						
Waite	19	0	98	1		(1)	12	1	22	0
Grimmett	20	0	102	3			20.5	0	122	6
Ward	5	0	42	0			15	4	61	2
Tregoning	3	0	9	1	1w					
Klose	5.4	1	23	4		(2)	7	1	37	2

New South Wales Bowling	O	M	R	W		O	M	R	W
Roper	14	0	83	1	3nb	3	0	26	1
Cheetham	15	1	80	1	2nb	7	0	33	1
O'Reilly	22.1	4	108	5	1nb	10	0	29	0
Pepper	9	0	56	1		8	0	31	1
Walsh	12	0	72	1		2.2	0	33	0

Umpires: A.G.Jenkins, J.D.Scott and H.C.Newman. Toss: New South Wales

Close of Play: 1st day: South Australia (1) 68-1 (Ridings 29*, Bradman 27*); 2nd day: New South Wales (2) 139-4 (Chipperfield 38*).

The match was scheduled for four days but completed in three. C.M.Solomon's 131 took 154 minutes and included 18 fours. D.G.Bradman's 251 took 272 minutes and included 38 fours and 2 sixes. H.C.Newman deputised for J.D.Scott. 12th Men: P.L.Ridings (SA) and R.H.Robinson (NSW).

VICTORIA v QUEENSLAND

Played at Melbourne Cricket Ground, December 15, 16, 18, 19, 1939.

Victoria won by seven wickets. (Points: Victoria 5, Queensland 0)

QUEENSLAND

1	*W.A.Brown	st Barnett b Ring	20	b Sievers	27
2	G.G.Cook	c Johnson b Ring	62	b Sievers	9
3	T.Allen	b Sievers	1	run out	3
4	R.E.Rogers	c Sievers b Johnson	53	b Fleetwood-Smith	39
5	G.G.Baker	b Ring	17	lbw b Fleetwood-Smith	25
6	†D.Tallon	c Johnson b Sievers	56	b Fleetwood-Smith	6
7	D.Watt	b Fleetwood-Smith	6	not out	59
8	L.W.T.Tallon	c Barnett b Scott	19	lbw b Fleetwood-Smith	1
9	P.L.Dixon	b Scott	4	(10) b Sievers	25
10	C.P.Christ	b Ring	18	(9) lbw b Johnson	32
11	J.A.Ellis	not out	14	run out	8
	Extras	b 4, lb 1, w 1, nb 3	9	b 1, lb 5, nb 2	8
			279		242

FoW (1): 1-33 (1), 2-34 (3), 3-111 (4), 4-150 (5), 5-167 (2), 6-198 (7), 7-228 (8), 8-243 (6), 9-243 (9), 10-279 (10)
FoW (2): 1-37 (2), 2-38 (1), 3-52 (3), 4-106 (4), 5-109 (5), 6-116 (6), 7-120 (8), 8-189 (9), 9-224 (10), 10-242 (11)

VICTORIA

1	I.S.Lee	lbw b Ellis	52	c Cook b Ellis	4
2	G.E.Tamblyn	c Cook b Ellis	107	b Ellis	0
3	A.L.Hassett	c D.Tallon b Dixon	83		
4	K.R.Miller	c and b Christ	41	not out	47
5	I.W.G.Johnson	c D.Tallon b Ellis	44	not out	37
6	D.H.Fothergill	st D.Tallon b Christ	5	(3) b Ellis	10
7	*†B.A.Barnett	b Ellis	37		
8	M.W.Sievers	c Watt b Cook	12		
9	D.T.Ring	c Baker b Cook	15		
10	R.B.Scott	not out	11		
11	L.O.Fleetwood-Smith	c D.Tallon b Ellis	0		
	Extras	b 3, lb 6, nb 2	11	lb 2, w 5	7
			418	(3 wickets)	105

FoW (1): 1-91 (1), 2-217 (2), 3-271 (3), 4-297 (4), 5-307 (6), 6-369 (5), 7-382 (7), 8-398 (8), 9-416 (9), 10-418 (11)
FoW (2): 1-1 (2), 2-14 (1), 3-15 (3)

Victoria Bowling

	O	M	R	W			O	M	R	W	
Scott	13	0	44	2	1w		7	0	42	0	2nb
Sievers	18	3	49	2	2nb		13	0	45	3	
Ring	20.2	3	74	4	1nb		14	0	50	0	
Fleetwood-Smith	15	0	71	1			18	1	77	4	
Johnson	11	1	32	1			6	0	20	1	

Queensland Bowling

	O	M	R	W			O	M	R	W	
Ellis	30.2	2	110	5	1nb		5	0	14	3	
Cook	21	4	69	2	1nb		7	0	36	0	
L.W.T.Tallon	12	0	85	0							
Dixon	16	5	52	1		(3)	4	1	10	0	
Christ	23	3	65	2		(4)	3	0	12	0	4w
Watt	3	0	24	0		(5)	2.2	0	16	0	
Baker	2	1	2	0							
Rogers						(6)	2	0	10	0	1w

Umpires: A.N.Barlow and W.J.Craddock. Toss: Queensland

Close of Play: 1st day: Victoria (1) 3-0 (Lee 3*, Tamblyn 0*); 2nd day: Victoria (1) 363-5 (Johnson 41*, Barnett 28*); 3rd day: Queensland (2) 238-9 (Watt 56*, Ellis 7*).

G.E.Tamblyn's 107 took 202 minutes and included 11 fours. 12th Men: P.J.Beames (Vic) and C.D.Hansen (Qld).

TRANSVAAL v NORTH EASTERN TRANSVAAL

Played at Old Wanderers, Johannesburg, December 16, 18, 1939.

Transvaal won by an innings and 201 runs.

TRANSVAAL

1	J.T.Seccombe	c Bromham b Brown	58
2	J.H.F.Fuller	c Bromham b Bock	22
3	O.E.Wynne	c Brown b Henderson	49
4	*A.W.Briscoe	c Henderson b Brown	172
5	C.Breakey	c Lance b Henderson	1
6	E.S.Newson	b Henderson	25
7	A.M.B.Rowan	c Dowling b Henderson	43
8	J.H.M.Pickerill	not out	72
9	R.N.E.Petersen	not out	43
10	F.J.Wickham		
11	†G.L.Allpass		
	Extras	b 10, lb 8, nb 5	23
		(7 wickets, declared)	508

FoW (1): 1-68 (2), 2-115 (1), 3-172 (3), 4-186 (5), 5-242 (6), 6-347, 7-401

NORTH EASTERN TRANSVAAL

1	D.G.Helfrich	c Allpass b Petersen	20	b Wickham	5
2	†C.G.Bromham	c Wynne b Wickham	0	b Newson	6
3	L.O.Waller	b Newson	3	lbw b Newson	0
4	*R.S.Martin	c Newson b Pickerill	32	b Rowan	47
5	R.C.Hicks	c Pickerill b Petersen	4	(6) not out	32
6	R.A.Edwards	b Rowan	15	(7) lbw b Rowan	20
7	D.F.Dowling	c Petersen b Wickham	20	(5) b Wickham	61
8	L.S.Brown	b Newson	12	b Rowan	0
9	E.G.Bock	c Seccombe b Wickham	3	c Pickerill b Petersen	2
10	W.A.Henderson	b Newson	5	c Pickerill b Rowan	6
11	W.P.Lance	not out	0	b Petersen	0
	Extras		9		5
			123		184

FoW (1): 1-0 (2), 2-5 (3), 3-60, 4-60, 5-69, 6-94, 7-111, 8-118, 9-119, 10-123
FoW (2): 1-11, 2-11, 3-11, 4-120, 5-128, 6-173, 7-173, 8-176, 9-183, 10-184

North Eastern Transvaal Bowling

	O	M	R	W
Lance	29	6	87	0
Henderson	29	0	120	4
Bock	21	2	85	1
Brown	32	5	129	2
Dowling	8	0	59	0
Helfrich	1	0	5	0

Transvaal Bowling

	O	M	R	W		O	M	R	W
Newson	12	2	29	3		9	2	49	2
Wickham	9	3	23	3		8	1	28	2
Petersen	11	4	21	2		5.2	1	18	2
Pickerill	6	1	22	1		2	0	11	0
Rowan	7	1	19	1		12	0	48	4
Breakey					(6)	2	0	25	0

Umpires: Toss: Transvaal

Close of Play: 1st day: Transvaal (1) 508-7 (Pickerill 72*, Petersen 43*).

The match was scheduled for three days but completed in two. A.W.Briscoe's 172 took 210 minutes and included 12 fours.

WESTERN PROVINCE v GRIQUALAND WEST

Played at Newlands, Cape Town, December 16, 18, 19, 1939.

Match drawn.

GRIQUALAND WEST					
1	*T.H.Boggan	lbw b Plimsoll	83	c Brinkhaus b Evans	75
2	S.Nicholls	b Cheetham	11	c Eayrs b Cheetham	22
3	A.P.C.Steyn	c van der Bijl b Plimsoll	10	lbw b Plimsoll	22
4	S.S.Smith	c and b Cheetham	21	st Reid b Evans	9
5	L.E.McNamara	b Brinkhaus	6	c Plimsoll b Evans	44
6	F.F.Flanagan	b Brinkhaus	101	b Plimsoll	11
7	†A.Schultze	b Plimsoll	15	st Reid b Evans	1
8	J.P.McNally	b Evans	46	not out	37
9	J.Pickup	c Eayrs b Evans	7	c Reid b Plimsoll	1
10	J.E.Waddington	run out	5	c Foley b Cheetham	12
11	A.Waddington	not out	6	lbw b Brinkhaus	7
	Extras	b 2, lb 3	5	lb 1	1
			316		242

FoW (1): 1-36 (2), 2-64 (3), 3-92 (4), 4-101 (5), 5-137 (1), 6-171 (7), 7-276 (8), 8-284 (9), 9-300 (10), 10-316 (6)
FoW (2): 1-50 (2), 2-105 (3), 3-129 (1), 4-130 (4), 5-181 (5), 6-183 (7), 7-187 (6), 8-193 (9), 9-214 (10), 10-242 (11)

WESTERN PROVINCE					
1	*P.G.V.van der Bijl	lbw b J.E.Waddington	59	b A.Waddington	22
2	S.Kiel	b A.Waddington	0	c and b J.E.Waddington	36
3	L.M.Manning	b J.E.Waddington	101	c and b McNamara	46
4	G.Georgeu	b J.E.Waddington	52	run out	112
5	W.B.H.Foley	c McNally b J.E.Waddington	1	b A.Waddington	22
6	J.E.Cheetham	not out	26	not out	9
7	L.L.M.Evans	b A.Waddington	4	not out	1
8	†A.B.J.Reid	c McNamara b J.E.Waddington	7		
9	D.Eayrs	b J.E.Waddington	0		
10	J.G.B.Brinkhaus	c and b J.E.Waddington	4		
11	J.B.Plimsoll	lbw b J.E.Waddington	0		
	Extras	b 2, lb 11	13	lb 6	6
			267	(5 wickets)	254

FoW (1): 1-1 (2), 2-150 (3), 3-182 (1), 4-184 (5), 5-235 (4), 6-248 (7), 7-257 (8), 8-259 (9), 9-267 (10), 10-267 (11)
FoW (2): 1-51 (1), 2-69 (2), 3-157 (3), 4-236 (5), 5-249 (4)

Western Province Bowling	O	M	R	W		O	M	R	W
Brinkhaus	28.1	4	101	2		9.3	0	45	1
Plimsoll	26	8	61	3		22	1	52	3
Eayrs	12	1	36	0	(4)	6	0	22	0
Cheetham	11	1	38	2	(3)	12	0	63	2
Evans	17	1	52	2		14	1	59	4
Georgeu	6	0	23	0					

Griqualand West Bowling	O	M	R	W		O	M	R	W
A.Waddington	28	4	90	2		29	4	81	2
Flanagan	3	0	20	0					
J.E.Waddington	23.4	4	50	8	(2)	31	8	94	1
Pickup	4	0	17	0					
McNally	20	2	77	0	(3)	8	0	40	0
McNamara					(4)	5	0	33	1

Umpires: D.V.Collins and G.L.Sickler. Toss: Griqualand West

Close of Play: 1st day: Western Province (1) 100-1 (van der Bijl 23*, Manning 73*); 2nd day: Western Province (2) 50-0 (van der Bijl 21*, Kiel 26*).

F.F.Flanagan's 101 took 219 minutes and included 10 fours. L.M.Manning's 101 took 138 minutes and included 12 fours. G.Georgeu's 112 took 118 minutes and included 12 fours.

ORANGE FREE STATE v NATAL

Played at Ramblers Cricket Club Ground, Bloemfontein, December 19, 20, 1939.

Natal won by seven wickets.

ORANGE FREE STATE					
1	*E.W.Warner	b Lowell	30	c Harvey b Law	5
2	C.J.Kaplan	c Collins b Dawson	6	b Dawson	12
3	J.C.Newton	st Yuill b Dawson	3	(6) lbw b Lowell	21
4	H.F.Wright	lbw b Dawson	1	(3) lbw b Dawson	10
5	F.B.Lee	b Law	33	(4) b Law	5
6	W.Wilkinson	c Law b Lowell	0	(5) c Harvey b Dawson	43
7	K.Hayward	c Law b Mann	0	c Collins b Law	5
8	L.Tuckett	not out	25	not out	28
9	†F.Griffiths	st Yuill b Law	4	(10) run out	21
10	J.G.Espinasse	b Law	9	(9) st Yuill b Law	11
11	C.F.B.Papenfus	b Mann	2	c Law b Mann	1
	Extras		3		14
			116		176

FoW (1): 1-12 (2), 2-18 (3), 3-22 (4), 4-55 (1), 5-55 (6), 6-56 (7), 7-77 (5), 8-81 (9), 9-103 (10), 10-116 (11)
FoW (2): 1-12 (1), 2-27, 3-34, 4-36, 5-75, 6-95, 7-109, 8-120, 9-172, 10-176

NATAL					
1	R.C.Collins	lbw b Tuckett	0	b Tuckett	3
2	D.R.Fell	lbw b Papenfus	64	lbw b Tuckett	2
3	R.L.Harvey	c Warner b Tuckett	15		
4	*A.D.Nourse	lbw b Wright	75		
5	†R.R.Yuill	b Espinasse	10	(3) lbw b Papenfus	4
6	O.C.Dawson	c Tuckett b Hayward	63		
7	G.W.Boyes	b Papenfus	3	(5) not out	6
8	R.Howden	lbw b Papenfus	0	(4) not out	3
9	C.J.Lowell	b Hayward	13		
10	N.B.F.Mann	run out	8		
11	G.B.Law	not out	1		
	Extras		19		5
			271	(3 wickets)	23

FoW (1): 1-10 (1), 2-40 (3), 3-113 (2), 4-137 (5), 5-190 (4), 6-206 (7), 7-211 (8), 8-261, 9-262, 10-271
FoW (2): 1-4, 2-12, 3-14

Natal Bowling	O	M	R	W	O	M	R	W
Law	10	3	27	3	15	0	53	4
Dawson	10	2	28	3	13	0	33	3
Mann	12	4	28	2	15.2	4	34	1
Lowell	9	3	30	2	10	0	42	1

Orange Free State Bowling	O	M	R	W	O	M	R	W
Papenfus	21	1	92	3	5	0	11	1
Tuckett	17	1	78	2	4	0	7	2
Hayward	11	1	19	2				
Espinasse	4	0	39	1				
Wright	4	0	24	1				

Umpires: Toss:

Close of Play: 1st day: Orange Free State (2) 19-1 (Kaplan 8*, Wright 4*).

The match was scheduled for three days but completed in two.

SOUTH AUSTRALIA v QUEENSLAND

Played at Adelaide Oval, December 22, 23, 25, 26, 1939.

South Australia won by an innings and 222 runs. (Points: South Australia 5, Queensland 0)

	SOUTH AUSTRALIA		
1	K.L.Ridings	lbw b Baker	151
2	T.E.Klose	c Ellis b Cook	13
3	*D.G.Bradman	c Hansen b Ellis	138
4	R.A.Hamence	lbw b Cook	6
5	C.L.Badcock	b Dixon	236
6	M.G.Waite	c and b Dixon	137
7	R.S.Whitington	c Rogers b Christ	67
8	P.L.Ridings	not out	44
9	†C.W.Walker		
10	C.V.Grimmett		
11	F.A.Ward		
	Extras	b 10, lb 17, nb 2	29
		(7 wickets, declared)	821

FoW (1): 1-36 (2), 2-232 (3), 3-268 (4), 4-404 (1), 5-685 (5), 6-713 (6), 7-821 (7)

	QUEENSLAND				
1	*W.A.Brown	b Grimmett	20	st Walker b Ward	156
2	G.G.Cook	st Walker b Ward	27	c Waite b Grimmett	15
3	T.Allen	c Klose b Ward	35	c Waite b Ward	22
4	R.E.Rogers	c Waite b Grimmett	49	c Klose b Grimmett	50
5	G.G.Baker	c Walker b Klose	0	lbw b Grimmett	52
6	†D.Tallon	c Badcock b Ward	70	c Waite b Ward	14
7	C.D.P.Hansen	b Grimmett	2	c Walker b Grimmett	15
8	D.Watt	c Waite b Grimmett	6	(9) lbw b Grimmett	8
9	C.P.Christ	c Walker b Ward	1	(8) b Ward	12
10	P.L.Dixon	not out	3	c Walker b Grimmett	17
11	J.A.Ellis	c Badcock b Ward	5	not out	1
	Extras	lb 3, nb 1	4	b 8, lb 3, w 1, nb 3	15
			222		377

FoW (1): 1-41 (1), 2-76 (2), 3-91 (3), 4-92 (5), 5-199 (4), 6-207 (6), 7-213 (7), 8-214 (8), 9-216 (9), 10-222 (11)
FoW (2): 1-27 (2), 2-84 (3), 3-205 (4), 4-291 (1), 5-311 (6), 6-329 (5), 7-348 (8), 8-350 (7), 9-364 (9), 10-377 (10)

Queensland Bowling

	O	M	R	W	
Ellis	14	0	95	1	
Cook	22	1	129	2	
Dixon	24	0	142	2	2nb
Christ	27.1	3	144	1	
Baker	22	0	127	1	
Watt	14	1	135	0	
Rogers	4	1	20	0	

South Australia Bowling

	O	M	R	W		O	M	R	W	
P.L.Ridings	5	0	29	0	1nb	11	1	48	0	1w,1nb
Waite	9	2	40	0		13	2	21	0	2nb
Grimmett	19	2	71	4		33.4	5	124	6	
Ward	16.7	2	62	5		30	3	165	4	
Klose	5	1	16	1		3	0	4	0	

Umpires: H.C.Newman and J.D.Scott. Toss: South Australia

Close of Play: 1st day: South Australia (1) 553-4 (Badcock 172*, Waite 57*); 2nd day: Queensland (1) 177-4 (Rogers 38*, Tallon 53*); 3rd day: Queensland (2) 346-6 (Hansen 13*, Christ 11*).

K.L.Ridings's 151 took 238 minutes and included 14 fours. D.G.Bradman's 138 took 115 minutes and included 22 fours. C.L.Badcock's 236 took 249 minutes and included 26 fours and 4 sixes. M.G.Waite's 137 took 204 minutes and included 14 fours. W.A.Brown's 156 took 230 minutes and included 23 fours. 12th Men: G.Burton (SA) and L.W.T.Tallon (Qld).

VICTORIA v NEW SOUTH WALES

Played at Melbourne Cricket Ground, December 22, 23, 26, 1939.

Victoria won by 72 runs. (Points: Victoria 5, New South Wales 0)

	VICTORIA				
1	I.S.Lee	c McCabe b Cheetham	4	lbw b Pepper	18
2	G.E.Tamblyn	b Pepper	58	lbw b O'Reilly	15
3	A.L.Hassett	c Chipperfield b Pepper	33	lbw b Pepper	57
4	K.R.Miller	b Pepper	14	c Sismey b O'Reilly	14
5	I.W.G.Johnson	lbw b O'Reilly	41	c Fingleton b O'Reilly	13
6	P.J.Beames	c Pepper b Cheetham	34	b Pepper	3
7	*†B.A.Barnett	c Cheetham b Chipperfield	21	c sub (J.E.Walsh) b O'Reilly	66
8	M.W.Sievers	b O'Reilly	53	c Solomon b Pepper	29
9	D.T.Ring	b O'Reilly	8	c Sismey b O'Reilly	4
10	R.B.Scott	c Sismey b O'Reilly	4	not out	13
11	L.O.Fleetwood-Smith	not out	0	b Pepper	1
	Extras	b 4, lb 2, w 1, nb 3	10	lb 6, nb 3	9
			280		242

FoW (1): 1-9 (1), 2-78 (3), 3-98 (4), 4-123 (2), 5-162 (6), 6-203 (7), 7-233 (5), 8-253 (9), 9-257 (10), 10-280 (8)
FoW (2): 1-33 (2), 2-37 (1), 3-76 (4), 4-100 (5), 5-115 (6), 6-126 (3), 7-205 (8), 8-217 (9), 9-234 (7), 10-242 (11)

	NEW SOUTH WALES				
1	*S.J.McCabe	c Scott b Fleetwood-Smith	52	(2) c Johnson b Scott	4
2	J.H.W.Fingleton	b Scott	0	(1) lbw b Sievers	3
3	C.M.Solomon	lbw b Ring	52	c Barnett b Scott	1
4	S.G.Barnes	c Fleetwood-Smith b Sievers	98	run out	1
5	A.G.Chipperfield	c Tamblyn b Ring	40	lbw b Sievers	68
6	R.H.Robinson	c Johnson b Scott	16	lbw b Scott	6
7	A.G.Cheetham	lbw b Ring	16	b Scott	23
8	C.G.Pepper	st Barnett b Fleetwood-Smith	19	c Barnett b Sievers	1
9	W.J.O'Reilly	c Miller b Ring	17	c Hassett b Ring	15
10	A.W.Roper	run out (Hassett)	0	c Sievers b Ring	0
11	†S.G.Sismey	not out	0	not out	4
	Extras	b 6, lb 5	11	b 2, lb 1	3
			321		129

FoW (1): 1-3 (2), 2-103 (1), 3-121 (3), 4-214 (5), 5-247 (6), 6-273 (4), 7-297 (7), 8-319 (8), 9-319 (10), 10-321 (9)
FoW (2): 1-5 (1), 2-8 (3), 3-9 (2), 4-9 (4), 5-30 (6), 6-102 (7), 7-103 (8), 8-110 (5), 9-124 (9), 10-129 (10)

New South Wales Bowling	O	M	R	W			O	M	R	W	
Roper	4	0	22	0	1w						
Cheetham	17	2	72	2	2nb	(1)	9	1	27	0	
O'Reilly	20.3	6	75	4	1nb	(4)	27	3	72	5	3nb
Pepper	20	0	91	3		(3)	31	6	114	5	
Chipperfield	7	1	10	1		(2)	4	0	16	0	
Barnes						(5)	1	0	4	0	

Victoria Bowling	O	M	R	W		O	M	R	W
Scott	11	0	71	2		10	1	35	4
Sievers	14	0	74	1		8	2	18	3
Ring	14.3	0	85	4	(4)	8.4	2	33	2
Fleetwood-Smith	9	0	61	2	(3)	7	0	40	0
Johnson	2	0	19	0					

Umpires: A.N.Barlow and W.J.Craddock. Toss: Victoria

Close of Play: 1st day: Victoria (1) 280 all out; 2nd day: Victoria (2) 99-3 (Hassett 35*, Johnson 13*).

The match was scheduled for four days but completed in three. 12th Men: D.H.Fothergill (Vic) and J.E.Walsh (NSW).

CANTERBURY v OTAGO

Played at Lancaster Park, Christchurch, December 23, 25, 26, 27, 1939.

Match drawn. (Points: Canterbury 4, Otago 2)

CANTERBURY					
1	*J.L.Kerr	c Mills b Lemin	0	c Mills b Lemin	4
2	M.P.Donnelly	c Mills b Begg	104	not out	20
3	F.P.O'Brien	c Monteath b Lemin	65	c Robertson b Lemin	0
4	W.A.Hadlee	c Mills b Lemin	58	not out	12
5	I.B.Cromb	c Mills b Lemin	1		
6	R.E.J.Menzies	c Chettleburgh b Robertson	14		
7	W.M.Anderson	not out	70		
8	A.W.Roberts	lbw b Robertson	10		
9	D.A.N.McRae	c Fraser b Moloney	15		
10	†R.C.Webb	run out	12		
11	H.Davis	b Lemin	20		
	Extras	b 4, lb 1	5		
			374	(2 wickets)	36

FoW (1): 1-3 (1), 2-140 (3), 3-208 (2), 4-213 (5), 5-238 (6), 6-256 (4), 7-273 (8), 8-304 (9), 9-331 (10), 10-374 (11)
FoW (2): 1-4 (1), 2-12 (3)

OTAGO			
1	G.J.Robertson	not out	83
2	V.J.T.Chettleburgh	c Webb b Davis	3
3	A.S.H.Cutler	c Kerr b McRae	13
4	*D.A.R.Moloney	b Davis	15
5	C.J.Elmes	st Webb b Cromb	16
6	A.P.J.Monteath	c Davis b McRae	12
7	T.C.Fraser	b McRae	47
8	†G.H.Mills	b Cromb	7
9	G.G.McGregor	b McRae	8
10	N.C.Begg	c McRae b Roberts	16
11	T.G.F.Lemin	b Roberts	6
	Extras	b 19, lb 4	23
			249

FoW (1): 1-15 (2), 2-45 (3), 3-49 (4), 4-68 (5), 5-80 (6), 6-168 (7), 7-195 (8), 8-206 (9), 9-227 (10), 10-249 (11)

Otago Bowling	O	M	R	W		O	M	R	W
Begg	10	3	52	1	(2)	2	0	14	0
Lemin	19.4	2	96	5	(1)	3	1	14	2
Moloney	18	0	85	1					
Robertson	17	1	87	2					
Elmes	3	0	34	0	(3)	1	0	8	0
Chettleburgh	2	0	15	0					

Canterbury Bowling	O	M	R	W
Davis	22	4	64	2
Roberts	15.4	2	35	2
McRae	23	5	58	4
Cromb	15	4	54	2
Donnelly	4	0	15	0

Umpires: T.W.Burgess and J.McGuinness. Toss: Canterbury

Close of Play: 1st day: Otago (1) 68-4 (Monteath 6*); 2nd day: Canterbury (2) 36-2 (Donnelly 20*, Hadlee 12*); 3rd day: No play.

There was no play on the final day. M.P.Donnelly's 104 took 150 minutes and included 12 fours. G.J.Robertson retired hurt with severe cramp in the Otago first innings having scored 10 (team had lost 1 wicket) - he returned when the score was 68-4.

EASTERN PROVINCE v GRIQUALAND WEST

Played at St George's Park, Port Elizabeth, December 23, 26, 1939.

Eastern Province won by nine wickets.

GRIQUALAND WEST					
1	*T.H.Boggan	b Leibbrandt	27	b Thwaits	40
2	S.Nicholls	c Leibbrandt b Lynch	0	b B.A.Smith	5
3	A.P.C.Steyn	b Lynch	10	b Hoskin	62
4	L.E.McNamara	b B.A.Smith	2	(7) st Marais b Hoskin	0
5	S.S.Smith	c Lynch b Leibbrandt	0	(6) c and b Hoskin	4
6	F.F.Flanagan	c Thwaits b Hartman	37	(5) c B.A.Smith b Hoskin	1
7	†A.Schultze	lbw b Hartman	34	(4) b Thwaits	4
8	J.Pickup	not out	33	not out	16
9	J.E.Waddington	b Thwaits	10	(10) b Southey	1
10	S.J.Evert	c Hartman b Thwaits	16	(11) c Marais b Southey	10
11	A.Waddington	c Marais b Hartman	0	(9) st Marais b Southey	6
	Extras	b 23, lb 6, w 1, nb 1	31	b 3, lb 1	4
			200		153

FoW (1): 1-2 (2), 2-22 (3), 3-25 (4), 4-41, 5-41, 6-123, 7-124, 8-164, 9-200, 10-200
FoW (2): 1-5 (2), 2-92, 3-100, 4-105, 5-113, 6-113, 7-122, 8-123, 9-141, 10-153

EASTERN PROVINCE					
1	†W.Marais	run out	15	c McNamara b A.Waddington	0
2	G.Hartman	c Schultze b Flanagan	1	not out	9
3	I.E.Drimmie	b J.E.Waddington	12	not out	20
4	F.W.R.Southey	b McNamara	17		
5	D.E.Dimbleby	st Schultze b A.Waddington	90		
6	J.M.Leibbrandt	c Steyn b A.Waddington	63		
7	W.C.Hoskin	b A.Waddington	32		
8	*C.S.Smith	c Steyn b A.Waddington	54		
9	B.C.Lynch	st Schultze b McNamara	15		
10	S.A.Thwaits	b McNamara	2		
11	B.A.Smith	not out	10		
	Extras	b 9, lb 5	14	w 1	1
			325	(1 wicket)	30

FoW (1): 1-4 (2), 2-27, 3-32, 4-72, 5-205, 6-209, 7-253, 8-290, 9-304, 10-325
FoW (2): 1-0 (1)

Eastern Province Bowling	O	M	R	W		O	M	R	W
B.A.Smith	13	0	40	1		8	2	21	1
Lynch	19	3	39	2		14	5	33	0
Leibbrandt	17	3	45	2		6	1	16	0
Thwaits	12	1	32	2	(5)	8	1	29	2
Hartman	8.5	4	13	3	(4)	4	0	8	0
Hoskin					(6)	8	1	30	4
Southey					(7)	4.1	1	12	3

Griqualand West Bowling	O	M	R	W	O	M	R	W
A.Waddington	32.6	7	98	4	4	2	5	1
Flanagan	4	1	10	1	2	0	14	0
J.E.Waddington	38	6	103	1	2	0	10	0
McNamara	18	0	74	3				
Evert	2	0	10	0				
Pickup	8	1	16	0				

Umpires: E.Coulridge and H.V.Dorrington. Toss: Griqualand West

Close of Play: 1st day: Eastern Province (1) 178-4 (Dimbleby 74*, Leibbrandt 55*).

The match was scheduled for three days but completed in two.

TRANSVAAL v NATAL

Played at Old Wanderers, Johannesburg, December 23, 26, 27, 1939.

Transvaal won by an innings and 168 runs.

NATAL					
1	D.R.Fell	c Mitchell b Newson	1	c and b Petersen	20
2	R.C.Collins	c Mitchell b Gordon	22	c Mitchell b Newson	2
3	R.L.Harvey	b Pickerill	3	c and b Newson	1
4	*A.D.Nourse	c Langton b Gordon	13	c E.A.B.Rowan b A.M.B.Rowan	57
5	†R.R.Yuill	b Gordon	40	b Gordon	4
6	O.C.Dawson	b Gordon	4	c Langton b Mitchell	129
7	J.R.Ellis	c Mitchell b Gordon	0	c A.M.B.Rowan b Gordon	62
8	R.Howden	b Gordon	18	b Gordon	0
9	C.J.Lowell	c Langton b Mitchell	25	st Grieveson b Mitchell	3
10	G.B.Law	not out	11	c Newson b Mitchell	2
11	N.B.F.Mann	b Langton	5	not out	5
	Extras	lb 5	5		8
			147		293

FoW (1): 1-10 (1), 2-13 (3), 3-37, 4-42, 5-48, 6-48, 7-72, 8-115, 9-138, 10-147
FoW (2): 1-5 (2), 2-19 (3), 3-31 (1), 4-47 (5), 5-117 (4), 6-267 (7), 7-267 (8), 8-287, 9-288, 10-293

TRANSVAAL			
1	S.H.Curnow	lbw b Dawson	135
2	E.A.B.Rowan	not out	306
3	*B.Mitchell	c Collins b Mann	24
4	A.W.Briscoe	st Yuill b Law	1
5	†R.E.Grieveson	b Mann	43
6	A.C.B.Langton	c Fell b Law	52
7	E.S.Newson	b Dawson	16
8	A.M.B.Rowan	not out	16
9	J.H.M.Pickerill		
10	N.Gordon		
11	R.N.E.Petersen		
	Extras		15
		(6 wickets, declared)	608

FoW (1): 1-221 (1), 2-296 (3), 3-299 (4), 4-389 (5), 5-529 (6), 6-548 (7)

Transvaal Bowling	O	M	R	W		O	M	R	W
Newson	5	3	8	1		11	1	44	2
Pickerill	6	0	11	1		6	0	19	0
Gordon	15	2	61	6	(5)	22	3	86	3
Langton	9.2	3	27	1	(3)	8	2	18	0
Mitchell	4	0	35	1	(7)	4.2	0	15	3
Petersen					(4)	12	2	38	1
A.M.B.Rowan					(6)	14	0	65	1

Natal Bowling	O	M	R	W
Law	33	0	171	2
Dawson	26	4	98	2
Mann	45	14	104	2
Lowell	13	0	96	0
Howden	5	0	27	0
Harvey	11	0	83	0
Ellis	1	0	14	0

Umpires: Toss:

Close of Play: 1st day: Transvaal (1) 296-2 (E.A.B.Rowan 128*); 2nd day: Natal (2) 198-5 (Dawson 76*, Ellis 31*).

S.H.Curnow's 135 took 189 minutes and included 18 fours and 1 six. E.A.B.Rowan's 306 took 462 minutes and included 28 fours and 1 six. O.C.Dawson's 129 took 237 minutes and included 14 fours.

WELLINGTON v AUCKLAND

Played at Basin Reserve, Wellington, December 23, 25, 26, 27, 1939.

Match drawn. (Points: Wellington 4, Auckland 2)

	AUCKLAND				
1	P.E.Whitelaw	c Wilson b Pritchard	2	lbw b Ashenden	0
2	H.T.Pearson	b Ashenden	6	b Pritchard	53
3	V.S.Sale	c Tindill b Lamason	14	b Pritchard	97
4	*W.M.Wallace	c du Chateau b Lamason	47	c McLeod b Pritchard	7
5	G.L.Weir	b Pritchard	10	b Pritchard	50
6	V.J.Scott	c Ashenden b Lamason	7	c Wilson b Ashenden	11
7	A.M.Matheson	c Wilson b Ashenden	8	b Ashenden	0
8	C.Burke	c Tindill b Pritchard	3	b Pritchard	5
9	†J.A.R.Blandford	not out	14	c Pritchard b Ashenden	11
10	D.C.Cleverley	c Tindill b Pritchard	2	not out	8
11	J.Cowie	run out	0	b Pritchard	24
	Extras	b 6, lb 9, w 2, nb 4	21	b 3, lb 4, w 1, nb 2	10
			134		276

FoW (1): 1-8 (1), 2-12 (2), 3-69 (3), 4-76 (4), 5-87 (5), 6-92 (6), 7-99 (8), 8-107 (7), 9-129 (10), 10-134 (11)
FoW (2): 1-1 (1), 2-147 (2), 3-161 (3), 4-178 (4), 5-222 (6), 6-222 (7), 7-232 (8), 8-238 (5), 9-246 (9), 10-276 (11)

	WELLINGTON				
1	V.H.du Chateau	c Cowie b Weir	19	(2) b Cowie	4
2	W.F.T.Hepburn	b Cleverley	26	(1) c Wallace b Weir	55
3	W.G.Rainbird	lbw b Cleverley	17	(4) run out	6
4	†E.W.T.Tindill	lbw b Weir	1	(3) c Matheson b Weir	29
5	J.A.Ongley	b Weir	1	c Matheson b Cowie	17
6	J.R.Lamason	c Pearson b Cleverley	25	b Cleverley	0
7	W.F.Airey	b Cleverley	11	c Cleverley b Weir	5
8	*E.G.McLeod	not out	20	not out	13
9	D.S.Wilson	c Blandford b Matheson	12	not out	23
10	T.L.Pritchard	c Wallace b Matheson	20		
11	J.G.Ashenden	c Cleverley b Cowie	0		
	Extras	b 7, lb 1, nb 4	12	b 5, lb 6	11
			164	(7 wickets)	163

FoW (1): 1-44 (2), 2-53 (1), 3-55 (4), 4-61 (5), 5-93 (3), 6-102 (6), 7-110 (7), 8-131 (9), 9-160 (10), 10-164 (11)
FoW (2): 1-19 (2), 2-86 (3), 3-97 (1), 4-111 (4), 5-111 (6), 6-122 (7), 7-128 (5)

Wellington Bowling	O	M	R	W			O	M	R	W	
Pritchard	13.7	0	45	4	1w,3nb		21.4	2	66	6	1w,4nb
Ashenden	8	1	29	2			19	4	83	4	
Lamason	6	1	24	3	1w	(5)	10	3	55	0	
Wilson	3	1	15	0		(3)	16	2	45	0	
McLeod						(4)	5	2	17	0	

Auckland Bowling	O	M	R	W		O	M	R	W
Cowie	7.1	0	35	1		12	2	37	2
Matheson	10	0	39	2	2nb	11	3	22	0
Cleverley	14	2	45	4	3nb	16	4	47	1
Weir	10	2	33	3		17	8	30	3
Burke	1	1	0	0		4	0	16	0

Umpires: C.W.Moore and J.B.Watson. Toss: Auckland

Close of Play: 1st day: Auckland (2) 18-1 (Pearson not out, Sale not out); 2nd day: Auckland (2) 254-9 (Cleverley 4*, Cowie 6*); 3rd day: Wellington (2) 163-7 (McLeod 13*, Wilson 23*).

There was no play on the final day.

ORANGE FREE STATE v BORDER

Played at South African Railways Club Old Ground, Bloemfontein, December 26, 27, 1939.

Border won by 191 runs.

BORDER					
1	F.Davidson	lbw b Tuckett	4	(2) lbw b Papenfus	3
2	†G.G.L.Mandy	b Papenfus	16	(1) lbw b Fraser	32
3	R.P.Richter	b Papenfus	10	b Papenfus	7
4	*S.L.White	c Griffiths b Papenfus	21	b Tuckett	29
5	R.R.Phillips	c and b Fraser	29	c Griffiths b Papenfus	42
6	G.V.Wienand	lbw b Hayward	32	b Tuckett	0
7	E.C.Holmes	c Hayward b Wright	16	lbw b Fraser	8
8	P.S.Hubbard	not out	17	c Griffiths b Hayward	17
9	D.W.Niland	b Fraser	10	b Wright	20
10	R.Beesly	c Francis b Papenfus	19	b Hayward	20
11	M.A.Hanley	b Papenfus	1	not out	8
	Extras	b 5, lb 10	15		14
			190		200

FoW (1): 1-10 (1), 2-35, 3-36, 4-87, 5-109, 6-140, 7-140, 8-155, 9-181, 10-190
FoW (2): 1-4, 2-19, 3-63, 4-97, 5-97, 6-112, 7-132, 8-159, 9-184, 10-200

ORANGE FREE STATE					
1	C.J.Kaplan	run out	22	(2) c Hubbard b Beesly	2
2	*E.W.Warner	b Niland	8	(1) run out	37
3	H.F.Wright	c Mandy b Beesly	12	b Niland	6
4	M.G.Francis	b Wienand	3	lbw b Wienand	13
5	L.Mendelsohn	b Hubbard	22	b Hubbard	11
6	W.Wilkinson	b Wienand	1	b Wienand	9
7	K.Hayward	b Wienand	8	st Mandy b Hubbard	5
8	L.Tuckett	lbw b Hubbard	5	c White b Hanley	4
9	†F.Griffiths	c Mandy b Hubbard	0	c Niland b Hanley	1
10	T.W.Fraser	b Hubbard	3	not out	4
11	C.F.B.Papenfus	not out	1	b Hubbard	1
	Extras	b 2, lb 1	3	b 10, lb 8	18
			88		111

FoW (1): 1-9 (2), 2-38 (3), 3-45 (4), 4-47 (1), 5-50 (6), 6-66 (7), 7-76 (8), 8-79 (9), 9-85 (5), 10-88 (10)
FoW (2): 1-8, 2-23, 3-47, 4-72, 5-91, 6-95, 7-102, 8-106, 9-106, 10-111

Orange Free State Bowling	O	M	R	W		O	M	R	W
Tuckett	15	1	33	1	(2)	12	0	45	2
Papenfus	15	2	39	5	(1)	15	3	63	3
Fraser	15	1	61	2		11	2	48	2
Hayward	7	1	24	1		3.4	0	21	2
Wright	5	1	18	1		4	0	9	1

Border Bowling	O	M	R	W		O	M	R	W
Beesly	6	0	21	1	(2)	6	0	28	1
Niland	9	1	28	1	(1)	7	1	24	1
Hanley	3	0	10	0	(5)	3	0	8	2
Wienand	9	2	18	3	(3)	8	1	13	2
Hubbard	3.1	1	8	4	(4)	8.1	0	20	3

Umpires: Toss: Orange Free State

Close of Play: 1st day: Orange Free State (1) 88 all out.

The match was scheduled for three days but completed in two.

WESTERN PROVINCE v NORTH EASTERN TRANSVAAL

Played at Newlands, Cape Town, December 26, 27, 28, 1939.

Western Province won by seven wickets.

WESTERN PROVINCE					
1	*P.G.V.van der Bijl	c Edwards b Brown	3	c Edwards b Brown	6
2	S.Kiel	c Bromham b Brown	12	not out	139
3	L.M.Manning	lbw b Brown	11	lbw b Dowling	25
4	G.Georgeu	c Bromham b Bock	154	c Edwards b Bock	3
5	A.R.M.Ralph	c Bromham b Brown	0	not out	53
6	J.E.Cheetham	c Bromham b Bock	11		
7	L.C.G.Whiteing	c Dowling b Bock	4		
8	L.S.Eckard	c Dowling b Lance	25		
9	†A.B.J.Reid	c Bromham b Bock	81		
10	D.Price	c Bromham b Henderson	22		
11	J.B.Plimsoll	not out	8		
	Extras	lb 6, nb 2	8	b 3, lb 4, nb 2	9
			339	(3 wickets)	235

FoW (1): 1-13 (1), 2-18 (2), 3-35 (3), 4-35 (5), 5-81 (6), 6-99 (7), 7-156 (8), 8-274 (4), 9-321 (10), 10-339 (9)
FoW (2): 1-11 (1), 2-83 (3), 3-94 (4)

NORTH EASTERN TRANSVAAL					
1	D.G.Helfrich	c Reid b Eckard	59	b Plimsoll	59
2	R.C.Hicks	c Georgeu b Price	2	c sub (G.E.Crighton) b Plimsoll	108
3	R.A.Edwards	c Manning b Price	7	(4) b Eckard	27
4	L.O.Waller	lbw b Price	14	(5) c Kiel b Cheetham	65
5	D.F.Dowling	c Ralph b Plimsoll	10	(3) b Plimsoll	0
6	*R.S.Martin	c Reid b Eckard	36	run out	37
7	†C.G.Bromham	c Reid b Price	23	st Reid b Eckard	32
8	L.S.Brown	b Eckard	0	c Ralph b Eckard	38
9	W.A.Henderson	c van der Bijl b Eckard	1	b Eckard	0
10	W.P.Lance	not out	1	(11) not out	5
11	E.G.Bock	b Eckard	0	(10) b Plimsoll	27
	Extras	b 7, lb 4	11	b 2, lb 8	10
			164		408

FoW (1): 1-10 (2), 2-23 (3), 3-76 (4), 4-91 (1), 5-110 (5), 6-158 (6), 7-158 (8), 8-162 (9), 9-162 (7), 10-164 (11)
FoW (2): 1-139 (1), 2-139 (3), 3-188 (2), 4-197 (4), 5-266 (6), 6-323 (5), 7-353 (7), 8-367 (9), 9-402 (10), 10-408 (8)

North Eastern Transvaal Bowling	O	M	R	W		O	M	R	W
Lance	23	4	80	1		9	1	25	0
Brown	18	5	57	4		12	0	55	1
Henderson	15	0	75	1		6	0	36	0
Bock	13.4	1	67	4		11	1	56	1
Dowling	3	0	24	0		7	0	24	1
Waller	1	0	5	0	(7)	1.5	0	16	0
Helfrich	4	0	23	0					
Martin					(6)	2	0	14	0

Western Province Bowling	O	M	R	W		O	M	R	W
Plimsoll	12	2	30	1		31	4	83	4
Price	20	7	40	4		19	2	68	0
Eckard	19.7	5	43	5		31.1	6	107	4
Cheetham	7	0	40	0	(6)	16	0	98	1
Georgeu					(4)	4	0	26	0
van der Bijl					(5)	5	1	14	0
Whiteing					(7)	1	0	2	0

Umpires: S.Collins and G.L.Sickler. Toss: Western Province
Close of Play: 1st day: North Eastern Transvaal (1) 97-4 (Dowling 3*, Martin 5*); 2nd day: North Eastern Transvaal (2) 245-4 (Waller 22*, Martin 26*).
G.Georgeu's 154 took 196 minutes and included 15 fours. R.C.Hicks's 108 took 180 minutes and included 11 fours. S.Kiel's 139 took 160 minutes and included 14 fours.

NEW SOUTH WALES v QUEENSLAND

Played at Sydney Cricket Ground, December 29, 30, 1939.

New South Wales won by an innings and 130 runs. (Points: New South Wales 5, Queensland 0)

QUEENSLAND

1	*W.A.Brown	c Chipperfield b Lush	24	(4) c Mudge b O'Reilly	14
2	G.G.Cook	lbw b O'Reilly	15	(3) c Sismey b Pepper	3
3	T.Allen	b O'Reilly	2	(2) lbw b Pepper	17
4	R.E.Rogers	c Sismey b O'Reilly	18	(1) b Cheetham	18
5	G.G.Baker	run out (Lush)	10	c Mudge b O'Reilly	51
6	†D.Tallon	b O'Reilly	16	c Solomon b O'Reilly	0
7	D.Watt	b O'Reilly	0	b O'Reilly	6
8	L.W.T.Tallon	b O'Reilly	3	(9) c Lush b O'Reilly	0
9	C.P.Christ	not out	5	(8) b Walsh	9
10	P.L.Dixon	b O'Reilly	2	c Mudge b O'Reilly	7
11	J.A.Ellis	b O'Reilly	2	not out	4
	Extras	b 7, nb 1	8	b 9, lb 4, nb 2	15
			105		144

FoW (1): 1-37 (1), 2-44 (2), 3-51 (3), 4-76 (4), 5-82 (5), 6-82 (7), 7-94 (8), 8-101 (6), 9-103 (10), 10-105 (11)
FoW (2): 1-31 (1), 2-47 (3), 3-48 (2), 4-104 (4), 5-104 (6), 6-116 (5), 7-125 (7), 8-125 (9), 9-140 (8), 10-144 (10)

NEW SOUTH WALES

1	*S.J.McCabe	c Brown b Ellis	13
2	H.Mudge	lbw b Baker	79
3	C.M.Solomon	b Dixon	24
4	S.G.Barnes	c Ellis b Baker	119
5	A.G.Chipperfield	b Cook	10
6	A.G.Cheetham	st D.Tallon b Christ	21
7	C.G.Pepper	st D.Tallon b Cook	8
8	J.G.Lush	b Ellis	54
9	W.J.O'Reilly	c and b Christ	26
10	†S.G.Sismey	c and b L.W.T.Tallon	5
11	J.E.Walsh	not out	10
	Extras	b 4, lb 5, nb 1	10
			379

FoW (1): 1-20 (1), 2-84 (3), 3-159 (2), 4-191 (5), 5-233 (6), 6-242 (7), 7-307 (4), 8-350 (9), 9-361 (10), 10-379 (8)

New South Wales Bowling

	O	M	R	W			O	M	R	W	
Lush	6	0	27	1			3	0	18	0	
Cheetham	4	1	10	0	1nb		5	0	18	1	2nb
Pepper	13	2	37	0		(4)	14	2	45	2	
O'Reilly	11.1	3	23	8		(3)	15.2	7	22	6	
Walsh						(5)	5	0	26	1	

Queensland Bowling

	O	M	R	W	
Ellis	16.3	0	60	2	1nb
Cook	12	0	67	2	
Baker	11	0	65	2	
Dixon	7	2	26	1	
L.W.T.Tallon	11	0	71	1	
Christ	12	0	53	2	
Watt	4	0	27	0	

Umpires: G.E.Borwick and R.McGrath. Toss: Queensland

Close of Play: 1st day: New South Wales (1) 240-5 (Barnes 78*, Pepper 7*).

The match was scheduled for four days but completed in two. S.G.Barnes's 119 took 159 minutes and included 13 fours. 12th Men: R.A.Saggers (NSW) and C.D.Hansen (Qld).

VICTORIA v SOUTH AUSTRALIA

Played at Melbourne Cricket Ground, December 29, 30, 1939, January 1, 2, 1940.

Match drawn. (Points: Victoria 1, South Australia 3)

VICTORIA					
1	I.S.Lee	b Klose	36	(7) c Grimmett b Ward	39
2	G.E.Tamblyn	c Walker b Ward	38	absent hurt	0
3	A.L.Hassett	st Walker b Grimmett	92	c and b Ward	66
4	K.R.Miller	c Bradman b Burton	108	c Bradman b Klose	1
5	I.W.G.Johnson	lbw b Waite	14	lbw b Klose	23
6	P.J.Beames	c and b Burton	104	b Burton	32
7	*†B.A.Barnett	b Burton	7	(1) lbw b Klose	46
8	M.W.Sievers	lbw b Burton	16	(2) c Badcock b Grimmett	36
9	D.T.Ring	st Walker b Grimmett	32	(8) not out	41
10	R.B.Scott	c Waite b Burton	7	(9) b Grimmett	17
11	L.O.Fleetwood-Smith	not out	11	(10) st Walker b Ward	4
	Extras	b 5, lb 5	10	b 5, lb 3	8
			475		313

FoW (1): 1-60 (1), 2-225 (3), 3-275 (4), 4-277 (5), 5-289 (7), 6-313 (8), 7-353 (2), 8-440 (9), 9-460 (6), 10-475 (10)
FoW (2): 1-74 (2), 2-96 (1), 3-102 (4), 4-178 (3), 5-178 (5), 6-239 (6), 7-261 (7), 8-298 (9), 9-313 (10)

SOUTH AUSTRALIA					
1	K.L.Ridings	c Johnson b Ring	56	not out	29
2	T.E.Klose	b Scott	54	lbw b Ring	15
3	*D.G.Bradman	c Johnson b Fleetwood-Smith	267		
4	C.L.Badcock	lbw b Ring	58		
5	R.A.Hamence	lbw b Fleetwood-Smith	20	(3) not out	11
6	R.S.Whitington	c Ring b Scott	41		
7	†C.W.Walker	lbw b Scott	1		
8	M.G.Waite	c Hassett b Ring	64		
9	F.A.Ward	c and b Ring	26		
10	C.V.Grimmett	c Sievers b Ring	6		
11	G.Burton	not out	1		
	Extras	b 6, lb 9, w 1	16	b 3, lb 1, nb 1	5
			610	(1 wicket)	60

FoW (1): 1-108 (1), 2-122 (2), 3-259 (4), 4-330 (5), 5-420 (6), 6-430 (7), 7-556 (3), 8-596 (8), 9-609 (9), 10-610 (10)
FoW (2): 1-36 (2)

South Australia Bowling	O	M	R	W			O	M	R	W	
Burton	20.2	0	99	5			11	1	44	1	
Waite	21	3	90	1			10	1	38	0	
Grimmett	33	2	136	2			21	2	78	2	
Klose	21	3	42	1			17	4	43	3	
Ward	19	0	98	1			14.4	2	102	3	

Victoria Bowling	O	M	R	W			O	M	R	W	
Scott	25	0	135	3	1w		3	0	9	0	
Sievers	29	1	120	0			3	0	12	0	
Ring	25.4	1	123	5		(4)	4	1	13	1	1nb
Fleetwood-Smith	27	0	156	2							
Johnson	13	0	60	0		(3)	5	2	14	0	
Hassett						(5)	1	0	7	0	

Umpires: A.N.Barlow and W.J.Craddock. Toss: Victoria

Close of Play: 1st day: Victoria (1) 289-5 (Beames 7*, Sievers 0*); 2nd day: South Australia (1) 213-2 (Bradman 52*, Badcock 41*); 3rd day: Victoria (2) 10-0 (Barnett 10*, Sievers 0*).

K.R.Miller's 108 took 169 minutes and included 7 fours. P.J.Beames's 104 took 143 minutes and included 8 fours. D.G.Bradman's 267 took 340 minutes and included 27 fours. G.E.Tamblyn retired hurt in the Victoria first innings having scored 21 (team score 64-1) - he returned when the score was 313-6. 12th Men: D.H.Fothergill (Vic) and P.L.Ridings (SA).

WELLINGTON v CANTERBURY

Played at Basin Reserve, Wellington, December 29, 30, 1939, January 1, 1940.

Canterbury won by an innings and 5 runs. (Points: Wellington 0, Canterbury 8)

WELLINGTON

1	V.H.du Chateau	c Davis b Cromb	25	c Anderson b Roberts	8
2	W.F.T.Hepburn	b Roberts	7	c Roberts b McRae	42
3	O.L.Wrigley	lbw b McRae	2	(4) c Harbridge b Roberts	12
4	†E.W.T.Tindill	c Anderson b Davis	69	(3) b Roberts	45
5	W.G.Rainbird	b Cromb	1	c Roberts b Davis	33
6	*E.G.McLeod	b Cromb	0	(8) not out	18
7	D.S.Wilson	c Davis b Roberts	10	(6) c Cromb b Donnelly	83
8	J.R.Lamason	c Roberts b Cromb	11	(9) b Davis	8
9	W.F.Airey	run out	28	(7) c Menzies b Roberts	13
10	T.L.Pritchard	not out	19	b Davis	0
11	J.G.Ashenden	b Cromb	13	b Donnelly	5
	Extras	b 3, lb 5, nb 2	10	b 13, lb 2	15
			195		282

FoW (1): 1-10 (2), 2-27 (3), 3-52 (1), 4-58 (5), 5-60 (6), 6-84 (7), 7-101 (8), 8-146 (9), 9-166 (4), 10-195 (11)
FoW (2): 1-18 (1), 2-94 (2), 3-112 (3), 4-113 (4), 5-190 (5), 6-218 (7), 7-262 (6), 8-275 (9), 9-277 (10), 10-282 (11)

CANTERBURY

1	*J.L.Kerr	c Lamason b Pritchard	0
2	M.P.Donnelly	c Tindill b Lamason	97
3	F.P.O'Brien	lbw b Lamason	81
4	W.A.Hadlee	b Pritchard	9
5	I.B.Cromb	run out	171
6	R.E.J.Menzies	c McLeod b Pritchard	28
7	W.M.Anderson	st Tindill b Ashenden	10
8	A.W.Roberts	c Hepburn b Ashenden	53
9	D.A.N.McRae	b Pritchard	8
10	†B.C.Harbridge	lbw b Ashenden	6
11	H.Davis	not out	3
	Extras	b 4, lb 9, nb 3	16
			482

FoW (1): 1-0 (1), 2-127 (3), 3-150 (4), 4-242 (2), 5-298 (6), 6-329 (7), 7-434 (8), 8-467 (5), 9-473 (9), 10-482 (10)

Canterbury Bowling

	O	M	R	W	O	M	R	W
Roberts	13	1	33	2	28	3	60	4
McRae	15	2	33	1	25	8	61	1
Davis	17	2	49	1	14	2	47	3
Cromb	22.3	3	66	5	17	3	56	0
Donnelly	2	0	4	0	12.5	3	43	2

Wellington Bowling

	O	M	R	W
Pritchard	33	4	118	4
Ashenden	25.6	2	127	3
Lamason	23	2	88	2
Wilson	17	0	75	0
McLeod	7	0	36	0
Hepburn	3	0	22	0

Umpires: W.A.Aldersley and J.B.Watson. Toss: Wellington

Close of Play: 1st day: Canterbury (1) 177-3 (Donnelly 68*, Cromb 11*); 2nd day: Wellington (2) 55-1 (Hepburn 27*, Tindill 16*).

The match was scheduled for four days but completed in three. I.B.Cromb's 171 included 7 fours.

AUCKLAND v OTAGO

Played at Eden Park, Auckland, December 30, 1939, January 1, 2, 1940.

Auckland won by an innings and 169 runs. (Points: Auckland 8, Otago 0)

	OTAGO				
1	G.J.Robertson	b Cowie	9	(2) b Cowie	17
2	V.J.T.Chettleburgh	b Matheson	1	absent hurt	0
3	A.S.H.Cutler	b Carson	51	c Blandford b Cowie	33
4	*D.A.R.Moloney	b Weir	4	b Cowie	6
5	C.J.Elmes	b Cowie	51	c Whitelaw b Burke	6
6	T.C.Fraser	b Carson	43	b Cowie	0
7	A.P.J.Monteath	lbw b Cowie	1	b Cowie	1
8	A.C.Holden	st Blandford b Burke	19	(1) c Blandford b Burke	36
9	†G.H.Mills	c Blandford b Carson	1	(8) b Cowie	11
10	N.C.Begg	run out	1	(9) not out	7
11	T.G.F.Lemin	not out	8	(10) c Scott b Burke	2
	Extras	b 2, lb 1, w 1, nb 1	5	b 12, lb 2	14
			194		133

FoW (1): 1-5 (2), 2-35 (1), 3-46 (4), 4-89 (3), 5-148, 6-150, 7-173, 8-175, 9-181, 10-194
FoW (2): 1-28 (2), 2-88 (3), 3-102, 4-108, 5-110, 6-110, 7-117, 8-130, 9-133

	AUCKLAND		
1	P.E.Whitelaw	lbw b Elmes	72
2	H.T.Pearson	st Mills b Elmes	50
3	V.S.Sale	c and b Robertson	23
4	*W.M.Wallace	lbw b Elmes	32
5	G.L.Weir	lbw b Moloney	49
6	W.N.Carson	c Fraser b Begg	12
7	V.J.Scott	c Elmes b Begg	100
8	A.M.Matheson	c and b Moloney	51
9	C.Burke	b Elmes	42
10	†J.A.R.Blandford	c Fraser b Elmes	36
11	J.Cowie	not out	2
	Extras	b 17, lb 6, w 1, nb 3	27
			496

FoW (1): 1-114 (1), 2-129 (2), 3-173 (3), 4-195 (4), 5-213 (6), 6-266 (5), 7-393, 8-425, 9-489, 10-496

Auckland Bowling	O	M	R	W		O	M	R	W
Cowie	15	1	36	3		21	2	44	6
Matheson	9	2	30	1	(3)	8	0	12	0
Weir	10	0	26	1	(5)	3	0	7	0
Burke	16.6	2	56	1	(2)	13.6	0	39	3
Carson	11	1	41	3	(4)	5	0	17	0

Otago Bowling	O	M	R	W
Lemin	13	1	62	0
Robertson	23	1	78	1
Begg	15	2	80	2
Elmes	45.3	10	133	5
Moloney	37	4	116	2

Umpires: O.R.Montgomery and R.H.Simmons. Toss: Otago

Close of Play: 1st day: Auckland (1) 144-2 (Sale 13*, Wallace 6*); 2nd day: Otago (2) 19-0 (Holden 7*, Robertson 10*).

The match was scheduled for four days but completed in three.

EASTERN PROVINCE v ORANGE FREE STATE

Played at St George's Park, Port Elizabeth, December 30, 1939, January 1, 2, 1940.

Orange Free State won by 226 runs.

ORANGE FREE STATE					
1	*E.W.Warner	c Lynch b Thwaits	16	lbw b Lynch	40
2	C.J.Kaplan	b Thwaits	77	b Lynch	48
3	J.C.Newton	run out	49	b Lynch	71
4	H.F.Wright	c Leibbrandt b Thwaits	5	b B.A.Smith	42
5	L.Mendelsohn	c B.A.Smith b Hartman	5	b Hartman	27
6	W.Wilkinson	b Thwaits	3	c Marais b Hartman	9
7	L.Tuckett	c and b Thwaits	11	not out	55
8	K.Hayward	c Robson b Thwaits	0	b Leibbrandt	41
9	†F.Griffiths	c Lynch b Thwaits	2		
10	T.W.Fraser	not out	9	(9) b Lynch	11
11	C.F.B.Papenfus	b Thwaits	1		
	Extras	b 11, lb 6, nb 1	18	b 10, lb 10, w 1	21
			196	(8 wickets, declared)	365

FoW (1): 1-60 (1), 2-151 (2), 3-156, 4-161, 5-173, 6-174, 7-174, 8-176, 9-194, 10-196
FoW (2): 1-99, 2-102, 3-207, 4-215, 5-237, 6-268, 7-347, 8-365

EASTERN PROVINCE					
1	G.Hartman	lbw b Papenfus	1	(7) c Papenfus b Fraser	8
2	†W.Marais	b Wright	69	c Kaplan b Fraser	34
3	I.E.Drimmie	b Papenfus	8	(8) c Tuckett b Fraser	1
4	R.W.Robson	b Tuckett	16	(3) b Papenfus	2
5	D.E.Dimbleby	lbw b Tuckett	2	(4) c Warner b Fraser	35
6	J.M.Leibbrandt	b Tuckett	4	(5) c Wright b Tuckett	0
7	W.C.Hoskin	b Tuckett	44	(6) b Fraser	13
8	B.C.Lynch	b Tuckett	14	(9) c Warner b Fraser	8
9	*C.S.Smith	lbw b Tuckett	15	(1) b Fraser	15
10	S.A.Thwaits	c Papenfus b Tuckett	12	c Tuckett b Fraser	3
11	B.A.Smith	not out	5	not out	7
	Extras	b 4, lb 9, w 1	14	b 3, lb 1, nb 1	5
			204		131

FoW (1): 1-1 (1), 2-21 (3), 3-70 (4), 4-78 (5), 5-98, 6-129, 7-151, 8-182, 9-191, 10-204
FoW (2): 1-23, 2-45, 3-68, 4-68, 5-69, 6-97, 7-110, 8-120, 9-120, 10-131

Eastern Province Bowling	O	M	R	W		O	M	R	W
B.A.Smith	10	1	29	0	(2)	20	3	67	1
Lynch	19	4	38	0	(1)	23.5	4	63	4
Leibbrandt	5	0	25	0	(4)	20	5	47	1
Thwaits	14.6	0	43	8	(5)	23	3	65	0
Hartman	12	3	27	1	(3)	13	2	43	2
Hoskin	3	1	16	0		9	0	42	0
Dimbleby					(7)	2	0	10	0
C.S.Smith					(8)	1	0	7	0

Orange Free State Bowling	O	M	R	W		O	M	R	W
Papenfus	9	3	30	2		17	6	21	1
Tuckett	25.1	2	74	7		11	0	29	1
Fraser	10	1	39	0		21	3	71	8
Hayward	16	5	44	0					
Wright	2	1	3	1	(4)	2	1	5	0

Umpires: E.Coulridge and H.L.Fielding. Toss: Orange Free State

Close of Play: 1st day: Eastern Province (1) 136-6 (Hoskin 4*, Lynch 6*); 2nd day: Orange Free State (2) 302-6 (Tuckett 26*, Hayward 23*).

NATAL v BORDER

Played at Kingsmead, Durban, December 30, 1939, January 1, 1940.

Natal won by six wickets.

BORDER

1	A.J.Lipke	c Harvey b Smith	4	(2) st Wade b Dawson	1
2	†G.G.L.Mandy	c Nourse b Dawson	0	(1) c Nourse b Smith	2
3	*S.L.White	c Nourse b Law	9	(5) b Smith	17
4	R.P.Richter	c Nourse b Smith	42	(3) c Wade b Dawson	5
5	R.R.Phillips	c Dawson b Harvey	61	(4) b Harvey	24
6	G.V.Wienand	c Fell b Law	31	lbw b Mann	52
7	P.S.Hubbard	b Harvey	9	c Turner b Mann	0
8	E.C.Holmes	c and b Harvey	11	not out	6
9	D.W.Niland	lbw b Harvey	0	b Smith	1
10	R.Beesly	not out	0	c Wade b Mann	1
11	M.A.Hanley	b Harvey	0	b Smith	3
	Extras		12		1
			179		113

FoW (1): 1-2 (2), 2-12 (1), 3-44 (3), 4-81, 5-151, 6-159, 7-176, 8-178, 9-179, 10-179
FoW (2): 1-3, 2-3, 3-15, 4-24, 5-102, 6-102, 7-102, 8-107, 9-110, 10-113

NATAL

1	D.R.Fell	c Phillips b Wienand	10	lbw b Niland	20
2	D.S.Turner	b Beesly	6	b Hanley	3
3	R.L.Harvey	b Wienand	6	c Mandy b Hanley	23
4	*A.D.Nourse	lbw b Wienand	19	b Hanley	66
5	†W.W.Wade	b Hanley	37	not out	32
6	O.C.Dawson	b Hanley	6	not out	9
7	R.R.Yuill	lbw b Wienand	1		
8	F.J.Smith	b Hanley	34		
9	G.B.Law	c Mandy b Niland	4		
10	N.B.F.Mann	lbw b Niland	2		
11	C.D.Lamble	not out	1		
	Extras		3		14
			129	(4 wickets)	167

FoW (1): 1-16 (1), 2-20 (2), 3-28 (3), 4-53 (4), 5-64 (6), 6-66 (7), 7-98 (5), 8-113 (9), 9-121 (10), 10-129 (8)
FoW (2): 1-21, 2-29, 3-88, 4-143

Natal Bowling

	O	M	R	W		O	M	R	W
Smith	14	3	41	2		14.3	4	39	4
Dawson	5	3	2	1		6	1	10	2
Lamble	9	2	46	0					
Law	13	4	32	2		4	0	25	0
Mann	11	3	25	0		10	3	15	3
Harvey	5.3	1	21	5	(3)	2	0	23	1

Border Bowling

	O	M	R	W		O	M	R	W
Niland	6	0	11	2		10.7	4	20	1
Beesly	7	2	17	1	(3)	8	1	37	0
Wienand	20	6	46	4	(4)	5	2	12	0
Hanley	17.3	4	46	3	(2)	22	2	71	3
Hubbard	1	0	6	0		4	0	13	0

Umpires: Toss: Border

Close of Play: 1st day: Natal (1) 91-6 (Wade 33*, Smith 8*).

The match was scheduled for three days but completed in two.

WESTERN PROVINCE v TRANSVAAL

Played at Newlands, Cape Town, December 30, 1939, January 1, 2, 1940.

Transvaal won by 12 runs.

TRANSVAAL					
1	S.H.Curnow	lbw b Eckard	31	run out	31
2	E.A.B.Rowan	c Eckard b Plimsoll	164	lbw b Plimsoll	12
3	J.T.Seccombe	b Price	1	b Price	35
4	*A.W.Briscoe	lbw b Price	8	c Plimsoll b Paull	4
5	†R.E.Somers Vine	run out (Price)	39	b Paull	4
6	O.E.Wynne	run out (Kiel/Paull)	71	c Reid b Plimsoll	16
7	A.M.B.Rowan	b Eckard	5	not out	71
8	J.H.M.Pickerill	lbw b Paull	13	c Georgeu b Price	44
9	R.N.E.Petersen	not out	30		
10	N.Gordon	st Reid b Paull	6		
11	J.G.Taylor	b Paull	4		
	Extras	b 4, lb 5, w 2	11	b 6, lb 2	8
			383	(7 wickets, declared)	225

FoW (1): 1-52 (1), 2-57 (3), 3-84 (4), 4-232 (5), 5-258 (2), 6-265 (7), 7-301 (8), 8-372 (6), 9-379 (10), 10-383 (11)
FoW (2): 1-25 (2), 2-66 (1), 3-75 (4), 4-85 (5), 5-95 (3), 6-132 (6), 7-225 (8)

WESTERN PROVINCE					
1	*P.G.V.van der Bijl	c Curnow b A.M.B.Rowan	33	b Gordon	89
2	S.Kiel	b Gordon	69	b Gordon	36
3	L.M.Manning	lbw b Taylor	33	b Petersen	2
4	G.Georgeu	c Pickerill b Gordon	1	lbw b Petersen	5
5	A.R.M.Ralph	not out	43	run out	140
6	W.C.Ross	c Somers Vine b Petersen	24	c Briscoe b Taylor	31
7	G.B.Paull	b Gordon	4	b Gordon	23
8	†A.B.J.Reid	b Gordon	2	(10) b A.M.B.Rowan	0
9	L.S.Eckard	b Gordon	7	(8) c Petersen b A.M.B.Rowan	1
10	D.Price	lbw b A.M.B.Rowan	5	(9) b A.M.B.Rowan	7
11	J.B.Plimsoll	c Gordon b A.M.B.Rowan	3	not out	6
	Extras	b 12, lb 3, nb 3	18	b 9, lb 4, w 1	14
			242		354

FoW (1): 1-73 (1), 2-134 (3), 3-137 (4), 4-144 (2), 5-180 (6), 6-195 (7), 7-203 (8), 8-215 (9), 9-234 (10), 10-242 (11)
FoW (2): 1-53 (2), 2-60 (3), 3-68 (4), 4-204 (1), 5-267 (6), 6-327 (7), 7-332 (8), 8-343 (9), 9-343 (10), 10-354 (5)

Western Province Bowling	O	M	R	W		O	M	R	W
Plimsoll	23	3	84	1		20	3	68	2
van der Bijl	1	0	4	0					
Price	21	4	94	2	(2)	15.6	2	65	2
Eckard	29	2	111	2	(3)	19	3	56	0
Paull	16.6	0	79	3	(4)	10	2	28	2

Transvaal Bowling	O	M	R	W		O	M	R	W
Pickerill	4	0	10	0	(2)	2	0	19	0
Petersen	8	4	11	1	(1)	18	1	77	2
Gordon	33	2	87	5		19.1	3	74	3
A.M.B.Rowan	17.5	3	53	3	(5)	23	3	96	3
Taylor	16	1	63	1	(4)	13	1	48	1
Wynne					(6)	4	0	26	0

Umpires: J.C.Niddrie and G.L.Sickler. Toss: Transvaal

Close of Play: 1st day: Western Province (1) 37-0 (van der Bijl 20*, Kiel 14*); 2nd day: Transvaal (2) 131-5 (Wynne 16*, A.M.B.Rowan 21*).

E.A.B.Rowan's 164 took 216 minutes and included 13 fours and 1 five. A.R.M.Ralph's 140 took 241 minutes and included 15 fours.

AUCKLAND v CANTERBURY

Played at Eden Park, Auckland, January 5, 6, 8, 9, 1940.

Auckland won by an innings and 140 runs. (Points: Auckland 8, Canterbury 0)

CANTERBURY					
1	*J.L.Kerr	b Burke	28	b Cowie	3
2	M.P.Donnelly	b Cowie	3	c and b Burke	78
3	F.P.O'Brien	c Blandford b Cowie	12	b Cleverley	86
4	W.A.Hadlee	b Cleverley	35	c Weir b Carson	23
5	I.B.Cromb	b Cleverley	51	c Blandford b Carson	15
6	R.E.J.Menzies	b Cleverley	9	(7) c Whitelaw b Burke	29
7	W.M.Anderson	c and b Burke	25	(8) st Blandford b Cleverley	2
8	A.W.Roberts	c Wallace b Cleverley	30	(9) b Cleverley	18
9	†V.James	b Cowie	4	(10) not out	2
10	D.A.N.McRae	b Cleverley	5	(11) b Cleverley	0
11	H.Davis	not out	2	(6) c Weir b Burke	33
	Extras	b 14, lb 9	23	b 31, lb 5, nb 1	37
			227		326

FoW (1): 1-3 (2), 2-25 (3), 3-68 (1), 4-100, 5-120, 6-173, 7-193, 8-216, 9-217, 10-227
FoW (2): 1-22, 2-181, 3-187, 4-216, 5-227, 6-278, 7-281, 8-325, 9-326, 10-326

AUCKLAND			
1	P.E.Whitelaw	b McRae	4
2	H.T.Pearson	c James b Davis	43
3	V.S.Sale	b McRae	0
4	*W.M.Wallace	st James b Donnelly	211
5	G.L.Weir	c James b Donnelly	73
6	W.N.Carson	c Roberts b Cromb	26
7	V.J.Scott	c and b Davis	198
8	C.Burke	run out	33
9	†J.A.R.Blandford	not out	58
10	D.C.Cleverley	c McRae b Davis	8
11	J.Cowie	not out	5
	Extras	b 14, lb 19, w 1	34
		(9 wickets, declared)	693

FoW (1): 1-7 (1), 2-9 (3), 3-116 (2), 4-276 (5), 5-334 (4), 6-389 (6), 7-503 (8), 8-646 (7), 9-683 (10)

Auckland Bowling	O	M	R	W	O	M	R	W
Cowie	22	4	54	3	23	6	70	1
Cleverley	21.4	2	67	5	27	1	94	4
Weir	13	4	23	0	3	1	11	0
Carson	5	1	14	0	7	0	31	2
Burke	14	3	46	2	32	4	83	3

Canterbury Bowling	O	M	R	W
Roberts	12	0	52	0
McRae	46	9	168	2
Davis	28	3	113	3
Cromb	21	0	107	1
Donnelly	42	6	145	2
O'Brien	7	0	38	0
Anderson	7	0	36	0

Umpires: R.W.Mitchell and O.R.Montgomery. Toss: Canterbury

Close of Play: 1st day: Auckland (1) 50-2 (Pearson 18*, Wallace 23*); 2nd day: Auckland (1) 545-7 (Scott 134*, Blandford 2*); 3rd day: Canterbury (2) 235-5 (Davis 8*, Menzies 2*).

W.M.Wallace's 211 took 292 minutes and included 16 fours and 3 sixes.

GRIQUALAND WEST v TRANSVAAL

Played at De Beers Stadium, Kimberley, January 5, 6, 1940.

Transvaal won by eight wickets.

GRIQUALAND WEST					
1	F.W.Whelan	b A.M.B.Rowan	35	(2) c Briscoe b Petersen	17
2	*T.H.Boggan	c Somers Vine b Gordon	14	(5) b Gordon	0
3	F.Nicholson	c A.M.B.Rowan b Taylor	8	lbw b Gordon	0
4	†A.P.C.Steyn	b A.M.B.Rowan	15	b Petersen	2
5	A.Dunn	c Pickerill b A.M.B.Rowan	0	(1) c Seccombe b Petersen	3
6	F.F.Flanagan	lbw b Taylor	0	lbw b Gordon	7
7	L.E.McNamara	c and b A.M.B.Rowan	54	b Gordon	0
8	J.P.McNally	b Gordon	4	c E.A.B.Rowan b A.M.B.Rowan	12
9	J.E.Waddington	c Wynne b Gordon	0	c and b A.M.B.Rowan	11
10	J.W.Robinson	not out	1	c and b A.M.B.Rowan	2
11	F.Cotty	run out	2	not out	3
	Extras		23		11
			156		68

FoW (1): 1-21 (2), 2-57, 3-77, 4-77, 5-80, 6-140, 7-151, 8-153, 9-156, 10-156
FoW (2): 1-3, 2-4, 3-11, 4-14, 5-33, 6-34, 7-34, 8-59, 9-64, 10-68

TRANSVAAL					
1	S.H.Curnow	c Boggan b Dunn	5	c Steyn b Waddington	16
2	E.A.B.Rowan	lbw b McNally	20		
3	†R.E.Somers Vine	c Dunn b McNally	90	not out	8
4	J.T.Seccombe	lbw b Waddington	17	(2) lbw b McNally	17
5	*A.W.Briscoe	hit wkt b Cotty	5		
6	O.E.Wynne	b McNamara	20	(4) not out	0
7	A.M.B.Rowan	b McNamara	6		
8	J.H.M.Pickerill	b McNamara	1		
9	R.N.E.Petersen	c McNamara b McNally	1		
10	N.Gordon	not out	4		
11	J.G.Taylor	b McNamara	0		
	Extras		7		8
			176	(2 wickets)	49

FoW (1): 1-23 (1), 2-44 (2), 3-96 (4), 4-111 (5), 5-156, 6-170, 7-170, 8-172, 9-175, 10-176
FoW (2): 1-41, 2-47

Transvaal Bowling	O	M	R	W		O	M	R	W
Pickerill	1	0	3	0					
Gordon	9	3	20	3		11	3	21	4
Petersen	2	1	6	0	(1)	9	2	26	3
A.M.B.Rowan	14.6	2	56	4	(3)	2.3	0	10	3
Taylor	8	0	48	2					

Griqualand West Bowling	O	M	R	W		O	M	R	W
Robinson	3	0	14	0		4	0	9	0
Dunn	3	1	26	1					
Waddington	13	1	38	1	(2)	5	1	10	1
McNally	14	2	46	3	(3)	3.2	0	15	1
McNamara	5.5	1	12	4					
Cotty	5	0	33	1					
Flanagan					(4)	2	0	7	0

Umpires: Toss:

Close of Play: 1st day: Griqualand West (2) 29-4 (Whelan 16*, Flanagan 7*).

The match was scheduled for three days but completed in two.

MAHARASHTRA v WESTERN INDIA

Played at Poona Club Ground, January 6, 7, 8, 1940.

Match drawn.

MAHARASHTRA					
1	K.V.Bhandarkar	lbw b Saeed Ahmed	27	c Rathod b Nyalchand	31
2	S.W.Sohoni	c Gandhi b Manavadar	31	retired out	109
3	S.Nazir Ali	c Barritt b Akbar Khan	62		
4	N.D.Nagarwala	lbw b Akbar Khan	10	(5) c Faiz Ahmed b Sukhvantrai	24
5	V.S.Hazare	c Faiz Ahmed b Manavadar	40		
6	*D.B.Deodhar	not out	157		
7	K.M.Rangnekar	c Faiz Ahmed b Rathod	102	not out	17
8	J.G.Harris	lbw b Nyalchand	58		
9	Raja of Jath	c Akbar Khan b Rathod	23	(3) c and b Nyalchand	2
10	†D.S.Doctor	not out	20	(6) not out	16
11	M.K.Patwardhan			(4) c Sukhvantrai b Faiz Ahmed	25
	Extras		13		3
		(8 wickets, declared)	543	(5 wickets, declared)	227

FoW (1): 1-36 (1), 2-98 (2), 3-111 (4), 4-166 (3), 5-178 (5), 6-328 (7), 7-435 (8), 8-497 (9)
FoW (2): 1-48 (1), 2-52 (3), 3-106 (4), 4-187, 5-198

WESTERN INDIA					
1	†Faiz Ahmed	lbw b Harris	61		
2	H.W.Barritt	lbw b Hazare	13	st Bhandarkar b Jath	28
3	Umar Khan	b Hazare	4	(1) lbw b Rangnekar	9
4	R.P.Rathod	b Hazare	1		
5	Nawab of Manavadar	b Hazare	59	c sub b Jath	4
6	*K.S.Abdul Khaliq	b Sohoni	17		
7	Saeed Ahmed	c Doctor b Hazare	15		
8	Sukhvantrai	b Hazare	3	(6) not out	0
9	Akbar Khan	b Patwardhan	56	(3) c Bhandarkar b Rangnekar	0
10	S.B.Gandhi	c Harris b Hazare	53	(4) not out	33
11	S.Nyalchand	not out	2		
	Extras		22		10
			306	(4 wickets)	84

FoW (1): 1-36 (2), 2-52 (3), 3-54 (4), 4-118 (1), 5-164 (6), 6-184 (5), 7-191 (7), 8-192 (8), 9-298 (9), 10-306 (10)
FoW (2): 1-20 (1), 2-24 (3), 3-76 (2), 4-80 (5)

Western India Bowling	O	M	R	W		O	M	R	W
Saeed Ahmed	45	0	114	1		1	0	5	0
Manavadar	23	2	86	2					
Gandhi	30	3	100	0					
Akbar Khan	33	7	83	2					
Nyalchand	14	5	41	1	(3)	10	1	28	2
Rathod	28	2	106	2					
Faiz Ahmed					(2)	19	2	73	1
Umar Khan					(4)	6	0	37	0
Barritt					(5)	7	0	48	0
Sukhvantrai					(6)	5	0	33	1

Maharashtra Bowling	O	M	R	W		O	M	R	W
Patwardhan	22	6	61	1					
Sohoni	10	2	39	1					
Hazare	45.4	13	94	7	(2)	2	0	7	0
Harris	27	9	39	1					
Jath	15	2	51	0	(4)	5	0	18	2
Rangnekar					(1)	8	2	28	2
Nazir Ali					(3)	5	2	8	0
Deodhar					(5)	4	0	13	0

Umpires: Toss: Maharashtra

Close of Play: 1st day: Maharashtra (1) 361-6 (Deodhar 66*, Harris 11*); 2nd day: Western India (1) 170-5 (Manavadar 55*, Saeed Ahmed 5*).

K.M.Rangnekar's 102 took 98 minutes and included 12 fours. S.W.Sohoni's 109 took 120 minutes. K.V.Bhandarkar kept wicket in the Western India second innings.

QUEENSLAND v SOUTH AUSTRALIA

Played at Brisbane Cricket Ground, Woolloongabba, Brisbane, January 6, 8, 9, 10, 1940.

Queensland won by two wickets. (Points: Queensland 5, South Australia 0)

SOUTH AUSTRALIA

1	K.L.Ridings	c Tallon b Stackpoole	35	b Stackpoole	1
2	T.E.Klose	c Tallon b Stackpoole	27	st Tallon b Christ	31
3	*D.G.Bradman	c Dixon b Stackpoole	0	(4) c Tallon b Cook	97
4	R.S.Whitington	b Gooma	38	(3) b Stackpoole	0
5	R.A.Hamence	c Stackpoole b Christ	26	(6) c Brown b Christ	2
6	M.G.Waite	c Christ b Stackpoole	13	(8) b Dixon	62
7	†C.W.Walker	b Stackpoole	37	(5) b Christ	18
8	E.J.R.Moyle	b Stackpoole	32	(7) b Dixon	6
9	F.A.Ward	c Tallon b Dixon	4	c Baker b Stackpoole	15
10	C.V.Grimmett	b Dixon	12	(11) not out	5
11	G.Burton	not out	2	(10) b Dixon	11
	Extras	lb 2, nb 2	4	b 1, lb 2, w 1	4
			230		252

FoW (1): 1-53 (2), 2-53 (3), 3-68 (1), 4-119 (5), 5-140 (4), 6-145 (6), 7-203 (8), 8-212 (9), 9-228 (10), 10-230 (7)
FoW (2): 1-8 (1), 2-8 (3), 3-61 (2), 4-107 (5), 5-121 (6), 6-130 (7), 7-173 (4), 8-229 (9), 9-245 (8), 10-252 (10)

QUEENSLAND

1	*W.A.Brown	c Walker b Ward	37	c Ward b Burton	111
2	G.G.Cook	c Walker b Grimmett	8	lbw b Ward	54
3	R.E.Rogers	run out (Whitington/Walker)	19	lbw b Waite	74
4	G.G.Baker	lbw b Burton	20	c Bradman b Klose	28
5	†D.Tallon	c Walker b Grimmett	41	b Waite	0
6	D.Watt	b Waite	6	not out	59
7	W.C.J.Bryce	lbw b Grimmett	0	b Grimmett	1
8	G.A.Gooma	b Grimmett	0	(9) c Klose b Grimmett	0
9	C.P.Christ	not out	0	(8) c Klose b Grimmett	3
10	P.L.Dixon	st Walker b Waite	1	not out	14
11	J.Stackpoole	b Waite	0		
	Extras	lb 1	1	b 4, lb 2	6
			133	(8 wickets)	350

FoW (1): 1-22 (2), 2-44 (3), 3-83 (4), 4-99 (1), 5-132 (5), 6-132 (7), 7-132 (8), 8-132 (6), 9-133 (10), 10-133 (11)
FoW (2): 1-143 (2), 2-214 (1), 3-255 (3), 4-261 (5), 5-294 (4), 6-295 (7), 7-305 (8), 8-305 (9)

Queensland Bowling

	O	M	R	W			O	M	R	W	
Stackpoole	18.1	0	72	6			14	1	66	3	
Cook	11	1	35	0	1nb		8	1	32	1	
Dixon	16	5	33	2	1nb		10.3	2	33	3	1w
Gooma	6	0	27	1		(5)	5	0	27	0	
Christ	16	3	53	1		(4)	25	2	87	3	
Baker	2	0	6	0			2	1	3	0	

South Australia Bowling

	O	M	R	W		O	M	R	W
Burton	11	1	33	1		12	0	54	1
Waite	16.3	6	25	3		25	2	89	2
Grimmett	20	3	52	4		38.1	6	116	3
Ward	4	0	15	1	(5)	13	0	47	1
Klose	3	2	7	0	(4)	19	6	38	1

Umpires: D.W.Given and S.Ryan. Toss: South Australia

Close of Play: 1st day: South Australia (1) 164-6 (Walker 10*, Moyle 12*); 2nd day: South Australia (2) 62-3 (Bradman 29*, Walker 0*); 3rd day: Queensland (2) 128-0 (Brown 81*, Cook 46*).

W.A.Brown's 111 took 213 minutes and included 12 fours. 12th Men: T.Allen (Qld) and P.L.Ridings (SA).

UNITED PROVINCES v CENTRAL INDIA

Played at Muir Central College Ground, Allahabad, January 6, 7, 1940.

United Provinces won by an innings and 96 runs.

UNITED PROVINCES			
1	Ranjit Singh	b Mushtaq Ali	22
2	*P.E.Palia	lbw b Mushtaq Ali	47
3	Shamim Khwaja	b Mushtaq Ali	125
4	Iqbal Ahmed Khan	b Mushtaq Ali	2
5	Shahabuddin	c Mushtaq Ali b Das	25
6	A.S.N.Murthy	lbw b Boga	19
7	B.K.Garudachar	lbw b Mushtaq Ali	20
8	Hasan	not out	25
9	E.Alexander	b Pavri	1
10	Masood Salahuddin	b Mushtaq Ali	1
11	†S.J.Dastoor	b Mushtaq Ali	15
	Extras		24
			326

FoW (1): 1-45 (1), 2-123 (2), 3-145 (4), 4-199 (5), 5-242 (6), 6-280 (7), 7-288 (3), 8-293 (9), 9-294 (10), 10-326 (11)

CENTRAL INDIA					
1	S.Mushtaq Ali	b Alexander	15	(5) b Garudachar	74
2	N.C.Pavri	lbw b Garudachar	12	lbw b Masood Salahuddin	0
3	S.Ishtiaq Ali	lbw b Garudachar	9	(1) b Garudachar	19
4	Abdul Salim	b Garudachar	10	(7) b Palia	2
5	J.N.Bhaya	c Palia b Garudachar	6	(6) b Alexander	41
6	B.Maneckshaw	lbw b Alexander	5	(4) lbw b Murthy	15
7	*R.N.Zutchi	b Alexander	1	(8) b Alexander	3
8	Har Swarup	b Garudachar	0	(3) c Dastoor b Alexander	0
9	N.Godrej	b Garudachar	0	b Garudachar	1
10	K.B.Boga	not out	1	(11) not out	1
11	V.P.Das	b Alexander	0	(10) b Garudachar	0
	Extras		5		10
			64		166

FoW (1): 1-22 (1), 2-30 (2), 3-45 (3), 4-56 (4), 5-57 (5), 6-59, 7-60, 8-62, 9-64, 10-64
FoW (2): 1-2 (2), 2-3 (3), 3-35 (4), 4-49 (1), 5-127 (5), 6- (7), 7-161 (6), 8- , 9- , 10-166

Central India Bowling	O	M	R	W
Boga	17	4	64	1
Pavri	15	2	57	1
Mushtaq Ali	39.1	11	108	7
Bhaya	13	1	39	0
Das	8	2	15	1
Zutchi	4	0	15	0
Ishtiaq Ali	1	0	4	0

United Provinces Bowling	O	M	R	W		O	M	R	W
Alexander	11.2	3	15	4		18	5	61	3
Masood Salahuddin	3	0	8	0		4	2	4	1
Garudachar	11	3	30	6		17.3	1	59	4
Palia	3	0	6	0	(5)	10	1	18	1
Murthy					(4)	4	0	14	1

Umpires: Toss: Central India

Close of Play: 1st day: United Provinces (1) 324-9 (Hasan 25*, Dastoor 13*).

The match was scheduled for three days but completed in two. Shamim Khwaja's 125 took 193 minutes and included 16 fours.

EUROPEANS v INDIANS

Played at Madras Cricket Club Ground, Chepauk, Madras, January 12, 13, 14, 1940.

Indians won by four wickets.

EUROPEANS					
1	A.W.Stansfeld	b Rangachari	18	c Nayudu b Ram Singh	7
2	†G.G.Cradock-Watson	b Rangachari	21	c Parthasarathi b Venkatesan	20
3	C.N.Reed	c Parankusam b Ram Singh	48	b Rangachari	0
4	*C.P.Johnstone	c Chari b Venkatesan	45	lbw b Nayudu	36
5	R.S.Nailer	st Chari b Ram Singh	56	b Ram Singh	91
6	H.P.Ward	b Ram Singh	0	(7) c Ramaswami b Ram Singh	30
7	P.J.Keen	c Chari b Ram Singh	1	(8) b Nayudu	0
8	H.W.Horton	b Nayudu	1	(9) st Chari b Ram Singh	3
9	J.S.Versey-Brown	c Venkatesan b Parankusam	36	(10) c Gopalan b Parthasarathi	7
10	F.F.Coldwell	b Ram Singh	2	(6) b Ram Singh	9
11	R.A.Spitteler	not out	11	not out	8
	Extras		20		2
			259		213

FoW (1): 1-36 (1), 2-57 (2), 3-129 (4), 4-196 (3), 5-202 (6), 6-207 (5), 7-208 (8), 8-212 (7), 9-216 (10), 10-259 (9)
FoW (2): 1-9 (1), 2-9 (3), 3-56 (4), 4-68 (2), 5-92 (6), 6-192 (7), 7-195 (8), 8-197 (5), 9-200 (9), 10-213 (10)

INDIANS					
1	A.V.Krishnaswami	lbw b Spitteler	20	c Cradock-Watson b Versey-Brown	43
2	B.S.R.Bhadradri	c Ward b Versey-Brown	23	lbw b Johnstone	6
3	A.G.Ram Singh	b Coldwell	47	c Cradock-Watson b Versey-Brown	3
4	N.J.Venkatesan	run out	3	(8) not out	25
5	C.K.Nayudu	lbw b Versey-Brown	46	(4) b Versey-Brown	4
6	C.Ramaswami	c Coldwell b Spitteler	105	(5) c Versey-Brown b Spitteler	0
7	G.Parthasarathi	c Ward b Spitteler	6	(6) c Cradock-Watson b Versey-Brown	35
8	*M.J.Gopalan	b Spitteler	32	(7) not out	21
9	†S.V.T.Chari	c and b Spitteler	9		
10	T.S.Parankusam	run out	0		
11	C.R.Rangachari	not out	1		
	Extras		36		9
			328	(6 wickets)	146

FoW (1): 1-38 (1), 2-49 (2), 3-57 (4), 4-125 (5), 5-185 (3), 6-198 (7), 7-306 (8), 8-327 (6), 9-327 (9), 10-328 (10)
FoW (2): 1-10 (2), 2-15 (3), 3-27 (4), 4-28 (5), 5-91 (1), 6-109 (6)

Indians Bowling	O	M	R	W		O	M	R	W
Gopalan	6	1	22	0		1	0	3	0
Ram Singh	22	2	78	5		24	5	72	5
Rangachari	20	5	50	2		12	3	38	1
Nayudu	19	1	61	1		12	0	36	2
Venkatesan	4	1	23	1		1	0	1	1
Parankusam	2.5	0	5	1		6	0	36	0
Parthasarathi					(7)	7.4	0	25	1

Europeans Bowling	O	M	R	W	O	M	R	W
Versey-Brown	26.4	4	72	2	22	4	57	4
Johnstone	8	1	29	0	7	0	19	1
Spitteler	29	6	91	5	18.3	3	49	1
Coldwell	17	0	69	1	3	0	12	0
Stansfeld	1	0	3	0				
Horton	6	1	16	0				
Nailer	3	0	12	0				

Umpires: Toss: Europeans

Close of Play: 1st day: Indians (1) 52-2 (Ram Singh 2*, Venkatesan 0*); 2nd day: Europeans (2) 70-4 (Nailer 5*, Coldwell 1*).

C.Ramaswami's 105 included 9 fours and 2 sixes.

BENGAL v UNITED PROVINCES

Played at Eden Gardens, Calcutta, January 13, 14, 15, 1940.

Match drawn.

BENGAL					
1	S.W.E.Behrend	c Palia b Masood Salahuddin	107	(9) b Palia	17
2	P.N.Miller	c and b Palia	40	(1) c Ranjit Singh b Aftab Ahmed	55
3	S.K.Ganguli	b Palia	0	(8) run out	5
4	*N.M.Bose	c Iqbal Ahmed Khan b Palia	0	(5) c Shamim Khwaja b Aftab Ahmed	0
5	N.C.Chatterjee	c Garudachar b Masood Salahuddin	64	(3) st Dastoor b Palia	26
6	A.Jabbar	lbw b Masood Salahuddin	0	c Dastoor b Aftab Ahmed	8
7	K.Bhattacharya	c Dastoor b Masood Salahuddin	0	(10) not out	16
8	A.N.Hammond	b Alexander	5	(4) c Masud Alam b Aftab Ahmed	0
9	†K.R.Roy	b Masood Salahuddin	6	(2) b Palia	19
10	F.E.Eccleston	not out	7	(7) b Palia	7
11	A.K.Dutt	c Alexander b Masood Salahuddin	7	c Ranjit Singh b Aftab Ahmed	8
	Extras		24		2
			260		163

FoW (1): 1-100 (2), 2-100 (3), 3-104 (4), 4-231 (1), 5-231 (6), 6-231 (7), 7-237 (8), 8-237 (5), 9-244 (9), 10-260 (11)
FoW (2): 1-51 (2), 2-79 (1), 3-79 (4), 4-84 (5), 5-99 (6), 6-114 (3), 7-121 (8), 8-121 (7), 9-150 (9), 10-163 (11)

UNITED PROVINCES					
1	Ranjit Singh	st Roy b Bhattacharya	11	run out	6
2	Masud Alam	b Bhattacharya	33	b Behrend	2
3	Aftab Ahmed	b Behrend	72	lbw b Hammond	9
4	*P.E.Palia	lbw b Behrend	71	b Bhattacharya	22
5	Masood Salahuddin	c and b Hammond	3	(7) b Chatterjee	38
6	Shamim Khwaja	c Bose b Eccleston	33	(5) c and b Behrend	11
7	A.S.N.Murthy	c Behrend b Bhattacharya	9	(8) b Chatterjee	11
8	B.K.Garudachar	st Roy b Bhattacharya	18	(9) not out	10
9	Iqbal Ahmed Khan	b Bhattacharya	13	(10) not out	5
10	E.Alexander	not out	16	(6) lbw b Eccleston	6
11	†S.J.Dastoor	st Roy b Eccleston	0		
	Extras		16		4
			295	(8 wickets)	124

FoW (1): 1-44 (1), 2-55 (2), 3-200 (3), 4-205 (5), 5-205 (4), 6-220 (7), 7-250 (8), 8-264 (9), 9-295 (6), 10-295 (11)
FoW (2): 1-4 (2), 2-17 (1), 3-39 (3), 4-39 (4), 5-48 (6), 6-80 (5), 7-105 (8), 8-110 (7)

United Provinces Bowling	O	M	R	W		O	M	R	W
Masood Salahuddin	23.4	6	62	6		4	0	21	0
Alexander	20	7	37	1	(4)	2	0	19	0
Palia	30	8	54	3	(2)	13	0	66	4
Garudachar	17	2	44	0					
Aftab Ahmed	9	3	22	0	(3)	11.2	0	55	5
Murthy	5	0	17	0					

Bengal Bowling	O	M	R	W		O	M	R	W
Behrend	19	2	56	2		11	2	28	2
Dutt	12	2	32	0	(3)	3	0	10	0
Bhattacharya	24	7	56	5	(4)	11	5	28	1
Hammond	22	2	72	1	(2)	11	2	25	1
Eccleston	7	0	37	2		7	1	20	1
Chatterjee	7	1	26	0		5	2	9	2

Umpires: M.Dutta Roy and P.Mukherjee. Toss: Bengal

Close of Play: 1st day: Bengal (1) 245-9 (Eccleston 0*, Dutt 1*); 2nd day: United Provinces (1) 271-8 (Shamim Khwaja 22*, Alexander 3*).

S.W.E.Behrend's 107 took 275 minutes and included 12 fours.

NEW SOUTH WALES v SOUTH AUSTRALIA

Played at Sydney Cricket Ground, January 13, 15, 16, 17, 1940.

New South Wales won by 237 runs. (Points: New South Wales 5, South Australia 0)

	NEW SOUTH WALES				
1	M.B.Cohen	c Walker b Klose	74	b Ward	70
2	H.Mudge	st Walker b Grimmett	14	c Bradman b Ward	57
3	*S.J.McCabe	st Walker b Grimmett	59	c Walker b Grimmett	55
4	S.G.Barnes	lbw b Grimmett	34	c Bradman b Grimmett	25
5	A.G.Chipperfield	lbw b Grimmett	0	st Walker b Grimmett	1
6	R.A.Saggers	c Walker b Klose	45	b Ward	57
7	A.G.Cheetham	lbw b Waite	14	b Grimmett	1
8	C.G.Pepper	lbw b Grimmett	9	c Waite b Burton	26
9	J.G.Lush	st Walker b Klose	1	st Walker b Grimmett	13
10	W.J.O'Reilly	st Walker b Grimmett	6	c Bradman b Ward	0
11	†S.G.Sismey	not out	2	not out	0
	Extras	b 6, lb 6	12	b 5, lb 1	6
			270		311

FoW (1): 1-22 (2), 2-130 (3), 3-189 (4), 4-189 (5), 5-189 (1), 6-223 (7), 7-238 (8), 8-249 (9), 9-262 (10), 10-270 (6)
FoW (2): 1-111 (1), 2-156 (2), 3-199 (4), 4-207 (5), 5-212 (3), 6-222 (7), 7-265 (8), 8-304 (9), 9-305 (10), 10-311 (6)

	SOUTH AUSTRALIA				
1	K.L.Ridings	b Lush	3	b Cheetham	1
2	T.E.Klose	c Sismey b Lush	0	b Pepper	13
3	R.S.Whitington	c Barnes b O'Reilly	37	c Chipperfield b Pepper	11
4	*D.G.Bradman	lbw b O'Reilly	39	c sub (D.K.Carmody) b Pepper	40
5	C.L.Badcock	c Mudge b O'Reilly	40	c Chipperfield b O'Reilly	20
6	R.A.Hamence	c Mudge b O'Reilly	43	c Cohen b O'Reilly	0
7	M.G.Waite	run out (Pepper)	9	c Mudge b Pepper	19
8	†C.W.Walker	lbw b O'Reilly	1	c McCabe b Pepper	10
9	F.A.Ward	b Pepper	17	b O'Reilly	1
10	C.V.Grimmett	not out	7	b O'Reilly	6
11	G.Burton	c McCabe b O'Reilly	7	not out	11
	Extras	b 5, lb 2, w 1	8	nb 1	1
			211		133

FoW (1): 1-1 (2), 2-8 (1), 3-77 (4), 4-103 (3), 5-140 (5), 6-156 (7), 7-162 (8), 8-187 (6), 9-201 (9), 10-211 (11)
FoW (2): 1-1 (1), 2-22 (3), 3-27 (2), 4-85 (5), 5-85 (6), 6-85 (4), 7-112 (8), 8-115 (7), 9-117 (9), 10-133 (10)

South Australia Bowling	O	M	R	W			O	M	R	W	
Burton	12	1	44	0			11	0	27	1	
Waite	13	0	43	1			7	0	32	0	
Grimmett	22	0	118	6			29	2	111	5	
Ward	3	0	32	0			22.1	1	120	4	
Klose	11.3	3	21	3			4	0	15	0	

New South Wales Bowling	O	M	R	W			O	M	R	W	
Lush	8	0	26	2	1w		4	0	13	0	
Cohen	5	2	9	0							
O'Reilly	24.5	7	77	6			13.7	2	62	4	1nb
Pepper	27	3	85	1			12	1	49	5	
Mudge	1	0	6	0							
Cheetham						(2)	5	1	8	1	

Umpires: G.E.Borwick and R.McGrath. Toss: New South Wales

Close of Play: 1st day: South Australia (1) 54-2 (Whitington 23*, Bradman 24*); 2nd day: New South Wales (2) 49-0 (Cohen 26*, Mudge 23*); 3rd day: South Australia (2) 74-3 (Bradman 35*, Badcock 14*).

12th Men: D.K.Carmody (NSW) and P.L.Ridings (SA).

QUEENSLAND v VICTORIA

Played at Brisbane Cricket Ground, Woolloongabba, Brisbane, January 19, 20, 22, 23, 1940.

Victoria won by nine wickets. (Points: Queensland 0, Victoria 5)

QUEENSLAND					
1	*W.A.Brown	c Scott b Ring	60	c and b Fleetwood-Smith	32
2	G.G.Cook	b Fleetwood-Smith	64	st Barnett b Fleetwood-Smith	24
3	R.E.Rogers	c Barnett b Ring	16	c Lee b Johnson	73
4	G.G.Baker	lbw b Johnson	34	lbw b Sievers	80
5	T.Allen	c Beames b Fleetwood-Smith	42	c Barnett b Johnson	4
6	†D.Tallon	lbw b Ring	0	c Hassett b Johnson	154
7	D.Watt	c Sievers b Scott	10	c Miller b Scott	29
8	C.P.Christ	b Johnson	5	not out	13
9	G.A.Gooma	c Miller b Johnson	2	b Ring	1
10	P.L.Dixon	c Hassett b Fleetwood-Smith	0	b Johnson	1
11	J.Stackpoole	not out	1	c Lee b Ring	0
	Extras	b 4, lb 5, w 1	10	b 5, lb 4	9
			244		420

FoW (1): 1-112 (1), 2-141 (2), 3-149 (3), 4-194 (4), 5-197 (6), 6-226 (7), 7-241 (8), 8-243 (9), 9-243 (10), 10-244 (5)
FoW (2): 1-50 (2), 2-71 (1), 3-177 (3), 4-183 (5), 5-255 (4), 6-370 (7), 7-413 (6), 8-419 (9), 9-420 (10), 10-420 (11)

VICTORIA					
1	I.S.Lee	c Watt b Dixon	90	c and b Stackpoole	93
2	*†B.A.Barnett	c Christ b Stackpoole	92	not out	104
3	A.L.Hassett	c Watt b Stackpoole	17		
4	K.R.Miller	b Cook	37		
5	I.W.G.Johnson	c Stackpoole b Cook	7		
6	P.J.Beames	st Tallon b Christ	55		
7	D.H.Fothergill	c Baker b Cook	0	(3) not out	26
8	M.W.Sievers	not out	55		
9	D.T.Ring	st Tallon b Watt	45		
10	R.B.Scott	c Brown b Gooma	33		
11	L.O.Fleetwood-Smith				
	Extras	b 2, lb 2	4	b 6, w 1	7
		(9 wickets, declared)	435	(1 wicket)	230

FoW (1): 1-152 (1), 2-180 (3), 3-230 (4), 4-243 (2), 5-248 (5), 6-252 (7), 7-325 (6), 8-398 (9), 9-435 (10)
FoW (2): 1-169 (1)

Victoria Bowling	O	M	R	W			O	M	R	W	
Scott	13	1	52	1			15	1	58	1	
Sievers	12	1	18	0			15	2	53	1	
Ring	19	1	71	3			19.5	0	108	2	
Fleetwood-Smith	19.5	3	77	3	1w		23	0	131	2	
Johnson	6	1	16	3			23	4	61	4	

Queensland Bowling	O	M	R	W			O	M	R	W	
Stackpoole	16	0	91	2			9.2	1	39	1	
Dixon	17	0	81	1			6	0	33	0	
Christ	19	2	73	1			7	0	23	0	
Cook	16	1	55	3			9	0	36	0	1w
Gooma	13.7	0	75	1			6	0	30	0	
Watt	10	1	51	1			4	0	25	0	
Baker	1	0	5	0			4	1	29	0	
Allen						(8)	2	0	8	0	

Umpires: D.W.Given and R.Weitemeyer. Toss: Queensland

Close of Play: 1st day: Victoria (1) 28-0 (Lee 12*, Barnett 15*); 2nd day: Victoria (1) 435-9 (Sievers 55*); 3rd day: Queensland (2) 343-5 (Tallon 103*, Watt 21*).

D.Tallon's 154 took 185 minutes and included 15 fours and 1 six. B.A.Barnett's 104 took 181 minutes and included 9 fours. 12th Men: W.C.J.Bryce (Qld) and F.L.O.Thorn (Vic).

NATAL v EASTERN PROVINCE

Played at City Oval, Pietermaritzburg, January 20, 22, 1940.

Natal won by an innings and 297 runs.

NATAL			
1	D.R.Fell	c Marais b Gardner	3
2	D.S.Turner	lbw b Gardner	64
3	R.L.Harvey	c Marais b Smith	1
4	*A.D.Nourse	c Smith b Leibbrandt	136
5	†W.W.Wade	c Leibbrandt b Coy	208
6	O.C.Dawson	c Coy b Southey	37
7	R.Howden	b Southey	64
8	F.J.Smith	c Leibbrandt b Coy	23
9	I.D.E.Anderson	st Marais b Coy	17
10	N.B.F.Mann	not out	15
11	C.D.Lamble	c Leibbrandt b Coy	15
	Extras	lb 4	4
			587

FoW (1): 1-5 (1), 2-6 (3), 3-192 (2), 4-225 (4), 5-337 (6), 6-516, 7-518, 8-546, 9-556, 10-587

EASTERN PROVINCE					
1	R.W.Robson	c Harvey b Smith	25	(2) b Dawson	0
2	†W.Marais	c Turner b Harvey	30	(1) lbw b Dawson	10
3	H.J.S.Gardner	c Wade b Lamble	1	b Smith	4
4	F.W.R.Southey	c Wade b Harvey	1	b Smith	1
5	S.A.Thwaits	b Anderson	17	(6) run out	0
6	J.M.Leibbrandt	lbw b Smith	1	(5) c Dawson b Harvey	71
7	G.Hartman	run out	3	c Dawson b Anderson	16
8	D.R.McAllister	run out	1	c and b Mann	5
9	J.M.Buchanan	c Turner b Harvey	5	b Mann	1
10	*A.H.Coy	not out	47	st Wade b Mann	18
11	B.A.Smith	b Lamble	23	not out	1
	Extras	b 1, lb 6	7	lb 2	2
			161		129

FoW (1): 1-49 (1), 2-56 (3), 3-57 (4), 4-66, 5-67, 6-71, 7-76, 8-82, 9-98, 10-161
FoW (2): 1-0 (2), 2-5 (3), 3-15 (4), 4-21 (1), 5-31 (6), 6-80 (7), 7-85 (8), 8-91 (9), 9-123 (5), 10-129 (10)

Eastern Province Bowling

	O	M	R	W
Smith	18	1	112	1
Gardner	10	0	60	2
Leibbrandt	19	2	101	1
Coy	18	2	87	4
Thwaits	10	0	55	0
Buchanan	7	0	68	0
Southey	12	1	75	2
Hartman	2	0	25	0

Natal Bowling

	O	M	R	W		O	M	R	W
Smith	18	7	45	2		7	2	23	2
Dawson	3	1	13	0		8	4	6	2
Harvey	20	5	47	3	(6)	5	0	19	1
Lamble	8	2	24	2	(3)	9	1	21	0
Anderson	7	1	25	1		8	0	28	1
Mann					(4)	20.5	7	30	3

Umpires: Toss: Natal

Close of Play: 1st day: Eastern Province (1) 57-2 (Marais 30*, Southey 0*).

The match was scheduled for three days but completed in two. A.D.Nourse's 136 included 17 fours. W.W.Wade's 208 included 25 fours.

MAHARASHTRA v BARODA

Played at Poona Club Ground, January 21, 22, 23, 1940.

Match drawn.

BARODA					
1	Y.E.Sheikh	c Doctor b Patwardhan	14		
2	V.M.Pandit	b Patwardhan	21	c Sohoni b Jath	11
3	M.M.Jagdale	b Hazare	38	(4) c and b Deodhar	9
4	H.R.Adhikari	c Doctor b Jath	68	(6) not out	23
5	C.S.Nayudu	c Doctor b Hazare	28	(3) st Doctor b Jath	6
6	R.B.Nimbalkar	b Patwardhan	63	(5) c Deodhar b Jath	78
7	*W.N.Ghorpade	c Jath b Sohoni	35		
8	M.M.Naidu	st Doctor b Patwardhan	15	(1) b Rangnekar	120
9	B.B.Nimbalkar	lbw b Patwardhan	5	(7) not out	22
10	K.S.Gaekwar	b Patwardhan	0		
11	†S.G.Powar	not out	10		
	Extras		6		14
			303	(5 wickets)	283

FoW (1): 1-22 (1), 2-39 (2), 3-123 (3), 4-159 (5), 5-187 (4), 6-271 (6), 7-271 (7), 8-278 (9), 9-278 (10), 10-303 (8)
FoW (2): 1-59 (2), 2-67 (3), 3-109 (4), 4-221 (5), 5-251 (1)

MAHARASHTRA			
1	K.V.Bhandarkar	run out	77
2	S.W.Sohoni	c Jagdale b Gaekwar	13
3	S.Nazir Ali	c Adhikari b Nayudu	9
4	Raja of Jath	st Powar b Nayudu	28
5	V.S.Hazare	not out	316
6	K.M.Rangnekar	c Jagdale b Nayudu	51
7	*D.B.Deodhar	st Powar b Nayudu	12
8	J.G.Harris	c Nayudu b Jagdale	8
9	†D.S.Doctor	b Jagdale	0
10	N.D.Nagarwala	b Gaekwar	98
11	M.K.Patwardhan	not out	23
	Extras		15
		(9 wickets, declared)	650

FoW (1): 1-41 (2), 2-62 (3), 3-129 (1), 4-141 (4), 5-243 (6), 6-301 (7), 7-324 (8), 8-324 (9), 9-569 (10)

Maharashtra Bowling	O	M	R	W		O	M	R	W
Hazare	29	11	48	2					
Patwardhan	30.3	5	103	6	(1)	17	4	51	0
Sohoni	18	1	76	1	(2)	12	2	46	0
Harris	14	2	32	0					
Jath	11	1	36	1	(4)	15	1	55	3
Rangnekar	1	0	2	0	(3)	10	0	49	1
Deodhar					(5)	5	1	20	1
Nazir Ali					(6)	2	0	14	0
Nagarwala					(7)	5	1	21	0
Bhandarkar					(8)	1	0	13	0

Baroda Bowling	O	M	R	W
Gaekwar	47	10	132	2
Jagdale	32	5	80	2
Nayudu	64	4	261	4
Sheikh	18	3	66	0
B.B.Nimbalkar	7	0	37	0
Adhikari	5	0	29	0
R.B.Nimbalkar	5	0	30	0

Umpires: D.K.Naik and Vali Ahmed. Toss: Baroda

Close of Play: 1st day: Maharashtra (1) 19-0 (Bhandarkar 15*, Sohoni 4*); 2nd day: Maharashtra (1) 410-8 (Hazare 165*, Nagarwala 32*).
V.S.Hazare's 316 took 387 minutes and included 37 fours. M.M.Naidu's 120 took 164 minutes and included 13 fours. V.S.Hazare added 151 before lunch on the third day.

TRANSVAAL v EASTERN PROVINCE

Played at Old Wanderers, Johannesburg, January 25, 26, 1940.

Transvaal won by an innings and 230 runs.

EASTERN PROVINCE					
1	R.W.Robson	c Petersen b Pickerill	3	c Mitchell b Chubb	27
2	†W.Marais	b Chubb	3	c Mitchell b Chubb	3
3	H.J.S.Gardner	b Chubb	0	(8) c Pickerill b Mitchell	5
4	J.M.Leibbrandt	b Pickerill	1	b Gordon	2
5	I.E.Drimmie	c Dacey b Petersen	16	(3) lbw b Gordon	79
6	F.W.R.Southey	c Cawood b Chubb	2	(7) c Mitchell b Chubb	4
7	*A.H.Coy	st Cawood b Chubb	3	(9) st Cawood b Gordon	21
8	S.A.Thwaits	lbw b Mitchell	28	(5) c and b Mitchell	9
9	G.Hartman	not out	27	(6) b Chubb	7
10	B.A.Smith	b Gordon	1	not out	3
11	J.M.Buchanan	b Mitchell	1	run out	6
	Extras	b 5, lb 4	9	lb 1, nb 1	2
			94		168

FoW (1): 1-4, 2-6, 3-7, 4-9, 5-17, 6-21, 7-39, 8-90, 9-93, 10-94
FoW (2): 1-18 (2), 2-34 (1), 3-39 (4), 4-70 (5), 5-90 (6), 6-100 (7), 7-107 (8), 8-155, 9-159, 10-168

TRANSVAAL			
1	J.T.Seccombe	lbw b Coy	26
2	L.S.Dacey	st Marais b Southey	58
3	O.E.Wynne	b Thwaits	8
4	*B.Mitchell	c Coy b Leibbrandt	88
5	E.A.B.Rowan	run out	88
6	C.H.K.Jones	run out	85
7	G.W.A.Chubb	not out	71
8	†C.H.Cawood	not out	53
9	R.N.E.Petersen		
10	J.H.M.Pickerill		
11	N.Gordon		
	Extras	b 11, lb 2, w 2	15
		(6 wickets, declared)	492

FoW (1): 1-57 (1), 2-89 (3), 3-117 (2), 4-262, 5-304, 6-413

Transvaal Bowling

	O	M	R	W		O	M	R	W
Pickerill	6	1	15	2	(5)	1	0	8	0
Chubb	10	0	24	4	(1)	15	4	43	4
Petersen	6	1	9	1	(2)	5	0	17	0
Gordon	7	0	17	1	(3)	15.1	2	52	3
Mitchell	5.2	0	20	2	(4)	16	0	46	2

Eastern Province Bowling

	O	M	R	W
Smith	10	0	68	0
Leibbrandt	13	0	83	1
Coy	13	1	63	1
Thwaits	24	2	125	1
Southey	7	0	36	1
Gardner	5	0	50	0
Hartman	4	0	34	0
Buchanan	2	0	18	0

Umpires: Toss: Eastern Province

Close of Play: 1st day: Transvaal (1) 492-6 (Chubb 71*, Cawood 53*, 78 overs).

The match was scheduled for three days but completed in two.

NEW SOUTH WALES v VICTORIA

Played at Sydney Cricket Ground, January 26, 27, 29, 30, 1940.

New South Wales won by 177 runs. (Points: New South Wales 5, Victoria 0)

NEW SOUTH WALES					
1	M.B.Cohen	run out (Scott/Barnett)	73	b Sievers	13
2	H.Mudge	c Scott b Ring	82	c and b Johnson	61
3	*S.J.McCabe	b Scott	49	c Beames b Ring	114
4	S.G.Barnes	c Ring b Sievers	17	not out	135
5	R.A.Saggers	lbw b Scott	0	c Sievers b Johnson	71
6	A.G.Chipperfield	c Lee b Johnson	8	lbw b Johnson	15
7	A.G.Cheetham	b Ring	55	not out	70
8	C.G.Pepper	c Fothergill b Ring	4		
9	J.G.Lush	run out (Fothergill)	5		
10	W.J.O'Reilly	c Barnett b Ring	8		
11	†S.G.Sismey	not out	1		
	Extras	b 1, lb 6	7	b 11, lb 2	13
			309	(5 wickets, declared)	492

FoW (1): 1-131 (1), 2-186 (2), 3-218 (4), 4-223 (5), 5-228 (3), 6-259 (6), 7-268 (8), 8-293 (9), 9-308 (10), 10-309 (7)
FoW (2): 1-25 (1), 2-171 (2), 3-217 (3), 4-329 (5), 5-359 (6)

VICTORIA					
1	I.S.Lee	run out (Lush/Sismey)	50	c O'Reilly b Cheetham	8
2	*†B.A.Barnett	c Sismey b Lush	6	(4) c Sismey b Pepper	11
3	M.W.Sievers	c Chipperfield b Pepper	30	(2) c McCabe b Pepper	54
4	A.L.Hassett	c Pepper b O'Reilly	122	(3) c Chipperfield b Lush	122
5	K.R.Miller	lbw b O'Reilly	1	run out	24
6	I.W.G.Johnson	c Barnes b O'Reilly	0	c Chipperfield b Lush	40
7	P.J.Beames	b O'Reilly	1	b O'Reilly	23
8	D.H.Fothergill	c Chipperfield b Mudge	32	not out	32
9	D.T.Ring	c Chipperfield b Cheetham	29	b O'Reilly	3
10	R.B.Scott	b O'Reilly	9	c Pepper b O'Reilly	0
11	L.O.Fleetwood-Smith	not out	4	b Pepper	0
	Extras	b 8, lb 4, nb 2	14	b 4, lb 4, nb 1	9
			298		326

FoW (1): 1-11 (2), 2-80 (1), 3-103 (3), 4-106 (5), 5-110 (6), 6-118 (7), 7-185 (8), 8-241 (9), 9-293 (4), 10-298 (10)
FoW (2): 1-9 (1), 2-89 (2), 3-120 (4), 4-192 (5), 5-259 (6), 6-266 (3), 7-317 (7), 8-325 (9), 9-325 (10), 10-326 (11)

Victoria Bowling	O	M	R	W			O	M	R	W	
Scott	16	0	60	2			17	0	82	0	
Sievers	13	1	37	1			18	1	94	1	
Johnson	20	0	84	1			23	0	142	3	
Fleetwood-Smith	12	0	58	0		(5)	10	0	77	0	
Ring	10.5	0	63	4		(4)	12	0	84	1	

New South Wales Bowling	O	M	R	W			O	M	R	W	
Lush	12	3	37	1			10	1	51	2	
Cheetham	9	0	54	1			8	0	30	1	1nb
O'Reilly	22.1	3	78	5	2nb	(4)	19	2	79	3	
Pepper	18	0	66	1		(5)	23.4	0	115	3	
Mudge	6	0	45	1							
Barnes	1	0	4	0			3	0	28	0	
Cohen						(3)	1	0	14	0	

Umpires: G.E.Borwick and R.McGrath. Toss: New South Wales

Close of Play: 1st day: Victoria (1) 18-1 (Lee 10*, Sievers 0*); 2nd day: New South Wales (2) 87-1 (Mudge 29*, McCabe 45*); 3rd day: Victoria (2) 89-2 (Hassett 23*, Barnett 0*).

A.L.Hassett's 122 took 173 minutes and included 16 fours. S.J.McCabe's 114 took 139 minutes and included 11 fours. S.G.Barnes's 135 took 170 minutes and included 16 fours. A.L.Hassett's 122 took 177 minutes and included 13 fours. 12th Men: V.E.Jackson (NSW) and F.L.O.Thorn (Vic).

SOUTHERN PUNJAB v NORTH WEST FRONTIER PROVINCE

Played at Baradari Ground, Patiala, January 29, 30, 31, 1940.

Southern Punjab won by five wickets.

NORTH WEST FRONTIER PROVINCE

1	Qazi Daud	b Murawwat Hussain	8	(2) b Murawwat Hussain	22
2	Jaswant Rai	b Amarnath	9	(3) lbw b Amarnath	2
3	Fazal Rahim	lbw b Amarnath	10	(5) c Abdur Rehman b Murawwat Hussain	1
4	Rajindernath	b Amarnath	0	(8) c Nazir Ali b Murawwat Hussain	3
5	G.C.Kapoor	c Shahabuddin b Amir Elahi	24	(4) c Azmat Hayat b Murawwat Hussain	1
6	*Abdul Rashid	c Roshan Lal b Patiala	30	c Azmat Hayat b Amarnath	0
7	Sardar Gul	b Bhalindra Singh	4	(9) c Amir Elahi b Amarnath	13
8	†Karim Baksh	b Patiala	58	(1) lbw b Amarnath	0
9	Abdul Latif	c Murawwat Hussain b Patiala	70	(7) c Patiala b Amarnath	4
10	B.C.Khanna	c and b Patiala	2	(11) c Amarnath b Patiala	11
11	Paramanand	not out	0	(10) not out	27
	Extras		13		8
			228		92

FoW (1): 1-13 (1), 2-28 (2), 3-28 (4), 4-31 (3), 5-82 (5), 6-91 (7), 7-98 (6), 8-223 (9), 9-225 (10), 10-228 (8)
FoW (2): 1-4 (1), 2-8 (3), 3-18 (4), 4-19 (5), 5-21 (6), 6-26 (7), 7-34 (8), 8-46 (2), 9-62 (9), 10-92 (11)

SOUTHERN PUNJAB

1	†Abdur Rehman	b Abdul Latif	4		
2	Roshan Lal	run out	31	(1) run out	9
3	Azmat Hayat	c Sardar Gul b Rajindernath	30		
4	L.Amarnath	c and b Abdul Latif	13	(3) lbw b Qazi Daud	3
5	S.Nazir Ali	b Abdul Latif	1	(6) lbw b Qazi Daud	12
6	Bhalindra Singh	b Rajindernath	5		
7	*Maharaja of Patiala	c Paramanand b Qazi Daud	23	not out	30
8	Murawwat Hussain	b Abdul Latif	11	(4) not out	36
9	Mohammad Saeed	c and b Abdul Latif	51	(5) c Khanna b Qazi Daud	4
10	Amir Elahi	c Kapoor b Abdul Latif	9	(2) c Paramanand b Qazi Daud	14
11	Shahabuddin	not out	0		
	Extras		27		8
			205	(5 wickets)	116

FoW (1): 1-7 (1), 2-80 (3), 3-89 (2), 4-96 (4), 5-97 (5), 6-107 (6), 7-131 (8), 8-155 (7), 9-186 (10), 10-205 (9)
FoW (2): 1-23 (2), 2-26 (1), 3-35 (3), 4-40 (5), 5-70 (6)

Southern Punjab Bowling

	O	M	R	W		O	M	R	W
Patiala	21	1	77	4		6.4	1	14	1
Amarnath	26	6	50	3		19	7	22	5
Murawwat Hussain	3	1	14	1		19	8	27	4
Amir Elahi	9	2	35	1	(5)	4	0	15	0
Bhalindra Singh	8	2	39	1					
Shahabuddin					(4)	2	0	6	0

North West Frontier Province Bowling

	O	M	R	W		O	M	R	W
Rajindernath	12	0	40	2		2	0	11	0
Abdul Latif	21.1	1	76	6		7	2	24	0
Kapoor	7	1	39	0					
Qazi Daud	3	0	17	1	(3)	16	4	54	4
Khanna	4	2	6	0	(4)	10	2	19	0

Umpires: Toss: Southern Punjab

Close of Play: 1st day: Southern Punjab (1) 77-1 (Roshan Lal 31*, Azmat Hayat 30*); 2nd day: North West Frontier Province (2) 70-9 (Paramanand 15*, Khanna 7*).

NORTH EASTERN TRANSVAAL v ORANGE FREE STATE

Played at Berea Park, Pretoria, February 2, 3, 4, 1940.

North Eastern Transvaal won by 83 runs.

NORTH EASTERN TRANSVAAL					
1	D.G.Helfrich	b Tuckett	28	c Kirsner b Papenfus	0
2	M.A.Wright	lbw b Papenfus	0	(4) b Glover	91
3	T.H.Woolley	c Kirsner b Papenfus	40	(2) b Papenfus	2
4	R.C.Hicks	lbw b Fraser	1	(3) c Papenfus b Jackson	47
5	L.O.Waller	lbw b Papenfus	21	(6) b Tuckett	10
6	D.F.Dowling	not out	91	(5) c Kirsner b Wright	74
7	†C.G.Bromham	b Papenfus	0	(9) not out	39
8	A.C.Vlok	b Papenfus	0	(7) c Kirsner b Tuckett	6
9	*L.S.Brown	c Kirsner b Tuckett	22	(8) st Kirsner b Tuckett	31
10	W.H.Douglas	c Wright b Fraser	6	not out	14
11	W.A.Henderson	b Papenfus	1		
	Extras		9		15
			219	(8 wickets, declared)	329

FoW (1): 1-13 (2), 2-44 (1), 3-47 (4), 4-93 (5), 5-102 (3), 6-102 (7), 7-102 (8), 8-157 (9), 9-201 (10), 10-213 (11)
FoW (2): 1-0 (1), 2-18 (2), 3-114 (3), 4-190, 5-229, 6-243, 7-245, 8-284

ORANGE FREE STATE					
1	*E.W.Warner	st Bromham b Henderson	33	c Bromham b Vlok	0
2	C.J.Kaplan	lbw b Vlok	7	b Henderson	9
3	H.F.Wright	b Vlok	2	c Bromham b Vlok	14
4	L.Mendelsohn	b Henderson	4	(6) lbw b Henderson	17
5	J.P.G.Glover	b Brown	25	(4) b Brown	24
6	A.W.Bayly	c Vlok b Brown	41	(9) b Brown	0
7	L.Tuckett	lbw b Brown	42	(5) c Hicks b Brown	101
8	G.F.K.Jackson	lbw b Brown	0	(7) c Bromham b Wright	31
9	T.W.Fraser	b Henderson	6	(8) c Henderson b Vlok	23
10	C.F.B.Papenfus	b Henderson	1	c Vlok b Brown	60
11	†I.Kirsner	not out	0	not out	6
	Extras		12		7
			173		292

FoW (1): 1-25 (2), 2-31 (3), 3-49 (4), 4-59 (1), 5-119, 6-128, 7-128, 8-147, 9-153, 10-173
FoW (2): 1-0 (1), 2-24, 3-28, 4-74, 5-119, 6-194, 7-216, 8-216, 9-234, 10-292

Orange Free State Bowling	O	M	R	W		O	M	R	W
Papenfus	24	1	88	6		22	2	89	2
Tuckett	14	1	35	2		26	3	82	3
Fraser	23	4	45	2		15	1	48	0
Wright	6	0	26	0		10	1	49	1
Glover	3	0	16	0	(6)	1	0	10	1
Jackson					(5)	5	0	36	1

North Eastern Transvaal Bowling	O	M	R	W		O	M	R	W
Vlok	9	1	32	2		18	4	61	3
Brown	21	2	64	4		24.1	3	105	4
Henderson	16	2	56	4		17	2	50	2
Douglas	5	2	7	0		6	0	26	0
Dowling	2	1	2	0		7	0	24	0
Waller					(6)	1	0	3	0
Wright					(7)	4	0	16	1

Umpires: Toss:
Close of Play: 1st day: Orange Free State (1) 59-4 (Glover 10*); 2nd day: North Eastern Transvaal (2) ?-?.

UNITED PROVINCES v HYDERABAD

Played at Maharaja of Benares Palace Ground, Benares, February 4, 5, 6, 7, 1940.
The BCCI awarded the match to United Provinces as Hyderabad would not play on the designated date.

BORDER v EASTERN PROVINCE

Played at Jan Smuts Ground, East London, February 9, 10, 1940.

Border won by an innings and 15 runs.

BORDER

1	†G.G.L.Mandy	b Lynch	13
2	R.P.Richter	b Gouldie	50
3	R.J.Evans	run out	23
4	R.R.Phillips	c Young b Gouldie	37
5	H.V.L.Whitfield	lbw b Gouldie	20
6	G.V.Wienand	c and b Leibbrandt	102
7	*H.D.Bowley	c Hartman b Gouldie	76
8	W.A.E.Ayres	c Young b Knight	28
9	P.S.Hubbard	not out	16
10	R.K.B.Morkel	st Riemer b Young	18
11	M.A.Hanley	c Leibbrandt b Young	4
	Extras	b 12, lb 5	17
			404

FoW (1): 1-50 (1), 2-73 (2), 3-102, 4-126, 5-175, 6-302, 7-347, 8-377, 9-399, 10-404

EASTERN PROVINCE

1	*C.S.Smith	b Morkel	4	b Hubbard	7
2	J.G.Sharp	lbw b Morkel	1	b Hubbard	29
3	G.Hartman	c Morkel b Wienand	3	b Ayres	8
4	J.O.Young	b Evans	23	b Evans	76
5	R.Rouse	b Hanley	44	c Morkel b Evans	25
6	J.M.Leibbrandt	b Hanley	20	(7) lbw b Hubbard	11
7	I.E.Drimmie	b Hubbard	26	(6) lbw b Hubbard	35
8	B.C.Lynch	c and b Evans	12	b Hubbard	0
9	†D.G.Riemer	b Hanley	21	st Mandy b Evans	1
10	R.S.Gouldie	b Hanley	4	b Evans	0
11	B.O.Knight	not out	3	not out	9
	Extras	b 11, lb 6	17	b 4, lb 5, nb 1	10
			178		211

FoW (1): 1-4, 2-8, 3-9, 4-54, 5-107, 6-109, 7-124, 8-156, 9-164, 10-178
FoW (2): 1-32 (1), 2-48, 3-62, 4-147, 5-162, 6-197, 7-197, 8-198, 9-198, 10-211

Eastern Province Bowling

	O	M	R	W
Lynch	14	1	64	1
Gouldie	21.6	2	96	4
Leibbrandt	7	0	47	1
Young	16	0	91	2
Knight	9	0	58	1
Hartman	3	0	24	0
Smith	1	0	7	0

Border Bowling

	O	M	R	W		O	M	R	W
Morkel	6	1	19	2		3	0	12	0
Wienand	9	2	25	1		3	0	13	0
Hanley	18	3	71	4	(5)	10	1	55	0
Evans	11	1	42	2	(6)	12	1	52	4
Hubbard	3.2	1	4	1	(3)	18.1	2	35	5
Ayres					(4)	8	1	34	1

Umpires: Toss:

Close of Play: 1st day: Eastern Province (1) 56-4 (Rouse 16*, Leibbrandt 0*).

G.V.Wienand's 102 took 150 minutes and included 1 six.

OTAGO v WELLINGTON

Played at Carisbrook, Dunedin, February 9, 10, 12, 13, 1940.

Otago won by 58 runs. (Points: Otago 8, Wellington 0)

OTAGO					
1	*D.A.R.Moloney	b Pritchard	12	lbw b Wilson	33
2	G.J.Robertson	c Tindill b Wilson	17	c Wrigley b Pritchard	11
3	A.S.H.Cutler	b Wilson	13	b Ashenden	16
4	C.J.Elmes	c Pritchard b Ashenden	0	b Pritchard	17
5	H.R.Cameron	b Pritchard	26	b Pritchard	18
6	T.C.Fraser	b Wilson	10	c Ashenden b Pritchard	118
7	V.J.T.Chettleburgh	c Wrigley b Pritchard	5	c Wilson b Whyte	5
8	C.D.G.Toomey	c McLeod b Pritchard	11	c du Chateau b McLeod	51
9	J.V.Leader	b Pritchard	17	c Wrigley b McLeod	9
10	†G.H.Mills	lbw b Wilson	11	c McLeod b Ashenden	50
11	T.G.F.Lemin	not out	3	not out	1
	Extras	lb 12, nb 1	13	b 8, lb 13, nb 1	22
			138		351

FoW (1): 1-17 (1), 2-42 (3), 3-43 (4), 4-45 (2), 5-82 (6), 6-84 (5), 7-100, 8-103, 9-124, 10-138
FoW (2): 1-28 (2), 2-50 (1), 3-81, 4-81, 5-110, 6-120, 7-263, 8-279, 9-319, 10-351

WELLINGTON					
1	†E.W.T.Tindill	lbw b Elmes	40	(9) not out	14
2	O.L.Wrigley	b Lemin	1	c Mills b Lemin	6
3	W.G.Rainbird	lbw b Lemin	13	c and b Moloney	46
4	J.A.Ongley	run out	37	c Cutler b Moloney	6
5	V.H.du Chateau	b Elmes	14	c Mills b Lemin	13
6	D.S.Wilson	c Robertson b Elmes	16	c Moloney b Elmes	32
7	*E.G.McLeod	not out	52	(1) c Elmes b Moloney	28
8	W.F.Airey	c Toomey b Leader	30	(7) b Lemin	2
9	T.L.Pritchard	b Leader	2	(8) b Moloney	7
10	G.L.Whyte	c Moloney b Leader	3	b Lemin	42
11	J.G.Ashenden	c Mills b Leader	5	c Toomey b Lemin	0
	Extras	b 6, lb 1	7	b 9, lb 3, nb 3	15
			220		211

FoW (1): 1-5 (2), 2-41 (3), 3-98 (4), 4-99 (1), 5-123 (6), 6-130 (5), 7-176 (8), 8-178 (9), 9-208 (10), 10-220 (11)
FoW (2): 1-15, 2-59, 3-67, 4-108, 5-115, 6-118, 7-152, 8-161, 9-211, 10-211

Wellington Bowling	O	M	R	W			O	M	R	W	
Pritchard	15	1	68	5	1nb		30	2	107	4	
Ashenden	8	1	19	1			25.7	3	97	2	
Wilson	12.3	3	38	4			16	2	73	1	1nb
Whyte						(4)	9	0	45	1	
McLeod						(5)	5	1	7	2	

Otago Bowling	O	M	R	W			O	M	R	W	
Lemin	20	1	72	2			12.5	2	21	5	1nb
Robertson	5	2	17	0			10	1	22	0	1nb
Leader	12.6	1	42	4		(4)	19	10	50	0	1nb
Elmes	15	4	35	3		(3)	25	8	44	1	
Moloney	7	1	39	0			20	2	59	4	
Chettleburgh	2	1	8	0							

Umpires: L.Diehl and G.McQueen. Toss: Otago

Close of Play: 1st day: Wellington (1) 191-8 (McLeod 31*, Whyte 0*); 2nd day: Otago (2) 287-8 (Fraser 105*, Mills 4*); 3rd day: Wellington (2) 175-8 (Tindill 6*, Whyte 14*).

T.C.Fraser's 118 took 253 minutes and included 7 fours. W.G.Rainbird took over as wicket-keeper at lunch on the second day (Otago 73/2) as E.W.T.Tindill was suffering from a chill in his back.

RAJPUTANA v SOUTHERN PUNJAB

Played at Mayo College Ground, Ajmer, February 10, 11, 12, 1940.

Southern Punjab won by an innings and 190 runs.

RAJPUTANA					
1	†A.Wahab	lbw b Amir Elahi	30	c Wazir Ali b Amir Elahi	31
2	K.B.Murad	c Abdur Rehman b Nissar	2	(9) lbw b Amir Elahi	2
3	*W.H.Bradshaw	b Amir Elahi	6	(8) c Nazir Ali b Roshan Lal	14
4	H.Vohra	b Amir Elahi	4	(11) not out	11
5	Attique Hussain	hit wkt b Nissar	3	(4) c Wazir Ali b Nissar	2
6	S.Abbas	c Murawwat Hussain b Amir Elahi	6	(5) b Amir Elahi	13
7	G.R.Naidoo	c Murawwat Hussain b Amir Elahi	0	(6) c Nazir Ali b Amir Elahi	12
8	N.P.Kesari	b Nissar	14	(7) c sub b Amir Elahi	4
9	M.A.McCanlis	b Amarnath	9	(10) c Azmat Hayat b Amir Elahi	6
10	Firasat Hussain	not out	10	(2) b Amarnath	0
11	Azim Khan	c Abdur Rehman b Murawwat Hussain	9	(3) b Amir Elahi	31
	Extras		12		7
			105		133

FoW (1): 1-15 (2), 2- , 3- , 4- , 5- , 6- , 7- , 8- , 9-80, 10-105
FoW (2): 1- (2), 2-64 (3), 3- , 4- , 5- , 6- , 7- , 8- , 9- , 10-133

SOUTHERN PUNJAB			
1	†Abdur Rehman	lbw b Firasat Hussain	6
2	Roshan Lal	c Kesari b Azim Khan	14
3	L.Amarnath	lbw b Kesari	103
4	*S.Wazir Ali	c Azim Khan b Firasat Hussain	2
5	S.Nazir Ali	c Abbas b Azim Khan	6
6	Azmat Hayat	c Naidoo b Firasat Hussain	112
7	Mohammad Saeed	lbw b Attique Hussain	54
8	Bhalindra Singh	lbw b Azim Khan	9
9	Murawwat Hussain	lbw b Bradshaw	50
10	Amir Elahi	b Naidoo	18
11	M.Nissar	not out	32
	Extras		22
			428

FoW (1): 1-21 (2), 2-23 (1), 3- (4), 4-61 (5), 5-171 (3), 6-269 (7), 7- (8), 8-353 (6), 9- (10), 10-428 (9)

Southern Punjab Bowling	O	M	R	W		O	M	R	W
Nissar	14	7	22	3		8	2	19	1
Amarnath	8	0	21	1		7	3	11	1
Murawwat Hussain	6	1	15	1	(6)	3	1	6	0
Nazir Ali	4	0	15	0	(3)	3	0	16	0
Amir Elahi	8	1	20	5		17	4	33	7
Bhalindra Singh					(4)	4	1	12	0
Wazir Ali					(7)	2	0	7	0
Azmat Hayat					(8)	3	0	13	0
Roshan Lal					(9)	4	0	9	1

Rajputana Bowling	O	M	R	W
Bradshaw	18.2	3	65	1
Kesari	18	5	58	1
Azim Khan	31	10	72	3
Firasat Hussain	18	2	76	3
Murad	3	0	7	0
Abbas	6	0	30	0
Naidoo	9	0	48	1
Attique Hussain	10	1	50	1

Umpires: Toss:

Close of Play: 1st day: Southern Punjab (1) 150-4 (Amarnath 84*, Azmat Hayat 27*); 2nd day: Rajputana (2) 64-2 (Wahab 29*).
L.Amarnath's 103 included 18 fours. Azmat Hayat's 112 took 250 minutes and included 15 fours.

WESTERN AUSTRALIA v SOUTH AUSTRALIA

Played at Western Australia Cricket Association Ground, Perth, February 10, 12, 13, 1940.

Match drawn.

SOUTH AUSTRALIA					
1	K.L.Ridings	c Bandy b Halcombe	46		
2	T.E.Klose	b MacGill	6		
3	R.A.Hamence	c Lovelock b Eyres	3	(4) c and b Eyres	14
4	*D.G.Bradman	c Lovelock b MacGill	42	(3) not out	209
5	L.Michael	c Eyres b MacGill	5	not out	27
6	M.G.Waite	lbw b MacGill	37		
7	V.R.Gibson	c J.A.Jeffreys b Zimbulis	35		
8	J.M.Kierse	c J.A.Jeffreys b Watt	23		
9	F.A.Ward	c K.S.Jeffreys b Halcombe	15	(2) b Eyres	12
10	C.V.Grimmett	c Inverarity b Zimbulis	14		
11	†C.W.Walker	not out	2	(1) c Inverarity b Zimbulis	34
	Extras	b 16, lb 2, w 1, nb 1	20	b 9, lb 1	10
			248	(3 wickets, declared)	306

FoW (1): 1-21, 2-28, 3-97, 4-103, 5-115, 6-155, 7-200, 8-227, 9-227, 10-248
FoW (2): 1-25, 2-83, 3-135

WESTERN AUSTRALIA					
1	C.W.T.MacGill	c Ward b Grimmett	78	run out	11
2	J.A.Jeffreys	c Klose b Ward	36	c Bradman b Kierse	8
3	A.D.Watt	st Walker b Ward	18	b Ridings	52
4	A.E.O.Barras	lbw b Klose	11		
5	L.H.Bandy	c Klose b Ward	1	(4) not out	20
6	K.S.Jeffreys	st Walker b Ward	7	(5) not out	27
7	*M.Inverarity	st Walker b Ward	57		
8	†O.I.Lovelock	b Grimmett	13		
9	A.G.Zimbulis	not out	42		
10	G.Eyres	c Ward b Grimmett	9		
11	R.A.Halcombe	b Ward	2		
	Extras	b 1	1	lb 3	3
			275	(3 wickets)	121

FoW (1): 1-69, 2-91, 3-123, 4-135, 5-151, 6-153, 7-188, 8-252, 9-265, 10-275
FoW (2): 1-15, 2-26, 3-91

Western Australia Bowling	O	M	R	W			O	M	R	W
Eyres	22	2	81	1	1nb		16	2	65	2
MacGill	18	1	49	4	1w		15	3	66	0
Halcombe	13	1	51	2		(4)	9	0	59	0
Zimbulis	9.1	0	36	2		(3)	5	0	50	1
Watt	3	1	6	1						
Barras	2	1	5	0		(5)	4	0	28	0
K.S.Jeffreys						(6)	2	0	28	0

South Australia Bowling	O	M	R	W		O	M	R	W
Waite	8	1	26	0					
Kierse	3	1	6	0	(1)	7	2	19	1
Grimmett	33	8	94	3		4	0	26	0
Klose	10	2	18	1	(6)	6	4	8	0
Gibson	12	3	25	0	(2)	7	1	21	0
Ward	26.3	1	105	6	(4)	7	1	32	0
Ridings					(5)	4	0	12	1

Umpires: J.P.Robbins and M.J.Troy. Toss: South Australia

Close of Play: 1st day: Western Australia (1) 7-0 (MacGill 4*, J.A.Jeffreys 3*); 2nd day: South Australia (2) 1-0 (Walker 0*, Ward 0*).

D.G.Bradman's 209 took 161 minutes and included 30 fours and 1 six. 12th Men: A.E.Read (WA) and F.L.Teisseire (SA).

WESTERN AUSTRALIA v SOUTH AUSTRALIA

Played at Western Australia Cricket Association Ground, Perth, February 16, 17, 19, 1940.

Match drawn.

WESTERN AUSTRALIA					
1	C.W.T.MacGill	b Klose	17	c Klose b Gibson	17
2	A.E.Read	c Teisseire b Grimmett	55	b Grimmett	46
3	A.D.Watt	c Walker b Grimmett	1	(8) b Grimmett	10
4	A.E.O.Barras	run out (Michael/Walker)	6	c Teisseire b Grimmett	23
5	*M.Inverarity	b Gibson	52	b Ward	3
6	K.S.Jeffreys	lbw b Grimmett	26	(9) not out	21
7	L.H.Bandy	c Klose b Ward	30	(6) st Walker b Grimmett	4
8	†O.I.Lovelock	c Walker b Grimmett	45	(7) c Klose b Ward	29
9	A.G.Zimbulis	c Michael b Klose	33	(3) c and b Ward	1
10	C.W.Puckett	c Walker b Grimmett	4	(11) lbw b Grimmett	2
11	G.Eyres	not out	1	(10) b Grimmett	39
	Extras	b 3, lb 2	5	b 7, lb 3, w 1	11
			275		206

FoW (1): 1-21, 2-24, 3-31, 4-133, 5-141, 6-189, 7-195, 8-270, 9-272, 10-275
FoW (2): 1-42, 2-45, 3-73, 4-82, 5-93, 6-94, 7-120, 8-147, 9-200, 10-206

SOUTH AUSTRALIA			
1	K.L.Ridings	c Barras b Zimbulis	34
2	T.E.Klose	c Zimbulis b Eyres	60
3	*D.G.Bradman	c Zimbulis b Eyres	135
4	R.A.Hamence	run out (MacGill)	63
5	L.Michael	c and b Zimbulis	10
6	F.L.Teisseire	b MacGill	56
7	M.G.Waite	c Eyres b Zimbulis	24
8	V.R.Gibson	c and b Puckett	21
9	†C.W.Walker	b Puckett	3
10	F.A.Ward	run out	8
11	C.V.Grimmett	not out	5
	Extras	b 4, lb 6	10
			429

FoW (1): 1-79, 2-113, 3-263, 4-303, 5-319, 6-355, 7-400, 8-410, 9-424, 10-429

South Australia Bowling	O	M	R	W		O	M	R	W	
Waite	17	4	43	0	(2)	6	0	26	0	1w
Gibson	15	5	39	1	(1)	9	5	20	1	
Klose	21	12	24	2	(6)	3	3	0	0	
Grimmett	33.6	6	67	5		19.2	6	57	6	
Ward	21	2	97	1	(3)	21	3	81	3	
Ridings					(5)	4	1	11	0	

Western Australia Bowling	O	M	R	W
Eyres	23	3	79	2
MacGill	22	3	108	1
Puckett	24.3	4	89	2
Zimbulis	22	0	131	3
Bandy	1	0	12	0

Umpires: J.P.Robbins and M.J.Troy. Toss: Western Australia

Close of Play: 1st day: Western Australia (1) 256-7 (Lovelock 40*, Zimbulis 24*); 2nd day: South Australia (1) 363-6 (Teisseire 25*, Gibson 3*).

D.G.Bradman's 135 took 148 minutes and included 14 fours. 12th Men: W.A.Roach (WA) and J.M.Kierse (SA).

MAHARASHTRA v SOUTHERN PUNJAB

Played at Poona Club Ground, February 17, 18, 19, 20, 1940.

Match drawn.

	SOUTHERN PUNJAB				
1	Roshan Lal	c Harris b Patwardhan	47	(9) not out	35
2	†Abdur Rehman	lbw b Patwardhan	4	(7) b Hazare	22
3	Azmat Hayat	c Hazare b Sohoni	40	(8) b Hazare	0
4	*S.Wazir Ali	c Jadhav b Sohoni	13	b Jadhav	152
5	S.Nazir Ali	c sub b Sohoni	151	c Bhandarkar b Jadhav	21
6	Mohammad Saeed	c Patwardhan b Deodhar	76	(1) b Hazare	17
7	Bhalindra Singh	b Hazare	23	(10) b Patwardhan	11
8	Murawwat Hussain	b Sohoni	6	(6) b Jadhav	2
9	Amir Elahi	b Harris	9	(2) b Hazare	32
10	Ahmed Saeed	b Hazare	36	(3) b Hazare	0
11	Shahabuddin	not out	2	not out	4
	Extras		22		13
			429	(9 wickets, declared)	309

FoW (1): 1-23 (2), 2-71 (3), 3-94 (4), 4-142 (1), 5-305 (6), 6-355 (7), 7-378 (5), 8-389 (8), 9-413 (9), 10-429 (10)
FoW (2): 1-31 (1), 2-39 (3), 3-89 (2), 4-136 (5), 5-140 (6), 6-207 (7), 7-207 (8), 8-270 (4), 9-295 (10)

	MAHARASHTRA				
1	†K.V.Bhandarkar	c Abdur Rehman b Amir Elahi	35	c and b Amir Elahi	15
2	S.W.Sohoni	run out	60	lbw b Nazir Ali	15
3	S.Nazir Ali	c Bhalindra Singh b Shahabuddin	21	lbw b Amir Elahi	0
4	*D.B.Deodhar	c Abdur Rehman b Shahabuddin	25	(6) c Azmat Hayat b Wazir Ali	51
5	V.S.Hazare	c Amir Elahi b Bhalindra Singh	155	st Ahmed Saeed b Azmat Hayat	55
6	K.M.Rangnekar	lbw b Nazir Ali	87	(7) not out	22
7	N.D.Nagarwala	st Abdur Rehman b Amir Elahi	22	(4) lbw b Bhalindra Singh	29
8	J.G.Harris	lbw b Nazir Ali	27	not out	1
9	D.S.Doctor	b Nazir Ali	8		
10	M.K.Patwardhan	b Bhalindra Singh	13		
11	K.M.Jadhav	not out	15		
	Extras		14		15
			482	(6 wickets)	203

FoW (1): 1-50 (1), 2-104 (3), 3-120 (2), 4-161 (4), 5-308 (6), 6-358 (7), 7-416 (8), 8-432 (9), 9-455 (5), 10-482 (10)
FoW (2): 1-19 (1), 2-19 (3), 3-39 (2), 4-72 (4), 5-174 (6), 6-198 (5)

Maharashtra Bowling	O	M	R	W		O	M	R	W
Patwardhan	39	7	113	2	(2)	8	0	44	1
Hazare	41.2	12	92	2	(1)	26	4	79	5
Harris	21	6	50	1	(7)	6	1	27	0
Sohoni	20	4	105	4	(3)	8	0	63	0
Jadhav	6	0	25	0	(4)	16	1	61	3
Deodhar	8	3	22	1	(5)	2	0	15	0
Rangnekar					(6)	2	0	7	0

Southern Punjab Bowling	O	M	R	W		O	M	R	W
Shahabuddin	27	2	113	2		9	2	20	0
Nazir Ali	22	2	71	3		9	1	32	1
Murawwat Hussain	23	4	78	0		4	2	3	0
Amir Elahi	35	4	131	2		26	5	80	2
Bhalindra Singh	26.4	4	63	2		11	2	29	1
Wazir Ali	1	0	7	0	(7)	4	1	3	1
Mohammad Saeed	2	0	5	0					
Abdur Rehman					(6)	4	0	15	0
Azmat Hayat					(8)	1	0	6	1

Umpires: S.Hassan Shah and M.Nagarkar. Toss: Southern Punjab

Close of Play: 1st day: Southern Punjab (1) 340-5 (Nazir Ali 129*, Bhalindra Singh 15*); 2nd day: Maharashtra (1) 264-4 (Hazare 61*, Rangnekar 56*); 3rd day: Southern Punjab (2) 135-3 (Wazir Ali 60*, Nazir Ali 21*).
S.Nazir Ali's 151 took 286 minutes and included 16 fours and 2 sixes. V.S.Hazare's 155 took 323 minutes and included 10 fours. S.Wazir Ali's 152 took 207 minutes and included 17 fours. Ahmed Saeed kept wicket in the Maharashtra second innings.

MAHARASHTRA v UNITED PROVINCES

Played at Poona Gymkhana Ground, February 24, 25, 26, 27, 1940.

Maharashtra won by ten wickets.

UNITED PROVINCES

1	Masud Alam	c Jadhav b Hazare	0	(9) lbw b Harris	0
2	A.S.N.Murthy	c Doctor b Sohoni	48	(1) b Hazare	1
3	*P.E.Palia	c Sohoni b Patwardhan	5	c Hazare b Jadhav	216
4	Aftab Ahmed	run out (Bhandarkar)	20	c Doctor b Hazare	19
5	Shamim Khwaja	run out	16	c Doctor b Sohoni	5
6	Akhtar Hussain	st Doctor b Sohoni	7	(7) b Sohoni	16
7	Masood Salahuddin	b Harris	34	(6) c Hazare b Sohoni	0
8	B.K.Garudachar	not out	63	run out	8
9	Iqbal Ahmed Khan	b Hazare	0	(10) not out	9
10	E.Alexander	run out	3	(2) c Deodhar b Jadhav	41
11	†S.J.Dastoor	c and b Sohoni	23	run out	16
	Extras		18		24
			237		355

FoW (1): 1-0 (1), 2-13 (3), 3-57 (4), 4-94 (2), 5-102 (6), 6-110 (5), 7-166 (7), 8-169 (9), 9-176 (10), 10-237 (11)
FoW (2): 1-1 (1), 2-142 (2), 3-218 (4), 4-240 (5), 5-241 (6), 6-287 (7), 7-312 (8), 8-313 (9), 9-338 (3), 10-355 (11)

MAHARASHTRA

1	K.V.Bhandarkar	b Palia	132	not out	7
2	S.W.Sohoni	c Alexander b Murthy	96	not out	1
3	N.D.Nagarwala	c Garudachar b Murthy	54		
4	*D.B.Deodhar	c Aftab Ahmed b Masood Salahuddin	60		
5	V.S.Hazare	c Murthy b Masood Salahuddin	53		
6	K.M.Rangnekar	c Masud Alam b Garudachar	45		
7	J.G.Harris	run out	62		
8	K.M.Jadhav	b Alexander	1		
9	R.G.Salvi	b Aftab Ahmed	33		
10	†D.S.Doctor	st Dastoor b Aftab Ahmed	8		
11	M.K.Patwardhan	not out	1		
	Extras		36		4
			581	(no wicket)	12

FoW (1): 1-188 (2), 2-275 (3), 3-321 (1), 4-417 (5), 5-448 (4), 6-477 (6), 7-480 (8), 8-540 (9), 9-555 (10), 10-581 (7)

Maharashtra Bowling

	O	M	R	W		O	M	R	W
Hazare	25	5	78	2	(2)	36	12	67	2
Patwardhan	10	0	34	1	(1)	12	1	32	0
Harris	15	5	29	1	(5)	17	3	58	1
Jadhav	10	0	45	0		18	3	58	2
Sohoni	5.5	0	32	3	(3)	31	5	97	3
Deodhar	1	0	1	0		8.3	3	19	0

United Provinces Bowling

	O	M	R	W		O	M	R	W
Alexander	33	5	98	1	8nb	1	0	1	0
Masood Salahuddin	22	2	90	2	9nb	0.5	0	7	0
Palia	46	14	95	1					
Aftab Ahmed	25	3	97	2					
Garudachar	11	0	45	1	1nb				
Murthy	27	0	112	2					
Iqbal Ahmed Khan	1	0	8	0					

Umpires: Toss: United Provinces

Close of Play: 1st day: Maharashtra (1) 131-0 (Bhandarkar 54*, Sohoni 67*); 2nd day: Maharashtra (1) 477-6 (Harris 9*, Jadhav 0*); 3rd day: United Provinces (2) 240-4 (Palia 156*).

K.V.Bhandarkar's 132 took 272 minutes and included 12 fours. P.E.Palia's 216 took 331 minutes and included 25 fours.

NATAL v WESTERN PROVINCE

Played at Kingsmead, Durban, March 2, 4, 5, 1940.

Match drawn.

NATAL

1	D.S.Turner	c Glantz b Brinkhaus	77
2	D.V.Dyer	c Cloete b Brinkhaus	185
3	R.L.Harvey	b Brinkhaus	80
4	*A.D.Nourse	c Glantz b Brinkhaus	87
5	W.W.Wade	c Ralph b Plimsoll	57
6	E.L.Dalton	c Manning b Plimsoll	10
7	O.C.Dawson	b Brinkhaus	7
8	†R.R.Yuill	not out	17
9	L.W.Payn	not out	7
10	N.B.F.Mann		
11	R.K.Moir		
	Extras		26
		(7 wickets, declared)	553

FoW (1): 1-183 (1), 2-331, 3-406, 4-475, 5-511, 6-523, 7-539

WESTERN PROVINCE

1	S.Kiel	b Dalton	43	b Moir	7
2	G.E.Crighton	c Dalton b Mann	40	run out	21
3	L.M.Manning	b Dalton	24	b Moir	11
4	G.Georgeu	b Dalton	50	c Harvey b Payn	13
5	*A.R.M.Ralph	not out	119	(6) c Yuill b Dalton	6
6	T.M.H.van der Spuy	run out (Harvey)	52	(5) not out	38
7	P.H.B.Cloete	b Payn	6	not out	14
8	†A.Glantz	c Payn b Mann	15		
9	L.S.Eckard	b Dalton	0		
10	J.G.B.Brinkhaus	b Dalton	0		
11	J.B.Plimsoll	c Dyer b Mann	5		
	Extras		4		14
			358	(5 wickets)	124

FoW (1): 1-76, 2-91, 3-128, 4-180, 5-306, 6-319, 7-348, 8-349, 9-351, 10-358
FoW (2): 1-18 (1), 2-44 (3), 3-46 (2), 4-67 (4), 5-94 (6)

Western Province Bowling

	O	M	R	W
Plimsoll	32	3	124	2
Brinkhaus	48	5	180	5
Eckard	21	1	59	0
Cloete	17	0	86	0
van der Spuy	6	0	28	0
Georgeu	2	0	10	0
Crighton	9	2	40	0

Natal Bowling

	O	M	R	W	O	M	R	W
Dawson	8	2	21	0	5	0	10	0
Moir	19	4	46	0	10	2	22	2
Dalton	36	8	113	5	8	3	16	1
Payn	33	10	77	1	10	2	23	1
Mann	43.1	15	67	3	5	1	15	0
Harvey	9	2	30	0	8	3	24	0

Umpires: Toss: Natal

Close of Play: 1st day: Natal (1) 434-3 (Nourse 57*, Wade 14*); 2nd day: Western Province (1) 177-3 (Georgeu 48*, Ralph 19*).

D.V.Dyer's 185 took 370 minutes. A.R.M.Ralph's 119 included 6 fours.

BORDER v WESTERN PROVINCE

Played at Jan Smuts Ground, East London, March 8, 9, 1940.

Western Province won by six wickets.

	BORDER				
1	S.L.White	c Glantz b Plimsoll	3	b Plimsoll	21
2	R.P.Richter	b Brinkhaus	29	lbw b Plimsoll	30
3	R.J.Evans	lbw b Brinkhaus	1	c Glantz b Plimsoll	5
4	R.R.Phillips	run out	29	b Plimsoll	22
5	H.V.L.Whitfield	lbw b Brinkhaus	37	c Glantz b Plimsoll	25
6	G.V.Wienand	b Brinkhaus	42	(7) b Brinkhaus	21
7	*H.D.Bowley	c Brinkhaus b Cloete	1	(6) st Glantz b Cloete	4
8	†G.G.L.Mandy	not out	27	b Cloete	8
9	P.S.Hubbard	b Brinkhaus	15	not out	11
10	D.W.Niland	b Brinkhaus	0	c van der Spuy b Cloete	5
11	M.A.Hanley	lbw b Brinkhaus	0	c Cheetham b Cloete	4
	Extras		5	b 3, lb 2, nb 1	6
			189		162

FoW (1): 1-7 (1), 2-8 (3), 3-46, 4-85, 5-140, 6-143, 7-155, 8-187, 9-189, 10-189
FoW (2): 1-46 (1), 2-58 (3), 3-73, 4-92, 5-113, 6-115, 7-123, 8-149, 9-158, 10-162

	WESTERN PROVINCE				
1	S.Kiel	c White b Wienand	3	b Hubbard	54
2	G.E.Crighton	st Mandy b Evans	28	c Whitfield b Evans	8
3	L.M.Manning	b Evans	29	c Evans b Hanley	0
4	G.Georgeu	st Mandy b Evans	19	not out	39
5	*A.R.M.Ralph	not out	68		
6	T.M.H.van der Spuy	b Hanley	12	(5) lbw b Hanley	14
7	J.E.Cheetham	b Whitfield	15	(6) not out	17
8	P.H.B.Cloete	c Hubbard b Whitfield	0		
9	†A.Glantz	lbw b Hubbard	1		
10	J.B.Plimsoll	c Hubbard b Hanley	18		
11	J.G.B.Brinkhaus				
	Extras		13	b 9, lb 4, nb 1	14
		(9 wickets, declared)	206	(4 wickets)	146

FoW (1): 1-15 (1), 2-59 (2), 3-78 (3), 4-89 (4), 5-124 (6), 6-173 (7), 7-175 (8), 8-176 (9), 9-206 (10)
FoW (2): 1-38 (2), 2-41 (3), 3-84 (1), 4-115 (5)

Western Province Bowling

	O	M	R	W		O	M	R	W
Brinkhaus	17.6	2	60	7		20	6	38	1
Plimsoll	14	0	42	1		25	7	60	5
Cloete	5	0	24	1		17.6	1	58	4
van der Spuy	5	0	35	0					
Cheetham	3	0	23	0					

Border Bowling

	O	M	R	W		O	M	R	W
Niland	4	0	16	0		7.6	0	24	0
Wienand	5	1	22	1					
Evans	18	1	68	3		8	1	29	1
Hanley	10.5	3	34	2		8	1	27	2
Hubbard	13	2	37	1	(6)	9	1	33	1
Whitfield	7	0	16	2	(5)	3	0	12	0
Richter					(2)	3	1	7	0

Umpires: Toss: Border

Close of Play: 1st day: Western Province (1) 206-9 (Ralph 68*).

The match was scheduled for three days but completed in two.

NEW SOUTH WALES v THE REST

Played at Sydney Cricket Ground, March 8, 9, 11, 1940.

New South Wales won by two wickets.

THE REST					
1	W.A.Brown	c Saggers b Pepper	35	run out	97
2	I.S.Lee	c and b Cheetham	0	c Saggers b Cheetham	14
3	*D.G.Bradman	c Saggers b O'Reilly	25	c McCool b Cheetham	2
4	A.L.Hassett	c Mudge b Cheetham	136	b Pepper	75
5	R.E.Rogers	c O'Reilly b Lush	25	c and b McCool	17
6	M.G.Waite	c McCabe b O'Reilly	5	c O'Reilly b Cohen	12
7	I.W.G.Johnson	b Pepper	12	c McCool b Cheetham	8
8	†D.Tallon	b Pepper	0	c and b Cohen	8
9	D.T.Ring	c Mudge b O'Reilly	2	c McCool b Cohen	14
10	C.V.Grimmett	c McCabe b Cheetham	27	c McCool b Cohen	0
11	R.B.Scott	not out	13	not out	2
	Extras	b 5, lb 3, nb 1	9	lb 2, nb 1	3
			289		252

FoW (1): 1-2, 2-64, 3-64, 4-108, 5-115, 6-142, 7-142, 8-166, 9-266, 10-289
FoW (2): 1-31, 2-37, 3-145, 4-196, 5-210, 6-227, 7-229, 8-247, 9-247, 10-252

NEW SOUTH WALES					
1	M.B.Cohen	b Waite	12	run out	67
2	H.Mudge	c and b Grimmett	21	b Grimmett	21
3	*S.J.McCabe	c Tallon b Grimmett	72	c Grimmett b Ring	96
4	S.G.Barnes	c and b Grimmett	2	lbw b Grimmett	46
5	C.M.Solomon	c Lee b Grimmett	20	b Waite	5
6	†R.A.Saggers	c Waite b Scott	3	c Johnson b Grimmett	32
7	A.G.Cheetham	c Bradman b Waite	58	c and b Grimmett	2
8	C.L.McCool	c and b Grimmett	19	c Johnson b Grimmett	15
9	C.G.Pepper	b Scott	4	not out	25
10	J.G.Lush	not out	2	not out	2
11	W.J.O'Reilly	b Waite	1		
	Extras	b 1, lb 4	5	b 2, lb 8, w 1, nb 1	12
			219	(8 wickets)	323

FoW (1): 1-17, 2-62, 3-64, 4-108, 5-119, 6-157, 7-203, 8-214, 9-216, 10-219
FoW (2): 1-36, 2-176, 3-236, 4-245, 5-247, 6-254, 7-294, 8-303

New South Wales Bowling	O	M	R	W			O	M	R	W	
Lush	6	0	34	1	1nb						
Cheetham	8.7	1	41	3		(1)	11	0	43	3	1nb
O'Reilly	18	4	78	3			8	0	49	0	
Pepper	17	1	102	3			14	0	81	1	
Cohen	2	0	25	0		(2)	7.7	1	25	4	
McCool						(5)	9	1	51	1	

The Rest Bowling	O	M	R	W			O	M	R	W	
Scott	14	0	57	2			11	0	63	0	1w,1nb
Waite	8.2	2	12	3			16	1	37	1	
Ring	12	0	54	0		(4)	8	0	48	1	
Grimmett	21	2	65	5		(3)	23.1	2	130	5	
Johnson	4	0	26	0			5	0	33	0	

Umpires: G.E.Borwick and R.McGrath. Toss: The Rest

Close of Play: 1st day: New South Wales (1) 137-5 (McCabe 67*, Cheetham 9*); 2nd day: New South Wales (2) 21-0 (Cohen 6*, Mudge 13*).

The match was scheduled for four days but completed in three. A.L.Hassett's 136 took 132 minutes and included 15 fours and 4 sixes. 12th Men: J.W.Chegwyn (NSW) and K.L.Ridings (Rest).

EASTERN PROVINCE v WESTERN PROVINCE

Played at St George's Park, Port Elizabeth, March 13, 14, 15, 1940.

Match drawn.

WESTERN PROVINCE					
1	S.Kiel	lbw b Leibbrandt	5	c Leibbrandt b Coy	120
2	G.E.Crighton	run out	18	c Gouldie b Leibbrandt	25
3	*L.M.Manning	c Gouldie b Leibbrandt	0	b Gouldie	9
4	T.M.H.van der Spuy	c Rouse b Coy	74	c Drimmie b Coy	33
5	G.Georgeu	c Holmes b Thwaits	28	lbw b Leibbrandt	7
6	J.E.Cheetham	c Drimmie b Leibbrandt	5	not out	108
7	P.H.B.Cloete	c Gouldie b Thwaits	29	c Leibbrandt b Coy	3
8	†A.Glantz	lbw b Thwaits	0	(11) not out	0
9	L.S.Eckard	not out	18	(8) c Marais b Coy	0
10	J.B.Plimsoll	b Leibbrandt	0	(9) b Coy	3
11	J.G.B.Brinkhaus	b Leibbrandt	4	(10) b Coy	0
	Extras	b 3, lb 3	6	b 7, lb 3	10
			187	(9 wickets, declared)	318

FoW (1): 1-23 (2), 2-23 (3), 3-30 (1), 4-78 (5), 5-85 (6), 6-137 (7), 7-137 (8), 8-183 (4), 9-183 (10), 10-187 (11)
FoW (2): 1-44 (2), 2-59 (3), 3-155 (4), 4-167 (5), 5-254 (1), 6-270 (7), 7-271 (8), 8-300 (9), 9-300 (10)

EASTERN PROVINCE					
1	†W.Marais	st Glantz b van der Spuy	42	not out	21
2	J.G.Sharp	lbw b Eckard	20	c Glantz b Brinkhaus	0
3	I.E.Drimmie	c Kiel b Plimsoll	25	not out	12
4	P.S.C.Johnson	lbw b Plimsoll	1		
5	P.L.Holmes	c and b van der Spuy	16		
6	J.M.Leibbrandt	b van der Spuy	19		
7	R.Rouse	c Glantz b Plimsoll	13		
8	S.A.Thwaits	c Manning b Plimsoll	15		
9	C.Bernstein	c Cloete b Plimsoll	3		
10	R.S.Gouldie	c Georgeu b Eckard	14		
11	*A.H.Coy	not out	19		
	Extras	b 5, lb 3	8	lb 5	5
			195	(1 wicket)	38

FoW (1): 1-48 (2), 2-75 (3), 3-89 (4), 4-90 (1), 5-127 (6), 6-134 (5), 7-150, 8-154, 9-161, 10-195
FoW (2): 1-1 (2)

Eastern Province Bowling	O	M	R	W		O	M	R	W
Leibbrandt	20	4	55	5		18	3	82	2
Gouldie	14	5	36	0		25	3	79	1
Coy	16	5	60	1		22	1	94	6
Thwaits	10	1	30	3		11	0	53	0

Western Province Bowling	O	M	R	W		O	M	R	W
Brinkhaus	9	0	38	0		4	0	7	1
Plimsoll	22	4	52	5		5	1	14	0
Eckard	10.3	2	31	2	(4)	1	0	2	0
Cloete	10	0	40	0	(5)	1	0	3	0
van der Spuy	7	0	26	3	(3)	1	0	7	0

Umpires: E.Coulridge and H.V.Dorrington. Toss: Eastern Province

Close of Play: 1st day: Eastern Province (1) 135-6 (Rouse 5*, Thwaits 1*); 2nd day: Western Province (2) 318-9 (Cheetham 108*, Glantz 0*).

S.Kiel's 120 took 180 minutes and included 8 fours.

EASTERN PROVINCE v BORDER

Played at St George's Park, Port Elizabeth, March 23, 25, 1940.

Eastern Province won by eight wickets.

	BORDER				
1	C.D.White	c Marais b Gouldie	4	c Marais b Gouldie	8
2	R.P.Richter	c Hoskin b Gouldie	7	c Holmes b Leibbrandt	3
3	A.J.Bauer	b Leibbrandt	19	c Marais b Gouldie	4
4	R.R.Phillips	c Procter b Gouldie	8	b Procter	30
5	*S.L.White	b Gouldie	47	c Marais b Hoskin	35
6	W.A.E.Ayres	st Marais b Procter	8	b Hoskin	15
7	A.W.D.Hanley	c Sharp b Thwaits	10	b Gouldie	25
8	†G.G.L.Mandy	hit wkt b Thwaits	4	run out	40
9	D.W.Niland	c Gouldie b Procter	29	c Marais b Procter	7
10	R.B.Gordon	not out	19	b Gouldie	2
11	M.A.Hanley	st Marais b Procter	0	not out	2
	Extras	lb 2, w 1	3	b 8, lb 6	14
			158		185

FoW (1): 1-7, 2-23, 3-39, 4-39, 5-68, 6-81, 7-87, 8-125, 9-158, 10-158
FoW (2): 1-11, 2-11, 3-21, 4-70, 5-94, 6-117, 7-149, 8-172, 9-179, 10-185

	EASTERN PROVINCE				
1	*†W.Marais	c Niland b M.A.Hanley	10		
2	J.G.Sharp	lbw b Gordon	8	st Mandy b Phillips	29
3	J.O.Young	c Mandy b Phillips	86	(1) b Phillips	29
4	I.E.Drimmie	c and b Gordon	8	(3) not out	13
5	J.M.Leibbrandt	c Mandy b Ayres	15	(4) not out	48
6	P.L.Holmes	b Niland	6		
7	R.Rouse	lbw b Phillips	30		
8	W.C.Hoskin	b Phillips	0		
9	S.A.Thwaits	st Mandy b Phillips	0		
10	R.S.Gouldie	b Phillips	14		
11	W.C.Procter	not out	35		
	Extras	b 5, lb 2	7	b 3, lb 6	9
			219	(2 wickets)	128

FoW (1): 1-15, 2-27, 3-69, 4-97, 5-118, 6-146, 7-146, 8-146, 9-172, 10-219
FoW (2): 1-62, 2-67

Eastern Province Bowling	O	M	R	W		O	M	R	W
Leibbrandt	16	3	45	1		18	1	44	1
Gouldie	22	4	54	4		15	1	47	4
Young	1	0	9	0		3	0	6	0
Procter	12.5	2	28	3		8.3	0	22	2
Thwaits	8	2	19	2		4	0	10	0
Hoskin					(6)	8	0	42	2

Border Bowling	O	M	R	W		O	M	R	W
Niland	17	3	36	1		5	1	14	0
M.A.Hanley	13	2	71	1		13	0	40	0
Ayres	4	0	27	1					
Richter	2	0	8	0	(3)	3	0	16	0
Gordon	10	1	32	2	(4)	1.5	0	30	0
Phillips	6.4	1	38	5	(5)	13	4	19	2

Umpires: Toss:

Close of Play: 1st day: Eastern Province (1) 173-9 (Rouse 19*, Procter 1*).

R.R.Phillips took a hat-trick in the Eastern Province first innings (Young, Hoskin, Thwaits).

INDEX OF 1939/40 MATCH SCORECARDS

1940/41

NAWANAGAR v WESTERN INDIA

Played at Ajitsinhji Ground, Jamnagar, November 8, 9, 1940.

Western India won by two wickets.

NAWANAGAR					
1	M.H.Mankad	b Saeed Ahmed	4	c Akbar Khan b Prithviraj	4
2	I.Oza	c Rajkot b Prithviraj	22	st Faiz Ahmed b Purshottam	18
3	S.N.Banerjee	c sub (Prataprai) b Nyalchand	13	(4) lbw b Nyalchand	16
4	S.H.M.Colah	c Akbar Khan b Nyalchand	35	(3) c Nyalchand b Akbar Khan	15
5	*R.K.Yadvendrasinhji	b Nyalchand	6	(6) lbw b Nyalchand	29
6	J.R.Oza	b Nyalchand	8	(7) c Faiz Ahmed b Prithviraj	1
7	K.Mankad	c Prithviraj b Nyalchand	11	(5) lbw b Prithviraj	15
8	Mubarak Ali	b Nyalchand	0	c Purshottam b Nyalchand	15
9	Prabhat Singh	not out	8	lbw b Akbar Khan	8
10	†K.Mehta	b Akbar Khan	2	c Barritt b Akbar Khan	0
11	Mulwantrai	b Nyalchand	2	not out	3
	Extras		6		16
			117		140

FoW (1): 1-15 (1), 2-30 (2), 3-49 (3), 4-67 (5), 5-81 (6), 6-102 (4), 7-102 (8), 8-105 (7), 9-110 (10), 10-117 (11)
FoW (2): 1- (1), 2- (2), 3- (3), 4-75 (5), 5-85 (4), 6-92 (7), 7-122 (6), 8- , 9- , 10-140

WESTERN INDIA					
1	†Faiz Ahmed	c J.R.Oza b Banerjee	14	lbw b Mubarak Ali	12
2	H.W.Barritt	b Mubarak Ali	1	c Mehta b Mubarak Ali	2
3	Umar Khan	c Colah b M.H.Mankad	12	b Mubarak Ali	16
4	Nawab of Manavadar	c Mehta b Banerjee	13	(5) c Mehta b Banerjee	1
5	Purshottam	c Mehta b Banerjee	2	(8) c I.Oza b Banerjee	31
6	Prithviraj	st Mehta b M.H.Mankad	0	(4) c M.H.Mankad b J.R.Oza	53
7	K.S.Abdul Khaliq	b M.H.Mankad	1	(10) not out	6
8	*Thakore Saheb of Rajkot	not out	3	(6) c Colah b J.R.Oza	42
9	Akbar Khan	b Banerjee	10	(7) c M.H.Mankad b Mubarak Ali	24
10	S.Nyalchand	c Mehta b Banerjee	0		
11	Saeed Ahmed	absent hurt	0	(9) not out	9
	Extras		1		7
			57	(8 wickets)	203

FoW (1): 1-8 (2), 2- , 3- , 4- , 5- , 6- , 7- , 8- , 9-57
FoW (2): 1-6 (2), 2-23 (1), 3-36 (3), 4-51 (5), 5-129 (4), 6-150 (6), 7-183 (7), 8-197 (8)

Western India Bowling	O	M	R	W		O	M	R	W
Saeed Ahmed	9	5	6	1					
Akbar Khan	22	4	42	1	(1)	14	4	28	3
Nyalchand	19.5	4	38	7	(2)	23.3	9	47	3
Prithviraj	8	2	25	1	(3)	13	2	34	3
Purshottam					(4)	4	0	15	1

Nawanagar Bowling	O	M	R	W		O	M	R	W
Banerjee	13.4	4	26	5		16	1	59	2
Mubarak Ali	7	2	6	1		17	0	86	4
M.H.Mankad	7	1	18	3		9	0	27	0
Mulwantrai	1	0	6	0					
Prabhat Singh					(4)	4	1	9	0
J.R.Oza					(5)	4	0	15	2

Umpires: Toss: Nawanagar

Close of Play: 1st day: Nawanagar (2) 46-3 (Banerjee 3*, K.Mankad 1*).
The match was scheduled for three days but completed in two.

HYDERABAD v CENTRAL PROVINCES AND BERAR

Played in November 1940.
Hyderabad won by a walk-over.
It is not known exactly when this match should have been played but it was reported in the newspaper on 18 November that Central Provinces and Berar would not play.

MAHARASHTRA v BOMBAY

Played at Poona Club Ground, November 15, 16, 17, 18, 19, 1940.

Match drawn.

MAHARASHTRA			
1	K.V.Bhandarkar	c and b Havewala	91
2	S.W.Sohoni	lbw b Hakim	120
3	R.V.Bhajekar	c Havewala b Ibrahim	0
4	*D.B.Deodhar	c sub b Havewala	246
5	V.S.Hazare	c Hindlekar b Rangnekar	76
6	†Y.N.Gokhale	run out	17
7	C.T.Sarwate	lbw b Hakim	14
8	B.J.Mohoni	hit wkt b Hakim	8
9	Ushaq Ahmed	lbw b Havewala	54
10	K.M.Jadhav	b Merchant	6
11	M.K.Patwardhan	not out	21
	Extras	b 14, lb 3, w 3, nb 2	22
			675

FoW (1): 1-204 (1), 2-205 (3), 3-216 (2), 4-371 (5), 5-393 (6), 6-429 (7), 7-441 (8), 8-588 (9), 9-632 (10), 10-675 (4)

BOMBAY			
1	†D.D.Hindlekar	c Mohoni b Patwardhan	0
2	L.B.Kenny	b Sohoni	67
3	A.A.Hakim	c Deodhar b Sohoni	23
4	S.M.Kadri	c Hazare b Sarwate	45
5	*V.M.Merchant	b Hazare	109
6	K.M.Rangnekar	c Mohoni b Sarwate	202
7	K.C.Ibrahim	st Gokhale b Mohoni	61
8	J.B.Khot	c Mohoni b Patwardhan	55
9	M.S.Naik	c Sohoni b Hazare	34
10	D.R.Havewala	c Deodhar b Hazare	14
11	K.K.Tarapore	not out	16
	Extras	b 18, lb 6	24
			650

FoW (1): 1-0 (1), 2-48 (3), 3-122 (4), 4-219 (2), 5-304 (5), 6-451 (7), 7-569 (6), 8-617 (8), 9-619 (9), 10-650 (10)

Bombay Bowling	O	M	R	W
Merchant	21	3	52	1
Hakim	41	6	153	3
Khot	19	3	66	0
Havewala	52.1	7	137	3
Tarapore	16	6	117	0
Ibrahim	18	4	47	1
Kenny	1	0	13	0
Rangnekar	19	1	58	1
Naik	2	0	10	0

Maharashtra Bowling	O	M	R	W
Patwardhan	30	8	72	2
Sohoni	58	12	139	2
Hazare	66.1	21	132	3
Ushaq Ahmed	40	11	80	0
Sarwate	73	13	154	2
Jadhav	12	1	34	0
Mohoni	3	0	9	1
Deodhar	4	0	6	0

Umpires: N.D.Marshall and D.K.Naik. Toss: Maharashtra

Close of Play: 1st day: Maharashtra (1) 385-4 (Deodhar 80*, Gokhale 9*); 2nd day: Bombay (1) 0-1 (Kenny 0*, Hakim 0*); 3rd day: Bombay (1) 215-3 (Kenny 67*, Merchant 69*); 4th day: Bombay (1) 501-6 (Rangnekar 160*, Khot 20*).
The match was scheduled for three days but extended to five. S.W.Sohoni's 120 took 165 minutes and included 13 fours. D.B.Deodhar's 246 included 19 fours. V.M.Merchant's 109 took 262 minutes and included 9 fours. K.M.Rangnekar's 202 took 365 minutes and included 22 fours. Deodhar had a runner from lunch on the second day when his score was 129*.

NORTH WEST FRONTIER PROVINCE v NORTHERN INDIA

Played at Peshawar Club Ground, November 15, 16, 17, 1940.

Northern India won by 229 runs.

NORTHERN INDIA

1	Nazar Mohammad	c Kapoor b Rajindernath	0	(2) lbw b Abdul Latif	21
2	Amir Hussain	b Abdul Latif	34	(1) b Faqir Hussain	1
3	R.P.Mehra	b Faqir Hussain	6	(4) c Paramanand b Faqir Hussain	85
4	Gul Mohammad	c Paramanand b Faqir Hussain	9	(5) c Abdul Latif b Faqir Hussain	8
5	Muzaffar Baig	b Abdul Latif	40	(3) b Rajindernath	3
6	†G.B.Bull	b Faqir Hussain	8	(7) b Qazi Daud	41
7	*M.Jahangir Khan	b Abdul Latif	3	(6) c Kapoor b Qazi Daud	25
8	Agha Sarfraz	c Rajindernath b Abdul Latif	6	b Abdul Latif	62
9	Habibullah	c Kapoor b Qazi Daud	8	c Hamid Tajak b Abdul Latif	25
10	D.R.Puri	not out	0	(11) not out	0
11	Mohammad Ramzan	lbw b Rajindernath	0	(10) b Rajindernath	0
	Extras		20		9
			134		280

FoW (1): 1-0 (1), 2- (3), 3- , 4- , 5- , 6- , 7- , 8- , 9- , 10-134
FoW (2): 1- , 2- , 3- , 4- , 5- , 6- , 7- , 8- , 9- , 10-280

NORTH WEST FRONTIER PROVINCE

1	Qazi Daud	lbw b Mohammad Ramzan	1	c Jahangir Khan b Habibullah	0
2	Hamid Tajak	b Mohammad Ramzan	1	c Habibullah b Mohammad Ramzan	25
3	Sita Ram	b Puri	0	(10) b Agha Sarfraz	0
4	Amin Hassan	lbw b Mohammad Ramzan	0	(6) not out	29
5	Sher Khan	b Jahangir Khan	14	b Habibullah	3
6	†G.C.Kapoor	run out	0	(4) c Nazar Mohammad b Mohammad Ramzan	7
7	B.C.Khanna	not out	38	(3) lbw b Mohammad Ramzan	5
8	Rajindernath	lbw b Agha Sarfraz	7	(7) lbw b Habibullah	1
9	*Abdul Latif	c Amir Hussain b Agha Sarfraz	6	(8) c Mehra b Mohammad Ramzan	3
10	Paramanand	b Habibullah	10	(9) lbw b Agha Sarfraz	7
11	Faqir Hussain	b Habibullah	0	lbw b Nazar Mohammad	1
	Extras		20		7
			97		88

FoW (1): 1-2, 2-8, 3-8, 4-8, 5-8, 6-39, 7-64, 8- , 9-97, 10-97
FoW (2): 1- , 2- , 3- , 4- , 5- , 6- , 7- , 8- , 9- , 10-88

North West Frontier Province Bowling

	O	M	R	W		O	M	R	W
Rajindernath	6.5	1	18	2		18	2	58	2
Faqir Hussain	15	3	44	3		14	1	68	3
Abdul Latif	11	1	46	4		15.2	1	53	3
Qazi Daud	1	0	6	1		14	1	53	2
Khanna					(5)	7	1	29	0
Paramanand					(6)	3	1	10	0

Northern India Bowling

	O	M	R	W		O	M	R	W
Mohammad Ramzan	14	7	24	3		21	8	43	4
Puri	5	4	1	1					
Habibullah	9.2	2	24	2		15	4	24	3
Jahangir Khan	10	7	6	1					
Agha Sarfraz	8	1	19	2	(4)	4	1	10	2
Muzaffar Baig	2	1	2	0					
Amir Hussain	2	1	1	0	(2)	2	1	1	0
Nazar Mohammad					(5)	1	0	3	1

Umpires: Toss: Northern India

Close of Play: 1st day: North West Frontier Province (1) 97 all out; 2nd day: North West Frontier Province (2) 6-0 (Qazi Daud not out, Hamid Tajak not out).

QUEENSLAND v NEW SOUTH WALES

Played at Brisbane Cricket Ground, Woolloongabba, Brisbane, November 15, 16, 18, 19, 1940.

New South Wales won by 27 runs.

NEW SOUTH WALES					
1	M.B.Cohen	b Ellis	7	c Tallon b Cook	11
2	D.K.Carmody	c Brown b Ellis	2	c and b Raymer	47
3	S.G.Barnes	c Brown b Ellis	0	lbw b Raymer	15
4	*S.J.McCabe	c Tallon b Stackpoole	88	b Ellis	57
5	J.W.Chegwyn	c Stackpoole b Cook	3	c Christ b Ellis	48
6	†R.A.Saggers	st Tallon b Raymer	22	run out	45
7	B.Cook	b Raymer	15	c Tallon b Ellis	1
8	V.E.Jackson	lbw b Raymer	19	not out	55
9	C.L.McCool	c Christ b Ellis	37	b Cook	6
10	V.Trumper	c Christ b Cook	18	b Raymer	3
11	W.J.O'Reilly	not out	1	c Allen b Stackpoole	15
	Extras			b 8, lb 6, w 1	15
			212		318

FoW (1): 1-7, 2-7, 3-20, 4-27, 5-105, 6-135, 7-137, 8-170, 9-204, 10-212
FoW (2): 1-29, 2-59, 3-124, 4-150, 5-230, 6-236, 7-236, 8-245, 9-275, 10-318

QUEENSLAND					
1	*W.A.Brown	b Trumper	1	c Saggers b Barnes	84
2	G.G.Cook	b Trumper	1	b Jackson	35
3	T.Allen	run out (Chegwyn/Saggers)	18	c McCabe b McCool	39
4	R.E.Rogers	st Saggers b McCool	31	lbw b Trumper	43
5	†D.Tallon	b McCool	55	b Jackson	6
6	G.G.Baker	st Saggers b McCool	58	st Saggers b McCool	1
7	D.Watt	b O'Reilly	34	c and b McCool	43
8	V.N.Raymer	c Jackson b O'Reilly	2	lbw b Trumper	20
9	J.A.Ellis	not out	13	c McCool b O'Reilly	0
10	C.P.Christ	lbw b O'Reilly	0	run out	0
11	J.Stackpoole	c Cook b O'Reilly	0	not out	5
	Extras	b 1, lb 5	6	b 5, lb 2, nb 1	8
			219		284

FoW (1): 1-2, 2-3, 3-32, 4-84, 5-144, 6-199, 7-202, 8-207, 9-207, 10-219
FoW (2): 1-115, 2-121, 3-186, 4-193, 5-208, 6-220, 7-254, 8-266, 9-267, 10-284

Queensland Bowling

	O	M	R	W		O	M	R	W	
Ellis	14.2	2	62	4		19	2	73	3	
Cook	8	2	21	2		18	4	58	2	1w
Stackpoole	7	0	28	1		10.5	1	63	1	
Christ	8	1	38	0	(5)	8	0	42	0	
Raymer	13	0	63	3	(4)	13	0	67	3	

New South Wales Bowling

	O	M	R	W		O	M	R	W	
Trumper	10	0	42	2		11	3	49	2	
Jackson	11	1	37	0		16	4	65	2	
O'Reilly	15.6	4	42	4		12	4	36	1	1nb
McCool	20	0	85	3		20.3	0	106	3	
McCabe	1	0	7	0						
Barnes					(5)	6	1	20	1	

Umpires: D.W.Given and R.Weitemeyer. Toss: New South Wales

Close of Play: 1st day: No play; 2nd day: Queensland (1) 144-4 (Tallon 55*, Baker 33*); 3rd day: New South Wales (2) 289-9 (Jackson 36*, O'Reilly 6*).

12th Men: J.E.McCarthy (Qld) and K.C.Gulliver (NSW).

SOUTHERN PUNJAB v DELHI

Played at Baradari Ground, Patiala, November 15, 16, 1940.

Southern Punjab won by an innings and 58 runs.

DELHI

1	Yusuf Nanjrani	run out	12	b Patiala	20
2	Jamilul Hai	b Nissar	1	b Patiala	5
3	M.H.Maqsood	c Amarnath b Patiala	29	c Amir Elahi b Patiala	6
4	Ishwar Lal	b Amir Elahi	0	lbw b Amir Elahi	20
5	Masud Yar Khan	c and b Amir Elahi	5	c Abdur Rehman b Patiala	11
6	Mohammad Ishaq	c Ram Kishen b Patiala	16	b Murawwat Hussain	15
7	Shujauddin	c Nissar b Patiala	4	st Abdur Rehman b Amir Elahi	13
8	J.Sen	lbw b Amir Elahi	9	b Amir Elahi	6
9	Mohammad Yunus Khan	c sub b Amir Elahi	2	st Abdur Rehman b Amir Elahi	1
10	*A.S.de Mello	b Amir Elahi	15	c Murawwat Hussain b Amir Elahi	0
11	†B.C.Mathur	not out	5	not out	2
	Extras		13		7
			111		106

FoW (1): 1-2 (2), 2-53 (1), 3-53 (4), 4-60 (5), 5-62 (3), 6-70 (7), 7-89 (6), 8-89 (8), 9-104 (9), 10-111 (10)
FoW (2): 1-17 (2), 2- (3), 3-48 (1), 4-62 (4), 5-84 (6), 6-86 (5), 7- , 8- , 9- , 10-106

SOUTHERN PUNJAB

1	†Abdur Rehman	b Mohammad Yunus Khan	34
2	Roshan Lal	lbw b Mohammad Yunus Khan	8
3	Murawwat Hussain	st Mathur b Sen	19
4	L.Amarnath	b Mohammad Yunus Khan	105
5	*Maharaja of Patiala	c Maqsood b Mohammad Ishaq	34
6	Amir Elahi	b Sen	41
7	Feroze Khan	b Mohammad Yunus Khan	13
8	M.Nissar	lbw b Shujauddin	15
9	Devinder Singh	b Sen	1
10	B.Ram Kishen	lbw b Mohammad Yunus Khan	0
11	Shahabuddin	not out	0
	Extras		5
			275

FoW (1): 1-10 (2), 2-61 (3), 3-63 (1), 4-116 (5), 5-181 (6), 6-218 (7), 7-248 (8), 8-251 (9), 9-265 (10), 10-275 (4)

Southern Punjab Bowling

	O	M	R	W		O	M	R	W
Nissar	5	2	10	1	(2)	6	2	7	0
Amarnath	7	3	5	0					
Shahabuddin	3	2	2	0	(4)	1	0	2	0
Patiala	11	3	25	3	(1)	23	8	38	4
Amir Elahi	15	1	45	5	(3)	10.3	1	29	5
Feroze Khan	1	0	11	0		1	0	2	0
Murawwat Hussain					(5)	7	1	21	1

Delhi Bowling

	O	M	R	W
de Mello	12	1	49	0
Mohammad Yunus Khan	20	3	59	5
Sen	26	0	82	3
Shujauddin	8	1	27	1
Maqsood	8	0	35	0
Mohammad Ishaq	4	0	18	1

Umpires: Toss: Southern Punjab

Close of Play: 1st day: Southern Punjab (1) 131-4 (Amarnath 29*, Amir Elahi 7*).

The match was scheduled for three days but completed in two. L.Amarnath's 105 included 10 fours.

QUEENSLAND AND VICTORIA v NEW SOUTH WALES

Played at Brisbane Cricket Ground, Woolloongabba, Brisbane, November 22, 23, 25, 26, 1940.

New South Wales won by one wicket.

QUEENSLAND AND VICTORIA

1	*W.A.Brown	c Chegwyn b Trumper	13	c Jackson b O'Reilly	43
2	G.G.Cook	b Jackson	5	c Saggers b Gulliver	22
3	R.E.Rogers	c and b O'Reilly	29	(4) c Saggers b Gulliver	34
4	†D.Tallon	c Chegwyn b O'Reilly	55	(5) c Trumper b Cohen	152
5	A.L.Hassett	c McCool b Trumper	14	(3) c Saggers b McCool	96
6	K.R.Miller	c Saggers b McCool	8	c Saggers b Jackson	24
7	G.G.Baker	c Gulliver b Trumper	22	c Saggers b Gulliver	12
8	M.W.Sievers	not out	23	c Saggers b Gulliver	25
9	V.N.Raymer	c Saggers b McCool	15	b Jackson	1
10	D.T.Ring	st Saggers b McCool	5	c Saggers b Gulliver	0
11	J.A.Ellis	c Chegwyn b O'Reilly	1	not out	1
	Extras	b 7, lb 4, nb 1	12	lb 5, w 1	6
			202		416

FoW (1): 1-14, 2-30, 3-108, 4-111, 5-129, 6-146, 7-157, 8-177, 9-187, 10-202
FoW (2): 1-58, 2-78, 3-147, 4-309, 5-364, 6-379, 7-397, 8-414, 9-414, 10-416

NEW SOUTH WALES

1	M.B.Cohen	c Tallon b Ellis	0	b Baker	34
2	D.K.Carmody	b Sievers	7	run out	36
3	S.G.Barnes	c Tallon b Ring	144	lbw b Baker	3
4	*S.J.McCabe	c Cook b Ring	43	(6) c Cook b Ring	53
5	J.W.Chegwyn	c Tallon b Sievers	37	(4) c and b Raymer	21
6	†R.A.Saggers	c Hassett b Raymer	58	(5) c Tallon b Baker	5
7	V.E.Jackson	c Rogers b Ring	7	lbw b Raymer	2
8	C.L.McCool	c Miller b Raymer	52	not out	27
9	K.C.Gulliver	not out	66	c Brown b Ring	0
10	V.Trumper	c Baker b Raymer	4	run out	0
11	W.J.O'Reilly	b Cook	4	not out	4
	Extras	b 4, lb 3	7	b 2, lb 5	7
			429	(9 wickets)	192

FoW (1): 1-0, 2-16, 3-83, 4-184, 5-278, 6-288, 7-309, 8-388, 9-415, 10-429
FoW (2): 1-69, 2-74, 3-85, 4-105, 5-105, 6-118, 7-177, 8-178, 9-182

New South Wales Bowling

	O	M	R	W			O	M	R	W	
Trumper	9	0	37	3	1nb		10	2	46	0	1w
Jackson	6	0	18	1			17.5	2	69	2	
O'Reilly	10.4	0	46	3		(5)	17	1	85	1	
Gulliver	7	0	44	0		(3)	16	0	80	5	
Barnes	1	0	6	0							
McCool	9	0	39	3			11	0	91	1	
Cohen						(4)	9	2	39	1	

Queensland and Victoria Bowling

	O	M	R	W		O	M	R	W
Ellis	20	5	76	1		10	3	26	0
Sievers	17	1	68	2	(3)	5	1	20	0
Ring	20	0	143	3	(4)	9.4	2	50	2
Cook	12.3	3	29	1	(2)	7	1	17	0
Raymer	19	0	85	3	(6)	9	0	55	2
Baker	3	0	21	0	(5)	9	1	17	3

Umpires: K.E.S.Fagg and D.W.Given. Toss: Queensland and Victoria

Close of Play: 1st day: New South Wales (1) 184-4 (Barnes 94*, Saggers 0*); 2nd day: Queensland and Victoria (2) 126-2 (Hassett 30*, Rogers 27*); 3rd day: New South Wales (2) 134-6 (McCabe 20*, McCool 7*).

S.G.Barnes's 144 took 225 minutes and included 16 fours. D.Tallon's 152 took 115 minutes and included 20 fours and 1 six. 12th Men: D.Watt (Comb XI) and B.Cook (NSW).

BIHAR v BENGAL

Played at Keenan Stadium, Jamshedpur, November 30, December 1, 2, 1940.

Match drawn.

BENGAL					
1	A.Jabbar	b Bose	6	c Mody b Khambatta	68
2	S.W.E.Behrend	b Khambatta	50		
3	S.Bose	c Naoroji b Khambatta	37		
4	*N.M.Bose	c Naoroji b Bose	31		
5	N.C.Chatterjee	lbw b Zahur Ahmed	11	(3) b Zahur Ahmed	61
6	A.S.Garbis	b Khambatta	8	(5) not out	18
7	H.M.Bose	not out	35		
8	B.Ramchandra	c and b Sen	51		
9	K.Bhattacharya	b Banerjee	9	(4) not out	35
10	†K.R.Roy	b Banerjee	1		
11	T.S.Bhattacharjee	b Banerjee	2	(2) run out	62
	Extras		16		18
			257	(3 wickets, declared)	262

FoW (1): 1-8 (1), 2- (3), 3- (4), 4- (2), 5- (5), 6- (6), 7-232 (8), 8- (9), 9- (10), 10-257 (11)
FoW (2): 1-95 (2), 2-198 (1), 3-220 (3)

BIHAR					
1	S.Bagchi	c N.M.Bose b Chatterjee	31	(7) lbw b Ramchandra	5
2	S.Chakravorty	c Bhattacharjee b Behrend	11		
3	S.Banerjee	c Roy b Behrend	8	(1) b Behrend	5
4	N.Vania	c Bhattacharya b Ramchandra	14	(2) c Bhattacharya b Bhattacharjee	12
5	E.Sanjana	c Bhattacharjee b Chatterjee	54	(4) b Behrend	11
6	B.Sen	c Roy b Bhattacharya	31	(3) not out	17
7	Zahur Ahmed	b Behrend	11	(5) b Behrend	0
8	*†K.A.D.Naoroji	c and b Bhattacharjee	21	(6) c Jabbar b Behrend	0
9	N.Mody	c Bhattacharya b Behrend	21	(8) not out	1
10	B.K.Bose	c Roy b Behrend	0		
11	D.S.Khambatta	not out	5		
	Extras		10		7
			217	(6 wickets)	58

FoW (1): 1-18 (2), 2-36 (3), 3-70 (4), 4-72 (1), 5-151 (5), 6-168 (7), 7-172 (6), 8-207 (9), 9-207 (10), 10-217 (8)
FoW (2): 1-20 (1), 2-22 (2), 3-40 (4), 4-40 (5), 5-44 (6), 6-57 (7)

Bihar Bowling	O	M	R	W		O	M	R	W
Khambatta	19	4	51	3	(2)	19	2	74	1
Bose	17	3	42	2	(1)	6	4	10	0
Zahur Ahmed	23	3	79	1		18	1	64	1
Chakravorty	9	1	24	0	(6)	13	2	45	0
Sen	3	0	19	1		5	0	18	0
Banerjee	3.2	1	7	3	(4)	6	2	13	0
Vania	8	2	19	0					
Sanjana					(7)	4	0	20	0

Bengal Bowling	O	M	R	W		O	M	R	W
Behrend	19	1	68	5		8	2	24	4
Bhattacharjee	7.4	2	20	1		5	0	24	1
Bhattacharya	18	7	39	1	(5)	1	0	2	0
Chatterjee	17	2	45	2	(3)	2	2	0	0
Ramchandra	11	4	30	1	(4)	2	1	1	1
Garbis	1	0	5	0					

Umpires: M.K.Banerjee, M.Dutta Roy and P.Misra. Toss: Bengal
Close of Play: 1st day: Bihar (1) 8-0 (Bagchi 3*, Chakravorty 1*); 2nd day: Bengal (2) 12-0 (Jabbar 4*, Bhattacharjee 6*).
P.Misra stood on the third day in place of M.Dutta Roy who had to return to Calcutta to attend to urgent business.

GUJARAT v BARODA

Played at Ahmedabad, November 30, December 1, 2, 1940.
Gujarat won by a walk-over.
Baroda conceded a walk-over due to the death of the Maharaja of Kolhapur.

WESTERN INDIA v SIND

Played at Municipal Stadium, Rajkot, December 1, 2, 3, 1940.

Western India won by six wickets.

SIND

1	Qamaruddin Sheikh	lbw b Saeed Ahmed	9	c Purshottam b Saeed Ahmed	66
2	Inam Khan	c Akbar Khan b Nyalchand	8	run out	2
3	†Abbas Khan	b Nyalchand	47	c Abdul Khaliq b Nyalchand	1
4	Daud Khan	lbw b Nyalchand	61	b Akbar Khan	15
5	G.Kishenchand	c Prithviraj b Nyalchand	50	(7) c Umar Khan b Nyalchand	33
6	*Naoomal Jaoomal	c Faiz Ahmed b Saeed Ahmed	11		
7	M.A.Gopaldas	b Saeed Ahmed	8		
8	Ibrahim Vazir	b Saeed Ahmed	0	(6) b Nyalchand	6
9	W.L.Mascarenhas	b Saeed Ahmed	1		
10	M.J.Mobed	not out	32	(8) not out	6
11	S.K.Girdhari	run out	7	(5) c Purshottam b Akbar Khan	34
	Extras		5		5
			239	(7 wickets, declared)	168

FoW (1): 1-17 (1), 2-17 (2), 3-127 (3), 4-132 (4), 5-153 (6), 6-173 (7), 7-173 (8), 8-198 (5), 9-200 (9), 10-239 (11)
FoW (2): 1- (2), 2- (3), 3- (4), 4- (1), 5- (6), 6- (5), 7-168 (7)

WESTERN INDIA

1	†Faiz Ahmed	b Gopaldas	0	c Mascarenhas b Qamaruddin Sheikh	12
2	H.W.Barritt	c Inam Khan b Naoomal Jaoomal	34	c Girdhari b Gopaldas	23
3	Umar Khan	c Mascarenhas b Ibrahim Vazir	50	(5) not out	40
4	Prithviraj	st Abbas Khan b Ibrahim Vazir	51	(6) not out	0
5	K.S.Abdul Khaliq	lbw b Mobed	10	(3) run out	3
6	*Thakore Saheb of Rajkot	c and b Girdhari	14		
7	Purshottam	b Mobed	10		
8	Nawab of Manavadar	c Daud Khan b Girdhari	34	(4) c sub (Vissuman) b Girdhari	69
9	Akbar Khan	b Girdhari	2		
10	S.Nyalchand	b Mobed	3		
11	Saeed Ahmed	not out	24		
	Extras		18		12
			250	(4 wickets)	159

FoW (1): 1-0 (1), 2-43 (2), 3- (4), 4- (5), 5- (3), 6- (6), 7- (7), 8- (9), 9- (8), 10-250 (10)
FoW (2): 1- (2), 2- (3), 3-43 (1), 4-155 (4)

Western India Bowling

	O	M	R	W		O	M	R	W
Saeed Ahmed	32	8	78	5		17	4	37	1
Nyalchand	26	5	73	4		27	7	63	3
Akbar Khan	19	6	44	0		16	1	44	2
Prithviraj	6.1	0	22	0		3	0	14	0
Purshottam	3	0	17	0					
Rajkot					(5)	3	0	5	0

Sind Bowling

	O	M	R	W		O	M	R	W
Gopaldas	11	4	23	1	(3)	12	3	23	1
Qamaruddin Sheikh	5	1	19	0	(1)	9	0	41	1
Ibrahim Vazir	19	2	49	2	(5)	6	2	7	0
Mascarenhas	18	6	28	0	(2)	3	1	4	0
Mobed	21.1	5	48	3	(6)	11	2	22	0
Girdhari	17	2	37	3	(4)	15	2	44	1
Naoomal Jaoomal	17	3	28	1		5	2	6	0

Umpires: H.D.Billimoria and D.K.Naik. Toss: Sind

Close of Play: 1st day: Western India (1) 43-2 (Umar Khan 9*); 2nd day: Sind (2) 35-2 (Qamaruddin Sheikh 24*, Daud Khan 6*).

NEW SOUTH WALES v SOUTH AUSTRALIA

Played at Sydney Cricket Ground, December 6, 7, 9, 1940.

New South Wales won by 374 runs.

	NEW SOUTH WALES				
1	M.B.Cohen	c Walker b Klose	20		
2	D.K.Carmody	c Walker b Waite	7	(1) c Walker b Grimmett	32
3	S.G.Barnes	c Roberts b Ward	108	st Walker b Ward	3
4	*S.J.McCabe	c and b Grimmett	18	c sub (P.L.Ridings) b Ward	9
5	†R.A.Saggers	st Walker b Ward	47	(2) b Roberts	29
6	V.E.Jackson	lbw b Ward	21	(5) c Cotton b Roberts	11
7	C.L.McCool	b Cotton	90	(6) not out	39
8	C.G.Pepper	c Waite b Ward	77	(7) b Cotton	35
9	W.J.O'Reilly	c Waite b Ward	12	(8) b Ward	3
10	V.Trumper	st Walker b Ward	0		
11	R.B.Scott	not out	1		
	Extras	b 1	1	b 5, lb 1	6
			402	(7 wickets, declared)	167

FoW (1): 1-27, 2-27, 3-59, 4-175, 5-217, 6-222, 7-355, 8-381, 9-392, 10-402
FoW (2): 1-45, 2-49, 3-65, 4-85, 5-94, 6-162, 7-167

	SOUTH AUSTRALIA				
1	K.L.Ridings	c Jackson b Trumper	4	c McCabe b Trumper	10
2	T.E.Klose	retired hurt	0	(8) c Barnes b O'Reilly	1
3	C.L.Badcock	c Scott b Pepper	38	(4) lbw b O'Reilly	17
4	R.A.Hamence	c O'Reilly b Scott	41	(5) c McCabe b Trumper	4
5	M.G.Waite	c Saggers b Scott	0	(6) lbw b O'Reilly	3
6	B.H.Leak	c Barnes b O'Reilly	8	(7) st Saggers b Pepper	1
7	W.M.Roberts	c McCool b O'Reilly	1	(9) b O'Reilly	2
8	*†C.W.Walker	st Saggers b O'Reilly	2	(2) b Scott	0
9	C.V.Grimmett	c Jackson b McCool	23	(10) c Barnes b O'Reilly	5
10	F.A.Ward	not out	24	(3) c McCool b Scott	2
11	H.N.J.Cotton	b McCool	0	not out	1
	Extras	b 6, lb 1	7	nb 1	1
			148		47

FoW (1): 1-5, 2-78, 3-78, 4-90, 5-94, 6-94, 7-104, 8-148, 9-148
FoW (2): 1-10, 2-12, 3-14, 4-20, 5-27, 6-36, 7-37, 8-39, 9-46, 10-47

South Australia Bowling	O	M	R	W		O	M	R	W
Cotton	13.4	0	42	1		6	0	23	1
Waite	6	0	46	1		6	1	13	0
Klose	15	4	56	1					
Grimmett	19	4	83	1	(3)	7	0	32	1
Ward	20	0	131	6	(4)	13	0	66	3
Roberts	11	1	43	0	(5)	6	1	27	2

New South Wales Bowling	O	M	R	W		O	M	R	W	
Scott	5	0	11	2		6	0	10	2	1nb
Trumper	5	1	15	1		6	2	14	2	
Jackson	10	0	34	0						
O'Reilly	12	1	28	3	(3)	6.4	2	11	5	
Pepper	15	1	51	1	(4)	6	2	11	1	
McCool	2.3	1	2	2						

Umpires: G.E.Borwick and R.McGrath. Toss: New South Wales

Close of Play: 1st day: New South Wales (1) 402 all out; 2nd day: New South Wales (2) 167-7 (McCool 39*).

The match was scheduled for four days but completed in three. S.G.Barnes's 108 took 164 minutes and included 15 fours. T.E.Klose retired hurt in the South Australia first innings having scored 0 (team score 1-0). 12th Men: J.W.Chegwyn (NSW) and P.L.Ridings (SA).

BENGAL v UNITED PROVINCES

Played at Eden Gardens, Calcutta, December 7, 8, 9, 1940.

United Provinces won by 144 runs.

UNITED PROVINCES					
1	E.Alexander	st Bedwell b Bhattacharya	21	b Bhattacharya	2
2	Firasat Hussain	lbw b Kendrew	0	(6) c Bhattacharya b Behrend	30
3	*P.E.Palia	b Bhattacharya	45	c and b Chatterjee	65
4	J.P.Phansalkar	lbw b Bhattacharjee	51	(5) lbw b Behrend	27
5	Shamim Khwaja	run out	27	(7) hit wkt b Chatterjee	21
6	†Dilawar Hussain	c Bedwell b Bhattacharya	2	(2) lbw b Bhattacharya	9
7	Aftab Ahmed	not out	21	(4) c Bhattacharya b Kendrew	0
8	Masood Salahuddin	b Bhattacharjee	4	(9) c Ramchandra b Bhattacharya	13
9	B.K.Garudachar	c Behrend b Bhattacharya	9	(8) b Behrend	39
10	Wahidullah	b Bhattacharya	1	not out	2
11	A.S.N.Murthy	b Bhattacharya	0	st Bedwell b Bhattacharya	4
	Extras		10		14
			191		226

FoW (1): 1-4 (2), 2-45 (1), 3-88 (3), 4-154 (4), 5-154 (5), 6-166 (6), 7-171 (8), 8-184 (9), 9-189 (10), 10-191 (11)
FoW (2): 1-10 (2), 2-18 (1), 3-21 (4), 4-97 (5), 5-141 (3), 6-150 (6), 7-201 (7), 8-215 (9), 9-221 (8), 10-226 (11)

BENGAL					
1	S.W.E.Behrend	b Firasat Hussain	20	(10) c and b Firasat Hussain	5
2	A.Jabbar	lbw b Firasat Hussain	5	(1) lbw b Alexander	9
3	K.Bhattacharya	b Alexander	4	(8) not out	30
4	S.Bose	b Palia	38	(3) b Alexander	0
5	*N.M.Bose	c Firasat Hussain b Aftab Ahmed	10	(4) c Dilawar Hussain b Alexander	4
6	N.C.Chatterjee	b Palia	1	(2) b Alexander	22
7	B.Ramchandra	b Masood Salahuddin	25	(5) c Murthy b Palia	17
8	A.Kamal	not out	31	(6) b Firasat Hussain	0
9	T.S.Bhattacharjee	b Masood Salahuddin	5	st Dilawar Hussain b Aftab Ahmed	5
10	†J.S.Bedwell	b Firasat Hussain	4	(11) c Firasat Hussain b Palia	1
11	N.A.Kendrew	b Palia	2	(7) b Firasat Hussain	23
	Extras		2		10
			147		126

FoW (1): 1-20 (2), 2-29 (3), 3-46 (1), 4-63 (5), 5-68 (6), 6-85 (4), 7-115 (7), 8-121 (9), 9-144 (10), 10-147 (11)
FoW (2): 1-33 (1), 2-33 (3), 3-38 (2), 4-39 (4), 5-42 (6), 6-66 (5), 7-91 (7), 8-112 (9), 9-123 (10), 10-126 (11)

Bengal Bowling	O	M	R	W		O	M	R	W
Behrend	10	0	34	0	(3)	17	3	71	3
Kendrew	11	6	20	1	(4)	11	0	27	1
Bhattacharya	23	4	41	6	(1)	32.3	5	60	4
Bhattacharjee	10	2	40	2	(2)	8	1	23	0
Ramchandra	6	0	20	0		4	0	10	0
Chatterjee	8	0	26	0		8	1	21	2

United Provinces Bowling	O	M	R	W		O	M	R	W
Alexander	10	2	32	1		6	0	20	4
Masood Salahuddin	13	6	17	2		2	0	18	0
Palia	14.5	3	30	3	(4)	5.1	1	25	2
Aftab Ahmed	6	0	23	1	(5)	3	0	14	1
Garudachar	1	0	7	0					
Firasat Hussain	22	9	36	3	(3)	12	1	39	3

Umpires: M.K.Banerjee and J.Subbuswami. Toss: United Provinces

Close of Play: 1st day: Bengal (1) 20-1 (Behrend 15*, Bhattacharya 0*); 2nd day: United Provinces (2) 97-4 (Palia 48*, Firasat Hussain 0*).

VICTORIA v SOUTH AUSTRALIA

Played at Melbourne Cricket Ground, December 13, 14, 16, 17, 1940.

Match drawn.

SOUTH AUSTRALIA					
1	K.L.Ridings	c Baker b Ring	69	lbw b Johnson	22
2	T.E.Klose	c Ring b Dudley	2		
3	C.L.Badcock	c Ring b Sievers	120	c Tamblyn b Sievers	102
4	*†C.W.Walker	c Johnson b Sievers	10		
5	R.A.Hamence	c Dudley b Sievers	130	(4) not out	103
6	M.G.Waite	hit wkt b Dempster	15		
7	B.H.Leak	b Dudley	79		
8	P.L.Ridings	lbw b Johnson	42		
9	C.V.Grimmett	st Baker b Johnson	14		
10	F.A.Ward	c Dempster b Johnson	7	(2) b Ring	10
11	H.N.J.Cotton	not out	7		
	Extras	b 5, lb 10, w 1, nb 4	20	b 6, lb 2	8
			515	(3 wickets, declared)	245

FoW (1): 1-9, 2-195, 3-206, 4-221, 5-264, 6-440, 7-444, 8-493, 9-506, 10-515
FoW (2): 1-30, 2-44, 3-245

VICTORIA					
1	I.S.Lee	b Cotton	93	(3) b Ward	41
2	G.E.Tamblyn	b Grimmett	32	(1) c and b Ward	29
3	R.A.Dempster	lbw b Grimmett	10	(2) lbw b Waite	2
4	K.R.Miller	b Grimmett	63	b Waite	16
5	*A.L.Hassett	c Waite b Grimmett	67	(6) not out	36
6	P.J.Beames	st Walker b Grimmett	42	(7) c Cotton b Grimmett	1
7	I.W.G.Johnson	c Klose b Grimmett	0	(8) c P.L.Ridings b Ward	9
8	M.W.Sievers	lbw b Waite	41	(5) b Ward	1
9	†E.A.Baker	lbw b Grimmett	15	not out	12
10	D.T.Ring	not out	12		
11	W.J.Dudley	c Cotton b Waite	4		
	Extras	b 1, lb 6, nb 3	10	b 12, lb 2	14
			389	(7 wickets)	161

FoW (1): 1-57, 2-85, 3-198, 4-214, 5-308, 6-312, 7-317, 8-371, 9-381, 10-389
FoW (2): 1-3, 2-70, 3-91, 4-95, 5-95, 6-102, 7-119

Victoria Bowling	O	M	R	W			O	M	R	W
Dudley	24	0	71	2	1w,1nb		10	0	45	0
Sievers	30	3	100	3	3nb		9.5	0	49	1
Johnson	26.1	0	117	3		(4)	12	0	50	1
Ring	27	1	139	1		(3)	14	4	56	1
Dempster	15	1	65	1			4	0	16	0
Miller	1	0	3	0						
Hassett						(6)	3	0	21	0

South Australia Bowling	O	M	R	W			O	M	R	W
Cotton	11	2	47	1	3nb		4	0	8	0
Waite	19.1	0	55	2			11	3	14	2
P.L.Ridings	7	0	23	0			4	1	11	0
Grimmett	38	6	114	7		(6)	7	1	36	1
Klose	14	3	46	0						
Ward	13	0	94	0		(4)	13	2	53	4
Hamence						(5)	4	0	25	0

Umpires: A.N.Barlow and W.J.Craddock. Toss: South Australia

Close of Play: 1st day: South Australia (1) 311-5 (Hamence 60*, Leak 20*); 2nd day: Victoria (1) 168-2 (Lee 70*, Miller 52*); 3rd day: South Australia (2) 65-2 (Badcock 12*, Hamence 20*).
C.L.Badcock's 120 took 174 minutes and included 9 fours. R.A.Hamence's 130 took 231 minutes and included 12 fours.
C.L.Badcock's 102 took 148 minutes and included 10 fours. R.A.Hamence's 103 took 130 minutes and included 8 fours.

MADRAS v MYSORE

Played at Marina Stadium, Madras, December 14, 15, 16, 1940.

Match drawn.

MYSORE			
1	P.G.Doraiswami	b Rangachari	11
2	M.B.Rama Rao	lbw b Ram Singh	36
3	K.Thimmappiah	lbw b Rangachari	15
4	C.J.Ramdev	b Krishna Rao	4
5	†F.K.Irani	c Doraiswami b Rangachari	53
6	B.V.Ramakrishnappa	b Ram Singh	0
7	B.Frank	b Ram Singh	0
8	M.G.Vijayasarathi	b Krishna Rao	7
9	*S.Darashah	c Ramaswami b Ram Singh	25
10	Y.S.Ramaswami	b Ram Singh	0
11	S.Rama Rao	not out	6
	Extras		14
			171

FoW (1): 1-16 (1), 2-56 (3), 3-73 (4), 4-81 (2), 5-81 (6), 6-81 (7), 7-107 (8), 8-145 (9), 9-145 (10), 10-171 (5)

MADRAS			
1	M.Swaminathan	run out	60
2	V.N.Madhava Rao	c Irani b Vijayasarathi	28
3	A.G.Ram Singh	c Irani b Vijayasarathi	12
4	B.S.R.Bhadradri	c M.B.RamaRao b Vijayasarathi	1
5	M.C.Karthikeyan	b Ramaswami	1
6	C.Ramaswami	c M.B.RamaRao b Vijayasarathi	13
7	M.S.Gopal	c Darashah b Ramaswami	3
8	*M.J.Gopalan	not out	39
9	†T.M.Doraiswami	not out	12
10	B.S.Krishna Rao		
11	C.R.Rangachari		
	Extras		5
		(7 wickets)	174

FoW (1): 1-53 (2), 2-69 (3), 3-73 (4), 4-79 (5), 5-102 (6), 6-119 (7), 7-139 (1)

Madras Bowling

	O	M	R	W
Gopalan	9	3	15	0
Ram Singh	15	6	38	5
Rangachari	13	3	37	3
Karthikeyan	3	0	8	0
Krishna Rao	13	0	59	2

Mysore Bowling

	O	M	R	W
S.Rama Rao	8	1	15	0
Darashah	30	16	30	0
Vijayasarathi	32	6	75	4
Ramaswami	22	5	40	2
Thimmappiah	2	0	3	0
Frank	1	0	6	0

Umpires: L.O'Callaghan and T.A.Ramachandran. Toss: Mysore

Close of Play: 1st day: Madras (1) 89-4 (Swaminathan 41*, Ramaswami 4*); 2nd day: No play.

MUSLIMS v PARSEES

Played at Brabourne Stadium, Bombay, December 14, 15, 16, 1940.

Match drawn.

PARSEES

1	M.F.Mistry	lbw b Amir Elahi	50	hit wkt b Chippa	33
2	K.K.Tarapore	st Abbas Khan b Amir Elahi	42	st Abbas Khan b Amir Elahi	15
3	E.B.Aibara	c Chippa b Amir Elahi	47	b Amir Elahi	27
4	*P.E.Palia	run out	6		
5	J.B.Khot	lbw b Amir Elahi	0	(6) b Ibrahim	20
6	J.N.Bhaya	b Amir Elahi	47	(7) not out	28
7	J.S.Lawyer	b Sheikh	8	(4) c Hakim b Amir Elahi	40
8	F.K.Nariman	lbw b Amir Elahi	2	(5) st Abbas Khan b Amir Elahi	8
9	M.J.Mobed	not out	28	(8) not out	1
10	†M.P.Engineer	lbw b Sheikh	7		
11	S.M.Palsetia	st Abbas Khan b Sheikh	3		
	Extras	b 5	5		4
			245	(6 wickets)	176

FoW (1): 1-94 (2), 2-104 (1), 3-120 (4), 4-126 (5), 5-196 (6), 6-197 (3), 7-203 (8), 8-209 (7), 9-227 (10), 10-245 (11)
FoW (2): 1-42 (2), 2-50 (1), 3-102 (3), 4-118 (5), 5-127 (4), 6-171 (6)

MUSLIMS

1	Y.E.Sheikh	b Tarapore	51
2	S.M.Kadri	b Palia	10
3	S.Mushtaq Ali	b Tarapore	79
4	*S.Wazir Ali	lbw b Tarapore	30
5	K.C.Ibrahim	c Engineer b Khot	22
6	S.M.Nasiruddin	b Mobed	64
7	†Abbas Khan	b Khot	7
8	Saeed Ahmed	c Engineer b Palsetia	36
9	Amir Elahi	b Palsetia	0
10	U.R.Chippa	b Palsetia	0
11	A.A.Hakim	not out	0
	Extras	b 3, lb 2	5
			304

FoW (1): 1-28 (2), 2-140 (3), 3-145 (1), 4-186 (5), 5-198 (4), 6-213 (7), 7-280 (8), 8-280 (9), 9-280 (10), 10-304 (6)

Muslims Bowling

	O	M	R	W		O	M	R	W
Hakim	2	1	1	0		14	2	35	0
Saeed Ahmed	16	5	32	0		7	1	11	0
Chippa	12	2	29	0	(5)	12	6	20	1
Sheikh	21.2	4	51	3					
Amir Elahi	32	4	122	6	(6)	23	2	64	4
Wazir Ali	1	0	1	0	(4)	3	0	8	0
Mushtaq Ali	6	2	4	0	(7)	3	1	2	0
Ibrahim					(3)	6	0	25	1
Nasiruddin					(8)	2	0	7	0

Parsees Bowling

	O	M	R	W
Palsetia	36	15	53	3
Palia	41	16	68	1
Nariman	4	3	6	0
Khot	28	8	45	2
Mobed	24.1	1	43	1
Tarapore	39	13	75	3
Bhaya	3	0	9	0

Umpires: G.S.Richards and Vali Ahmed. Toss: Parsees

Close of Play: 1st day: Muslims (1) 21-0 (Sheikh 13*, Kadri 8*); 2nd day: Muslims (1) 238-6 (Nasiruddin 24*, Saeed Ahmed 11*).

EUROPEANS v THE REST

Played at Brabourne Stadium, Bombay, December 20, 21, 22, 1940.

Match drawn.

THE REST

1	J.O.Gonsalves	c Williams b Tomlinson	93
2	A.C.Pereira	b Williams	2
3	M.B.Cohen	c Tomlinson b Hall	29
4	A.B.Fernandes	b Pearson	0
5	V.S.Hazare	c Sturgess b Anson	182
6	*J.G.Harris	lbw b Pearson	5
7	G.S.Richards	c Binny b Williams	42
8	S.R.Arolkar	st Sturgess b Hall	48
9	†P.P.Fernandes	lbw b Tomlinson	4
10	W.L.Mascarenhas	b Williams	25
11	E.Alexander	not out	6
	Extras	b 6, lb 2, w 1	9
			445

FoW (1): 1-9 (2), 2-81 (3), 3-92 (4), 4-171 (1), 5-188 (6), 6-254 (7), 7-364 (8), 8-379 (9), 9-428 (5), 10-445 (10)

EUROPEANS

1	F.S.Tomlinson	b Harris	78	(3) st P.P.Fernandes b Arolkar	20
2	H.W.Barritt	c Hazare b Richards	15	b Hazare	53
3	D.J.Rimmer	lbw b Harris	3	(4) b Mascarenhas	120
4	K.G.Anson	b Harris	1	(5) b Harris	4
5	*J.E.Tew	b Hazare	76	(6) b Mascarenhas	48
6	J.Walters	c Mascarenhas b Harris	9	(7) c and b Cohen	59
7	H.P.Hall	not out	14	(1) b Hazare	11
8	R.A.W.Binny	b Alexander	4	(9) b Alexander	9
9	P.C.Williams	c Hazare b Richards	14	(8) b Mascarenhas	0
10	†T.M.Sturgess	b Hazare	0	b Alexander	4
11	C.L.Pearson	b Hazare	0	not out	27
	Extras	b 15, lb 3, w 1, nb 4	23	b 16, w 2, nb 1	19
			237		374

FoW (1): 1-30 (2), 2-38 (3), 3-40 (4), 4-166 (5), 5-187 (6), 6-200 (1), 7-204 (8), 8-232 (9), 9-237 (10), 10-237 (11)
FoW (2): 1-34 (1), 2-75 (3), 3-141 (2), 4-154 (5), 5-247 (4), 6-286 (6), 7-286 (8), 8-297 (9), 9-310 (10), 10-374 (7)

Europeans Bowling

	O	M	R	W
Williams	28.4	4	88	3
Hall	30	8	83	2
Tomlinson	27	5	74	2
Binny	9	2	46	0
Pearson	21	0	101	2
Anson	11	0	44	1

The Rest Bowling

	O	M	R	W		O	M	R	W
Richards	27	3	64	2					
Alexander	13	1	40	1	(8)	4	0	39	2
Hazare	26	9	41	3	(1)	17	1	58	2
Arolkar	20	4	36	0	(4)	10	2	38	1
Harris	21	6	30	4	(3)	14	4	52	1
Mascarenhas	2	1	3	0	(2)	19	1	83	3
P.P.Fernandes					(5)	2	0	7	0
Gonsalves					(6)	10	1	57	0
Cohen					(7)	3.1	0	21	1

Umpires: J.R.Patel and Vali Ahmed. Toss: The Rest

Close of Play: 1st day: The Rest (1) 384-8 (Hazare 152*, Mascarenhas 0*); 2nd day: Europeans (1) 200-6 (Hall 4*, Binny 0*).

V.S.Hazare's 182 took 270 minutes and included 14 fours. D.J.Rimmer's 120 took 95 minutes and included 13 fours and 1 six.

MADRAS v CEYLON

Played at Madras Cricket Club Ground, Chepauk, Madras, December 20, 21, 22, 1940.

Ceylon won by three wickets.

MADRAS					
1	*C.P.Johnstone	b A.H.Gooneratne	51	c Navaratne b Porritt	26
2	V.N.Madhava Rao	lbw b Kelaart	5	st Navaratne b Jayawickreme	19
3	A.G.Ram Singh	lbw b A.H.Gooneratne	65	c Navaratne b A.H.Gooneratne	103
4	M.S.Gopal	lbw b A.H.Gooneratne	7	c and b A.H.Gooneratne	20
5	R.S.Nailer	lbw b Jayasundera	37	b Jayasundera	35
6	N.J.Venkatesan	not out	15	(7) c Jayawickreme b Jayasundera	6
7	M.J.Gopalan	lbw b Jayasundera	0	(6) c Porritt b G.J.D.Gooneratne	9
8	†T.M.Doraiswami	b Jayasundera	0	run out	10
9	J.S.Versey-Brown	b Jayasundera	0	(10) lbw b Kelaart	2
10	B.S.Krishna Rao	b A.H.Gooneratne	3	(9) b A.H.Gooneratne	6
11	C.R.Rangachari	b A.H.Gooneratne	2	not out	0
	Extras		4		7
			189		243

FoW (1): 1-12 (2), 2-106 (1), 3-114 (4), 4-149 (3), 5-178 (5), 6-178 (7), 7-178 (8), 8-178 (9), 9-187 (10), 10-189 (11)
FoW (2): 1-38 (1), 2-66 (2), 3-114 (4), 4-167 (5), 5-189 (6), 6-205 (7), 7-223 (8), 8-230 (9), 9-242 (10), 10-243 (3)

CEYLON					
1	J.E.Pulle	c Nailer b Venkatesan	18	(2) c and b Krishna Rao	9
2	W.L.Mendis	c Johnstone b Venkatesan	25	(1) lbw b Gopalan	10
3	R.A.K.Solomons	b Venkatesan	12	(4) c and b Johnstone	27
4	A.M.H.Kelaart	c Gopalan b Ram Singh	50	(3) lbw b Versey-Brown	14
5	G.J.D.Gooneratne	b Krishna Rao	58	(6) b Ram Singh	28
6	*S.S.Jayawickreme	c and b Gopalan	42	(5) b Versey-Brown	2
7	F.W.E.Porritt	c Rangachari b Krishna Rao	0	(8) not out	25
8	A.H.Gooneratne	st Doraiswami b Krishna Rao	6	(7) st Doraiswami b Gopalan	45
9	H.S.Roberts	c Versey-Brown b Krishna Rao	22	not out	10
10	†B.Navaratne	lbw b Rangachari	6		
11	D.S.Jayasundera	not out	0		
	Extras		16		14
			255	(7 wickets)	184

FoW (1): 1-39 (1), 2-51 (2), 3-63 (3), 4-155 (4), 5-186 (5), 6-186 (7), 7-203 (8), 8-237 (9), 9-253 (10), 10-255 (6)
FoW (2): 1-16 (1), 2-24 (2), 3-40 (3), 4-44 (5), 5-77 (4), 6-120 (6), 7-174 (7)

Ceylon Bowling	O	M	R	W		O	M	R	W
Jayasundera	17	4	33	4		20	3	42	2
Kelaart	20	6	41	1		26	6	64	1
Porritt	26	4	74	0		16	4	42	1
Jayawickreme	9	4	12	0		8	2	19	1
Solomons	2	0	7	0		2	0	5	0
A.H.Gooneratne	10.1	3	18	5		12.3	2	45	3
G.J.D.Gooneratne					(7)	6	1	19	1

Madras Bowling	O	M	R	W		O	M	R	W
Versey-Brown	8	2	15	0	(3)	14	0	42	2
Rangachari	9	0	28	1		5	1	14	0
Ram Singh	16	2	36	1	(4)	14	3	44	1
Venkatesan	20	0	58	3	(5)	7	0	23	0
Krishna Rao	16	0	63	4	(6)	8	1	23	1
Johnstone	5	0	21	0	(7)	3	0	7	1
Gopalan	7	1	18	1	(1)	6	2	17	2

Umpires: L.O'Callaghan and J.Subbuswami. Toss: Madras

Close of Play: 1st day: Ceylon (1) 76-3 (Kelaart 6*, G.J.D.Gooneratne 11*); 2nd day: Madras (2) 100-2 (Ram Singh 30*, Gopal 19*).

A.G.Ram Singh's 103 took 210 minutes and included 12 fours. Ceylon batted on after winning.

MUSLIMS v THE REST

Played at Brabourne Stadium, Bombay, December 24, 25, 26, 27, 1940.

Muslims won by seven wickets.

	THE REST				
1	J.O.Gonsalves	b Saeed Ahmed	16	c Masood Salahuddin b Amir Elahi	26
2	†M.B.Cohen	lbw b Saeed Ahmed	38	(3) c Dilawar Hussain b Amir Elahi	24
3	B.P.Kadam	b Masood Salahuddin	21	(5) b Amir Elahi	4
4	S.R.Arolkar	st Dilawar Hussain b Amir Elahi	15	(8) st Dilawar Hussain b Amir Elahi	1
5	W.L.Mascarenhas	c Abbas Khan b Amir Elahi	0	(9) b Saeed Ahmed	49
6	V.S.Hazare	st Dilawar Hussain b Amir Elahi	2	(4) st Dilawar Hussain b Amir Elahi	17
7	*J.G.Harris	c Masood Salahuddin b Amir Elahi	82	(6) not out	12
8	A.B.Fernandes	st Dilawar Hussain b Amir Elahi	0	(10) b Saeed Ahmed	9
9	P.P.Fernandes	lbw b Amir Elahi	13	(7) lbw b Saeed Ahmed	43
10	E.Alexander	c Sheikh b Amir Elahi	0	(2) lbw b Amir Elahi	26
11	A.K.Bhalerao	not out	0	st Dilawar Hussain b Amir Elahi	0
	Extras	b 12, lb 2, nb 1	15	b 3, lb 8, w 2, nb 2	15
			202		226

FoW (1): 1-27 (1), 2-76 (2), 3-95 (4), 4-95 (5), 5-98 (6), 6-121 (3), 7-126 (8), 8-166 (9), 9-192 (10), 10-202 (7)
FoW (2): 1-47 (1), 2-64 (2), 3-96 (3), 4-103 (4), 5-112 (5), 6-130 (8), 7-188 (7), 8-214 (10), 9-223 (9), 10-226 (11)

	MUSLIMS				
1	Y.E.Sheikh	st Cohen b Bhalerao	1		
2	S.M.Kadri	b Harris	26	c Gonsalves b Hazare	10
3	S.Mushtaq Ali	c Mascarenhas b Bhalerao	110		
4	*S.Wazir Ali	b Alexander	59	(1) b Hazare	7
5	K.C.Ibrahim	lbw b Harris	17	(4) not out	16
6	S.M.Nasiruddin	c Alexander b Hazare	44	(3) st Cohen b Bhalerao	10
7	†Dilawar Hussain	lbw b Harris	54		
8	Abbas Khan	b Hazare	37		
9	Saeed Ahmed	run out	2		
10	Amir Elahi	not out	10		
11	Masood Salahuddin	lbw b Harris	5	(5) not out	3
	Extras	lb 8, nb 8	16	b 1, nb 1	2
			381	(3 wickets)	48

FoW (1): 1-10 (1), 2-83 (2), 3-193 (3), 4-204 (4), 5-228 (5), 6-291 (6), 7-361 (8), 8-363 (7), 9-363 (9), 10-381 (11)
FoW (2): 1-13 (1), 2-18 (2), 3-45 (3)

Muslims Bowling	O	M	R	W		O	M	R	W
Saeed Ahmed	24	7	29	2		26	13	34	3
Masood Salahuddin	14	2	44	1		12	0	41	0
Amir Elahi	27.4	3	88	7	(5)	30.1	4	104	7
Sheikh	5	0	14	0		7	1	29	0
Mushtaq Ali	3	0	12	0					
Ibrahim					(3)	3	3	0	0
Wazir Ali					(6)	1	0	3	0

The Rest Bowling	O	M	R	W	O	M	R	W
Alexander	21	7	55	1	7	2	15	0
Hazare	40	8	81	2	11	6	15	2
Bhalerao	22	1	89	2	3.5	2	7	1
Harris	26	8	40	4	1	1	0	0
Arolkar	24	2	74	0	2	0	9	0
Mascarenhas	6	1	26	0				

Umpires: H.D.Billimoria and J.R.Patel. Toss: The Rest

Close of Play: 1st day: Muslims (1) 75-1 (Kadri 26*, Mushtaq Ali 42*); 2nd day: Muslims (1) 377-9 (Amir Elahi 10*, Masood Salahuddin 1*); 3rd day: Muslims (2) 18-2 (Nasiruddin 1*).

J.G.Harris retired ill in the The Rest second innings having scored 8 (team score 129-5) - he returned when the score was 214-8.

CANTERBURY v OTAGO

Played at Lancaster Park, Christchurch, December 25, 26, 27, 1940.

Canterbury won by seven wickets.

OTAGO					
1	A.R.Knight	lbw b Burgess	43	b Westwood	54
2	S.F.Duncan	lbw b Cromb	27	c Moynihan b Westwood	52
3	G.J.Robertson	c James b Burgess	27	b Scott	56
4	L.D.Smith	b Cromb	49	c Scott b Burgess	25
5	A.J.Edwards	b Westwood	16	b Burgess	0
6	*V.J.T.Chettleburgh	b Westwood	2	(9) not out	7
7	C.J.Elmes	c Hadlee b Burgess	14	c Hadlee b Roberts	1
8	C.D.G.Toomey	c and b Burgess	29	c Anderson b Scott	26
9	†G.H.Mills	not out	26	(6) lbw b Burgess	0
10	J.V.Leader	b Burgess	24	not out	6
11	N.C.Begg	c O'Brien b Burgess	6		
	Extras	b 23, lb 11, nb 1	35	b 9, lb 5	14
			298	(8 wickets, declared)	241

FoW (1): 1-72, 2-99, 3-142, 4-173, 5-175, 6-197, 7-200, 8-242, 9-286, 10-298
FoW (2): 1-104, 2-117, 3-179, 4-179, 5-179, 6-192, 7-220, 8-231

CANTERBURY					
1	K.F.M.Uttley	c Robertson b Smith	35	c Knight b Elmes	16
2	*W.A.Hadlee	c Knight b Elmes	9	st Mills b Chettleburgh	144
3	F.P.O'Brien	c and b Smith	18	c Begg b Robertson	101
4	W.M.Anderson	c Duncan b Elmes	39	(5) not out	18
5	I.B.Cromb	st Mills b Chettleburgh	28	(4) not out	22
6	T.D.Moynihan	b Smith	19		
7	†V.James	b Begg	12		
8	A.W.Roberts	not out	59		
9	A.T.Burgess	b Smith	4		
10	R.H.Scott	c Mills b Leader	0		
11	R.J.Westwood	c Robertson b Begg	12		
	Extras	lb 2	2	b 4, lb 1	5
			237	(3 wickets)	306

FoW (1): 1-28, 2-52, 3-67, 4-119, 5-141, 6-157, 7-165, 8-192, 9-193, 10-237
FoW (2): 1-46 (1), 2-256, 3-277

Canterbury Bowling	O	M	R	W		O	M	R	W
Roberts	29	8	44	0		12	0	41	1
Westwood	20	4	64	2		12	1	44	2
Scott	18	3	58	0	(6)	12	1	53	2
Cromb	15	3	45	2	(5)	6	1	20	0
Burgess	20.7	5	52	6	(3)	19	2	61	3
Anderson					(4)	1	0	4	0
O'Brien					(7)	1	0	4	0

Otago Bowling	O	M	R	W		O	M	R	W
Begg	9.6	1	43	2		7	1	49	0
Elmes	8	1	30	2		7	0	61	1
Robertson	1	0	11	0		8	0	50	1
Leader	14	3	31	1	(5)	5	0	48	0
Smith	17	0	94	4	(4)	3	0	30	0
Chettleburgh	5	0	26	1		3.5	0	41	1
Knight					(7)	1	0	22	0

Umpires: T.W.Burgess and A.Winter. Toss: Otago

Close of Play: 1st day: Otago (1) 203-7 (Toomey 2*, Mills 2*); 2nd day: Otago (2) 41-0 (Knight 28*, Duncan 11*).

W.A.Hadlee's 144 included 14 fours and 1 five. F.P.O'Brien's 101 included 10 fours and 1 six.

SOUTH AUSTRALIA v VICTORIA

Played at Adelaide Oval, December 25, 26, 27, 28, 1940.

South Australia won by 175 runs.

SOUTH AUSTRALIA					
1	C.L.Badcock	c Sievers b Dempster	25	c Dudley b Sievers	172
2	K.L.Ridings	run out (Hassett/Baker)	0	c Hassett b Sievers	17
3	*D.G.Bradman	c Sievers b Dudley	0	b Sievers	6
4	R.A.Hamence	c Baker b Dudley	85	c Baker b Dempster	62
5	B.H.Leak	c Ring b Sievers	12	b Dudley	6
6	M.G.Waite	lbw b Sievers	2	c Johnson b Dempster	20
7	P.L.Ridings	lbw b Ring	2	lbw b Ring	90
8	†C.W.Walker	c Baker b Johnson	40	c Meikle b Ring	4
9	C.V.Grimmett	run out	2	(10) c and b Johnson	31
10	F.A.Ward	c Hassett b Sievers	10	(9) c Baker b Dempster	4
11	H.N.J.Cotton	not out	9	not out	2
	Extras	b 1, lb 2, nb 1	4	b 1, lb 4, nb 2	7
			191		421

FoW (1): 1-1, 2-1, 3-61, 4-97, 5-101, 6-106, 7-154, 8-173, 9-175, 10-191
FoW (2): 1-30, 2-36, 3-222, 4-240, 5-281, 6-303, 7-314, 8-323, 9-385, 10-421

VICTORIA					
1	I.S.Lee	b Waite	0	c Badcock b P.L.Ridings	1
2	G.E.Tamblyn	c Waite b Cotton	0	st Walker b Grimmett	10
3	D.T.Ring	c Cotton b Grimmett	72	(9) run out	24
4	R.A.Dempster	lbw b Cotton	3	(3) c Waite b Grimmett	10
5	*A.L.Hassett	b Cotton	7	(4) b Ward	113
6	D.H.Fothergill	c Walker b P.L.Ridings	18	(5) b Ward	14
7	M.W.Sievers	st Walker b Ward	14	(8) c Waite b Ward	31
8	G.S.Meikle	lbw b Grimmett	12	(6) c Leak b Waite	13
9	I.W.G.Johnson	c Walker b Cotton	29	(7) b Grimmett	27
10	†E.A.Baker	not out	13	not out	14
11	W.J.Dudley	c Leak b Grimmett	0	b Grimmett	5
	Extras	b 1, lb 3	4	lb 2, nb 1	3
			172		265

FoW (1): 1-1, 2-7, 3-12, 4-26, 5-56, 6-79, 7-100, 8-152, 9-172, 10-172
FoW (2): 1-5, 2-22, 3-23, 4-82, 5-109, 6-189, 7-195, 8-231, 9-253, 10-265

Victoria Bowling	O	M	R	W			O	M	R	W	
Dudley	7	0	34	2			11	2	38	1	1nb
Sievers	11.4	1	45	3	1nb		25	1	104	3	1nb
Ring	9	1	32	1		(5)	11	0	67	2	
Johnson	3	0	8	1			8	0	66	1	
Dempster	6	0	21	1		(3)	15	1	66	3	
Meikle	8	0	47	0			4	0	26	0	
Fothergill						(7)	6	0	40	0	
Hassett						(8)	1	0	7	0	

South Australia Bowling	O	M	R	W			O	M	R	W	
Cotton	11	0	39	4		(5)	8	0	30	0	
Waite	7	2	15	1			14	2	37	1	
Grimmett	12.7	1	54	3			24.3	3	75	4	
P.L.Ridings	3	1	5	1		(1)	8	1	34	1	1nb
Ward	10	0	55	1		(4)	22	3	86	3	

Umpires: J.D.Scott and L.A.Smith. Toss: South Australia

Close of Play: 1st day: Victoria (1) 7-2 (Ring 6*); 2nd day: South Australia (2) 222-3 (Badcock 133*, Leak 0*); 3rd day: Victoria (2) 77-3 (Hassett 41*, Fothergill 14*).

C.L.Badcock's 172 took 217 minutes and included 21 fours and 1 six. A.L.Hassett's 113 took 142 minutes and included 4 fours and 1 six. 12th Men: T.E.Klose (SA) and M.R.Harvey (Vic).

WELLINGTON v AUCKLAND

Played at Basin Reserve, Wellington, December 25, 26, 27, 1940.

Auckland won by eight wickets.

	WELLINGTON				
1	J.A.Standidge	c Burke b Andrews	25	st Blandford b Cleverley	4
2	H.W.Osborn	lbw b Cleverley	13	b Weir	0
3	P.D.Wilson	c Blandford b Weir	32	c Cleverley b Andrews	12
4	*J.R.Lamason	b Andrews	0	(7) st Blandford b Burke	7
5	†W.E.Norris	c Andrews b Cleverley	16	(4) c Cleal b Weir	48
6	D.S.Wilson	c and b Weir	17	(5) c Blandford b Andrews	16
7	N.S.H.Burnette	c and b Weir	8	(6) lbw b Andrews	44
8	T.S.Russ	b Cleverley	2	lbw b Burke	0
9	C.K.Parsloe	c Cleal b Weir	9	b Weir	1
10	G.O.Rabone	b Cleverley	11	c Blandford b Andrews	8
11	T.A.Downes	not out	1	not out	2
	Extras	b 1, lb 8	9	b 4, lb 3, w 1	8
			143		150

FoW (1): 1-40 (2), 2-40 (1), 3-40 (4), 4-91, 5-103, 6-119, 7-120, 8-130, 9-136, 10-143
FoW (2): 1-2 (2), 2-5 (1), 3-27 (3), 4-57 (5), 5-110 (4), 6-119 (7), 7-119, 8-120, 9-147, 10-150

	AUCKLAND				
1	P.E.Whitelaw	lbw b Parsloe	1	c Norris b Parsloe	17
2	G.C.Burgess	c Norris b Lamason	21	c Norris b D.S.Wilson	26
3	H.T.Pearson	b Parsloe	70	(4) not out	0
4	*G.L.Weir	b Lamason	0		
5	V.J.Scott	c Parsloe b Downes	21	(3) not out	28
6	O.C.Cleal	c Burnette b Parsloe	58		
7	†J.A.R.Blandford	b Downes	8		
8	H.J.H.Harrison	lbw b Parsloe	0		
9	C.Burke	b Downes	2		
10	D.C.Cleverley	run out	5		
11	F.M.Andrews	not out	17		
	Extras	b 11, lb 5, nb 3	19	b 2	2
			222	(2 wickets)	73

FoW (1): 1-2 (1), 2-44 (2), 3-44 (4), 4-94 (5), 5-185 (6), 6-196 (3), 7-196 (8), 8-197 (7), 9-200 (9), 10-222 (10)
FoW (2): 1-28 (1), 2-67 (2)

Auckland Bowling	O	M	R	W		O	M	R	W
Cleverley	14.7	1	61	4		11	0	39	1
Weir	7	0	25	4		13	4	30	3
Andrews	10	1	25	2		12.4	1	45	4
Burke	5	1	13	0		10	2	26	2
Harrison	3	1	10	0		0.4	0	2	0

Wellington Bowling	O	M	R	W		O	M	R	W
Parsloe	21.5	3	62	4		6	0	20	1
Downes	21	4	74	3		5	0	25	0
Lamason	8	0	30	2					
Rabone	4	0	14	0	(3)	3.2	0	19	0
D.S.Wilson	4	0	23	0	(4)	3	0	7	1

Umpires: W.A.Aldersley and C.W.Moore. Toss: Auckland

Close of Play: 1st day: Auckland (1) 48-3 (Pearson 19*, Scott 2*); 2nd day: Auckland (2) 10-0 (Whitelaw 5*, Burgess 5*).

INDIAN XI v CEYLON

Played at Eden Gardens, Calcutta, December 26, 27, 28, 1940.

Match drawn.

INDIAN XI					
1	S.K.Ganguli	lbw b Kelaart	69	c Porritt b Jayasundera	64
2	M.Toufiq	lbw b Kelaart	0	b Jayasundera	4
3	P.E.Palia	c Navaratne b M.O.Gooneratne	38	(4) lbw b Kelaart	37
4	*C.K.Nayudu	c Mendis b Porritt	29	(5) b Porritt	50
5	N.C.Chatterjee	st Navaratne b M.O.Gooneratne	53	(6) not out	73
6	S.N.Banerjee	c A.H.Gooneratne b Kelaart	43	(7) not out	25
7	S.Bose	b Kelaart	2		
8	A.Jabbar	lbw b M.O.Gooneratne	4	(3) c Kelaart b Jayawickreme	21
9	K.Bhattacharya	c Navaratne b M.O.Gooneratne	1		
10	†L.E.Hunt	lbw b Porritt	10		
11	J.Nuttall	not out	0		
	Extras		2		19
			251	(5 wickets, declared)	293

FoW (1): 1-1 (2), 2-69 (3), 3-116 (4), 4-164 (1), 5-197 (5), 6-200 (7), 7-207 (8), 8-211 (9), 9-247 (10), 10-251 (6)
FoW (2): 1-9 (2), 2-61 (3), 3-122 (1), 4-180 (4), 5-209 (5)

CEYLON					
1	W.L.Mendis	c Nayudu b Palia	12	not out	22
2	J.E.Pulle	c Hunt b Banerjee	4	c Toufiq b Nuttall	35
3	A.M.H.Kelaart	lbw b Bhattacharya	0	c Nuttall b Chatterjee	1
4	*S.S.Jayawickreme	c Nayudu b Banerjee	138		
5	G.J.D.Gooneratne	lbw b Bhattacharya	44		
6	A.H.Gooneratne	lbw b Banerjee	34	(4) not out	13
7	F.W.E.Porritt	c Palia b Bhattacharya	49		
8	H.S.Roberts	b Nayudu	16		
9	M.O.Gooneratne	c Palia b Nayudu	0		
10	†B.Navaratne	lbw b Palia	18		
11	D.S.Jayasundera	not out	37		
	Extras		20		11
			372	(2 wickets)	82

FoW (1): 1-7 (2), 2-8 (3), 3-24 (1), 4-176 (5), 5-233 (4), 6-259 (6), 7-276 (8), 8-276 (9), 9-315 (10), 10-372 (7)
FoW (2): 1-57 (2), 2-58 (3)

Ceylon Bowling	O	M	R	W		O	M	R	W
Jayasundera	4	2	9	0		24	4	78	2
Kelaart	20.3	2	70	4		36	12	83	1
A.H.Gooneratne	3	0	17	0		3	0	11	0
Jayawickreme	5	2	28	0		17	8	33	1
M.O.Gooneratne	16	1	79	4		4	0	21	0
Porritt	5	0	19	2		17	2	48	1
G.J.D.Gooneratne	3	0	27	0					

Indian XI Bowling	O	M	R	W		O	M	R	W
Banerjee	28	3	114	3		6	0	17	0
Nayudu	30	4	83	2		2	0	12	0
Bhattacharya	19.4	5	49	3		4	1	7	0
Palia	27	6	58	2					
Nuttall	3	0	11	0	(4)	7	3	17	1
Chatterjee	8	0	37	0	(5)	6	1	18	1

Umpires: Toss: Indian XI

Close of Play: 1st day: Ceylon (1) 96-3 (Jayawickreme 56*, G.J.D.Gooneratne 18*); 2nd day: Indian XI (2) 42-1 (Ganguli 23*, Jabbar 8*).

S.S.Jayawickreme's 138 took 189 minutes and included 15 fours.

NEW SOUTH WALES v QUEENSLAND

Played at Sydney Cricket Ground, December 26, 27, 28, 30, 1940.

New South Wales won by 404 runs.

NEW SOUTH WALES					
1	M.B.Cohen	c Christ b Ellis	5	b Cox	118
2	A.R.Morris	b McCarthy	148	c Ellis b Watt	111
3	S.G.Barnes	c McCarthy b Cook	133	c Tallon b Cook	5
4	*S.J.McCabe	c Rogers b Watt	75		
5	C.L.McCool	lbw b Christ	45	(4) lbw b Ellis	0
6	†R.A.Saggers	b Christ	1	(5) c Tallon b Cox	33
7	V.E.Jackson	c McCarthy b Ellis	47	(6) not out	47
8	C.G.Pepper	c Brown b Watt	7	(7) st Tallon b Watt	6
9	W.J.O'Reilly	b Cook	30	(8) c Baker b Watt	13
10	V.Trumper	not out	5	(9) c Ellis b Watt	11
11	R.B.Scott	run out	4	(10) c Brown b Cox	2
	Extras	b 13, lb 3	16	b 14, lb 8, nb 1	23
			516	(9 wickets, declared)	369

FoW (1): 1-6, 2-267, 3-309, 4-408, 5-409, 6-410, 7-435, 8-497, 9-499, 10-516
FoW (2): 1-200, 2-215, 3-216, 4-276, 5-299, 6-316, 7-338, 8-366, 9-369

QUEENSLAND					
1	*W.A.Brown	c Pepper b Trumper	7	c Scott b Pepper	57
2	G.G.Cook	b Scott	4	run out	25
3	R.E.Rogers	c Pepper b Jackson	114	b Pepper	26
4	†D.Tallon	lbw b O'Reilly	34	c and b Pepper	0
5	G.G.Baker	b Jackson	48	c Barnes b Pepper	3
6	D.Watt	b Pepper	13	c Trumper b Pepper	0
7	V.N.Raymer	not out	41	b Pepper	10
8	J.E.McCarthy	run out	18	lbw b O'Reilly	4
9	D.E.Cox	b McCool	16	b O'Reilly	14
10	J.A.Ellis	st Saggers b McCool	0	not out	1
11	C.P.Christ	b Jackson	18	st Saggers b O'Reilly	0
	Extras	b 10, lb 6, w 1, nb 4	21	b 6, lb 1	7
			334		147

FoW (1): 1-7, 2-13, 3-80, 4-211, 5-219, 6-231, 7-272, 8-301, 9-301, 10-334
FoW (2): 1-62, 2-94, 3-94, 4-115, 5-115, 6-127, 7-132, 8-146, 9-147, 10-147

Queensland Bowling	O	M	R	W			O	M	R	W	
Ellis	17	1	82	2			12	1	54	1	
Cook	13.7	0	67	2			12	0	66	1	1nb
Cox	10	1	73	0		(5)	10.5	0	63	3	
Christ	17	0	78	2			5	0	23	0	
Raymer	5	0	46	0		(7)	4	0	23	0	
Watt	11	0	110	2			10	0	90	4	
McCarthy	9	1	44	1		(3)	5	1	27	0	

New South Wales Bowling	O	M	R	W			O	M	R	W
Scott	8	1	36	1	1w,3nb		4	0	12	0
Trumper	7	0	34	1			3	0	13	0
Jackson	9.6	1	30	3			7	2	15	0
Pepper	16	2	82	1		(5)	13	1	57	6
O'Reilly	7	1	34	1	1nb	(4)	13.6	2	43	3
McCool	12	0	96	2						
Cohen	3	2	1	0						

Umpires: G.E.Borwick and R.McGrath. Toss: New South Wales

Close of Play: 1st day: New South Wales (1) 489-7 (Jackson 41*, O'Reilly 26*); 2nd day: New South Wales (2) 32-0 (Cohen 11*, Morris 15*); 3rd day: Queensland (2) 50-0 (Brown 27*, Cook 22*).

A.R.Morris's 148 took 214 minutes and included 18 fours. S.G.Barnes's 133 took 176 minutes and included 14 fours. R.E.Rogers's 114 took 143 minutes and included 15 fours. M.B.Cohen's 118 took 192 minutes and included 5 fours. A.R.Morris's 111 took 142 minutes and included 7 fours. 12th Men: D.K.Carmody (NSW) and J.Stackpoole (Qld).

MADRAS v HYDERABAD

Played at Madras Cricket Club Ground, Chepauk, Madras, December 30, 31, 1940, January 1, 1941.

Madras won by 254 runs.

MADRAS					
1	*C.P.Johnstone	c Asadullah Qureshi b Bhupathi	94	(2) b Khanna	13
2	M.Swaminathan	run out	17	(1) b Khanna	24
3	A.G.Ram Singh	b Khanna	27	c Isa Khan b Bhupathi	53
4	R.S.Nailer	b Bhupathi	11	c and b Zahiruddin	78
5	C.Ramaswami	lbw b Khanna	0	c Dittia b Bhupathi	2
6	N.J.Venkatesan	b Bhupathi	18	(8) not out	24
7	M.J.Gopalan	c Hadi b Mehta	10	(6) c Isa Khan b Khanna	39
8	G.Parthasarathi	c Patel b Khanna	31	(7) c Isa Khan b Khanna	7
9	†T.M.Doraiswami	run out	14		
10	B.S.Krishna Rao	lbw b Khanna	0	b Khanna	1
11	C.R.Rangachari	not out	0	(9) c and b Zahiruddin	5
	Extras		5		11
			227	(9 wickets, declared)	257

FoW (1): 1-70 (2), 2-135 (1), 3-142 (3), 4-142 (5), 5-152 (4), 6-163 (7), 7-196 (6), 8-227 (9), 9-227 (8), 10-227 (10)
FoW (2): 1-17 (2), 2-93 (1), 3-97 (3), 4-121 (5), 5-216 (6), 6-222 (4), 7-237 (7), 8-249 (9), 9-257 (10)

HYDERABAD					
1	†Isa Khan	b Ram Singh	1	(9) c and b Ram Singh	18
2	F.D.Dittia	st Doraiswami b Ram Singh	20	c Rangachari b Ram Singh	0
3	Asadullah Qureshi	b Ram Singh	2	b Gopalan	1
4	S.R.Mehta	c Johnstone b Rangachari	2	(1) lbw b Ram Singh	0
5	E.B.Aibara	c Rangachari b Ram Singh	17	(4) c Rangachari b Krishna Rao	25
6	*S.M.Hadi	st Doraiswami b Ram Singh	2	(8) c Johnstone b Ram Singh	16
7	B.Zahiruddin	c Rangachari b Ram Singh	3	lbw b Rangachari	8
8	B.R.Patel	st Doraiswami b Venkatesan	20	(6) b Krishna Rao	6
9	B.C.Khanna	not out	22	(5) c Rangachari b Krishna Rao	40
10	Ghulam Ahmed	lbw b Venkatesan	1	b Rangachari	3
11	A.R.Bhupathi	st Doraiswami b Krishna Rao	0	not out	8
	Extras		8		7
			98		132

FoW (1): 1-1 (1), 2-3 (3), 3-12 (4), 4-36 (2), 5-49 (5), 6-55 (6), 7-59 (7), 8-91 (8), 9-95 (10), 10-98 (11)
FoW (2): 1-2 (1), 2-3 (3), 3-16 (2), 4-47 (4), 5-76 (6), 6-83 (5), 7-91 (7), 8-109 (8), 9-120 (10), 10-132 (9)

Hyderabad Bowling	O	M	R	W		O	M	R	W
Khanna	20	5	47	4		31.5	6	85	5
Patel	1	0	3	0					
Mehta	13	1	36	1	(4)	5	1	24	0
Zahiruddin	15	2	39	0	(2)	18	2	56	2
Bhupathi	28	4	68	3	(3)	18	3	49	2
Ghulam Ahmed	4	0	11	0					
Asadullah Qureshi	6	0	18	0	(5)	9	0	30	0
Aibara					(6)	1	0	2	0

Madras Bowling	O	M	R	W	O	M	R	W
Gopalan	3	1	2	0	4	1	11	1
Ram Singh	17	6	30	6	9.1	1	26	4
Rangachari	9	2	20	1	11	0	41	2
Venkatesan	8	1	30	2	4	1	9	0
Krishna Rao	1.3	0	8	1	9	1	38	3

Umpires: B.V.Ramakrishnappa and M.G.Vijayasarathi. Toss: Madras

Close of Play: 1st day: Hyderabad (1) 6-2 (Dittia 1*, Mehta 2*); 2nd day: Madras (2) 210-4 (Nailer 73*, Gopalan 34*).

INDIAN XI v CEYLON

Played at Brabourne Stadium, Bombay, December 31, 1940, January 1, 2, 1941.

Indian XI won by an innings and 110 runs.

	CEYLON				
1	W.L.Mendis	c Deodhar b Nayudu	42	c Adhikari b Hazare	1
2	J.E.Pulle	b Saeed Ahmed	3	b Hazare	9
3	G.J.D.Gooneratne	b Saeed Ahmed	96	b Nayudu	29
4	R.A.K.Solomons	b Chippa	1	b Chippa	22
5	*S.S.Jayawickreme	st Engineer b Chippa	3	(7) b Hazare	0
6	A.H.Gooneratne	run out	6	(5) b Sohoni	37
7	F.W.E.Porritt	b Chippa	19	(6) b Hazare	10
8	A.M.H.Kelaart	c Engineer b Chippa	0	st Engineer b Nayudu	13
9	M.O.Gooneratne	b Saeed Ahmed	22	c Deodhar b Nayudu	0
10	†B.Navaratne	not out	23	c Deodhar b Sohoni	0
11	D.S.Jayasundera	b Chippa	8	not out	0
	Extras		11		13
			234		134

FoW (1): 1-11 (2), 2-82 (1), 3-85 (4), 4-91 (5), 5-113 (6), 6-154 (7), 7-158 (8), 8-201 (9), 9-206 (3), 10-234 (11)
FoW (2): 1-2 (1), 2-32 (2), 3-56 (3), 4-80 (4), 5-115 (6), 6-115 (7), 7-134 (8), 8-134 (5), 9-134 (9), 10-134 (10)

	INDIAN XI		
1	V.M.Merchant	run out	137
2	S.W.Sohoni	b Porritt	18
3	H.R.Adhikari	lbw b Jayasundera	90
4	V.S.Hazare	b Jayasundera	13
5	*D.B.Deodhar	c and b Porritt	69
6	K.M.Rangnekar	c Mendis b Porritt	117
7	C.S.Nayudu	c A.H.Gooneratne b Kelaart	18
8	K.C.Ibrahim	not out	0
9	Saeed Ahmed		
10	U.R.Chippa		
11	†M.P.Engineer		
	Extras		16
		(7 wickets, declared)	478

FoW (1): 1-52 (2), 2-245 (1), 3-253 (3), 4-288 (4), 5-448 (5), 6-475 (7), 7-478 (6)

Indian XI Bowling	O	M	R	W	O	M	R	W
Saeed Ahmed	19	3	49	3	4	1	15	0
Hazare	14	3	48	0	16	5	34	4
Nayudu	26	5	58	1	11	1	32	3
Sohoni	10	2	30	0	7.1	1	22	2
Chippa	17.4	2	38	5	14	7	18	1

Ceylon Bowling	O	M	R	W
Jayasundera	15	1	50	2
Kelaart	30	6	90	1
Jayawickreme	5	0	39	0
M.O.Gooneratne	17	1	74	0
Porritt	21.2	0	107	3
A.H.Gooneratne	5	0	31	0
G.J.D.Gooneratne	9	0	33	0
Solomons	9	1	38	0

Umpires: D.K.Naik and Vali Ahmed. Toss: Ceylon

Close of Play: 1st day: Indian XI (1) 82-1 (Merchant 52*, Adhikari 9*); 2nd day: Ceylon (2) 113-4 (A.H.Gooneratne 30*, Porritt 9*).

V.M.Merchant's 137 took 165 minutes and included 16 fours. K.M.Rangnekar's 117 took 107 minutes and included 11 fours.

CANTERBURY v WELLINGTON

Played at Lancaster Park, Christchurch, January 1, 2, 3, 1941.

Wellington won by four wickets.

CANTERBURY					
1	K.F.M.Uttley	c Donnelly b Ashenden	78	c Norris b Pritchard	13
2	D.A.R.Moloney	c Lamason b Pritchard	12	b Pritchard	3
3	F.P.O'Brien	b Pritchard	2	(4) lbw b D.S.Wilson	11
4	W.M.Anderson	lbw b Pritchard	86	(5) c Lamason b D.S.Wilson	116
5	*I.B.Cromb	b Rabone	9	(3) c Lamason b Pritchard	17
6	T.D.Moynihan	b Pritchard	21	b D.S.Wilson	1
7	†V.James	c Burnette b Pritchard	1	b Pritchard	20
8	A.W.Roberts	not out	94	c Ashenden b Pritchard	12
9	A.T.Burgess	b Rabone	15	b Ashenden	10
10	W.O.Mapplebeck	c Donnelly b Rabone	17	not out	18
11	R.J.Westwood	st Norris b Donnelly	14	b D.S.Wilson	0
	Extras	b 5, lb 5	10	b 6, lb 6	12
			359		233

FoW (1): 1-31 (2), 2-33 (3), 3-167, 4-178, 5-205, 6-206, 7-243, 8-278, 9-330, 10-359
FoW (2): 1-15, 2-32, 3-39, 4-70, 5-82, 6-107, 7-125, 8-181, 9-233, 10-233

WELLINGTON					
1	M.P.Donnelly	c Anderson b Burgess	68	not out	138
2	H.W.Osborn	lbw b Westwood	17	c sub b Mapplebeck	8
3	P.D.Wilson	c Westwood b Mapplebeck	9	c and b Cromb	25
4	†W.E.Norris	b Cromb	36	b Cromb	13
5	N.S.H.Burnette	c Burgess b Mapplebeck	22	(6) lbw b Cromb	23
6	D.S.Wilson	c Mapplebeck b Westwood	72	(7) c Moloney b Cromb	31
7	*J.R.Lamason	c Roberts b Mapplebeck	0	(5) c Cromb b Burgess	17
8	T.S.Russ	b Mapplebeck	24		
9	G.O.Rabone	c Westwood b Moloney	27		
10	T.L.Pritchard	not out	22	(8) not out	11
11	J.G.Ashenden	c Moloney b Cromb	5		
	Extras	b 4, lb 10	14	b 6, lb 7	13
			316	(6 wickets)	279

FoW (1): 1-57 (2), 2-79 (3), 3-124 (1), 4-148 (4), 5-188 (5), 6-188 (7), 7-255, 8-265, 9-309, 10-316
FoW (2): 1-11 (2), 2-79 (3), 3-107 (4), 4-138 (5), 5-191 (6), 6-237 (7)

Wellington Bowling	O	M	R	W		O	M	R	W
Pritchard	22	2	87	5		22	3	87	5
Ashenden	12	1	55	1		16	2	58	1
D.S.Wilson	11	0	54	0		20	1	54	4
Lamason	9	1	50	0					
P.D.Wilson	1	0	9	0					
Rabone	15	1	74	3	(4)	6	0	22	0
Donnelly	5	0	20	1					

Canterbury Bowling	O	M	R	W		O	M	R	W
Mapplebeck	23	4	105	4		4	0	32	1
Westwood	15	3	41	2		8	0	35	0
Roberts	14.1	1	42	0					
Burgess	14	2	54	1		20	0	99	1
Cromb	15	3	34	2	(3)	24	2	100	4
Moloney	4	0	26	1					

Umpires: J.McGuinness and C.H.Rowe. Toss: Canterbury

Close of Play: 1st day: Wellington (1) 71-1 (Donnelly 41*, P.D.Wilson 7*); 2nd day: Canterbury (2) 102-5 (Anderson 32*, James 15*).

M.P.Donnelly's 138 took 180 minutes and included 20 fours.

D.G.BRADMAN'S XI v S.J.MCCABE'S XI

Played at Melbourne Cricket Ground, January 1, 2, 3, 4, 1941.

S.J.McCabe's XI won by an innings and 103 runs.

S.J.MCCABE'S XI

1	I.S.Lee	b Waite	14
2	C.L.Badcock	b Waite	105
3	S.G.Barnes	c Hamence b Jackson	137
4	R.E.Rogers	lbw b Waite	16
5	*S.J.McCabe	lbw b Pepper	7
6	†D.Tallon	b Pepper	21
7	K.R.Miller	b Scott	29
8	M.W.Sievers	not out	55
9	C.V.Grimmett	b Jackson	5
10	W.J.O'Reilly	c Saggers b Scott	5
11	J.A.Ellis	not out	19
	Extras	b 19, lb 6, w 4, nb 7	36
		(9 wickets, declared)	449

FoW (1): 1-29, 2-241, 3-295, 4-300, 5-322, 6-331, 7-387, 8-398, 9-407

D.G.BRADMAN'S XI

1	W.A.Brown	c O'Reilly b Ellis	13	c Barnes b O'Reilly	16
2	K.L.Ridings	lbw b Ellis	50	c Tallon b Miller	5
3	*D.G.Bradman	c sub (G.E.Tamblyn) b Ellis	0	b O'Reilly	12
4	R.A.Hamence	c Lee b O'Reilly	73	st Tallon b Grimmett	35
5	A.L.Hassett	c Rogers b Grimmett	31	c Ellis b Grimmett	20
6	†R.A.Saggers	not out	13	lbw b Grimmett	5
7	M.G.Waite	c Miller b O'Reilly	15	c Barnes b O'Reilly	18
8	V.E.Jackson	lbw b O'Reilly	0	c sub (K.L.Ridings) b Grimmett	14
9	C.G.Pepper	c Badcock b O'Reilly	1	lbw b O'Reilly	10
10	R.B.Scott	st Tallon b Grimmett	1	lbw b O'Reilly	0
11	V.Trumper	lbw b Grimmett	0	not out	1
	Extras	b 3, lb 3, nb 2	8	b 2, lb 1, w 1, nb 1	5
			205		141

FoW (1): 1-25, 2-25, 3-118, 4-169, 5-173, 6-195, 7-196, 8-200, 9-205, 10-205
FoW (2): 1-10, 2-35, 3-36, 4-66, 5-75, 6-104, 7-122, 8-135, 9-135, 10-141

D.G.Bradman's XI Bowling

	O	M	R	W	
Scott	23	1	87	2	1w,6nb
Trumper	14	1	60	0	3w,1nb
Waite	24	2	84	3	
Jackson	22	3	97	2	
Pepper	12	0	85	2	

S.J.McCabe's XI Bowling

	O	M	R	W			O	M	R	W	
Ellis	10	2	23	3			4	0	13	0	1w
McCabe	5	1	10	0							
Grimmett	22.2	1	100	3		(4)	8	0	46	4	
O'Reilly	14	2	41	4	2nb	(3)	10	1	53	5	1nb
Barnes	5	0	23	0							
Miller						(2)	6	0	24	1	

Umpires: A.N.Barlow and W.J.Craddock. Toss: S.J.McCabe's XI

Close of Play: 1st day: S.J.McCabe's XI (1) 393-7 (Sievers 30*, Grimmett 0*); 2nd day: No play; 3rd day: D.G.Bradman's XI (1) 118-3 (Hamence 54*).

C.L.Badcock's 105 took 226 minutes and included 9 fours. S.G.Barnes's 137 took 204 minutes and included 15 fours.

VICEROY'S XI v BENGAL GOVERNOR'S XI

Played at Eden Gardens, Calcutta, January 3, 4, 5, 1941.

Viceroy's XI won by three wickets.

BENGAL GOVERNOR'S XI

1	S.K.Ganguli	c Nissar b Amir Elahi	28	(2) lbw b Nissar	1
2	S.Mushtaq Ali	c Azmat Hayat b Amir Elahi	59	(1) b Amarnath	2
3	P.E.Palia	c Hindlekar b Mankad	28	c Amir Elahi b Nazir Ali	21
4	*C.K.Nayudu	c Nissar b Mankad	13	lbw b Amarnath	3
5	N.C.Chatterjee	b Mankad	0	st Hindlekar b Nazir Ali	2
6	†Dilawar Hussain	c Nazir Ali b Amarnath	31	lbw b Amir Elahi	10
7	S.N.Banerjee	st Hindlekar b Amir Elahi	62	c Nissar b Amarnath	29
8	T.C.Longfield	b Mankad	18	c Murawwat Hussain b Amarnath	14
9	A.G.Ram Singh	c and b Amir Elahi	45	lbw b Mankad	0
10	M.Jahangir Khan	c Qamaruddin Sheikh b Amir Elahi	60	c Nazir Ali b Amir Elahi	18
11	K.Bhattacharya	not out	7	not out	7
	Extras		13		16
			364		123

FoW (1): 1-69 (2), 2-100 (1), 3-132 (4), 4-132 (5), 5-135 (3), 6-220 (6), 7-244 (7), 8-260 (8), 9-350 (10), 10-364 (9)
FoW (2): 1-3 (1), 2-4 (2), 3- (4), 4-37 (3), 5-38 (5), 6-59 (6), 7-92 (8), 8-92 (9), 9-94 (7), 10-123 (10)

VICEROY'S XI

1	†D.D.Hindlekar	c Dilawar Hussain b Longfield	8	b Nayudu	39
2	M.H.Mankad	c Longfield b Palia	11	c sub b Nayudu	26
3	Murawwat Hussain	lbw b Banerjee	6	(7) c Ganguli b Nayudu	2
4	Qamaruddin Sheikh	c Dilawar Hussain b Jahangir Khan	42	(3) lbw b Longfield	2
5	L.Amarnath	c Dilawar Hussain b Jahangir Khan	62	(4) b Longfield	0
6	S.Nazir Ali	run out	26	(5) c Dilawar Hussain b Nayudu	7
7	*Maharaja of Patiala	b Ram Singh	24	(8) c Nayudu b Longfield	24
8	Azmat Hayat	c Palia b Ram Singh	65	(6) not out	61
9	Bhalindra Singh	c Chatterjee b Banerjee	18	not out	18
10	Amir Elahi	c Banerjee b Ram Singh	29		
11	M.Nissar	not out	1		
	Extras		10		10
			302	(7 wickets)	189

FoW (1): 1-9 (1), 2-16 (3), 3-44 (2), 4-86 (4), 5-151 (6), 6-183 (7), 7-185 (5), 8-240 (9), 9-299 (10), 10-302 (8)
FoW (2): 1-48 (2), 2-51 (3), 3-51 (4), 4-70 (5), 5-77 (1), 6-82 (7), 7-121 (8)

Viceroy's XI Bowling

	O	M	R	W		O	M	R	W
Nissar	9	3	29	0	(2)	2	0	9	1
Amarnath	10	2	34	1	(1)	14	3	30	4
Amir Elahi	30.2	0	160	5	(4)	6.5	0	44	2
Murawwat Hussain	2	0	16	0					
Mankad	22	1	95	4		3	1	10	1
Patiala	4	1	17	0					
Nazir Ali					(3)	5	1	14	2

Bengal Governor's XI Bowling

	O	M	R	W		O	M	R	W
Banerjee	21	4	64	2		4	0	17	0
Jahangir Khan	26	9	57	2		6	1	18	0
Longfield	9	1	25	1	(4)	14	1	37	3
Nayudu	7	0	20	0	(5)	27.5	6	67	4
Palia	11	2	24	1	(6)	1	0	6	0
Ram Singh	22.3	4	63	3	(3)	9	0	28	0
Bhattacharya	5	0	27	0					
Chatterjee	2	0	12	0					
Mushtaq Ali					(7)	1	0	6	0

Umpires: M.Dutta Roy and P.Mukherjee. Toss: Bengal Governor's XI

Close of Play: 1st day: Viceroy's XI (1) 19-2 (Mankad 5*, Qamaruddin Sheikh 0*); 2nd day: Viceroy's XI (1) 302 all out.

GUJARAT v MAHARASHTRA

Played at Gujarat College Ground, Ahmedabad, January 11, 12, 13, 1941.

Match drawn.

MAHARASHTRA			
1	S.G.Powar	c Modi b Baloch	0
2	S.W.Sohoni	b Baloch	134
3	R.B.Nimbalkar	b C.M.Patel	66
4	*D.B.Deodhar	b Baloch	19
5	V.S.Hazare	c Sahana b Baloch	117
6	M.M.Naidu	lbw b Bhagwandas	20
7	†Y.N.Gokhale	c Cambhatta b Baloch	4
8	K.M.Jadhav	c Baloch b C.M.Patel	38
9	Ushaq Ahmed	c Sahana b Baloch	38
10	C.T.Sarwate	not out	36
11	B.J.Mohoni	c Bhagwandas b Baloch	15
	Extras		31
			518

FoW (1): 1-0 (1), 2-107 (3), 3-152 (4), 4-305 (2), 5-366 (6), 6-373 (7), 7-404 (5), 8-449 (8), 9-488 (9), 10-518 (11)

GUJARAT			
1	†J.M.Sahana	c Sohoni b Hazare	8
2	M.K.Pathan	b Sohoni	6
3	R.M.Patel	b Hazare	64
4	M.Bhagwandas	c Nimbalkar b Hazare	10
5	*S.Mushtaq Ali	c Sohoni b Sarwate	156
6	P.N.Cambhatta	b Sohoni	42
7	C.F.Parmar	st Gokhale b Sarwate	1
8	Modi	c Nimbalkar b Sarwate	0
9	U.R.Chippa	c Sohoni b Sarwate	0
10	C.M.Patel	b Sarwate	11
11	M.S.Baloch	not out	23
	Extras		14
			335

FoW (1): 1-8 (2), 2-46 (1), 3-64 (4), 4-207 (3), 5-277 (5), 6-292 (7), 7-292 (8), 8- , 9- , 10-335

Gujarat Bowling	O	M	R	W
Baloch	68.1	25	124	7
Bhagwandas	29	8	84	1
Chippa	36	6	113	0
R.M.Patel	20	2	59	0
C.M.Patel	22	6	70	2
Mushtaq Ali	9	2	20	0
Parmar	4	1	17	0

Maharashtra Bowling	O	M	R	W
Hazare	30	10	72	3
Sohoni	19	2	60	2
Ushaq Ahmed	16	2	66	0
Jadhav	14	3	52	0
Sarwate	18.1	1	71	5

Umpires: Toss:

Close of Play: 1st day: Maharashtra (1) 295-3 (Sohoni 130*, Hazare 67*); 2nd day: Gujarat (1) 45-1 (Sahana 7*, R.M.Patel 22*).

S.W.Sohoni's 134 took 330 minutes and included 15 fours. S.Mushtaq Ali's 156 took 137 minutes and included 19 fours and 1 six.

NORTHERN INDIA v SOUTHERN PUNJAB

Played at Lahore, January 11, 12, 13, 1941.
Northern India won by a walk-over.

EUROPEANS v INDIANS

Played at Madras Cricket Club Ground, Chepauk, Madras, January 12, 13, 14, 1941.

Indians won by 97 runs.

INDIANS					
1	V.N.Madhava Rao	c Law b McHatton	19	b Johnstone	55
2	M.Swaminathan	c Johnstone b Spitteler	14	c Johnstone b Versey-Brown	6
3	A.G.Ram Singh	c Johnstone b Versey-Brown	44	c Law b Versey-Brown	6
4	B.S.R.Bhadradri	lbw b Johnstone	11	run out	54
5	T.D.Narayanaswami Rao	b McHatton	1	c McHatton b Johnstone	4
6	G.Parthasarathi	b Spitteler	32	c Law b Johnstone	1
7	*M.J.Gopalan	b Versey-Brown	51	c Law b Versey-Brown	25
8	N.J.Venkatesan	c Johnstone b Versey-Brown	4	c O'Callaghan b Versey-Brown	3
9	†M.O.Srinivasan	not out	7	c Nailer b Versey-Brown	0
10	B.S.Krishna Rao	b Versey-Brown	11	c and b Spitteler	2
11	C.R.Rangachari	c O'Callaghan b Versey-Brown	0	not out	2
	Extras		15		10
			209		168

FoW (1): 1-29 (1), 2-47 (2), 3-86 (4), 4-87 (5), 5-108 (3), 6-162 (6), 7-179 (8), 8-191 (7), 9-209 (10), 10-209 (11)
FoW (2): 1-13 (2), 2-21 (3), 3-109 (1), 4-123 (5), 5-125 (6), 6-142 (4), 7-150 (8), 8-152 (9), 9-154 (10), 10-168 (7)

EUROPEANS					
1	*C.P.Johnstone	c Srinivasan b Ram Singh	39	b Ram Singh	16
2	J.A.G.C.Law	c Srinivasan b Rangachari	1	c Gopalan b Ram Singh	17
3	C.N.Reed	c Bhadradri b Rangachari	59	c Rangachari b Ram Singh	14
4	H.B.McHatton	c Madhava Rao b Krishna Rao	14	(7) c Ram Singh b Rangachari	0
5	R.S.Nailer	c Parthasarathi b Krishna Rao	2	(4) b Rangachari	21
6	†H.P.Ward	c Parthasarathi b Rangachari	24	(5) st Srinivasan b Ram Singh	39
7	D.A.S.Day	st Srinivasan b Rangachari	3	(6) b Rangachari	0
8	L.O'Callaghan	c Ram Singh b Rangachari	6	c Krishna Rao b Ram Singh	3
9	J.R.Shadwell	c Narayanaswami Rao b Ram Singh	1	c and b Ram Singh	1
10	J.S.Versey-Brown	b Ram Singh	0	not out	0
11	R.A.Spitteler	not out	0	b Rangachari	1
	Extras		15		4
			164		116

FoW (1): 1-23 (2), 2-55 (1), 3-106 (4), 4-110 (5), 5-146 (3), 6-151 (7), 7-157 (6), 8-164 (8), 9-164 (9), 10-164 (10)
FoW (2): 1-29 (1), 2-36 (2), 3-63 (3), 4-73 (4), 5-73 (6), 6-89 (7), 7-93 (8), 8-96 (9), 9-115 (5), 10-116 (11)

Europeans Bowling	O	M	R	W		O	M	R	W
Versey-Brown	22.2	7	47	5		24.5	5	64	5
O'Callaghan	11	4	18	0		7	0	13	0
Spitteler	24	6	86	2		15	2	43	1
McHatton	12	3	26	2		7	2	17	0
Johnstone	7	0	17	1		14	7	17	3
Day					(6)	2	0	4	0

Indians Bowling	O	M	R	W	O	M	R	W
Gopalan	3	1	10	0	2	0	4	0
Ram Singh	28.2	8	57	3	22	6	59	6
Venkatesan	12	2	24	0	6	3	10	0
Rangachari	19	4	41	5	15.4	4	30	4
Krishna Rao	5	0	17	2	1	0	9	0

Umpires: V.S.Natarajan and J.Subbuswami. Toss: Indians

Close of Play: 1st day: Europeans (1) 58-2 (Reed 18*, McHatton 0*); 2nd day: Indians (2) 144-6 (Gopalan 6*, Venkatesan 2*).

BARODA v MAHARASHTRA

Played at Central College Ground, Baroda, January 15, 16, 17, 1941.

Match drawn.

MAHARASHTRA

1	C.V.Gupte	c Ghorpade b Adhikari	32	b Patel	21
2	S.W.Sohoni	lbw b Patel	2	c Sheikh b Nayudu	27
3	S.Mushtaq Ali	b Adhikari	37	lbw b Gai	24
4	*D.B.Deodhar	c Adhikari b Nayudu	11	b Patel	6
5	V.S.Hazare	lbw b Nayudu	4	b Adhikari	141
6	Raja of Jath	b Gai	12	st Powar b Adhikari	21
7	K.M.Jadhav	c Pandit b Vinod	58	c Vinod b Adhikari	5
8	C.T.Sarwate	lbw b Sheikh	23	b Patel	12
9	B.J.Mohoni	c and b Patel	15	c and b Nayudu	8
10	S.G.Shinde	not out	15	c Nayudu b Patel	12
11	†D.K.Yarde	b Nayudu	3	not out	4
	Extras		14		14
			226		295

FoW (1): 1-3, 2-64, 3-83, 4-85, 5-96, 6-102, 7-157, 8-189, 9-219, 10-226
FoW (2): 1- , 2- , 3- , 4- , 5- , 6- , 7- , 8- , 9- , 10-295

BARODA

1	V.M.Pandit	b Hazare	2	not out	30
2	†S.G.Powar	c Mushtaq Ali b Sohoni	11	lbw b Shinde	53
3	H.R.Adhikari	c Gupte b Jadhav	91	c Yarde b Shinde	29
4	R.B.Nimbalkar	c Jath b Sarwate	29	b Hazare	77
5	C.S.Nayudu	b Jadhav	17	lbw b Hazare	21
6	*W.N.Ghorpade	b Jadhav	0	b Sarwate	42
7	M.S.Indulkar	lbw b Hazare	0	b Hazare	0
8	Y.E.Sheikh	c Yarde b Hazare	15	b Mohoni	24
9	T.B.Vinod	lbw b Sarwate	5	b Hazare	11
10	A.Patel	c Mohoni b Hazare	3		
11	E.B.Gai	not out	10		
	Extras		15		16
			198	(8 wickets)	303

FoW (1): 1-16, 2-28, 3-97, 4- , 5- , 6- , 7- , 8- , 9- , 10-198
FoW (2): 1- , 2- , 3- , 4- , 5- , 6- , 7- , 8-303

Baroda Bowling

	O	M	R	W		O	M	R	W
Patel	10	1	42	2		20	5	100	4
Gai	13	3	33	1		19	2	54	1
Nayudu	20.5	2	73	3		21	1	78	2
Vinod	9	2	15	1		8	3	14	0
Adhikari	9	1	31	2		7.1	0	27	3
Sheikh	5	1	18	1		4	0	8	0

Maharashtra Bowling

	O	M	R	W		O	M	R	W
Hazare	18	3	64	4		26.3	4	80	4
Sohoni	18	1	21	1		19	3	61	0
Sarwate	8.3	0	26	2		8	0	32	1
Shinde	3	0	25	0		12	1	53	2
Jath	3	0	22	0					
Jadhav	9	2	25	3	(5)	3	0	11	0
Mohoni					(6)	10	3	31	1
Mushtaq Ali					(7)	6	1	19	0

Umpires: Toss:

Close of Play: 1st day: ; 2nd day: .

QUEENSLAND v VICTORIA

Played at Brisbane Cricket Ground, Woolloongabba, Brisbane, January 18, 20, 21, 22, 1941.

Match drawn.

QUEENSLAND					
1	R.E.Rogers	c Johnson b Ring	92	c Harvey b Johnson	103
2	G.G.Cook	b Johnson	117	lbw b Dempster	24
3	†D.Tallon	c Dudley b Johnson	18	b Johnson	38
4	G.G.Baker	b Dudley	5	b Sievers	3
5	*W.A.Brown	c Baker b Dudley	26	c Baker b Dudley	47
6	D.Watt	c Lee b Sievers	9	c sub (D.H.Fothergill) b Meikle	55
7	J.F.Barnes	c Dudley b Dempster	8	run out	7
8	H.F.Bendixen	b Dempster	1	retired hurt	0
9	V.N.Raymer	c Ring b Johnson	50	not out	23
10	T.E.Thwaites	b Johnson	0	not out	24
11	J.A.Ellis	not out	7		
	Extras	b 1, lb 2	3	b 10, lb 2	12
			336	(7 wickets)	336

FoW (1): 1-117, 2-146, 3-152, 4-210, 5-229, 6-240, 7-246, 8-309, 9-309, 10-336
FoW (2): 1-65, 2-145, 3-152, 4-190, 5-246, 6-258, 7-300

VICTORIA			
1	*I.S.Lee	c Cook b Ellis	0
2	G.E.Tamblyn	b Ellis	136
3	M.R.Harvey	c Tallon b Ellis	25
4	R.A.Dempster	c and b Watt	15
5	I.W.G.Johnson	c Tallon b Ellis	85
6	M.W.Sievers	lbw b Ellis	5
7	T.K.Sarovich	b Ellis	78
8	G.S.Meikle	run out	42
9	D.T.Ring	b Ellis	60
10	†E.A.Baker	b Bendixen	4
11	W.J.Dudley	not out	0
	Extras	b 9, lb 1	10
			460

FoW (1): 1-0, 2-28, 3-55, 4-206, 5-214, 6-297, 7-367, 8-455, 9-460, 10-460

Victoria Bowling	O	M	R	W		O	M	R	W
Dudley	16	1	59	2		13	0	60	1
Sievers	17	4	42	1		11	0	54	1
Dempster	11	1	27	2	(4)	9	0	25	1
Ring	32	2	107	1	(3)	9	0	34	0
Johnson	17	0	73	4		13	1	79	2
Meikle	5	0	25	0		9	0	46	1
Lee					(7)	2	0	26	0

Queensland Bowling	O	M	R	W
Ellis	22.5	2	86	7
Cook	14	2	25	0
Bendixen	23	1	75	1
Watt	16	1	94	1
Baker	9	2	32	0
Raymer	9	0	61	0
Thwaites	12	2	58	0
Rogers	3	0	19	0

Umpires: K.E.S.Fagg and R.Weitemeyer. Toss: Queensland

Close of Play: 1st day: Queensland (1) 54-0 (Rogers 48*, Cook 5*); 2nd day: Victoria (1) 26-1 (Tamblyn 1*, Harvey 25*); 3rd day: Victoria (1) 436-7 (Sarovich 68*, Ring 50*).

G.G.Cook's 117 took 335 minutes and included 6 fours. G.E.Tamblyn's 136 took 259 minutes and included 15 fours. R.E.Rogers's 103 took 139 minutes and included 8 fours. H.F.Bendixen retired hurt in the Queensland second innings having scored 0 (team score 258-6). 12th Men: D.E.Cox (Qld) and D.H.Fothergill (Vic).

NEW SOUTH WALES v VICTORIA

Played at Sydney Cricket Ground, January 25, 27, 28, 29, 1941.

Victoria won by 24 runs.

VICTORIA					
1	M.R.Harvey	c Barnes b O'Reilly	35	b O'Reilly	70
2	G.E.Tamblyn	lbw b Pepper	36	b Gulliver	48
3	T.K.Sarovich	lbw b Pepper	13	c Barnes b Gulliver	4
4	*I.S.Lee	b O'Reilly	14	(5) b Pepper	4
5	I.W.G.Johnson	c Saggers b O'Reilly	22	(6) c Cohen b Jackson	40
6	M.W.Sievers	c Saggers b O'Reilly	24	(4) b O'Reilly	18
7	R.A.Dempster	lbw b Pepper	2	(8) not out	87
8	D.H.Fothergill	not out	30	(7) c Trumper b O'Reilly	86
9	G.S.Meikle	c Saggers b Pepper	46	b Gulliver	2
10	D.T.Ring	st Saggers b Pepper	0	c Saggers b O'Reilly	31
11	†E.A.Baker	b Pepper	7	c Barnes b O'Reilly	0
	Extras	b 1, lb 3, nb 3	7	b 2, lb 4, w 3, nb 4	13
			236		403

FoW (1): 1-75, 2-75, 3-102, 4-104, 5-143, 6-152, 7-152, 8-218, 9-218, 10-236
FoW (2): 1-115, 2-125, 3-146, 4-146, 5-180, 6-205, 7-314, 8-320, 9-401, 10-403

NEW SOUTH WALES					
1	M.B.Cohen	b Sievers	5	b Sievers	12
2	A.R.Morris	c Meikle b Johnson	37	b Sievers	1
3	S.G.Barnes	c Sarovich b Sievers	132	c Fothergill b Johnson	55
4	D.K.Carmody	lbw b Johnson	21	c Baker b Sievers	7
5	†R.A.Saggers	c Ring b Sievers	35	b Johnson	4
6	V.E.Jackson	c Ring b Meikle	54	(7) c Baker b Sievers	11
7	C.G.Pepper	c Tamblyn b Ring	62	(6) c Dempster b Ring	30
8	K.C.Gulliver	not out	49	b Johnson	9
9	*W.J.O'Reilly	c Meikle b Johnson	4	c Lee b Ring	14
10	R.B.Scott	c Ring b Johnson	9	not out	11
11	V.Trumper	run out	14	c Fothergill b Ring	13
	Extras	b 11, lb 6, w 1	18	b 3, lb 5	8
			440		175

FoW (1): 1-15, 2-70, 3-126, 4-233, 5-240, 6-339, 7-388, 8-400, 9-419, 10-440
FoW (2): 1-3, 2-16, 3-48, 4-57, 5-92, 6-105, 7-127, 8-140, 9-152, 10-175

New South Wales Bowling	O	M	R	W			O	M	R	W	
Scott	9	2	32	0	2nb		9	0	66	0	1w,3nb
Trumper	4	0	22	0			7	0	48	0	1w
Jackson	5	0	25	0		(6)	9	0	32	1	
O'Reilly	22	8	43	4	1nb		20.7	6	56	5	
Pepper	24	2	85	6		(3)	18	0	99	1	1w
Gulliver	4	0	22	0		(5)	15	0	76	3	1nb
Barnes						(7)	2	0	13	0	

Victoria Bowling	O	M	R	W			O	M	R	W
Sievers	16	1	74	3			15	1	44	4
Dempster	11	3	31	0	1w		5	0	16	0
Meikle	7	0	58	1						
Ring	25	0	118	1			8.7	0	55	3
Johnson	31.4	2	117	4		(3)	12	1	52	3
Fothergill	2	0	24	0						

Umpires: G.E.Borwick and R.McGrath. Toss: Victoria

Close of Play: 1st day: Victoria (1) 229-9 (Fothergill 27*, Baker 3*); 2nd day: New South Wales (1) 417-8 (Gulliver 41*, Scott 8*); 3rd day: Victoria (2) 403 all out.

S.G.Barnes's 132 took 167 minutes and included 6 fours and 1 six. 12th Men: J.W.Chegwyn (NSW) and W.J.Dudley (Vic).

HINDUS v THE REST

Played at Alexandra Ground, Amritsar, February 1, 2, 3, 1941.

Match drawn.

HINDUS

1	D.Jagdish Lal	c Majithia b Inayat Khan	3	(2) c Quayle b Tarapore	48
2	†D.D.Hindlekar	b Hazare	8	(1) b Tarapore	7
3	Roshan Lal	b Tarapore	8	b Majithia	18
4	*C.K.Nayudu	c Imtinan b Tarapore	10	(5) c Gurbachan Singh b Tarapore	9
5	Naoomal Jaoomal	c Quayle b Hazare	51	(4) c Quayle b Majithia	1
6	R.P.Mehra	run out	34	c Tarapore b Imtinan	21
7	Gian Prakash	not out	28	c Bhaya b Tarapore	7
8	Shiv Dayal	b Hazare	7	(9) not out	5
9	D.R.Puri	b Inayat Khan	14	(8) c Kewal Krishnan b Imtinan	0
10	Om Prakash	b Hazare	0	not out	0
11	Ram Labhaya	st Quayle b Hazare	0		
	Extras		17		3
			180	(8 wickets)	119

FoW (1): 1-3 (1), 2-19 (2), 3-21 (3), 4-36 (4), 5-118 (6), 6-126 (5), 7-146 (8), 8-171 (9), 9-172 (10), 10-180 (11)
FoW (2): 1-32 (1), 2-71 (2), 3-74 (4), 4-81 (3), 5-87 (5), 6-114 (7), 7-114 (6), 8-114 (8)

THE REST

1	Gurbachan Singh	lbw b Nayudu	0
2	Imtinan	c Naoomal Jaoomal b Nayudu	83
3	K.K.Tarapore	c Jagdish Lal b Shiv Dayal	4
4	V.S.Hazare	c Jagdish Lal b Puri	171
5	J.N.Bhaya	c Hindlekar b Naoomal Jaoomal	23
6	*S.S.Majithia	c Nayudu b Shiv Dayal	14
7	H.C.W.Westwood	b Naoomal Jaoomal	9
8	†H.D.M.Quayle	lbw b Nayudu	18
9	Ashraf	b Shiv Dayal	107
10	Inayat Khan	c Jagdish Lal b Nayudu	4
11	Kewal Krishnan	not out	3
	Extras		10
			446

FoW (1): 1-2 (1), 2-40 (3), 3-108 (2), 4-143 (5), 5-178 (6), 6-194 (7), 7-243 (8), 8-414 (4), 9-432 (10), 10-446 (9)

The Rest Bowling

	O	M	R	W		O	M	R	W
Hazare	33.5	14	54	5		8	3	23	0
Inayat Khan	17	6	31	2	(6)	6	5	6	0
Tarapore	23	6	49	2		23	8	44	4
Westwood	4	1	6	0	(2)	6	2	12	0
Bhaya	11	3	23	0	(4)	9	3	22	0
Majithia					(5)	8	5	7	2
Imtinan					(7)	3	1	2	2

Hindus Bowling

	O	M	R	W
Puri	23	4	70	1
Nayudu	47	11	157	4
Naoomal Jaoomal	36	1	123	2
Shiv Dayal	23.3	1	80	3
Ram Labhaya	3	1	6	0

Umpires: Toss: Hindus

Close of Play: 1st day: The Rest (1) 1-0 (Gurbachan Singh 0*, Imtinan 1*); 2nd day: The Rest (1) 340-7 (Hazare 129*, Ashraf 51*).

V.S.Hazare's 171 took 240 minutes and included 15 fours.

TRINIDAD v BARBADOS

Played at Queen's Park Oval, Port of Spain, February 1, 3, 4, 5, 1941.

Match drawn.

TRINIDAD					
1	*V.H.Stollmeyer	b Parris	37	c Bourne b Williams	9
2	D.Merry	c and b Clarke	47	lbw b Griffith	80
3	N.S.Asgarali	run out	33	c Bourne b Crick	0
4	G.E.Gomez	run out	10	(6) lbw b Williams	11
5	S.A.H.Niamat	b Crick	3	(4) b Sealy	31
6	C.Persaud	c Carew b Williams	58	(5) c Blackman b Sealy	18
7	R.P.Tang Choon	c Blackman b Crick	83	b Crick	16
8	†S.Samaroo	c Bourne b Carew	18	b Griffith	0
9	S.M.Ali	b Carew	1	not out	5
10	J.Hendrickson	b Williams	14	c Walcott b Griffith	8
11	L.R.Pierre	not out	6	b Crick	0
	Extras	b 15, lb 2, w 1, nb 4	22	b 9, lb 1, w 1, nb 2	13
			332		191

FoW (1): 1-81, 2-95, 3-110, 4-116, 5-163, 6-253, 7-301, 8-306, 9-312, 10-332
FoW (2): 1-16, 2-22, 3-90, 4-133, 5-151, 6-176, 7-176, 8-178, 9-191, 10-191

BARBADOS					
1	†C.L.Bourne	b Pierre	22	b Pierre	0
2	G.M.Carew	run out	41	not out	40
3	R.G.Blackman	c Asgarali b Pierre	47	b Hendrickson	12
4	G.Waithe	run out	0	(5) b Ali	2
5	J.E.D.Sealy	b Pierre	71	(4) c Stollmeyer b Pierre	3
6	E.A.V.Williams	c Merry b Tang Choon	2	b Ali	1
7	M.I.C.Clarke	c Stollmeyer b Tang Choon	153	lbw b Tang Choon	4
8	K.E.Walcott	b Pierre	0	not out	21
9	J.L.Parris	c Pierre b Persaud	21		
10	C.O.Crick	not out	13		
11	*H.C.Griffith	not out	0		
	Extras	b 3, lb 4	7	b 4, lb 2	6
		(9 wickets, declared)	377	(6 wickets)	89

FoW (1): 1-28, 2-97, 3-97, 4-123, 5-148, 6-219, 7-219, 8-270, 9-377
FoW (2): 1-0, 2-23, 3-26, 4-40, 5-42, 6-47

Barbados Bowling	O	M	R	W		O	M	R	W
Crick	17	1	73	2		17.3	0	59	3
Williams	12.1	1	51	2		9	0	21	2
Clarke	16	5	29	1		3	2	7	0
Parris	17	0	105	1		4	0	30	0
Walcott	2	0	12	0					
Griffith	3	0	14	0	(5)	13	2	38	3
Carew	5	0	26	2	(6)	3	0	10	0
Sealy					(7)	6	0	13	2

Trinidad Bowling	O	M	R	W		O	M	R	W
Pierre	13	1	79	4		7	0	41	2
Hendrickson	9	0	39	0		4	1	7	1
Persaud	10	1	71	1					
Tang Choon	13	1	81	2	(3)	5	0	11	1
Ali	15	1	67	0	(4)	6	2	11	2
Stollmeyer	4	0	33	0	(5)	1	0	13	0

Umpires: Toss: Trinidad

Close of Play: 1st day: Trinidad (1) 262-6 (Tang Choon 54*, Samaroo 6*); 2nd day: Barbados (1) 235-7 (Clarke 38*, Parris not out); 3rd day: Trinidad (2) 90-2 (Merry 39*, Niamat 31*).

MUSLIMS v THE REST

Played at Alexandra Ground, Amritsar, February 5, 6, 7, 1941.

Match drawn.

THE REST

1	*K.K.Tarapore	b Ahmed Khan	18	run out	2
2	Imtinan	c Jahangir Khan b Nazir Ali	9	c Gul Mohammad b Amir Elahi	19
3	Ashraf	c Abdur Rehman b Amir Elahi	45	b Nissar	0
4	L.Amarnath	lbw b Ahmed Khan	29	c Gul Mohammad b Ahmed Khan	12
5	J.N.Bhaya	c Nissar b Amir Elahi	27	b Ahmed Khan	116
6	K.Rai Singh	c Gul Mohammad b Amir Elahi	26	lbw b Ahmed Khan	57
7	Hazara Singh	b Ahmed Khan	5	b Amir Elahi	9
8	†H.D.M.Quayle	st Abdur Rehman b Amir Elahi	29	c Ahmed Khan b Amir Elahi	5
9	R.D.B.Robathan	b Nazar Mohammad	1	b Nazar Mohammad	1
10	H.C.W.Westwood	c Ahmed Khan b Amir Elahi	0	(11) not out	23
11	J.M.Gwyn	not out	5	(10) c Nissar b Amir Elahi	6
	Extras		7		24
			201		274

FoW (1): 1-12 (2), 2-71 (1), 3-81 (3), 4-122 (4), 5-142 (5), 6-164 (6), 7-165 (7), 8-169 (9), 9-174 (10), 10-201 (8)
FoW (2): 1-3 (1), 2-3 (3), 3-28 (2), 4-40 (4), 5-204 (6), 6-231 (7), 7-231 (5), 8- , 9- , 10-274

MUSLIMS

1	Nazar Mohammad	c Tarapore b Amarnath	43	(3) lbw b Tarapore	1
2	†Abdur Rehman	c and b Amarnath	12	(1) c Rai Singh b Amarnath	3
3	Gul Mohammad	c sub (Inayat Khan) b Tarapore	115	(5) not out	3
4	M.Nissar	b Amarnath	1		
5	*S.Wazir Ali	lbw b Imtinan	23		
6	S.Nazir Ali	c Bhaya b Tarapore	56		
7	Anwar Hussain	b Rai Singh	29		
8	Murawwat Hussain	not out	35		
9	Amir Elahi	c Westwood b Tarapore	17	(4) not out	32
10	Ahmed Khan	c Hazara Singh b Tarapore	31	(2) run out	7
11	M.Jahangir Khan	b Bhaya	12		
	Extras		25		8
			399	(3 wickets)	54

FoW (1): 1-53 (2), 2-84 (1), 3-88 (4), 4-141 (5), 5-250 (3), 6-272 (6), 7-309 (7), 8-334 (9), 9- (10), 10-399 (11)
FoW (2): 1- , 2- , 3-

Muslims Bowling

	O	M	R	W		O	M	R	W
Nissar	13	3	25	0		16	4	43	1
Nazir Ali	10	2	24	1		3	0	7	0
Murawwat Hussain	4	0	23	0					
Ahmed Khan	17	6	35	3	(3)	24	8	43	3
Amir Elahi	24.2	5	74	5	(4)	30.2	2	107	4
Nazar Mohammad	2	0	4	1	(5)	8	1	35	1
Wazir Ali	2	0	9	0					
Anwar Hussain					(6)	5	0	15	0

The Rest Bowling

	O	M	R	W		O	M	R	W
Amarnath	57	14	152	3		6	1	26	1
Westwood	5	1	12	0					
Tarapore	32	4	122	4	(2)	3	0	11	1
Bhaya	11.3	2	28	1					
Imtinan	5	0	38	1					
Hazara Singh	4	1	5	0					
Gwyn	2	0	13	0					
Rai Singh	2	0	4	1	(3)	2	0	9	0

Umpires: Toss: The Rest

Close of Play: 1st day: Muslims (1) 52-0 (Nazar Mohammad 32*, Abdur Rehman 12*); 2nd day: Muslims (1) 399 all out.
J.N.Bhaya's 116 included 12 fours.

MADRAS v UNITED PROVINCES

Played at Madras Cricket Club Ground, Chepauk, Madras, February 7, 8, 9, 1941.

Madras won by 25 runs.

MADRAS					
1	*C.P.Johnstone	b Aftab Ahmed	37	b Masood Salahuddin	1
2	V.N.Madhava Rao	c Maqbool Alam b Masood Salahuddin	10	b Alexander	5
3	A.G.Ram Singh	c Alexander b Aftab Ahmed	91	(8) c and b Alexander	9
4	B.S.R.Bhadradri	c Maqbool Alam b Aftab Ahmed	3	c Firasat Hussain b Alexander	1
5	R.S.Nailer	lbw b Aftab Ahmed	10	c Aftab Ahmed b Alexander	55
6	M.J.Gopalan	not out	101	lbw b Alexander	6
7	G.Parthasarathi	lbw b Palia	3	c Garudachar b Aftab Ahmed	9
8	N.J.Venkatesan	b Palia	0	(9) b Alexander	21
9	†J.A.G.C.Law	lbw b Aftab Ahmed	0	(3) c Phansalkar b Alexander	17
10	B.S.Krishna Rao	c Maqbool Alam b Masood Salahuddin	7	run out	8
11	C.R.Rangachari	b Palia	0	not out	7
	Extras		9		19
			271		158

FoW (1): 1-24 (2), 2-72 (1), 3-78 (4), 4-101 (5), 5-194 (3), 6-197 (7), 7-197 (8), 8-206 (9), 9-244 (10), 10-271 (11)
FoW (2): 1-2 (1), 2-12 (2), 3-15 (4), 4-84 (5), 5-96 (6), 6-99 (3), 7-109 (7), 8-136 (8), 9-145 (9), 10-158 (10)

UNITED PROVINCES					
1	E.Alexander	c Nailer b Ram Singh	0	lbw b Venkatesan	14
2	A.S.N.Murthy	c Law b Rangachari	26	b Rangachari	4
3	B.K.Garudachar	b Rangachari	44	(4) c Rangachari b Krishna Rao	20
4	*P.E.Palia	not out	110	(3) b Rangachari	8
5	J.P.Phansalkar	c Krishna Rao b Parthasarathi	17	(9) b Rangachari	9
6	Aftab Ahmed	c Law b Rangachari	1	(8) b Parthasarathi	25
7	Shamim Khwaja	lbw b Parthasarathi	6	(10) not out	30
8	†Maqbool Alam	c Law b Rangachari	26	(5) b Venkatesan	6
9	Masood Salahuddin	b Rangachari	3	(6) st Law b Krishna Rao	0
10	Firasat Hussain	b Krishna Rao	15	(7) b Venkatesan	5
11	Abdul Hamid	b Krishna Rao	0	b Parthasarathi	10
	Extras		7		18
			255		149

FoW (1): 1-1 (1), 2-37 (2), 3-106 (3), 4-153 (5), 5-160 (6), 6-183 (7), 7-216 (8), 8-220 (9), 9-255 (10), 10-255 (11)
FoW (2): 1-13 (2), 2-23 (3), 3-48 (1), 4-52 (4), 5-52 (6), 6-66 (5), 7-73 (7), 8-93 (9), 9-131 (8), 10-149 (11)

United Provinces Bowling	O	M	R	W		O	M	R	W
Alexander	15	1	46	0		21	8	29	7
Masood Salahuddin	12	1	40	2		12	4	25	1
Firasat Hussain	11	1	29	0	(4)	7	3	15	0
Palia	23.5	11	41	3					
Aftab Ahmed	27	4	96	5	(3)	11	1	35	1
Murthy	3	1	10	0	(5)	9	2	27	0
Garudachar					(6)	2	0	8	0

Madras Bowling	O	M	R	W		O	M	R	W
Gopalan	10	5	8	0	(2)	5	1	11	0
Ram Singh	2	1	1	1					
Parthasarathi	11	0	56	2	(6)	2.5	0	13	2
Rangachari	22	1	75	5	(1)	10	1	31	3
Krishna Rao	14.5	0	66	2	(4)	15	2	52	2
Venkatesan	8	0	39	0	(3)	14	5	22	3
Johnstone	2	1	3	0	(5)	2	1	2	0

Umpires: B.V.Ramakrishnappa and M.G.Vijayasarathi. Toss: Madras

Close of Play: 1st day: United Provinces (1) 2-1 (Murthy 2*, Garudachar 0*); 2nd day: Madras (2) 84-3 (Law 13*, Nailer 54*).

M.J.Gopalan's 101 took 185 minutes and included 9 fours and 2 sixes. P.E.Palia's 110 took 160 minutes and included 7 fours.

OTAGO v CANTERBURY

Played at Carisbrook, Dunedin, February 7, 8, 10, 1941.

Canterbury won by an innings and 18 runs.

CANTERBURY

1	*W.A.Hadlee	c Groves b Knight	6
2	I.B.Cromb	c D.J.Blakely b Chettleburgh	96
3	F.P.O'Brien	c D.J.Blakely b Robertson	112
4	W.M.Anderson	lbw b Robertson	8
5	V.James	not out	155
6	T.D.Moynihan	c Leader b J.W.Blakely	46
7	A.W.Roberts	c and b Leader	69
8	W.O.Mapplebeck	not out	7
9	†B.C.Harbridge		
10	S.M.Cameron		
11	A.T.Burgess		
	Extras	b 2, lb 6	8
		(6 wickets, declared)	507

FoW (1): 1-9 (1), 2-169 (2), 3-179 (4), 4-249 (3), 5-363 (6), 6-497 (7)

OTAGO

1	A.R.Knight	b Cromb	56	b Burgess	152
2	S.F.Duncan	c Harbridge b Mapplebeck	18	(6) lbw b Cromb	0
3	G.J.Robertson	b Mapplebeck	6	c Burgess b Cameron	0
4	L.D.Smith	b Roberts	2	(5) c Roberts b Cromb	10
5	T.F.C.Geary	c Cromb b Burgess	12	(7) c James b Cromb	1
6	J.W.Blakely	b Burgess	1	(11) not out	5
7	†G.H.Mills	b Roberts	8	(4) c Cromb b Roberts	16
8	*V.J.T.Chettleburgh	b Burgess	44	st Harbridge b Cromb	64
9	L.J.Groves	c Roberts b Cromb	21	(10) c Cromb b Anderson	11
10	D.J.Blakely	c Roberts b Cromb	8	(9) c Cameron b Burgess	28
11	J.V.Leader	not out	2	(2) b Roberts	2
	Extras	b 7, lb 1, nb 1	9	b 6, lb 4, nb 3	13
			187		302

FoW (1): 1-24 (2), 2-34 (3), 3-37 (4), 4-64 (5), 5-72 (6), 6-85 (7), 7-149, 8-157, 9-170, 10-187
FoW (2): 1-4 (2), 2-7 (3), 3-39 (4), 4-58 (5), 5-58 (6), 6-63 (7), 7-192 (8), 8-279, 9-296, 10-302

Otago Bowling

	O	M	R	W
Robertson	16	2	69	2
Knight	17	6	62	1
Leader	20	4	58	1
Geary	8	0	60	0
Groves	12	1	91	0
Smith	8	0	44	0
Chettleburgh	11	0	59	1
J.W.Blakely	6	0	32	1
Duncan	5	0	24	0

Canterbury Bowling

	O	M	R	W		O	M	R	W
Roberts	15	3	36	2		20	2	38	2
Mapplebeck	7	1	32	2					
Cromb	7.1	0	22	3	(2)	20	3	72	4
Cameron	10	0	39	0	(3)	12	0	65	1
Burgess	15	4	49	3	(4)	20.4	7	49	2
Anderson					(5)	8	0	58	1
Hadlee					(6)	3	1	7	0

Umpires: L.Diehl and G.McQueen. Toss: Canterbury

Close of Play: 1st day: Canterbury (1) 507-6 (James 155*, Mapplebeck 7*); 2nd day: Otago (2) 118-6 (Knight 52*, Chettleburgh 30*).
I.B.Cromb hit three consecutive sixes in one over from L.J.Groves.

TRINIDAD v BARBADOS

Played at Queen's Park Oval, Port of Spain, February 8, 10, 11, 12, 1941.

Trinidad won by nine wickets.

	BARBADOS				
1	†C.L.Bourne	b Pierre	0	c Tang Choon b J.B.Stollmeyer	65
2	G.M.Carew	c and b V.H.Stollmeyer	100	b Ali	10
3	G.Waithe	c Sealey b Pierre	6	(7) b Ali	0
4	R.G.Blackman	c and b V.H.Stollmeyer	69	(3) c Ganteaume b Tang Choon	140
5	J.E.D.Sealy	run out	17	(4) run out	6
6	M.I.C.Clarke	b Pierre	42	(5) c V.H.Stollmeyer b Jones	13
7	S.S.Gill	b Jones	1	(8) c Tang Choon b Ali	5
8	E.A.V.Williams	not out	39	(6) c and b Ali	67
9	*H.C.Griffith	b J.B.Stollmeyer	16	b Tang Choon	2
10	C.O.Crick	lbw b J.B.Stollmeyer	6	b Ali	3
11	N.E.Marshall	lbw b V.H.Stollmeyer	0	not out	0
	Extras	b 3, lb 2	5	b 12, lb 6, w 1, nb 2	21
			301		332

FoW (1): 1-0, 2-6, 3-172, 4-179, 5-217, 6-218, 7-258, 8-288, 9-290, 10-301
FoW (2): 1-30, 2-113, 3-131, 4-164, 5-305, 6-305, 7-311, 8-327, 9-328, 10-332

	TRINIDAD				
1	*V.H.Stollmeyer	b Sealy	41	not out	86
2	J.B.Stollmeyer	c Bourne b Williams	84	lbw b Crick	92
3	D.Merry	lbw b Sealy	4	not out	4
4	G.E.Gomez	run out	51		
5	L.Harbin	lbw b Crick	16		
6	B.J.Sealey	c sub b Crick	32		
7	R.P.Tang Choon	c Clarke b Carew	38		
8	†A.G.Ganteaume	b Crick	87		
9	P.E.W.Jones	b Griffith	43		
10	S.M.Ali	c Williams b Crick	33		
11	L.R.Pierre	not out	1		
	Extras	b 6, lb 12, w 2, nb 2	22		
			452	(1 wicket)	182

FoW (1): 1-129, 2-129, 3-134, 4-161, 5-232, 6-244, 7-306, 8-409, 9-451, 10-452
FoW (2): 1-170

Trinidad Bowling	O	M	R	W		O	M	R	W
Pierre	12	1	50	3		12	2	42	0
Jones	14	0	55	1		11	0	41	1
Tang Choon	8	0	36	0		8	0	49	2
Ali	7	0	50	0		9.7	2	63	5
Harbin	6	0	19	0		6	0	31	0
Sealey	3	0	22	0		2	0	8	0
J.B.Stollmeyer	10	2	26	2		10	0	55	1
V.H.Stollmeyer	7.3	0	38	3		3	0	12	0
Gomez					(9)	3	0	10	0

Barbados Bowling	O	M	R	W		O	M	R	W
Crick	19.7	0	84	4		2	0	11	1
Williams	12	2	52	1		3	1	17	0
Clarke	10	1	37	0					
Gill	10	1	30	0	(3)	8	0	41	0
Griffith	13	0	88	1	(4)	1	0	9	0
Marshall	6	0	30	0	(5)	9	0	70	0
Sealy	15	2	68	2					
Carew	9	1	41	1	(6)	2.2	0	15	0
Blackman					(7)	2	0	19	0

Umpires: Toss: Barbados

Close of Play: 1st day: Trinidad (1) 6-0 (V.H.Stollmeyer 4*, J.B.Stollmeyer 2*); 2nd day: Trinidad (1) 357-7 (Ganteaume 60*, Jones 22*); 3rd day: Barbados (2) 263-4 (Blackman 105*, Williams 50*).

R.G.Blackman's 140 took 257 minutes.

WESTERN INDIA v MAHARASHTRA

Played at Municipal Stadium, Rajkot, February 8, 9, 10, 1941.

Match drawn.

WESTERN INDIA			
1	†Faiz Ahmed	c Jadhav b Sohoni	7
2	H.W.Barritt	b Jadhav	34
3	Umar Khan	c Gokhale b Hazare	15
4	*K.S.Abdul Khaliq	c Deodhar b Sarwate	36
5	S.M.Nasiruddin	st Gokhale b Sarwate	30
6	Prithviraj	c Sohoni b Jadhav	45
7	Nawab of Manavadar	c Sohoni b Sarwate	62
8	S.B.Gandhi	b Hazare	41
9	Akbar Khan	c Mohoni b Sarwate	57
10	Saeed Ahmed	not out	80
11	S.Nyalchand	c and b Sohoni	20
	Extras		32
			459

FoW (1): 1-19 (1), 2-46 (3), 3-80 (2), 4-123 (4), 5-132 (5), 6-206 (6), 7-276 (7), 8-306 (8), 9-394 (9), 10-459 (11)

MAHARASHTRA			
1	S.W.Sohoni	not out	218
2	R.V.Bhajekar	b Nyalchand	35
3	R.B.Nimbalkar	c Gandhi b Saeed Ahmed	16
4	*D.B.Deodhar	b Akbar Khan	4
5	V.S.Hazare	not out	164
6	Ushaq Ahmed		
7	K.M.Jadhav		
8	†Y.N.Gokhale		
9	M.M.Naidu		
10	C.T.Sarwate		
11	B.J.Mohoni		
	Extras		23
		(3 wickets)	460

FoW (1): 1-76 (2), 2-100 (3), 3-118 (4)

Maharashtra Bowling

	O	M	R	W
Hazare	37	8	110	2
Sohoni	37	5	126	2
Jadhav	14	3	39	2
Ushaq Ahmed	8	1	39	0
Sarwate	37	7	107	4
Mohoni	2	0	6	0

Western India Bowling

	O	M	R	W
Saeed Ahmed	46	9	76	1
Akbar Khan	41	12	123	1
Gandhi	25	4	74	0
Nyalchand	39	13	96	1
Prithviraj	16	2	44	0
Umar Khan	2	0	5	0
Manavadar	2	0	11	0
Barritt	1	0	8	0

Umpires: Toss: Western India

Close of Play: 1st day: Western India (1) 344-8 (Akbar Khan 33*, Saeed Ahmed 18*); 2nd day: Maharashtra (1) 168-3 (Sohoni 72*, Hazare 27*).

S.W.Sohoni's 218 took 503 minutes.

AUCKLAND v WELLINGTON

Played at Eden Park, Auckland, February 14, 15, 17, 18, 1941.

Auckland won by an innings and 24 runs.

WELLINGTON					
1	W.F.T.Hepburn	c Jackman b Burke	6	b Weir	5
2	*E.G.McLeod	c Pearson b Andrews	85	b Burke	26
3	P.D.Wilson	c Jackman b Burke	18	b Cleverley	0
4	F.R.Crawford	run out	14	b Weir	0
5	D.S.Wilson	c Cleal b Burke	37	(6) c Jackman b Weir	0
6	†W.E.Norris	c Cleverley b Burke	9	(5) c and b Weir	5
7	N.S.H.Burnette	b Andrews	1	c and b Weir	49
8	R.J.Duffy	lbw b Burke	3	not out	59
9	T.L.Pritchard	b Andrews	6	b Andrews	14
10	J.G.Ashenden	c Burke b Andrews	7	c Burgess b Weir	17
11	T.A.Downes	not out	0	b Andrews	11
	Extras	b 5, lb 4	9	b 11, lb 1	12
			195		198

FoW (1): 1-19 (1), 2-50 (3), 3-89 (4), 4-157, 5-174, 6-178, 7-178, 8-185, 9-195, 10-195
FoW (2): 1-15 (1), 2-16 (3), 3-17 (4), 4-29 (5), 5-31 (6), 6-46 (2), 7-135 (7), 8-164 (9), 9-183 (10), 10-198 (11)

AUCKLAND			
1	P.E.Whitelaw	b D.S.Wilson	95
2	G.C.Burgess	b Ashenden	13
3	H.T.Pearson	b Ashenden	14
4	W.M.Wallace	c D.S.Wilson b Ashenden	1
5	V.J.Scott	c and b D.S.Wilson	133
6	*G.L.Weir	b D.S.Wilson	1
7	O.C.Cleal	c and b D.S.Wilson	98
8	C.Burke	b Ashenden	28
9	†C.K.Q.Jackman	b D.S.Wilson	0
10	D.C.Cleverley	not out	16
11	F.M.Andrews	not out	2
	Extras	b 4, lb 12	16
		(9 wickets, declared)	417

FoW (1): 1-30 (2), 2-62 (3), 3-64 (4), 4-189 (1), 5-193 (6), 6-369, 7-372, 8-384, 9-414

Auckland Bowling	O	M	R	W		O	M	R	W
Cleverley	16	0	44	0		18	5	37	1
Weir	7	1	22	0		23	2	56	6
Burke	28.5	4	71	5		15	5	37	1
Andrews	19	4	49	4		17.4	1	46	2
Scott					(5)	5	1	10	0

Wellington Bowling	O	M	R	W
Pritchard	24	1	90	0
Downes	15	1	63	0
Ashenden	21	1	94	4
D.S.Wilson	21	2	86	5
Duffy	7	2	21	0
Crawford	4	0	30	0
Hepburn	3	0	17	0

Umpires: R.W.Mitchell and O.R.Montgomery. Toss: Wellington

Close of Play: 1st day: Wellington (1) 28-1 (McLeod 13*, P.D.Wilson 5*); 2nd day: Auckland (1) 133-3 (Whitelaw 71*, Scott 31*); 3rd day: Wellington (2) 71-6 (Burnette 23*, Duffy 8*).

The match was played for the Centennial Cup.

VICTORIA v NEW SOUTH WALES

Played at Melbourne Cricket Ground, February 14, 15, 17, 18, 1941.

New South Wales won by 235 runs.

NEW SOUTH WALES

1	M.B.Cohen	c Lee b Dempster	13	c Dudley b Johnson	19
2	A.R.Morris	lbw b Ring	25	c Baker b Sievers	31
3	S.G.Barnes	b Sievers	185	b Dempster	79
4	*S.J.McCabe	c Sarovich b Meikle	82	absent hurt	0
5	J.W.Chegwyn	b Dudley	78	absent hurt	0
6	C.L.McCool	not out	20	(4) b Johnson	0
7	†R.A.Saggers	hit wkt b Johnson	6	(5) c Meikle b Ring	47
8	V.E.Jackson	c Baker b Johnson	0	(6) c Sievers b Ring	57
9	C.G.Pepper	lbw b Dudley	1	(7) c Baker b Sievers	32
10	W.J.O'Reilly	c Sievers b Johnson	0	(8) c Sievers b Johnson	26
11	V.Trumper	c Baker b Dudley	0	(9) not out	5
	Extras	b 3, nb 3	6	b 4, lb 3, nb 1	8
			416		304

FoW (1): 1-21, 2-57, 3-195, 4-378, 5-393, 6-402, 7-402, 8-403, 9-412, 10-416
FoW (2): 1-49, 2-53, 3-54, 4-169, 5-185, 6-239, 7-293, 8-304

VICTORIA

1	*I.S.Lee	c Pepper b Trumper	67	absent hurt	0
2	M.R.Harvey	b O'Reilly	14	(1) c sub (K.C.Gulliver) b Pepper	38
3	T.K.Sarovich	b Pepper	7	b O'Reilly	0
4	I.W.G.Johnson	c Morris b Pepper	60	c Morris b O'Reilly	20
5	R.A.Dempster	lbw b O'Reilly	11	(2) b O'Reilly	16
6	D.H.Fothergill	c Barnes b O'Reilly	63	(5) lbw b Pepper	1
7	G.S.Meikle	lbw b O'Reilly	31	(8) c O'Reilly b McCool	4
8	M.W.Sievers	b Pepper	29	(7) b McCool	37
9	D.T.Ring	b O'Reilly	7	lbw b McCool	4
10	†E.A.Baker	c Saggers b O'Reilly	8	(6) st Saggers b McCool	20
11	W.J.Dudley	not out	9	(10) not out	11
	Extras	b 8, lb 6, w 3, nb 3	20	b 7, lb 1	8
			326		159

FoW (1): 1-49, 2-73, 3-144, 4-176, 5-178, 6-261, 7-284, 8-307, 9-311, 10-326
FoW (2): 1-54, 2-54, 3-60, 4-70, 5-94, 6-128, 7-140, 8-144, 9-159

Victoria Bowling

	O	M	R	W			O	M	R	W	
Dudley	12.6	2	46	3			12	1	49	0	
Sievers	19	0	94	1			15	0	64	2	1nb
Dempster	14	0	63	1	1nb	(5)	6	0	12	1	
Ring	16	0	112	1		(3)	18.4	0	92	2	
Johnson	12	0	49	3		(4)	19	0	79	3	
Meikle	5	0	46	1							

New South Wales Bowling

	O	M	R	W			O	M	R	W
Trumper	10	0	36	1	2w		5	1	17	0
Jackson	10	2	51	0			4	0	32	0
O'Reilly	24	2	60	6	3nb		10	5	17	3
Pepper	23	1	106	3	1w		14	1	56	2
Cohen	3	1	6	0						
McCool	5	0	39	0		(5)	6.5	0	29	4
Barnes	2	0	8	0						

Umpires: A.N.Barlow and W.J.Craddock. Toss: New South Wales

Close of Play: 1st day: New South Wales (1) 416 all out; 2nd day: New South Wales (2) 18-0 (Cohen 7*, Morris 11*); 3rd day: Victoria (2) 73-4 (Johnson 10*, Baker 1*).

S.G.Barnes's 185 took 233 minutes and included 16 fours. 12th Men: I.R.Porter (Vic) and K.C.Gulliver (NSW).

SOUTH AUSTRALIA v NEW SOUTH WALES

Played at Adelaide Oval, February 21, 22, 24, 1941.

New South Wales won by an innings and 45 runs.

	SOUTH AUSTRALIA				
1	K.L.Ridings	b Pepper	11	st Saggers b McCool	62
2	C.L.Badcock	b O'Reilly	40	b Pepper	40
3	R.A.Hamence	st Saggers b Gulliver	31	lbw b O'Reilly	5
4	B.H.Leak	st Saggers b McCool	21	b O'Reilly	1
5	M.G.Waite	c Morris b Gulliver	3	(7) b Pepper	94
6	R.S.Holman	b O'Reilly	1	hit wkt b McCool	3
7	L.D.Duldig	run out	9	(5) c Saggers b McCool	23
8	P.L.Ridings	c Barnes b O'Reilly	4	c Stapleton b Gulliver	21
9	*C.V.Grimmett	b O'Reilly	9	c O'Reilly b McCool	67
10	†H.V.Heairfield	b O'Reilly	0	not out	4
11	H.N.J.Cotton	not out	0	c Stapleton b McCool	8
	Extras	nb 3	3	b 3, w 1, nb 3	7
			132		335

FoW (1): 1-42, 2-68, 3-99, 4-102, 5-112, 6-112, 7-123, 8-123, 9-123, 10-132
FoW (2): 1-61, 2-66, 3-72, 4-134, 5-135, 6-138, 7-183, 8-313, 9-327, 10-335

	NEW SOUTH WALES		
1	M.B.Cohen	lbw b Waite	21
2	A.R.Morris	b Grimmett	33
3	S.G.Barnes	c K.L.Ridings b P.L.Ridings	51
4	J.W.Chegwyn	c P.L.Ridings b Cotton	103
5	C.L.McCool	c Leak b Cotton	100
6	†R.A.Saggers	c P.L.Ridings b Cotton	63
7	H.V.Stapleton	lbw b Cotton	1
8	V.E.Jackson	c Cotton b Waite	70
9	K.C.Gulliver	b P.L.Ridings	29
10	C.G.Pepper	not out	25
11	*W.J.O'Reilly	c Heairfield b P.L.Ridings	1
	Extras	b 7, lb 3, w 1, nb 4	15
			512

FoW (1): 1-23, 2-102, 3-124, 4-284, 5-353, 6-362, 7-412, 8-477, 9-509, 10-512

New South Wales Bowling	O	M	R	W			O	M	R	W	
Jackson	7	0	17	0			11	2	39	0	
Stapleton	4	1	9	0			6	0	29	0	
Pepper	9	0	47	1	1nb		16	0	89	2	1w
O'Reilly	9.3	1	28	5	2nb		25	9	61	2	2nb
McCool	2	0	12	1		(6)	13.7	0	65	5	
Gulliver	5	1	16	2		(5)	8	1	45	1	1nb

South Australia Bowling	O	M	R	W	
Cotton	15	2	85	4	
Waite	27	4	111	2	
P.L.Ridings	10.6	1	76	3	
Grimmett	24	1	128	1	
K.L.Ridings	19	0	97	0	1w

Umpires: J.D.Scott and L.A.Smith. Toss: South Australia

Close of Play: 1st day: New South Wales (1) 284-3 (Chegwyn 103*, McCool 69*); 2nd day: South Australia (2) 108-3 (K.L.Ridings 46*, Duldig 15*).

The match was scheduled for four days but completed in three. J.W.Chegwyn's 103 took 110 minutes and included 13 fours. C.L.McCool's 100 took 158 minutes and included 7 fours. 12th Men: F.L.Teisseire (SA) and V.Trumper, jun. (NSW).

MAHARASHTRA v NORTHERN INDIA

Played at Poona Club Ground, February 22, 23, 24, 25, 1941.

Match drawn.

MAHARASHTRA			
1	R.V.Bhajekar	b Habibullah	120
2	S.W.Sohoni	c Gul Mohammad b Habibullah	68
3	M.M.Naidu	b Habibullah	3
4	R.B.Nimbalkar	b Agha Sarfraz	0
5	V.S.Hazare	c sub (Ahmed Saeed) b Gul Mohammad	65
6	C.T.Sarwate	b Mohammad Ramzan	63
7	*D.B.Deodhar	b Gul Mohammad	196
8	†Y.N.Gokhale	b Gul Mohammad	75
9	K.M.Jadhav	c sub (Ahmed Saeed) b Agha Sarfraz	115
10	Raja of Jath	not out	27
11	M.K.Patwardhan	lbw b Habibullah	10
	Extras		56
			798

FoW (1): 1-158 (2), 2-164 (3), 3-165 (4), 4-277 (5), 5-277 (1), 6-430 (6), 7-601 (8), 8-733 (7), 9-764 (9), 10-798 (11)

NORTHERN INDIA			
1	D.Jagdish Lal	b Hazare	5
2	Nazar Mohammad	b Hazare	21
3	Amir Hussain	c Gokhale b Sarwate	12
4	*R.P.Mehra	not out	209
5	Gul Mohammad	b Sarwate	1
6	Mohammad Sharif	b Hazare	118
7	†Anwar Hussain	c Nimbalkar b Sarwate	25
8	Agha Sarfraz	b Sarwate	11
9	Ahmed Khan	b Patwardhan	16
10	Habibullah	c sub (B.J.Mohoni) b Sohoni	0
11	Mohammad Ramzan	c Jadhav b Sohoni	4
	Extras		20
			442

FoW (1): 1-11 (1), 2-30 (2), 3-69 (3), 4-81 (5), 5-298 (6), 6-353 (7), 7-374 (8), 8-427 (9), 9-436 (10), 10-442 (11)

Northern India Bowling	O	M	R	W
Mohammad Ramzan	41	14	103	1
Amir Hussain	14	4	41	0
Ahmed Khan	44	10	80	0
Agha Sarfraz	45	11	149	2
Habibullah	70.5	19	174	4
Gul Mohammad	26	5	122	3
Mohammad Sharif	14	0	46	0
Nazar Mohammad	8	1	17	0
Mehra	1	0	10	0

Maharashtra Bowling	O	M	R	W
Patwardhan	37	17	47	1
Hazare	42	7	116	3
Sohoni	24.5	4	70	2
Sarwate	46	19	69	4
Jadhav	17	4	44	0
Jath	14	0	49	0
Bhajekar	2	0	13	0
Deodhar	8	3	14	0

Umpires: Toss: Maharashtra

Close of Play: 1st day: Maharashtra (1) 277-4 (Bhajekar 120*, Sarwate 0*); 2nd day: Maharashtra (1) 612-7 (Deodhar 164*, Jadhav 16*); 3rd day: Northern India (1) 188-4 (Mehra 69*, Mohammad Sharif 66*).

The match was scheduled for three days but extended to four. R.V.Bhajekar's 120 took 310 minutes and included 15 fours. D.B.Deodhar's 196 took 390 minutes and included 24 fours. K.M.Jadhav's 115 took 115 minutes and included 16 fours and 1 six. R.P.Mehra's 209 took 456 minutes and included 17 fours. Mohammad Sharif's 118 took 313 minutes and included 12 fours. R.V.Bhajekar kept wicket from 40 minutes after lunch on the fourth day when Y.N.Gokhale injured a finger.

UNITED PROVINCES GOVERNOR'S XI v C.K.NAYUDU'S XI

Played at Alfred Park, Allahabad, February 22, 23, 24, 1941.

United Provinces Governor's XI won by 13 runs.

	UNITED PROVINCES GOVERNOR'S XI				
1	A.S.N.Murthy	c Bhattacharya b Mushtaq Ali	0	(10) b Bhattacharya	24
2	L.Amarnath	lbw b Dutt	2	(4) b Nayudu	29
3	J.P.Phansalkar	lbw b Dutt	0	(9) lbw b Bhattacharya	9
4	Shamim Khwaja	lbw b Bhattacharya	8	(7) c Ganguli b Mushtaq Ali	12
5	E.Alexander	c Hindlekar b Bhattacharya	22	(1) c Bhattacharya b Mushtaq Ali	2
6	B.K.Garudachar	c Ramchandra b Nayudu	12	(2) c Ganguli b Mushtaq Ali	89
7	*J.Smyth	b Bhattacharya	1	(8) c Dutt b Bhattacharya	10
8	Wahidullah	c and b Mushtaq Ali	16	(3) c and b Bhattacharya	16
9	Amir Elahi	c Dutt b Mushtaq Ali	36	(6) b Dutt	8
10	Iqbal Ahmed Khan	st Hindlekar b Bhattacharya	1	(11) not out	6
11	Maqbool Alam	not out	4	(5) c Bhaya b Dutt	24
	Extras		16		14
			118		243

FoW (1): 1- , 2- , 3- , 4- , 5- , 6- , 7- , 8- , 9- , 10-118
FoW (2): 1-6, 2-56, 3-105, 4-164, 5-169, 6-180, 7-189, 8-212, 9-212, 10-243

	C.K.NAYUDU'S XI				
1	S.K.Ganguli	c Amarnath b Alexander	4	lbw b Alexander	4
2	S.Mushtaq Ali	b Amarnath	7	(5) lbw b Amarnath	100
3	†D.D.Hindlekar	lbw b Amarnath	8	(4) b Garudachar	21
4	*C.K.Nayudu	c Amir Elahi b Amarnath	14	absent ill	0
5	J.N.Bhaya	c Smyth b Amarnath	9	(7) c Murthy b Amarnath	47
6	S.Ishtiaq Ali	b Amarnath	0	(2) b Alexander	12
7	Naoomal Jaoomal	lbw b Amir Elahi	31	(6) b Amarnath	15
8	K.Bhattacharya	b Amir Elahi	10	c Smyth b Amir Elahi	4
9	B.Ramchandra	c Iqbal Ahmed Khan b Amir Elahi	8	not out	1
10	Ramaiyagam	b Amir Elahi	0	b Amir Elahi	19
11	P.D.Dutt	not out	13	(3) b Amir Elahi	3
	Extras		8		10
			112		236

FoW (1): 1- , 2- , 3- , 4- , 5- , 6- , 7- , 8- , 9- , 10-112
FoW (2): 1-6, 2-32, 3-38, 4-69, 5-93, 6-199, 7-212, 8-217, 9-236

C.K.Nayudu's XI Bowling

	O	M	R	W		O	M	R	W
Dutt	11	2	32	2	(4)	14	3	49	2
Mushtaq Ali	10.2	5	16	3		14	2	69	3
Nayudu	9	1	14	1	(1)	10	2	43	1
Bhattacharya	9	1	40	4	(3)	13.4	0	49	4
Ramchandra					(5)	2	0	8	0
Naoomal Jaoomal					(6)	3	0	11	0

United Provinces Governor's XI Bowling

	O	M	R	W		O	M	R	W
Amarnath	23	8	36	5		34	1	86	3
Alexander	10	2	30	1	(4)	14	4	49	2
Amir Elahi	13	2	38	4	(2)	14	0	62	3
Garudachar					(3)	6	0	29	1

Umpires: Toss: United Provinces Governor's XI

Close of Play: 1st day: C.K.Nayudu's XI (1) 112 all out; 2nd day: C.K.Nayudu's XI (2) 57-3 (Hindlekar 21*, Mushtaq Ali 13*).

S.Mushtaq Ali's 100 took 120 minutes and included 7 fours. The match was played for the United Provinces War Purposes Fund.

WELLINGTON v CANTERBURY

Played at Basin Reserve, Wellington, February 28, March 1, 3, 1941.

Wellington won by 127 runs.

WELLINGTON					
1	H.W.Osborn	c Harbridge b Anderson	48	c Cromb b Westwood	116
2	O.L.Wrigley	b Mapplebeck	6	c Burgess b Westwood	0
3	W.Burton	c Cromb b Mapplebeck	3	(8) c O'Brien b Cromb	7
4	R.T.Morgan	b Cameron	1	c Menzies b Westwood	63
5	D.S.Wilson	b Cromb	17	c James b Anderson	13
6	N.S.H.Burnette	c Burgess b Mapplebeck	8	c and b Westwood	55
7	*†W.E.Norris	c Harbridge b Cameron	14	c Harbridge b Mapplebeck	0
8	R.J.Duffy	c Cromb b Mapplebeck	7	(3) lbw b Mapplebeck	11
9	T.L.Pritchard	c James b Mapplebeck	43	c Menzies b Cromb	38
10	J.G.Ashenden	c Menzies b Westwood	2	b Cromb	12
11	T.A.Downes	not out	4	not out	2
	Extras	b 7, lb 1, w 1, nb 2	11	b 10, lb 5, w 2, nb 3	20
			164		337

FoW (1): 1-28 (2), 2-32 (3), 3-33 (4), 4-60 (5), 5-85 (6), 6-101 (1), 7-110 (7), 8-139 (8), 9-142 (10), 10-164 (9)
FoW (2): 1-2 (2), 2-23 (3), 3-114 (4), 4-139 (5), 5-248 (6), 6-253 (7), 7-279 (1), 8-292 (8), 9-329 (9), 10-337 (10)

CANTERBURY					
1	I.B.Cromb	c Norris b Pritchard	66	c Norris b Pritchard	0
2	*F.P.O'Brien	c Norris b Ashenden	9	(4) st Norris b Ashenden	3
3	W.M.Anderson	lbw b Ashenden	66	(2) lbw b Ashenden	24
4	V.James	b Pritchard	1	(5) c Ashenden b Downes	7
5	R.E.J.Menzies	lbw b Pritchard	1	(3) b Downes	26
6	T.D.Moynihan	c Ashenden b Wilson	21	c Downes b Wilson	5
7	A.T.Burgess	not out	61	c Morgan b Wilson	24
8	W.O.Mapplebeck	b Ashenden	0	(9) b Ashenden	0
9	†B.C.Harbridge	b Downes	23	(8) b Ashenden	12
10	S.M.Cameron	b Morgan	6	run out	5
11	R.J.Westwood	c Morgan b Pritchard	1	not out	0
	Extras	b 7, lb 2	9	lb 3, nb 1	4
			264		110

FoW (1): 1-12 (2), 2-118 (1), 3-140 (4), 4-142 (5), 5-158 (3), 6-174 (6), 7-175 (8), 8-232 (9), 9-263 (10), 10-264 (11)
FoW (2): 1-0 (1), 2-44 (3), 3-47 (4), 4-62 (5), 5-62 (2), 6-80 (6), 7-101 (8), 8-101 (9), 9-110 (10), 10-110 (7)

Canterbury Bowling	O	M	R	W		O	M	R	W
Mapplebeck	13.5	0	59	5		18	3	64	2
Westwood	6	2	32	1		15	3	35	4
Cameron	10	3	27	2	(4)	9	3	34	0
Cromb	7	1	17	1	(5)	16.6	1	61	3
Burgess	6	2	13	0	(3)	12	1	57	0
Anderson	2	1	5	1		11	0	66	1

Wellington Bowling	O	M	R	W		O	M	R	W
Pritchard	13.1	0	71	4		8	2	25	1
Wilson	11	2	33	1	(4)	5.2	2	4	2
Ashenden	15	0	79	3	(2)	12	2	38	4
Downes	13	0	67	1	(3)	10	0	35	2
Morgan	2	0	5	1		2	0	4	0

Umpires: C.W.Moore and S.L.Searell. Toss: Wellington

Close of Play: 1st day: Canterbury (1) 232-8 (Burgess 38*); 2nd day: Wellington (2) 337 all out.

MADRAS v MAHARASHTRA

Played at Madras Cricket Club Ground, Chepauk, Madras, March 7, 8, 9, 10, 1941.

Maharashtra won by six wickets.

MADRAS					
1	*C.P.Johnstone	c Sohoni b Patwardhan	4	c Gokhale b Sarwate	49
2	V.N.Madhava Rao	c Gokhale b Sohoni	12	(3) run out	34
3	A.G.RamSingh	c Naidu b Patwardhan	0	(4) c Bhajekar b Jadhav	71
4	R.S.Nailer	b Jadhav	19	(5) c Sohoni b Sarwate	54
5	C.Ramaswami	b Jadhav	14	(6) c sub (B.J.Mohoni) b Hazare	1
6	M.J.Gopalan	c Gokhale b Jadhav	1	(7) c Deodhar b Sarwate	43
7	G.Parthasarathi	b Sarwate	11	(8) not out	18
8	†J.A.G.C.Law	c and b Sarwate	3	(2) c Naidu b Sarwate	33
9	N.J.Venkatesan	c Hazare b Sarwate	31	c Naidu b Sarwate	10
10	B.S.Krishna Rao	not out	29	b Hazare	2
11	C.R.Rangachari	b Jadhav	8	b Sarwate	0
	Extras		13		32
			145		347

FoW (1): 1-4 (1), 2-4 (3), 3-36 (4), 4-50 (2), 5-54 (5), 6-57 (6), 7-66 (8), 8-77 (7), 9-136 (9), 10-145 (11)
FoW (2): 1-78 (1), 2-93 (2), 3-174 (3), 4-249 (4), 5-257 (6), 6-285 (5), 7-318 (7), 8-339 (9), 9-346 (10), 10-347 (11)

MAHARASHTRA					
1	R.V.Bhajekar	b Rangachari	27	b Ram Singh	26
2	S.W.Sohoni	c Johnstone b Rangachari	11	c Johnstone b Ram Singh	104
3	R.B.Nimbalkar	lbw b Ram Singh	5	c Law b Rangachari	21
4	*D.B.Deodhar	lbw b Rangachari	11	lbw b Ram Singh	32
5	M.M.Naidu	c Johnstone b Krishna Rao	0		
6	V.S.Hazare	c Johnstone b Venkatesan	137	(5) not out	6
7	K.M.Jadhav	c Johnstone b Ram Singh	15	(6) not out	2
8	C.T.Sarwate	b Venkatesan	33		
9	†Y.N.Gokhale	c Ramaswami b Rangachari	14		
10	S.G.Shinde	not out	22		
11	M.K.Patwardhan	c and b Venkatesan	0		
	Extras		9		19
			284	(4 wickets)	210

FoW (1): 1-18 (2), 2-36 (3), 3-50 (1), 4-55 (4), 5-56 (5), 6-90 (7), 7-149 (8), 8-216 (9), 9-284 (6), 10-284 (11)
FoW (2): 1-90 (1), 2-129 (3), 3-194 (2), 4-204 (4)

Maharashtra Bowling	O	M	R	W		O	M	R	W
Patwardhan	13	3	39	2		11	2	31	0
Hazare	14	6	27	0		19	4	38	2
Jadhav	9.4	1	23	4		20	4	51	1
Sohoni	10	1	15	1		20	3	49	0
Shinde	1	0	2	0	(6)	26	7	56	0
Sarwate	11	2	26	3	(5)	32.2	9	83	6
Deodhar					(7)	1	0	7	0

Madras Bowling	O	M	R	W	O	M	R	W
Gopalan	8	1	29	0	2	0	8	0
Ram Singh	25	5	57	2	21.1	6	54	3
Rangachari	20	2	71	4	9	0	33	1
Venkatesan	18.4	1	60	3	22	5	49	0
Krishna Rao	12	0	36	1	14	3	39	0
Parthasarathi	4	0	22	0	2	0	8	0

Umpires: Vali Ahmed and M.G.Vijayasarathi. Toss: Madras

Close of Play: 1st day: Maharashtra (1) 113-6 (Hazare 27*, Sarwate 16*); 2nd day: Madras (2) 107-2 (Madhava Rao 14*, Ram Singh 4*); 3rd day: Maharashtra (2) 52-0 (Bhajekar 20*, Sohoni 28*).

V.S.Hazare's 137 took 220 minutes and included 8 fours. S.W.Sohoni's 104 took 200 minutes and included 6 fours. R.V.Bhajekar kept wicket on the third day in place of Y.N.Gokhale who was injured.

REST OF INDIA v MAHARASHTRA

Played at Brabourne Stadium, Bombay, April 10, 11, 12, 13, 1941.

Rest of India won by nine wickets.

REST OF INDIA					
1	M.H.Mankad	c Gokhale b Sohoni	105	not out	53
2	S.N.Banerjee	b Hazare	3	b Shinde	10
3	S.Mushtaq Ali	run out	90	not out	54
4	L.Amarnath	st Gokhale b Sarwate	50		
5	K.M.Rangnekar	c Gokhale b Sohoni	135		
6	*C.K.Nayudu	b Shinde	1		
7	J.N.Bhaya	b Hazare	27		
8	Gul Mohammad	c Sarwate b Hazare	23		
9	Saeed Ahmed	lbw b Hazare	0		
10	Amir Elahi	st Gokhale b Sarwate	40		
11	†M.P.Engineer	not out	4		
	Extras		9		2
			487	(1 wicket)	119

FoW (1): 1-7 (2), 2-185 (3), 3-229 (1), 4-286 (4), 5-291 (6), 6-354 (7), 7-414 (8), 8-414 (9), 9-474 (5), 10-487 (10)
FoW (2): 1-49 (2)

MAHARASHTRA					
1	R.V.Bhajekar	b Saeed Ahmed	26	c Engineer b Banerjee	12
2	S.W.Sohoni	run out	101	lbw b Banerjee	5
3	R.B.Nimbalkar	c Mankad b Nayudu	52	c Nayudu b Saeed Ahmed	78
4	C.T.Sarwate	b Banerjee	0	(8) lbw b Banerjee	3
5	V.S.Hazare	c Amarnath b Banerjee	40	lbw b Amir Elahi	4
6	*D.B.Deodhar	st Engineer b Amir Elahi	33	(4) st Engineer b Amir Elahi	69
7	M.M.Naidu	c Amarnath b Banerjee	1	(6) c Saeed Ahmed b Banerjee	22
8	K.M.Jadhav	b Banerjee	4	(7) b Saeed Ahmed	39
9	†Y.N.Gokhale	b Mankad	14	b Banerjee	24
10	S.G.Shinde	c Banerjee b Mankad	7	not out	8
11	M.K.Patwardhan	not out	0	c sub (F.K.Nariman) b Banerjee	2
	Extras		30		29
			308		295

FoW (1): 1-39 (1), 2-150 (3), 3-158 (4), 4-237 (5), 5-258 (2), 6-259 (7), 7-264 (8), 8-296 (9), 9-308 (10), 10-308 (6)
FoW (2): 1-15 (1), 2-20 (2), 3-168 (3), 4-179 (5), 5-188 (4), 6-242 (7), 7-250 (6), 8-261 (8), 9-291 (9), 10-295 (11)

Maharashtra Bowling	O	M	R	W		O	M	R	W
Patwardhan	21	3	84	0		3	0	13	0
Hazare	35	13	118	4		7	0	20	0
Jadhav	14	6	50	0		4	1	21	0
Sarwate	29.3	2	98	2		7	0	21	0
Sohoni	22	1	72	2					
Shinde	12	2	56	1	(5)	5	0	31	1
Deodhar					(6)	0.5	0	11	0

Rest of India Bowling	O	M	R	W	O	M	R	W
Banerjee	22	6	73	4	21.1	5	69	6
Amarnath	19	4	39	0	12	4	29	0
Saeed Ahmed	12	3	20	1	19	3	51	2
Mankad	20	3	55	2	6	3	11	0
Amir Elahi	25.1	7	64	1	19	3	81	2
Nayudu	6	1	26	1	7	1	25	0
Gul Mohammad	1	0	1	0				

Umpires: D.K.Naik and Vali Ahmed. Toss: Rest of India

Close of Play: 1st day: Rest of India (1) 310-5 (Rangnekar 43*, Bhaya 12*); 2nd day: Maharashtra (1) 154-2 (Sohoni 59*, Sarwate 0*); 3rd day: Maharashtra (2) 64-2 (Nimbalkar 22*, Deodhar 21*).
K.M.Rangnekar's 135 took 187 minutes. S.W.Sohoni's 101 took 260 minutes and included 8 fours. It was announced on Day 3 that the teams had agreed to extend the match into a fifth day but this was not required.

INDEX OF 1940/41 MATCH SCORECARDS

1941/42

MAHARASHTRA v BARODA

Played at Deccan Gymkhana Ground, Poona, October 10, 11, 12, 1941.

Baroda won by 194 runs.

BARODA

1	M.M.Naidu	lbw b Sarwate	59	c and b Sarwate	42
2	V.M.Pandit	b Patwardhan	10	lbw b Jadhav	14
3	C.S.Nayudu	st Gokhale b Sarwate	60	b Shinde	35
4	M.S.Indulkar	c and b Sarwate	24	lbw b Patwardhan	19
5	V.S.Hazare	c Chari b Patwardhan	55	lbw b Sarwate	16
6	Y.E.Sheikh	st Gokhale b Sarwate	13		
7	*W.N.Ghorpade	st Gokhale b Sarwate	18	(8) c and b Sohoni	24
8	K.P.Kesari	c Chari b Sarwate	10	(6) b Patwardhan	1
9	M.V.Bobjee	b Sarwate	0	(7) not out	32
10	†D.S.Doctor	not out	0	(9) b Sohoni	9
11	A.Patel	b Patwardhan	1		
	Extras		4		8
			254	(8 wickets, declared)	200

FoW (1): 1-23 (2), 2-113 (3), 3-138 (1), 4-173 (4), 5-213 (6), 6- , 7- , 8- , 9- , 10-254
FoW (2): 1-31 (2), 2-78 (1), 3-92 (3), 4- , 5- , 6- , 7- , 8-200

MAHARASHTRA

1	S.W.Sohoni	c Doctor b Hazare	3	b Hazare	3
2	R.V.Bhajekar	lbw b Hazare	5	lbw b Hazare	14
3	C.T.Sarwate	c and b Hazare	11	(9) st Doctor b Nayudu	9
4	B.B.Nimbalkar	c Nayudu b Hazare	12	(6) lbw b Hazare	0
5	K.N.V.Chari	c Naidu b Nayudu	43	(4) c Doctor b Nayudu	4
6	*D.B.Deodhar	c Indulkar b Nayudu	1	(5) b Patel	23
7	K.M.Jadhav	c Naidu b Hazare	8	(8) not out	64
8	†Y.N.Gokhale	c Naidu b Hazare	8	(7) c Patel b Hazare	0
9	M.N.Paranjpe	b Hazare	0	(3) c Pandit b Hazare	27
10	S.G.Shinde	c Naidu b Nayudu	10	run out	0
11	M.K.Patwardhan	not out	1	c Naidu b Nayudu	1
	Extras		5		8
			107		153

FoW (1): 1- , 2- , 3- , 4- , 5- , 6- , 7- , 8- , 9-106, 10-107
FoW (2): 1- , 2- , 3- , 4- , 5- , 6- , 7- , 8- , 9- , 10-153

Maharashtra Bowling

	O	M	R	W	O	M	R	W
Patwardhan	21	5	54	3	16	1	48	2
Jadhav	21	3	50	0	13	0	33	1
Sohoni	13	2	38	0	14.1	4	51	2
Sarwate	23	1	81	7	10	1	32	2
Shinde	5	0	27	0	9	0	28	1

Baroda Bowling

	O	M	R	W	O	M	R	W
Hazare	17	5	40	7	19	7	35	5
Patel	4	1	10	0	8	0	35	1
Nayudu	13	0	52	3	17.2	2	75	3

Umpires: Toss: Baroda

Close of Play: 1st day: Baroda (1) 173-4 (Hazare 19*); 2nd day: Maharashtra (1) 106-9 (Shinde 10*).

V.S.Hazare took a hat-trick in the Maharashtra second innings (Paranjpe, Nimbalkar, Gokhale).

SIND v MAHARASHTRA

Played at Karachi Gymkhana Ground, October 20, 21, 22, 23, 1941.

Sind won by 160 runs.

SIND					
1	B.S.Ambep	lbw b Jadhav	1	c Gokhale b Jadhav	4
2	Qamaruddin Sheikh	b Jadhav	2	(3) lbw b Sarwate	19
3	F.S.R.Johnson	lbw b Mohoni	24	(2) lbw b Sohoni	18
4	G.Kishenchand	c and b Sarwate	38	c Sohoni b Sarwate	74
5	†Abbas Khan	run out	0	c Chari b Sarwate	2
6	Naoomal Jaoomal	b Jadhav	37	c Deshmukh b Sarwate	66
7	Daud Khan	c Gokhale b Deodhar	46	b Sohoni	9
8	*M.J.Mobed	b Jadhav	60	(9) b Jadhav	13
9	P.P.Fernandes	b Deshmukh	40	(8) lbw b Sarwate	0
10	S.K.Girdhari	not out	3	c Jadhav b Sarwate	93
11	Ibrahim Vazir	c Deodhar b Sarwate	1	not out	19
	Extras		21		3
			273		320

FoW (1): 1-1 (1), 2-9 (2), 3-52 (3), 4-52 (5), 5- (4), 6-129 (6), 7-189 (7), 8-250 (9), 9-272 (8), 10-273 (11)
FoW (2): 1-8 (1), 2-39 (3), 3-41 (2), 4-54 (5), 5-159 (4), 6- (6), 7-187 (8), 8- (7), 9-266 (9), 10-320 (10)

MAHARASHTRA					
1	R.V.Bhajekar	b Naoomal Jaoomal	17	c Mobed b Qamaruddin Sheikh	17
2	S.W.Sohoni	b Mobed	23	lbw b Ibrahim Vazir	37
3	S.Nazir Ali	c and b Girdhari	33	st Abbas Khan b Girdhari	40
4	K.N.V.Chari	st Abbas Khan b Naoomal Jaoomal	0	(7) run out	38
5	*D.B.Deodhar	b Mobed	1	lbw b Qamaruddin Sheikh	67
6	K.M.Jadhav	c and b Naoomal Jaoomal	5	c Qamaruddin Sheikh b Ibrahim Vazir	3
7	C.T.Sarwate	not out	12	(4) c Mobed b Ibrahim Vazir	11
8	B.B.Nimbalkar	c and b Naoomal Jaoomal	5	(9) not out	42
9	†Y.N.Gokhale	c Fernandes b Girdhari	8	(8) lbw b Mobed	49
10	B.J.Mohoni	b Mobed	4	c Abbas Khan b Girdhari	6
11	M.A.Deshmukh	b Mobed	0	b Girdhari	0
	Extras		2		13
			110		323

FoW (1): 1-40 (1), 2-51 (2), 3- (4), 4- (5), 5- (6), 6-83 (3), 7-91 (8), 8-105 (9), 9-110 (10), 10-110 (11)
FoW (2): 1- (1), 2-57 (2), 3- (4), 4- (3), 5- (6), 6- (7), 7-228 (5), 8- (8), 9-323 (10), 10-323 (11)

Maharashtra Bowling	O	M	R	W		O	M	R	W
Deshmukh	22	7	35	1		10	3	27	0
Jadhav	27	8	63	4		26	5	91	2
Sohoni	15	3	51	0		17	4	51	2
Mohoni	7	0	21	1		2	0	3	0
Sarwate	22	8	48	2		36	3	121	6
Nazir Ali	10	2	25	0		6	2	9	0
Deodhar	6	2	9	1		3	0	9	0
Nimbalkar					(8)	3	1	6	0

Sind Bowling	O	M	R	W		O	M	R	W
Qamaruddin Sheikh	6	1	14	0		29	8	56	2
Ibrahim Vazir	6	2	7	0		35	11	66	3
Mobed	16	5	25	4		25	6	49	1
Girdhari	6	1	17	2		29	4	75	3
Naoomal Jaoomal	10	1	45	4		13	2	40	0
Kishenchand					(6)	7	0	18	0
Fernandes					(7)	2	0	6	0

Umpires: Toss: Sind

Close of Play: 1st day: Sind (1) 272-8 (Mobed 60*, Girdhari 3*); 2nd day: Sind (2) 111-4 (Kishenchand 38*, Naoomal Jaoomal 30*); 3rd day: Maharashtra (2) 89-2 (Nazir Ali 21*, Sarwate 9*).
The match was played for the War Fund.

BARODA v GUJARAT

Played at Central College Ground, Baroda, November 8, 9, 10, 1941.

Baroda won by a concession.

BARODA					
1	M.S.Indulkar	b Baloch	22	c Kadri b Bhatt	1
2	V.M.Pandit	b Baloch	5	b Baloch	22
3	C.S.Nayudu	b Baloch	8	(4) c Sheikh b Chippa	3
4	H.R.Adhikari	c Baloch b Chippa	88	(3) hit wkt b Prajapati	106
5	V.S.Hazare	lbw b Baloch	38	(6) b Baloch	66
6	†R.B.Nimbalkar	c Baloch b Chippa	40	(5) c Prajapati b Bhatt	34
7	M.M.Naidu	b Baloch	38		
8	*W.N.Ghorpade	c Kadri b Chippa	9		
9	Y.E.Sheikh	lbw b Chippa	4		
10	M.V.Bobjee	not out	22	(7) not out	8
11	A.Patel	b Baloch	17		
	Extras		21		17
			312	(6 wickets, declared)	257

FoW (1): 1-21 (2), 2-36 (1), 3-52 (3), 4-154 (5), 5-208 (4), 6-229 (6), 7- (8), 8- (9), 9-269 (7), 10-312 (11)
FoW (2): 1-7 (1), 2-35 (2), 3-39 (4), 4-105 (5), 5-231 (6), 6-257 (3)

GUJARAT					
1	R.C.Thakore	b Hazare	13	b Hazare	2
2	†H.M.Kadri	lbw b Nayudu	14	(3) not out	0
3	R.M.Patel	c Indulkar b Nayudu	28		
4	P.N.Cambhatta	b Hazare	20	(2) b Patel	21
5	U.R.Chippa	c Pandit b Hazare	6		
6	M.K.Pathan	not out	35		
7	K.A.Sheikh	lbw b Hazare	1		
8	M.L.Prajapati	c Patel b Nayudu	6		
9	M.J.Bhatt	c Indulkar b Hazare	5		
10	*M.S.Baloch	c Nimbalkar b Hazare	1		
11	C.M.Patel	b Hazare	9		
	Extras		12		
			150	(2 wickets)	23

FoW (1): 1-18 (1), 2-42 (2), 3-69 (3), 4-81 (5), 5-92 (4), 6-100 (7), 7-111 (8), 8- (9), 9- (10), 10-150 (11)
FoW (2): 1-23 (2), 2-23 (1)

Gujarat Bowling	O	M	R	W		O	M	R	W
Baloch	42	7	85	6		24	4	68	2
Bhatt	18	2	43	0		17	3	47	2
Chippa	33	5	122	4		20	4	43	1
Sheikh	10	2	19	0		12	1	38	0
C.M.Patel	4	0	22	0		4	1	14	0
R.M.Patel					(6)	5	0	26	0
Prajapati					(7)	1	0	4	1

Baroda Bowling	O	M	R	W	O	M	R	W
Hazare	25.3	9	62	7	2.1	0	5	1
Patel	3	1	12	0	2	0	18	1
Nayudu	22	3	64	3				

Umpires: Toss: Baroda

Close of Play: 1st day: Baroda (1) 239-6 (Naidu 19*, Ghorpade 6*); 2nd day: Baroda (2) 64-3 (Adhikari 17*, Nimbalkar 11*).

H.R.Adhikari's 106 took 214 minutes and included 7 fours and 1 six. Gujarat declared their second innings as there was only two hours to go.

BOMBAY v WESTERN INDIA

Played at Brabourne Stadium, Bombay, November 8, 9, 10, 1941.

Match drawn.

BOMBAY			
1	L.B.Kenny	run out	19
2	V.N.Raiji	run out	7
3	K.K.Tarapore	lbw b Akbar Khan	0
4	K.C.Ibrahim	not out	230
5	*V.M.Merchant	run out	12
6	K.M.Rangnekar	c and b Adhyaram	22
7	J.B.Khot	b Saeed Ahmed	101
8	S.R.Arolkar	c Sukhvantrai b Adhyaram	13
9	M.N.Raiji	lbw b Nyalchand	31
10	R.S.Irani	b Nyalchand	9
11	†M.P.Engineer	lbw b Nyalchand	0
	Extras	b 12, lb 6	18
			462

FoW (1): 1-7 (2), 2-8 (3), 3-60 (1), 4-93 (5), 5-140 (6), 6-346 (7), 7-376 (8), 8-432 (9), 9-454 (10), 10-462 (11)

WESTERN INDIA					
1	†Faiz Ahmed	c Engineer b Khot	3		
2	H.W.Barritt	c M.N.Raiji b Tarapore	12	b Irani	1
3	S.M.Nasiruddin	b Tarapore	9	(4) c Engineer b Khot	12
4	Sukhvantrai	lbw b Khot	15	(5) b Irani	6
5	Saeed Ahmed	c Engineer b Tarapore	13	(3) lbw b M.N.Raiji	58
6	Umar Khan	lbw b Khot	2	lbw b Irani	0
7	*Sheikh Sahib of Mangrol	b Tarapore	18		
8	Prithviraj	not out	16	(1) not out	86
9	Akbar Khan	c Ibrahim b M.N.Raiji	0	(7) not out	0
10	S.Nyalchand	b M.N.Raiji	4		
11	H.Adhyaram	b M.N.Raiji	0		
	Extras	lb 3	3	b 3, w 1	4
			95	(5 wickets)	167

FoW (1): 1-12 (1), 2-18 (2), 3-30 (3), 4-45 (4), 5-53 (6), 6-61 (5), 7-79 (7), 8-80 (9), 9-95 (10), 10-95 (11)
FoW (2): 1-1 (2), 2-100 (3), 3-119 (4), 4-151 (5), 5-161 (6)

Western India Bowling	O	M	R	W
Saeed Ahmed	55	21	96	1
Akbar Khan	62	23	87	1
Nyalchand	31.4	6	95	3
Adhyaram	31	6	90	2
Prithviraj	23	1	63	0
Umar Khan	3	0	13	0

Bombay Bowling	O	M	R	W		O	M	R	W
Khot	15	11	9	3		10	7	5	1
Irani	13	4	27	0		22	10	43	3
Tarapore	22	12	24	4		7	3	7	0
M.N.Raiji	20.3	3	32	3		17	3	48	1
Rangnekar	1	1	0	0		5	1	11	0
Arolkar					(6)	15	4	40	0
Kenny					(7)	5	0	9	0

Umpires: L.O'Callaghan and M.G.Vijayasarathi. Toss: Bombay

Close of Play: 1st day: Bombay (1) 254-5 (Ibrahim 128*, Khot 56*); 2nd day: Western India (1) 45-4 (Saeed Ahmed 5*, Umar Khan 0*).

K.C.Ibrahim's 230 took 492 minutes and included 20 fours. J.B.Khot's 101 took 235 minutes and included 5 fours.

HOLKAR v UNITED PROVINCES

Played at Yeshwant Club Ground, Indore, November 8, 9, 10, 1941.

Match drawn.

UNITED PROVINCES					
1	E.Alexander	st Bhandarkar b Nayudu	7	(4) b Jagdale	4
2	A.S.N.Murthy	c and b Ishtiaq Ali	40	(6) b Jagdale	70
3	*P.E.Palia	lbw b Jagdale	8	c Nayudu b Surendrasingh	0
4	J.P.Phansalkar	run out	14	(7) c Ishtiaq Ali b Mukherjee	29
5	Aftab Ahmed	lbw b Nayudu	3	(8) c Subramaniam b Nayudu	17
6	Shamim Khwaja	c Yarde b Subramaniam	81	(5) c Surendrasingh b Jagdale	2
7	B.P.Telang	c Ishtiaq Ali b Bhaya	53	(2) c Surendrasingh b Jagdale	5
8	P.Shadwell	lbw b Bhaya	0	(11) not out	15
9	S.K.Bahry	lbw b Mukherjee	16	(10) b Jagdale	0
10	Firasat Hussain	c Nayudu b Subramaniam	33	(1) b Jagdale	11
11	†Wahidullah	not out	34	(9) b Bhaya	26
	Extras		18		13
			307		192

FoW (1): 1-33 (1), 2-46 (3), 3-75 (2), 4-80 (4), 5-88 (5), 6-212 (7), 7-212 (8), 8-230 (6), 9-241 (9), 10-307 (10)
FoW (2): 1-16 (2), 2-17 (1), 3-20 (3), 4-29 (4), 5-31 (5), 6-108 (7), 7-150 (8), 8-154 (6), 9-154 (10), 10-192 (9)

HOLKAR					
1	S.Ishtiaq Ali	c Telang b Palia	9		
2	†K.V.Bhandarkar	c Murthy b Alexander	0	(1) c Shamim Khwaja b Palia	22
3	S.Mushtaq Ali	c Telang b Alexander	0	(2) c Shadwell b Alexander	36
4	D.K.Yarde	b Firasat Hussain	19		
5	M.M.Jagdale	c Wahidullah b Alexander	6		
6	*C.K.Nayudu	c Murthy b Alexander	35	(3) c Shamim Khwaja b Palia	54
7	J.N.Bhaya	c Firasat Hussain b Alexander	60	(4) not out	43
8	Surendrasingh	not out	71		
9	R.Subramaniam	c Murthy b Alexander	9	(5) not out	7
10	S.Kothane	st Wahidullah b Palia	24		
11	M.Mukherjee	lbw b Palia	4		
	Extras		9		7
			246	(3 wickets)	169

FoW (1): 1-10 (1), 2-13 (2), 3-13 (3), 4-40 (4), 5-54 (5), 6-85 (6), 7-150 (7), 8-173 (9), 9-240 (10), 10-246 (11)
FoW (2): 1-58 (2), 2-59 (1), 3-146 (3)

Holkar Bowling	O	M	R	W		O	M	R	W
Jagdale	16	2	37	1		35	14	65	6
Mushtaq Ali	11	3	36	0		4	2	10	0
Nayudu	33	5	91	2		18	7	48	1
Subramaniam	6.5	1	22	2	(7)	3	0	13	0
Ishtiaq Ali	16	1	52	1					
Bhaya	21	4	39	2	(4)	5.3	1	9	1
Mukherjee	10	2	12	1	(5)	2	1	4	1
Surendrasingh					(6)	17	5	30	1

United Provinces Bowling	O	M	R	W	O	M	R	W
Alexander	34	6	88	6	13	0	68	1
Palia	36.5	8	79	3	13	0	88	2
Firasat Hussain	14	2	46	1	1	0	6	0
Telang	2	1	7	0				
Aftab Ahmed	2	0	11	0				
Shadwell	3	1	6	0				

Umpires: Toss: United Provinces

Close of Play: 1st day: United Provinces (1) 307 all out; 2nd day: United Provinces (2) 2-0 (Firasat Hussain 2*, Telang 0*).

NAWANAGAR v MAHARASHTRA

Played at Ajitsinhji Ground, Jamnagar, November 15, 16, 1941.

Nawanagar won by eight wickets.

MAHARASHTRA					
1	†R.V.Bhajekar	c Mehta b Banerjee	1	c Banerjee b M.H.Mankad	42
2	S.W.Sohoni	c Samarsinhji b Banerjee	0	lbw b M.H.Mankad	16
3	S.Nazir Ali	c M.H.Mankad b Mubarak Ali	0	st Mehta b M.H.Mankad	4
4	B.B.Nimbalkar	c Mehta b Mubarak Ali	8	b M.H.Mankad	20
5	*D.B.Deodhar	b Banerjee	11	(6) b Banerjee	1
6	K.L.Dalaya	b Banerjee	0	(10) c Mulwantrai b Oza	1
7	C.T.Sarwate	c Samarsinhji b Banerjee	0	(5) c Banerjee b M.H.Mankad	1
8	K.M.Jadhav	b Banerjee	3	(7) c Mulwantrai b Oza	63
9	K.N.V.Chari	hit wkt b Banerjee	9	(8) c Mulwantrai b Mubarak Ali	3
10	M.N.Paranjpe	not out	6	(9) c and b Banerjee	32
11	S.G.Shinde	c Colah b Banerjee	0	not out	6
	Extras		1		
			39		189

FoW (1): 1-1 (2), 2-2 (3), 3-2 (1), 4-16 (5), 5-18 (6), 6-18 (7), 7-24 (8), 8-24 (4), 9-39 (9), 10-39 (11)
FoW (2): 1-54 (2), 2-58 (3), 3-63 (1), 4-69 (5), 5-70 (6), 6-118 (4), 7-135 (8), 8-152 (7), 9-154 (10), 10-189 (9)

NAWANAGAR					
1	M.H.Mankad	b Sohoni	29	c and b Jadhav	20
2	J.R.Oza	b Jadhav	2	c and b Jadhav	10
3	S.H.M.Colah	c Bhajekar b Jadhav	25	not out	12
4	*R.K.Indravijaysinhji	lbw b Sohoni	0		
5	R.K.Yadvendrasinhji	b Sohoni	4		
6	S.N.Banerjee	run out	48	(4) not out	24
7	K.Mankad	b Sarwate	15		
8	M.S.Samarsinhji	c Shinde b Sarwate	13		
9	Mubarak Ali	c Chari b Sarwate	4		
10	Mulwantrai	st Bhajekar b Shinde	10		
11	†K.Mehta	not out	1		
	Extras		8		7
			159	(2 wickets)	73

FoW (1): 1-13 (2), 2-52 (3), 3-57 (4), 4-60 (1), 5-61 (5), 6-78 (7), 7-101 (8), 8-106 (9), 9-131 (10), 10-159 (6)
FoW (2): 1-29 (2), 2-34 (1)

Nawanagar Bowling	O	M	R	W		O	M	R	W
Banerjee	9.2	3	25	8		10.1	3	31	2
Mubarak Ali	9	3	13	2		16	2	63	1
Mulwantrai					(3)	3	0	7	0
Oza					(4)	3	0	20	2
M.H.Mankad					(5)	22	7	68	5

Maharashtra Bowling	O	M	R	W	O	M	R	W
Sohoni	12	3	61	3	8.4	2	25	0
Jadhav	12.2	3	25	2	9	2	28	2
Sarwate	12	0	40	3	3	0	13	0
Nimbalkar	1	0	6	0				
Shinde	3	0	19	1				

Umpires: D.K.Naik and Vali Ahmed. Toss: Maharashtra

Close of Play: 1st day: Maharashtra (2) 67-3 (Nimbalkar 5*, Sarwate 0*).

The match was scheduled for three days but completed in two.

QUEENSLAND v NEW SOUTH WALES

Played at Brisbane Cricket Ground, Woolloongabba, Brisbane, November 28, 29, December 1, 1941.

Queensland won by 19 runs.

QUEENSLAND					
1	R.E.Rogers	b Collins	16	c Lindwall b O'Reilly	20
2	G.G.Cook	c McCabe b Cristofani	68	b Lindwall	1
3	E.C.la Frantz	b O'Reilly	6	b Lindwall	7
4	†D.Tallon	c and b Cristofani	13	(6) c and b O'Reilly	0
5	*W.A.Brown	c Horsfield b Powell	56	lbw b O'Reilly	69
6	G.G.Baker	lbw b O'Reilly	40	(4) b Lindwall	4
7	D.Watt	b Cristofani	50	(8) lbw b O'Reilly	47
8	V.N.Raymer	not out	53	(7) c Livingston b Cristofani	77
9	C.P.Christ	b Collins	3	c Collins b O'Reilly	3
10	J.A.Ellis	c Horsfield b Cristofani	7	not out	5
11	A.H.McGinn	b O'Reilly	5	c and b O'Reilly	2
	Extras	b 2, lb 3, nb 12	17	b 7, lb 4, nb 3	14
			334		249

FoW (1): 1-20, 2-31, 3-50, 4-135, 5-204, 6-215, 7-301, 8-307, 9-314, 10-334
FoW (2): 1-3, 2-13, 3-20, 4-62, 5-62, 6-143, 7-231, 8-240, 9-247, 10-249

NEW SOUTH WALES					
1	†L.Livingston	c Brown b Christ	46	c Tallon b Ellis	7
2	L.J.Fallowfield	c Ellis b McGinn	0	st Tallon b Watt	42
3	*S.J.McCabe	c Baker b McGinn	8	b Ellis	41
4	J.W.Chegwyn	c and b Watt	61	lbw b McGinn	24
5	G.C.Horsfield	run out (sub [J.E.McCarthy]/Tallon)	43	run out (sub [J.E.McCarthy]/Tallon)	35
6	R.V.James	c Tallon b Cook	44	c sub (J.E.McCarthy) b Raymer	46
7	G.Powell	c Tallon b Watt	47	lbw b Baker	0
8	V.A.Collins	not out	29	c Ellis b Cook	20
9	D.R.Cristofani	b Watt	10	b Cook	10
10	R.R.Lindwall	b Ellis	1	b Ellis	10
11	W.J.O'Reilly	c Rogers b Watt	4	not out	7
	Extras	b 10, lb 7	17	b 11, lb 1	12
			310		254

FoW (1): 1-4, 2-12, 3-80, 4-153, 5-180, 6-235, 7-284, 8-298, 9-301, 10-310
FoW (2): 1-8, 2-58, 3-100, 4-128, 5-202, 6-202, 7-210, 8-235, 9-238, 10-254

New South Wales Bowling	O	M	R	W			O	M	R	W	
Lindwall	15	0	81	0	6nb		7	0	36	3	2nb
Collins	11	2	33	2			4	0	16	0	
O'Reilly	16.2	5	35	3	6nb		21.7	2	89	6	1nb
Cristofani	21	2	97	4			15	1	67	1	
Powell	9	0	71	1			3	0	27	0	

Queensland Bowling	O	M	R	W		O	M	R	W
Ellis	20	2	81	1		16.1	1	61	3
McGinn	10	1	46	2		7	0	34	1
Cook	8	0	41	1		10	2	38	2
Christ	6	3	5	1					
Raymer	12	1	51	0		7	0	35	1
Baker	3	0	6	0	(7)	4	2	6	1
Watt	8.5	0	40	4	(4)	10	0	57	1
la Frantz	4	0	23	0	(6)	2	0	11	0

Umpires: C.V.Pengelly and R.Weitemeyer. Toss: Queensland

Close of Play: 1st day: New South Wales (1) 80-3 (Chegwyn 25*, Horsfield 0*); 2nd day: Queensland (2) 169-6 (Raymer 51*, Watt 5*).

12th Men: J.E.McCarthy (Qld) and S.J.Carroll (NSW).

CENTRAL PROVINCES AND BERAR v MADRAS

Played at Central Provinces Gymkhana Ground, Nagpur, November 29, 30, December 1, 1941.

Madras won by four wickets.

CENTRAL PROVINCES AND BERAR

1	P.R.Naidu	b Ram Singh	0	c Varadan b Ram Singh	41
2	V.V.Deo	b Ram Singh	1	b Venkatesan	6
3	E.G.Mane	b Varadan	42	b Venkatesan	10
4	C.M.Pandurangam	c Kannan b Ram Singh	42	b Venkatesan	26
5	*D.R.Rutnam	c Kannan b Ram Singh	0	c Mohanakrishnan b Varadan	6
6	H.G.Gaekwad	b Kannan	0	c Madhava Rao b Venkatesan	4
7	S.Ishaq Ali	c Mohanakrishnan b Ram Singh	11	b Venkatesan	6
8	S.A.Lateef	lbw b Venkatesan	8	b Venkatesan	0
9	Mohammad Hussain	not out	49	lbw b Ram Singh	7
10	†U.N.Kondra	b Varadan	1	not out	5
11	N.D.Sane	b Venkatesan	18	c Rangachari b Venkatesan	10
	Extras		20		7
			192		128

FoW (1): 1-0 (1), 2-1 (2), 3-67 (4), 4-67 (5), 5-70 (6), 6-91 (7), 7-106 (8), 8- (3), 9- (10), 10-192 (11)
FoW (2): 1-16 (2), 2-34 (3), 3- (4), 4- (5), 5- (6), 6-101 (7), 7-101 (8), 8-112 (9), 9-113 (1), 10-128 (11)

MADRAS

1	N.Suryanarayan	c Mohammad Hussain b Pandurangam	2	(7) c Kondra b Mohammad Hussain	0
2	K.Mohanakrishnan	c Kondra b Mohammad Hussain	23	b Pandurangam	24
3	M.Swaminathan	c Rutnam b Mohammad Hussain	4	b Lateef	4
4	*A.G.Ram Singh	run out	58	(5) not out	15
5	C.K.Nainakannu	lbw b Lateef	53	(4) st Kondra b Lateef	23
6	V.N.Madhava Rao	c Kondra b Lateef	1	run out	10
7	†J.A.G.C.Law	c Kondra b Lateef	24	(1) c Pandurangam b Lateef	24
8	P.V.Varadan	c Kondra b Lateef	9	not out	0
9	N.J.Venkatesan	c Pandurangam b Lateef	11		
10	K.S.Kannan	not out	17		
11	C.R.Rangachari	b Gaekwad	0		
	Extras		15		4
			217	(6 wickets)	104

FoW (1): 1-23 (1), 2-36 (2), 3-36 (3), 4-140 (5), 5-150 (6), 6-157 (4), 7-167 (8), 8-189 (9), 9-203 (7), 10-217 (11)
FoW (2): 1-36 (2), 2-45 (3), 3-75 (4), 4-76 (1), 5-95 (6), 6-101 (7)

Madras Bowling

	O	M	R	W		O	M	R	W
Ram Singh	24	11	45	5		22	8	40	2
Rangachari	15	2	45	0		6	3	11	0
Venkatesan	11.1	1	31	2		23.5	5	56	7
Kannan	14	2	44	1		3	1	6	0
Varadan	2	0	7	2		2	0	3	1
Swaminathan					(6)	1	0	5	0

Central Provinces and Berar Bowling

	O	M	R	W	O	M	R	W
Mohammad Hussain	16	2	51	2	9.2	0	26	1
Sane	12	1	32	0	3	0	5	0
Pandurangam	7	1	10	1	11	4	21	1
Gaekwad	21.3	5	43	1	1	1	0	0
Lateef	23	7	66	5	21	8	48	3

Umpires: Toss: Central Provinces and Berar

Close of Play: 1st day: Madras (1) 64-3 (Ram Singh not out, Nainakannu not out); 2nd day: Central Provinces and Berar (2) 84-5 (Naidu 26*, Ishaq Ali 1*).

MYSORE v HYDERABAD

Played at Central College Ground, Bangalore, November 29, 30, December 1, 1941.

Mysore won by 111 runs.

MYSORE					
1	M.B.Krishna Rao	c Mehta b Hyder Ali	13	lbw b Mehta	10
2	T.V.Parthasarathi	c Hyder Ali b Zahiruddin	0	(8) c Mehta b Vajubha	53
3	K.Thimmappiah	run out (Ushaq Ahmed)	8	st Kanakasabhapathi b Asadullah Qureshi	29
4	B.K.Garudachar	c Dittia b Zahiruddin	6	c Zahiruddin b Asadullah Qureshi	56
5	C.J.Ramdev	b Hyder Ali	71	b Hyder Ali	41
6	B.V.Ramakrishnappa	c Ghulam Ahmed b Mehta	1	c Khanna b Hyder Ali	36
7	B.Frank	b Khanna	62	c and b Hyder Ali	37
8	†F.K.Irani	b Khanna	0	(10) b Ghulam Ahmed	47
9	*S.Darashah	st Kanakasabhapathi b Khanna	12	b Ghulam Ahmed	13
10	S.Rama Rao	c and b Hyder Ali	12	(11) not out	1
11	Y.S.Ramaswami	not out	11	(2) lbw b Mehta	13
	Extras		3		16
			199		352

FoW (1): 1-4 (2), 2-16 (3), 3-28 (4), 4-42 (1), 5-47 (6), 6-151 (7), 7-157 (8), 8-176 (9), 9-176 (5), 10-199 (10)
FoW (2): 1-22 (1), 2-31 (2), 3-112 (4), 4-114 (3), 5-178 (5), 6-224 (6), 7-245 (7), 8-263 (9), 9-350 (10), 10-352 (8)

HYDERABAD					
1	S.R.Mehta	lbw b Garudachar	14	c Irani b Garudachar	29
2	†Kanakasabhapathi	c Irani b Rama Rao	0	c Irani b Garudachar	12
3	E.B.Aibara	c Thimmappiah b Rama Rao	0	(4) b Rama Rao	110
4	Asadullah Qureshi	c Irani b Garudachar	66	(5) lbw b Garudachar	10
5	F.D.Dittia	b Garudachar	39	(6) c Irani b Rama Rao	27
6	B.C.Khanna	c Parthasarathi b Ramaswami	7	(7) lbw b Garudachar	10
7	*Ushaq Ahmed	lbw b Garudachar	6	(9) run out	17
8	B.Zahiruddin	c Garudachar b Ramaswami	1	not out	33
9	Vajubha	c Frank b Garudachar	7	(10) b Darashah	2
10	Hyder Ali	b Garudachar	8	(3) b Garudachar	0
11	Ghulam Ahmed	not out	1	c Darashah b Rama Rao	8
	Extras		20		13
			169		271

FoW (1): 1- (2), 2- (3), 3- (1), 4- (4), 5- , 6- , 7- , 8- , 9- , 10-169
FoW (2): 1-29 (2), 2-29 (3), 3-95 (1), 4-119 (5), 5-182 (6), 6-201 (4), 7-209 (7), 8-236 (9), 9-255 (10), 10-271 (11)

Hyderabad Bowling	O	M	R	W		O	M	R	W
Khanna	13	4	31	3		12	3	29	0
Zahiruddin	11	1	38	2		14	1	45	0
Hyder Ali	20	8	45	3		25	6	84	3
Mehta	9	2	28	1		19	3	65	2
Ghulam Ahmed	8	1	29	0		13	1	43	2
Vajubha	3	0	18	0		7.1	1	22	1
Ushaq Ahmed	1	0	7	0		4	0	12	0
Asadullah Qureshi					(8)	11	0	36	2

Mysore Bowling	O	M	R	W		O	M	R	W
Thimmappiah	3	2	9	0					
Rama Rao	9	1	25	2	(1)	15.5	2	60	3
Darashah	7	2	20	0	(2)	13	1	46	1
Garudachar	21.2	4	46	6	(3)	20	1	78	5
Ramaswami	18	4	49	2	(4)	22	2	74	0

Umpires: Toss: Mysore

Close of Play: 1st day: Hyderabad (1) 137-4 (Dittia 39*, Khanna 3*); 2nd day: Mysore (2) 301-8 (Parthasarathi 32*, Irani 23*).

E.B.Aibara's 110 took 119 minutes.

NAWANAGAR v BOMBAY

Played at Ajitsinhji Ground, Jamnagar, November 29, 30, December 1, 1941.

Match drawn.

NAWANAGAR					
1	M.H.Mankad	c Hakim b Havewala	1	c Khot b Rangnekar	18
2	J.R.Oza	b Havewala	48	not out	12
3	S.N.Banerjee	run out	40		
4	S.H.M.Colah	c Hindlekar b Khot	11	(3) b Hakim	7
5	*R.K.Indravijaysinhji	run out	47		
6	R.K.Yadvendrasinhji	c Rangnekar b Tarapore	43		
7	K.Mankad	st Hindlekar b Havewala	46	(4) not out	7
8	M.S.Samarsinhji	c Hindlekar b V.M.Merchant	23		
9	Mubarak Ali	c U.M.Merchant b Tarapore	8		
10	Mulwantrai	c Hakim b Havewala	5		
11	†K.Mehta	not out	0		
	Extras	b 11, lb 1	12	lb 4	4
			284	(2 wickets)	48

FoW (1): 1-7 (1), 2-87 (3), 3-111 (4), 4-111 (2), 5-198 (6), 6-208 (5), 7-266 (8), 8-278 (7), 9-278 (9), 10-284 (10)
FoW (2): 1-18 (1), 2-37 (3)

BOMBAY			
1	†D.D.Hindlekar	c M.H.Mankad b Banerjee	6
2	L.B.Kenny	c Colah b Mubarak Ali	15
3	A.A.Hakim	c Colah b Banerjee	63
4	K.C.Ibrahim	c M.H.Mankad b Mubarak Ali	9
5	*V.M.Merchant	not out	170
6	K.M.Rangnekar	b Mubarak Ali	31
7	D.R.Havewala	b Mubarak Ali	8
8	L.P.Jai	st Mehta b Oza	81
9	J.B.Khot	c and b Mulwantrai	50
10	U.M.Merchant	not out	6
11	K.K.Tarapore		
	Extras	b 8, lb 15	23
		(8 wickets, declared)	462

FoW (1): 1-12 (1), 2-52 (2), 3-74 (4), 4-119 (3), 5-195 (6), 6-211 (7), 7-342 (8), 8-447 (9)

Bombay Bowling	O	M	R	W		O	M	R	W
Hakim	17	5	40	0		7	3	11	1
Havewala	41.1	14	92	4					
Khot	28	9	52	1					
Tarapore	37	7	74	2					
Rangnekar	5	1	9	0	(2)	11	2	32	1
Kenny	1	1	0	0					
Ibrahim	3	2	1	0	(3)	4	3	1	0
V.M.Merchant	4	0	4	1					

Nawanagar Bowling	O	M	R	W
Banerjee	36	9	82	2
Mubarak Ali	51	5	148	4
M.H.Mankad	50	7	148	0
Oza	8	1	39	1
K.Mankad	2	0	8	0
Mulwantrai	4	1	14	1

Umpires: M.G.Bhave and Vali Ahmed. Toss: Bombay

Close of Play: 1st day: Nawanagar (1) 225-6 (K.Mankad 23*, Samarsinhji 1*); 2nd day: Bombay (1) 168-4 (V.M.Merchant 40*, Rangnekar 24*).

V.M.Merchant's 170 took 340 minutes and included 18 fours.

NORTHERN INDIA v NORTH WEST FRONTIER PROVINCE

Played at Aitchison College Ground, Lahore, December 5, 6, 7, 1941.

Northern India won by an innings and 405 runs.

NORTHERN INDIA			
1	Nazar Mohammad	c Mohammad Danish b Faqir Hussain	175
2	D.Jagdish Lal	lbw b Khanna	130
3	Aslam Khokhar	lbw b Kapoor	18
4	R.P.Mehra	c Mohammad Danish b Kapoor	0
5	Gul Mohammad	c Faqir Hussain b Khanna	32
6	Mohammad Sharif	b Kapoor	93
7	Agha Sarfraz	b Abdul Latif	2
8	*M.Jahangir Khan	not out	125
9	Habibullah		
10	†G.B.Bull		
11	Chuni Lal		
	Extras		38
		(7 wickets, declared)	613

FoW (1): 1-273 (2), 2-314 (3), 3-322 (4), 4-365 (5), 5-407 (1), 6-414 (7), 7-613 (6)

NORTH WEST FRONTIER PROVINCE					
1	*R.L.Holdsworth	b Chuni Lal	2	(4) b Agha Sarfraz	0
2	Mohammad Danish	b Chuni Lal	6	(1) c Nazar Mohammad b Chuni Lal	0
3	Razzaq	c Agha Sarfraz b Chuni Lal	17	(5) lbw b Agha Sarfraz	5
4	B.C.Khanna	c Mohammad Sharif b Chuni Lal	0	(6) c Bull b Aslam Khokhar	11
5	Fazal Rahim	c Habibullah b Agha Sarfraz	27	(2) c Aslam Khokhar b Habibullah	13
6	G.C.Kapoor	b Agha Sarfraz	0	(7) c Mohammad Sharif b Aslam Khokhar	0
7	Abdul Latif	b Agha Sarfraz	0	(8) c Chuni Lal b Aslam Khokhar	22
8	Rajindernath	lbw b Chuni Lal	18	(9) st Bull b Aslam Khokhar	2
9	†Karim Baksh	c Agha Sarfraz b Chuni Lal	2	(10) c Bull b Aslam Khokhar	7
10	Qazi Daud	c and b Agha Sarfraz	7	(11) not out	2
11	Faqir Hussain	not out	1	(3) st Bull b Aslam Khokhar	42
	Extras		10		14
			90		118

FoW (1): 1-2 (1), 2-23 (2), 3-23 (4), 4-42 (3), 5-51 (6), 6-51 (7), 7-64 (5), 8-77 (9), 9- (10), 10-90 (8)
FoW (2): 1-0 (1), 2- , 3- , 4- , 5- , 6- , 7- , 8- , 9- , 10-118

North West Frontier Province Bowling	O	M	R	W
Faqir Hussain	23	3	107	1
Rajindernath	14	1	64	0
Abdul Latif	36	4	156	1
Qazi Daud	10	0	40	0
Kapoor	26.2	4	98	3
Khanna	34	0	110	2

Northern India Bowling	O	M	R	W		O	M	R	W
Chuni Lal	18.5	5	42	6		6	0	19	1
Habibullah	5	1	8	0	(4)	4	2	4	1
Agha Sarfraz	8	1	26	4		11	1	45	2
Jahangir Khan	5	2	4	0	(2)	5	3	10	0
Aslam Khokhar					(5)	6.2	0	26	6

Umpires: Toss: Northern India

Close of Play: 1st day: Northern India (1) 375-4 (Nazar Mohammad 158*, Mohammad Sharif 10*); 2nd day: North West Frontier Province (2) 4-1 (Fazal Rahim 0*, Faqir Hussain 4*).

Nazar Mohammad's 175 included 15 fours. D.Jagdish Lal's 130 took 207 minutes and included 14 fours. M.Jahangir Khan's 125 included 21 fours and 1 six.

BIHAR v BENGAL

Played at Keenan Stadium, Jamshedpur, December 6, 7, 8, 1941.

Match drawn.

BENGAL

1	K.Bhattacharya	c Sanjana b Chowdhury	0	(3) b Chowdhury	12
2	A.Jabbar	b Chowdhury	26	(1) lbw b Khambatta	26
3	S.Bose	c Sanjana b Chowdhury	9	(4) c Mukherjee b Bose	6
4	N.C.Chatterjee	c Bose b Khambatta	17	(5) b Chowdhury	5
5	*N.M.Bose	b Bose	107	(7) run out	43
6	B.Ramchandra	lbw b Chowdhury	16	c Mukherjee b Banerjee	39
7	A.K.Das	lbw b Chowdhury	9	(8) not out	84
8	†A.K.Deb	b Chowdhury	10	(9) lbw b Bose	50
9	M.Obaidullah	b Chowdhury	41	(10) c Sen b Chowdhury	17
10	S.Dutt	c Sen b Bose	0	(2) b Kumar	5
11	S.A.Banerjee	not out	0	lbw b Chowdhury	1
	Extras		28		6
			263		294

FoW (1): 1-6 (1), 2-30 (3), 3-45 (2), 4-63 (4), 5-102 (6), 6-112 (7), 7-158 (8), 8-261 (5), 9-263 (10), 10-263 (9)
FoW (2): 1-8 (2), 2-29 (3), 3-36 (4), 4-47 (5), 5-69 (1), 6-138 (6), 7-141 (7), 8-221 (9), 9-283 (10), 10-294 (11)

BIHAR

1	S.Bagchi	c Bhattacharya b Obaidullah	9	not out	7
2	B.Mukherjee	c Deb b Banerjee	2	b Banerjee	6
3	B.Sen	b Bhattacharya	14		
4	M.Dastoor	c Dutt b Bhattacharya	32		
5	*S.K.Roy	c Deb b Ramchandra	15		
6	S.Banerjee	c Deb b Banerjee	73	(3) not out	22
7	N.Kumar	c and b Dutt	15		
8	†E.Sanjana	c Jabbar b Dutt	4		
9	B.K.Bose	c Jabbar b Dutt	66		
10	D.S.Khambatta	run out	14		
11	N.R.Chowdhury	not out	6		
	Extras		12		2
			262	(1 wicket)	37

FoW (1): 1-5 (2), 2-21 (1), 3-28 (3), 4-67 (4), 5-91 (5), 6-128 (7), 7-149 (8), 8-210 (6), 9-243 (10), 10-262 (9)
FoW (2): 1-10 (2)

Bihar Bowling

	O	M	R	W		O	M	R	W
Chowdhury	24	4	79	7		20.2	2	86	4
Bose	23	5	75	2		17	3	78	2
Khambatta	13	2	25	1	(5)	10	1	58	1
Banerjee	11	3	32	0		6	1	32	1
Kumar	5	0	24	0	(3)	6	1	29	1
Sen					(6)	2	0	5	0

Bengal Bowling

	O	M	R	W		O	M	R	W
Banerjee	22	4	62	2	(2)	7	1	11	1
Ramchandra	22	3	57	1	(1)	8	2	16	0
Obaidullah	7	2	17	1		3	0	8	0
Bhattacharya	15	0	34	2					
Dutt	15.4	0	67	3					
Chatterjee	2	0	13	0					

Umpires: Toss: Bengal

Close of Play: 1st day: Bihar (1) 5-1 (Bagchi 3*); 2nd day: Bengal (2) 7-0 (Jabbar 3*, Dutt 4*).

SIND v BARODA

Played at Karachi Gymkhana Ground, December 6, 7, 8, 1941.

Sind won by eight wickets.

BARODA					
1	M.S.Indulkar	lbw b Mobed	8	(6) b Mobed	29
2	V.M.Pandit	c Girdhari b Lakda	45	run out	6
3	H.R.Adhikari	c Mobed b Lakda	44	c Abdul Shakoor b Qamaruddin Sheikh	3
4	†R.B.Nimbalkar	c and b Girdhari	5	(1) c Mobed b Abdul Shakoor	23
5	V.S.Hazare	c Naoomal Jaoomal b Girdhari	3	b Girdhari	12
6	C.S.Nayudu	b Mobed	25	(4) st Abbas Khan b Girdhari	17
7	M.M.Naidu	lbw b Mobed	6	(9) st Abbas Khan b Lakda	12
8	*W.N.Ghorpade	c Ibrahim Vazir b Lakda	0	c Daud Khan b Mobed	0
9	Y.E.Sheikh	run out	14	(7) c and b Naoomal Jaoomal	22
10	A.Patel	b Mobed	17	not out	1
11	E.B.Gai	not out	0	absent ill	0
	Extras		11		1
			178		126

FoW (1): 1-31 (1), 2-83 (2), 3- (4), 4-102 (5), 5-120 (3), 6- (7), 7-137 (8), 8-141 (6), 9-172 (10), 10-178 (9)
FoW (2): 1- , 2- , 3- , 4- , 5- , 6- , 7- , 8- , 9-126

SIND					
1	F.S.R.Johnson	c Sheikh b Hazare	29	st Nimbalkar b Nayudu	18
2	F.G.Lakda	c Adhikari b Hazare	10	c Nayudu b Hazare	1
3	Qamaruddin Sheikh	b Nayudu	2	not out	43
4	G.Kishenchand	c Sheikh b Hazare	92	not out	5
5	Abdul Shakoor	c Hazare b Nayudu	4		
6	†Abbas Khan	c and b Nayudu	1		
7	Naoomal Jaoomal	c Sheikh b Nayudu	5		
8	Daud Khan	run out	55		
9	*M.J.Mobed	c sub b Hazare	18		
10	S.K.Girdhari	b Hazare	1		
11	Ibrahim Vazir	not out	5		
	Extras		15		1
			237	(2 wickets)	68

FoW (1): 1-23 (2), 2-26 (3), 3-73 (1), 4- , 5- , 6- , 7- , 8- , 9- , 10-237
FoW (2): 1- , 2-

Sind Bowling

	O	M	R	W		O	M	R	W
Qamaruddin Sheikh	4	0	12	0		6	0	29	1
Abdul Shakoor	4	1	7	0		4	1	23	1
Ibrahim Vazir	12	2	30	0		2	0	9	0
Mobed	12	5	20	4		10	3	26	2
Girdhari	14	2	52	2		10	3	27	2
Naoomal Jaoomal	1	0	7	0		2	0	4	1
Lakda	14	2	39	3		2	0	7	1

Baroda Bowling

	O	M	R	W		O	M	R	W
Hazare	56	26	64	5		13	5	27	1
Patel	6	2	20	0		7	3	14	0
Gai	13	6	14	0					
Nayudu	46	7	113	4	(3)	8	1	17	1
Sheikh	7	3	5	0					
Adhikari	2	0	6	0	(4)	3	0	9	0

Umpires: Toss: Baroda

Close of Play: 1st day: Sind (1) 78-3 (Kishenchand 30*, Abdul Shakoor 4*); 2nd day: Baroda (2) 126 all out.

MUSLIMS v THE REST

Played at Brabourne Stadium, Bombay, December 13, 14, 15, 1941.

Match drawn.

THE REST					
1	B.P.Kadam	b Chippa	36	c and b Chippa	49
2	J.O.Gonsalves	lbw b Hakim	0		
3	E.Alexander	b Saeed Ahmed	6	(7) run out	0
4	A.C.Pereira	c Sheikh b Chippa	6		
5	S.R.Arolkar	c Nakhuda b Chippa	32	(6) c sub b Sheikh	49
6	V.S.Hazare	b Hakim	74	(4) not out	101
7	P.S.D'Souza	run out	15	(3) b Chippa	33
8	B.Frank	c Nakhuda b Sheikh	0	(5) b Latiff	19
9	*G.S.Richards	b Saeed Ahmed	26	(8) not out	7
10	A.K.Bhalerao	lbw b Sheikh	2		
11	†V.Dias	not out	10	(2) b Hakim	14
	Extras	b 7, lb 3	10	b 10	10
			217	(6 wickets)	282

FoW (1): 1-6 (2), 2-25 (3), 3-51 (1), 4-56 (4), 5-98 (5), 6-130 (7), 7-130 (8), 8-164 (9), 9-176 (10), 10-217 (6)
FoW (2): 1-26 (2), 2-86 (3), 3-128 (1), 4-165 (5), 5-249 (6), 6-262 (7)

MUSLIMS			
1	Nazar Mohammad	b Richards	30
2	*S.M.Kadri	c Richards b Hazare	76
3	Y.E.Sheikh	b Bhalerao	96
4	K.C.Ibrahim	lbw b Bhalerao	27
5	Gul Mohammad	st Dias b Bhalerao	0
6	A.A.Hakim	b Alexander	1
7	Saeed Ahmed	c Hazare b Bhalerao	52
8	†H.A.Nakhuda	lbw b Bhalerao	6
9	E.A.Alloo	b Hazare	21
10	U.R.Chippa	c Richards b Bhalerao	22
11	M.A.Latiff	not out	3
	Extras	b 19, lb 4, nb 2	25
			359

FoW (1): 1-51 (1), 2-180 (2), 3-236 (3), 4-236 (5), 5-239 (6), 6-239 (4), 7-264 (8), 8-324, 9-342, 10-359

Muslims Bowling

	O	M	R	W		O	M	R	W
Saeed Ahmed	27	5	63	2		5	0	12	0
Hakim	10.1	1	37	2		16	0	62	1
Sheikh	23	7	38	2	(5)	26	3	77	1
Chippa	24	6	46	3		21	4	52	2
Latiff	10	2	20	0	(6)	16	2	32	1
Gul Mohammad	2	1	3	0	(3)	4	0	20	0
Ibrahim					(7)	5	2	13	0
Alloo					(8)	1	0	4	0

The Rest Bowling

	O	M	R	W
Alexander	25	4	39	1
Hazare	43	16	78	2
Richards	30	5	72	1
Arolkar	8	1	27	0
Bhalerao	54.3	15	99	6
Frank	3	0	16	0
Gonsalves	2	1	3	0

Umpires: D.K.Kapadia and D.K.Naik. Toss: The Rest

Close of Play: 1st day: Muslims (1) 56-1 (Kadri 18*, Sheikh 1*); 2nd day: Muslims (1) 306-7 (Saeed Ahmed 39*, Alloo 10*).

V.S.Hazare's 101 took 171 minutes and included 8 fours.

EUROPEANS v PARSEES

Played at Brabourne Stadium, Bombay, December 16, 17, 18, 1941.

Parsees won by an innings and 262 runs.

PARSEES

1	†K.R.Meherhomji	c Rice b Buckland	5
2	M.F.Mistry	retired out	152
3	J.H.Wadia	c Moss b Coleman	4
4	E.B.Aibara	c Gifford b Buckland	59
5	R.S.Modi	c Mischler b Buckland	144
6	J.B.Khot	not out	103
7	R.S.Cooper	not out	24
8	D.R.Havewala		
9	*P.E.Palia		
10	M.J.Mobed		
11	K.K.Tarapore		
	Extras	b 29, lb 4, w 4, nb 4	41
		(5 wickets, declared)	532

FoW (1): 1-7 (1), 2-18 (3), 3-125 (4), 4-356 (5), 5-433 (2)

EUROPEANS

1	P.L.G.Child	b Palia	27	b Khot	4
2	S.I.Philips	b Palia	26	run out	42
3	R.F.Moss	b Havewala	42	b Mobed	9
4	†N.M.Mischler	b Palia	0	not out	75
5	*J.E.Tew	b Khot	13	c and b Mobed	9
6	S.W.E.Behrend	b Palia	0	b Mobed	0
7	H.M.Rice	c Palia b Khot	4	b Palia	6
8	C.W.E.U'ren	lbw b Mobed	3	c Mistry b Palia	0
9	W.P.Buckland	not out	0	b Tarapore	6
10	A.A.K.Gifford	b Tarapore	1	c and b Havewala	0
11	R.Coleman	b Tarapore	0	b Tarapore	1
	Extras	lb 1	1	b 1	1
			117		153

FoW (1): 1-47 (2), 2-60 (1), 3-62 (4), 4-99 (5), 5-100 (6), 6-107 (7), 7-115 (8), 8-115 (3), 9-117 (10), 10-117 (11)
FoW (2): 1-14 (1), 2-32 (3), 3-71 (2), 4-90 (5), 5-90 (6), 6-107 (7), 7-111 (8), 8-151 (9), 9-152 (10), 10-153 (11)

Europeans Bowling

	O	M	R	W
Coleman	8	1	43	1
Buckland	25	1	100	3
Behrend	14	1	60	0
Gifford	39	3	107	0
Rice	18	0	74	0
U'ren	18	1	88	0
Child	5	0	19	0

Parsees Bowling

	O	M	R	W	O	M	R	W
Khot	17	5	36	2	4	0	13	1
Palia	31	11	32	4	11	0	39	2
Havewala	17	3	24	1	11	4	19	1
Mobed	13	6	10	1	18	2	40	3
Tarapore	7	3	7	2	13.2	1	27	2
Cooper	6	1	7	0	7	2	14	0

Umpires: D.K.Naik and Vali Ahmed. Toss:

Close of Play: 1st day: Parsees (1) 348-3 (Mistry 116*, Modi 136*); 2nd day: Europeans (1) 90-3 (Moss 30*, Tew 7*).

M.F.Mistry's 152 took 404 minutes and included 8 fours. R.S.Modi's 144 took 234 minutes and included 9 fours. J.B.Khot's 103 took 129 minutes and included 10 fours.

HINDUS v MUSLIMS

Played at Brabourne Stadium, Bombay, December 19, 20, 21, 1941.

Match drawn.

HINDUS					
1	†D.D.Hindlekar	b Peerbhoy	13	lbw b Baloch	91
2	S.W.Sohoni	b Peerbhoy	30	retired hurt	7
3	M.N.Raiji	c and b Peerbhoy	26		
4	*V.M.Merchant	not out	243		
5	K.M.Rangnekar	lbw b Saeed Ahmed	28		
6	H.R.Adhikari	c Ibrahim b Hakim	88		
7	C.S.Nayudu	not out	7	(5) c Hakim b Sheikh	15
8	U.M.Merchant			(4) not out	38
9	C.T.Sarwate			(3) retired out	51
10	K.M.Jadhav			(6) not out	27
11	S.R.Godambe				
	Extras	b 7, lb 1	8	b 15, lb 2	17
		(5 wickets, declared)	443	(3 wickets)	246

FoW (1): 1-41 (2), 2-44 (1), 3-99 (3), 4-170 (5), 5-404 (6)
FoW (2): 1-155 (1), 2-175 (3), 3-205 (5)

MUSLIMS			
1	Nazar Mohammad	st Hindlekar b Sarwate	27
2	*S.M.Kadri	c Sohoni b Jadhav	3
3	Y.E.Sheikh	lbw b Nayudu	15
4	K.C.Ibrahim	b Sarwate	14
5	Gul Mohammad	b Nayudu	101
6	A.A.Hakim	c Adhikari b Nayudu	16
7	Saeed Ahmed	not out	67
8	M.S.Baloch	lbw b Nayudu	1
9	U.R.Chippa	b Jadhav	9
10	A.A.Peerbhoy	b Jadhav	0
11	†E.S.Maka	c Adhikari b Nayudu	8
	Extras	b 4, lb 3, nb 2	9
			270

FoW (1): 1-7 (2), 2-45 (3), 3-51 (1), 4-78 (4), 5-125 (6), 6-240 (5), 7-242 (8), 8-252 (9), 9-257 (10), 10-270 (11)

Muslims Bowling	O	M	R	W		O	M	R	W
Saeed Ahmed	50	13	95	1		4	1	14	0
Hakim	20	2	56	1					
Baloch	33	9	55	0	(2)	16	2	62	1
Chippa	22	2	45	0	(3)	8	1	27	0
Peerbhoy	39	2	115	3	(4)	6	0	21	0
Sheikh	10	2	26	0	(5)	13	0	73	1
Gul Mohammad	1	0	1	0	(6)	3	0	15	0
Ibrahim	2	0	7	0					
Nazar Mohammad	9	0	27	0	(7)	3	0	11	0
Kadri	1	0	8	0	(8)	2	0	6	0

Hindus Bowling	O	M	R	W
Jadhav	25	10	43	3
Godambe	11	4	15	0
Nayudu	38.3	4	116	5
Sohoni	5	2	12	0
Sarwate	20	3	54	2
Raiji	5	0	19	0
V.M.Merchant	3	2	2	0

Umpires: D.K.Kapadia and J.R.Patel. Toss: Hindus

Close of Play: 1st day: Hindus (1) 247-4 (V.M.Merchant 104*, Adhikari 37*); 2nd day: Muslims (1) 125-4 (Gul Mohammad 48*, Hakim 16*).

V.M.Merchant's 243 took 430 minutes and included 18 fours. Gul Mohammad's 101 took 180 minutes and included 9 fours.

S.W.Sohoni retired hurt with a strained thigh muscle in the Hindus second innings having scored 7 (team score 40-0). Gul Mohammad kept wicket after tea on the third day.

HINDUS v PARSEES

Played at Brabourne Stadium, Bombay, December 23, 24, 25, 26, 1941.

Hindus won by ten wickets.

HINDUS					
1	†D.D.Hindlekar	run out	14	not out	15
2	S.W.Sohoni	b Palia	3	not out	26
3	M.N.Raiji	c Meherhomji b Khot	2		
4	V.M.Merchant	c Palia b Havewala	221		
5	C.T.Sarwate	c Mistry b Mobed	5		
6	K.M.Rangnekar	b Mobed	117		
7	*L.P.Jai	lbw b Tarapore	27		
8	U.M.Merchant	c and b Khot	47		
9	R.J.Gharat	run out	7		
10	K.M.Jadhav	lbw b Havewala	9		
11	S.K.Girdhari	not out	9		
	Extras	b 12, lb 1	13		
			474	(no wicket)	41

FoW (1): 1-6 (2), 2-9 (3), 3-46 (1), 4-67 (5), 5-292 (6), 6-359 (7), 7-426 (4), 8-450 (8), 9-461, 10-474

PARSEES					
1	†K.R.Meherhomji	c Sarwate b Sohoni	19	(9) lbw b Jadhav	71
2	M.F.Mistry	c Jai b Sarwate	5	(1) lbw b Raiji	36
3	E.B.Aibara	b Sarwate	5	(8) b Raiji	57
4	R.S.Modi	c Hindlekar b Sohoni	34	c Sarwate b Raiji	13
5	H.A.Printer	b Girdhari	15	(2) lbw b Sarwate	28
6	J.B.Khot	c Raiji b Jadhav	38	(5) b Sarwate	7
7	K.K.Tarapore	run out	39	(6) st Hindlekar b Raiji	24
8	*P.E.Palia	lbw b Sarwate	3	(7) b Sarwate	16
9	R.S.Cooper	not out	31	(3) c Jai b Sarwate	0
10	D.R.Havewala	c and b Girdhari	2	b Raiji	14
11	M.J.Mobed	b Girdhari	0	not out	4
	Extras	b 9, lb 3	12	b 31, lb 8	39
			203		309

FoW (1): 1-19 (2), 2-31 (3), 3-31 (1), 4-55 (5), 5-97 (4), 6-133 (6), 7-136 (8), 8-198 (7), 9-203 (10), 10-203 (11)
FoW (2): 1-69 (2), 2-69 (3), 3-92 (4), 4-95 (1), 5-131 (5), 6-135 (6), 7-155 (7), 8-265 (9), 9-296 (10), 10-309 (8)

Parsees Bowling	O	M	R	W		O	M	R	W
Khot	34	8	84	2		2	0	6	0
Palia	54	20	90	1					
Mobed	41	6	113	2					
Tarapore	31	7	85	1					
Havewala	19	2	78	2	(2)	4	0	20	0
Cooper	2	0	11	0					
Printer					(3)	2.1	0	15	0

Hindus Bowling	O	M	R	W		O	M	R	W
Jadhav	9	0	26	1		12	7	27	1
Sohoni	19	4	50	2		16	6	45	0
V.M.Merchant	1	0	1	0					
Sarwate	22	5	41	3	(3)	31	10	77	4
Girdhari	19.4	6	30	3	(4)	19	4	47	0
Rangnekar	3	0	11	0					
Raiji	5	1	14	0	(5)	31.4	4	54	5
Gharat	7	0	18	0	(6)	9	1	20	0

Umpires: H.E.Choudhury and Vali Ahmed. Toss: Hindus

Close of Play: 1st day: Hindus (1) 299-5 (V.M.Merchant 145*, Jai 4*); 2nd day: Parsees (1) 103-5 (Khot 20*, Tarapore 2*); 3rd day: Parsees (2) 106-4 (Khot 2*, Tarapore 6*).

V.M.Merchant's 221 took 450 minutes and included 17 fours. K.M.Rangnekar's 117 took 187 minutes and included 12 fours.

MADRAS v MADRAS GOVERNOR'S XI

Played at Madras Cricket Club Ground, Chepauk, Madras, December 26, 27, 28, 1941.

Madras Governor's XI won by nine wickets.

MADRAS					
1	*C.P.Johnstone	c Hazare b Versey-Brown	20	(2) c Ward b Nayudu	24
2	V.N.Madhava Rao	b Versey-Brown	7	(1) b Hazare	1
3	A.G.Ram Singh	c Gul Mohammad b Versey-Brown	66	(5) b Khanna	51
4	C.K.Nainakannu	c Hazare b Khanna	4	b Versey-Brown	10
5	C.Ramaswami	b Hazare	2	(3) c Hazare b Khanna	42
6	R.S.Nailer	b Jayasundera	35	(8) c Adhikari b Hazare	47
7	M.J.Gopalan	c Ward b Hazare	0	(9) c Ward b Hazare	15
8	N.J.Venkatesan	b Nayudu	16	(6) c Ward b Khanna	0
9	†M.O.Srinivasan	lbw b Versey-Brown	0	(7) c Nayudu b Adhikari	15
10	C.R.Rangachari	b Versey-Brown	0	c Nayudu b Hazare	2
11	P.S.Ramachandran	not out	1	not out	0
	Extras		10		14
			161		221

FoW (1): 1-21 (2), 2-40 (1), 3-54 (4), 4-57 (5), 5-112 (6), 6-121 (7), 7-160 (3), 8-160 (8), 9-160 (9), 10-161 (10)
FoW (2): 1-6 (1), 2-55 (2), 3-72 (4), 4-102 (3), 5-102 (6), 6-136, 7- , 8-204, 9-206, 10-221

MADRAS GOVERNOR'S XI					
1	Raja of Ramnad	run out	15	(2) not out	31
2	B.C.Khanna	st Srinivasan b Ram Singh	40	(1) c Madhava Rao b Johnstone	4
3	H.R.Adhikari	st Srinivasan b Ram Singh	17		
4	V.S.Hazare	c Rangachari b Venkatesan	24		
5	Gul Mohammad	st Srinivasan b Venkatesan	25	(3) not out	21
6	C.S.Nayudu	c Rangachari b Ram Singh	79		
7	C.K.Haridas	c Gopalan b Rangachari	4		
8	K.S.Kannan	c Ramaswami b Gopalan	16		
9	*†H.P.Ward	st Srinivasan b Ram Singh	54		
10	D.S.Jayasundera	st Srinivasan b Venkatesan	47		
11	J.S.Versey-Brown	not out	0		
	Extras		8		1
			329	(1 wicket)	57

FoW (1): 1-46 (1), 2-75 (2), 3-76 (3), 4-117 (5), 5-136 (4), 6-160 (7), 7-218 (8), 8-220 (6), 9-329 (9), 10-329 (10)
FoW (2): 1- (1)

Madras Governor's XI Bowling

	O	M	R	W		O	M	R	W
Jayasundera	13	5	16	1		11	1	32	0
Khanna	14	5	20	1		14	6	30	3
Versey-Brown	7.3	3	14	5		7	0	21	1
Nayudu	11	1	46	1		11	1	55	1
Hazare	12	2	40	2		14.2	1	37	4
Kannan	2	0	15	0		6	1	15	0
Adhikari					(7)	4	0	17	1

Madras Bowling

	O	M	R	W		O	M	R	W
Ramachandran	5	0	24	0					
Ram Singh	33	4	123	4					
Rangachari	14	1	66	1					
Venkatesan	18.3	0	74	3					
Gopalan	4	0	17	1					
Johnstone	2	0	17	0	(1)				1

Umpires: V.S.Natarajan and T.A.Ramachandran. Toss: Madras

Close of Play: 1st day: Madras Governor's XI (1) 81-3 (Hazare 4*, Gul Mohammad 1*); 2nd day: Madras (2) 104-5 (Ram Singh 13*, Srinivasan 1*).

This match was played in aid of the Red Cross Fund.

NORTHERN INDIA v SOUTHERN PUNJAB

Played at Aitchison College Ground, Lahore, December 27, 28, 29, 1941.

Northern India won by 74 runs.

NORTHERN INDIA					
1	Nazar Mohammad	b Bhalindra Singh	16	st Balindu Shah b Nazir Ali	1
2	D.Jagdish Lal	b Murawwat Hussain	9	b Nazir Ali	4
3	Gulzar Mir	run out	47	c Muni Lal b Nazir Ali	0
4	R.P.Mehra	c Amir Elahi b Amarnath	44	st Balindu Shah b Amir Elahi	34
5	Mohammad Sharif	st Balindu Shah b Amarnath	36	b Amir Elahi	7
6	*†G.E.B.Abell	c Muni Lal b Amir Elahi	11	b Amir Elahi	2
7	Anwar Hussain	c and b Amir Elahi	50	st Balindu Shah b Amir Elahi	51
8	M.Jahangir Khan	c Amarnath b Amir Elahi	16	b Amir Elahi	9
9	Agha Sarfraz	not out	37	b Amarnath	7
10	Chuni Lal	run out	4	c Amir Elahi b Amarnath	0
11	Habibullah	lbw b Amir Elahi	2	not out	6
	Extras		13		7
			285		128

FoW (1): 1-12 (2), 2-35 (1), 3-92 (3), 4-154 (5), 5-167 (4), 6-175 (6), 7-198 (8), 8-269 (7), 9-274 (10), 10-285 (11)
FoW (2): 1- (1), 2- (2), 3- (3), 4- (5), 5-22 (6), 6-85 (4), 7-105 (8), 8-118 (9), 9-118 (10), 10-128 (7)

SOUTHERN PUNJAB					
1	D.Muni Lal	b Chuni Lal	2	lbw b Habibullah	5
2	Daljinder Singh	b Habibullah	7	c Mehra b Jahangir Khan	2
3	Abdur Rehman	b Chuni Lal	4	(10) c Nazar Mohammad b Chuni Lal	2
4	L.Amarnath	c Nazar Mohammad b Habibullah	79	(5) c Abell b Chuni Lal	11
5	S.Nazir Ali	c Habibullah b Agha Sarfraz	12	(6) c Abell b Jahangir Khan	78
6	K.Rai Singh	st Abell b Habibullah	19	(8) b Chuni Lal	15
7	*Bhalindra Singh	not out	13	b Chuni Lal	20
8	Roshan Lal	b Habibullah	0	(4) lbw b Habibullah	6
9	Murawwat Hussain	run out	2	(3) c Habibullah b Chuni Lal	1
10	Amir Elahi	lbw b Habibullah	7	(9) c and b Chuni Lal	27
11	†Balindu Shah	c Mohammad Sharif b Habibullah	1	not out	2
	Extras		12		12
			158		181

FoW (1): 1-2 (1), 2-12 (2), 3-36 (3), 4-74 (5), 5-128 (4), 6-129 (6), 7-129 (8), 8-133 (9), 9-142 (10), 10-158 (11)
FoW (2): 1-5 (1), 2-6 (3), 3-8 (2), 4-21 (4), 5-29 (5), 6-88 (7), 7-126 (8), 8-157 (6), 9-170 (10), 10-181 (9)

Southern Punjab Bowling	O	M	R	W		O	M	R	W
Murawwat Hussain	13	4	30	1		3	0	10	0
Amarnath	26	4	60	2	(3)	14	3	25	2
Nazir Ali	11	5	17	0	(2)	11	3	21	3
Bhalindra Singh	14	1	68	1					
Amir Elahi	33.1	4	97	4	(4)	18.1	4	65	5

Northern India Bowling	O	M	R	W		O	M	R	W
Jahangir Khan	17	6	34	0	(3)	13	6	15	2
Chuni Lal	18	2	50	2		31.5	10	94	6
Habibullah	15	7	17	6	(1)	24	8	37	2
Agha Sarfraz	13	1	45	1		4	0	10	0
Nazar Mohammad					(5)	2	0	13	0

Umpires: Toss: Northern India

Close of Play: 1st day: Southern Punjab (1) 12-2 (Abdur Rehman 2*); 2nd day: Southern Punjab (2) 8-2 (Daljinder Singh 2*, Roshan Lal 0*).

BOMBAY v SIND

Played at Brabourne Stadium, Bombay, December 29, 30, 31, 1941.

Match drawn.

BOMBAY

1	†D.D.Hindlekar	b Girdhari	9
2	S.M.Kadri	b Kishenchand	59
3	V.N.Raiji	lbw b Ibrahim Vazir	20
4	K.C.Ibrahim	st Abbas Khan b Naoomal Jaoomal	20
5	*V.M.Merchant	not out	153
6	K.M.Rangnekar	run out	58
7	L.P.Jai	c and b Naoomal Jaoomal	43
8	J.B.Khot	c Ibrahim Vazir b Naoomal Jaoomal	13
9	D.R.Havewala	st Abbas Khan b Naoomal Jaoomal	2
10	M.N.Raiji	b Girdhari	1
11	K.K.Tarapore	c Daud Khan b Naoomal Jaoomal	16
	Extras	b 6, lb 2, w 1, nb 2	11
			405

FoW (1): 1-23 (1), 2-67 (3), 3-104 (2), 4-120 (4), 5-249 (6), 6-328 (7), 7-350 (8), 8-356 (9), 9-357 (10), 10-405 (11)

SIND

1	F.S.R.Johnson	lbw b Tarapore	39
2	F.G.Lakda	st Hindlekar b Tarapore	13
3	†Abbas Khan	b M.N.Raiji	15
4	G.Kishenchand	not out	131
5	Naoomal Jaoomal	b Tarapore	16
6	S.K.Girdhari	lbw b Tarapore	12
7	Daud Khan	lbw b Rangnekar	65
8	P.P.Fernandes	lbw b M.N.Raiji	0
9	M.A.Gopaldas	c Jai b M.N.Raiji	0
10	*M.J.Mobed	lbw b M.N.Raiji	13
11	Ibrahim Vazir	st Hindlekar b Merchant	0
	Extras	b 8, lb 12, nb 2	22
			326

FoW (1): 1-46 (2), 2-69 (1), 3-75 (3), 4-118 (5), 5-146 (6), 6-289 (7), 7-290 (8), 8-290 (9), 9-321 (10), 10-326 (11)

Sind Bowling

	O	M	R	W
Gopaldas	11	4	16	0
Ibrahim Vazir	22	5	53	1
Mobed	24	4	55	0
Girdhari	32	11	56	2
Naoomal Jaoomal	37.2	2	121	5
Lakda	23	3	66	0
Kishenchand	8	0	27	1

Bombay Bowling

	O	M	R	W
Havewala	28	7	41	0
Khot	18	8	34	0
Merchant	12.4	3	20	1
Tarapore	54	20	60	4
M.N.Raiji	50	3	142	4
Rangnekar	4	3	6	1
Ibrahim	1	0	1	0

Umpires: D.K.Naik and J.R.Patel. Toss: Bombay

Close of Play: 1st day: Bombay (1) 248-4 (Merchant 73*, Rangnekar 58*); 2nd day: Sind (1) 118-4 (Kishenchand 30*, Girdhari 10*).

V.M.Merchant's 153 took 304 minutes and included 18 fours. G.Kishenchand's 131 took 340 minutes and included 8 fours.

MYSORE v MADRAS

Played at Central College Ground, Bangalore, December 31, 1941, January 1, 2, 1942.

Mysore won by 22 runs.

MYSORE					
1	T.V.Parthasarathi	c Nailer b Rangachari	8	c Gopalan b Rangachari	8
2	Y.S.Ramaswami	c Srinivasan b Ram Singh	0	lbw b Rangachari	1
3	K.Thimmappiah	c Srinivasan b Gopalan	16	c Srinivasan b Gopalan	127
4	B.K.Garudachar	c Parthasarathi b Rangachari	57	c Ram Singh b Gopalan	13
5	C.J.Ramdev	b Ram Singh	18	c Srinivasan b Ram Singh	3
6	B.Frank	b Rangachari	15	c Ram Singh b Rangachari	38
7	†F.K.Irani	b Rangachari	7	(9) st Srinivasan b Ram Singh	31
8	*S.Darashah	c Parthasarathi b Ram Singh	12	(7) c Srinivasan b Rangachari	0
9	M.R.Alasingrachar	b Rangachari	1	(8) c and b Ram Singh	12
10	S.Rama Rao	st Srinivasan b Ram Singh	6	b Ram Singh	0
11	H.D.Rangaiyengar	not out	1	not out	4
	Extras		6		9
			147		246

FoW (1): 1-4, 2-28, 3-30, 4-37, 5-116, 6- , 7-137, 8- , 9- , 10-147
FoW (2): 1-12, 2-15, 3-25, 4-35, 5-103, 6-103, 7-206, 8-214, 9- , 10-246

MADRAS					
1	†M.O.Srinivasan	c Ramdev b Rama Rao	1	(10) run out	2
2	Raja of Ramnad	b Garudachar	17	b Garudachar	27
3	A.G.Ram Singh	c Frank b Rangaiyengar	0	c Irani b Rama Rao	3
4	C.K.Haridas	st Irani b Ramaswami	18	b Garudachar	0
5	R.S.Nailer	b Garudachar	25	b Garudachar	1
6	G.Parthasarathi	c Darashah b Garudachar	24	c Irani b Garudachar	19
7	*M.J.Gopalan	b Garudachar	14	st Irani b Garudachar	46
8	S.G.Deenan	b Garudachar	6	c Thimmappiah b Garudachar	21
9	N.J.Venkatesan	b Garudachar	12	b Garudachar	31
10	K.S.Kannan	not out	15	(1) c and b Garudachar	43
11	C.R.Rangachari	c Frank b Rama Rao	2	not out	0
	Extras		20		24
			154		217

FoW (1): 1-3, 2-4, 3-44, 4-48, 5-85, 6-102, 7-119, 8-130, 9-151, 10-154
FoW (2): 1-83 (1), 2-91 (2), 3-91 (3), 4-91 (4), 5-93 (5), 6-155 (6), 7-166 (7), 8-197 (8), 9-216 (10), 10-217 (9)

Madras Bowling	O	M	R	W		O	M	R	W
Gopalan	6	1	18	1		24	1	60	2
Ram Singh	20.4	2	47	4		24.4	2	80	4
Rangachari	13	4	36	5		18	0	62	4
Venkatesan	3	0	17	0		1	0	9	0
Parthasarathi	5	0	23	0		5	1	14	0
Kannan					(6)	2	0	12	0

Mysore Bowling	O	M	R	W		O	M	R	W
Rama Rao	16.4	3	45	2	(2)	23	8	43	1
Rangaiyengar	3	2	2	1	(3)	6	1	6	0
Garudachar	23	2	56	6	(1)	31.3	2	99	8
Ramaswami	10	2	31	1		2	1	3	0
Darashah					(5)	9	0	28	0
Alasingrachar					(6)	4	0	14	0

Umpires: H.D.Billimoria and Vali Ahmed. Toss: Mysore

Close of Play: 1st day: Madras (1) 153-9 (Kannan 14*, Rangachari 2*); 2nd day: Madras (2) 83-1 (Ramnad 23*).

K.Thimmappiah's 127 took 186 minutes and included 13 fours.

WESTERN PROVINCE v TRANSVAAL

Played at Newlands, Cape Town, January 1, 2, 3, 1942.

Match drawn.

WESTERN PROVINCE					
1	R.Lofthouse	c Pickerill b Warne	28	b Gordon	4
2	S.Kiel	run out	12	not out	128
3	K.G.Fismer	c Dacey b Langton	54	c Langton b Warne	4
4	T.M.H.van der Spuy	c Bromham b Gordon	7	lbw b Langton	7
5	*A.R.M.Ralph	c Georgeu b Gordon	2	c Bromham b Warne	19
6	J.E.Cheetham	run out	37	b Langton	0
7	A.W.Marshall	b Heaney	6	(8) lbw b Gordon	0
8	A.D.Keen	lbw b Warne	44	(7) c Petersen b Gordon	45
9	L.S.Eckard	run out	8	(10) not out	9
10	†A.B.J.Reid	c Bromham b Langton	16	(9) b Gordon	0
11	D.Eayrs	not out	0		
	Extras	b 15, lb 8	23	b 10, lb 10	20
			237	(8 wickets, declared)	236

FoW (1): 1-20 (2), 2-63 (1), 3-90 (4), 4-96 (5), 5-146, 6-156, 7-170, 8-184, 9-237, 10-237
FoW (2): 1-20 (1), 2-35 (3), 3-48 (4), 4-99 (5), 5-100 (6), 6-197 (7), 7-197 (8), 8-197 (9)

TRANSVAAL					
1	F.W.Smith	c Reid b Lofthouse	5	lbw b Eckard	9
2	R.N.E.Petersen	run out	0	c and b Eayrs	11
3	*L.S.Dacey	b Lofthouse	8	c Reid b Eckard	9
4	J.H.M.Pickerill	c Eckard b Keen	71	c Keen b Lofthouse	21
5	G.Georgeu	run out	20	not out	68
6	F.B.Warne	run out	66		
7	A.C.B.Langton	c Cheetham b Lofthouse	50	(6) b Lofthouse	39
8	†C.G.Bromham	b Lofthouse	18		
9	F.G.Turner	not out	2	(7) st Reid b van der Spuy	1
10	N.Gordon				
11	L.J.Heaney				
	Extras	b 6, lb 5	11	b 5, lb 2, nb 1	8
		(8 wickets, declared)	251	(6 wickets)	166

FoW (1): 1-3 (2), 2-6 (1), 3-19 (3), 4-56 (5), 5-169, 6-171, 7-240, 8-251
FoW (2): 1-24, 2-32, 3-38, 4-84, 5-152, 6-166

Transvaal Bowling	O	M	R	W		O	M	R	W
Heaney	23	7	47	1		5	0	13	0
Petersen	11	4	25	0		2	0	9	0
Langton	17	4	41	2		16	2	66	2
Gordon	12	4	53	2		21	3	63	4
Warne	16.1	0	48	2		20	3	65	2

Western Province Bowling	O	M	R	W		O	M	R	W
Kiel	2	0	7	0		2	1	3	0
Lofthouse	19.6	3	63	4		13	1	32	2
Eckard	19	1	57	0		13	3	39	2
Keen	14	4	23	1		3	0	28	0
Eayrs	17	3	42	0		17	2	49	1
Cheetham	5	0	24	0					
Fismer	3	0	15	0					
van der Spuy	2	0	9	0	(6)	0.5	0	7	1

Umpires: D.V.Collins and G.L.Sickler. Toss: Western Province

Close of Play: 1st day: Transvaal (1) 6-2 (Dacey 0*); 2nd day: Western Province (2) 20-1 (Kiel 15*).

S.Kiel's 128 included 9 fours.

BENGAL GOVERNOR'S XI v MAHARASHTRA

Played at Eden Gardens, Calcutta, January 3, 4, 5, 1942.

Match drawn.

	BENGAL GOVERNOR'S XI				
1	S.N.Banerjee	c Nimbalkar b Hazare	17		
2	S.Mushtaq Ali	run out	31	b Girdhari	45
3	H.R.Adhikari	b Girdhari	27	(6) c Chari b Baloch	76
4	N.C.Chatterjee	b Sarwate	0	lbw b Girdhari	0
5	C.S.Nayudu	b Naoomal Jaoomal	55	(7) c and b Hazare	7
6	†D.D.Hindlekar	c Deodhar b Girdhari	32	(1) b Hazare	10
7	N.M.Bose	not out	55	(5) not out	86
8	M.Jahangir Khan	c Chari b Girdhari	3	b Girdhari	21
9	*T.C.Longfield	lbw b Sarwate	1		
10	B.Ramchandra	b Sarwate	0		
11	A.K.Deb	b Hazare	13	(3) b Baloch	18
	Extras		23		12
			257	(7 wickets, declared)	275

FoW (1): 1-24 (1), 2-66 (2), 3-71 (4), 4-97 (3), 5-165 (5), 6-189 (6), 7-199 (8), 8-200 (9), 9-200 (10), 10-257 (11)
FoW (2): 1-39 (1), 2-67 (2), 3-67 (4), 4-78 (3), 5-220 (6), 6-238 (7), 7-275 (8)

	MAHARASHTRA				
1	†B.B.Nimbalkar	b Banerjee	27	b Banerjee	4
2	M.S.Baloch	lbw b Banerjee	0		
3	M.N.Paranjpe	b Jahangir Khan	4	(7) not out	0
4	G.Kishenchand	c Nayudu b Jahangir Khan	17	(3) lbw b Mushtaq Ali	28
5	V.S.Hazare	lbw b Banerjee	83	b Adhikari	34
6	K.M.Rangnekar	c Mushtaq Ali b Banerjee	8	(4) c and b Mushtaq Ali	12
7	*D.B.Deodhar	c Deb b Longfield	38	(6) not out	24
8	Naoomal Jaoomal	lbw b Nayudu	39		
9	C.T.Sarwate	c and b Nayudu	37	(2) b Jahangir Khan	38
10	S.K.Girdhari	lbw b Nayudu	35		
11	K.N.V.Chari	not out	5		
	Extras		15		13
			308	(5 wickets)	153

FoW (1): 1-15 (2), 2-21 (3), 3-51 (1), 4-55 (4), 5-73 (6), 6-136 (7), 7-213 (5), 8-246 (8), 9-291 (9), 10-308 (10)
FoW (2): 1-10 (1), 2-71 (2), 3-91 (3), 4-92 (4), 5-153 (5)

Maharashtra Bowling	O	M	R	W		O	M	R	W
Hazare	13	1	44	2		26	6	65	2
Baloch	17	1	55	0		21	4	51	2
Sarwate	16	1	57	3	(4)	14	2	69	0
Girdhari	15	2	51	3	(3)	14.2	2	45	3
Naoomal Jaoomal	5	0	24	1		5	0	23	0
Rangnekar	1	0	3	0					
Kishenchand					(6)	1	0	10	0

Bengal Governor's XI Bowling	O	M	R	W		O	M	R	W
Banerjee	22	5	91	4		10	1	40	1
Jahangir Khan	19	9	23	2		16	6	24	1
Longfield	17	2	30	1		6	1	10	0
Nayudu	19	0	103	3		9	1	27	0
Ramchandra	10	1	36	0		4	0	16	0
Chatterjee	2	0	10	0					
Mushtaq Ali					(6)	4	0	13	2
Adhikari					(7)	3	1	10	1

Umpires: N.Roy and L.A.Weston. Toss: Bengal Governor's XI

Close of Play: 1st day: Maharashtra (1) 15-1 (Nimbalkar 13*); 2nd day: Bengal Governor's XI (2) 74-3 (Deb 16*, Bose 2*).
The match was played for the War Fund. L.Amarnath was supposed to have played but he wired that his daughter was ill and so he was unable to come and B.Ramchandra played in his place.

UNITED PROVINCES v BENGAL

Played at Maharaja of Benares Palace Ground, Benares, January 10, 11, 12, 1942.

Match drawn.

BENGAL

1	S.K.Ganguli	b Aftab Ahmed	63
2	D.R.Das	b Firasat Hussain	19
3	K.Bhattacharya	b Palia	71
4	A.K.Das	c Wahidullah b Alexander	20
5	*N.M.Bose	b Alexander	7
6	B.Ramchandra	c Salim b Firasat Hussain	2
7	†A.K.Deb	b Firasat Hussain	128
8	S.K.Mustafi	b Alexander	101
9	M.Obaidullah	st Wahidullah b Aftab Ahmed	25
10	S.Dutt	b Firasat Hussain	2
11	J.Nuttall	not out	1
	Extras		34
			473

FoW (1): 1-45 (2), 2-130 (1), 3-169 (4), 4-185 (5), 5-188 (6), 6-236 (3), 7-394 (8), 8-421 (9), 9-452 (10), 10-473 (7)

UNITED PROVINCES

1	E.Alexander	lbw b Bhattacharya	13
2	Firasat Hussain	c Dutt b Obaidullah	55
3	*P.E.Palia	c Deb b Obaidullah	53
4	J.P.Phansalkar	b Nuttall	13
5	Shamim Khwaja	c Ganguli b Dutt	58
6	A.S.N.Murthy	run out	3
7	Aftab Ahmed	b Nuttall	23
8	Salim	b Ramchandra	92
9	†Wahidullah	c Ganguli b Bhattacharya	55
10	K.Mahinder Singh	st Deb b Dutt	10
11	S.N.Gandhi	not out	15
	Extras		36
			426

FoW (1): 1-54 (1), 2-127 (3), 3-136 (2), 4-173 (4), 5- (6), 6-228 (5), 7-231 (7), 8-321 (9), 9-378 (10), 10-426 (8)

United Provinces Bowling

	O	M	R	W
Alexander	43	2	158	3
Mahinder Singh	8	2	30	0
Palia	30	8	66	1
Aftab Ahmed	23	3	73	2
Firasat Hussain	31.4	5	87	4
Gandhi	4	0	14	0
Shamim Khwaja	1	0	2	0
Phansalkar	2	0	9	0

Bengal Bowling

	O	M	R	W
Mustafi	15	3	32	0
Bhattacharya	27	6	65	2
Ramchandra	31	6	88	1
Nuttall	13	2	53	2
Obaidullah	15	3	39	2
Dutt	39	10	104	2
Bose	6	2	9	0

Umpires: Toss: Bengal

Close of Play: 1st day: Bengal (1) 320-6 (Deb 61*, Mustafi 47*); 2nd day: United Provinces (1) 144-3 (Phansalkar 6*, Shamim Khwaja 7*).

WESTERN INDIA STATES v REST OF INDIA

Played at Poona Club Ground, January 11, 12, 13, 14, 1942.

Match drawn.

REST OF INDIA					
1	S.Mushtaq Ali	c Naoomal Jaoomal b Sohoni	38	(4) st Hindlekar b Sarwate	22
2	Nazar Mohammad	c Sarwate b Banerjee	25	(1) b Nayudu	83
3	A.G.Ram Singh	run out	69		
4	R.P.Mehra	lbw b Banerjee	25		
5	Gul Mohammad	b Sarwate	116	c Hindlekar b Hazare	25
6	J.N.Bhaya	c Mankad b Banerjee	36	(7) not out	35
7	*C.Ramaswami	b Sarwate	75		
8	L.Amarnath	lbw b Nayudu	17	(6) not out	75
9	Amir Elahi	b Sarwate	16		
10	N.J.Venkatesan	lbw b Sarwate	1	(2) b Banerjee	0
11	Mubarak Ali	c Kishenchand b Sarwate	0		
12	†M.O.Srinivasan	not out	0	(3) c Naoomal Jaoomal b Mankad	34
	Extras		13		24
			431	(5 wickets, declared)	298

(9) FoW (1): 1-53 (2), 2-79 (1), 3-138 (4), 4-182 (3), 5-244 (6), 6-383 (5), 7-406 (7), 8-422 (8), 9-423 (10), 10-423 (11), 11-431
FoW (2): 1-10 (2), 2-111, 3-144, 4-174, 5-221

WESTERN INDIA STATES					
1	†D.D.Hindlekar	c and b Amir Elahi	44		
2	M.H.Mankad	lbw b Venkatesan	47		
3	G.Kishenchand	c Srinivasan b Ram Singh	19	(5) not out	6
4	H.R.Adhikari	c Srinivasan b Mubarak Ali	83		
5	V.S.Hazare	b Amarnath	25	(3) not out	43
6	*D.B.Deodhar	b Amir Elahi	35	(1) b Nazar Mohammad	74
7	K.C.Ibrahim	c Ram Singh b Amarnath	63		
8	C.S.Nayudu	b Amir Elahi	17	(2) c Mushtaq Ali b Mubarak Ali	3
9	Naoomal Jaoomal	not out	74		
10	C.T.Sarwate	b Amarnath	59		
11	S.N.Banerjee	run out	10	(4) c Amir Elahi b Venkatesan	2
12	S.W.Sohoni				
	Extras		14		18
		(10 wickets, declared)	490	(3 wickets)	146

FoW (1): 1-84 (2), 2-107 (1), 3-137 (3), 4-223 (5), 5-239 (4), 6-293 (6), 7-313 (8), 8-363 (7), 9-468 (10), 10-490 (11)
FoW (2): 1-12 (2), 2-127 (1), 3-130 (4)

Western India States Bowling	O	M	R	W		O	M	R	W
Banerjee	28	1	137	3	(2)	14	0	62	1
Hazare	28	6	79	0	(1)	14	2	55	1
Sarwate	26	3	54	5		25	5	68	1
Sohoni	6	2	16	1					
Nayudu	19	1	92	1		13	1	54	1
Mankad	5	0	14	0	(4)	11	3	35	1
Naoomal Jaoomal	5	0	19	0					
Deodhar	1	0	7	0					

Rest of India Bowling	O	M	R	W		O	M	R	W
Amarnath	68	21	136	3		12	3	32	0
Mubarak Ali	22	4	66	1		5	0	23	1
Ram Singh	26	4	73	1					
Venkatesan	8	0	37	1	(6)	1	0	11	1
Amir Elahi	45	10	119	3	(4)	5	0	32	0
Gul Mohammad	5	1	28	0					
Mushtaq Ali	7	2	17	0	(3)	4	1	18	0
Nazar Mohammad					(5)	3	0	12	1

Umpires: D.K.Naik and Vali Ahmed. Toss: Rest of India

Close of Play: 1st day: Rest of India (1) 346-5 (Gul Mohammad 100*, Ramaswami 41*); 2nd day: Western India States (1) 213-3 (Adhikari 74*, Hazare 20*); 3rd day: Rest of India (2) 25-1 (Nazar Mohammad 8*, Srinivasan 9*).

The match was played to celebrate the 51st birthday of D.B.Deodhar of Maharashtra.

TRINIDAD v BARBADOS

Played at Queen's Park Oval, Port of Spain, January 17, 19, 20, 21, 1942.

Trinidad won by two wickets.

BARBADOS					
1	G.M.Carew	c V.H.Stollmeyer b Jones	5	b Skeete	46
2	C.L.Walcott	b Pierre	8	(4) c Gomez b Jones	0
3	R.G.Blackman	c Samaroo b Pierre	74	st Samaroo b Skeete	12
4	†C.L.Bourne	b Jones	8	(11) c J.B.Stollmeyer b Pierre	42
5	J.E.D.Sealy	lbw b Pierre	30	lbw b Ali	4
6	E.A.V.Williams	c J.B.Stollmeyer b Skeete	39	b J.B.Stollmeyer	5
7	J.D.C.Goddard	c Samaroo b Ali	4	(9) not out	98
8	K.E.Walcott	b Pierre	48	(7) c J.B.Stollmeyer b Ali	0
9	H.A.O.Skinner	b Pierre	2	(8) b Ali	1
10	*T.N.M.Peirce	not out	45	(2) c Skeete b Pierre	1
11	F.M.M.Worrell	c Tang Choon b Pierre	29	(10) c Ali b Skeete	6
	Extras	b 2, lb 5	7	lb 11	11
			299		226

FoW (1): 1-15, 2-15, 3-27, 4-68, 5-129, 6-139, 7-200, 8-204, 9-243, 10-299
FoW (2): 1-3, 2-18, 3-37, 4-43, 5-44, 6-46, 7-107, 8-121, 9-129, 10-226

TRINIDAD					
1	*V.H.Stollmeyer	c sub (A.M.Taylor) b Worrell	71	c Bourne b Williams	20
2	J.B.Stollmeyer	b Williams	6	c Carew b Sealy	13
3	P.B.Burke	c Worrell b Sealy	1	c K.E.Walcott b Worrell	12
4	G.E.Gomez	b Worrell	37	not out	133
5	N.S.Asgarali	c Williams b Peirce	32	c Bourne b Worrell	8
6	R.P.Tang Choon	c Sealy b Worrell	30	run out	50
7	†S.Samaroo	lbw b Peirce	1	(8) c Worrell b Carew	14
8	C.C.R.Skeete	not out	41	(7) lbw b Worrell	13
9	P.E.W.Jones	c Peirce b Williams	14	lbw b Williams	12
10	S.M.Ali	c sub (A.M.Taylor) b Williams	0	not out	2
11	L.R.Pierre	st sub (A.M.Taylor) b Williams	0		
	Extras	b 5, lb 1, nb 1	7	b 4, lb 3, nb 2	9
			240	(8 wickets)	286

FoW (1): 1-15, 2-20, 3-110, 4-154, 5-155, 6-162, 7-204, 8-234, 9-234, 10-240
FoW (2): 1-15, 2-45, 3-49, 4-59, 5-198, 6-223, 7-256, 8-282

Trinidad Bowling	O	M	R	W		O	M	R	W
Pierre	18.6	1	68	6		16.2	1	62	2
Jones	14	2	61	2		11	1	25	1
Tang Choon	10	0	49	0	(6)	2	0	9	0
Ali	17	2	66	1	(3)	15	2	52	3
J.B.Stollmeyer	1	0	2	0	(4)	7	1	26	1
Skeete	8	0	46	1	(5)	7	0	31	3
V.H.Stollmeyer					(7)	2	0	10	0

Barbados Bowling	O	M	R	W		O	M	R	W
Williams	15.3	2	49	4		23.5	1	79	2
Sealy	9	0	48	1		11	0	38	1
Goddard	6	0	25	0	(4)	4	0	17	0
Skinner	3	1	19	0					
Worrell	14	0	58	3	(3)	15	1	70	3
Peirce	7	1	34	2	(5)	3	0	30	0
Carew					(6)	11	1	43	1

Umpires: M.Achong, D.de la Rosa and V.Guillen. Toss: Trinidad

Close of Play: 1st day: Barbados (1) 282-9 (Peirce 35*, Worrell 23*); 2nd day: Barbados (2) 3-1 (Carew 1*); 3rd day: Trinidad (2) 8-0 (V.H.Stollmeyer 1*, J.B.Stollmeyer 6*).

M.Achong stood in place of D.de la Rosa on the third day.

TRINIDAD v BARBADOS

Played at Queen's Park Oval, Port of Spain, January 24, 26, 27, 28, 1942.

Trinidad won by ten wickets.

BARBADOS					
1	G.M.Carew	c Gomez b Jones	4	lbw b Ali	18
2	†C.L.Bourne	lbw b Skeete	53	c Samaroo b Tang Choon	28
3	R.G.Blackman	c Skeete b Trestrail	50	st Samaroo b Tang Choon	1
4	J.E.D.Sealy	c Samaroo b Trestrail	35	(5) b Pierre	87
5	A.M.Taylor	lbw b Jones	3	(4) b Skeete	11
6	E.A.V.Williams	b Ali	13	(7) c V.H.Stollmeyer b Pierre	4
7	K.E.Walcott	c Trestrail b Jones	3	(8) b Pierre	0
8	J.D.C.Goddard	lbw b Pierre	12	(9) not out	67
9	*T.N.M.Peirce	b Pierre	15	(10) c J.B.Stollmeyer b Pierre	2
10	F.M.M.Worrell	not out	34	(6) c J.B.Stollmeyer b Pierre	1
11	W.M.Foster	c Hutcheon b Pierre	2	b Skeete	13
	Extras	b 4, lb 1	5	b 5, lb 4	9
			229		241

FoW (1): 1-6, 2-99, 3-141, 4-144, 5-148, 6-157, 7-172, 8-174, 9-227, 10-229
FoW (2): 1-34, 2-35, 3-48, 4-90, 5-101, 6-108, 7-109, 8-204, 9-220, 10-241

TRINIDAD					
1	*V.H.Stollmeyer	c Williams b Carew	121	not out	52
2	J.B.Stollmeyer	b Peirce	106	not out	43
3	G.E.Gomez	c Walcott b Peirce	0		
4	R.A.Hutcheon	c Bourne b Williams	14		
5	R.P.Tang Choon	c Bourne b Carew	16		
6	A.L.Trestrail	lbw b Sealy	7		
7	C.C.R.Skeete	b Worrell	68		
8	†S.Samaroo	lbw b Sealy	1		
9	P.E.W.Jones	st Bourne b Peirce	12		
10	S.M.Ali	not out	11		
11	L.R.Pierre	st Bourne b Williams	0		
	Extras	b 6, lb 5	11	b 4, lb 5, w 1	10
			367	(no wicket)	105

FoW (1): 1-224, 2-224, 3-230, 4-250, 5-263, 6-275, 7-278, 8-316, 9-366, 10-367

Trinidad Bowling	O	M	R	W		O	M	R	W
Pierre	16	3	34	3		15	0	62	5
Jones	12	3	44	3		9	1	28	0
J.B.Stollmeyer	4	0	21	0	(7)	2	0	17	0
Ali	14	5	32	1	(3)	10	1	51	1
Hutcheon	1	0	3	0	(9)	1	0	10	0
Skeete	7	0	42	1	(5)	3.4	0	26	2
Tang Choon	4	0	16	0	(4)	4	1	18	2
Trestrail	9	0	32	2	(6)	4	1	7	0
V.H.Stollmeyer					(8)	3	0	13	0

Barbados Bowling	O	M	R	W		O	M	R	W
Williams	13.5	0	60	2		3	0	19	0
Sealy	6	1	21	2		3	0	10	0
Worrell	11	0	48	1		2	0	16	0
Foster	3	0	27	0	(6)	2	1	4	0
Taylor	2	0	12	0					
Blackman	4	0	39	0					
Peirce	18	1	114	3	(4)	4	0	22	0
Carew	10	1	35	2	(5)	4	0	24	0

Umpires: D.de la Rosa and V.Guillen. Toss: Barbados

Close of Play: 1st day: Barbados (1) 227-8 (Peirce 15*, Worrell 34*); 2nd day: Trinidad (1) 349-8 (Skeete 54*, Ali 10*); 3rd day: Barbados (2) 241 all out.

V.H.Stollmeyer's 121 took 143 minutes and included 18 fours. J.B.Stollmeyer's 106 included 9 fours.

BENGAL v MYSORE

Played at Eden Gardens, Calcutta, January 31, February 1, 2, 3, 1942.

Mysore won by 17 runs.

MYSORE

1	P.G.Doraiswami	b Puri	8	b Puri	0
2	†T.V.Parthasarathi	c and b Sumption	46	c Puri b Ramchandra	28
3	K.Thimmappiah	b Ramchandra	26	lbw b Mustafi	0
4	B.K.Garudachar	b Ramchandra	46	(5) c Mustafi b Ramchandra	8
5	C.J.Ramdev	not out	105	(6) b Bhattacharya	57
6	B.Frank	b Ramchandra	13	(8) c sub b Puri	48
7	M.G.Vijayasarathi	c Puri b Ramchandra	1	(9) c Puri b Mustafi	25
8	*S.Darashah	c Deb b Ramchandra	30	(7) c Mustafi b Puri	0
9	M.R.Alasingrachar	c Deb b Puri	6	(10) b Puri	14
10	K.S.Rangaraj	lbw b Ramchandra	9	(4) b Ramchandra	14
11	H.D.Rangaiyengar	b Ramchandra	2	not out	3
	Extras		15		11
			307		208

FoW (1): 1-20 (1), 2-73 (2), 3-116 (3), 4-141 (4), 5-177 (6), 6-184 (7), 7-263 (8), 8-273 (9), 9-302 (10), 10-307 (11)
FoW (2): 1-2 (1), 2-3 (3), 3-47 (2), 4-51 (4), 5-58 (5), 6-66 (7), 7-150 (8), 8-175 (6), 9-204 (10), 10-208 (9)

BENGAL

1	A.Jabbar	c Darashah b Vijayasarathi	14	(2) b Darashah	2
2	S.K.Ganguli	b Rangaraj	4	(1) c Frank b Rangaiyengar	11
3	K.Bhattacharya	c Darashah b Rangaiyengar	16	lbw b Garudachar	65
4	A.K.Das	b Garudachar	9	c and b Vijayasarathi	29
5	*N.M.Bose	run out	19	(6) b Rangaiyengar	11
6	†A.K.Deb	b Darashah	13	(7) b Rangaraj	36
7	S.K.Mustafi	c Parthasarathi b Rangaraj	2	(9) b Garudachar	2
8	B.Ramchandra	not out	97	(5) c and b Garudachar	5
9	D.R.Puri	b Rangaiyengar	58	(8) not out	42
10	C.E.Sumption	b Rangaiyengar	30	b Garudachar	4
11	M.Obaidullah	lbw b Rangaiyengar	1	c and b Garudachar	0
	Extras		16		12
			279		219

FoW (1): 1-7 (2), 2-24 (3), 3-35 (4), 4-47 (1), 5-70 (6), 6-76 (7), 7-87 (5), 8-188 (9), 9-263 (10), 10-279 (11)
FoW (2): 1-13 (1), 2-13 (2), 3-82 (4), 4-91 (5), 5-119 (6), 6-142 (3), 7-185 (7), 8-206 (9), 9-219 (10), 10-219 (11)

Bengal Bowling

	O	M	R	W		O	M	R	W
Puri	18	2	55	2		19	1	71	4
Mustafi	13	0	62	0		6.4	1	25	2
Bhattacharya	33	5	46	0	(4)	12	0	38	1
Sumption	11	1	48	1	(5)	3	0	9	0
Ramchandra	20.2	5	52	7	(3)	28	10	53	3
Obaidullah	6	1	29	0		1	0	1	0

Mysore Bowling

	O	M	R	W		O	M	R	W
Rangaraj	13	5	25	2		9	3	35	1
Rangaiyengar	13.4	9	39	4		14	1	45	2
Thimmappiah	4	2	7	0					
Garudachar	18	4	65	1		25	1	68	5
Vijayasarathi	20	3	78	1		14	7	20	1
Darashah	8	1	25	1	(3)	13	0	39	1
Alasingrachar	1	0	9	0					
Frank	1	0	15	0					

Umpires: M.K.Banerjee, M.Dutta Roy and T.A.Ramachandran. Toss: Mysore

Close of Play: 1st day: Bengal (1) 6-0 (Jabbar 3*, Ganguli 3*); 2nd day: Mysore (2) 49-3 (Rangaraj 14*, Garudachar 0*); 3rd day: Bengal (2) 125-5 (Bhattacharya 57*, Deb 3*).

T.A.Ramachandran was ill and was replaced as umpire by M.Dutta Roy after an hour's play on the first day.

AUCKLAND v WELLINGTON

Played at Eden Park, Auckland, February 6, 7, 9, 1942.

Auckland won by eight wickets.

AUCKLAND					
1	N.Ellis	b Wilson	69	c sub b Allen	61
2	H.G.Walters	b Andrews	81	st Mooney b Riddolls	39
3	*H.T.Pearson	c and b Wilson	8		
4	W.H.Cooper	c Menzies b Allen	28	(3) not out	11
5	B.Sutcliffe	st Mooney b Andrews	11		
6	G.F.Wallace	c Mooney b Osborn	62	(4) not out	7
7	A.C.Kerr	st Mooney b Allen	122		
8	D.R.Garrard	b Andrews	16		
9	H.J.H.Harrison	c Wilson b Duffy	15		
10	†C.K.Q.Jackman	lbw b Duffy	0		
11	H.C.Nottman	not out	24		
	Extras	b 28, lb 4, nb 1	33	b 7	7
			469	(2 wickets)	125

FoW (1): 1-137 (1), 2-153 (3), 3-187, 4-209, 5-209, 6-316, 7-341, 8-372, 9-372, 10-469
FoW (2): 1-93, 2-117

WELLINGTON					
1	R.J.Duffy	lbw b Garrard	26	(5) st Jackman b Kerr	11
2	H.W.Osborn	st Jackman b Sutcliffe	58	(1) run out	25
3	R.E.J.Menzies	c Kerr b Nottman	74	c and b Harrison	76
4	M.A.O'Brien	c Jackman b Kerr	18	c Ellis b Kerr	42
5	*D.S.Wilson	b Garrard	2	(6) c Jackman b Garrard	24
6	†F.L.H.Mooney	c Pearson b Nottman	44	(2) b Kerr	16
7	F.B.Rogers	b Nottman	21	b Nottman	0
8	C.McCarthy	b Nottman	17	c Jackman b Harrison	23
9	A.W.Riddolls	b Harrison	7	b Nottman	23
10	F.M.Andrews	c and b Kerr	20	b Nottman	26
11	R.Allen	not out	2	not out	1
	Extras	b 14, lb 3, nb 1	18	b 11, lb 8	19
			307		286

FoW (1): 1-56, 2-113, 3-149, 4-152, 5-216, 6-245, 7-266, 8-273, 9-301, 10-307
FoW (2): 1-47, 2-50, 3-110, 4-129, 5-169, 6-170, 7-224, 8-237, 9-285, 10-286

Wellington Bowling	O	M	R	W		O	M	R	W
Wilson	23	1	104	2		5	0	31	0
Andrews	30	4	108	3		6	0	30	0
Riddolls	16	0	70	0		6	0	36	1
Allen	14.3	1	97	2		4	0	21	1
Osborn	3	0	26	1					
Duffy	6	0	31	2					

Auckland Bowling	O	M	R	W		O	M	R	W
Nottman	22	0	60	4		22	2	60	3
Kerr	25.5	4	59	2		22	1	100	3
Garrard	26	0	82	2		11	0	42	1
Sutcliffe	3	1	14	1					
Harrison	23	1	74	1	(4)	16	2	44	2
Cooper					(5)	7	2	21	0

Umpires: O.R.Montgomery and R.H.Simmons. Toss: Auckland

Close of Play: 1st day: Wellington (1) 21-0 (Duffy 8*, Osborn 11*); 2nd day: Wellington (2) 14-0 (Osborn 9*, Mooney 0*).

The match was played for the Centennial Cup.

NORTHERN INDIA v BOMBAY

Played at Lawrence Gardens, Lahore, February 13, 14, 15, 16, 1942.

Bombay won by seven wickets.

NORTHERN INDIA

1	Nazar Mohammad	c Raiji b Rangnekar	5	st Mantri b Bhalerao	38
2	D.Jagdish Lal	c Raiji b Rangnekar	7	c Raiji b Tarapore	36
3	Gulzar Mir	c U.M.Merchant b V.M.Merchant	33	st Mantri b Bhalerao	0
4	R.P.Mehra	run out	93	(6) c Mantri b Bhalerao	28
5	Mohammad Sharif	st Mantri b Khot	18	(4) c Khot b Tarapore	0
6	†Anwar Hussain	lbw b Tarapore	22	(5) c and b Tarapore	4
7	*M.Jahangir Khan	c Mantri b Tarapore	5	lbw b Tarapore	29
8	Agha Sarfraz	st Mantri b Khot	2	c Mantri b Tarapore	2
9	Habibullah	c and b Tarapore	9	(10) c Mantri b Khot	44
10	Chuni Lal	st Mantri b Raiji	10	(11) not out	10
11	D.C.Nation	not out	0	(9) lbw b Bhalerao	26
	Extras	b 2, lb 2, w 3	7	lb 7, w 1	8
			211		225

FoW (1): 1-12 (2), 2-20 (1), 3-93 (3), 4-126 (5), 5-165 (6), 6-171 (7), 7-178 (8), 8-196 (4), 9-211 (10), 10-211 (9)
FoW (2): 1-75 (1), 2-75 (2), 3-75 (4), 4-75 (3), 5-90 (5), 6-140 (7), 7-140 (6), 8-144 (8), 9-194 (9), 10-225 (10)

BOMBAY

1	M.F.Mistry	b Chuni Lal	1	run out	9
2	S.M.Kadri	c Mohammad Sharif b Jahangir Khan	2	c Nazar Mohammad b Jahangir Khan	28
3	†M.K.Mantri	b Chuni Lal	35	b Agha Sarfraz	13
4	K.C.Ibrahim	c Mehra b Jahangir Khan	24	not out	69
5	K.K.Tarapore	lbw b Habibullah	10		
6	*V.M.Merchant	c Agha Sarfraz b Jahangir Khan	25	(5) not out	48
7	K.M.Rangnekar	c Chuni Lal b Jahangir Khan	0		
8	J.B.Khot	c Mehra b Chuni Lal	95		
9	U.M.Merchant	b Jahangir Khan	43		
10	M.N.Raiji	not out	1		
11	A.K.Bhalerao	run out	3		
	Extras	b 14, lb 4	18	b 14, lb 3	17
			257	(3 wickets)	184

FoW (1): 1-1 (1), 2-5 (2), 3-74 (4), 4-76 (3), 5-112 (5), 6-112 (6), 7-117 (7), 8-217 (9), 9-253 (8), 10-257 (11)
FoW (2): 1-12 (1), 2-44 (3), 3-70 (2)

Bombay Bowling

	O	M	R	W		O	M	R	W
V.M.Merchant	8	3	19	1		7	0	28	0
Khot	18	4	36	2		14.2	4	31	1
Rangnekar	11	2	31	2		3	0	5	0
Tarapore	18.4	3	46	3		34	7	85	5
Raiji	9	0	50	1		3	0	15	0
Bhalerao	4	0	22	0		27	9	53	4

Northern India Bowling

	O	M	R	W		O	M	R	W
Jahangir Khan	28	9	50	5		24	12	30	1
Chuni Lal	34.5	11	81	3		18	2	52	0
Habibullah	24	6	77	1		12	3	24	0
Agha Sarfraz	9	0	31	0		14	1	42	1
Nazar Mohammad					(5)	4	0	12	0
Mohammad Sharif					(6)	3	1	7	0
Anwar Hussain					(7)	1	1	0	0

Umpires: M.G.Bhave and T.A.Ramachandran. Toss: Northern India

Close of Play: 1st day: Bombay (1) 76-3 (Mantri 35*, Tarapore 1*); 2nd day: Northern India (2) 92-5 (Mehra 11*, Jahangir Khan 2*); 3rd day: Bombay (2) 136-3 (Ibrahim 48*, V.M.Merchant 23*).

UNITED PROVINCES v UNITED PROVINCES GOVERNOR'S XI

Played at Railways Recreation Ground, Lucknow, February 28, March 1, 2, 1942.

United Provinces won by 12 runs.

UNITED PROVINCES					
1	S.Mushtaq Ali	lbw b Nissar	25	c and b Amir Elahi	30
2	E.Alexander	c Amir Elahi b Nissar	10	lbw b Nissar	5
3	*P.E.Palia	c Nazir Ali b Saifuddin	30	lbw b Amarnath	2
4	A.S.N.Murthy	c Maqsood Ali b Saifuddin	6	lbw b Amir Elahi	0
5	J.N.Bhaya	c Amarnath b Amir Elahi	50	(6) run out	5
6	Shamim Khwaja	c Saifuddin b Nissar	30	(5) c Nissar b Amarnath	16
7	Firasat Hussain	c Nissar b Amir Elahi	1	c Amarnath b Amir Elahi	6
8	†S.Mohammad Khan	c Nissar b Amarnath	20	(9) c Rajendra Singh b Amarnath	0
9	S.Murthy	c Aslam Khokhar b Maqsood Ali	37	(8) st Rajendra Singh b Amir Elahi	24
10	Abdul Hamid	b Amir Elahi	7	b Amarnath	4
11	Roop Lal	not out	2	not out	0
	Extras		16		14
			234		106

FoW (1): 1-44, 2-44, 3-83, 4-87, 5-146, 6-149, 7-182, 8-187, 9-231, 10-234
FoW (2): 1-16, 2-33, 3-34, 4-43, 5-59, 6-67, 7-87, 8-92, 9-101, 10-106

UNITED PROVINCES GOVERNOR'S XI					
1	†Rajendra Singh	c sub b S.Murthy	12	(2) c and b Firasat Hussain	13
2	R.Balbhadra Singh	b Firasat Hussain	4	(10) b Palia	0
3	M.M.Jagdale	c Firasat Hussain b Palia	9	(6) lbw b Firasat Hussain	13
4	Aslam Khokhar	c Mushtaq Ali b Palia	38	(1) run out	54
5	S.Nazir Ali	lbw b Firasat Hussain	1	c Alexander b Palia	0
6	Gul Mohammad	c and b Firasat Hussain	8	(4) c Shamim Khwaja b Palia	68
7	L.Amarnath	not out	9	(3) c Mohammad Khan b Palia	43
8	Amir Elahi	c and b Firasat Hussain	1	(7) b Palia	2
9	M.Nissar	run out	0	not out	7
10	Maqsood Ali	st Mohammad Khan b Palia	1	(8) c Shamim Khwaja b Palia	18
11	Saifuddin	b Firasat Hussain	0	run out	0
	Extras		16		11
			99		229

FoW (1): 1-31, 2-36, 3-70, 4-75, 5-85, 6-87, 7-91, 8-91, 9-96, 10-99
FoW (2): 1-31, 2-115, 3-115, 4-115, 5-130, 6-130, 7-220, 8-224, 9-228, 10-229

United Provinces Governor's XI Bowling	O	M	R	W		O	M	R	W
Nissar	17	2	56	3		4	0	19	1
Amarnath	18	2	33	1		18.3	4	37	4
Nazir Ali	6	1	16	0					
Amir Elahi	18.1	0	72	3	(3)	15	4	36	4
Saifuddin	7	2	28	2					
Aslam Khokhar	5	0	11	0					
Maqsood Ali	2	0	2	1					

United Provinces Bowling	O	M	R	W		O	M	R	W
S.Murthy	2	1	5	1		2	0	13	0
Firasat Hussain	17	3	33	5		32	10	66	2
Palia	16	9	12	3		33.5	6	91	6
Alexander	11	3	23	0		5	1	14	0
Mushtaq Ali	2	1	5	0		7	1	31	0
Mohammad Khan	4	1	5	0					
Shamim Khwaja					(6)	1	0	3	0

Umpires: Toss: United Provinces

Close of Play: 1st day: United Provinces Governor's XI (1) 54-2 (Jagdale 7*, Aslam Khokhar 16*); 2nd day: United Provinces Governor's XI (2) 115-3 (Gul Mohammad 0*).

BOMBAY v MYSORE

Played at Brabourne Stadium, Bombay, March 7, 8, 9, 1942.

Bombay won by an innings and 281 runs.

MYSORE					
1	M.B.Rama Rao	c Mantri b Khot	6	st Mantri b Khot	15
2	Y.S.Ramaswami	c Raiji b Khot	4	c Mantri b Khot	7
3	K.Thimmappiah	run out	0	(6) b Bhalerao	2
4	C.J.Ramdev	not out	28	b Bhalerao	28
5	B.K.Garudachar	b Khot	0	b Khot	0
6	B.Frank	c U.M.Merchant b Khot	4	(7) b Khot	61
7	M.G.Vijayasarathi	b Rangnekar	1	(8) c Raiji b Khot	11
8	*†S.Darashah	b Khot	18	(3) b Bhalerao	16
9	G.M.Rajasekhar	c U.M.Merchant b Khot	4	b Bhalerao	3
10	S.Rama Rao	b Raiji	1	b Bhalerao	5
11	H.D.Rangaiyengar	lbw b Raiji	1	not out	4
	Extras	lb 1	1	b 4, w 1	5
			68		157

FoW (1): 1-10 (2), 2-10 (3), 3-11 (1), 4-11 (5), 5-15 (6), 6-18 (7), 7-53 (8), 8-65 (9), 9-66 (10), 10-68 (11)
FoW (2): 1-10 (2), 2-30 (3), 3-47 (1), 4-47 (5), 5-54 (6), 6-119 (4), 7-143 (7), 8-148 (8), 9-148 (9), 10-157 (10)

BOMBAY			
1	M.F.Mistry	c Vijayasarathi b S.RamaRao	93
2	S.M.Kadri	b Rangaiyengar	29
3	†M.K.Mantri	c Vijayasarathi b Garudachar	65
4	K.C.Ibrahim	st M.B.RamaRao b Thimmappiah	117
5	*V.M.Merchant	c Ramdev b Garudachar	60
6	K.M.Rangnekar	b Garudachar	26
7	U.M.Merchant	b Ramaswami	22
8	M.N.Raiji	not out	29
9	A.K.Bhalerao	b Rajasekhar	18
10	J.B.Khot	c Frank b Rajasekhar	3
11	K.K.Tarapore	not out	1
	Extras	b 31, lb 8, nb 4	43
		(9 wickets, declared)	506

FoW (1): 1-61 (2), 2-201 (3), 3-209 (1), 4-335 (5), 5-390 (6), 6-439 (7), 7-456 (4), 8-495 (9), 9-499 (10)

Bombay Bowling	O	M	R	W		O	M	R	W
V.M.Merchant	4	0	9	0		3	0	9	0
Khot	19	8	19	6		19	9	40	5
Rangnekar	7	5	8	1		8	2	23	0
Tarapore	5	1	9	0					
Bhalerao	3	0	10	0	(4)	18.4	3	46	5
Raiji	8.2	5	12	2	(5)	13	3	34	0

Mysore Bowling	O	M	R	W
Garudachar	49	6	161	3
S.RamaRao	20	2	70	1
Rangaiyengar	24	1	66	1
Ramaswami	24	1	81	1
Vijayasarathi	18	2	59	0
Darashah	5	0	13	0
Thimmappiah	2	1	3	1
Frank	1	0	4	0
Rajasekhar	2	0	6	2

Umpires: M.G.Bhave and T.A.Ramachandran. Toss: Mysore

Close of Play: 1st day: Bombay (1) 206-2 (Mistry 93*, Ibrahim 1*); 2nd day: Mysore (2) 33-2 (M.B.RamaRao 7*, Ramdev 2*).

The match was scheduled for five days but completed in three. K.C.Ibrahim's 117 took 205 minutes and included 5 fours.
M.B.Rama Rao took over as wicket-keeper at lunch on the second day.

VICTORIA v QUEENSLAND

Played at Melbourne Cricket Ground, December 19, 20, 22, 1941.

Match cancelled due to war.

SOUTH AUSTRALIA v QUEENSLAND

Played at Adelaide Oval, December 25, 26, 27, 1941.

Match cancelled due to war.

VICTORIA v NEW SOUTH WALES

Played at Melbourne Cricket Ground, December 25, 26, 27, 1941.

Match cancelled due to war.

NEW SOUTH WALES v QUEENSLAND

Played at Sydney Cricket Ground, January 1, 2, 3, 1942.

Match cancelled due to war.

VICTORIA v SOUTH AUSTRALIA

Played at Melbourne Cricket Ground, January 1, 2, 3, 1942.

Match cancelled due to war.

QUEENSLAND v VICTORIA

Played at Brisbane Cricket Ground, Woolloongabba, Brisbane, January 16, 17, 19, 1942.

Match cancelled due to war.

NEW SOUTH WALES v VICTORIA

Played at Sydney Cricket Ground, January 23, 24, 26, 1942.

Match cancelled due to war.

INDEX OF 1941/42 MATCH SCORECARDS

1942

BARBADOS v TRINIDAD

Played at Kensington Oval, Bridgetown, July 18, 20, 21, 1942.

Barbados won by an innings and 178 runs.

BARBADOS

1	G.M.Carew	c Samaroo b Pierre	95
2	†S.O.Gittens	run out	23
3	T.S.Birkett	c Skeete b Jones	17
4	J.E.D.Sealy	b Pierre	36
5	J.D.C.Goddard	b Pierre	7
6	E.A.V.Williams	b J.B.Stollmeyer	13
7	C.L.Walcott	c Tang Choon b Jones	70
8	C.L.Bourne	c Gomez b Pierre	14
9	F.M.M.Worrell	c Samaroo b Jones	48
10	*T.N.M.Peirce	c Pierre b Jones	3
11	L.F.Harris	not out	0
	Extras	b 7, lb 4, w 1, nb 1	13
			339

FoW (1): 1-39, 2-94, 3-161, 4-169, 5-189, 6-204, 7-229, 8-329, 9-337, 10-339

TRINIDAD

1	*V.H.Stollmeyer	b Sealy	4	b Sealy	0
2	A.G.Ganteaume	c Carew b Sealy	9	(3) c Peirce b Sealy	2
3	†S.Samaroo	c Peirce b Sealy	0	(10) c Goddard b Williams	4
4	H.J.B.Burnett	c Peirce b Sealy	0	(8) b Harris	5
5	C.C.R.Skeete	c Goddard b Sealy	0	(6) c Peirce b Williams	21
6	R.P.Tang Choon	b Williams	0	(7) c Goddard b Worrell	1
7	J.B.Stollmeyer	b Williams	0	(2) c Williams b Worrell	36
8	G.E.Gomez	not out	3	(4) c Carew b Williams	47
9	W.F.Waller	c Peirce b Sealy	0	(5) c Gittens b Williams	1
10	P.E.W.Jones	c Peirce b Sealy	0	(9) b Harris	15
11	L.R.Pierre	c Peirce b Sealy	0	not out	4
	Extras			lb 8, nb 1	9
			16		145

FoW (1): 1-6 (1), 2-6 (3), 3-7 (4), 4-7 (5), 5-12 (6), 6-12 (7), 7-16 (2), 8-16 (9), 9-16 (10), 10-16 (11)
FoW (2): 1-0 (1), 2-4 (3), 3-91, 4-93, 5-93, 6-99, 7-116, 8-123, 9-129, 10-145

Trinidad Bowling

	O	M	R	W
Pierre	18	3	67	4
Jones	14.3	1	65	4
Burnett	6	1	27	0
J.B.Stollmeyer	14	1	69	1
Skeete	12	1	59	0
Gomez	4	1	15	0
Tang Choon	3	0	24	0

Barbados Bowling

	O	M	R	W		O	M	R	W
Sealy	6.7	2	8	8		11	2	20	2
Williams	6	2	8	2		11	1	33	4
Goddard					(3)	3	0	16	0
Harris					(4)	8.7	1	29	2
Worrell					(5)	8	0	33	2
Walcott					(6)	3	0	5	0

Umpires: H.C.Griffith and E.L.Ward. Toss: Barbados

Close of Play: 1st day: Barbados (1) 329-7 (Walcott 64*, Worrell 48*); 2nd day: Trinidad (2) 129-8 (Jones 4*, Samaroo 4*).

The match was scheduled for four days but completed in three.

BARBADOS v TRINIDAD

Played at Kensington Oval, Bridgetown, July 25, 27, 28, 29, 1942.

Barbados won by 115 runs.

BARBADOS					
1	G.M.Carew	b Jones	9	(2) c Gomez b J.B.Stollmeyer	13
2	†S.O.Gittens	b Jones	11	(1) lbw b Jones	78
3	C.L.Walcott	c Tang Choon b Ali	67	run out	50
4	J.E.D.Sealy	c Ganteaume b Ali	42	c Tang Choon b Skeete	29
5	J.D.C.Goddard	b Pierre	59	c Samaroo b Jones	29
6	E.A.V.Williams	c Ganteaume b Ali	18		
7	K.E.Walcott	b Pierre	8	not out	19
8	F.M.M.Worrell	b Jones	9	(6) not out	7
9	*T.N.M.Peirce	c Gomez b J.B.Stollmeyer	25		
10	B.D.Inniss	c J.B.Stollmeyer b V.H.Stollmeyer	33		
11	L.F.Harris	not out	3		
	Extras	b 6, lb 3, nb 14	23	b 5	5
			307	(5 wickets, declared)	230

FoW (1): 1-16, 2-30, 3-110, 4-150, 5-194, 6-208, 7-223, 8-266, 9-303, 10-307
FoW (2): 1-38 (2), 2-142, 3-142, 4-196, 5-204

TRINIDAD					
1	*V.H.Stollmeyer	lbw b Williams	42	b Harris	104
2	J.B.Stollmeyer	b Harris	43	(8) st Gittens b Peirce	9
3	A.G.Ganteaume	lbw b Harris	13	(2) st Gittens b Peirce	37
4	G.E.Gomez	lbw b Harris	36	c C.L.Walcott b Peirce	13
5	N.Sarkar	b Worrell	1	(3) lbw b Worrell	5
6	C.C.R.Skeete	lbw b Worrell	0	(5) c and b Peirce	3
7	R.P.Tang Choon	c and b Worrell	41	(6) c and b Harris	13
8	P.E.W.Jones	lbw b Worrell	11	(7) c Gittens b Peirce	10
9	†S.Samaroo	not out	6	c Peirce b Goddard	13
10	S.M.Ali	b Worrell	0	run out	0
11	L.R.Pierre	lbw b Harris	6	not out	0
	Extras	lb 3	3	b 5, lb 1, w 4, nb 3	13
			202		220

FoW (1): 1-80, 2-93, 3-106, 4-109, 5-109, 6-167, 7-190, 8-193, 9-202, 10-202
FoW (2): 1-94 (2), 2-103 (3), 3-128 (4), 4-139 (5), 5-163 (6), 6-180 (7), 7-198 (1), 8-218 (9), 9-219 (10), 10-220 (8)

Trinidad Bowling	O	M	R	W		O	M	R	W
Pierre	17	0	68	2		3	0	22	0
Jones	20	2	66	3		13	2	38	2
J.B.Stollmeyer	8	1	26	1		10.5	1	54	1
Ali	25	5	99	3		8	0	25	0
Skeete	8	1	18	0		6	0	34	1
V.H.Stollmeyer	1.4	0	7	1		3	0	23	0
Gomez					(7)	5	0	29	0

Barbados Bowling	O	M	R	W		O	M	R	W
Sealy	6	0	21	0		8	2	18	0
Williams	12	1	40	1		9	0	35	0
Inniss	8	0	30	0	(4)	2	0	6	0
Worrell	18	7	47	5	(3)	10	1	28	1
Harris	17.5	3	55	4		10	0	44	2
Peirce	1	0	6	0	(7)	16.3	2	54	5
C.L.Walcott					(6)	2	0	15	0
Carew					(8)	2	1	4	0
Goddard					(9)	3	1	3	1

Umpires: H.C.Griffith and E.L.Ward. Toss: Barbados

Close of Play: 1st day: Barbados (1) 242-7 (Goddard 51*, Peirce 7*); 2nd day: Trinidad (1) 80-1 (J.B.Stollmeyer 36*, Ganteaume 0*); 3rd day: Barbados (2) 175-3 (Sealy 17*, Goddard 15*).
S.M.Ali was no-balled for throwing by E.L.Ward 3 times in his first over, 5 times in his first over after lunch (during which he switched to underarm for a few deliveries), 8 times in his next over, and 26 times in all during the innings.

INDEX OF 1942 MATCH SCORECARDS

1942/43

RAJPUTANA v DELHI

Played at Mayo College Ground, Ajmer, November 20, 21, 22, 1942.

Rajputana won by 150 runs.

RAJPUTANA					
1	J.Solomon	run out	5	lbw b Shujauddin	29
2	†D.Mathur	c Ejaz Ahmed b Idrees Baig	5	lbw b Ejaz Ahmed	0
3	Basant Singh	c Idrees Baig b Kamal	13	not out	110
4	H.Vohra	b Idrees Baig	90	lbw b Ejaz Ahmed	11
5	Attique Hussain	b Ejaz Ahmed	23	lbw b Ejaz Ahmed	0
6	G.R.Naidoo	b Ejaz Ahmed	8	lbw b Ejaz Ahmed	35
7	Ahmed Ali Khan	c Idrees Baig b Ejaz Ahmed	12	b Shujauddin	1
8	*N.P.Kesari	lbw b Idrees Baig	9	c Ejaz Ahmed b Sen	4
9	Azimuddin	lbw b Idrees Baig	0	lbw b Idrees Baig	5
10	Ghulam Mohiuddin	c Idrees Baig b Ejaz Ahmed	4	lbw b Idrees Baig	0
11	Maula Bux	not out	4	st Khalil-ur-Rehman b Ejaz Ahmed	1
	Extras		7		11
			180		207

FoW (1): 1- , 2- , 3- , 4- , 5- , 6- , 7- , 8- , 9- , 10-180
FoW (2): 1- , 2- , 3- , 4- , 5- , 6- , 7- , 8- , 9- , 10-207

DELHI					
1	F.S.R.Johnson	b Kesari	3	(6) lbw b Ahmed Ali Khan	0
2	Saleem	c Mathur b Kesari	13	(1) run out	47
3	A.Kamal	lbw b Kesari	19	(7) lbw b Ahmed Ali Khan	0
4	Idrees Baig	b Naidoo	39	not out	45
5	Ejaz Ahmed	b Maula Bux	6	c Naidoo b Attique Hussain	2
6	M.H.Maqsood	c Attique Hussain b Maula Bux	7	(3) lbw b Naidoo	4
7	Ishwar Lal	c Mathur b Naidoo	1	(8) lbw b Ahmed Ali Khan	1
8	Shujauddin	not out	13	(10) c Kesari b Attique Hussain	0
9	J.Sen	c Solomon b Kesari	6	b Ahmed Ali Khan	0
10	†Khalil-ur-Rehman	run out	1	(2) lbw b Maula Bux	0
11	*A.S.de Mello	b Kesari	4	c Attique Hussain b Naidoo	4
	Extras		12		10
			124		113

FoW (1): 1- , 2- , 3- , 4- , 5- , 6- , 7- , 8- , 9- , 10-124
FoW (2): 1- , 2- , 3- , 4- , 5- , 6- , 7- , 8- , 9- , 10-113

Delhi Bowling	O	M	R	W		O	M	R	W
Idrees Baig	17.5	4	36	4	(2)	26	6	46	2
Ejaz Ahmed	16	2	65	4	(1)	24.1	3	67	5
de Mello	3	1	10	0					
Shujauddin	3	1	3	0		15	3	37	2
Sen	6	0	29	0	(3)	8	0	26	1
Kamal	3	0	15	1	(5)	4	0	13	0
Maqsood	4	0	15	0	(6)	3	0	7	0

Rajputana Bowling	O	M	R	W		O	M	R	W
Maula Bux	15	1	53	2		8	0	23	1
Kesari	15.1	4	33	5		6	0	24	0
Naidoo	6	3	5	2		5.4	0	14	2
Attique Hussain	4	0	21	0	(5)	10	1	24	2
Ghulam Mohiuddin	1	1	0	0	(6)	1	1	0	0
Ahmed Ali Khan					(4)	8	3	18	4

Umpires: Toss: Delhi

Close of Play: 1st day: Delhi (1) 109-7 (Shujauddin 9*, Sen 4*); 2nd day: Delhi (2) ?-?.

Basant Singh's 110 included 11 fours.

WESTERN INDIA v NAWANAGAR

Played at Jafar Maidan, Junagadh, November 28, 29, 30, 1942.

Western India won by eight wickets.

NAWANAGAR					
1	I.Oza	b Gandhi	8	(2) b Saeed Ahmed	18
2	J.R.Oza	c Prataprai b Saeed Ahmed	47	(1) c Kishenchand b Jayantilal Vora	32
3	R.K.Yadvendrasinhji	b Saeed Ahmed	26	(8) c Prataprai b Kishenchand	2
4	R.K.Indravijaysinhji	lbw b Saeed Ahmed	16	st Prataprai b Kishenchand	4
5	K.Mankad	b Saeed Ahmed	2	c Umar Khan b Chippa	33
6	*M.S.Samarsinhji	b Saeed Ahmed	25	c Chippa b Kishenchand	18
7	Bhagwat Singh	b Saeed Ahmed	5	(3) c Gandhi b Chippa	42
8	Mangal Singh	c Gandhi b Dilawar Khanji	2	(9) b Gandhi	27
9	†K.Mehta	c Kishenchand b Dilawar Khanji	4	(11) not out	14
10	Mubarak Ali	not out	64	(7) c Jayantilal Vora b Kishenchand	0
11	Hira Singh	run out	0	(10) c Umar Khan b Kishenchand	0
	Extras		26		17
			225		207

FoW (1): 1- , 2- , 3- , 4- , 5- , 6- , 7- , 8- , 9- , 10-225
FoW (2): 1- , 2- , 3- , 4- , 5- , 6- , 7- , 8- , 9- , 10-207

WESTERN INDIA					
1	†Prataprai	b Hira Singh	28	c Bhagwat Singh b J.R.Oza	30
2	Jayantilal Vora	b J.R.Oza	27		
3	Umar Khan	c Bhagwat Singh b J.R.Oza	79	(2) not out	24
4	G.Kishenchand	c Indravijaysinhji b J.R.Oza	17	not out	5
5	*M.DilawarKhanji	c Bhagwat Singh b J.R.Oza	1		
6	Prithviraj	c Mubarak Ali b Mangal Singh	109		
7	Saeed Ahmed	lbw b Bhagwat Singh	31		
8	S.B.Gandhi	c Mehta b Mubarak Ali	14		
9	Purshottam	c Mankad b Mubarak Ali	24		
10	Gatoor	not out	10	(3) c Mankad b Mubarak Ali	27
11	U.R.Chippa	c Mangal Singh b J.R.Oza	1		
	Extras		9		2
			350	(2 wickets)	88

FoW (1): 1- , 2- , 3- , 4- , 5- , 6- , 7- , 8- , 9- , 10-350
FoW (2): 1- , 2-

Western India Bowling	O	M	R	W		O	M	R	W
Dilawar Khanji	7	0	48	2		3	1	8	0
Saeed Ahmed	27	8	61	6		16	10	15	1
Chippa	29	13	61	0		34	14	54	2
Gandhi	7	1	16	1		9.2	0	22	1
Kishenchand	5	0	9	0		16	1	67	5
Jayantilal Vora	3	1	4	0		11	6	14	1
Purshottam					(7)	2	0	10	0

Nawanagar Bowling	O	M	R	W		O	M	R	W
Mubarak Ali	27	4	93	2		6	0	34	1
Mangal Singh	13	4	43	1		1	0	16	0
J.R.Oza	58.5	23	93	5		7	1	28	1
Hira Singh	29	10	70	1					
Bhagwat Singh	13	4	33	1	(4)	2	1	8	0
Mankad	1	0	9	0					

Umpires: M.J.Abdulla and Vali Ahmed. Toss: Nawanagar

Close of Play: 1st day: Western India (1) 81-2 (Umar Khan not out, Kishenchand not out); 2nd day: Nawanagar (2) 17-0 (J.R.Oza not out, I.Oza not out).

Prithviraj's 109 included 16 fours.

BENGAL v BIHAR

Played at Eden Gardens, Calcutta, December 12, 13, 14, 1942.

Match drawn.

BIHAR

1	S.Bagchi	lbw b P.D.Dutt	75	c Ganguli b Cooch Behar	0
2	H.D.Edmunds	lbw b Bhattacharya	1	b S.Dutt	22
3	K.Bose	c Tamplin b P.D.Dutt	24	(5) c Harvey-Johnston b Cooch Behar	21
4	*S.N.Banerjee	lbw b Chatterjee	15	(3) c Mustafi b Bhattacharya	21
5	S.Banerjee	c S.Dutt b Cooch Behar	34	(4) b S.Dutt	28
6	B.Sen	not out	56	(8) not out	26
7	N.Kumar	b Mustafi	3	(6) lbw b Cooch Behar	15
8	K.Ghosh	c Mustafi b Cooch Behar	36	(7) st Tamplin b S.Dutt	5
9	D.S.Khambatta	c Mustafi b Cooch Behar	0	(10) run out	21
10	N.R.Chowdhury	st Tamplin b S.Dutt	1	(11) not out	3
11	†Lunn	c Tamplin b P.D.Dutt	0	(9) c Bhattacharya b Cooch Behar	1
	Extras		26		13
			271	(9 wickets, declared)	176

FoW (1): 1-18 (2), 2-93 (3), 3-124 (4), 4-128 (1), 5-194 (5), 6-214 (7), 7-255 (8), 8-255 (9), 9-270 (10), 10-271 (11)
FoW (2): 1-0 (1), 2-41 (3), 3-79 (4), 4-80 (2), 5-103 (6), 6-110 (7), 7-128 (5), 8-140 (9), 9-169 (10)

BENGAL

1	A.Jabbar	b S.N.Banerjee	2	(2) b Ghosh	21
2	S.K.Ganguli	c Lunn b Chowdhury	0	(1) c Lunn b Chowdhury	9
3	K.Bhattacharya	b Chowdhury	11	c S.Banerjee b Chowdhury	6
4	N.C.Chatterjee	c Lunn b Chowdhury	104	not out	64
5	E.C.Harvey-Johnston	c Khambatta b Chowdhury	87	not out	8
6	*N.M.Bose	c Edmunds b S.N.Banerjee	5		
7	Maharaja of Cooch Behar	not out	71		
8	S.K.Mustafi	lbw b S.N.Banerjee	6		
9	P.D.Dutt	c S.Banerjee b Chowdhury	11		
10	†C.Tamplin	c Bose b Chowdhury	0		
11	S.Dutt	b Chowdhury	4		
	Extras		11		12
			312	(3 wickets)	120

FoW (1): 1-0 (2), 2-4 (1), 3-18 (3), 4-179 (5), 5-188 (6), 6-242 (4), 7-253 (8), 8-302 (9), 9-302 (10), 10-312 (11)
FoW (2): 1-14 (1), 2-20 (3), 3-76 (2)

Bengal Bowling

	O	M	R	W		O	M	R	W
Mustafi	23	8	50	1	(2)	3	0	12	0
Cooch Behar	23	14	29	3	(1)	16	3	42	4
Bhattacharya	14	1	37	1		9	0	43	1
P.D.Dutt	22	6	38	3		6	0	23	0
S.Dutt	15	3	56	1		10	1	43	3
Chatterjee	12	2	35	1					

Bihar Bowling

	O	M	R	W		O	M	R	W
S.N.Banerjee	25	3	92	3		6	0	30	0
S.Banerjee	14	1	49	0		6	2	24	0
Bagchi	3	0	25	0					
Chowdhury	27.4	3	100	7	(3)	10	2	16	2
Khambatta	6	1	17	0	(4)	2	1	1	0
Edmunds	2	0	18	0					
Kumar					(5)	5	1	11	0
Ghosh					(6)	3	0	26	1

Umpires: M.K.Banerjee and K.Chatterjee. Toss: Bihar

Close of Play: 1st day: Bihar (1) 247-6 (Sen 47*, Ghosh 29*); 2nd day: Bengal (1) 280-7 (Cooch Behar 49*, P.D.Dutt 7*).

N.C.Chatterjee's 104 included 10 fours.

SIND v WESTERN INDIA

Played at Karachi Gymkhana Ground, December 18, 19, 1942.

Western India won by nine wickets.

SIND					
1	F.G.Lakda	b Gandhi	0	(11) b Gandhi	0
2	†J.K.Irani	c Prithviraj b Nyalchand	8	(1) c Prataprai b Chippa	28
3	Qamaruddin Sheikh	b Jayantilal Vora	47	c Gandhi b Chippa	11
4	Naoomal Jaoomal	c Prataprai b Chippa	5	(6) c Prataprai b Chippa	21
5	Daud Khan	c Kishenchand b Chippa	1	(8) b Gandhi	17
6	H.M.Asha	not out	20	(5) run out	14
7	*M.J.Mobed	run out	5	(10) not out	7
8	S.K.Girdhari	c Prithviraj b Gandhi	0	(4) c Prithviraj b Nyalchand	0
9	Hyder Ali	lbw b Gandhi	8	b Gandhi	0
10	V.K.Samtani	c Kishenchand b Chippa	22	(7) b Nyalchand	0
11	Ibrahim Vazir	b Gandhi	0	(2) c Umar Khan b Gandhi	6
	Extras		2		2
			118		106

FoW (1): 1-0 (1), 2-16 (2), 3-29 (4), 4-63 (3), 5-66 (5), 6- (7), 7- (8), 8- (9), 9- (10), 10-118 (11)
FoW (2): 1-9 (2), 2-38 (3), 3-39 (4), 4-51 (1), 5-72 (5), 6-73 (7), 7-94 (6), 8- (9), 9- (8), 10-106 (11)

WESTERN INDIA					
1	†Prataprai	lbw b Ibrahim Vazir	11	c Daud Khan b Hyder Ali	1
2	Jayantilal Vora	c Girdhari b Samtani	4		
3	Umar Khan	c Irani b Hyder Ali	46		
4	Gatoor	c Qamaruddin Sheikh b Samtani	23		
5	G.Kishenchand	not out	57		
6	Prithviraj	b Lakda	22		
7	*K.S.G.Limbdi	c and b Lakda	9		
8	Purshottam	b Samtani	2	(2) not out	12
9	S.B.Gandhi	c Qamaruddin Sheikh b Samtani	1	(3) not out	12
10	U.R.Chippa	c Mobed b Hyder Ali	6		
11	S.Nyalchand	b Hyder Ali	0		
	Extras		19		2
			200	(1 wicket)	27

FoW (1): 1-9 (2), 2- (1), 3-94 (4), 4-104 (3), 5-147 (6), 6-163 (7), 7-175 (8), 8-183 (9), 9- (10), 10-200 (11)
FoW (2): 1- (1)

Western India Bowling	O	M	R	W		O	M	R	W
Gandhi	14.2	4	34	4		8	1	27	4
Nyalchand	19	8	39	1		11	4	39	2
Chippa	27	11	41	3		10	3	25	3
Jayantilal Vora	3	2	2	1					
Purshottam					(4)	5	1	13	0

Sind Bowling	O	M	R	W		O	M	R	W
Samtani	23	6	49	4		3	0	10	0
Hyder Ali	24	10	39	3		3	1	6	1
Mobed	9	5	13	0					
Naoomal Jaoomal	5	4	3	0					
Ibrahim Vazir	16	3	34	1	(4)	1	0	4	0
Lakda	16	4	31	2	(3)	1	0	5	0
Girdhari	5	1	12	0					

Umpires: D.K.Naik and J.R.Patel. Toss:

Close of Play: 1st day: Western India (1) 93-2 (Umar Khan 40*, Gatoor 23*).

The match was scheduled for three days but completed in two. 35 runs were added for the 9th wicket in the Sind first innings (H.M.Asha and V.K.Samtani).

AIR FORCE XI v THE REST

Played at Old Wanderers, Johannesburg, December 26, 27, 1942.

The Rest won by five wickets.

AIR FORCE XI					
1	†G.M.Larkin	lbw b Heaney	24	c Fullerton b Gordon	38
2	O.W.Grinaker	c Georgeu b Gordon	15	c Somers Vine b Petersen	73
3	A.F.Townsend	b Gordon	14	lbw b Gordon	0
4	E.W.Sturgess	b Heaney	0	c Heaney b Warne	45
5	*W.R.Hammond	lbw b Gordon	60	c Georgeu b Petersen	18
6	E.V.Witte	not out	38	b Petersen	9
7	T.A.Harris	b Gordon	2	b Heaney	41
8	W.A.Sime	c Fullerton b Gordon	1	not out	39
9	C.L.Vincent	lbw b Warne	4	not out	1
10	W.N.Mercer	hit wkt b Warne	0		
11	J.Sant	st Fullerton b Warne	1		
	Extras		13		2
			172	(7 wickets, declared)	266

FoW (1): 1-39, 2-39, 3-39, 4-77, 5-137, 6- , 7-147, 8- , 9- , 10-172
FoW (2): 1-58 (1), 2-58 (3), 3-153, 4-175, 5-175, 6-195, 7-263

THE REST					
1	S.H.Curnow	c Hammond b Sturgess	117	b Sturgess	30
2	F.B.Warne	b Vincent	108	c Harris b Sturgess	2
3	†G.M.Fullerton	c and b Mercer	9	b Sturgess	13
4	E.D.Jenkins	c Hammond b Vincent	23	not out	41
5	*R.E.Somers Vine	lbw b Sturgess	3	b Vincent	8
6	G.Georgeu	not out	42	b Vincent	8
7	F.F.Flanagan	b Sturgess	0	not out	15
8	S.F.Viljoen	b Vincent	12		
9	R.N.E.Petersen	c Mercer b Sime	5		
10	L.J.Heaney	b Mercer	1		
11	N.Gordon	st Larkin b Mercer	0		
	Extras		3		
			323	(5 wickets)	117

FoW (1): 1-206 (2), 2-227 (1), 3-240 (3), 4-260, 5-262, 6-267, 7-305, 8-319, 9-323, 10-323
FoW (2): 1-22 (2), 2-45, 3-46, 4-66, 5-84

The Rest Bowling	O	M	R	W		O	M	R	W
Viljoen	5	2	13	0		3	0	13	0
Petersen	4	1	16	0	(7)	7	0	39	3
Heaney	11	0	33	2	(2)	14	2	48	1
Gordon	16	2	61	5	(3)	16.3	2	50	2
Warne	8.1	1	25	3	(4)	13	0	84	1
Jenkins	3	0	11	0		4	0	18	0
Somers Vine					(5)	3	0	12	0

Air Force XI Bowling	O	M	R	W		O	M	R	W
Sime	13	1	74	1					
Sturgess	19	1	82	3		6	0	39	3
Hammond	2	1	5	0					
Vincent	20	4	79	3	(3)	3	0	34	2
Witte	12	1	36	0	(1)	9.3	1	44	0
Mercer	4.4	0	31	3					
Harris	3	0	13	0					

Umpires: Toss: Air Force XI

Close of Play: 1st day: The Rest (1) 249-3 (Jenkins not out, Somers Vine not out).

S.H.Curnow's 117 included 18 fours and 1 six. F.B.Warne's 108 took 145 minutes and included 15 fours.

EUROPEANS v INDIANS

Played at Madras Cricket Club Ground, Chepauk, Madras, December 26, 27, 1942.

Europeans won by eight wickets.

INDIANS					
1	V.N.Madhava Rao	c Johnstone b Versey-Brown	13	b Versey-Brown	2
2	M.Swaminathan	c Robinson b Weymouth	56	c Nailer b Robinson	15
3	Raja of Ramnad	c de Kretser b Robinson	8	c Nailer b Blunt	4
4	C.K.Nainakannu	b Weymouth	13	c Edge b Blunt	0
5	A.G.Ram Singh	c Johnstone b Blunt	54	lbw b Robinson	27
6	K.S.Kannan	b Weymouth	4	c Mischler b Weymouth	8
7	N.J.Venkatesan	c Law b Blunt	16	(8) st Edge b Robinson	5
8	*M.J.Gopalan	st Mischler b Weymouth	87	(7) b Robinson	2
9	†M.O.Srinivasan	c Edge b Robinson	10	c Lindley-Jones b Robinson	23
10	T.S.Parankusam	not out	0	run out	27
11	C.R.Rangachari	c and b Robinson	0	not out	1
	Extras		7		3
			268		117

FoW (1): 1-18 (1), 2-57 (3), 3-76 (4), 4-124 (2), 5-149 (5), 6-153 (6), 7-223 (7), 8-266 (8), 9-268 (9), 10-268 (11)
FoW (2): 1-2 (1), 2-12 (3), 3-16 (4), 4-40 (2), 5-57 (5), 6-59 (6), 7-62 (7), 8-67 (8), 9-114 (9), 10-117 (10)

EUROPEANS					
1	*C.P.Johnstone	run out	75	st Srinivasan b Ram Singh	51
2	G.B.Edge	b Rangachari	4	c and b Parankusam	31
3	E.F.E.de Kretser	b Ram Singh	43		
4	M.Robinson	st Srinivasan b Venkatesan	32	(3) not out	27
5	R.S.Nailer	c Ram Singh b Parankusam	4	(4) not out	31
6	†N.M.Mischler	b Ram Singh	38		
7	J.A.G.C.Law	c Madhava Rao b Ram Singh	11		
8	H.M.Lindley-Jones	b Rangachari	3		
9	E.W.Weymouth	not out	14		
10	J.S.Versey-Brown	st Srinivasan b Ram Singh	3		
11	L.Blunt	c Srinivasan b Rangachari	0		
	Extras		15		4
			242	(2 wickets)	144

FoW (1): 1-38 (2), 2-115 (1), 3-139 (3), 4-145 (5), 5-175 (4), 6-213 (6), 7-220 (7), 8-226 (8), 9-242 (10), 10-242 (11)
FoW (2): 1-51 (2), 2-96 (1)

Europeans Bowling	O	M	R	W		O	M	R	W
Versey-Brown	22	7	50	1		8	0	31	1
Blunt	21	4	53	2		12	1	28	2
Johnstone	6	0	31	0		3	1	5	0
Robinson	12	0	45	3		13.1	5	27	5
Weymouth	19	2	54	4		6	0	23	1
de Kretser	5	0	28	0					

Indians Bowling	O	M	R	W		O	M	R	W
Ram Singh	22	1	60	4		7	1	30	1
Rangachari	25.2	7	68	3		7	0	29	0
Kannan	6	2	12	0		3	0	13	0
Venkatesan	11	0	51	1		3	0	21	0
Parankusam	12	3	26	1		5	0	24	1
Swaminathan	1	0	10	0					
Gopalan					(6)	10	1	23	0

Umpires: L.O'Callaghan and T.A.Ramachandran. Toss: Indians

Close of Play: 1st day: Europeans (1) 115-1 (Johnstone 75*, de Kretser 30*).

The match was scheduled for three days but completed in two. G.B.Edge kept wicket in the Indians second innings.

BARODA v MAHARASHTRA

Played at Central College Ground, Baroda, January 2, 3, 4, 1943.

Baroda won by eight wickets.

MAHARASHTRA					
1	†M.K.Mantri	c Indulkar b Vijay S.Hazare	12	(7) c Adhikari b Sheikh	7
2	S.W.Sohoni	c Naidu b Vijay S.Hazare	82	c Indulkar b Sheikh	56
3	V.M.Pandit	c Indulkar b Vivek S.Hazare	13	(1) c Nimbalkar b Gaekwar	6
4	C.T.Sarwate	lbw b Nayudu	12	(9) st Nimbalkar b Nayudu	7
5	*D.B.Deodhar	b Nayudu	49	(4) c Adhikari b Nayudu	64
6	D.G.Phadkar	run out	30	(8) not out	15
7	M.N.Paranjpe	c Indulkar b Vijay S.Hazare	8	(3) b Vijay S.Hazare	27
8	S.R.Arolkar	c and b Nayudu	11	(6) run out	3
9	D.S.Doctor	c Nayudu b Vijay S.Hazare	18	(5) run out	23
10	M.E.Z.Ghazali	c Vijay S.Hazare b Vivek S.Hazare	15	st Nimbalkar b Nayudu	11
11	S.G.Shinde	not out	7	c Sheikh b Nayudu	0
	Extras		5		5
			262		224

FoW (1): 1- , 2- , 3-89, 4-165, 5- , 6- , 7- , 8- , 9- , 10-262
FoW (2): 1-17, 2-60, 3-134, 4-170, 5-176, 6-190, 7-195, 8-206, 9-224, 10-224

BARODA					
1	Y.E.Sheikh	lbw b Shinde	25	lbw b Shinde	24
2	M.S.Indulkar	c Mantri b Phadkar	11		
3	M.M.Naidu	c Pandit b Sohoni	5		
4	†R.B.Nimbalkar	c Sohoni b Sarwate	20	(3) not out	100
5	Vijay S.Hazare	c Ghazali b Phadkar	44	(4) not out	32
6	H.R.Adhikari	run out	44		
7	C.S.Nayudu	c Sohoni b Sarwate	16		
8	*W.N.Ghorpade	not out	60		
9	S.G.Powar	lbw b Shinde	19	(2) lbw b Shinde	22
10	K.S.Gaekwar	run out	3		
11	Vivek S.Hazare	c Ghazali b Sohoni	10		
	Extras		51		8
			308	(2 wickets)	186

FoW (1): 1- , 2- , 3- , 4-81, 5-158, 6-189, 7- , 8- , 9- , 10-308
FoW (2): 1-50, 2-60

Baroda Bowling	O	M	R	W		O	M	R	W
Gaekwar	16	7	38	0		6	0	23	1
Vijay S.Hazare	35	12	57	4		9	0	55	1
Nayudu	40	5	129	3		17.3	0	75	4
Vivek S.Hazare	9	0	16	2		3	0	13	0
Adhikari	3	0	7	0					
Sheikh	7	2	10	0	(5)	12	0	53	2

Maharashtra Bowling	O	M	R	W		O	M	R	W
Sohoni	19.1	5	42	2		7	1	25	0
Phadkar	12	4	17	2		3	1	9	0
Sarwate	40	8	85	2	(5)	16	2	53	0
Shinde	32	4	87	2		18	4	36	2
Ghazali	7	1	18	0	(3)	8	2	31	0
Arolkar	2	0	8	0		4	1	11	0
Deodhar					(7)	2.1	0	13	0

Umpires: Toss:

Close of Play: 1st day: Baroda (1) 17-2; 2nd day: Maharashtra (2) 19-1 (Sohoni 11*, Paranjpe 2*).

R.B.Nimbalkar's 100 took 86 minutes and included 9 fours and 1 six. Baroda batted on after winning so that Nimbalkar could reach his century. The score details at the point of winning are not known.

HYDERABAD v MYSORE

Played at Railways Recreation Club Ground, Secunderabad, January 9, 10, 11, 1943.

Hyderabad won by 162 runs.

HYDERABAD					
1	Asadullah Qureshi	b Garudachar	22	c Krishnaswamy b Darashah	16
2	S.R.Mehta	b Garudachar	48	c Frank b Rama Rao	8
3	E.B.Aibara	b Darashah	12	lbw b Garudachar	17
4	B.C.Khanna	b Garudachar	74	c Garudachar b Darashah	2
5	*S.M.Hussain	run out	0	(6) c Darashah b Rama Rao	23
6	Asghar Ali	c Garudachar b Vijayasarathi	17	(5) c Garudachar b Rama Rao	22
7	Ushaq Ahmed	lbw b Garudachar	0	(8) b Darashah	9
8	†I.Sanjiva Rao	lbw b Garudachar	1	(9) b Darashah	12
9	R.K.Rao	c and b Ethinder	17	(7) b Garudachar	13
10	Ghulam Ahmed	lbw b Garudachar	27	c Rama Rao b Darashah	13
11	A.R.Bhupathi	not out	13	not out	0
	Extras		29		18
			260		153

FoW (1): 1-57 (1), 2-74 (3), 3-120 (2), 4-120 (5), 5-173 (6), 6- (7), 7- (8), 8-205 (4), 9- (9), 10-260 (10)
FoW (2): 1- , 2- , 3- , 4- , 5- , 6- , 7- , 8- , 9- , 10-153

MYSORE					
1	M.B.Krishna Rao	lbw b Mehta	13	b Ushaq Ahmed	13
2	P.G.Doraiswami	lbw b Ghulam Ahmed	18	(5) b Mehta	0
3	A.Ethinder	not out	68	c Mehta b Ghulam Ahmed	2
4	B.K.Garudachar	c Ghulam Ahmed b Bhupathi	56	(6) lbw b Mehta	12
5	B.Frank	lbw b Bhupathi	0	(7) c Asadullah Qureshi b Bhupathi	9
6	K.Thimmappiah	c Hussain b Ghulam Ahmed	12	(8) not out	11
7	M.G.Vijayasarathi	b Ghulam Ahmed	0	(9) b Mehta	0
8	*S.Darashah	b Ghulam Ahmed	0	(2) c Asadullah Qureshi b Bhupathi	12
9	K.L.Ranganath	c Sanjiva Rao b Bhupathi	0	(4) c Sanjiva Rao b Mehta	0
10	S.Rama Rao	b Mehta	9	c Hussain b Bhupathi	2
11	E.Krishnaswamy	b Ghulam Ahmed	2	b Bhupathi	0
	Extras		5		7
			183		68

FoW (1): 1-30 (1), 2-32 (2), 3-118, 4- , 5- , 6- , 7- , 8- , 9- , 10-183
FoW (2): 1- , 2- , 3- , 4- , 5- , 6- , 7- , 8- , 9- , 10-68

Mysore Bowling	O	M	R	W	O	M	R	W
Darashah	21	4	61	1	16.5	2	44	5
Rama Rao	14	6	33	0	12	3	22	3
Garudachar	28.2	5	69	6	21	3	53	2
Vijayasarathi	20	6	47	1	4	1	11	0
Ethinder	4	0	16	1	1	0	5	0
Thimmappiah	1	0	5	0				

Hyderabad Bowling	O	M	R	W	O	M	R	W
Ghulam Ahmed	21.2	6	45	5	5	2	10	1
Bhupathi	28	4	70	3	11.2	5	18	4
Mehta	16	3	30	2	15	5	18	4
Ushaq Ahmed	4	1	6	0	4	1	6	1
Khanna	11	4	21	0	3	0	9	0
Asadullah Qureshi	5	1	6	0				

Umpires: Toss: Hyderabad

Close of Play: 1st day: Mysore (1) 32-2 (Ethinder 1*); 2nd day: Hyderabad (2) 152-8.

UNITED PROVINCES v HOLKAR

Played at Railways Recreation Ground, Lucknow, January 9, 10, 11, 1943.

Holkar won by seven wickets.

UNITED PROVINCES					
1	Firasat Hussain	lbw b Jagdale	67	c Dotiwala b Jagdale	0
2	*P.E.Palia	c Nayudu b Jagdale	16	c Nayudu b Jagdale	2
3	B.P.Telang	b Nayudu	9	c sub b Jagdale	0
4	J.P.Phansalkar	b Nayudu	28	b Jagdale	50
5	Shamim Khwaja	st Navle b Nayudu	41	c Yarde b Salim Khan	23
6	Abdul Hamid	c Singh b Salim Khan	22	(8) c Ishtiaq Ali b Jagdale	36
7	H.A.Butler	c Singh b Jagdale	1	(10) c Salim Khan b Jagdale	11
8	†Wahidullah	lbw b Nayudu	1	(7) c Nayudu b Jagdale	32
9	B.Ramchandra	not out	4	(6) run out	1
10	Fazal Halim	b Salim Khan	0	(9) lbw b Nayudu	9
11	E.Alexander	run out	0	not out	1
	Extras		23		13
			212		178

FoW (1): 1- , 2- , 3- , 4- , 5- , 6- , 7- , 8- , 9- , 10-212
FoW (2): 1- , 2- , 3- , 4- , 5- , 6- , 7- , 8- , 9- , 10-178

HOLKAR					
1	D.K.Yarde	lbw b Alexander	0	lbw b Palia	7
2	S.Dotiwala	c Firasat Hussain b Ramchandra	4		
3	S.Ishtiaq Ali	c Firasat Hussain b Ramchandra	0		
4	S.R.Kale	c Wahidullah b Palia	21	(2) b Palia	0
5	S.Mushtaq Ali	not out	66	(3) b Alexander	113
6	M.M.Jagdale	c Phansalkar b Alexander	1	(4) not out	70
7	*C.K.Nayudu	b Alexander	7	(5) not out	81
8	J.N.Bhaya	c Palia b Alexander	1		
9	†J.G.Navle	c Wahidullah b Alexander	2		
10	R.P.Singh	b Firasat Hussain	5		
11	M.Salim Khan	b Alexander	0		
	Extras		2		11
			109	(3 wickets)	282

FoW (1): 1- , 2- , 3-9, 4- , 5- , 6- , 7- , 8- , 9- , 10-109
FoW (2): 1-1 (2), 2-75 (1), 3-164 (3)

Holkar Bowling	O	M	R	W		O	M	R	W
Jagdale	27	6	47	3		25.3	3	65	7
Mushtaq Ali	16	8	21	0	(3)	5	3	5	0
Nayudu	28.5	5	68	4	(2)	19	4	59	1
Salim Khan	20	2	52	2		13	2	36	1
Singh	1	0	1	0					

United Provinces Bowling	O	M	R	W		O	M	R	W
Alexander	19.3	2	55	6		25	2	94	1
Ramchandra	5	0	15	2		10	4	11	0
Firasat Hussain	12	3	22	1	(4)	22	4	61	0
Palia	6	0	15	1	(3)	31	8	82	2
Telang					(5)	3	0	23	0

Umpires: M.K.Banerjee and M.Dutta Roy. Toss:

Close of Play: 1st day: Holkar (1) 9-3 (Kale 5*); 2nd day: Holkar (2) 1-0 (Yarde 0*, Kale 0*, 4 overs).

WESTERN INDIA v BARODA

Played at European Gymkhana Ground, Rajkot, January 29, 30, 31, 1943.

Baroda won by 4 runs.

BARODA					
1	Y.E.Sheikh	c Dilawar Khanji b Saeed Ahmed	33	lbw b Saeed Ahmed	15
2	†R.B.Nimbalkar	c and b Kishenchand	71	(5) c Dilawar Khanji b Chippa	10
3	H.R.Adhikari	c Umar Khan b Saeed Ahmed	14	lbw b Nyalchand	10
4	Vijay S.Hazare	c Prithviraj b Gandhi	73	c Prataprai b Chippa	43
5	C.S.Nayudu	c Gandhi b Nyalchand	3	(6) c Umar Khan b Chippa	7
6	*W.N.Ghorpade	b Nyalchand	1	(7) c Umar Khan b Nyalchand	6
7	M.S.Indulkar	b Nyalchand	2	(2) c Kishenchand b Gandhi	3
8	M.M.Naidu	b Nyalchand	20	c Umar Khan b Nyalchand	2
9	S.G.Powar	b Nyalchand	13	not out	28
10	A.Patel	b Nyalchand	0	(11) st Prataprai b Nyalchand	0
11	Vivek S.Hazare	not out	0	(10) b Nyalchand	0
	Extras		15		11
			245		135

FoW (1): 1-101 (2), 2- (1), 3- (3), 4- (5), 5- (6), 6- (7), 7- (8), 8- (9), 9- (10), 10-245 (4)
FoW (2): 1-17 (2), 2-22 (1), 3-36 (3), 4-59 (5), 5-72 (6), 6-79 (7), 7-83 (8), 8-123 (4), 9-125 (10), 10-135 (11)

WESTERN INDIA					
1	†Prataprai	b Vijay S.Hazare	21	c Vivek S.Hazare b Nayudu	2
2	Gatoor	lbw b Nayudu	16	run out	0
3	Umar Khan	lbw b Vijay S.Hazare	9	c Adhikari b Nayudu	15
4	G.Kishenchand	c Nimbalkar b Nayudu	10	(5) b Nayudu	55
5	Prithviraj	c Indulkar b Vijay S.Hazare	3	(6) b Vivek S.Hazare	47
6	Saeed Ahmed	c Vijay S.Hazare b Nayudu	22	(8) lbw b Nayudu	8
7	*M.Dilawar Khanji	c Sheikh b Nayudu	0	(9) b Vijay S.Hazare	8
8	S.B.Gandhi	b Vivek S.Hazare	52	(7) st Nimbalkar b Vijay S.Hazare	48
9	Purshottam	c Indulkar b Nayudu	4	(10) c Nayudu b Vijay S.Hazare	16
10	U.R.Chippa	not out	11	(4) st Nimbalkar b Nayudu	1
11	S.Nyalchand	c Nayudu b Vivek S.Hazare	2	not out	0
	Extras		18		8
			168		208

FoW (1): 1-28 (2), 2-50 (1), 3-59 (3), 4-65 (5), 5-69 (4), 6-69 (7), 7-114 (6), 8-142 (9), 9-162 (8), 10-168 (11)
FoW (2): 1-1, 2-17, 3-18, 4-19, 5-104, 6-130, 7-153, 8-170, 9-208, 10-208

Western India Bowling	O	M	R	W		O	M	R	W
Saeed Ahmed	42	21	49	2		15	8	12	1
Dilawar Khanji	6	0	25	0					
Gandhi	3.2	0	12	1		2	1	1	1
Chippa	19	4	71	0	(5)	26	6	42	3
Nyalchand	35	13	63	6	(2)	24.2	11	53	5
Kishenchand	4	1	10	1	(4)	4	0	16	0

Baroda Bowling	O	M	R	W		O	M	R	W
Vijay S.Hazare	31	10	45	3		20.2	5	46	3
Patel	3	0	12	0		3	2	5	0
Vivek S.Hazare	5.2	1	8	2	(5)	13	1	42	1
Nayudu	30	6	85	5	(3)	30	4	88	5
Sheikh					(4)	6	1	19	0

Umpires: M.G.Bhave and Vali Ahmed. Toss: Baroda

Close of Play: 1st day: Baroda (1) 245 all out; 2nd day: Baroda (2) 73-5 (Vijay S.Hazare 20*, Ghorpade 2*).

S.B.Gandhi was stumped going for a big hit assuming it was to be the last ball of the match as M.G.Bhave had called time was up, but under the Laws the over would have been completed. Western India protested to the BCCI but this was rejected.

HOLKAR v BENGAL

Played at Yeshwant Club Ground, Indore, February 6, 7, 8, 1943.

Match drawn.

HOLKAR			
1	†D.K.Yarde	run out	45
2	V.R.Ghetge	b Dutt	10
3	S.Mushtaq Ali	c Bhattacharya b Cooper	119
4	M.M.Jagdale	c Cooch Behar b Bhattacharya	29
5	*C.K.Nayudu	c Dutt b Bhattacharya	102
6	B.B.Nimbalkar	c and b Bhattacharya	178
7	J.N.Bhaya	b Dutt	0
8	S.Ishtiaq Ali	not out	52
9	S.Mohammad Khan	c Cooch Behar b Mustafi	68
10	R.P.Singh	b Cooch Behar	2
11	M.SalimKhan	b Cooch Behar	0
	Extras		13
			618

FoW (1): 1-33 (2), 2-101 (1), 3-190 (4), 4-225 (3), 5-399 (5), 6-404 (7), 7-512 (6), 8-615 (9), 9-618 (10), 10-618 (11)

BENGAL			
1	K.Bhattacharya	st Yarde b Mushtaq Ali	40
2	J.B.Madan	b Nimbalkar	5
3	N.C.Chatterjee	b Nayudu	46
4	Maharaja of Cooch Behar	c Mushtaq Ali b Nayudu	13
5	E.C.Harvey-Johnston	c Jagdale b Mushtaq Ali	3
6	*N.M.Bose	c Salim Khan b Jagdale	34
7	†A.K.Deb	c Nimbalkar b Nayudu	0
8	H.M.Bose	c Salim Khan b Nimbalkar	13
9	P.D.Dutt	c and b Singh	22
10	S.K.Mustafi	c Nayudu b Ishtiaq Ali	34
11	D.Cooper	not out	2
	Extras		9
			221

FoW (1): 1-16 (2), 2-71 (1), 3-93 (4), 4-100 (5), 5-130 (3), 6-130 (7), 7-160 (6), 8-165 (8), 9-219 (10), 10-221 (9)

Bengal Bowling

	O	M	R	W
Cooch Behar	28.2	7	82	2
Mustafi	32	6	97	1
Bhattacharya	60	21	109	3
Dutt	51	7	124	2
Chatterjee	34	4	94	0
Cooper	27	5	86	1
H.M.Bose	3	0	13	0

Holkar Bowling

	O	M	R	W
Jagdale	16	5	38	1
Nayudu	18	7	41	3
Salim Khan	5	0	13	0
Bhaya	2	0	7	0
Nimbalkar	13	2	48	2
Mushtaq Ali	19	3	53	2
Ishtiaq Ali	2	0	8	1
Singh	1.5	0	4	1

Umpires: Toss: Holkar

Close of Play: 1st day: Holkar (1) 299-4 (Nayudu 59*, Nimbalkar 32*); 2nd day: Holkar (1) 610-7 (Ishtiaq Ali 48*, Mohammad Khan 67*).

S.Mushtaq Ali's 119 took 180 minutes. C.K.Nayudu's 102 took 220 minutes and included 14 fours. B.B.Nimbalkar's 178 took 300 minutes.

BENGAL GOVERNOR'S XI v MAHARAJA OF COOCH-BEHAR'S XI

Played at Eden Gardens, Calcutta, February 13, 14, 15, 1943.

Bengal Governor's XI won by 149 runs.

BENGAL GOVERNOR'S XI					
1	S.K.Ganguli	lbw b Mushtaq Ali	62	c Roy b Bhattacharya	98
2	A.Sen	lbw b Rangaraj	8	c Nimbalkar b Rangaraj	1
3	E.C.Harvey-Johnston	c Das b Bhattacharya	8	c Phansalkar b Mushtaq Ali	1
4	N.M.Bose	c Mitra b Bhattacharya	72		
5	*C.K.Nayudu	c Phansalkar b Mitra	5	not out	112
6	A.G.Ram Singh	b Horn	13	not out	1
7	N.C.Chatterjee	st Edwards b Mushtaq Ali	38	(4) lbw b Greene	26
8	Shamim Khwaja	not out	37		
9	S.K.Mustafi	b Greene	3		
10	†T.M.Doraiswami	lbw b Mushtaq Ali	0		
11	B.K.Mitra	c and b Mushtaq Ali	1		
	Extras		34		7
			281	(4 wickets, declared)	246

FoW (1): 1-33 (2), 2-57 (3), 3-131 (1), 4-145 (5), 5-187 (6), 6-197 (4), 7-256 (7), 8- (9), 9- (10), 10-281 (11)
FoW (2): 1-5 (2), 2-24 (3), 3-68 (4), 4-232 (1)

MAHARAJA OF COOCH-BEHAR'S XI					
1	P.Rangaraj	c Harvey-Johnston b Nayudu	13	(7) c Doraiswami b Sen	3
2	S.K.Roy	c Harvey-Johnston b Ram Singh	13	(8) c Doraiswami b Nayudu	33
3	R.Greene	b Ram Singh	41	(2) c Chatterjee b Sen	0
4	S.Mushtaq Ali	c Ganguli b Mitra	20	(1) b Mitra	15
5	B.B.Nimbalkar	b Ram Singh	19	(3) c Sen b Mitra	8
6	K.Bhattacharya	lbw b Sen	15	lbw b Ram Singh	13
7	J.P.Phansalkar	c Doraiswami b Mitra	26	(5) c Doraiswami b Nayudu	28
8	*†A.R.G.M.Edwards	lbw b Nayudu	7	(10) st Doraiswami b Ram Singh	30
9	D.R.Das	c Ganguli b Nayudu	36	(4) b Sen	2
10	H.W.Horn	c Mitra b Nayudu	22	(9) b Nayudu	3
11	S.Mitra	not out	0	not out	7
	Extras		19		5
			231		147

FoW (1): 1- (1), 2-35 (2), 3-80 (4), 4-116 (3), 5-133 (6), 6-143 (5), 7-173 (8), 8-175 (7), 9-231 (9), 10-231 (10)
FoW (2): 1-4 (2), 2-22 (3), 3-28 (1), 4-32 (4), 5-47 (6), 6-52 (7), 7-85 (5), 8-91 (9), 9-119 (8), 10-147 (10)

Maharaja of Cooch-Behar's XI Bowling	O	M	R	W		O	M	R	W
Rangaraj	9	1	15	1		6	3	6	1
Horn	16	3	61	1	(6)	7	0	35	0
Mushtaq Ali	19	5	77	4		17	3	61	1
Nimbalkar	10	0	27	0	(2)	13	2	51	0
Bhattacharya	11	4	22	2	(4)	19	4	45	1
Mitra	8	0	24	1	(7)	1	0	6	0
Greene	6	0	21	1	(5)	7	0	35	1

Bengal Governor's XI Bowling	O	M	R	W		O	M	R	W
Mitra	18	4	50	2		7	0	24	2
Ram Singh	20	1	56	3	(3)	10.5	0	44	2
Chatterjee	5	0	11	0					
Mustafi	6	3	10	0					
Nayudu	16.5	2	67	4	(4)	7	0	37	3
Sen	6	1	18	1	(2)	10	1	37	3

Umpires: Toss: Bengal Governor's XI

Close of Play: 1st day: Maharaja of Cooch-Behar's XI (1) 29-1 (Roy 13*, Greene 1*); 2nd day: Bengal Governor's XI (2) 103-3 (Ganguli 52*, Nayudu 21*).

C.K.Nayudu's 112 included 15 fours and 1 six. This match was played in aid of the Midnapore Cyclone Relief Fund.

TRINIDAD v BARBADOS

Played at Queen's Park Oval, Port of Spain, February 13, 15, 16, 17, 1943.

Trinidad won by ten wickets.

TRINIDAD					
1	*V.H.Stollmeyer	c Carew b Graham	10	not out	27
2	J.B.Stollmeyer	lbw b Sealy	107	not out	25
3	A.G.Ganteaume	lbw b Worrell	3		
4	G.E.Gomez	not out	216		
5	H.J.B.Burnett	b Parris	11		
6	C.C.R.Skeete	b Parris	2		
7	R.P.Tang Choon	b Goddard	8		
8	E.Constantine	c Goddard b Peirce	30		
9	P.E.W.Jones	lbw b Graham	47		
10	†S.Samaroo	not out	5		
11	L.R.Pierre				
	Extras		10		2
		(8 wickets, declared)	449	(no wicket)	54

FoW (1): 1-30 (1), 2-36 (3), 3-221, 4-254, 5-260, 6-282, 7-345, 8-440

BARBADOS					
1	G.M.Carew	b Jones	7	c Tang Choon b Skeete	55
2	†S.O.Gittens	b J.B.Stollmeyer	19	c Tang Choon b Burnett	17
3	C.L.Walcott	b Jones	58	b Pierre	56
4	J.E.D.Sealy	lbw b Jones	42	lbw b Pierre	1
5	J.D.C.Goddard	lbw b Tang Choon	25	c Jones b Tang Choon	21
6	F.M.M.Worrell	not out	64	b Pierre	2
7	K.E.Walcott	b Tang Choon	21	b Burnett	25
8	O.S.Graham	lbw b Burnett	8	lbw b Pierre	12
9	*T.N.M.Peirce	lbw b Pierre	7	not out	5
10	J.L.Parris	run out	9	lbw b Pierre	0
11	N.E.Marshall	run out	14	c Samaroo b Pierre	0
	Extras		14		18
			288		212

FoW (1): 1-18, 2-27, 3-124, 4-133, 5-179, 6-214, 7-223, 8-246, 9-261, 10-288
FoW (2): 1-44, 2-107, 3-110, 4-144, 5-148, 6-191, 7-197, 8-210, 9-210, 10-212

Barbados Bowling	O	M	R	W		O	M	R	W
Sealy	13	3	41	1		4.1	0	22	0
Graham	17	0	55	2		2	0	10	0
Goddard	15	2	41	1					
Worrell	14	3	45	1	(3)	2	0	20	0
Parris	21	1	105	2					
Peirce	11	0	76	1					
Marshall	12	1	50	0					
Carew	6	2	26	0					

Trinidad Bowling	O	M	R	W		O	M	R	W
Pierre	17	1	69	1		10.3	0	47	6
Jones	17.6	1	59	3		9	0	49	0
J.B.Stollmeyer	9	1	28	1		4	0	20	0
Constantine	5	1	19	0					
Skeete	4	0	14	0	(4)	5	0	23	1
Tang Choon	12	0	54	2	(5)	12	1	25	1
Burnett	11	0	31	1	(6)	12	4	30	2

Umpires: Toss: Barbados

Close of Play: 1st day: Trinidad (1) 265-5 (Gomez 124*, Tang Choon 2*); 2nd day: Barbados (1) 45-2 (C.L.Walcott 15*, Sealy 3*); 3rd day: Barbados (1) 288 all out.

G.E.Gomez's 216 included 26 fours.

NORTH ISLAND ARMY v SOUTH ISLAND ARMY

Played at Basin Reserve, Wellington, February 19, 20, 22, 1943.

South Island Army won by 31 runs.

SOUTH ISLAND ARMY

1	*I.B.Cromb	c Norris b Pritchard	35	lbw b Andrews	6
2	M.L.Page	c Lamason b Andrews	14	c Andrews b Matthews	70
3	W.M.Anderson	c Lamason b Andrews	6	(4) c and b Pritchard	57
4	L.A.Milnes	b Partridge	41	(3) b Pritchard	6
5	F.B.Smith	c Lamason b Pritchard	6	c Norris b Partridge	8
6	L.Watt	c Coupland b Pritchard	0	(8) c Matthews b Andrews	11
7	D.W.Monaghan	c O'Brien b Lamason	10	(6) c Norris b Pritchard	9
8	R.H.Scott	c Lamason b Partridge	12	(7) b Pritchard	0
9	†D.M.Dunnet	c Lamason b Partridge	0	b Andrews	5
10	R.F.Cook	not out	2	b Pritchard	1
11	E.Mulcock	run out	0	not out	1
	Extras	b 3, lb 1	4	b 11, lb 6	17
			130		191

FoW (1): 1-50, 2-52, 3-59, 4-69, 5-69, 6-113, 7-116, 8-116, 9-129, 10-130
FoW (2): 1-25, 2-46, 3-109, 4-124, 5-159, 6-174, 7-174, 8-179, 9-190, 10-191

NORTH ISLAND ARMY

1	A.J.Postles	c Page b Scott	22	c Cromb b Scott	37
2	S.G.Haliday	c Watt b Mulcock	36	lbw b Mulcock	3
3	R.J.M.Coupland	b Cromb	10	c and b Cromb	7
4	M.A.O'Brien	st Dunnet b Cromb	0	c Milnes b Scott	25
5	S.J.Matthews	b Cromb	3	(8) b Cromb	15
6	G.H.Hook	c Milnes b Cromb	12	(7) not out	54
7	†W.E.Norris	run out	1	(5) b Cromb	25
8	*J.R.Lamason	c Watt b Cromb	10	(6) c Page b Cook	9
9	L.E.Partridge	c Scott b Cromb	5	c and b Cromb	0
10	T.L.Pritchard	b Cromb	0	b Scott	13
11	F.M.Andrews	not out	0	c and b Cromb	0
	Extras	b 1	1	b 2	2
			100		190

FoW (1): 1-38, 2-68, 3-68, 4-68, 5-72, 6-83, 7-93, 8-100, 9-100, 10-100
FoW (2): 1-7 (2), 2-19 (3), 3-69 (4), 4-84 (1), 5-107 (5), 6-107 (6), 7-151 (8), 8-159 (9), 9-185 (10), 10-190 (11)

North Island Army Bowling

	O	M	R	W		O	M	R	W
Pritchard	11	1	30	3		17.6	2	53	5
Partridge	7	1	23	3		6	1	23	1
Andrews	12	2	50	2		17	6	45	3
Lamason	8.1	3	23	1		6	0	21	0
Matthews					(5)	8	1	32	1

South Island Army Bowling

	O	M	R	W		O	M	R	W
Scott	9	2	26	1		15	2	56	3
Cook	6	1	16	0	(4)	14	2	42	1
Mulcock	13	4	36	1	(2)	13	2	16	1
Cromb	16.7	3	21	7	(3)	18.6	1	74	5

Umpires: C.W.Moore and M.F.Pengelly. Toss: South Island Army

Close of Play: 1st day: North Island Army (1) 14-0 (Postles 11*, Haliday 3*); 2nd day: North Island Army (2) 30-2 (Postles 16*, O'Brien 3*).

TRINIDAD v BARBADOS

Played at Queen's Park Oval, Port of Spain, February 20, 22, 23, 24, 1943.

Match drawn.

BARBADOS					
1	G.M.Carew	run out	40	c J.B.Stollmeyer b Jones	14
2	†S.O.Gittens	c and b Burnett	19	b Pierre	6
3	C.L.Walcott	c J.B.Stollmeyer b Tang Choon	6	lbw b Tang Choon	28
4	J.E.D.Sealy	c Gomez b Tang Choon	9	c Samaroo b Pierre	1
5	J.D.C.Goddard	c V.H.Stollmeyer b Tang Choon	62	not out	101
6	F.M.M.Worrell	c J.B.Stollmeyer b Pierre	188	st Ganteaume b V.H.Stollmeyer	68
7	*T.N.M.Peirce	b Jones	14		
8	K.E.Walcott	c V.H.Stollmeyer b J.B.Stollmeyer	72	(7) not out	42
9	E.A.V.Williams	lbw b Burnett	7		
10	J.L.Parris	not out	18		
11	O.S.Graham	c Jones b Pierre	6		
	Extras		11		13
			452	(5 wickets, declared)	273

FoW (1): 1-55, 2-66, 3-68, 4-78, 5-189, 6-242, 7-364, 8-396, 9-442, 10-452
FoW (2): 1-18, 2-22, 3-23, 4-56, 5-189

TRINIDAD					
1	*V.H.Stollmeyer	c Peirce b Sealy	83	c Gittens b Goddard	7
2	J.B.Stollmeyer	b Sealy	0	not out	77
3	A.G.Ganteaume	c Gittens b Williams	4	c Peirce b Goddard	9
4	G.E.Gomez	b Sealy	117		
5	H.J.B.Burnett	c K.E.Walcott b Carew	61		
6	W.F.Waller	lbw b Goddard	10	(4) not out	20
7	R.P.Tang Choon	lbw b C.L.Walcott	47		
8	W.Ferguson	c Sealy b Peirce	37		
9	P.E.W.Jones	not out	48		
10	†S.Samaroo	c and b Peirce	7		
11	L.R.Pierre	c Worrell b Peirce	0		
	Extras		14		1
			428	(2 wickets)	114

FoW (1): 1-1 (2), 2-25 (3), 3-208, 4-215, 5-243, 6-324, 7-350, 8-396, 9-412, 10-428
FoW (2): 1-18, 2-32

Trinidad Bowling	O	M	R	W		O	M	R	W
Pierre	23.4	1	109	2		15	1	75	2
Jones	14	0	83	1		9	1	36	1
Burnett	24	4	59	2		9	0	34	0
Tang Choon	19	2	86	3		7	0	32	1
Ferguson	8	0	38	0		5	0	23	0
J.B.Stollmeyer	9	0	52	1					
Gomez	3	0	14	0	(6)	5	0	35	0
V.H.Stollmeyer					(7)	5	0	25	1

Barbados Bowling	O	M	R	W		O	M	R	W
Sealy	10	1	34	3		2	0	9	0
Graham	10	1	32	0		2	0	8	0
Goddard	14	4	45	1		3	0	12	2
Williams	17	3	65	1		4	0	13	0
Parris	12	0	62	0		3	0	15	0
Peirce	13.4	0	80	3		1	0	10	0
Worrell	11	3	25	0		3	0	20	0
C.L.Walcott	4	0	24	1					
Carew	10	1	47	1					
K.E.Walcott					(8)	3	0	26	0

Umpires: V.Guillen and L.Maing. Toss: Trinidad

Close of Play: 1st day: Barbados (1) 249-6 (Worrell 84*, K.E.Walcott 4*); 2nd day: Trinidad (1) 143-2 (V.H.Stollmeyer 60*, Gomez 72*); 3rd day: Barbados (2) 23-3 (C.L.Walcott 3*).

F.M.M.Worrell's 188 took 300 minutes.

BARODA v RAJPUTANA

Played at Maharaja Pratapsingh Coronation Gymkhana Ground, Baroda, February 26, 27, 28, 1943.

Baroda won by an innings and 356 runs.

RAJPUTANA					
1	†Raghbir Singh	b Nayudu	10	st Nimbalkar b Nayudu	28
2	A.Wahab	c Nimbalkar b Vijay S.Hazare	1	c Sheikh b Nayudu	24
3	Alimuddin	c Naidu b Nayudu	13	st Nimbalkar b Nayudu	27
4	H.Vohra	run out	2	b Adhikari	12
5	Attique Hussain	b Nayudu	0	c Vivek S.Hazare b Vijay S.Hazare	11
6	M.S.Baloch	b Vijay S.Hazare	9	c Carey b Nayudu	4
7	Iftikhar Hussain	b Nayudu	2	c Adhikari b Nayudu	0
8	*N.P.Kesari	not out	7	c Naidu b Vijay S.Hazare	5
9	Ahmed Ali Khan	b Vijay S.Hazare	0	c Carey b Nayudu	3
10	Masoom Ali Khan	c Indulkar b Nayudu	4	b Nayudu	10
11	M.Dayal	b Vijay S.Hazare	2	not out	1
	Extras		4		8
			54		133

FoW (1): 1-1 (2), 2-21, 3-23, 4- , 5- , 6- , 7- , 8- , 9- , 10-54
FoW (2): 1-54 (2), 2- , 3- , 4- , 5- , 6- , 7- , 8- , 9- , 10-133

BARODA			
1	Y.E.Sheikh	b Masoom Ali Khan	3
2	†R.B.Nimbalkar	c Raghbir Singh b Masoom Ali Khan	9
3	H.R.Adhikari	b Kesari	6
4	Vijay S.Hazare	c Raghbir Singh b Alimuddin	28
5	M.M.Naidu	b Baloch	199
6	C.S.Nayudu	b Masoom Ali Khan	127
7	*W.N.Ghorpade	run out	97
8	M.S.Indulkar	c Raghbir Singh b Ahmed Ali Khan	42
9	R.G.Powar	lbw b Ahmed Ali Khan	10
10	P.A.H.Carey	b Masoom Ali Khan	6
11	Vivek S.Hazare	not out	2
	Extras		14
			543

FoW (1): 1-11 (2), 2-14 (1), 3-23 (3), 4-67 (4), 5-306 (6), 6-399 (5), 7-494 (8), 8-522 (9), 9-540 (10), 10-543 (7)

Baroda Bowling	O	M	R	W		O	M	R	W
Vijay S.Hazare	14.2	4	17	4		15	5	32	2
Carey	7	1	8	0		9	3	27	0
Vivek S.Hazare	5	1	5	0	(4)	2	0	4	0
Nayudu	10	2	20	5	(3)	20.1	2	36	7
Adhikari					(5)	7	0	26	1

Rajputana Bowling	O	M	R	W
Masoom Ali Khan	33	7	143	4
Dayal	11	5	31	0
Baloch	32	12	71	1
Kesari	28.4	4	82	1
Attique Hussain	29	3	122	0
Alimuddin	5	0	39	1
Iftikhar Hussain	2	0	12	0
Ahmed Ali Khan	7	1	29	2

Umpires: J.R.Patel and Vali Ahmed. Toss:

Close of Play: 1st day: Baroda (1) 188-4 (Naidu 91*, Nayudu 47*); 2nd day: Baroda (1) 522-8 (Ghorpade 89*, Carey 0*).

The match was scheduled for four days but completed in three. M.M.Naidu's 199 took 300 minutes and included 31 fours and 4 sixes. C.S.Nayudu's 127 took 170 minutes and included 12 fours.

HYDERABAD v HOLKAR

Played at Railways Recreation Club Ground, Secunderabad, February 26, 27, 28, March 1, 1943.

Hyderabad won by 187 runs.

HYDERABAD					
1	S.R.Mehta	b Nimbalkar	7	b Nimbalkar	5
2	Asadullah Qureshi	b Mushtaq Ali	148	c Nayudu b Jagdale	78
3	E.B.Aibara	lbw b Jagdale	48	c Jagdale b Nayudu	15
4	B.C.Khanna	b Nimbalkar	57	c Jagdale b Nimbalkar	22
5	*S.M.Hussain	c Nayudu b Nimbalkar	10	(6) lbw b Mushtaq Ali	14
6	Asghar Ali	lbw b Jagdale	0	(7) b Nimbalkar	14
7	S.Ali Abbas	c Yarde b Jagdale	24	(5) c Yarde b Nimbalkar	63
8	Ibrahim Khan	lbw b Nayudu	27	c Salim Khan b Nayudu	28
9	Ghulam Ahmed	c Nimbalkar b Mushtaq Ali	0	c Salim Khan b Mushtaq Ali	10
10	†Qutubuddin	b Nayudu	0	st Yarde b Nayudu	9
11	A.R.Bhupathi	not out	3	not out	0
	Extras		31		19
			355		277

FoW (1): 1-8 (1), 2-90 (3), 3-235 (4), 4-249 (5), 5-260 (6), 6-300 (7), 7-351 (2), 8-351 (9), 9-352 (10), 10-355 (8)
FoW (2): 1-21 (1), 2-41 (3), 3-105 (4), 4-166 (2), 5-186 (6), 6-217 (7), 7-230 (5), 8-257 (8), 9-268 (9), 10-277 (10)

HOLKAR					
1	†D.K.Yarde	c sub b Mehta	15	(9) b Ghulam Ahmed	8
2	V.R.Ghetge	c Qutubuddin b Ghulam Ahmed	2	(11) b Mehta	6
3	S.Mushtaq Ali	st Qutubuddin b Ghulam Ahmed	72	b Mehta	20
4	M.M.Jagdale	lbw b Ghulam Ahmed	27	(1) hit wkt b Ibrahim Khan	24
5	*C.K.Nayudu	lbw b Ghulam Ahmed	0	(4) b Ghulam Ahmed	3
6	B.B.Nimbalkar	b Mehta	61	(2) c Ghulam Ahmed b Mehta	18
7	J.N.Bhaya	lbw b Mehta	35	(5) c Asadullah Qureshi b Mehta	6
8	S.Ishtiaq Ali	b Mehta	8	(6) b Ghulam Ahmed	0
9	R.P.Singh	lbw b Ghulam Ahmed	4	(8) not out	48
10	S.R.Kale	not out	5	(7) b Bhupathi	25
11	M.Salim Khan	c Asadullah Qureshi b Ghulam Ahmed	2	(10) st Qutubuddin b Ghulam Ahmed	4
	Extras		37		15
			268		177

FoW (1): 1-10 (2), 2-80 (1), 3-127 (4), 4-127 (5), 5-150 (3), 6-226 (7), 7-245 (8), 8-260 (6), 9-266 (9), 10-268 (11)
FoW (2): 1-31 (1), 2-53 (2), 3-66 (3), 4-78 (4), 5-78 (6), 6-78 (5), 7-126 (7), 8-143 (9), 9-151 (10), 10-177 (11)

Holkar Bowling	O	M	R	W		O	M	R	W
Nayudu	36.4	6	103	2		21.2	7	39	3
Jagdale	33	11	59	3		18	3	57	1
Nimbalkar	23	4	70	3		19	2	56	4
Mushtaq Ali	26	5	62	2		18	5	42	2
Salim Khan	6	2	18	0		4	0	19	0
Ishtiaq Ali	1	0	2	0		12	0	40	0
Singh	3	0	10	0					
Bhaya					(7)	3	1	5	0

Hyderabad Bowling	O	M	R	W		O	M	R	W
Ibrahim Khan	15	3	27	0	(3)	9	1	38	1
Khanna	11	4	16	0	(4)	15	3	37	0
Ghulam Ahmed	41.4	11	58	6	(1)	16	2	50	4
Bhupathi	27	5	80	0	(6)	7	2	8	1
Mehta	24	6	40	4	(2)	13.5	4	23	4
Asadullah Qureshi	2	0	10	0	(5)	2	0	6	0

Umpires: Toss: Hyderabad

Close of Play: 1st day: Hyderabad (1) 300-6 (Asadullah Qureshi 127*); 2nd day: Holkar (1) 182-5 (Nimbalkar 19*, Bhaya 11*); 3rd day: Hyderabad (2) 214-5 (Ali Abbas 55*, Asghar Ali 13*).

Asadullah Qureshi's 148 took 380 minutes and included 21 fours.

FIRST SOUTH AFRICAN DIVISION v THE REST

Played at Old Wanderers, Johannesburg, March 13, 14, 1943.

Match drawn.

FIRST SOUTH AFRICAN DIVISION

1	E.A.B.Rowan	b Sturgess	15	c Melville b Heaney	84
2	*P.G.V.van der Bijl	lbw b Plimsoll	111		
3	B.Mitchell	c Melville b Warne	64	(2) c Sturgess b Heaney	20
4	R.S.Martin	b Heaney	21		
5	O.C.Dawson	lbw b Gordon	13	(4) c sub b Sturgess	57
6	†D.M.Ovenstone	b Heaney	0		
7	R.E.Somers Vine	b Warne	25	not out	8
8	H.G.O.Owen-Smith	lbw b Gordon	0	(3) b Warne	13
9	A.M.B.Rowan	lbw b Gordon	8		
10	A.W.Keightley-Smith	not out	20	(5) lbw b Warne	21
11	L.S.Brown	c Melville b Warne	18	(6) b Plimsoll	12
	Extras		16		9
			311	(6 wickets, declared)	224

FoW (1): 1-25, 2-166, 3-224, 4-229, 5-229, 6- , 7-253, 8-270, 9- , 10-311
FoW (2): 1-43, 2-62, 3-160, 4-200, 5-215, 6-224

THE REST

1	S.H.Curnow	st Ovenstone b Mitchell	40	lbw b Dawson	7
2	F.B.Warne	b Dawson	21	(8) not out	42
3	†G.M.Larkin	c Mitchell b Brown	32	(2) c and b Keightley-Smith	1
4	A.D.Nourse	not out	141	b Keightley-Smith	30
5	G.Georgeu	b Brown	0	b Keightley-Smith	0
6	F.F.Flanagan	b Brown	5	(7) c Mitchell b Brown	31
7	*A.Melville	c Somers Vine b Dawson	23	(6) lbw b Keightley-Smith	0
8	E.W.Sturgess	c Dawson b Brown	43	(3) b Keightley-Smith	8
9	J.B.Plimsoll	b Brown	4	c Ovenstone b Brown	3
10	N.Gordon	c Owen-Smith b Mitchell	11		
11	L.J.Heaney	b Brown	8	(10) c Ovenstone b Brown	18
	Extras		11		1
			339	(9 wickets)	141

FoW (1): 1-30, 2-95, 3-95, 4-95, 5-121, 6-170, 7-274, 8-296, 9-323, 10-339
FoW (2): 1-6, 2-12, 3-40, 4-42, 5-42, 6-47, 7-101, 8-113, 9-141

The Rest Bowling

	O	M	R	W		O	M	R	W
Heaney	15	2	56	2		11.3	0	74	2
Sturgess	13	0	53	1		9	0	67	1
Plimsoll	10	1	34	1		4	0	25	1
Gordon	17	1	55	3		2	0	9	0
Warne	18	0	97	3		10	1	40	2

First South African Division Bowling

	O	M	R	W		O	M	R	W
Dawson	13	0	82	2		8	0	31	1
Keightley-Smith	13	0	51	0		10	0	32	5
A.M.B.Rowan	23	3	69	0					
Brown	20.7	4	78	6	(3)	6.3	0	32	3
Mitchell	4	0	32	2	(4)	4	0	45	0
Owen-Smith	2	0	16	0					

Umpires: Toss:

Close of Play: 1st day: The Rest (1) 116-4 (Nourse 19*, Flanagan 2*).

P.G.V.van der Bijl's 111 included 6 fours and 1 six. A.D.Nourse's 141 included 22 fours. P.G.V.van der Bijl was 98* at lunch on the first day.

BIJAPUR FAMINE XI v BENGAL CYCLONE XI

Played at Brabourne Stadium, Bombay, March 19, 20, 21, 22, 1943.

Match drawn.

	BENGAL CYCLONE XI				
1	M.H.Mankad	b Amarnath	6		
2	†M.K.Mantri	c Meherhomji b Sarwate	44	b Amir Elahi	53
3	S.Mushtaq Ali	c V.M.Merchant b Sohoni	7	(1) b Sarwate	25
4	V.S.Hazare	st Meherhomji b Amir Elahi	264		
5	Gul Mohammad	c Amarnath b Amir Elahi	144		
6	H.R.Adhikari	c V.M.Merchant b Sohoni	18	(3) not out	53
7	*C.K.Nayudu	c U.M.Merchant b Amir Elahi	26	(5) b Sarwate	0
8	G.Kishenchand	c Deodhar b Garudachar	55	(6) not out	15
9	C.S.Nayudu	run out	57	(4) st Meherhomji b Sarwate	0
10	Naoomal Jaoomal	lbw b Sarwate	25		
11	J.N.Bhaya	not out	3		
	Extras		54		10
			703	(4 wickets, declared)	156

FoW (1): 1-12 (1), 2-19 (3), 3-102 (2), 4-404 (5), 5-452 (6), 6-552 (4), 7-559 (7), 8-650 (9), 9-678 (8), 10-703 (10)
FoW (2): 1- , 2- , 3- , 4-

	BIJAPUR FAMINE XI				
1	†K.R.Meherhomji	c Naoomal Jaoomal b C.S.Nayudu	5	(3) st Mantri b Naoomal Jaoomal	21
2	S.W.Sohoni	c Mantri b C.K.Nayudu	94	(6) b C.S.Nayudu	0
3	C.T.Sarwate	c and b C.S.Nayudu	21	(4) b C.S.Nayudu	15
4	L.Amarnath	c C.K.Nayudu b C.S.Nayudu	0	(1) c Adhikari b Naoomal Jaoomal	36
5	V.M.Merchant	b Mankad	1	(2) b Hazare	6
6	K.C.Ibrahim	c Hazare b Naoomal Jaoomal	250		
7	*D.B.Deodhar	b Mankad	106	not out	5
8	K.M.Rangnekar	b Naoomal Jaoomal	138		
9	U.M.Merchant	c Kishenchand b Naoomal Jaoomal	6	(5) c Mantri b Naoomal Jaoomal	27
10	Amir Elahi	c Mankad b Naoomal Jaoomal	33		
11	B.K.Garudachar	not out	2		
	Extras	b 1, lb 14, nb 2	17		5
			673	(6 wickets)	115

FoW (1): 1-35 (1), 2-90 (3), 3-90 (4), 4-93 (5), 5-128 (2), 6-336 (7), 7-610 (8), 8-624 (9), 9-669 (10), 10-673 (6)
FoW (2): 1- , 2- , 3- , 4- , 5- , 6-115

Bijapur Famine XI Bowling	O	M	R	W		O	M	R	W
Amarnath	47	12	100	1		5	0	15	0
Sohoni	19	1	82	2	(5)	2	1	14	0
Garudachar	27	4	111	1	(6)	3	1	9	0
Amir Elahi	49	7	180	3	(3)	12	0	56	1
Sarwate	40.1	3	139	2	(4)	11	1	34	3
Rangnekar	4	0	15	0					
Deodhar	4	0	22	0					
V.M.Merchant					(2)	6	1	18	0

Bengal Cyclone XI Bowling	O	M	R	W		O	M	R	W
C.K.Nayudu	43	5	149	1	(2)	4	0	16	0
Hazare	14	0	46	0	(1)	4	0	27	1
Gul Mohammad	19	1	99	0					
C.S.Nayudu	61	9	177	3	(3)	10	1	32	2
Mankad	40	6	87	2					
Naoomal Jaoomal	27.5	3	76	4	(4)	9.2	1	35	3
Kishenchand	1	0	8	0					
Mushtaq Ali	3	2	1	0					
Adhikari	3	0	13	0					

Umpires: D.K.Naik and Vali Ahmed. Toss: Bengal Cyclone XI

Close of Play: 1st day: Bengal Cyclone XI (1) 446-4 (Hazare 203*, Adhikari 12*); 2nd day: Bijapur Famine XI (1) 151-5 (Ibrahim 20*, Deodhar 7*); 3rd day: Bijapur Famine XI (1) 529-6 (Ibrahim 187*, Rangnekar 99*).

V.S.Hazare's 264 took 420 minutes and included 30 fours. Gul Mohammad's 144 took 210 minutes and included 14 fours. K.C.Ibrahim's 250 took 568 minutes and included 18 fours. D.B.Deodhar's 106 took 185 minutes and included 10 fours. K.M.Rangnekar's 138 took 275 minutes and included 5 fours. The match was played in aid of the Bengal Cyclone Fund and the Bijapur Felief Fund.

HYDERABAD v BARODA

Played at Railways Recreation Club Ground, Secunderabad, March 26, 27, 28, 29, 30, 1943.

Baroda won by 307 runs.

BARODA

1	†R.B.Nimbalkar	c Mehta b Bhupathi	16	b Mehta	17
2	Y.E.Sheikh	c Hussain b Bhupathi	36	b Bhupathi	35
3	V.S.Hazare	c Qutubuddin b Mehta	81	(4) b Bhupathi	97
4	H.R.Adhikari	b Khanna	56	(3) c Ghulam Ahmed b Khanna	70
5	M.M.Naidu	b Ghulam Ahmed	15	lbw b Ibrahim Khan	2
6	C.S.Nayudu	b Ghulam Ahmed	45	c Ibrahim Khan b Ghulam Ahmed	17
7	*W.N.Ghorpade	c Qutubuddin b Ghulam Ahmed	7	b Mehta	19
8	M.S.Indulkar	c and b Ghulam Ahmed	1	(9) not out	26
9	S.G.Powar	b Ghulam Ahmed	20	(8) c Ghulam Ahmed b Mehta	9
10	R.G.Powar	c Qutubuddin b Ghulam Ahmed	10	lbw b Mehta	3
11	P.A.H.Carey	not out	3	b Mehta	10
	Extras		18		16
			308		321

FoW (1): 1-36 (1), 2-63 (2), 3-167 (4), 4-192 (5), 5-246 (3), 6-270 (6), 7-273, 8-276, 9-295, 10-308
FoW (2): 1-36 (1), 2-76 (2), 3-187 (3), 4-192 (5), 5-225 (6), 6-259 (4), 7-278 (7), 8-291 (8), 9-301 (10), 10-321 (11)

HYDERABAD

1	S.R.Mehta	b Hazare	1	(6) b Hazare	1
2	Asadullah Qureshi	c Nimbalkar b Hazare	50	c Nayudu b Carey	0
3	E.B.Aibara	c R.G.Powar b Nayudu	37	st Nimbalkar b Nayudu	43
4	B.C.Khanna	c Naidu b Nayudu	75	(5) b Nayudu	5
5	*S.M.Hussain	c Sheikh b Hazare	15	(7) c Nayudu b Hazare	1
6	S.Ali Abbas	lbw b Nayudu	0	(8) c Adhikari b Hazare	5
7	Ushaq Ahmed	lbw b Nayudu	2	(1) c Adhikari b Hazare	30
8	Ibrahim Khan	c S.G.Powar b Nayudu	13	(4) lbw b Nayudu	2
9	Ghulam Ahmed	b Hazare	1	b Nayudu	3
10	A.R.Bhupathi	c Sheikh b Nayudu	2	(11) b Nayudu	0
11	†Qutubuddin	not out	0	(10) not out	1
	Extras		19		16
			215		107

FoW (1): 1-6 (1), 2-60 (3), 3-161 (2), 4-185 (4), 5-185 (6), 6-187 (5), 7-206 (8), 8-208 (9), 9-215 (10), 10-215 (7)
FoW (2): 1-0 (2), 2-74 (3), 3-78 (4), 4-88, 5-89, 6-91, 7-101, 8-106, 9-106, 10-107

Hyderabad Bowling

	O	M	R	W		O	M	R	W
Khanna	7	1	11	1		7	2	20	1
Ghulam Ahmed	27.3	7	114	6	(4)	35	7	67	1
Mehta	28	8	46	1		36	2	103	5
Bhupathi	25	7	68	2	(7)	24	2	69	2
Ibrahim Khan	8	2	22	0	(2)	9	1	20	1
Asadullah Qureshi	3	0	12	0	(5)	2	0	14	0
Ushaq Ahmed	3	0	17	0	(6)	2	0	12	0

Baroda Bowling

	O	M	R	W	O	M	R	W
Hazare	40	17	59	4	28	11	42	4
Carey	13	3	39	0	6	1	21	1
Nayudu	33.5	8	60	6	25.2	15	21	5
Sheikh	6	1	12	0	5	1	7	0
Adhikari	6	0	26	0				

Umpires: M.G.Bhave and T.A.Ramachandran. Toss: Baroda

Close of Play: 1st day: Baroda (1) 213-4 (Hazare 59*, Nayudu 18*); 2nd day: Hyderabad (1) 136-2 (Asadullah Qureshi 45*, Khanna 49*); 3rd day: Baroda (2) 109-2 (Adhikari 70*, Hazare 58*); 4th day: Hyderabad (2) 77-2 (Ushaq Ahmed 20*, Ibrahim Khan 1*).

NEW ZEALAND ARMY v NEW ZEALAND AIR FORCE

Played at Lancaster Park, Christchurch, April 1, 2, 3, 1943.

New Zealand Army won by 203 runs.

NEW ZEALAND ARMY					
1	M.L.Page	c Crawford b Lemin	11	c Crawford b Hoar	75
2	*I.B.Cromb	lbw b Lemin	51	c Parkin b Crawford	66
3	S.G.Haliday	lbw b Parkin	11	(8) c Crawford b Dustin	5
4	L.A.Milnes	c and b Bird	46	c and b Lemin	14
5	J.L.Kerr	c Bird b Parkin	51	run out	62
6	G.H.Hook	b Bird	0	(3) b Parkin	3
7	W.M.Anderson	run out	70	(6) b Lemin	30
8	G.L.Weir	b Bird	8	(7) not out	43
9	L.E.Partridge	b Bird	0		
10	T.L.Pritchard	c Churchill b Lemin	16		
11	†D.M.Dunnet	not out	15		
	Extras	b 5, lb 9, nb 1	15	b 15, lb 2	17
			294	(7 wickets, declared)	315

FoW (1): 1-34, 2-68, 3-88, 4-179, 5-179, 6-185, 7-208, 8-208, 9-239, 10-294
FoW (2): 1-116, 2-125, 3-151, 4-167, 5-218, 6-293, 7-315

NEW ZEALAND AIR FORCE					
1	A.C.Kerr	c Dunnet b Pritchard	5	c Kerr b Pritchard	0
2	W.H.Dustin	run out	1	(3) c Cromb b Anderson	12
3	O.L.Wrigley	run out	2	(5) c and b Cromb	52
4	F.R.Crawford	b Weir	30	st Dunnet b Cromb	7
5	E.F.Bezzant	c Dunnet b Cromb	63	(2) c Kerr b Pritchard	78
6	K.Parkin	b Partridge	11	c Cromb b Pritchard	0
7	†G.A.Churchill	run out	2	b Pritchard	0
8	*C.J.Oliver	c Weir b Pritchard	1	(9) not out	17
9	N.R.Hoar	c Page b Pritchard	1	(8) c Dunnet b Anderson	67
10	T.G.F.Lemin	b Pritchard	1	(11) run out	0
11	W.G.Bird	not out	0	(10) c Partridge b Pritchard	14
	Extras	b 3, lb 7, nb 1	11	b 16, lb 12, nb 3	31
			128		278

FoW (1): 1-6, 2-7, 3-9, 4-67, 5-97, 6-115, 7-124, 8-124, 9-128, 10-128
FoW (2): 1-3, 2-20, 3-40, 4-133, 5-133, 6-139, 7-228, 8-247, 9-276, 10-278

New Zealand Air Force Bowling	O	M	R	W		O	M	R	W
Hoar	14	2	45	0		10	0	54	1
Lemin	20	4	84	3		16	3	67	2
Parkin	13	0	61	2		6	0	52	1
Kerr	5	0	27	0		4	0	37	0
Bird	13.6	1	58	4		5	0	38	0
Dustin	1	0	4	0		1.6	0	11	1
Crawford					(7)	6	0	39	1

New Zealand Army Bowling	O	M	R	W		O	M	R	W
Pritchard	14.6	5	33	4		24	6	50	5
Weir	10	1	30	1		5	1	7	0
Partridge	9	3	18	1		14	1	35	0
Cromb	13	3	36	1		26	8	77	2
Anderson					(5)	10	2	30	2
Page					(6)	11	0	48	0

Umpires: G.E.Falgar and H.Wilson. Toss: New Zealand Army

Close of Play: 1st day: New Zealand Air Force (1) 62-3 (Crawford 30*, Bezzant 22*); 2nd day: New Zealand Army (2) 315-7 (Weir 43*).

INDEX OF 1942/43 SCORECARDS

1943/44

MUSLIMS v PARSEES

Played at Brabourne Stadium, Bombay, November 23, 24, 25, 1943.

Match drawn.

PARSEES

1	M.F.Mistry	b Hakim	1	c Nakhuda b Hakim	10
2	†K.R.Meherhomji	b Hakim	7	(7) st Nakhuda b Amir Elahi	46
3	E.B.Aibara	c Nazar Mohammad b Hakim	15	c Saeed Ahmed b Ghazali	20
4	R.S.Modi	lbw b Saeed Ahmed	4	not out	72
5	R.S.Cooper	b Amir Elahi	40	c and b Amir Elahi	51
6	J.B.Khot	b Saeed Ahmed	64	lbw b Amir Elahi	0
7	N.H.Colah	c Nazar Mohammad b Amir Elahi	5		
8	K.H.Dastur	lbw b Amir Elahi	0	(2) c Ibrahim b Hakim	4
9	*M.J.Mobed	not out	32		
10	S.R.Mehta	lbw b Saeed Ahmed	0		
11	K.K.Tarapore	st Nakhuda b Amir Elahi	15		
	Extras	b 2, lb 1, w 1	4	b 9, nb 1	10
			187	(6 wickets)	213

FoW (1): 1-4 (1), 2-11 (2), 3-20 (4), 4-32 (3), 5-121 (5), 6-135 (7), 7-135 (8), 8-137 (6), 9-137 (10), 10-187 (11)
FoW (2): 1-8 (2), 2-35 (1), 3-35 (3), 4-131 (5), 5-131 (6), 6-213 (7)

MUSLIMS

1	*S.M.Kadri	b Colah	3
2	Nazar Mohammad	st Meherhomji b Mobed	61
3	Anwar Hussain	b Modi	59
4	K.C.Ibrahim	c Mobed b Khot	56
5	M.I.Merchant	lbw b Khot	55
6	Gul Mohammad	c Dastur b Tarapore	23
7	M.E.Z.Ghazali	lbw b Modi	32
8	†H.A.Nakhuda	lbw b Mobed	12
9	Amir Elahi	lbw b Khot	69
10	A.A.Hakim	not out	30
11	Saeed Ahmed	not out	16
	Extras	b 11, lb 2, nb 1	14
		(9 wickets, declared)	430

FoW (1): 1-12 (1), 2-104 (3), 3-160 (2), 4-207 (4), 5-246 (6), 6-293 (7), 7-305 (5), 8-335 (8), 9-398 (9)

Muslims Bowling

	O	M	R	W		O	M	R	W
Saeed Ahmed	34	10	50	3		13	2	22	0
Hakim	14	3	42	3		11	3	30	2
Anwar Hussain	2	0	5	0	(6)	12	3	31	0
Amir Elahi	31.3	8	61	4		29.4	6	68	3
Nazar Mohammad	2	0	15	0					
Ghazali	4	0	10	0	(3)	17	2	43	1
Gul Mohammad					(5)	4	1	9	0

Parsees Bowling

	O	M	R	W
Khot	39	10	95	3
Colah	15	3	32	1
Mehta	13	5	23	0
Tarapore	52	17	91	1
Mobed	32	4	85	2
Modi	32	6	78	2
Cooper	4	1	12	0

Umpires: J.Birtwistle and D.K.Naik. Toss: Parsees

Close of Play: 1st day: Muslims (1) 75-1 (Nazar Mohammad 38*, Anwar Hussain 34*); 2nd day: Muslims (1) 326-7 (Nakhuda 9*, Amir Elahi 16*).

EUROPEANS v HINDUS

Played at Brabourne Stadium, Bombay, November 26, 27, 28, 1943.

Hindus won by an innings and 209 runs.

HINDUS			
1	S.W.Sohoni	c Skinner b Legard	6
2	M.H.Mankad	c Sturgess b Legard	91
3	H.R.Adhikari	c Marshall b Legard	59
4	*V.M.Merchant	c Sturgess b Smith	62
5	G.Kishenchand	retired out	111
6	K.M.Rangnekar	c Legard b U'ren	17
7	R.P.Mehra	not out	116
8	C.S.Nayudu	c Harris b Legard	32
9	S.N.Banerjee	not out	7
10	†M.K.Mantri		
11	C.T.Sarwate		
	Extras	b 11, lb 1, nb 2	14
		(7 wickets, declared)	515

FoW (1): 1-6 (1), 2-92 (3), 3-212 (4), 4-234 (2), 5-251 (6), 6-434 (5), 7-492 (8)

EUROPEANS					
1	A.G.Skinner	b Sohoni	9	(4) c Banerjee b Sohoni	40
2	F.S.Tomlinson	b Banerjee	3	c Nayudu b Sohoni	19
3	M.Robinson	c Mankad b Banerjee	27	lbw b Banerjee	24
4	K.W.Marshall	b Banerjee	7	(5) b Banerjee	2
5	L.O.Waller	b Banerjee	32	(6) b Nayudu	18
6	J.A.B.Dickson	not out	39	(1) b Sohoni	14
7	C.W.E.U'ren	c Banerjee b Nayudu	1	(8) not out	10
8	D.E.B.Harris	c Adhikari b Mankad	4	(9) c Sarwate b Nayudu	0
9	F.S.W.Smith	lbw b Sarwate	0	(7) b Banerjee	14
10	*†T.M.Sturgess	c Sarwate b Nayudu	5	c Rangnekar b Nayudu	18
11	A.R.Legard	b Sarwate	2	st Mantri b Sarwate	2
	Extras	b 4, lb 5, nb 2	11	b 4, lb 1	5
			140		166

FoW (1): 1-6 (2), 2-28 (1), 3-46 (4), 4-51 (3), 5-105 (5), 6-115 (7), 7-122 (8), 8-124 (9), 9-133 (10), 10-140 (11)
FoW (2): 1-37 (2), 2-38 (1), 3-87 (3), 4-93 (5), 5-104 (4), 6-132, 7-138, 8-138, 9-162, 10-166

Europeans Bowling	O	M	R	W
Legard	54	28	96	4
U'ren	29	5	93	1
Robinson	17	2	91	0
Marshall	17	1	68	0
Waller	10	0	44	0
Tomlinson	7	1	20	0
Smith	21	1	82	1
Skinner	1	0	7	0

Hindus Bowling	O	M	R	W		O	M	R	W
Banerjee	10	2	19	4	(8)	11	1	25	3
Merchant	1	1	0	0		5	3	2	0
Sohoni	9	0	24	1	(6)	14	4	38	3
Mankad	10	2	16	1	(3)	8	3	5	0
Nayudu	16	5	32	2	(7)	18	3	54	3
Sarwate	13.5	2	38	2	(5)	14.4	5	27	1
Rangnekar					(1)	6	3	9	0
Kishenchand					(4)	2	1	1	0

Umpires: J.R.Patel and Vali Ahmed. Toss: Hindus

Close of Play: 1st day: Hindus (1) 372-5 (Kishenchand 79*, Mehra 48*); 2nd day: Europeans (2) 13-0 (Dickson 3*, Tomlinson 10*).
G.Kishenchand's 111 took 197 minutes and included 13 fours. R.P.Mehra's 116 took 204 minutes and included 12 fours.

MUSLIMS v THE REST

Played at Brabourne Stadium, Bombay, November 29, 30, December 1, 1943.

Match drawn.

MUSLIMS					
1	Nazar Mohammad	b Bhalerao	154		
2	*S.M.Kadri	c Dias b Roach	0		
3	Anwar Hussain	c Dias b Vijay S.Hazare	22	(2) lbw b Roach	16
4	K.C.Ibrahim	c Vijay S.Hazare b Shaw	20	(3) not out	71
5	Gul Mohammad	hit wkt b Arolkar	42	(1) st Kadam b Bhalerao	36
6	A.A.Hakim	b Roach	25		
7	Inayat Khan	b Frank	7	(4) c Kadam b Bhalerao	34
8	†H.A.Nakhuda	run out	3	(5) not out	2
9	Amir Elahi	c Arolkar b Roach	29		
10	Saeed Ahmed	c D'Souza b Bhalerao	41		
11	U.R.Chippa	not out	2		
	Extras	b 6, lb 1, nb 1	8	b 4	4
			353	(3 wickets)	163

FoW (1): 1-5 (2), 2-36 (3), 3-92 (4), 4-148 (5), 5-189 (6), 6-218 (7), 7-237 (8), 8-289 (9), 9-342 (1), 10-353 (10)
FoW (2): 1-43 (2), 2-62 (1), 3-137 (4)

THE REST			
1	B.P.Kadam	b Amir Elahi	15
2	†V.Dias	b Saeed Ahmed	1
3	P.S.D'Souza	c Gul Mohammad b Amir Elahi	10
4	Vijay S.Hazare	c and b Amir Elahi	248
5	B.Frank	c Nazar Mohammad b Amir Elahi	22
6	S.R.Arolkar	c Saeed Ahmed b Amir Elahi	66
7	E.Shaw	lbw b Amir Elahi	0
8	Vivek S.Hazare	c sub b Amir Elahi	21
9	*P.A.D'Avoine	lbw b Amir Elahi	0
10	A.K.Bhalerao	not out	1
11	J.Roach	b Chippa	0
	Extras	b 2, lb 5, nb 4	11
			395

FoW (1): 1-7 (2), 2-27 (1), 3-30 (3), 4-67 (5), 5-275 (6), 6-289 (7), 7-391 (8), 8-391 (9), 9-394 (4), 10-395 (11)

The Rest Bowling	O	M	R	W		O	M	R	W
Roach	40	3	111	3		10	1	37	1
Vijay S.Hazare	32	14	37	1					
Bhalerao	24.1	2	63	2	(4)	12	1	43	2
Shaw	16	0	44	1	(6)	4	0	13	0
Arolkar	11	0	50	1	(3)	9	2	19	0
Frank	16	4	38	1	(2)	2	0	18	0
D'Avoine	3	2	2	0	(5)	6	0	29	0

Muslims Bowling	O	M	R	W
Saeed Ahmed	45	17	58	1
Hakim	10	1	27	0
Anwar Hussain	5	0	11	0
Amir Elahi	53	7	160	8
Chippa	22.3	3	46	1
Inayat Khan	22	3	49	0
Gul Mohammad	8	2	10	0
Nazar Mohammad	3	0	11	0
Ibrahim	4	0	12	0

Umpires: D.K.Naik and J.R.Patel. Toss: Muslims

Close of Play: 1st day: Muslims (1) 336-8 (Nazar Mohammad 141*, Saeed Ahmed 9*); 2nd day: The Rest (1) 225-4 (Vijay S.Hazare 119*, Arolkar 31*).
Nazar Mohammad's 154 took 390 minutes and included 11 fours. Vijay S.Hazare's 248 took 452 minutes and included 21 fours.

HINDUS v THE REST

Played at Brabourne Stadium, Bombay, December 3, 4, 5, 6, 1943.

Hindus won by an innings and 61 runs.

HINDUS			
1	S.W.Sohoni	b Roach	57
2	M.H.Mankad	lbw b Harris	13
3	H.R.Adhikari	b Vijay S.Hazare	186
4	*V.M.Merchant	not out	250
5	K.M.Rangnekar	c Dias b Vijay S.Hazare	22
6	C.S.Nayudu	b Vijay S.Hazare	18
7	G.Kishenchand	not out	15
8	R.P.Mehra		
9	S.N.Banerjee		
10	†M.K.Mantri		
11	C.T.Sarwate		
	Extras	b 16, lb 3, nb 1	20
		(5 wickets, declared)	581

FoW (1): 1-39 (2), 2-114 (1), 3-459 (3), 4-503 (5), 5-545 (6)

THE REST					
1	P.S.D'Souza	c Rangnekar b Banerjee	1	b Banerjee	8
2	†V.Dias	lbw b Banerjee	41	b Sohoni	6
3	E.G.Mane	b Sohoni	5	(6) b Sarwate	5
4	Vijay S.Hazare	c and b Sarwate	59	c and b Nayudu	309
5	B.Frank	c Mankad b Nayudu	0	lbw b Sarwate	1
6	S.R.Arolkar	b Sarwate	3	(3) st Mantri b Nayudu	16
7	J.G.Harris	c Mankad b Nayudu	6	(9) c Kishenchand b Sarwate	1
8	Vivek S.Hazare	not out	8	(7) c Merchant b Nayudu	21
9	*P.A.D'Avoine	c Banerjee b Nayudu	2	(10) lbw b Nayudu	0
10	J.Roach	c Mantri b Sarwate	1	(11) not out	1
11	A.K.Bhalerao	c Banerjee b Nayudu	0	(8) lbw b Nayudu	0
	Extras	b 1, lb 4, w 1, nb 1	7	b 8, lb 7, w 2, nb 2	19
			133		387

FoW (1): 1-16 (1), 2-29 (3), 3-103 (2), 4-104 (5), 5-114 (4), 6-115 (6), 7-123 (7), 8-127 (9), 9-128 (10), 10-133 (11)
FoW (2): 1-14 (2), 2-14 (1), 3-45 (3), 4-46 (5), 5-60 (6), 6-360 (7), 7-362 (8), 8-365 (9), 9-372 (10), 10-387 (4)

The Rest Bowling	O	M	R	W
Roach	29	5	83	1
Vijay S.Hazare	51	8	119	3
Harris	23	5	67	1
Bhalerao	33	2	123	0
Vivek S.Hazare	15	1	77	0
Frank	13	2	37	0
Arolkar	22	6	51	0
Mane	1	0	4	0

Hindus Bowling	O	M	R	W		O	M	R	W
Banerjee	18	7	38	2		21	3	92	1
Sohoni	11	0	36	1		26	3	78	1
Rangnekar	1	1	0	0	(9)	3	0	7	0
Nayudu	23.2	6	46	4		32.1	4	90	5
Sarwate	6	1	6	3	(3)	32	9	65	3
Mankad					(5)	2	0	2	0
Adhikari					(6)	7	5	2	0
Merchant					(7)	11	4	17	0
Kishenchand					(8)	4	1	15	0

Umpires: J.Birtwistle and J.R.Patel. Toss: Hindus

Close of Play: 1st day: Hindus (1) 319-2 (Adhikari 123*, Merchant 112*); 2nd day: The Rest (1) 81-2 (Dias 37*, Vijay S.Hazare 32*); 3rd day: The Rest (2) 189-5 (Vijay S.Hazare 125*, Vivek S.Hazare 14*).

H.R.Adhikari's 186 took 393 minutes and included 14 fours. V.M.Merchant's 250 took 435 minutes and included 31 fours. Vijay S.Hazare's 309 took 417 minutes and included 32 fours and 1 six. Vijay S.Hazare scored 122 runs before lunch on the fourth day. Vijay S.Hazare scored 266 of the 300 run partnership.

NAWANAGAR v WESTERN INDIA

Played at Ajitsinhji Ground, Jamnagar, December 10, 11, 12, 1943.

Match drawn.

WESTERN INDIA					
1	*H.W.Barritt	c and b J.R.Oza	19	c Indravijaysinhji b Mulwantrai	8
2	†Prataprai	c J.R.Oza b Mulwantrai	5	c Jayendrasinhji b Man Singh	31
3	K.S.Abdul Kadir	st Mehta b Mangal Singh	10	b Mulwantrai	62
4	Umar Khan	lbw b Man Singh	58	not out	3
5	Prithviraj	b J.R.Oza	36	not out	6
6	Saeed Ahmed	st Mehta b Mangal Singh	0		
7	Purshottam	c J.R.Oza b Mulwantrai	33		
8	S.B.Gandhi	b Mulwantrai	80		
9	Sukhvantrai	c Indravijaysinhji b Mangal Singh	32		
10	Akbar Khan	not out	41		
11	Jayantilal Vora	run out	4		
	Extras		18		6
			336	(3 wickets, declared)	116

FoW (1): 1-10, 2-35, 3-39, 4-107, 5-112, 6-153, 7-177, 8-236, 9- , 10-336
FoW (2): 1- , 2- , 3-

NAWANAGAR					
1	I.Oza	b Saeed Ahmed	8	run out	34
2	J.Oza	b Purshottam	27	b Saeed Ahmed	1
3	R.K.Yadvendrasinhji	c Jayantilal Vora b Saeed Ahmed	49	c Gandhi b Saeed Ahmed	0
4	R.K.Indravijaysinhji	c Jayantilal Vora b Akbar Khan	48	(5) not out	7
5	J.R.Oza	b Saeed Ahmed	13	(6) c and b Abdul Kadir	1
6	*M.S.Samarsinhji	c Gandhi b Saeed Ahmed	2		
7	R.K.Jayendrasinhji	c Saeed Ahmed b Gandhi	22	(4) st Prataprai b Abdul Kadir	25
8	Mangal Singh	not out	22		
9	†K.Mehta	st Prataprai b Gandhi	2		
10	Mulwantrai	c Prataprai b Gandhi	0		
11	A.ManSingh	b Akbar Khan	1		
	Extras		27		2
			221	(5 wickets)	70

FoW (1): 1- , 2- , 3- , 4- , 5- , 6- , 7- , 8- , 9- , 10-221
FoW (2): 1- , 2- , 3- , 4- , 5-70

Nawanagar Bowling	O	M	R	W		O	M	R	W
Man Singh	29	7	51	1		14	4	28	1
Mulwantrai	46	15	94	3		12.4	2	23	2
Mangal Singh	26	9	75	3	(4)	7	1	22	0
J.R.Oza	39.4	7	96	2	(3)	16	3	37	0
Yadvendrasinhji	1	0	2	0					

Western India Bowling	O	M	R	W		O	M	R	W
Saeed Ahmed	41	13	60	4		6	4	4	2
Akbar Khan	34.2	2	44	2		5	2	12	0
Jayantilal Vora	21	9	24	0					
Purshottam	18	0	53	1					
Gandhi	9	1	13	3					
Sukhvantrai					(3)	3	1	3	0
Prithviraj					(4)	2	0	15	0
Abdul Kadir					(5)	4	0	10	2
Barritt					(6)	3	0	24	0

Umpires: M.J.Abdulla and Vali Ahmed. Toss:

Close of Play: 1st day: Western India (1) 274-8 (Gandhi 58*, Akbar Khan 10*); 2nd day: Nawanagar (1) 162-3 (Yadvendrasinhji 47*, J.R.Oza 9*).

BOMBAY v BARODA

Played at Brabourne Stadium, Bombay, December 11, 12, 13, 1943.

Match drawn.

BOMBAY

1	†M.K.Mantri	b Vijay S.Hazare	0
2	Anwar Hussain	b Nayudu	53
3	C.T.Sarwate	run out	16
4	R.S.Modi	b Nayudu	1
5	K.C.Ibrahim	c Nimbalkar b Nayudu	3
6	*V.M.Merchant	b Nayudu	141
7	K.M.Rangnekar	b Nayudu	98
8	J.B.Khot	b Nayudu	4
9	R.S.Cooper	b Vinod	73
10	M.N.Raiji	not out	81
11	B.K.Garudachar	lbw b Nayudu	0
	Extras	b 10, lb 7	17
			487

FoW (1): 1-10 (1), 2-69 (3), 3-75 (4), 4-76 (2), 5-89 (5), 6-279 (7), 7-317 (8), 8-342 (6), 9-486 (9), 10-487 (11)

BARODA

1	M.M.Naidu	c Garudachar b Khot	0
2	†R.B.Nimbalkar	c Mantri b Khot	65
3	H.R.Adhikari	b Sarwate	79
4	Vijay S.Hazare	c Khot b Garudachar	101
5	Vivek S.Hazare	b Khot	2
6	C.S.Nayudu	b Khot	0
7	M.S.Indulkar	b Khot	0
8	*W.N.Ghorpade	lbw b Sarwate	6
9	T.B.Vinod	b Garudachar	5
10	A.Patel	lbw b Sarwate	7
11	S.G.Gupte	not out	2
	Extras	b 17, lb 12, nb 1	30
			297

FoW (1): 1-0 (1), 2-123 (2), 3-195 (3), 4-210 (5), 5-210 (6), 6-210 (7), 7-238 (8), 8-275 (9), 9-293 (10), 10-297 (4)

Baroda Bowling

	O	M	R	W
Vijay S.Hazare	42	16	85	1
Patel	14	4	44	0
Nayudu	75	16	166	7
Gupte	8	0	37	0
Vivek S.Hazare	26	3	74	0
Vinod	4	1	5	1
Adhikari	22	2	59	0

Bombay Bowling

	O	M	R	W
Khot	42	12	113	5
Anwar Hussain	12	1	22	0
Rangnekar	3	0	12	0
Merchant	2	0	9	0
Garudachar	24.3	4	55	2
Sarwate	30	7	42	3
Raiji	4	0	14	0

Umpires: M.G.Bhave and T.A.Ramachandran. Toss: Bombay

Close of Play: 1st day: Bombay (1) 259-5 (Merchant 88*, Rangnekar 86*); 2nd day: Baroda (1) 75-1 (Nimbalkar 43*, Adhikari 31*).

V.M.Merchant's 141 took 339 minutes and included 11 fours. Vijay S.Hazare's 101 took 219 minutes and included 10 fours. J.B.Khot took a hat-trick in the Baroda first innings (Vivek S.Hazare, Nayudu, Indulkar).

SIND v GUJARAT

Played at Karachi Gymkhana Ground, December 11, 12, 13, 1943.

Sind won by nine wickets.

GUJARAT					
1	G.G.Desai	b Parsram	9	c Jamnadas b Samtani	13
2	†E.S.Maka	c Naoomal Jaoomal b Samtani	6	(8) not out	16
3	R.M.Patel	c Narottam b Samtani	2	(2) c Parsram b Girdhari	19
4	P.N.Cambhatta	st Jamnadas b Parsram	37	c Parsram b Girdhari	15
5	B.G.Patel	c Dipchand b Parsram	40	c and b Girdhari	0
6	K.L.Dalaya	b Parsram	0	(3) b Lakda	30
7	D.K.Contractor	b Samtani	0	b Girdhari	8
8	J.M.Patel	c Girdhari b Samtani	4	(10) c Dipchand b Girdhari	2
9	M.J.Bhatt	c Dipchand b Parsram	10	(6) c Samtani b Lakda	7
10	U.R.Chippa	c Samtani b Parsram	0	(11) run out	0
11	*M.S.Baloch	not out	1	(9) c Samtani b Girdhari	12
	Extras		11		14
			120		136

FoW (1): 1- , 2- , 3-20, 4-100, 5- , 6- , 7- , 8- , 9- , 10-120
FoW (2): 1- , 2- , 3- , 4- , 5- , 6- , 7- , 8- , 9- , 10-136

SIND					
1	P.H.Punjabi	b Bhatt	22	c Bhatt b Chippa	4
2	D.Narottam	b Bhatt	0	not out	40
3	†L.Jamnadas	b Bhatt	25	not out	33
4	Qamaruddin Sheikh	b Bhatt	12		
5	S.K.Girdhari	b J.M.Patel	9		
6	*Naoomal Jaoomal	c Contractor b J.M.Patel	0		
7	Daud Khan	lbw b Bhatt	27		
8	A.Dipchand	c Contractor b J.M.Patel	12		
9	F.G.Lakda	c Baloch b Bhatt	18		
10	V.K.Samtani	st Maka b Baloch	24		
11	J.Parsram	not out	14		
	Extras		12		6
			175	(1 wicket)	83

FoW (1): 1- , 2- , 3- , 4- , 5- , 6- , 7-107, 8- , 9- , 10-175
FoW (2): 1-

Sind Bowling	O	M	R	W		O	M	R	W
Samtani	18	3	40	4		10	2	23	1
Parsram	19	6	24	6		10	4	14	0
Girdhari	7	1	14	0		15	1	48	6
Lakda	7	1	16	0		15.4	3	37	2
Naoomal Jaoomal	5	0	15	0					

Gujarat Bowling	O	M	R	W		O	M	R	W
Baloch	24.1	10	43	1		4	1	12	0
Bhatt	22	7	49	6		8	0	22	0
Chippa	18	4	35	0		11	2	21	1
Contractor	1	0	4	0					
J.M.Patel	17	3	32	3	(4)	4.2	0	22	0

Umpires: D.K.Naik and J.R.Patel. Toss:

Close of Play: 1st day: Sind (1) 90-6 (Daud Khan 16*, Dipchand 1*); 2nd day: Sind (2) 47-1 (Narottam 25*, Jamnadas 14*).

HOLKAR v UNITED PROVINCES

Played at Yeshwant Club Ground, Indore, December 17, 18, 19, 1943.

Holkar won by 299 runs.

HOLKAR					
1	S.Ishtiaq Ali	c Asundi b Abbas	1	(6) c Wahidullah b Gandhi	5
2	S.Mohammad Khan	c Ramchandra b Gandhi	26	(1) b Saidullah	26
3	S.Mushtaq Ali	c Shamim Khwaja b Gandhi	34	c Shamim Khwaja b Saidullah	163
4	*C.K.Nayudu	c Wahidullah b Saidullah	102	(5) b Gandhi	16
5	†J.N.Bhaya	c Balendu Shah b Gandhi	15		
6	M.M.Jagdale	b Abbas	14	(7) c Balendu Shah b Saidullah	67
7	B.B.Nimbalkar	c Balendu Shah b Saidullah	10	(4) b Asundi	54
8	C.E.Holkar	b Saidullah	4	(2) c sub b Asundi	41
9	R.Subramaniam	b Saidullah	3		
10	R.P.Singh	c Balendu Shah b Saidullah	0	(8) not out	31
11	P.Tata Rao	not out	0		
	Extras		13		17
			222	(7 wickets, declared)	420

FoW (1): 1- (1), 2-48 (3), 3- (4), 4- (5), 5- , 6- , 7- , 8- , 9- , 10-222
FoW (2): 1-65 (1), 2- (2), 3- (4), 4- (3), 5- (6), 6-322 (5), 7-420 (7)

UNITED PROVINCES					
1	*†M.K.Balendu Shah	st Bhaya b Ishtiaq Ali	68	c Mushtaq Ali b Jagdale	0
2	K.R.Asundi	b Nimbalkar	0	c Nayudu b Tata Rao	13
3	B.P.Telang	c Bhaya b Mushtaq Ali	4	(8) b Jagdale	0
4	Shamim Khwaja	c Nayudu b Tata Rao	7	(5) c Mohammad Khan b Nayudu	33
5	J.P.Phansalkar	lbw b Nayudu	12	(6) c Mushtaq Ali b Nayudu	78
6	Wahidullah	c Bhaya b Nayudu	2	(4) c Nayudu b Mushtaq Ali	25
7	Abbas	lbw b Ishtiaq Ali	7	absent hurt	0
8	B.Ramchandra	c and b Ishtiaq Ali	0	(7) lbw b Nayudu	24
9	S.N.Gandhi	c and b Nayudu	2	not out	27
10	Saidullah	c Nimbalkar b Nayudu	1	lbw b Nayudu	4
11	Iqbal Ahmed Khan	not out	6	(3) c Jagdale b Subramaniam	9
	Extras		7		14
			116		227

FoW (1): 1-0 (2), 2-29 (3), 3-40 (4), 4- (5), 5- (6), 6- (7), 7- (8), 8- (9), 9- (1), 10-116 (10)
FoW (2): 1-0, 2- , 3- , 4-66, 5-132, 6- , 7- , 8- , 9-227

United Provinces Bowling	O	M	R	W		O	M	R	W
Ramchandra	18	6	42	0		17	4	37	0
Abbas	16	5	33	2					
Gandhi	29	6	68	3	(2)	39.4	7	109	2
Saidullah	29.4	7	66	5	(3)	42	11	155	3
Iqbal Ahmed Khan					(4)	9	2	23	0
Asundi					(5)	8	2	26	2
Wahidullah					(6)	4	0	11	0
Shamim Khwaja					(7)	18	4	42	0

Holkar Bowling	O	M	R	W		O	M	R	W
Jagdale	5	2	10	0		24	4	53	2
Nimbalkar	7	3	11	1		9	2	23	0
Mushtaq Ali	15	6	28	1		25	8	41	1
Tata Rao	11	2	23	1		19	4	33	1
Nayudu	19.4	7	33	4		11	7	37	4
Ishtiaq Ali	5	3	4	3		2	0	11	0
Subramaniam					(7)	4.3	0	15	1

Umpires: Toss: Holkar

Close of Play: 1st day: United Provinces (1) 55-3 (Balendu Shah 36*, Phansalkar 2*); 2nd day: Holkar (2) 306-4 (Nayudu 7*, Ishtiaq Ali 2*).

176 runs were added for the 3rd wicket in the Holkar second innings (S.Mushtaq Ali and B.B.Nimbalkar). C.K.Nayudu's 102 took 105 minutes. S.Mushtaq Ali's 163 included 20 fours.

BENGAL v BIHAR

Played at Eden Gardens, Calcutta, December 18, 19, 20, 1943.

Match drawn.

BIHAR					
1	S.Ghosh	run out	3	lbw b Chatterjee	63
2	†Lunn	run out	0	c Chatterjee b Mitra	1
3	A.K.Das Gupta	b Mitra	23	c Mustafi b Dutt	8
4	*S.N.Banerjee	c Sen b Bhattacharya	26	c Mustafi b Dutt	0
5	S.Banerjee	c Sen b Mitra	2	not out	101
6	Patankar	run out	3		
7	B.K.Bose	c and b Bhattacharya	4	(8) b Mitra	16
8	K.Ghosh	b Bhattacharya	45	(6) b Banerjee	14
9	T.P.Sweeney	c Mitra b Bhattacharya	3	not out	35
10	N.R.Chowdhury	st Sen b Bhattacharya	2		
11	S.Patel	not out	30	(7) lbw b Banerjee	0
	Extras	b 2, lb 8, w 8	18		23
			159	(7 wickets, declared)	261

FoW (1): 1-2 (2), 2-11 (1), 3-53 (4), 4-59 (5), 5-68 (3), 6-75 (6), 7-75 (7), 8-85 (9), 9-100 (10), 10-159 (8)
FoW (2): 1-5 (2), 2-31 (3), 3-37 (4), 4-131 (1), 5- (6), 6- (7), 7-205 (8)

BENGAL					
1	A.Jabbar	c S.N.Banerjee b Chowdhury	3	(4) b Chowdhury	15
2	†P.K.Sen	c S.Banerjee b S.N.Banerjee	13	c S.Ghosh b Chowdhury	2
3	P.D.Dutt	c Das Gupta b Chowdhury	11	b Chowdhury	14
4	N.M.Bose	b Chowdhury	1	(10) not out	0
5	E.C.Harvey-Johnston	b Chowdhury	2	(6) c Sweeney b Bose	4
6	N.C.Chatterjee	b Bose	78	(5) b Chowdhury	4
7	K.Bhattacharya	lbw b Bose	15	(1) b Bose	0
8	*Maharaja of Cooch Behar	b S.N.Banerjee	33	(7) c Das Gupta b Bose	16
9	S.K.Mustafi	b Chowdhury	77	not out	18
10	S.A.Banerjee	not out	8	(8) lbw b S.N.Banerjee	5
11	B.K.Mitra	c S.N.Banerjee b Chowdhury	0		
	Extras		8		10
			249	(8 wickets)	88

FoW (1): 1-9 (1), 2-27 (2), 3-28 (4), 4-30 (5), 5-35 (3), 6-72 (7), 7-120 (8), 8-201 (6), 9-249 (9), 10-249 (11)
FoW (2): 1-1 (1), 2-2 (2), 3-20, 4-24, 5-35, 6-40, 7-56, 8-88

Bengal Bowling	O	M	R	W		O	M	R	W
Mitra	13	6	29	2		17	6	46	2
Mustafi	8	4	5	0		6	2	27	0
Banerjee	18	11	13	0		22	3	76	2
Dutt	7	3	13	0		12	3	32	2
Cooch Behar	6	0	24	0					
Bhattacharya	24.3	4	57	5	(5)	10	3	31	0
Chatterjee					(6)	6	0	26	1

Bihar Bowling	O	M	R	W		O	M	R	W
S.N.Banerjee	21	5	89	2		8	7	1	1
Chowdhury	19.4	3	75	6		15	3	52	4
Bose	8	3	24	2		8	2	24	3
Sweeney	9	1	34	0		2	2	0	0
Das Gupta	1	0	11	0					
S.Banerjee	2	0	8	0	(5)	2	1	1	0
Patel					(6)	2	2	0	0

Umpires: M.G.Bhave and T.A.Ramachandran. Toss: Bihar

Close of Play: 1st day: Bengal (1) 26-1 (Sen 12*, Dutt 11*); 2nd day: Bihar (2) 60-3 (S.Ghosh 35*, S.Banerjee 10*).
S.Banerjee's 101 took 202 minutes. Lieutenant Patankar was involved in a motor accident after play on the second day and so was absent on the third day. A.K.Deb was supposed to keep wicket for Bengal but was ill on the day of the match so P.K.Sen was sent for with E.C.Harvey-Johnston keeping until Sen arrived. S.Ghosh kept wicket in the Bengal second innings.

GWALIOR v DELHI

Played at Laxmibai College of Physical Education Ground, Gwalior, December 20, 21, 22, 1943.

Delhi won by 419 runs.

DELHI

1	†Suraj Narain	c Mathur b Shankar	13	lbw b Mathur	27
2	Gurbaksh Singh	b Shankar	78	c Kunzru b Shankar	5
3	Idrees Baig	c Ram Singh b Afzal Ahmed	2	c Kunzru b Afzal Ahmed	106
4	*M.R.Bhide	c Roop Singh b Shankar	3	c Khanwilkar b Ram Singh	25
5	Ejaz Ahmed	lbw b Shankar	0	st Navle b Yarde	27
6	K.Bahadur	c Khanwilkar b Afzal Ahmed	3	b Afzal Ahmed	84
7	M.H.Maqsood	b Khanwilkar	21	st Navle b Mathur	10
8	Manzoor	lbw b Afzal Ahmed	45	b Shankar	20
9	Shujauddin	c Mathur b Shankar	3	not out	41
10	Mohammad Yunus Khan	c and b Shankar	0	lbw b Khanwilkar	12
11	Hargopal Singh	not out	6	c Afzal Ahmed b Shankar	22
	Extras		5		14
			179		393

FoW (1): 1- (1), 2- (3), 3- (4), 4- (5), 5-23 (6), 6-76 (7), 7-155 (8), 8- (9), 9- (10), 10-179 (2)
FoW (2): 1-18, 2-52, 3-74, 4- , 5- , 6- , 7- , 8- , 9- , 10-393

GWALIOR

1	R.D.Mathur	c Idrees Baig b Shujauddin	30	b Ejaz Ahmed	5
2	R.Balbhadra Singh	b Hargopal Singh	10	c Suraj Narain b Ejaz Ahmed	5
3	Roop Singh	st Suraj Narain b Bahadur	4	run out	0
4	†J.G.Navle	lbw b Mohammad Yunus Khan	27	lbw b Hargopal Singh	10
5	D.K.Yarde	b Hargopal Singh	0	lbw b Mohammad Yunus Khan	0
6	S.N.Kunzru	b Hargopal Singh	0	b Hargopal Singh	1
7	D.Shankar	b Hargopal Singh	1	b Bahadur	18
8	*Ram Singh	b Shujauddin	0	b Hargopal Singh	6
9	C.N.Haksar	b Mohammad Yunus Khan	2	c and b Bahadur	2
10	Khanwilkar	b Hargopal Singh	6	b Bahadur	2
11	Afzal Ahmed	not out	0	not out	3
	Extras		12		9
			92		61

FoW (1): 1-26 (2), 2- , 3- , 4- , 5- , 6- , 7- , 8- , 9- , 10-92
FoW (2): 1- , 2- , 3- , 4- , 5- , 6- , 7- , 8- , 9- , 10-61

Gwalior Bowling

	O	M	R	W		O	M	R	W
Afzal Ahmed	21	2	64	3		22	0	72	2
Shankar	18	1	57	6		28	1	103	3
Khanwilkar	7	0	34	1		17	2	63	1
Mathur	5	0	10	0		16	0	65	2
Haksar	4	1	9	0	(6)	2	0	16	0
Ram Singh					(5)	8	0	34	1
Yarde					(7)	4	0	14	1
Balbhadra Singh					(8)	2	0	12	0

Delhi Bowling

	O	M	R	W		O	M	R	W
Ejaz Ahmed	6	1	11	0		10	3	13	2
Mohammad Yunus Khan	10	3	14	2		6	1	8	1
Hargopal Singh	20.1	7	33	5		10	2	20	3
Shujauddin	8	2	12	2					
Bahadur	6	3	3	1	(4)	7	2	11	3
Idrees Baig	3	0	7	0					

Umpires: Toss:

Close of Play: 1st day: Gwalior (1) 92 all out; 2nd day: Delhi (2) 393 all out.

CANTERBURY v OTAGO

Played at Lancaster Park, Christchurch, December 25, 27, 28, 1943.

Canterbury won by an innings and 67 runs.

CANTERBURY

1	I.B.Cromb	c Knight b Mulcock	25
2	K.F.M.Uttley	c D.G.Watt b Mulcock	7
3	L.A.Butterfield	b Freeman	25
4	*W.A.Hadlee	b Toomey	105
5	W.M.Anderson	b Freeman	21
6	F.P.O'Brien	run out	164
7	J.Smith	lbw b Freeman	47
8	M.K.Lohrey	b Mulcock	6
9	R.H.Scott	not out	60
10	T.B.Burtt	b Mulcock	30
11	†D.M.Dunnet	b Mulcock	0
	Extras	b 15, lb 5	20
			510

FoW (1): 1-13 (2), 2-51 (1), 3-69 (3), 4-119 (5), 5-248 (4), 6-388 (7), 7-405 (8), 8-424 (6), 9-510 (10), 10-510 (11)

OTAGO

1	D.G.Watt	st Dunnet b Burtt	15	(3) c Anderson b Burtt	105
2	D.H.Murdoch	st Dunnet b Burtt	28	b Anderson	22
3	*C.D.G.Toomey	c Cromb b Burtt	13	(4) run out	9
4	J.C.Scandrett	c Scott b Burtt	22	(5) b Anderson	1
5	A.R.Knight	b Scott	2	(6) b Anderson	0
6	L.D.Smith	run out	19	(7) b Anderson	7
7	G.H.Mills	c Dunnet b Lohrey	21	(8) lbw b Anderson	6
8	L.Watt	lbw b Burtt	29	(9) b Burtt	1
9	†O.J.N.Everson	not out	26	(1) st Dunnet b Burtt	28
10	T.A.Freeman	b Scott	3	b Cromb	38
11	E.Mulcock	c and b Burtt	1	not out	4
	Extras	b 11, lb 7, nb 4	22	b 6, lb 7, nb 8	21
			201		242

FoW (1): 1-37 (1), 2-55 (3), 3-77 (2), 4-80 (5), 5-96 (4), 6-112 (6), 7-156 (7), 8-185 (8), 9-196 (10), 10-201 (11)
FoW (2): 1-55 (1), 2-55 (2), 3-93 (4), 4-99 (5), 5-103 (6), 6-125 (7), 7-145 (8), 8-152 (9), 9-230 (10), 10-242 (3)

Otago Bowling

	O	M	R	W
Mulcock	45.4	2	166	5
Freeman	34	2	157	3
Toomey	5	0	37	1
Smith	16	2	83	0
Knight	5	0	31	0
Mills	1	0	16	0

Canterbury Bowling

	O	M	R	W	O	M	R	W
Scott	20	5	53	2	6	0	17	0
Lohrey	16	2	46	1	8	2	11	0
Hadlee	3	1	6	0	4	0	10	0
Burtt	23.3	4	56	6	18	2	69	3
Anderson	4	0	10	0	16	1	90	5
Cromb	4	2	8	0	5	0	24	1

Umpires: Toss: Canterbury

Close of Play: 1st day: Canterbury (1) 291-5 (O'Brien 75*, Smith 18*); 2nd day: Otago (1) 201-9 (Everson 26*, Mulcock 1*).

F.P.O'Brien's 164 took 239 minutes and included 14 fours. D.G.Watt's 105 included 14 fours.

EUROPEANS v INDIANS

Played at Madras Cricket Club Ground, Chepauk, Madras, December 25, 26, 1943.

Match drawn.

INDIANS

1	M.Swaminathan	c Law b Barmby	6
2	K.S.Kannan	c Law b Robinson	29
3	*A.G.Ram Singh	lbw b Johnstone	72
4	T.V.Parthasarathi	lbw b Johnstone	38
5	Raja of Ramnad	c Law b Johnstone	27
6	A.Ananthanarayanan	st Law b Richardson	25
7	M.J.Gopalan	c Law b Johnstone	57
8	B.S.R.Bhadradri	b Robinson	5
9	N.J.Venkatesan	b Robinson	4
10	†M.O.Srinivasan	not out	15
11	C.R.Rangachari	not out	15
	Extras		12
		(9 wickets, declared)	305

FoW (1): 1-20 (1), 2-58 (2), 3-150 (4), 4-151 (3), 5-186 (6), 6-254 (5), 7-267 (7), 8-273 (8), 9-281 (9)

EUROPEANS

1	*C.P.Johnstone	c Bhadradri b Ram Singh	20	lbw b Gopalan	72
2	†J.A.G.C.Law	c Srinivasan b Kannan	35	b Rangachari	2
3	C.N.Reed	c Srinivasan b Ram Singh	45	c Kannan b Ram Singh	43
4	M.Robinson	b Kannan	0	not out	18
5	F.F.Richardson	c Kannan b Ram Singh	28	not out	7
6	N.M.Mischler	run out	0		
7	H.P.Ward	b Kannan	34		
8	G.A.Orford	lbw b Ram Singh	4		
9	C.Hitchen	c Rangachari b Ram Singh	0		
10	A.G.Barmby	lbw b Kannan	0		
11	G.C.Dallimore	not out	0		
	Extras		9		4
			175	(3 wickets)	146

FoW (1): 1-29 (1), 2-90 (2), 3-94 (4), 4-111 (3), 5-111 (6), 6-154 (5), 7-171 (8), 8-175 (7), 9-175 (10), 10-175 (9)
FoW (2): 1-9 (2), 2-88 (3), 3-136 (1)

Europeans Bowling

	O	M	R	W
Hitchen	15	4	36	0
Dallimore	10	2	22	0
Barmby	37	12	64	1
Johnstone	27	9	48	4
Robinson	33	6	93	3
Richardson	14	3	30	1

Indians Bowling

	O	M	R	W		O	M	R	W
Gopalan	12	5	16	0		15	2	32	1
Ram Singh	26.2	2	67	5		14	3	39	1
Rangachari	10	3	22	0		8	2	16	1
Venkatesan	15	0	49	0		4	0	24	0
Kannan	9	3	12	4		9	2	20	0
Swaminathan					(6)	3	0	11	0

Umpires: V.S.Natarajan and T.A.Ramachandran. Toss: Europeans

Close of Play: 1st day: Indians (1) 305-9 (Srinivasan 15*, Rangachari 15*).

WELLINGTON v AUCKLAND

Played at Basin Reserve, Wellington, December 25, 27, 28, 1943.

Auckland won by eight wickets.

AUCKLAND					
1	D.C.Ritchie	st Mooney b Allen	30	not out	46
2	N.Ellis	b Buchan	63	c Knapp b Buchan	11
3	*H.T.Pearson	c Tindill b Knapp	7	(4) not out	13
4	B.Sutcliffe	b Dickinson	146	(3) c sub b Buchan	5
5	W.H.Cooper	lbw b Allen	52		
6	A.C.Kerr	b Knapp	72		
7	R.W.G.Emery	b Dickinson	21		
8	†L.A.W.Kent	not out	11		
9	R.G.Sorenson	not out	15		
10	H.J.H.Harrison				
11	C.Burke				
	Extras	b 15, lb 2, w 2, nb 2	21	b 6, lb 1	7
		(7 wickets, declared)	438	(2 wickets)	82

FoW (1): 1-73 (1), 2-80 (3), 3-121 (2), 4-277 (5), 5-351 (4), 6-393 (7), 7-415 (6)
FoW (2): 1-43 (2), 2-51 (3)

WELLINGTON					
1	E.F.Bezzant	b Emery	3	(4) st Kent b Kerr	25
2	*E.W.T.Tindill	c Sutcliffe b Sorenson	21	(3) c and b Kerr	15
3	R.E.J.Menzies	b Burke	1	(5) b Kerr	7
4	G.H.Stringer	c and b Emery	47	(1) b Harrison	7
5	W.H.Dustin	c Emery b Sorenson	20	(2) c Ellis b Emery	2
6	C.A.Muir	lbw b Burke	18	b Kerr	0
7	†F.L.H.Mooney	c Kent b Burke	0	c Sorenson b Harrison	180
8	G.R.Dickinson	c Emery b Sorenson	10	c Sutcliffe b Sorenson	39
9	R.Allen	b Emery	18	b Sorenson	0
10	R.Buchan	lbw b Emery	16	b Kerr	34
11	E.C.Knapp	not out	5	not out	21
	Extras	b 3, lb 5	8	b 12, lb 6, nb 3	21
			167		351

FoW (1): 1-18 (1), 2-19 (3), 3-37, 4-70, 5-98, 6-100, 7-119, 8-145, 9-150, 10-167
FoW (2): 1-10 (1), 2-10 (2), 3-39 (3), 4-53 (5), 5-53 (6), 6-62 (4), 7-106 (8), 8-111 (9), 9-238 (10), 10-351 (7)

Wellington Bowling	O	M	R	W			O	M	R	W
Dickinson	23	1	91	2	2w,2nb		5	0	22	0
Buchan	20	1	65	1			7.5	0	30	2
Knapp	24	0	102	2			3	0	23	0
Allen	26	2	107	2						
Muir	8	2	40	0						
Dustin	2	0	12	0						

Auckland Bowling	O	M	R	W			O	M	R	W
Harrison	9	2	23	0			21.3	4	44	2
Emery	15.7	2	41	4			15	2	31	1
Burke	16	1	37	3		(4)	14	1	54	0
Sorenson	14	2	43	3		(3)	18	2	74	2
Kerr	5	1	15	0			27	4	80	5
Sutcliffe						(6)	2	0	15	0
Cooper						(7)	6	1	32	0

Umpires: M.F.Pengelly and C.A.Webb. Toss: Auckland

Close of Play: 1st day: Auckland (1) 337-4 (Sutcliffe 144*, Kerr 27*); 2nd day: Wellington (2) 26-2 (Tindill 7*, Bezzant 8*).

B.Sutcliffe's 146 included 16 fours and 1 six. F.L.H.Mooney's 180 took 251 minutes and included 25 fours.

WESTERN INDIA v SIND

Played at Municipal Stadium, Rajkot, December 28, 29, 30, 1943.

Match drawn.

WESTERN INDIA

1	†Prataprai	b Lakda	31	c Daud Khan b Samtani	16
2	*H.W.Barritt	c Jamnadas b Parsram	2	(8) c Jamnadas b Narottam	49
3	Umar Khan	b Girdhari	47	(6) c Qamaruddin Sheikh b Lakda	0
4	Prithviraj	run out	85	b Lakda	24
5	S.B.Gandhi	c Dipchand b Girdhari	7	(7) b Lakda	123
6	Saeed Ahmed	lbw b Girdhari	0	(9) c and b Girdhari	11
7	Purshottam	st Jamnadas b Lakda	53	(5) st Jamnadas b Girdhari	20
8	Sukhvantrai	c Qamaruddin Sheikh b Lakda	13	(10) not out	1
9	Akbar Khan	c Dipchand b Girdhari	8	(11) st Jamnadas b Girdhari	2
10	K.S.Abdul Kadir	run out	20	(3) c Jamnadas b Samtani	2
11	Jayantilal Vora	not out	5	(2) c Qamaruddin Sheikh b Samtani	6
	Extras		3		31
			274		285

FoW (1): 1- , 2-38, 3-121, 4- , 5- , 6- , 7- , 8- , 9- , 10-274
FoW (2): 1- (2), 2- (3), 3- , 4-71, 5- , 6-97, 7-243, 8- , 9- , 10-285

SIND

1	D.Narottam	c Prataprai b Saeed Ahmed	18	(2) c Prataprai b Saeed Ahmed	1
2	J.Parsram'	b Saeed Ahmed	37	(3) st Prataprai b Purshottam	19
3	†L.Jamnadas	b Akbar Khan	5	(1) c Sukhvantrai b Saeed Ahmed	19
4	Qamaruddin Sheikh	lbw b Saeed Ahmed	4	b Saeed Ahmed	0
5	H.M.Asha	b Gandhi	8	(6) not out	50
6	*Naoomal Jaoomal	b Gandhi	44	(8) not out	36
7	Daud Khan	b Saeed Ahmed	2	(5) c Purshottam b Jayantilal Vora	17
8	A.Dipchand	b Saeed Ahmed	1	(7) c Gandhi b Saeed Ahmed	9
9	S.K.Girdhari	c Purshottam b Saeed Ahmed	13		
10	V.K.Samtani	lbw b Akbar Khan	13		
11	F.G.Lakda	not out	10		
	Extras		17		7
			172	(6 wickets)	158

FoW (1): 1- , 2- , 3- , 4- , 5- , 6- , 7-96, 8-146, 9- , 10-172
FoW (2): 1- , 2- , 3-32, 4- , 5- , 6-72

Sind Bowling

	O	M	R	W		O	M	R	W
Samtani	18	5	40	0		10	6	16	3
Parsram	21	2	83	1		2	0	10	0
Lakda	19	3	43	3		24	3	65	3
Girdhari	21	2	82	4		23.4	6	63	3
Naoomal Jaoomal	16.1	6	23	0		8	0	30	0
Daud Khan					(6)	2	0	14	0
Narottam					(7)	7	0	18	1
Qamaruddin Sheikh					(8)	14	2	38	0

Western India Bowling

	O	M	R	W		O	M	R	W
Saeed Ahmed	25	5	45	6		14	7	26	4
Akbar Khan	17.5	4	45	2		9	0	30	0
Jayantilal Vora	5	1	10	0		8	1	21	1
Purshottam	11	1	29	0		9	1	31	1
Gandhi	15	3	26	2					
Prithviraj					(5)	3	0	24	0
Abdul Kadir					(6)	3	0	7	0
Barritt					(7)	3	0	12	0

Umpires: N.D.Karmarkar and J.R.Patel. Toss:

Close of Play: 1st day: Sind (1) 1-0 (Narottam 0*, Jamnadas 1*); 2nd day: Western India (2) 83-5 (Purshottam 15*, Gandhi 5*).
S.B.Gandhi's 123 included 14 fours. J.Parsram retired hurt after being hit on the jaw by a ball from Saeed Ahmed in the Sind first innings having scored 0 (team score 0-0) and later returned.

BOMBAY v MAHARASHTRA

Played at Brabourne Stadium, Bombay, December 31, 1943, January 1, 2, 3, 1944.

Match drawn.

BOMBAY			
1	†M.K.Mantri	c Phadkar b Sohoni	14
2	C.T.Sarwate	st Bhandarkar b Shinde	41
3	Anwar Hussain	run out	1
4	K.C.Ibrahim	lbw b Shinde	8
5	*V.M.Merchant	not out	359
6	K.M.Rangnekar	b Sohoni	8
7	R.S.Modi	b Jadhav	168
8	J.B.Khot	c Bhandarkar b Ghazali	15
9	R.S.Cooper	c and b Shinde	89
10	M.N.Raiji	c Deodhar b Shinde	5
11	B.K.Garudachar	st Bhandarkar b Shinde	2
	Extras	b 17, lb 4, w 2, nb 2	25
			735

FoW (1): 1-42 (1), 2-43 (3), 3-68 (4), 4-79 (2), 5-90 (6), 6-461 (7), 7-497 (8), 8-707 (9), 9-733 (10), 10-735 (11)

MAHARASHTRA			
1	S.W.Sohoni	lbw b Sarwate	43
2	†K.V.Bhandarkar	c Raiji b Sarwate	4
3	M.H.Mankad	c Mantri b Khot	48
4	*D.B.Deodhar	lbw b Sarwate	7
5	D.G.Phadkar	c Sarwate b Raiji	88
6	M.N.Paranjpe	c Rangnekar b Khot	49
7	M.E.Z.Ghazali	hit wkt b Sarwate	4
8	K.M.Jadhav	b Raiji	8
9	R.R.Chandorkar	c Khot b Sarwate	9
10	S.G.Shinde	not out	14
11	V.M.Pandit	absent ill	0
	Extras	b 8, lb 16	24
			298

FoW (1): 1-20 (2), 2-78 (1), 3-94 (4), 4-136 (3), 5-216 (6), 6-232 (7), 7-247 (8), 8-274 (9), 9-298 (5)

Maharashtra Bowling

	O	M	R	W
Phadkar	23	4	84	0
Sohoni	58	9	176	2
Jadhav	30	3	134	1
Shinde	75.5	10	186	5
Mankad	42	11	63	0
Ghazali	28	8	52	1
Deodhar	8	3	15	0

Bombay Bowling

	O	M	R	W
Khot	29	9	59	2
Anwar Hussain	4	2	12	0
Merchant	3	1	6	0
Sarwate	38	8	104	5
Garudachar	11	2	37	0
Raiji	21	3	42	2
Modi	3	0	10	0
Ibrahim	2	0	4	0

Umpires: J.Birtwistle and Vali Ahmed. Toss: Bombay

Close of Play: 1st day: Bombay (1) 308-5 (Merchant 119*, Modi 102*); 2nd day: Bombay (1) 665-7 (Merchant 322*, Cooper 67*); 3rd day: Maharashtra (1) 272-7 (Phadkar 77*, Chandorkar 8*).

The match was scheduled for three days but extended to four. V.M.Merchant's 359 took 640 minutes and included 31 fours. R.S.Modi's 168 took 361 minutes and included 19 fours.

CENTRAL PROVINCES AND BERAR v HYDERABAD

Played at Central Provinces Gymkhana Ground, Nagpur, December 31, 1943, January 1, 2, 1944.

Hyderabad won by 10 runs.

HYDERABAD					
1	Asadullah Qureshi	c Kesari b Lateef	52	c Lateef b Kesari	1
2	†I.Sanjiva Rao	c T.S.Naidu b Athar Khan	0	(10) not out	9
3	E.B.Aibara	run out	8	c Lokhande b Lateef	19
4	Venkataswami	c Kesari b Lokhande	6	(7) lbw b Lokhande	2
5	*B.C.Khanna	b Lateef	29	(4) c P.R.Naidu b Lateef	29
6	Asghar Ali	lbw b Lokhande	1	c T.S.Naidu b Lateef	4
7	S.R.Mehta	b Lokhande	6	(5) st Kondra b Ishaq Ali	2
8	Ushaq Ahmed	not out	18	(2) c T.S.Naidu b Lateef	22
9	M.Robinson	b Lokhande	1	(8) st Kondra b Lokhande	2
10	Ghulam Ahmed	c Poonawalla b Athar Khan	18	(9) b Lateef	10
11	A.R.Bhupathi	c Kondra b Athar Khan	2	lbw b Lokhande	1
	Extras		19		8
			160		109

FoW (1): 1-1 (2), 2- , 3- , 4- , 5- , 6- , 7- , 8- , 9- , 10-160
FoW (2): 1- , 2- , 3- , 4- , 5- , 6- , 7- , 8- , 9- , 10-109

CENTRAL PROVINCES AND BERAR					
1	†U.N.Kondra	lbw b Khanna	0	c Sanjiva Rao b Khanna	4
2	P.R.Naidu	c Robinson b Ghulam Ahmed	9	(7) b Ghulam Ahmed	5
3	T.S.Naidu	lbw b Ghulam Ahmed	16	(5) lbw b Ghulam Ahmed	3
4	Athar Khan	b Mehta	28	(6) c Bhupathi b Ghulam Ahmed	0
5	K.P.Kesari	lbw b Ghulam Ahmed	40	(9) c Sanjiva Rao b Mehta	8
6	S.J.Poonawalla	st Sanjiva Rao b Khanna	47	(10) not out	29
7	*E.G.Mane	c Bhupathi b Ghulam Ahmed	1	(11) b Ghulam Ahmed	35
8	S.Ishaq Ali	c Asadullah Qureshi b Mehta	1	(2) c Bhupathi b Mehta	0
9	D.L.Thompson	c Ghulam Ahmed b Mehta	3	(4) c Ghulam Ahmed b Khanna	0
10	S.A.Lateef	b Ghulam Ahmed	12	(8) b Mehta	7
11	M.L.Lokhande	not out	5	(3) c and b Mehta	2
	Extras		4		
			166		93

FoW (1): 1- , 2- , 3- , 4- , 5- , 6- , 7- , 8- , 9- , 10-166
FoW (2): 1- , 2- , 3- , 4- , 5- , 6-10, 7- , 8- , 9-47, 10-93

Central Provinces and Berar Bowling	O	M	R	W		O	M	R	W
Athar Khan	8.5	3	22	3		3	1	13	0
Kesari	12	4	16	0		7	1	14	1
Lokhande	21	6	39	4		9.3	3	15	3
Lateef	26	11	35	2		20	8	44	5
Ishaq Ali	15	4	29	0		7	1	15	1

Hyderabad Bowling	O	M	R	W		O	M	R	W
Khanna	11	5	23	2		3	1	5	2
Mehta	21	4	42	3		20	10	33	4
Ghulam Ahmed	22.5	6	54	5		18.1	0	41	4
Ushaq Ahmed	5	1	19	0					
Bhupathi	10	2	21	0	(4)	2	0	14	0
Asadullah Qureshi	1	0	3	0					

Umpires: V.S.Natarajan and S.Sriraman. Toss: Hyderabad

Close of Play: 1st day: Central Provinces and Berar (1) 52-2 (T.S.Naidu 15*, Athar Khan 28*); 2nd day: Central Provinces and Berar (2) 12-6 (P.R.Naidu not out, Lateef not out).

MYSORE v MADRAS

Played at Central College Ground, Bangalore, December 31, 1943, January 1, 2, 1944.

Match drawn.

MYSORE			
1	A.Ethinder	c G.Parthasarathi b Gopalan	81
2	Y.S.Ramaswami	c Ram Singh b Rangachari	0
3	K.Thimmappiah	c Gopalan b Rangachari	2
4	C.J.Ramdev	c Srinivasan b Rangachari	14
5	B.Frank	c Gopalan b Ram Singh	86
6	J.R.Snaize	b Gopalan	17
7	S.Rama Rao	c Gopalan b Ram Singh	33
8	†F.K.Irani	b Gopalan	0
9	*S.Darashah	c Gopalan b Ram Singh	54
10	G.M.Rajasekhar	st Srinivasan b Ram Singh	58
11	M.R.Alasingrachar	not out	5
	Extras		9
			359

FoW (1): 1-0 (2), 2-4 (3), 3-29 (4), 4-160 (5), 5-186 (6), 6-236 (7), 7-237 (1), 8-237 (8), 9-354 (10), 10-359 (9)

MADRAS			
1	T.V.Parthasarathi	c Irani b Frank	36
2	K.S.Kannan	lbw b Frank	47
3	A.G.Ram Singh	c Irani b Frank	80
4	A.Ananthanarayanan	b Darashah	21
5	F.F.Richardson	lbw b Frank	64
6	*M.J.Gopalan	c Darashah b Rama Rao	6
7	G.Parthasarathi	lbw b Darashah	19
8	N.J.Venkatesan	c Snaize b Thimmappiah	26
9	R.S.Nailer	c Thimmappiah b Rama Rao	17
10	†M.O.Srinivasan	c Snaize b Rama Rao	27
11	C.R.Rangachari	not out	8
	Extras		14
			365

FoW (1): 1-80 (2), 2-97 (1), 3-122 (4), 4-252 (3), 5-267 (5), 6-267 (6), 7-309 (8), 8-327 (7), 9-327 (9), 10-365 (10)

Madras Bowling

	O	M	R	W
Gopalan	21	3	58	3
Rangachari	24	3	95	3
Ram Singh	33.1	6	95	4
Venkatesan	12	1	46	0
G.Parthasarathi	8	0	45	0
Kannan	6	2	11	0

Mysore Bowling

	O	M	R	W
Darashah	29	6	83	2
Frank	38	15	79	4
Rama Rao	41.1	14	77	3
Ramaswami	17	4	64	0
Alasingrachar	2	0	9	0
Thimmappiah	9	2	19	1
Snaize	2	0	4	0
Rajasekhar	2	0	16	0

Umpires: L.O'Callaghan and M.G.Vijayasarathi. Toss: Mysore

Close of Play: 1st day: Mysore (1) 359 all out; 2nd day: Madras (1) 293-6 (G.Parthasarathi 9*, Venkatesan 16*).

CANTERBURY v AUCKLAND

Played at Lancaster Park, Christchurch, January 1, 3, 1944.

Canterbury won by eight wickets.

AUCKLAND					
1	D.C.Ritchie	c Cromb b Scott	9	c T.B.Burtt b Scott	30
2	N.Ellis	run out	17	c Scott b Butterfield	1
3	B.Sutcliffe	c Cromb b Scott	4	b Scott	6
4	*H.T.Pearson	b N.V.Burtt	19	b Butterfield	58
5	W.H.Cooper	lbw b N.V.Burtt	4	c Cromb b N.V.Burtt	4
6	A.C.Kerr	c O'Brien b Butterfield	20	c Cromb b Butterfield	81
7	R.W.G.Emery	c Hadlee b T.B.Burtt	8	c Dunnet b Butterfield	1
8	†L.A.W.Kent	run out	8	c Hadlee b N.V.Burtt	0
9	R.G.Sorenson	b T.B.Burtt	14	run out	29
10	H.J.H.Harrison	not out	7	c and b Butterfield	14
11	C.Burke	b Scott	18	not out	11
	Extras	b 6, lb 2, nb 2	10	b 12, nb 3	15
			138		250

FoW (1): 1-25, 2-25, 3-39, 4-52, 5-62, 6-73, 7-96, 8-96, 9-114, 10-138
FoW (2): 1-5 (2), 2-21 (3), 3-65 (1), 4-78 (5), 5-147, 6-155, 7-160, 8-216, 9-227, 10-250

CANTERBURY					
1	K.F.M.Uttley	c Pearson b Emery	55	c Harrison b Kerr	46
2	I.B.Cromb	c Sutcliffe b Burke	29	c Harrison b Kerr	16
3	L.A.Butterfield	b Kerr	0	not out	19
4	*W.A.Hadlee	c Kerr b Burke	16	not out	6
5	W.M.Anderson	c Kerr b Burke	64		
6	F.P.O'Brien	c Burke b Cooper	1		
7	J.Smith	c Sorenson b Kerr	19		
8	R.H.Scott	not out	71		
9	T.B.Burtt	c Kent b Burke	1		
10	†D.M.Dunnet	b Burke	1		
11	N.V.Burtt	b Sorenson	18		
	Extras	b 10, lb 8, nb 3	21	b 7, lb 3	10
			296	(2 wickets)	97

FoW (1): 1-58, 2-60, 3-94, 4-118, 5-139, 6-189, 7-227, 8-236, 9-238, 10-296
FoW (2): 1-39 (2), 2-79 (1)

Canterbury Bowling	O	M	R	W	O	M	R	W
Scott	15.4	2	36	3	23	3	70	2
Butterfield	12	3	21	1	15.4	8	24	5
T.B.Burtt	11	3	25	2	15	1	69	0
N.V.Burtt	9	0	46	2	8	0	72	2

Auckland Bowling	O	M	R	W	O	M	R	W
Emery	15	2	65	1	3	0	17	0
Harrison	18	2	58	0	4	0	15	0
Sorenson	11.7	0	55	1	3	0	18	0
Burke	12	2	52	5	3	0	11	0
Kerr	9	0	42	2	6.1	1	26	2
Cooper	2	1	3	1				

Umpires: G.E.Falgar and H.W.Gourlay. Toss: Auckland

Close of Play: 1st day: Canterbury (1) 251-9 (Scott 39*, N.V.Burtt 7*).

The match was scheduled for three days but completed in two.

BENGAL v HOLKAR

Played at Eden Gardens, Calcutta, January 7, 8, 9, 1944.

Bengal won by ten wickets.

BENGAL

1	A.Jabbar	c Nimbalkar b Nayudu	36		
2	A.C.Chatterjee	lbw b Subramaniam	47	not out	15
3	†P.K.Sen	b Tata Rao	142		
4	N.C.Chatterjee	c Subramaniam b Tata Rao	79		
5	K.Bhattacharya	c Mushtaq Ali b Nayudu	25		
6	S.K.Mustafi	c Nimbalkar b Tata Rao	6		
7	A.Sen	run out	2	(1) not out	3
8	*Maharaja of Cooch Behar	c Nayudu b Gaekwad	26		
9	S.A.Banerjee	run out	1		
10	S.Dutt	b Tata Rao	0		
11	B.K.Mitra	not out	0		
	Extras		23		3
			387	(no wicket)	21

FoW (1): 1-41 (1), 2-157 (2), 3-299 (3), 4-330 (4), 5-354 (6), 6-354 (5), 7-369 (7), 8- (9), 9- (10), 10-387 (8)

HOLKAR

1	S.R.Kale	b Mitra	4	c and b Banerjee	0
2	C.E.Holkar	c Dutt b Bhattacharya	29	(11) not out	0
3	S.Mushtaq Ali	c Mustafi b Bhattacharya	33	b Bhattacharya	70
4	*C.K.Nayudu	c Bhattacharya b Mitra	7	c Bhattacharya b Dutt	18
5	B.B.Nimbalkar	c Bhattacharya b Banerjee	9	(6) c A.C.Chatterjee b Mitra	57
6	†J.N.Bhaya	not out	19	(5) run out	20
7	H.G.Gaekwad	b Bhattacharya	1	b Banerjee	0
8	S.Ishtiaq Ali	b Bhattacharya	2	(10) b A.C.Chatterjee	21
9	R.Subramaniam	c Mustafi b Bhattacharya	0	(2) c P.K.Sen b Bhattacharya	15
10	R.P.Singh	b Bhattacharya	3	(9) c A.C.Chatterjee b Mitra	36
11	P.Tata Rao	st P.K.Sen b Dutt	12	(8) b Dutt	7
	Extras		19		22
			138		266

FoW (1): 1-9 (1), 2-66 (3), 3-74 (4), 4-93 (5), 5-95 (2), 6-99 (7), 7-113 (8), 8-113 (9), 9-125 (10), 10-138 (11)
FoW (2): 1-1 (1), 2-43 (2), 3-111 (4), 4-111 (3), 5-144 (5), 6-144 (7), 7-171 (8), 8-219 (6), 9-258 (9), 10-266 (10)

Holkar Bowling

	O	M	R	W		O	M	R	W
Gaekwad	37.1	11	84	1	(3)	2	1	2	0
Nimbalkar	2	2	0	0	(1)	5	3	7	0
Mushtaq Ali	18	4	57	0	(2)	2.2	1	9	0
Nayudu	27	2	117	2					
Ishtiaq Ali	2	0	7	0					
Tata Rao	23	7	46	4					
Subramaniam	5	0	27	1					
Singh	6	0	26	0					

Bengal Bowling

	O	M	R	W		O	M	R	W
Mitra	11	3	24	2		17	4	47	2
Banerjee	21	3	46	1		16	6	42	2
Cooch Behar	4	3	7	0		2	0	10	0
Bhattacharya	14	5	26	6		16	2	53	2
A.Sen	2	1	3	0		4	1	7	0
Dutt	5.3	1	13	1		9.4	0	52	2
Mustafi					(7)	2	0	15	0
N.C.Chatterjee					(8)	3	0	14	0
A.C.Chatterjee					(9)	0.5	0	4	1

Umpires: J.R.Patel and T.A.Ramachandran. Toss: Bengal

Close of Play: 1st day: Bengal (1) 377-7 (Cooch Behar 16*, Banerjee 1*); 2nd day: Holkar (2) 143-4 (Bhaya 19*, Nimbalkar 13*).
P.K.Sen's 142 took 225 minutes and included 16 fours and 1 five.

WESTERN INDIA v BOMBAY

Played at Rajkot Cricket Club Ground, January 14, 15, 16, 1944.

Match drawn.

BOMBAY			
1	M.F.Mistry	c Gandhi b Jayantilal Vora	3
2	C.T.Sarwate	c Saeed Ahmed b Jayantilal Vora	6
3	Anwar Hussain	c Akbar Khan b Jayantilal Vora	3
4	R.S.Modi	c Saeed Ahmed b Akbar Khan	128
5	*V.M.Merchant	c Prataprai b Jayantilal Vora	53
6	K.C.Ibrahim	c Prithviraj b Jayantilal Vora	9
7	J.B.Khot	c Gandhi b Saeed Ahmed	2
8	K.M.Rangnekar	b Saeed Ahmed	0
9	M.N.Raiji	lbw b Saeed Ahmed	5
10	†M.K.Mantri	b Saeed Ahmed	17
11	B.K.Garudachar	not out	16
	Extras	b 8, lb 4, nb 1	13
			255

FoW (1): 1-9 (1), 2-12 (2), 3-13 (3), 4-139 (5), 5-166 (6), 6-171 (7), 7-171 (8), 8-203 (9), 9-232 (4), 10-255 (10)

WESTERN INDIA			
1	†Prataprai	c Rangnekar b Sarwate	17
2	Jayantilal Vora	run out	0
3	Umar Khan	c Raiji b Merchant	136
4	Prithviraj	c Mantri b Merchant	174
5	Saeed Ahmed	not out	12
6	S.B.Gandhi	not out	8
7	Sukhvantrai		
8	*H.W.Barritt		
9	Purshottam		
10	K.S.Abdul Kadir		
11	Akbar Khan		
	Extras	b 14, lb 1, nb 1	16
		(4 wickets)	363

FoW (1): 1-1 (2), 2-28 (1), 3-341 (3), 4-346 (4)

Western India Bowling

	O	M	R	W
Saeed Ahmed	63	38	57	4
Jayantilal Vora	56	19	74	5
Akbar Khan	42	21	45	1
Gandhi	17	3	47	0
Purshottam	10	1	19	0

Bombay Bowling

	O	M	R	W
Khot	35	14	46	0
Merchant	29	10	52	2
Anwar Hussain	1	1	0	0
Sarwate	42	10	97	1
Ibrahim	5	1	24	0
Raiji	19	3	46	0
Garudachar	20	1	64	0
Rangnekar	9	2	18	0

Umpires: M.G.Bhave and M.G.Vijayasarathi. Toss: Bombay

Close of Play: 1st day: Bombay (1) 165-4 (Modi 84*, Ibrahim 8*); 2nd day: Western India (1) 150-2 (Umar Khan 55*, Prithviraj 70*).

R.S.Modi's 128 took 423 minutes and included 11 fours. Umar Khan's 136 took 385 minutes and included 14 fours. Prithviraj's 174 took 348 minutes and included 16 fours.

HYDERABAD v MADRAS

Played at Gymkhana Ground, Secunderabad, January 28, 29, 30, 1944.

Match drawn.

MADRAS

1	A.V.Krishnaswami	b Mehta	3	c Bhupathi b Ushaq Ahmed	0
2	K.S.Kannan	c Mistry b Mehta	7	lbw b Mehta	16
3	A.G.Ram Singh	c Aibara b Ghulam Ahmed	89	run out	59
4	M.S.Gopal	c Mistry b Mehta	0	lbw b Mehta	32
5	T.Ramachandran	b Bhupathi	12	lbw b Bhupathi	29
6	A.Ananthanarayanan	st Mistry b Ghulam Ahmed	101	b Mehta	8
7	*M.J.Gopalan	lbw b Mehta	31	(8) st Mistry b Mehta	3
8	E.C.Phillip	c Bhupathi b Ghulam Ahmed	44	(7) b Mehta	6
9	N.J.Venkatesan	lbw b Mehta	1	(10) b Ghulam Ahmed	1
10	†M.O.Srinivasan	lbw b Bhupathi	27	(11) not out	16
11	C.R.Rangachari	not out	0	(9) b Mehta	11
	Extras		34		10
			349		191

FoW (1): 1-5 (1), 2-11 (2), 3-11 (4), 4-28 (5), 5-184 (3), 6-258 (7), 7-288 (6), 8-289 (9), 9-349 (10), 10-349 (8)
FoW (2): 1-0 (1), 2-26 (2), 3-110 (4), 4-110 (3), 5-123 (6), 6-135 (7), 7-141 (8), 8-153 (9), 9-154 (10), 10-191 (5)

HYDERABAD

1	Ali Hussain	b Rangachari	17	st Srinivasan b Kannan	0
2	Asadullah Qureshi	c Ramachandran b Kannan	25	not out	52
3	*B.C.Khanna	c Venkatesan b Rangachari	3		
4	Ushaq Ahmed	c Rangachari b Ram Singh	5		
5	Asghar Ali	c Krishnaswami b Gopalan	70	(4) not out	86
6	E.B.Aibara	b Ram Singh	5		
7	S.R.Mehta	b Rangachari	4		
8	G.D.Qureshi	c Ram Singh b Venkatesan	10	(3) lbw b Kannan	0
9	Ghulam Ahmed	b Rangachari	28		
10	†F.Mistry	not out	4		
11	A.R.Bhupathi	b Rangachari	6		
	Extras		6		3
			183	(2 wickets)	141

FoW (1): 1-43 (1), 2-43 (2), 3-53 (3), 4-57 (4), 5-82 (6), 6-91 (7), 7-112 (8), 8-171 (5), 9-171 (9), 10-183 (11)
FoW (2): 1-0 (1), 2-2 (3)

Hyderabad Bowling

	O	M	R	W		O	M	R	W
Khanna	18	5	29	0	(6)	5	1	5	0
Mehta	54	21	93	5	(3)	25	4	50	6
Ghulam Ahmed	59.3	25	99	3	(4)	17	3	54	1
Bhupathi	21	10	74	2	(5)	12.4	4	30	1
Asadullah Qureshi	3	0	13	0	(7)	2	0	19	0
Ushaq Ahmed	3	0	7	0	(1)	2	1	7	1
G.D.Qureshi					(2)	4	1	16	0

Madras Bowling

	O	M	R	W	O	M	R	W
Gopalan	21	10	28	1	3	1	12	0
Rangachari	27.4	6	64	5	5	1	20	0
Ram Singh	35	12	63	2	6	1	20	0
Venkatesan	5	2	15	1	12	0	39	0
Kannan	7	3	7	1	12	1	47	2

Umpires: H.D.Billimoria and D.K.Naik. Toss:

Close of Play: 1st day: Madras (1) 280-6 (Ananthanarayanan 100*, Phillip 10*); 2nd day: Hyderabad (1) 169-7 (Asghar Ali 69*, Ghulam Ahmed 27*).

DELHI v SOUTHERN PUNJAB

Played at Feroz Shah Kotla, Delhi, January 29, 30, 1944.

Southern Punjab won by an innings and 201 runs.

DELHI

1	†Suraj Narain	run out	15	c Murawwat Hussain b Shahabuddin	4
2	Gurbaksh Singh	b Amarnath	0	b Shahabuddin	2
3	Idrees Baig	c sub b Amarnath	11	b Shahabuddin	21
4	H.Kishenchand	b Amarnath	0	(5) run out	18
5	K.Bahadur	b Badaruddin Malik	0	(4) b Shahabuddin	3
6	*M.R.Bhide	b Badaruddin Malik	2	(7) c and b Bhalindra Singh	6
7	Leach	lbw b Amarnath	9	(8) b Shahabuddin	0
8	Ejaz Ahmed	lbw b Badaruddin Malik	3	(6) lbw b Bhalindra Singh	2
9	Shujauddin	b Inderjit Barhoke	8	c Gian Prakash b Inderjit Barhoke	15
10	Hargopal Singh	c sub b Inderjit Barhoke	18	c sub b Bhalindra Singh	21
11	Mohammad Yunus Khan	not out	0	not out	0
	Extras		18		11
			84		103

FoW (1): 1-5 (2), 2- , 3- , 4- , 5- , 6- , 7- , 8-48, 9- , 10-84
FoW (2): 1- , 2- , 3-16, 4- , 5- , 6- , 7- , 8- , 9- , 10-103

SOUTHERN PUNJAB

1	Murawwat Hussain	c Suraj Narain b Ejaz Ahmed	89
2	D.MuniLal	b Ejaz Ahmed	3
3	L.Amarnath	c Suraj Narain b Ejaz Ahmed	148
4	K.Rai Singh	lbw b Shujauddin	24
5	*Bhalindra Singh	c and b Shujauddin	13
6	Roshan Lal	b Shujauddin	29
7	Inderjit Barhoke	b Ejaz Ahmed	8
8	Badaruddin Malik	lbw b Shujauddin	0
9	Padminder Singh	b Ejaz Ahmed	18
10	Gian Prakash	not out	10
11	Shahabuddin	c Kishenchand b Shujauddin	27
	Extras		19
			388

FoW (1): 1-3 (2), 2-199 (1), 3-257 (4), 4- (5), 5- (3), 6- (7), 7- (8), 8-351 (6), 9-351 (9), 10-388 (11)

Southern Punjab Bowling

	O	M	R	W		O	M	R	W
Amarnath	11	5	18	4		6	3	14	0
Shahabuddin	3	0	13	0		8	2	31	5
Badaruddin Malik	9	0	28	3					
Inderjit Barhoke	2.1	1	4	2	(3)	5.4	1	16	1
Murawwat Hussain	1	0	3	0					
Bhalindra Singh					(4)	9	0	31	3

Delhi Bowling

	O	M	R	W
Ejaz Ahmed	39	9	95	5
Mohammad Yunus Khan	12	1	31	0
Hargopal Singh	21	4	57	0
Shujauddin	42.4	5	96	5
Bahadur	18	5	33	0
Leach	7	4	12	0
Idrees Baig	11	1	35	0
Gurbaksh Singh	3	0	10	0

Umpires: Toss: Delhi

Close of Play: 1st day: Southern Punjab (1) 208-2 (Amarnath 104*, Rai Singh 2*).

The match was scheduled for three days but completed in two. L.Amarnath's 148 took 330 minutes and included 10 fours. Shujauddin and Hargopal Singh added 36 for the 9th wicket in the Delhi second innings.

BARBADOS v TRINIDAD

Played at Kensington Oval, Bridgetown, February 5, 7, 8, 1944.

Barbados won by 101 runs.

BARBADOS					
1	G.M.Carew	c Tang Choon b Pierre	1	c Sealy b Jones	13
2	†S.O.Gittens	c Jones b Pouchet	31	run out	33
3	C.L.Walcott	c Jones b Sealy	22	c Ganteaume b Sealy	23
4	F.M.M.Worrell	b Pouchet	2	c Stollmeyer b Jones	37
5	J.D.C.Goddard	b Pouchet	21	c Gomez b Stollmeyer	43
6	H.L.V.Griffith	c and b Jones	37	c Pierre b Stollmeyer	21
7	N.E.Marshall	c Pouchet b Stollmeyer	44	not out	33
8	E.A.V.Williams	run out	11	c Gomez b Jones	10
9	*T.N.M.Peirce	run out	3	c Ganteaume b Jones	1
10	L.F.Harris	not out	27	c Ganteaume b Jones	11
11	E.A.Greene	c and b Sealy	22	c Ganteaume b Jones	1
	Extras	lb 2, w 1, nb 2	5		6
			226		232

FoW (1): 1-6, 2-47, 3-51, 4-73, 5-86, 6-154, 7-168, 8-174, 9-183, 10-226
FoW (2): 1-19, 2-69, 3-72, 4-135, 5-172, 6-181, 7-200, 8-202, 9-206, 10-232

TRINIDAD					
1	A.G.Ganteaume	lbw b Williams	18	(2) lbw b Greene	20
2	J.B.Stollmeyer	b Greene	49	(1) b Worrell	32
3	H.J.B.Burnett	b Worrell	18	(6) lbw b Worrell	2
4	*G.E.Gomez	lbw b Greene	13	(5) c and b Worrell	40
5	J.E.D.Sealy	c and b Peirce	46	(4) c Griffith b Greene	2
6	N.S.Asgarali	lbw b Worrell	0	(3) lbw b Worrell	4
7	R.P.Tang Choon	run out	39	c Williams b Harris	15
8	†D.A.Galt	lbw b Worrell	7	c sub (K.E.Walcott) b Williams	3
9	P.E.W.Jones	b Worrell	0	c and b Worrell	11
10	L.R.Pierre	c Worrell b Greene	3	st Walcott b Harris	3
11	C.L.Pouchet	not out	5	not out	1
	Extras	b 11, lb 1, nb 1	13		13
			211		146

FoW (1): 1-38, 2-71, 3-90, 4-97, 5-106, 6-197, 7-199, 8-199, 9-200, 10-211
FoW (2): 1-37, 2-56, 3-67, 4-67, 5-70, 6-106, 7-109, 8-138, 9-142, 10-146

Trinidad Bowling	O	M	R	W		O	M	R	W	
Pierre	9	2	25	1		4	0	29	0	
Jones	12	1	46	1		16.7	0	66	6	
Sealy	9	0	36	2	(4)	15	1	56	1	
Pouchet	12	0	69	3	(5)	10	1	26	0	
Stollmeyer	8	0	45	1	(3)	9	0	49	2	1nb

Barbados Bowling	O	M	R	W		O	M	R	W	
Goddard	4	1	7	0	(2)	2	0	13	0	
Williams	9	0	34	1	(1)	7	1	27	1	2nb
Greene	12.7	2	60	3		9	0	36	2	
Harris	7	0	32	0	(5)	6	0	25	2	
Worrell	11	2	32	4	(4)	9	1	32	5	
Marshall	2	0	18	0						
Peirce	2	0	15	1						

Umpires: H.C.Griffith and E.L.Ward. Toss: Trinidad

Close of Play: 1st day: Trinidad (1) 8-0 (Ganteaume 4*, Stollmeyer 4*); 2nd day: Barbados (2) 115-3 (Worrell 23*, Goddard 18*).

The match was scheduled for four days but completed in three. A.Ganteaume kept wicket in the Barbados second innings as D.A.Galt was injured. C.L.Walcott kept wicket in the Trinidad second innings as S.D.Gittens was injured.

WESTERN INDIA STATES v REST OF INDIA

Played at Poona Club Ground, February 5, 6, 7, 8, 1944.
Match drawn.

WESTERN INDIA STATES

1	S.Mushtaq Ali	b Sarwate	54	(4) st Hindlekar b Modi	3
2	Prithviraj	c Modi b Banerjee	2	(1) c Deodhar b Sohoni	27
3	H.R.Adhikari	c Hindlekar b Banerjee	3	(2) b Modi	14
4	V.S.Hazare	b Sohoni	223	(6) b Modi	87
5	G.Kishenchand	c Hindlekar b Sohoni	63	(3) c Hindlekar b Sohoni	1
6	C.K.Nayudu	st Hindlekar b Sarwate	19	(5) b Sohoni	5
7	*Nawab of Pataudi	b Sarwate	8	(8) b Sarwate	29
8	R.K.Indravijaysinhji	b Shinde	52	(7) c Deodhar b Raiji	38
9	Amir Elahi	retired hurt	18		
	M.N.Paranjpe			(11) c Sarwate b Shinde	28
10	Mubarak Ali	b Shinde	15	(9) st Hindlekar b Raiji	16
11	†D.S.Doctor	not out	5	(10) not out	18
	Extras		15		14
			477		280

FoW (1): 1-19 (2), 2-54 (3), 3-108 (1), 4-224 (5), 5-256 (6), 6-290 (7), 7-395 (8), 8-447 (4), 9-477 (10)
FoW (2): 1-40 (2), 2-41 (3), 3-44 (4), 4-49 (5), 5-56 (1), 6-129 (7), 7-187 (8), 8-217 (9), 9-226 (6), 10-280 (11)

REST OF INDIA

1	†D.D.Hindlekar	b Hazare	56		
2	S.W.Sohoni	b Mubarak Ali	3	(1) b Mubarak Ali	0
3	C.T.Sarwate	c Doctor b Mushtaq Ali	95		
4	R.S.Modi	c Doctor b Mubarak Ali	35		
5	*D.B.Deodhar	c Mubarak Ali b Mushtaq Ali	0	(3) not out	75
6	K.M.Rangnekar	b Mubarak Ali	17	(2) c and b Mushtaq Ali	25
7	K.C.Ibrahim	c Hazare b Mubarak Ali	55	(4) c Indravijaysinhji b Nayudu	18
8	R.S.Cooper	c Hazare b Nayudu	122	(7) not out	8
9	S.N.Banerjee	c Nayudu b Mubarak Ali	109		
10	V.M.Merchant				
	M.N.Raiji	lbw b Nayudu	19	(6) b Adhikari	7
11	S.G.Shinde	not out	16	(5) st Doctor b Nayudu	15
	Extras		11		3
			538	(5 wickets)	151

FoW (1): 1-7 (2), 2-117 (1), 3-189 (3), 4-191 (5), 5-210 (6), 6-211 (4), 7-323 (7), 8-441 (8), 9-484 (10), 10-538 (9)
FoW (2): 1-0 (1), 2-36 (2), 3-79 (4), 4-109 (5), 5-119 (6)

Rest of India Bowling	O	M	R	W		O	M	R	W
Banerjee	29	2	114	2					
Sohoni	24	2	120	2	(1)	20	4	72	3
Modi	7	0	29	0	(2)	11	2	29	3
Shinde	27.2	3	96	2	(3)	16.2	3	59	1
Sarwate	29	5	91	3	(4)	20	0	78	1
Rangnekar	3	0	9	0	(5)	1	0	2	0
Deodhar	2	0	3	0					
Raiji					(6)	11	0	26	2

Western India States Bowling	O	M	R	W		O	M	R	W
Mubarak Ali	36.3	8	104	5		6	1	22	1
Hazare	43	18	90	1					
Nayudu	55	7	161	2	(2)	12	0	66	2
Mushtaq Ali	45	5	118	2	(3)	9	1	24	1
Indravijaysinhji	3	1	9	0					
Adhikari	14	3	33	0	(4)	8	0	36	1
Kishenchand	2	0	12	0					

Umpires: J.R.Patel and Vali Ahmed. Toss: Western India States

Close of Play: 1st day: Western India States (1) 398-7 (Hazare 184*, Amir Elahi 1*); 2nd day: Rest of India (1) 197-4 (Modi 34*, Rangnekar 4*); 3rd day: Western India States (2) 31-0 (Prithviraj 21*, Adhikari 9*).

M.N.Raiji was a full substitute for Rest of India, replacing V.M.Merchant who was injured while attempting a catch from VS.Hazare during the first hour of play. M.N.Paranjpe was a full substitute for Western India States, replacing the injured Amir Elahi. V.S.Hazare's 223 took 350 minutes and included 32 fours. R.S.Cooper's 122 took 190 minutes and included 14 fours. S.N.Banerjee's 109 took 150 minutes and included 10 fours. Amir Elahi retired hurt in the Western India States first innings having scored 18 (team had lost 8 wickets). He was struck in the face by a bouncer from S.W.Sohoni and then by a similar ball from S.N.Banerjee. This match was in aid of the Bengal Famine Relief Fund and the Patiala Memorial Fund.

INDIAN XI v SERVICES XI

Played at Brabourne Stadium, Bombay, February 11, 12, 13, 14, 1944.

Indian XI won by six wickets.

SERVICES XI					
1	H.R.Adhikari	b Hazare	23	run out	81
2	S.J.Cray	c Amir Elahi b Nayudu	12	c Mushtaq Ali b Amir Elahi	18
3	Mohammad Saeed	c Gul Mohammad b Amir Elahi	47	b Amir Elahi	37
4	J.Hardstaff	c Srinivasan b Modi	41	(5) c Sohoni b Modi	129
5	*D.R.Jardine	run out	43	(4) c Nazar Mohammad b Nayudu	13
6	P.A.H.Carey	b Banerjee	40	c Kishenchand b Nayudu	1
7	A.G.Skinner	not out	30	c and b Nayudu	2
8	R.G.Hunt	b Banerjee	2	c and b Amir Elahi	19
9	T.C.Dodds	lbw b Banerjee	2	c Sohoni b Hazare	14
10	†H.D.King	b Amir Elahi	6	not out	17
11	H.J.Butler	b Banerjee	23	st Srinivasan b Amir Elahi	4
	Extras		34		6
			303		341

FoW (1): 1-36 (2), 2-48 (1), 3-109 (3), 4-166 (4), 5-221 (5), 6-221 (6), 7-229 (8), 8-235 (9), 9-266 (10), 10-303 (11)
FoW (2): 1-75 (2), 2-125 (3), 3-147 (1), 4-156 (4), 5-174 (6), 6-182 (7), 7-230 (8), 8-293 (9), 9-328 (5), 10-341 (11)

INDIAN XI					
1	Nazar Mohammad	lbw b Butler	11	lbw b Butler	21
2	S.W.Sohoni	b Butler	74	lbw b Carey	16
3	*S.Mushtaq Ali	c Jardine b Skinner	77	lbw b Carey	8
4	V.S.Hazare	c and b Carey	39		
5	G.Kishenchand	c Butler b Carey	13	not out	42
6	Gul Mohammad	not out	144	(4) b Butler	8
7	R.S.Modi	lbw b Dodds	75		
8	C.S.Nayudu	c Skinner b Carey	32		
9	S.N.Banerjee	not out	13		
10	Amir Elahi			(6) not out	48
11	†M.O.Srinivasan				
	Extras		24		4
		(7 wickets, declared)	502	(4 wickets)	147

FoW (1): 1-34 (1), 2-151 (2), 3-192 (3), 4-218 (5), 5-233 (4), 6-418 (7), 7-477 (8)
FoW (2): 1-31 (2), 2-45 (3), 3-49 (1), 4-68 (4)

Indian XI Bowling	O	M	R	W		O	M	R	W
Banerjee	19.4	6	37	4		20	3	67	0
Sohoni	21	8	54	0		14	4	30	0
Hazare	19	8	33	1	(4)	20	7	44	1
Nayudu	21	5	55	1	(3)	25	5	70	3
Amir Elahi	24	4	79	2	(6)	30.3	5	85	4
Modi	4	0	11	1	(7)	6	1	12	1
Gul Mohammad					(5)	6	2	18	0
Nazar Mohammad					(8)	4	0	9	0

Services XI Bowling	O	M	R	W		O	M	R	W
Butler	43	10	114	2		12	4	38	2
Carey	34	10	108	3		11	2	47	2
Dodds	11	0	73	1					
Skinner	26	2	92	1		2	0	26	0
Hunt	2	0	16	0					
Adhikari	16	2	48	0	(5)	1.4	0	18	0
Mohammad Saeed	6	2	18	0					
Hardstaff	3	0	9	0	(3)	1	0	14	0

Umpires: J.Birtwistle and D.K.Naik. Toss: Services XI

Close of Play: 1st day: Services XI (1) 303-9 (Skinner 30*, Butler 23*); 2nd day: Indian XI (1) 342-5 (Gul Mohammad 70*, Modi 40*); 3rd day: Services XI (2) 134-2 (Adhikari 74*, Jardine 3*).
Gul Mohammad's 144 took 310 minutes and included 12 fours. J.Hardstaff's 129 took 196 minutes and included 11 fours. This match was played for the Red Cross Fund.

BARBADOS v TRINIDAD

Played at Kensington Oval, Bridgetown, February 12, 14, 15, 16, 1944.

Match drawn.

TRINIDAD

1	†A.G.Ganteaume	lbw b Worrell	28	b Greene	9
2	J.B.Stollmeyer	lbw b C.L.Walcott	210	b Greene	5
3	J.E.D.Sealy	run out	7		
4	*G.E.Gomez	lbw b Greene	94		
5	H.J.B.Burnett	c Harris b Marshall	9	not out	0
6	D.Fitzpatrick	run out	1	(3) c Goddard b Marshall	37
7	R.P.Tang Choon	lbw b Griffith	22		
8	A.L.Trestrail	b Marshall	44	(4) b Goddard	18
9	P.E.W.Jones	not out	60		
10	L.R.Pierre				
11	C.L.Pouchet				
	Extras	b 9, lb 5, nb 1	15	nb 1	1
		(8 wickets, declared)	490	(4 wickets)	70

FoW (1): 1-58 (1), 2-66 (3), 3-227, 4-242, 5-247, 6-303, 7-385, 8-490
FoW (2): 1-11, 2-18, 3-70, 4-70

BARBADOS

1	G.M.Carew	lbw b Pouchet	36
2	O.M.Robinson	lbw b Pouchet	19
3	†C.L.Walcott	b Pierre	55
4	F.M.M.Worrell	not out	308
5	J.D.C.Goddard	not out	218
6	H.L.V.Griffith		
7	N.E.Marshall		
8	K.E.Walcott		
9	*T.N.M.Peirce		
10	L.F.Harris		
11	E.A.Greene		
	Extras	b 4, lb 6, w 2, nb 2	14
		(3 wickets, declared)	650

FoW (1): 1-36 (2), 2-75 (1), 3-148 (3)

Barbados Bowling	O	M	R	W		O	M	R	W
Greene	22	0	91	1		8	1	19	2
Goddard	9	0	40	0	(7)	4.7	1	12	1
Marshall	22	0	88	2		6	2	5	1
Worrell	23	0	75	1		3	0	6	0
Harris	9	0	41	0		2	0	9	0
Peirce	9	0	61	0		2	0	7	0
Carew	3	0	26	0					
Griffith	5	0	29	1					
K.E.Walcott	5	0	23	0					
C.L.Walcott	0.7	0	1	1	(2)	4	0	11	0

Trinidad Bowling	O	M	R	W
Pierre	17	0	93	1
Jones	22	2	78	0
Sealy	14	2	67	0
Pouchet	27	3	107	2
Stollmeyer	12	0	68	0
Trestrail	21	0	92	0
Fitzpatrick	4	0	29	0
Gomez	2	0	16	0
Burnett	8	0	45	0
Tang Choon	9	0	41	0

Umpires: H.C.Griffith and E.L.Ward. Toss: Trinidad

Close of Play: 1st day: Trinidad (1) 359-6 (Stollmeyer 153*, Trestrail 30*); 2nd day: Barbados (1) 155-3 (Worrell 39*, Goddard 1*); 3rd day: Barbados (1) 463-3 (Worrell 200*, Goddard 139*).

J.D.C.Goddard's 218 took 404 minutes.

BENGAL v MADRAS

Played at Eden Gardens, Calcutta, February 19, 20, 21, 22, 1944.

Bengal won by 134 runs.

BENGAL

1	A.Jabbar	c Srinivasan b Rangachari	80	c Rangachari b Ram Singh	23
2	A.C.Chatterjee	b Rangachari	0	st Srinivasan b Ram Singh	53
3	†P.K.Sen	c Rangachari b Ram Singh	9	(6) c sub (J.Sydney) b Ram Singh	0
4	N.C.Chatterjee	c Rangachari b Ram Singh	4	lbw b Rangachari	112
5	D.R.Das	c Parankusam b Ram Singh	2	(3) b Rangachari	23
6	K.Bhattacharya	b Rangachari	67	(8) run out	2
7	S.K.Mustafi	c Parankusam b Ram Singh	17	lbw b Ram Singh	4
8	*Maharaja of Cooch Behar	c Gopalan b Ram Singh	16	(9) not out	12
9	A.Sen	not out	16	(5) b Ram Singh	20
10	S.A.Banerjee	b Ram Singh	6	st Srinivasan b Ram Singh	10
11	B.K.Mitra	c and b Ram Singh	10	b Ram Singh	1
	Extras		8		6
			235		266

FoW (1): 1-0 (2), 2-13 (3), 3-17 (4), 4-31 (5), 5-152 (6), 6-173 (7), 7-185 (1), 8-209 (8), 9-217 (10), 10-235 (11)
FoW (2): 1-40 (1), 2-73 (3), 3-161 (2), 4-203 (5), 5-203 (6), 6-241 (4), 7-241 (7), 8-245 (8), 9-260 (10), 10-266 (11)

MADRAS

1	C.V.Krishnaswami	b Banerjee	2	c P.K.Sen b Bhattacharya	32
2	K.S.Kannan	c Mitra b Banerjee	6	c A.Sen b Bhattacharya	8
3	B.S.R.Bhadradri	c N.C.Chatterjee b Bhattacharya	23	c Mustafi b Banerjee	32
4	†M.O.Srinivasan	b A.Sen	7	(9) c Mustafi b Bhattacharya	11
5	A.G.Ram Singh	lbw b Mitra	36	b Mitra	13
6	M.S.Gopal	c A.Sen b Banerjee	1	(4) c Mustafi b Bhattacharya	14
7	F.F.Richardson	b Mitra	9	(6) c Mitra b Bhattacharya	62
8	*M.J.Gopalan	b Banerjee	0	(7) c Bhattacharya b Banerjee	76
9	N.J.Venkatesan	c Mustafi b Banerjee	1	(8) b Bhattacharya	0
10	C.R.Rangachari	b Mitra	4	c Mustafi b Bhattacharya	0
11	T.S.Parankusam	not out	0	not out	2
	Extras		13		15
			102		265

FoW (1): 1-8 (2), 2-11 (1), 3-31 (4), 4-56 (3), 5-71 (6), 6-92 (5), 7-95 (7), 8-96 (9), 9-102 (8), 10-102 (10)
FoW (2): 1-46 (2), 2-47 (1), 3-73 (4), 4-93 (5), 5-117 (3), 6-247 (6), 7-251 (7), 8-251 (8), 9-254 (10), 10-265 (9)

Madras Bowling

	O	M	R	W		O	M	R	W
Gopalan	8	5	13	0		8	3	14	0
Rangachari	29	9	61	3		31	14	66	2
Ram Singh	34.3	5	104	7	(5)	27.5	5	90	7
Venkatesan	3	0	19	0	(6)	7	0	35	0
Kannan	4	1	4	0	(4)	16	4	36	0
Parankusam	6	0	26	0	(3)	5	1	19	0

Bengal Bowling

	O	M	R	W		O	M	R	W
Mitra	13.1	3	23	3		15	4	58	1
Banerjee	25	17	27	5		25	9	52	2
Bhattacharya	23	13	27	1		23.5	2	83	7
A.Sen	8	1	12	1		10	2	22	0
N.C.Chatterjee	3	3	0	0	(7)	1	0	6	0
Cooch Behar					(5)	1	0	8	0
A.C.Chatterjee					(6)	2	0	13	0
Mustafi					(8)	4	0	8	0

Umpires: M.K.Banerjee and J.R.Patel. Toss: Bengal

Close of Play: 1st day: Madras (1) 14-2 (Bhadradri 4*, Srinivasan 2*); 2nd day: Bengal (2) 147-2 (A.C.Chatterjee 51*, N.C.Chatterjee 49*); 3rd day: Madras (2) 183-5 (Richardson 32*, Gopalan 42*).

N.C.Chatterjee's 112 included 16 fours.

WELLINGTON v CANTERBURY

Played at Basin Reserve, Wellington, February 25, 26, 1944.

Canterbury won by eight wickets.

WELLINGTON					
1	S.A.McVicar	run out	13	c Uttley b McRae	11
2	W.G.C.Bain	b McRae	0	b Scott	1
3	G.H.Stringer	c Dunnet b Butterfield	24	c Butterfield b McRae	12
4	F.R.Crawford	c Butterfield b McRae	17	c Cromb b Scott	6
5	E.F.Bezzant	st Dunnet b Butterfield	36	(6) lbw b Cromb	1
6	†F.L.H.Mooney	b Butterfield	1	(7) b Cromb	4
7	*E.W.T.Tindill	c Cromb b Butterfield	25	(5) run out	2
8	H.Chapman	c Uttley b Scott	0	b Scott	0
9	R.Buchan	c Dunnet b Butterfield	17	not out	9
10	J.G.Ashenden	c Cromb b Burtt	21	b McRae	27
11	R.Allen	not out	2	lbw b McRae	9
	Extras	b 15, lb 2, nb 6	23	lb 1, nb 2	3
			179		85

FoW (1): 1-0 (2), 2-38 (1), 3-49 (3), 4-58 (4), 5-63 (6), 6-111, 7-112, 8-144, 9-175, 10-179
FoW (2): 1-1 (2), 2-27 (1), 3-28 (3), 4-33, 5-34, 6-36, 7-36, 8-42, 9-69, 10-85

CANTERBURY					
1	I.B.Cromb	c Crawford b Ashenden	27	c Bain b Ashenden	4
2	K.F.M.Uttley	st Mooney b Allen	75	c Mooney b Chapman	17
3	L.A.Butterfield	c Mooney b Ashenden	6		
4	*W.A.Hadlee	c Crawford b Chapman	18	(3) not out	12
5	W.M.Anderson	c and b Buchan	3		
6	F.P.O'Brien	run out	22	(4) not out	1
7	J.Smith	run out (Allen)	43		
8	R.H.Scott	c Bain b Allen	0		
9	D.A.N.McRae	c Crawford b Allen	16		
10	N.V.Burtt	c Chapman b Allen	4		
11	†D.M.Dunnet	not out	4		
	Extras	b 6, lb 4	10	b 4, nb 1	5
			228	(2 wickets)	39

FoW (1): 1-53 (1), 2-63 (3), 3-94 (4), 4-97 (5), 5-144 (6), 6-182 (2), 7-182 (8), 8-219 (9), 9-220 (7), 10-228 (10)
FoW (2): 1-11 (1), 2-33 (2)

Canterbury Bowling	O	M	R	W		O	M	R	W
Scott	18	5	28	1	(2)	14	2	34	3
McRae	13	4	30	2	(1)	12.4	4	15	4
Burtt	20	5	51	1					
Butterfield	20	2	47	5					
Cromb					(3)	7	2	33	2

Wellington Bowling	O	M	R	W		O	M	R	W
Chapman	15	2	66	1	(2)	4	0	20	1
Ashenden	11	1	39	2	(1)	4	0	14	1
Allen	15.2	3	59	4					
Buchan	19	3	40	1					
Crawford	2	0	14	0					

Umpires: C.W.Moore and M.F.Pengelly. Toss: Wellington

Close of Play: 1st day: Canterbury (1) 144-4 (Uttley 62*, O'Brien 22*).

The match was scheduled for three days but completed in two. J.Smith was run out by R.Allen when backing up too far after a previous warning.

SOUTHERN PUNJAB v NORTHERN INDIA

Played at Baradari Ground, Patiala, March 4, 5, 6, 1944.

Match drawn.

NORTHERN INDIA

1	Abdul Hafeez	c Rai Singh b Badaruddin Malik	94	run out	14
2	Asghar Ali	lbw b Amarnath	34	hit wkt b Murawwat Hussain	18
3	Aslam Khokhar	run out	5	c sub b Amarnath	7
4	R.P.Mehra	lbw b Badaruddin Malik	0	lbw b Bhalindra Singh	10
5	Gul Mohammad	b Amarnath	35	c Nisar Ahmed b Badaruddin Malik	28
6	A.A.Qureshi	c and b Amarnath	1	c sub b Amarnath	1
7	*M.Jahangir Khan	c sub b Bhalindra Singh	31	c Muni Lal b Amarnath	2
8	Amir Elahi	b Badaruddin Malik	20	(10) lbw b Badaruddin Malik	12
9	†V.Rajindernath	c Patiala b Badaruddin Malik	41	(8) lbw b Amarnath	14
10	Chuni Lal	st Nisar Ahmed b Bhalindra Singh	21	(11) not out	6
11	Fazal Mahmood	not out	38	(9) c Badaruddin Malik b Amarnath	2
	Extras		9		13
			329		127

FoW (1): 1-113 (2), 2-122 (3), 3-122 (4), 4-151 (1), 5-159 (6), 6-176 (5), 7-211, 8-241, 9-264, 10-329
FoW (2): 1- , 2- , 3- , 4- , 5- , 6- , 7- , 8- , 9- , 10-127

SOUTHERN PUNJAB

1	Daljinder Singh	b Abdul Hafeez	27	(10) not out	1
2	†Nisar Ahmed	lbw b Abdul Hafeez	14	(9) c Abdul Hafeez b Amir Elahi	0
3	L.Amarnath	c Jahangir Khan b Fazal Mahmood	37	(1) b Jahangir Khan	28
4	K.Rai Singh	c sub b Jahangir Khan	69	st Rajindernath b Amir Elahi	24
5	Bhalindra Singh	lbw b Asghar Ali	109	(8) run out	1
6	Murawwat Hussain	c Qureshi b Asghar Ali	8	(3) c Aslam Khokhar b Fazal Mahmood	12
7	D.Muni Lal	b Jahangir Khan	4	(2) c Gul Mohammad b Jahangir Khan	23
8	*Maharaja of Patiala	lbw b Jahangir Khan	7	(6) run out	0
9	Roshan Lal	c Qureshi b Jahangir Khan	20	(7) not out	3
10	Badaruddin Malik	lbw b Asghar Ali	6	(5) c Abdul Hafeez b Fazal Mahmood	3
11	Shahabuddin	not out	3		
	Extras		22		9
			326	(8 wickets)	104

FoW (1): 1-41 (2), 2-44 (1), 3-99 (3), 4-230 (4), 5-274 (6), 6-285 (7), 7-291 (5), 8-297 (8), 9-304 (10), 10-326 (9)
FoW (2): 1-50, 2- , 3- , 4- , 5- , 6- , 7- , 8-

Southern Punjab Bowling

	O	M	R	W		O	M	R	W
Amarnath	36	10	91	3		15	3	29	5
Shahabuddin	3	2	3	0					
Bhalindra Singh	14	0	58	2	(4)	11	2	37	1
Badaruddin Malik	29.5	3	112	4	(2)	12	2	30	2
Murawwat Hussain	11	3	32	0	(3)	9	1	18	1
Patiala	10	3	24	0					

Northern India Bowling

	O	M	R	W		O	M	R	W
Chuni Lal	22	11	38	0		4	0	23	0
Jahangir Khan	33	15	57	4		9	0	40	2
Abdul Hafeez	24	10	47	2					
Amir Elahi	38	7	105	0		1	0	3	2
Fazal Mahmood	12	4	22	1	(3)	4	0	29	2
Gul Mohammad	9	3	10	0					
Asghar Ali	18	5	25	3					

Umpires: Feroze Khan and H.W.Hunt. Toss: Northern India

Close of Play: 1st day: Southern Punjab (1) 20-0 (Daljinder Singh 13*, Nisar Ahmed 6*); 2nd day: Southern Punjab (1) 264-4 (Bhalindra Singh 90*, Murawwat Hussain 8*).

D.B.DEODHAR'S XI v C.K.NAYUDU'S XI

Played at Maharaja Pratapsingh Coronation Gymkhana Ground, Baroda, March 11, 12, 13, 14, 1944.
Match drawn.

D.B DEODHAR'S XI					
1	S.W.Sohoni	c Mushtaq Ali b C.S.Nayudu	46	c Kishenchand b Banerjee	16
2	M.H.Mankad	c Mushtaq Ali b Gaekwad	4	run out	6
3	H.R.Adhikari	c C.K.Nayudu b C.S.Nayudu	52	(6) lbw b Banerjee	3
4	V.S.Hazare	b C.S.Nayudu	74	(5) not out	45
5	R.S.Modi	b C.S.Nayudu	37		
6	†R.B.Nimbalkar	c Hindlekar b C.S.Nayudu	42		
7	*D.B.Deodhar	lbw b C.S.Nayudu	9	(3) c Gul Mohammad b C.S.Nayudu	6
8	M.N.Paranjpe	c Naoomal Jaoomal b C.K.Nayudu	82	(7) not out	52
9	M.M.Naidu	st Hindlekar b C.K.Nayudu	53		
10	M.N.Raiji	not out	17	(4) c C.K.Nayudu b Banerjee	2
11	D.K.Gaekwad	b C.K.Nayudu	5		
12	Amir Elahi	c Mushtaq Ali b C.S.Nayudu	3		
	Extras		23		7
			447	(5 wickets, declared)	137

FoW (1): 1-20 (2), 2-109 (1), 3-112 (3), 4-188 (5), 5-262 (6), 6-269 (4), 7-284 (7), 8-409 (9), 9-425 (8), 10-441 (11), 11-447 (12)
FoW (2): 1-22 (1), 2-22 (2), 3-29 (4), 4-35 (3), 5-47 (6)

C.K.NAYUDU'S XI					
1	†D.D.Hindlekar	lbw b Hazare	5		
2	Prithviraj	c Sohoni b Hazare	12	(4) not out	0
3	S.Mushtaq Ali	c Amir Elahi b Mankad	40		
4	Gul Mohammad	c Sohoni b Mankad	14		
5	G.Kishenchand	retired out	204		
6	C.S.Nayudu	st sub (D.D.Hindlekar) b Mankad	104	(3) st sub (S.G.Powar) b Mankad	0
7	*C.K.Nayudu	c Hazare b Amir Elahi	43	(2) st sub (S.G.Powar) b Mankad	19
8	Naoomal Jaoomal	lbw b Hazare	35		
9	Maharaja of Baroda	c Gaekwad b Deodhar	5		
10	S.N.Banerjee	c Sohoni b Deodhar	16	(1) not out	28
11	S.G.Powar	c Raiji b Gaekwad	12		
12	H.G.Gaekwad	not out	3		
	Extras		27		
			520	(2 wickets)	47

FoW (1): 1-13 (1), 2-36 (2), 3-63 (4), 4-74 (3), 5-250 (6), 6-386 (7), 7-469 (8), 8-479 (5), 9-479 (9), 10-503 (10), 11-520 (11)
FoW (2): 1-46 (2), 2-46 (3)

C.K.Nayudu's XI Bowling	O	M	R	W		O	M	R	W
Banerjee	31	9	74	0		17	2	53	3
Gaekwad	23	9	32	1					
C.S.Nayudu	52.3	4	177	7		19	5	41	1
Naoomal Jaoomal	16	2	57	0					
C.K.Nayudu	29	4	80	3	(2)	7	2	21	0
Mushtaq Ali	3	3	0	0					
Baroda	6	3	4	0	(5)	1	0	4	0
Kishenchand					(4)	2	0	11	0

D.B.Deodhar's XI Bowling	O	M	R	W		O	M	R	W
Sohoni	34	7	120	0		3	0	24	0
Hazare	40	7	115	3		4	0	22	0
Amir Elahi	34	12	62	1					
Mankad	25	2	63	3	(3)	1	0	1	2
Raiji	13	2	33	0					
Adhikari	11	0	39	0					
Gaekwad	10.2	0	37	1					
Deodhar	10	2	24	2					

Umpires: M.G.Bhave and J.R.Patel. Toss: D.B.Deodhar's XI
Close of Play: 1st day: D.B.Deodhar's XI (1) 296-7 (Paranjpe 12*, Naidu 3*); 2nd day: C.K.Nayudu's XI (1) 89-4 (Kishenchand 8*, C.S.Nayudu 10*); 3rd day: C.K.Nayudu's XI (1) 429-6 (Kishenchand 174*, Naoomal Jaoomal 15*).

G.Kishenchand's 204 took 409 minutes and included 24 fours. C.S.Nayudu's 104 took 150 minutes and included 10 fours. It was decided on the night before the game to make the match 12-a-side and add a young cricketer to each side (D.K.Gaekwad and Yuvraj of Baroda). S.G.Powar kept wicket in both second innings. The match was played for the Red Cross Fund.

TRINIDAD v BRITISH GUIANA

Played at Queen's Park Oval, Port of Spain, March 11, 13, 14, 15, 1944.

Trinidad won by 101 runs.

TRINIDAD					
1	*V.H.Stollmeyer	lbw b Trim	92	c Bayley b Gaskin	57
2	J.B.Stollmeyer	b Christiani	88	c McWatt b Gaskin	13
3	I.R.Ashtine	run out	19	c Trim b Gaskin	1
4	†A.G.Ganteaume	c Outridge b Gaskin	13	c Bayley b Gaskin	97
5	G.E.Gomez	c McWatt b Trim	12		
6	J.E.D.Sealy	lbw b Haynes	40	(5) lbw b Christiani	3
7	R.P.Tang Choon	b Haynes	17	(6) not out	44
8	E.Constantine	c Bayley b de Freitas	51	(7) not out	29
9	A.L.Trestrail	c Bayley b Haynes	3		
10	L.R.Pierre	not out	11		
11	C.L.Pouchet	c McKenzie b Haynes	0		
	Extras		4		7
			350	(5 wickets, declared)	251

FoW (1): 1-169, 2-195, 3-212, 4-221, 5-227, 6-258, 7-331, 8-335, 9-348, 10-350
FoW (2): 1-16 (2), 2-34 (3), 3-128 (1), 4-135 (5), 5-216 (4)

BRITISH GUIANA					
1	A.Dummett	c Trestrail b Sealy	7	lbw b V.H.Stollmeyer	23
2	U.B.McKenzie	lbw b Sealy	1	not out	115
3	*H.P.Bayley	b Sealy	16	b J.B.Stollmeyer	7
4	R.J.Christiani	c Ashtine b Sealy	126	c Ashtine b Pouchet	54
5	†C.A.McWatt	c and b Pouchet	6	(7) c Sealy b Pierre	46
6	H.W.de Freitas	c Pouchet b J.B.Stollmeyer	6	(5) lbw b Pierre	13
7	A.S.Outridge	c Pierre b Pouchet	3	(8) b Pierre	0
8	C.N.Haynes	c Trestrail b Pouchet	0	(9) b Constantine	9
9	D.Hill	run out	5	(10) run out	7
10	B.B.M.Gaskin	not out	30	(6) lbw b J.B.Stollmeyer	5
11	J.Trim	b Sealy	0	run out	0
	Extras	b 3, lb 4, nb 1	8		13
			208		292

FoW (1): 1-6 (2), 2-9 (1), 3-35 (3), 4-52 (5), 5-59 (6), 6-62 (7), 7-63 (8), 8-106 (9), 9-208 (4), 10-208 (11)
FoW (2): 1-57 (1), 2-64 (3), 3-158 (4), 4-183 (5), 5-202 (6), 6-261 (7), 7-261 (8), 8-272 (9), 9-292 (10), 10-292 (11)

British Guiana Bowling	O	M	R	W		O	M	R	W
Trim	17	2	79	2		9	1	55	0
Hill	16	3	47	0	(3)	9	1	40	0
Gaskin	25	2	90	1	(2)	16	4	55	4
de Freitas	17	3	54	1	(5)	7	1	33	0
Haynes	14.4	0	53	4	(4)	4	0	23	0
Christiani	3	0	16	1		6	1	38	1
McKenzie	3	0	7	0					

Trinidad Bowling	O	M	R	W		O	M	R	W
Pierre	10	1	36	0		14	0	67	3
Sealy	9.5	1	33	5		8	0	40	0
Pouchet	6	2	32	3	(4)	7	1	14	1
J.B.Stollmeyer	10	3	35	1	(6)	15	1	70	2
Trestrail	4	0	19	0	(3)	2	0	6	0
V.H.Stollmeyer	2	0	16	0	(5)	7	0	33	1
Constantine	4	0	8	0	(8)	6.2	1	12	1
Tang Choon	4	0	21	0	(7)	6	0	37	0

Umpires: A.L.Green and V.Guillen. Toss: Trinidad

Close of Play: 1st day: Trinidad (1) 258-6 (Sealy 14*); 2nd day: British Guiana (1) 200-8 (Christiani 122*, Gaskin 28*); 3rd day: British Guiana (2) 2-0 (Dummett 0*, McKenzie 1*).

WESTERN INDIA v NORTHERN INDIA

Played at European Gymkhana Ground, Rajkot, March 17, 18, 19, 20, 1944.

Western India won by seven wickets.

NORTHERN INDIA

1	Asghar Ali	b Gandhi	21	run out	5
2	Khwaja Bashir	c Jayantilal Vora b Gandhi	17	(7) run out	2
3	Aslam Khokhar	b Gandhi	0	(2) b Akbar Khan	3
4	*R.P.Mehra	b Saeed Ahmed	13	(5) lbw b Akbar Khan	2
5	Abdul Hafeez	b Gandhi	12	(3) b Saeed Ahmed	143
6	Inayat Khan	b Purshottam	25	(4) b Jayantilal Vora	33
7	Gulzar Mir	c and b Saeed Ahmed	2	(6) c Prataprai b Jayantilal Vora	5
8	†Zafar Ahmed	c Prithviraj b Gandhi	16	(10) not out	66
9	Fazal Mahmood	not out	19	b Akbar Khan	11
10	Ahmed Khan	c Jayantilal Vora b Gandhi	2	(8) c Saeed Ahmed b Gandhi	2
11	Salahuddin Ahmed	run out	1	b Akbar Khan	1
	Extras		17		10
			145		283

FoW (1): 1-37 (1), 2-37 (3), 3-53 (4), 4-75 (2), 5-76 (5), 6-86 (7), 7-120 (6), 8-120 (8), 9-126 (10), 10-145 (11)
FoW (2): 1-8 (2), 2-11 (1), 3-96 (4), 4-103 (5), 5-118 (6), 6-132 (7), 7-136 (8), 8-168 (9), 9-272 (3), 10-283 (11)

WESTERN INDIA

1	†Prataprai	c Gulzar Mir b Abdul Hafeez	16	lbw b Asghar Ali	16
2	Jayantilal Vora	lbw b Fazal Mahmood	19	c Khwaja Bashir b Fazal Mahmood	7
3	Umar Khan	b Asghar Ali	27	not out	66
4	Prithviraj	b Fazal Mahmood	37	c Mehra b Fazal Mahmood	43
5	Saeed Ahmed	c Zafar Ahmed b Fazal Mahmood	39	not out	23
6	S.B.Gandhi	b Asghar Ali	1		
7	Purshottam	lbw b Asghar Ali	1		
8	Sukhvantrai	lbw b Fazal Mahmood	45		
9	*H.W.Barritt	c Khwaja Bashir b Fazal Mahmood	2		
10	Akbar Khan	b Fazal Mahmood	25		
11	Basant Singh	not out	2		
	Extras		40		20
			254	(3 wickets)	175

FoW (1): 1-30 (1), 2-48 (2), 3-124 (4), 4-125 (3), 5-127 (6), 6-135 (7), 7-212 (8), 8-218 (9), 9-235 (5), 10-254 (10)
FoW (2): 1-13 (2), 2-39 (1), 3-118 (4)

Western India Bowling

	O	M	R	W		O	M	R	W
Saeed Ahmed	27	15	25	2		32	13	62	1
Jayantilal Vora	25	12	29	0	(3)	22	4	56	2
Akbar Khan	18	11	13	0	(2)	28	5	65	4
Gandhi	18.3	5	37	6		16	2	43	1
Purshottam	7	0	24	1		14	3	34	0
Basant Singh					(6)	2	0	10	0
Barritt					(7)	1	0	3	0

Northern India Bowling

	O	M	R	W		O	M	R	W
Abdul Hafeez	18	8	28	1		17	8	35	0
Inayat Khan	13	8	12	0		9	4	14	0
Fazal Mahmood	36.5	11	65	6	(4)	36	12	59	2
Asghar Ali	37	17	62	3	(5)	20	6	37	1
Aslam Khokhar	13	4	34	0	(6)	2	1	1	0
Ahmed Khan	7	3	13	0	(3)	7	3	9	0

Umpires: D.K.Naik and Vali Ahmed. Toss: Northern India

Close of Play: 1st day: Western India (1) 19-0 (Prataprai 8*, Jayantilal Vora 10*); 2nd day: Western India (1) 254 all out; 3rd day: Northern India (2) 265-8 (Abdul Hafeez 140*, Zafar Ahmed 52*).

Abdul Hafeez's 143 took 327 minutes and included 8 fours. Amir Elahi and Gul Mohammad who had been playing for Northern India in previous rounds were forbidden by their employer (Manavadar State) to play against Western India.

TRINIDAD v BRITISH GUIANA

Played at Queen's Park Oval, Port of Spain, March 20, 21, 22, 1944.

Trinidad won by an innings and 217 runs.

BRITISH GUIANA					
1	A.Dummett	c Ferguson b Burnett	15	lbw b Burnett	34
2	U.B.McKenzie	b Ferguson	8	run out	0
3	*H.P.Bayley	c Ganteaume b Ferguson	7	lbw b Pierre	2
4	R.J.Christiani	c Ganteaume b Burnett	12	c Ganteaume b Pierre	0
5	†C.A.McWatt	c Ganteaume b Lashley	29	(7) c and b Ferguson	9
6	G.A.Camacho	b J.B.Stollmeyer	15	(5) c Ferguson b Burnett	16
7	B.B.M.Gaskin	c J.B.Stollmeyer b Burnett	11	(6) c Tang Choon b Ferguson	5
8	D.Hill	c V.H.Stollmeyer b Ferguson	4	c Tang Choon b Ferguson	5
9	J.Bahadur	c Constantine b Ferguson	6	c Ganteaume b Ferguson	0
10	C.N.Haynes	not out	8	not out	0
11	J.Trim	b Ferguson	17	c Tang Choon b Burnett	0
	Extras		11	lb 3, w 1	4
			143		75

FoW (1): 1-23, 2-23, 3-43, 4-51, 5-96, 6-109, 7-112, 8-129, 9-129, 10-143
FoW (2): 1-7, 2-9, 3-11, 4-44, 5-49, 6-61, 7-73, 8-75, 9-75, 10-75

TRINIDAD			
1	*V.H.Stollmeyer	c Christiani b Trim	1
2	J.B.Stollmeyer	c McKenzie b Gaskin	0
3	†A.G.Ganteaume	lbw b Gaskin	42
4	I.R.Ashtine	run out	38
5	K.B.Trestrail	st McWatt b Hill	85
6	R.P.Tang Choon	c and b Hill	20
7	H.J.B.Burnett	lbw b Gaskin	31
8	E.Constantine	c Christiani b Trim	139
9	W.Ferguson	c Camacho b Bahadur	60
10	L.R.Pierre	b Trim	1
11	O.E.Lashley	not out	2
	Extras		16
			435

FoW (1): 1-1 (1), 2-3 (2), 3-70, 4-107, 5-143, 6-213, 7-244, 8-380, 9-414, 10-435

Trinidad Bowling	O	M	R	W		O	M	R	W
Pierre	3	0	12	0		5	1	23	2
Constantine	3	1	7	0		1	0	2	0
Ferguson	18	1	61	5	(5)	5	0	22	4
Burnett	17	4	27	3		5.7	0	7	3
J.B.Stollmeyer	5	0	17	1					
Lashley	5	0	8	1	(3)	3	0	17	0

British Guiana Bowling	O	M	R	W
Gaskin	33	3	89	3
Trim	20.5	3	94	3
Hill	23	4	79	2
Christiani	7	1	35	0
Haynes	18	3	65	0
Bahadur	8	0	49	1
McKenzie	2	0	8	0

Umpires: Toss: Trinidad

Close of Play: 1st day: Trinidad (1) 34-2 (Ganteaume 25*, Ashtine 7*); 2nd day: Trinidad (1) 310-7 (Constantine 54*, Ferguson 27*).

The match was scheduled for four days but completed in three.

NEW ZEALAND SERVICES v NEW ZEALAND XI

Played at Basin Reserve, Wellington, March 24, 25, 27, 1944.

Match drawn.

NEW ZEALAND SERVICES

1	S.A.McVicar	st Mooney b Burtt	3	b Butterfield	50
2	*H.T.Pearson	c Cromb b McRae	27	b McRae	10
3	J.A.Ongley	c Burtt b McRae	2	c and b Burtt	4
4	A.C.Kerr	b Burtt	8	b Burtt	1
5	F.R.Crawford	not out	35	b Cowie	7
6	E.F.Bezzant	c Cromb b Sutcliffe	2	b Cowie	10
7	M.A.O'Brien	c Sutcliffe b McRae	8	st Mooney b Burtt	15
8	R.H.Scott	c Cromb b McRae	1	c Mooney b Burtt	36
9	L.D.Smith	b McRae	0	not out	4
10	N.R.Hoar	c Cromb b Burtt	5	not out	1
11	†D.M.Dunnet	c McRae b Burtt	0		
	Extras	b 3, lb 2, nb 3	8	b 8, lb 1	9
			99	(8 wickets)	147

FoW (1): 1-7 (1), 2-26 (3), 3-37 (4), 4-49 (2), 5-59 (6), 6-80 (7), 7-84 (8), 8-84 (9), 9-96 (10), 10-99 (11)
FoW (2): 1-11 (2), 2-20 (3), 3-28 (4), 4-40 (5), 5-60 (6), 6-94, 7-120, 8-146

NEW ZEALAND XI

1	I.B.Cromb	lbw b Kerr	30
2	K.F.M.Uttley	lbw b Scott	60
3	*W.A.Hadlee	lbw b Kerr	10
4	W.M.Wallace	b Scott	5
5	B.Sutcliffe	b Hoar	2
6	F.P.O'Brien	b Hoar	0
7	†F.L.H.Mooney	b Smith	43
8	D.A.N.McRae	b Scott	10
9	L.A.Butterfield	b Smith	40
10	T.B.Burtt	c O'Brien b Smith	7
11	J.Cowie	not out	0
	Extras	b 13, lb 7, w 2, nb 4	26
			233

FoW (1): 1-93 (1), 2-108 (3), 3-121 (2), 4-124 (4), 5-124 (5), 6-124 (6), 7-138 (8), 8-219 (7), 9-233 (10), 10-233 (9)

New Zealand XI Bowling

	O	M	R	W		O	M	R	W
Cowie	6	0	26	0		13	2	26	2
McRae	17	9	20	5		17	6	30	1
Burtt	18	3	37	4		18	3	52	4
Sutcliffe	3	2	5	1					
Butterfield	4	2	3	0	(4)	10	2	19	1
Cromb					(5)	4	1	11	0

New Zealand Services Bowling

	O	M	R	W
Hoar	12	1	53	2
Scott	12	5	29	3
Kerr	10	0	44	2
Smith	6.3	0	44	3
O'Brien	9	2	23	0
Crawford	2	0	14	0

Umpires: Chapman and F.W.Harris-Daw. Toss: New Zealand Services

Close of Play: 1st day: New Zealand XI (1) 233 all out; 2nd day: New Zealand Services (2) 147-8 (Smith 4*, Hoar 1*).

There was no play on the final day.

MYSORE COMBINED XI v BARODA

Played at Central College Ground, Bangalore, April 1, 2, 4, 5, 1944.

Baroda won by six wickets.

MYSORE COMBINED XI					
1	*†D.D.Hindlekar	c Gul Mohammad b Amir Elahi	16	lbw b Gul Mohammad	16
2	A.Ethinder	c Paranjpe b Hazare	6	c Gul Mohammad b Adhikari	30
3	B.K.Garudachar	c Powar b Gul Mohammad	94	(4) c and b Amir Elahi	26
4	C.J.Ramdev	b Amir Elahi	0	(5) st Powar b Amir Elahi	63
5	B.Frank	c and b Amir Elahi	0	(7) b Hazare	109
6	B.G.Patel	b Amir Elahi	2	(3) lbw b Gul Mohammad	2
7	S.Rama Rao	c Hazare b Amir Elahi	0	(9) not out	15
8	M.R.Alasingrachar	lbw b Amir Elahi	40	(6) lbw b Gul Mohammad	23
9	S.Darashah	not out	18	(8) st Powar b Hazare	2
10	U.R.Chippa	st Powar b Amir Elahi	3	(11) c Patel b Amir Elahi	6
11	H.D.Rangaiyengar	c Powar b Gul Mohammad	1	(10) b Hazare	1
	Extras		13		14
			193		307

FoW (1): 1-23 (2), 2-35 (1), 3-35 (4), 4-35 (5), 5-41 (6), 6-41 (7), 7-161 (3), 8- (8), 9- (10), 10-193 (11)
FoW (2): 1- , 2- , 3- , 4- , 5-111, 6-249, 7- , 8- , 9- , 10-307

BARODA					
1	V.M.Pandit	c Darashah b Rama Rao	6	(5) b Chippa	10
2	†S.G.Powar	c Hindlekar b Rangaiyengar	0	(1) b Rama Rao	13
3	H.R.Adhikari	lbw b Rangaiyengar	31	c Hindlekar b Rama Rao	2
4	V.S.Hazare	not out	193	not out	45
5	Gul Mohammad	c Chippa b Rangaiyengar	33		
6	M.N.Paranjpe	b Rangaiyengar	80	not out	1
7	Amir Elahi	b Rangaiyengar	6		
8	*W.N.Ghorpade	b Rangaiyengar	4		
9	S.K.Vichare	lbw b Garudachar	9	(2) b Chippa	25
10	M.M.Naidu	c Darashah b Garudachar	11		
11	A.Patel	c Alasingrachar b Garudachar	0		
	Extras		30		3
			403	(4 wickets)	99

FoW (1): 1-5 (2), 2-11 (1), 3- (3), 4- (5), 5- (6), 6- (7), 7- (8), 8- (9), 9- (10), 10-403 (11)
FoW (2): 1- , 2- , 3- , 4-

Baroda Bowling	O	M	R	W		O	M	R	W
Amir Elahi	20	3	67	7		35.3	7	81	3
Gul Mohammad	16.2	5	30	2		21	4	74	3
Hazare	22	8	43	1		12	4	14	3
Adhikari	3	0	12	0		10	1	53	1
Patel	10	3	28	0		20	3	57	0
Naidu					(6)	3	0	13	0
Ghorpade					(7)	2	1	1	0

Mysore Combined XI Bowling	O	M	R	W		O	M	R	W
Rangaiyengar	26	8	54	6		9	1	31	0
Garudachar	21.5	0	100	3					
Rama Rao	23	7	83	1	(2)	10	1	31	2
Chippa	26	8	59	0	(3)	6	3	8	2
Patel	6	1	23	0					
Darashah	7	0	15	0					
Frank	6	1	22	0	(4)	1	0	11	0
Alasingrachar	2	0	17	0	(5)	1.3	0	15	0

Umpires: Toss: Mysore Combined XI

Close of Play: 1st day: Baroda (1) 55-2 (Adhikari 29*, Hazare 9*); 2nd day: Baroda (1) 322-7 (Hazare 133*, Vichare 1*); 3rd day: Mysore Combined XI (2) 239-5 (Ramdev 51*, Frank 77*).

175 runs were added for the 5th wicket in the Baroda first innings (V.S.Hazare and M.N.Paranjpe). V.S.Hazare's 193 took 415 minutes and included 20 fours. April 3rd was a rest day due to the Ration Census.

BENGAL v WESTERN INDIA

Played at Brabourne Stadium, Bombay, April 7, 8, 9, 10, 1944.

Western India won by an innings and 23 runs.

	BENGAL				
1	A.Jabbar	b Gandhi	35	c Jayantilal Vora b Saeed Ahmed	1
2	A.C.Chatterjee	b Purshottam	68	b Akbar Khan	6
3	†P.K.Sen	run out	61	lbw b Saeed Ahmed	1
4	N.C.Chatterjee	lbw b Saeed Ahmed	40	lbw b Saeed Ahmed	71
5	A.K.Deb	st Prataprai b Kishenchand	1	(7) c Barritt b Kishenchand	39
6	*Maharaja of Cooch Behar	c Jayantilal Vora b Gandhi	8	b Purshottam	17
7	K.Bhattacharya	b Gandhi	0	(8) b Purshottam	13
8	S.K.Mustafi	c Prataprai b Gandhi	3	(5) lbw b Saeed Ahmed	0
9	A.Sen	b Gandhi	0	b Purshottam	0
10	S.A.Banerjee	b Gandhi	3	c Kishenchand b Purshottam	11
11	B.K.Mitra	not out	3	not out	0
	Extras		12		17
			234		176

FoW (1): 1-70 (1), 2-138 (2), 3-182 (3), 4-191 (5), 5-222 (6), 6-222 (7), 7-226 (8), 8-226 (9), 9-226 (4), 10-234 (10)
FoW (2): 1-8 (1), 2-8 (2), 3-12 (3), 4-12 (5), 5-67 (6), 6-111 (4), 7-140 (8), 8-140 (9), 9-176 (7), 10-176 (10)

	WESTERN INDIA		
1	†Prataprai	b Mitra	0
2	Jayantilal Vora	lbw b A.C.Chatterjee	41
3	Umar Khan	c Mustafi b Mitra	75
4	G.Kishenchand	c Mustafi b Mitra	111
5	Prithviraj	b Banerjee	3
6	Saeed Ahmed	not out	84
7	S.B.Gandhi	b Mitra	2
8	Purshottam	lbw b A.Sen	56
9	Sukhvantrai	c N.C.Chatterjee b Banerjee	27
10	*H.W.Barritt	c Mustafi b Bhattacharya	3
11	Akbar Khan	b Bhattacharya	1
	Extras		30
			433

FoW (1): 1-6 (1), 2-95 (2), 3-208 (3), 4-215 (5), 5-269 (4), 6-281 (7), 7-373 (8), 8-417 (9), 9-427 (10), 10-433 (11)

Western India Bowling

	O	M	R	W		O	M	R	W
Saeed Ahmed	28	17	20	1		21	7	23	4
Akbar Khan	25	10	28	0		17	4	34	1
Jayantilal Vora	18	8	41	0	(6)	5	2	18	0
Purshottam	22	9	29	1		19.2	3	50	4
Kishenchand	15	0	54	1		4	1	18	1
Gandhi	22.2	8	50	6	(3)	13	7	16	0

Bengal Bowling

	O	M	R	W
Mitra	27	6	80	4
Banerjee	34	9	70	2
Bhattacharya	48.5	14	83	2
A.Sen	10	0	33	1
A.C.Chatterjee	6	0	30	1
Mustafi	7	2	27	0
Cooch Behar	8	0	42	0
N.C.Chatterjee	13	3	38	0

Umpires: M.G.Bhave and D.K.Naik. Toss: Bengal

Close of Play: 1st day: Bengal (1) 224-6 (N.C.Chatterjee 40*, Mustafi 1*); 2nd day: Western India (1) 260-4 (Kishenchand 104*, Saeed Ahmed 22*); 3rd day: Bengal (2) 120-6 (Deb 13*, Bhattacharya 3*).

G.Kishenchand's 111 took 180 minutes and included 10 fours.

INDEX OF 1943/44 MATCH SCORECARDS

1944/45

BRITISH GUIANA v BARBADOS

Played at Bourda, Georgetown, September 30, October 2, 3, 4, 1944.

Match drawn.

BRITISH GUIANA

1	U.B.McKenzie	c C.L.Walcott b Goddard	127	b Goddard	3
2	C.C.Reece	c Griffith b Worrell	92	b Marshall	20
3	L.S.Birkett	run out	34	c Worrell b Marshall	18
4	R.J.Christiani	b Greene	28	c Griffith b Marshall	7
5	*H.P.Bayley	c C.L.Walcott b Goddard	4	c and b Worrell	2
6	G.A.Camacho	c sub (O.M.Robinson) b Goddard	2	b Hoad	36
7	G.Lord	b Greene	21	c and b Peirce	40
8	†C.A.McWatt	c Hoad b Greene	26	c and b Hoad	38
9	J.Trim	lbw b Greene	5	not out	15
10	B.B.M.Gaskin	lbw b Goddard	5		
11	H.A.Vigilance	not out	0		
	Extras		2		6
			346	(8 wickets)	185

FoW (1): 1-191 (2), 2-245 (3), 3-266 (1), 4-287, 5-289, 6-289, 7-323, 8-329, 9-346, 10-346
FoW (2): 1-6 (1), 2-41, 3-46, 4-51, 5-53, 6-116, 7-141, 8-185

BARBADOS

1	G.M.Carew	lbw b Gaskin	33
2	M.C.Frederick	b Trim	8
3	†C.L.Walcott	lbw b Trim	24
4	F.M.M.Worrell	b Trim	41
5	J.D.C.Goddard	c McKenzie b Gaskin	179
6	H.L.V.Griffith	b Christiani	56
7	K.E.Walcott	c and b Trim	52
8	N.E.Marshall	b Gaskin	80
9	*T.N.M.Peirce	c Birkett b Gaskin	21
10	E.L.G.Hoad	not out	5
11	E.A.Greene	not out	1
	Extras		16
		(9 wickets, declared)	516

FoW (1): 1-19, 2-51, 3-92, 4-125, 5-271, 6-371, 7-446, 8-507, 9-510

Barbados Bowling

	O	M	R	W	O	M	R	W
Greene	22.2	2	82	4	10	0	43	0
Goddard	17	0	63	4	11	2	32	1
Worrell	10	1	39	1	14	3	43	1
Peirce	4	0	37	0	3	0	14	1
Marshall	16	0	50	0	10	3	22	3
Hoad	10	0	33	0	5.4	0	25	2
Carew	2	0	22	0				
Griffith	4	0	18	0				

British Guiana Bowling

	O	M	R	W
Trim	31	3	158	4
Vigilance	31	5	108	0
Gaskin	32	8	108	4
McKenzie	29	4	79	0
Christiani	5	0	25	1
Birkett	5	1	12	0
Bayley	1	0	10	0

Umpires: B.Menzies and J.M.Neblett. Toss: British Guiana

Close of Play: 1st day: British Guiana (1) 266-3 (Christiani 12*); 2nd day: Barbados (1) 121-3 (Worrell 37*, Goddard 18*); 3rd day: Barbados (1) 441-6 (Goddard 178*, Marshall 37*).

BRITISH GUIANA v BARBADOS

Played at Bourda, Georgetown, October 7, 9, 10, 11, 12, 1944.

Barbados won by 72 runs.

BARBADOS					
1	G.M.Carew	lbw b Naipaul	97	lbw b Gaskin	2
2	†O.M.Robinson	c Griffith b Naipaul	51	b Griffith	7
3	C.L.Walcott	lbw b Christiani	26	c McKenzie b Gaskin	125
4	F.M.M.Worrell	b Gaskin	20	lbw b Gaskin	16
5	J.D.C.Goddard	b Griffith	7	c Elvis b McKenzie	51
6	H.L.V.Griffith	lbw b Griffith	4	(8) c Christiani b Griffith	0
7	K.E.Walcott	c Naipaul b Griffith	0	(9) b Griffith	40
8	N.E.Marshall	c Christiani b Griffith	32	(6) c Christiani b Gaskin	22
9	*T.N.M.Peirce	b Naipaul	27	(7) lbw b Griffith	2
10	E.A.V.Williams	c Camacho b Gaskin	29	c McKenzie b Trim	48
11	E.A.Greene	not out	5	not out	0
	Extras		11		12
			309		325

FoW (1): 1-108, 2-173, 3-187, 4-207, 5-207, 6-215, 7-216, 8-270, 9-277, 10-309
FoW (2): 1-2 (1), 2-42 (2), 3-85 (4), 4-208, 5-222, 6-229, 7-229, 8-237, 9-317, 10-325

BRITISH GUIANA					
1	U.B.McKenzie	c Marshall b Williams	12	b Williams	0
2	C.C.Reece	lbw b Williams	55	b Williams	9
3	*H.P.Bayley	b Worrell	21	c K.E.Walcott b Worrell	61
4	†C.A.McWatt	b Goddard	64	c K.E.Walcott b Goddard	4
5	R.J.Christiani	c Peirce b Worrell	5	b Marshall	128
6	G.A.Camacho	c Griffith b Williams	40	c Carew b Griffith	31
7	J.Elvis	b Goddard	0	(8) st C.L.Walcott b Peirce	34
8	B.B.M.Gaskin	c Robinson b Goddard	3	(7) b Worrell	14
9	J.Trim	c C.L.Walcott b Worrell	16	(10) lbw b Williams	0
10	W.G.Griffith	st Robinson b Worrell	16	(9) b Williams	4
11	J.Naipaul	not out	8	not out	7
	Extras	b 10, lb 9, w 1, nb 1	21		9
			261		301

FoW (1): 1-26, 2-75, 3-131, 4-142, 5-214, 6-218, 7-218, 8-246, 9-261, 10-261
FoW (2): 1-0 (1), 2-16 (2), 3-21 (4), 4-168, 5-232, 6-242, 7-266, 8-281, 9-281, 10-301

British Guiana Bowling	O	M	R	W			O	M	R	W
Gaskin	21.2	3	58	2			18	1	81	4
Griffith	19	4	51	4			13.3	1	79	4
Trim	17	0	90	0			7	0	40	1
Naipaul	25	2	87	3	1w		15	0	52	0
Christiani	3	0	12	1			2	0	22	0
Elvis						(6)	6	0	29	0
McKenzie						(7)	4	0	10	1

Barbados Bowling	O	M	R	W		O	M	R	W
Williams	18	2	51	3	1nb	16	0	64	4
Goddard	12	0	42	3		15	1	63	1
Greene	12	2	24	0		4	0	12	0
Marshall	10	1	35	0		22	7	50	1
Worrell	15.3	3	45	4		20	4	76	2
Peirce	3	0	24	0		2.2	0	15	1
Griffith	6	1	19	0	1w	3	0	12	1

Umpires: B.Menzies and J.M.Neblett. Toss: Barbados

Close of Play: 1st day: Barbados (1) 253-7 (Marshall 25*, Peirce 12*); 2nd day: British Guiana (1) 175-4 (McWatt 48*, Camacho 17*); 3rd day: Barbados (2) 221-4 (C.L.Walcott 124*, Marshall 11*); 4th day: British Guiana (2) 153-3 (Bayley 58*, Christiani 79*).

SIND v BOMBAY

Played at Karachi Gymkhana Ground, November 3, 4, 5, 6, 1944.

Match drawn.

BOMBAY

1	K.C.Ibrahim	c Daud Khan b Narottam	55	not out	6
2	†M.K.Mantri	c Samtani b Narottam	32	c Ambep b Samtani	0
3	R.S.Modi	c Samtani b Inayat Khan	160		
4	*V.M.Merchant	b Qamaruddin Sheikh	84		
5	D.G.Phadkar	c Abbas Khan b Narottam	23		
6	R.S.Cooper	b Inayat Khan	7		
7	K.M.Rangnekar	c Samtani b Naoomal Jaoomal	9		
8	J.B.Khot	b Narottam	13		
9	Anwar Hussain	lbw b Inayat Khan	1	(3) not out	8
10	M.N.Raiji	st Irani b Narottam	4		
11	J.J.Kore	not out	11		
	Extras	b 24, lb 9	33		2
			432	(1 wicket)	16

FoW (1): 1-93 (1), 2-100 (2), 3-305 (4), 4-352 (3), 5-362 (6), 6-377 (7), 7-412 (5), 8-415 (9), 9-417 (8), 10-432 (10)
FoW (2): 1-3 (2)

SIND

1	R.T.Simpson	b Merchant	88	c and b Kore	63
2	B.S.Ambep	c Raiji b Kore	31	b Kore	51
3	D.Narottam	run out	5	b Anwar Hussain	58
4	Abbas Khan	b Kore	4	(5) c Mantri b Anwar Hussain	0
5	Qamaruddin Sheikh	c Ibrahim b Kore	0	(4) not out	47
6	*Naoomal Jaoomal	run out	0		
7	Daud Khan	c Mantri b Phadkar	53		
8	Inayat Khan	c Phadkar b Kore	51		
9	V.K.Samtani	b Kore	9		
10	†J.K.Irani	not out	9	(6) not out	23
11	F.G.Lakda	c Phadkar b Kore	1		
	Extras	b 6, lb 6, nb 1	13		2
			264	(4 wickets, declared)	244

FoW (1): 1-54 (2), 2-60 (3), 3-86 (4), 4-86 (5), 5-86 (6), 6-148 (1), 7-245 (7), 8-249 (8), 9-259 (9), 10-264 (11)
FoW (2): 1-105 (2), 2-122 (1), 3-194 (3), 4-210 (5)

Sind Bowling	O	M	R	W		O	M	R	W
Samtani	33	11	68	0		4	1	10	1
Narottam	54.4	16	85	5		3	2	4	0
Qamaruddin Sheikh	15	2	38	1					
Lakda	37	7	75	0					
Inayat Khan	55	29	59	3					
Naoomal Jaoomal	31	6	74	1					

Bombay Bowling	O	M	R	W		O	M	R	W
Phadkar	23	6	47	1	(8)	7	1	15	0
Khot	29	13	34	0		22	3	61	0
Anwar Hussain	12	7	9	0	(1)	12	3	45	2
Merchant	15	6	21	1	(3)	15	3	39	0
Rangnekar	3	0	10	0	(6)	6	0	17	0
Kore	45	10	90	6	(4)	11	1	42	2
Raiji	13	2	37	0	(5)	5	0	12	0
Modi	2	0	2	0					
Ibrahim	1	0	1	0	(7)	1	0	11	0

Umpires: M.G.Bhave and ?. Toss:

Close of Play: 1st day: Bombay (1) 201-2 (Modi 56*, Merchant 51*); 2nd day: Bombay (1) 432 all out; 3rd day: Sind (1) 228-6 (Daud Khan 51*, Inayat Khan 46*).
R.S.Modi's 160 took 315 minutes and included 10 fours and 1 six.

EUROPEANS v PARSEES

Played at Brabourne Stadium, Bombay, November 15, 16, 17, 1944.

Match drawn.

EUROPEANS

1	R.T.Simpson	c Palia b Satha	69	(2) b Tarapore	24
2	N.S.Hotchkin	c Satha b Modi	7		
3	D.C.S.Compton	b Colah	7	not out	79
4	*J.Hardstaff	c Meherhomji b Tarapore	150	not out	76
5	R.D.Fairbairn	b Khot	13	(1) b Palia	1
6	R.Howorth	b Khot	0		
7	P.Cranmer	b Palia	17		
8	P.F.Judge	run out	0		
9	P.A.H.Carey	not out	10		
10	†P.Corrall	lbw b Tarapore	0		
11	G.P.M.Blackmore	c Cooper b Palia	8		
	Extras	b 10, lb 9	19		
			300	(2 wickets)	180

FoW (1): 1-27 (2), 2-34 (3), 3-176 (1), 4-217 (5), 5-229 (6), 6-263 (7), 7-270 (8), 8-287 (4), 9-287 (10), 10-300 (11)
FoW (2): 1-12 (1), 2-39 (2)

PARSEES

1	N.H.Colah	b Compton	24
2	*P.E.Palia	c Fairbairn b Carey	5
3	M.F.Mistry	c Compton b Carey	1
4	R.S.Modi	b Carey	215
5	R.S.Cooper	b Carey	73
6	J.B.Khot	c Cranmer b Carey	2
7	D.B.Satha	b Howorth	70
8	P.N.Cambhatta	not out	25
9	E.B.Aibara	b Carey	0
10	†K.R.Meherhomji	lbw b Hardstaff	38
11	K.K.Tarapore	lbw b Compton	6
	Extras	b 14, lb 3, nb 3	20
			479

FoW (1): 1-12 (2), 2-16 (3), 3-66 (1), 4-217 (5), 5-225 (6), 6-392 (7), 7-412 (4), 8-412 (9), 9-468 (10), 10-479 (11)

Parsees Bowling

	O	M	R	W		O	M	R	W
Palia	37.3	10	53	2	(2)	16	6	25	1
Khot	22	6	45	2	(1)	11	2	28	0
Modi	27	5	74	1		4	0	13	0
Colah	6	0	32	1		6	1	11	0
Tarapore	24	2	60	2		18	8	32	1
Satha	9	2	17	1		15	2	54	0
Cooper					(7)	3	0	17	0

Europeans Bowling

	O	M	R	W
Judge	41	6	153	0
Carey	37	5	139	6
Blackmore	17	2	63	0
Compton	23.4	5	51	2
Howorth	27	10	35	1
Hardstaff	6	1	18	1

Umpires: D.K.Naik and Vali Ahmed. Toss: Europeans

Close of Play: 1st day: Europeans (1) 300 all out; 2nd day: Parsees (1) 311-5 (Modi 156*, Satha 34*).

J.Hardstaff's 150 took 284 minutes and included 8 fours and 1 five. R.S.Modi's 215 took 410 minutes and included 12 fours.

MUSLIMS v THE REST

Played at Brabourne Stadium, Bombay, November 18, 19, 20, 1944.

Match drawn.

THE REST

1	†V.Dias	c Maka b Amir Elahi	27	lbw b Baloch	6
2	B.P.Kadam	b Saeed Ahmed	6	c Maka b Inayat Khan	10
3	P.S.D'Souza	c Maka b Baloch	30	b Amir Elahi	15
4	*Vijay S.Hazare	lbw b Baloch	69	b Abdul Hafeez	11
5	M.Sathasivam	b Saeed Ahmed	101	c Gul Mohammad b Abdul Hafeez	0
6	S.S.Jayawickreme	c Gul Mohammad b Saeed Ahmed	39	(8) not out	14
7	B.Frank	b Saeed Ahmed	14	c Baloch b Abdul Hafeez	2
8	Vivek S.Hazare	c Maka b Ibrahim	11	(6) not out	3
9	A.B.Fernandes	b Amir Elahi	0		
10	A.K.Bhalerao	lbw b Amir Elahi	0		
11	J.Roach	not out	0		
	Extras	b 6, nb 5	11		5
			308	(6 wickets)	66

FoW (1): 1-12 (2), 2-53 (1), 3-67 (3), 4-238 (4), 5-238 (5), 6-260 (7), 7-288 (8), 8-290 (9), 9-298 (10), 10-308 (6)
FoW (2): 1-12 (1), 2-29 (2), 3-43 (4), 4-47 (3), 5-47 (5), 6-49 (7)

MUSLIMS

1	K.C.Ibrahim	c D'Souza b Vivek S.Hazare	31
2	Nazar Mohammad	lbw b Vijay S.Hazare	38
3	Abdul Hafeez	b Vivek S.Hazare	19
4	*S.Mushtaq Ali	lbw b Vijay S.Hazare	27
5	Gul Mohammad	b Roach	106
6	M.E.Z.Ghazali	not out	108
7	Saeed Ahmed	lbw b Vijay S.Hazare	11
8	Amir Elahi	lbw b Frank	13
9	Inayat Khan	not out	5
10	†E.S.Maka		
11	M.S.Baloch		
	Extras	b 12, lb 4, nb 4	20
		(7 wickets, declared)	378

FoW (1): 1-71 (1), 2-75 (2), 3-100 (3), 4-138 (4), 5-306 (5), 6-336 (7), 7-365 (8)

Muslims Bowling

	O	M	R	W		O	M	R	W
Saeed Ahmed	34.3	9	60	4		4	1	4	0
Baloch	28	7	57	2		4	2	9	1
Inayat Khan	6	1	11	0	(4)	7	3	9	1
Abdul Hafeez	6	1	14	0	(5)	9	2	13	3
Amir Elahi	34	7	105	3	(3)	16	6	26	1
Ghazali	9	0	33	0					
Ibrahim	2	1	2	1					
Mushtaq Ali	2	0	9	0					
Gul Mohammad	1	0	6	0					

The Rest Bowling

	O	M	R	W
Roach	26	6	56	1
Vijay S.Hazare	48	17	76	3
Jayawickreme	35	10	60	0
Frank	19	7	38	1
Bhalerao	14	4	47	0
Vivek S.Hazare	46	14	68	2
Sathasivam	3	0	13	0

Umpires: H.D.Billimoria and J.R.Patel. Toss: The Rest
Close of Play: 1st day: The Rest (1) 238-3 (Vijay S.Hazare 69*, Sathasivam 101*); 2nd day: Muslims (1) 211-4 (Gul Mohammad 39*, Ghazali 40*).
M.Sathasivam's 101 took 169 minutes and included 7 fours. Gul Mohammad's 106 took 317 minutes and included 9 fours.
M.E.Z.Ghazali's 108 took 358 minutes.

HINDUS v PARSEES

Played at Brabourne Stadium, Bombay, November 21, 22, 23, 1944.

Match drawn.

HINDUS

1	M.H.Mankad	c Satha b Tarapore	128		
2	S.W.Sohoni	lbw b Tarapore	38		
3	G.Kishenchand	lbw b Tarapore	0	(4) not out	23
4	*V.M.Merchant	not out	221		
5	C.S.Nayudu	b Palia	21		
6	K.M.Rangnekar	b Modi	51		
7	D.G.Phadkar	not out	0	(5) not out	9
8	C.T.Sarwate			(2) b Patel	12
9	U.M.Merchant			(3) c Cambhatta b Patel	21
10	S.N.Banerjee			(1) b Patel	1
11	†M.K.Mantri				
	Extras	b 8, lb 7	15		
		(5 wickets, declared)	474	(3 wickets)	66

FoW (1): 1-70 (2), 2-70 (3), 3-300 (1), 4-332 (5), 5-426 (6)
FoW (2): 1-1 (1), 2-33 (3), 3-44 (2)

PARSEES

1	N.H.Colah	c Mankad b Nayudu	36
2	J.A.Dadyseth	b Banerjee	46
3	J.B.Patel	c Nayudu b Banerjee	36
4	R.S.Modi	b Nayudu	31
5	K.K.Tarapore	c Rangnekar b Nayudu	28
6	R.S.Cooper	not out	58
7	D.B.Satha	b Nayudu	1
8	P.R.Umrigar	lbw b Banerjee	9
9	†K.R.Meherhomji	b Banerjee	0
10	P.N.Cambhatta	c Mankad b Sarwate	2
11	*P.E.Palia	b Sarwate	12
	Extras	b 27, lb 4, w 13, nb 5	49
			308

FoW (1): 1-79 (2), 2-88 (1), 3-140 (4), 4-208 (3), 5-242 (5), 6-244 (7), 7-272 (8), 8-272 (9), 9-275 (10), 10-308 (11)

Parsees Bowling

	O	M	R	W		O	M	R	W
Palia	45	13	84	1					
Modi	19	0	81	1	(1)	4	1	4	0
Umrigar	19	5	52	0		7	2	17	0
Patel	10	2	44	0	(2)	13	1	36	3
Colah	1	0	15	0					
Tarapore	53	14	141	3					
Satha	10	3	42	0	(4)	3	0	9	0

Hindus Bowling

	O	M	R	W
Banerjee	27	8	60	4
Phadkar	12	4	22	0
Sohoni	22	8	41	0
Sarwate	29	7	52	2
Nayudu	48	20	82	4
V.M.Merchant	3	2	2	0
Mankad	2	2	0	0

Umpires: J.Birtwistle and Vali Ahmed. Toss: Hindus

Close of Play: 1st day: Hindus (1) 313-3 (V.M.Merchant 126*, Nayudu 8*); 2nd day: Parsees (1) 144-3 (Patel 20*, Tarapore 2*).

M.H.Mankad's 128 took 330 minutes and included 16 fours and 1 six. V.M.Merchant's 221 took 383 minutes and included 21 fours. J.A.Dadyseth took over as wicket-keeper shortly before lunch on the first day as K.R.Meherhomji had injured a finger.

HINDUS v MUSLIMS

Played at Brabourne Stadium, Bombay, November 25, 26, 27, 28, 1944.

Muslims won by one wicket.

HINDUS					
1	S.W.Sohoni	lbw b Saeed Ahmed	0	(6) run out	8
2	M.H.Mankad	c Saeed Ahmed b Amir Elahi	52	lbw b Amir Elahi	17
3	C.T.Sarwate	b Saeed Ahmed	0	(9) b Saeed Ahmed	25
4	H.R.Adhikari	c Mushtaq Ali b Amir Elahi	14	(3) b Amir Elahi	20
5	*V.M.Merchant	c Maka b Inayat Khan	1	(4) c Maka b Saeed Ahmed	60
6	G.Kishenchand	c Mushtaq Ali b Amir Elahi	72	(5) not out	118
7	D.G.Phadkar	b Inayat Khan	26	(8) lbw b Amir Elahi	6
8	K.M.Rangnekar	c Inayat Khan b Baloch	2	(7) lbw b Baloch	0
9	C.S.Nayudu	b Amir Elahi	26	(10) lbw b Inayat Khan	11
10	†D.D.Hindlekar	lbw b Amir Elahi	1	(1) run out	4
11	S.N.Banerjee	not out	1	c sub (Mamsa) b Amir Elahi	12
	Extras	lb 6, nb 2	8	b 17, lb 11, nb 6	34
			203		315

FoW (1): 1-2 (1), 2-2 (3), 3-55 (4), 4-60 (5), 5-68 (2), 6-134 (7), 7-138 (8), 8-186 (9), 9-200 (10), 10-203 (6)
FoW (2): 1-9 (1), 2-36 (2), 3-60 (3), 4-154 (4), 5-169 (6), 6-182 (7), 7-197 (8), 8-256 (9), 9-283 (10), 10-315 (11)

MUSLIMS					
1	K.C.Ibrahim	c Sohoni b Banerjee	52	not out	137
2	Anwar Hussain	b Banerjee	38	c Hindlekar b Nayudu	4
3	*S.Mushtaq Ali	st Hindlekar b Nayudu	9	(7) b Sarwate	36
4	M.E.Z.Ghazali	c and b Nayudu	27	(5) lbw b Banerjee	3
5	Gul Mohammad	c Rangnekar b Nayudu	46	(4) c sub (M.K.Mantri) b Banerjee	42
6	Saeed Ahmed	c Kishenchand b Nayudu	0	(8) lbw b Sarwate	0
7	Abdul Hafeez	c Phadkar b Sarwate	10	(9) run out	35
8	Inayat Khan	lbw b Sarwate	0	(6) c Merchant b Nayudu	0
9	Amir Elahi	b Sarwate	12	(10) c Nayudu b Sarwate	30
10	†E.S.Maka	not out	10	(3) b Nayudu	0
11	M.S.Baloch	c and b Nayudu	4	not out	3
	Extras	b 6, lb 6, nb 1	13	b 2, lb 4, nb 2	8
			221	(9 wickets)	298

FoW (1): 1-90 (2), 2-107 (3), 3-109 (1), 4-171 (4), 5-171 (6), 6-189 (5), 7-193 (8), 8-194 (7), 9-209 (9), 10-221 (11)
FoW (2): 1-12 (2), 2-19 (3), 3-102 (4), 4-112 (5), 5-113 (6), 6-162 (7), 7-164 (8), 8-247 (9), 9-294 (10)

Muslims Bowling	O	M	R	W		O	M	R	W
Saeed Ahmed	17	10	22	2		38	22	37	2
Baloch	24	8	46	1		28	9	38	1
Anwar Hussain	1	0	2	0		1	1	0	0
Ghazali	1	0	6	0					
Inayat Khan	26	10	43	2		22	9	36	1
Amir Elahi	22.1	3	76	5	(4)	66.5	19	147	4
Abdul Hafeez					(6)	11	5	19	0
Gul Mohammad					(7)	1	0	4	0

Hindus Bowling	O	M	R	W		O	M	R	W
Banerjee	13	2	34	2		19	2	50	2
Sohoni	5	1	13	0					
Nayudu	30.1	3	93	5		45	5	134	3
Sarwate	22	5	62	3		29	4	72	3
Mankad	2	1	3	0		2	0	5	0
Merchant	3	1	3	0		2	0	10	0
Phadkar					(2)	6	1	19	0

Umpires: J.Birtwistle and J.R.Patel. Toss: Hindus

Close of Play: 1st day: Muslims (1) 75-0 (Ibrahim 41*, Anwar Hussain 27*); 2nd day: Hindus (2) 86-3 (Merchant 23*, Kishenchand 12*); 3rd day: Muslims (2) 13-1 (Ibrahim 7*, Maka 0*).
G.Kishenchand's 118 took 347 minutes and included 11 fours. K.C.Ibrahim's 137 took 349 minutes.

CRICKET CLUB OF INDIA v SERVICES XI

Played at Brabourne Stadium, Bombay, December 1, 2, 3, 4, 1944.

Cricket Club of India won by an innings and 35 runs.

SERVICES XI					
1	N.S.Hotchkin	b Nayudu	42	(8) c Merchant b Amir Elahi	1
2	R.T.Simpson	b Banerjee	2	(1) st Maka b Amir Elahi	50
3	S.Mushtaq Ali	c Maka b Banerjee	90	b Hazare	5
4	J.Hardstaff	b Amir Elahi	27	b Nayudu	21
5	D.C.S.Compton	c Modi b Banerjee	16	(2) st Maka b Amir Elahi	120
6	*C.K.Nayudu	c and b Mankad	91	(5) c sub b Amir Elahi	2
7	P.Cranmer	b Nayudu	24	(6) c Sohoni b Nayudu	22
8	P.A.H.Carey	b Banerjee	4	(9) b Nayudu	10
9	P.F.Judge	b Nayudu	26	(7) b Amir Elahi	2
10	H.J.Butler	not out	5	absent hurt	0
11	†P.Corrall	b Amir Elahi	2	(10) not out	3
	Extras		13	b 1, lb 1	2
			342		238

FoW (1): 1-5 (2), 2-137 (3), 3-165 (5), 4-193 (4), 5-220 (7), 6-236 (8), 7-320 (6), 8-334 (9), 9-335 (1), 10-342 (11)
FoW (2): 1-93 (1), 2-104 (3), 3-136 (4), 4-139 (5), 5-173 (6), 6-177 (7), 7-187 (8), 8-220 (9), 9-238 (2)

CRICKET CLUB OF INDIA			
1	M.H.Mankad	lbw b Judge	65
2	S.W.Sohoni	c Corrall b Carey	82
3	R.S.Modi	c Nayudu b Judge	14
4	V.S.Hazare	not out	200
5	*V.M.Merchant	retired out	201
6	Gul Mohammad	not out	17
7	C.T.Sarwate		
8	C.S.Nayudu		
9	S.N.Banerjee		
10	Amir Elahi		
11	†E.S.Maka		
	Extras		36
		(4 wickets, declared)	615

FoW (1): 1-143 (1), 2-168 (2), 3-188 (3), 4-570 (5)

Cricket Club of India Bowling	O	M	R	W		O	M	R	W
Banerjee	22	3	80	4		8	1	28	0
Hazare	11	1	34	0	(6)	7	0	32	1
Sohoni	12	2	47	0	(2)	3	0	20	0
Amir Elahi	30	3	77	2		28.4	4	109	5
Nayudu	16	3	72	3		15	2	43	3
Mankad	7	1	19	1					
Sarwate					(3)	2	0	4	0

Services XI Bowling	O	M	R	W
Butler	41	10	87	0
Judge	57	13	171	2
Carey	30	6	110	1
Compton	18	1	80	0
Mushtaq Ali	18	8	33	0
Hardstaff	12	1	50	0
Nayudu	6	0	37	0
Cranmer	1	0	11	0

Umpires: D.K.Naik and Vali Ahmed. Toss:

Close of Play: 1st day: Services XI (1) 342 all out; 2nd day: Cricket Club of India (1) 260-3 (Hazare 31*, Merchant 33*); 3rd day: Services XI (2) 50-0 (Simpson 29*, Compton 21*).
V.S.Hazare's 200 took 400 minutes and included 19 fours. V.M.Merchant's 201 took 338 minutes and included 18 fours. D.C.S.Compton's 120 took 195 minutes and included 16 fours. N.S.Hotchkin retired hurt when hit on the temple by a ball from S.N.Banerjee in the Services XI first innings having scored 35 (team score 128-1) - he returned when the score was 320-7. The match was played in aid of the Indian Red Cross Amenities Fund.

BENGAL v UNITED PROVINCES

Played at Eden Gardens, Calcutta, December 9, 10, 11, 12, 1944.

Bengal won by 75 runs.

BENGAL					
1	P.B.Datta	b Gandhi	58	b Gandhi	10
2	A.C.Chatterjee	b Majeed	0	b Gandhi	16
3	P.K.Sen	c Rajindernath b Gandhi	63	c Rajindernath b Majeed	12
4	F.Harker	c Balendu Shah b Gandhi	0	(5) b Mehra	16
5	N.C.Chatterjee	c Saidullah b Majeed	6	(4) c Rajindernath b Jalaluddin	2
6	*Maharaja of Cooch Behar	st Rajindernath b Gandhi	27	(7) b Mehra	14
7	†T.V.Parthasarathi	c Phansalkar b Majeed	21	(10) c Telang b Majeed	30
8	K.Bhattacharya	b Gandhi	31	(9) not out	24
9	A.Sen	b Majeed	4	(6) c Phansalkar b Mehra	12
10	P.A.H.Carey	b Ramchandra	23	(8) c Balendu Shah b Gandhi	0
11	N.R.Chowdhury	not out	1	b Gandhi	0
	Extras		14		21
			248		157

FoW (1): 1-1 (2), 2-125 (1), 3-128 (4), 4-133 (3), 5-166 (5), 6-166 (6), 7-215 (7), 8-223 (8), 9-233 (9), 10-248 (10)
FoW (2): 1-24 (3), 2-27 (4), 3-42 (2), 4-47 (1), 5-74 (6), 6-89 (5), 7-90 (8), 8-98 (7), 9-156 (10), 10-157 (11)

UNITED PROVINCES					
1	*M.K.Balendu Shah	c Chowdhury b Carey	20	c Bhattacharya b Chowdhury	11
2	†V.Rajindernath	c P.K.Sen b Carey	0	(4) lbw b A.Sen	25
3	S.N.Gandhi	b A.Sen	29	lbw b Chowdhury	0
4	Shamim Khwaja	b Chowdhury	1	(6) lbw b Bhattacharya	34
5	J.P.Phansalkar	c A.Sen b Chowdhury	0	(7) not out	40
6	B.P.Telang	c Bhattacharya b Chowdhury	2	(5) b A.Sen	5
7	B.Ramchandra	c A.Sen b Bhattacharya	32	(8) c Carey b Chowdhury	13
8	M.Jalaluddin	b Carey	29	(11) c Cooch Behar b Chowdhury	1
9	A.Majeed	b Harker	32	lbw b A.Sen	1
10	Saidullah	not out	14	c Cooch Behar b Chowdhury	3
11	J.Mehra	b Bhattacharya	8	(2) c Carey b Bhattacharya	15
	Extras		9		6
			176		154

FoW (1): 1-1 (2), 2-28 (1), 3-29 (4), 4-46 (5), 5- (6), 6-61 (3), 7-98 (7), 8-130 (8), 9-167 (9), 10-176 (11)
FoW (2): 1-24 (1), 2-24 (3), 3-50 (2), 4-56 (4), 5-67 (5), 6-109 (6), 7-131 (8), 8-132 (9), 9-149 (10), 10-154 (11)

United Provinces Bowling	O	M	R	W		O	M	R	W
Majeed	24	9	25	4		23	7	58	2
Jalaluddin	1	1	0	0		8	3	14	1
Gandhi	36	7	97	5	(4)	27.3	7	44	4
Ramchandra	26.3	11	55	1	(3)	1	0	1	0
Saidullah	9	1	33	0					
Mehra	3	0	12	0	(5)	11	5	19	3
Telang	2	0	12	0					

Bengal Bowling	O	M	R	W		O	M	R	W
Carey	14	5	48	3	(3)	14	4	37	0
Chowdhury	13	3	40	3	(1)	20.1	8	49	5
A.Sen	6	0	28	1	(2)	15	1	28	3
Datta	3	0	10	0					
Bhattacharya	7.3	2	25	2	(4)	13	1	34	2
Harker	4	0	16	1					

Umpires: H.D.Billimoria and Vali Ahmed. Toss: Bengal

Close of Play: 1st day: Bengal (1) 248 all out; 2nd day: Bengal (2) 74-5 (Harker 14*); 3rd day: United Provinces (2) 149-9 (Phansalkar 37*).

P.B.Datta retired hurt in the Bengal second innings having scored 0 (team score 0-0) - he returned when the score was 27-2. He was hit on the knee by a ball from A.Majeed.

MAHARASHTRA v NAWANAGAR

Played at Poona Club Ground, December 9, 10, 11, 1944.

Maharashtra won by 489 runs.

MAHARASHTRA					
1	S.W.Sohoni	c Mehta b Mubarak Ali	3	(6) c I.Oza b Man Singh	1
2	V.M.Pandit	b Man Singh	10	(1) lbw b Man Singh	10
3	S.K.Banerjee	c Man Singh b Mubarak Ali	11	b J.R.Oza	24
4	M.E.Z.Ghazali	c Yadvendrasinhji b Mubarak Ali	9	lbw b Mubarak Ali	46
5	*D.B.Deodhar	lbw b Man Singh	105	(8) st Mehta b Mubarak Ali	141
6	R.R.Chandorkar	c J.Oza b Mubarak Ali	7	(5) lbw b Mubarak Ali	36
7	†Y.N.Gokhale	c I.Oza b J.R.Oza	58		
8	M.N.Paranjpe	c Mehta b Mubarak Ali	18	(7) not out	65
9	M.R.Rege	st Mehta b Yadvendrasinhji	52	(2) st Mehta b Jadeja	25
10	K.M.Jadhav	not out	84		
11	S.G.Shinde	c Mehta b Mubarak Ali	9		
	Extras		6		15
			372	(7 wickets, declared)	363

FoW (1): 1-6 (1), 2-22 (3), 3-34 (2), 4-34 (4), 5-46 (6), 6-181 (7), 7-214 (5), 8-239 (8), 9-335 (9), 10-372 (11)
FoW (2): 1-23 (1), 2-62 (2), 3-66 (3), 4-146 (4), 5-147 (6), 6-147 (5), 7-363 (8)

NAWANAGAR					
1	J.Oza	b Ghazali	10	lbw b Shinde	29
2	L.R.Jadeja	b Sohoni	26	b Ghazali	2
3	I.Oza	c Pandit b Jadhav	9	b Ghazali	3
4	R.K.Yadvendrasinhji	c sub (K.N.V.Chari) b Rege	42	lbw b Jadhav	5
5	K.Mankad	run out	0	c Jadhav b Shinde	5
6	*M.S.Samarsinhji	lbw b Shinde	8	b Jadhav	28
7	J.R.Oza	c Banerjee b Shinde	10	c Jadhav b Shinde	0
8	Bhagwat Singh	not out	5	st Gokhale b Chandorkar	3
9	Mubarak Ali	b Shinde	0	b Shinde	23
10	†K.Mehta	b Shinde	0	not out	5
11	A.Man Singh	c Chandorkar b Shinde	9	c Paranjpe b Chandorkar	0
	Extras		12		12
			131		115

FoW (1): 1-25 (1), 2-40 (3), 3-68 (2), 4-71 (5), 5-91 (6), 6-103 (7), 7-119 (4), 8-119 (9), 9-119 (10), 10-131 (11)
FoW (2): 1-2, 2-32, 3-43, 4-49, 5-70, 6-74, 7-78, 8-107, 9-115, 10-115

Nawanagar Bowling	O	M	R	W		O	M	R	W
Man Singh	36	10	92	2	(2)	24	3	91	2
Mubarak Ali	38.3	9	96	6	(1)	25	3	102	3
J.R.Oza	24	4	80	1		22	4	67	1
Bhagwat Singh	10	0	44	0	(5)	8	3	22	0
Yadvendrasinhji	4	0	32	1					
Jadeja	3	0	22	0	(4)	16	3	66	1

Maharashtra Bowling	O	M	R	W		O	M	R	W
Sohoni	15	3	32	1		5	1	26	0
Ghazali	17	7	23	1		9	6	4	2
Jadhav	12	3	31	1		10	2	38	2
Shinde	13.4	4	17	5		9	4	29	4
Rege	4	1	16	1		2	0	6	0
Chandorkar					(6)	1.5	1	0	2

Umpires: D.K.Naik and J.R.Patel. Toss:

Close of Play: 1st day: Maharashtra (1) 358-9 (Jadhav 72*, Shinde 7*); 2nd day: Maharashtra (2) 118-3 (Ghazali 30*, Chandorkar 24*).

The match was scheduled for four days but completed in three. D.B.Deodhar's 105 took 161 minutes and included 12 fours. D.B.Deodhar's 141 took 120 minutes and included 22 fours and 1 six.

NORTHERN INDIA v DELHI

Played at Minto Park, Lahore, December 9, 10, 11, 1944.

Northern India won by an innings and 220 runs.

NORTHERN INDIA

1	Nazar Mohammad	lbw b Mazhar Hussain	13
2	D.Muni Lal	b Salahuddin Khan	30
3	Mohammad Saeed	c Maqsood b Salahuddin Khan	56
4	Abdul Hafeez	run out	68
5	*M.R.Bhide	st Shiv Narain b Salahuddin Khan	114
6	†Imtiaz Ahmed	b Mohammad Yunus Khan	1
7	Fazal Mahmood	b Mohammad Yunus Khan	15
8	M.Jahangir Khan	not out	24
9	D.R.Puri	not out	18
10	Mohammad Amin		
11	Gian Sagar		
	Extras		19
		(7 wickets, declared)	358

FoW (1): 1-24 (1), 2-91 (2), 3-114 (3), 4-262 (4), 5-270 (6), 6-301 (7), 7-330 (5)

DELHI

1	Mazhar Hussain	c Puri b Abdul Hafeez	12	(2) c Nazar Mohammad b Fazal Mahmood	21
2	Abdur Rauf	c Imtiaz Ahmed b Abdul Hafeez	9	(1) c Fazal Mahmood b Abdul Hafeez	25
3	Salahuddin Khan	st Imtiaz Ahmed b Fazal Mahmood	12	b Fazal Mahmood	0
4	Jamilul Hai	b Abdul Hafeez	0	c Imtiaz Ahmed b Mohammad Amin	19
5	Mohammad Ishaq	b Abdul Hafeez	0	(8) c Puri b Abdul Hafeez	0
6	Shujauddin	b Abdul Hafeez	0	(7) c Abdul Hafeez b Mohammad Amin	0
7	I.Dayal	lbw b Abdul Hafeez	6	(6) c and b Mohammad Amin	0
8	*M.H.Maqsood	not out	0	(5) c Imtiaz Ahmed b Mohammad Amin	0
9	†Shiv Narain	c Imtiaz Ahmed b Abdul Hafeez	0	b Abdul Hafeez	10
10	Hargopal Singh	run out	11	c Abdul Hafeez b Mohammad Amin	3
11	Mohammad Yunus Khan	c Nazar Mohammad b Fazal Mahmood	0	not out	0
	Extras		2		8
			52		86

FoW (1): 1-21 (2), 2-26 (1), 3-26 (4), 4-30 (5), 5-30 (6), 6-41 (7), 7-41 (3), 8-41 (9), 9-52 (10), 10-52 (11)
FoW (2): 1-45, 2-48, 3-54, 4-55, 5-59, 6-67, 7-68, 8-74, 9-86, 10-86

Delhi Bowling

	O	M	R	W
Mazhar Hussain	36	9	87	1
Mohammad Yunus Khan	19	3	57	2
Shujauddin	21	4	46	0
Hargopal Singh	16	3	45	0
Salahuddin Khan	27	4	87	3
Jamilul Hai	3	0	17	0

Northern India Bowling

	O	M	R	W		O	M	R	W
Puri	4	1	10	0	(2)	5	1	10	0
Abdul Hafeez	17	9	25	7	(1)	20	3	24	3
Fazal Mahmood	13.4	7	15	2	(4)	11	9	3	2
Jahangir Khan					(3)	4	1	8	0
Mohammad Amin					(5)	22	8	33	5

Umpires: Toss: Delhi

Close of Play: 1st day: Northern India (1) 301-6 (Bhide 100*); 2nd day: Delhi (1) 52 all out.

The match was scheduled for four days but completed in three. M.R.Bhide's 114 included 7 fours and 1 six.

BIHAR v HOLKAR

Played at Keenan Stadium, Jamshedpur, December 15, 16, 1944.

Holkar won by an innings and 140 runs.

HOLKAR

1	M.M.Jagdale	c Banerjee b S.Bose	142
2	K.V.Bhandarkar	c B.K.Bose b Banerjee	1
3	S.Mushtaq Ali	c Banerjee b Das Gupta	41
4	C.S.Nayudu	c Sen b Hydes	33
5	*C.K.Nayudu	c Bagchi b Banerjee	42
6	†B.B.Nimbalkar	b Banerjee	17
7	C.T.Sarwate	hit wkt b Das Gupta	71
8	J.N.Bhaya	c Mitter b Banerjee	11
9	H.G.Gaekwad	c Mitter b Banerjee	0
10	O.P.Rawal	not out	20
11	R.K.Vaid	run out	2
	Extras		9
			389

FoW (1): 1-1 (2), 2-46 (3), 3-104 (4), 4-159 (5), 5-200 (6), 6-316 (7), 7-353, 8-353, 9-375, 10-389

BIHAR

1	D.Madan	c Jagdale b C.S.Nayudu	16	c Sarwate b Mushtaq Ali	8
2	A.Mitter	st Nimbalkar b C.S.Nayudu	4	b C.S.Nayudu	5
3	S.Bagchi	c C.S.Nayudu b Sarwate	10	b Sarwate	25
4	A.Dey Sarkar	b Sarwate	46	st Nimbalkar b Sarwate	8
5	*S.N.Banerjee	st Nimbalkar b Sarwate	3	(9) not out	3
6	B.Sen	b C.S.Nayudu	2	(10) c Bhaya b Sarwate	0
7	A.K.Das Gupta	c and b C.S.Nayudu	5	c Bhandarkar b C.S.Nayudu	15
8	M.Guha	c and b Sarwate	9	(6) c Jagdale b Sarwate	1
9	B.K.Bose	b C.S.Nayudu	34	(8) st Nimbalkar b Sarwate	2
10	S.Bose	not out	6	(5) c C.K.Nayudu b C.S.Nayudu	9
11	Hydes	c Nimbalkar b C.S.Nayudu	2	run out	1
	Extras		21		14
			158		91

FoW (1): 1-24, 2-25, 3-45, 4-55, 5-64, 6-82, 7-100, 8-145, 9-147, 10-158
FoW (2): 1-8, 2-46, 3-54, 4-60, 5-68, 6-72, 7-87, 8-89, 9-89, 10-91

Bihar Bowling

	O	M	R	W
Banerjee	30	6	108	5
S.Bose	17	2	57	1
B.K.Bose	12	0	69	0
Hydes	12	2	38	1
Das Gupta	24	2	76	2
Madan	7	0	32	0

Holkar Bowling

	O	M	R	W		O	M	R	W
Jagdale	3	0	8	0					
Gaekwad	2	0	8	0					
Vaid	1	1	0	0					
C.S.Nayudu	21.4	4	79	6		8.2	2	16	3
Sarwate	21	7	42	4	(3)	9	1	35	5
Mushtaq Ali					(1)	4	0	20	1
Rawal					(2)	3	0	6	0

Umpires: H.D.Billimoria and Vali Ahmed. Toss: Holkar

Close of Play: 1st day: Holkar (1) 339-6 (Jagdale 119*, Bhaya 7*).

The match was scheduled for four days but completed in two. M.M.Jagdale's 142 included 11 fours and 4 sixes.

GUJARAT v WESTERN INDIA

Played at Gujarat College Ground, Ahmedabad, December 15, 16, 17, 18, 1944.

Western India won by 200 runs.

WESTERN INDIA					
1	†Prataprai	c Cambhatta b Baloch	4	lbw b J.M.Patel	23
2	Jayantilal Vora	c Prithviraj b Baloch	4	c Hazare b Chippa	11
3	Ramniklal	b J.M.Patel	13	lbw b J.M.Patel	24
4	S.B.Gandhi	c J.M.Patel b Chippa	33	run out	4
5	Purshottam	b Baloch	22	c Cambhatta b J.M.Patel	0
6	*Sukhvantrai	b Chippa	8	(8) lbw b Mankad	1
7	S.K.Girdhari	lbw b Kesari	44	(6) c Baloch b Kesari	149
8	R.P.Rathod	b Baloch	48	(7) b Baloch	30
9	Ismail	c Prithviraj b Kesari	0	(10) c Alimuddin b Chippa	10
10	S.Nyalchand	not out	19	(11) not out	3
11	Bhawanishankar	lbw b Baloch	15	(9) lbw b J.M.Patel	1
	Extras		14		15
			224		271

FoW (1): 1-4, 2-8, 3- , 4- , 5- , 6- , 7- , 8- , 9- , 10-224
FoW (2): 1- , 2- , 3- , 4- , 5- , 6- , 7- , 8- , 9- , 10-271

GUJARAT					
1	V.T.Parekh	b Nyalchand	19	c Prataprai b Nyalchand	33
2	Alimuddin	c Gandhi b Jayantilal Vora	54	b Nyalchand	14
3	Prithviraj	lbw b Jayantilal Vora	3	(4) c Gandhi b Jayantilal Vora	14
4	P.N.Cambhatta	b Jayantilal Vora	0	(8) lbw b Girdhari	7
5	*M.H.Mankad	c Ismail b Jayantilal Vora	1	(3) lbw b Jayantilal Vora	19
6	K.P.Kesari	b Nyalchand	1	(7) not out	22
7	B.G.Patel	b Jayantilal Vora	21	(9) c and b Girdhari	1
8	M.S.Baloch	c Girdhari b Nyalchand	1	(6) c Gandhi b Girdhari	15
9	†R.G.Hazare	b Nyalchand	0	(5) st Prataprai b Nyalchand	7
10	U.R.Chippa	not out	12	st Prataprai b Girdhari	0
11	J.M.Patel	c Jayantilal Vora b Girdhari	4	st Prataprai b Girdhari	6
	Extras		24		17
			140		155

FoW (1): 1- , 2- , 3- , 4- , 5- , 6- , 7- , 8- , 9- , 10-140
FoW (2): 1- , 2- , 3- , 4- , 5- , 6- , 7- , 8- , 9- , 10-155

Gujarat Bowling	O	M	R	W		O	M	R	W
Baloch	35	10	74	5		26	6	70	1
Kesari	14	4	30	2		4.4	1	15	1
J.M.Patel	16	3	49	1	(4)	22	2	58	4
Mankad	7	2	22	0	(5)	19	1	43	1
Chippa	10	3	34	2	(3)	17	3	49	2
Alimuddin	1	0	1	0					
Prithviraj					(6)	1	0	21	0

Western India Bowling	O	M	R	W		O	M	R	W
Gandhi	11	1	27	0		10	4	14	0
Jayantilal Vora	23	7	37	5		29	9	46	2
Girdhari	14	6	19	1	(4)	19.5	10	23	5
Nyalchand	23	7	33	4	(3)	36	13	48	3
Ismail					(5)	4	1	7	0

Umpires: M.J.Abdulla and J.R.Patel. Toss:

Close of Play: 1st day: Gujarat (1) 17-0 (Parekh 11*, Alimuddin 6*); 2nd day: Western India (2) 129-5 (Girdhari 37*, Rathod 19*); 3rd day: Gujarat (2) 96-4 (Hazare not out, Baloch not out).

43 runs were added for the 4th wicket in the Western India first innings. 49 runs were added for the 7th wicket in the Western India first innings. S.K.Girdhari took his score from 37* to 144* before lunch on the third day.

BENGAL GOVERNOR'S XI v SERVICES XI

Played at Eden Gardens, Calcutta, December 16, 17, 18, 1944.

Services XI won by an innings and 1 run.

BENGAL GOVERNOR'S XI

1	*T.C.Longfield	c Simpson b Carey	0	(7) lbw b Carey	31
2	P.B.Datta	lbw b Judge	4	(1) c Ingram-Johnson b Carey	7
3	A.C.Chatterjee	b Cranmer	36	(2) run out	6
4	N.C.Chatterjee	b Cranmer	36	lbw b Compton	115
5	†P.K.Sen	lbw b Judge	7	(3) c Ingram-Johnson b Hardstaff	37
6	D.J.Rimmer	c Hardstaff b Cranmer	14	(9) lbw b Judge	37
7	Maharaja of Cooch Behar	c Ingram-Johnson b Cranmer	1	(5) c Cray b Judge	3
8	C.W.Langford	lbw b Cranmer	0	c Prescott b Judge	11
9	A.Sen	not out	15	(6) lbw b Compton	29
10	S.Mitra	lbw b Cranmer	14	c Prescott b Judge	9
11	N.R.Chowdhury	b Cranmer	7	not out	30
	Extras		9		12
			143		327

FoW (1): 1-1 (1), 2-13 (2), 3-72, 4-81, 5-97, 6-99, 7-99, 8-100, 9-133, 10-143
FoW (2): 1-12 (2), 2-39 (1), 3-79 (3), 4-98 (5), 5-191 (6), 6-206 (4), 7-226 (8), 8-255 (7), 9-268 (10), 10-327 (9)

SERVICES XI

1	N.S.Hotchkin	c and b Mitra	74
2	R.T.Simpson	c A.Sen b Chowdhury	68
3	D.C.S.Compton	st sub (T.V.Parthasarathi) b Mitra	109
4	J.Hardstaff	b Chowdhury	153
5	S.J.Cray	b Chowdhury	20
6	R.F.Kettle	lbw b Chowdhury	2
7	*†R.E.S.Ingram-Johnson	b Langford	3
8	P.Cranmer	b Longfield	0
9	P.A.H.Carey	lbw b Chowdhury	5
10	P.F.Judge	b Langford	9
11	T.E.Prescott	not out	1
	Extras		27
			471

FoW (1): 1-144 (2), 2-167 (1), 3-373 (3), 4-436 (5), 5-443 (4), 6-448 (6), 7-448 (7), 8-450 (8), 9-469 (10), 10-471 (9)

Services XI Bowling

	O	M	R	W		O	M	R	W
Judge	17	5	42	2		28.3	7	90	4
Carey	5	1	12	1	(3)	17	4	48	2
Cranmer	19	5	52	7	(2)	8	1	35	0
Prescott	4	0	19	0	(6)	6	1	17	0
Compton	3	1	9	0	(7)	13	1	63	2
Hardstaff					(4)	7	1	41	1
Kettle					(5)	2	0	21	0

Bengal Governor's XI Bowling

	O	M	R	W
Chowdhury	22.4	2	104	5
Langford	15	1	60	2
A.Sen	16	1	93	0
Cooch Behar	7	0	27	0
Longfield	15	1	77	1
N.C.Chatterjee	1	0	6	0
Mitra	14	2	77	2

Umpires: Toss: Bengal Governor's XI

Close of Play: 1st day: Services XI (1) 125-0 (Hotchkin 53*, Simpson 59*); 2nd day: Bengal Governor's XI (2) 98-3 (N.C.Chatterjee 40*, Cooch Behar 3*).

T.V.Parthasarathi took over as wicket-keeper when P.K.Sen injured a finger. This match was played for the Troops Amenities Fund.

MAHARASHTRA v BARODA

Played at Poona Club Ground, December 16, 17, 18, 19, 1944.

Baroda won by 354 runs.

BARODA					
1	Y.E.Sheikh	b Sohoni	7	(3) st Gokhale b Shinde	2
2	V.N.Raiji	lbw b Jadhav	68	(1) lbw b Deodhar	53
3	H.R.Adhikari	lbw b Jadhav	7	(4) not out	164
4	Vijay S.Hazare	c Gokhale b Jadhav	127	(5) not out	162
5	Gul Mohammad	run out	26		
6	*R.B.Nimbalkar	b Ghazali	2	(2) c Pandit b Shinde	117
7	H.M.Asha	c Deodhar b Sohoni	16		
8	†S.G.Powar	c Pandit b Shinde	10		
9	M.M.Naidu	c Deodhar b Shinde	17		
10	Vivek S.Hazare	lbw b Shinde	4		
11	Amir Elahi	not out	23		
	Extras		7		14
			314	(3 wickets, declared)	512

FoW (1): 1-20 (1), 2-41 (3), 3-139 (2), 4-186 (5), 5-190 (6), 6-243 (7), 7-259 (4), 8-284 (8), 9-287 (9), 10-314 (10)
FoW (2): 1-128 (1), 2-131 (3), 3-209 (2)

MAHARASHTRA					
1	V.M.Pandit	b Vijay S.Hazare	0	(8) b Adhikari	12
2	M.R.Rege	lbw b Vivek S.Hazare	72	c Gul Mohammad b Vivek S.Hazare	25
3	M.E.Z.Ghazali	c Powar b Vijay S.Hazare	15	b Vivek S.Hazare	17
4	S.W.Sohoni	c Powar b Gul Mohammad	33	(1) st Powar b Vivek S.Hazare	27
5	*D.B.Deodhar	c Nimbalkar b Vijay S.Hazare	39	(4) hit wkt b Sheikh	60
6	M.N.Paranjpe	c Adhikari b Gul Mohammad	10	(5) lbw b Adhikari	63
7	K.M.Jadhav	b Amir Elahi	26	lbw b Amir Elahi	8
8	R.R.Chandorkar	lbw b Amir Elahi	0	absent ill	0
9	†Y.N.Gokhale	not out	2	(6) c and b Amir Elahi	10
10	S.K.Banerjee	b Amir Elahi	0	(9) not out	28
11	S.G.Shinde	run out	4	(10) lbw b Vijay S.Hazare	8
	Extras		4		9
			205		267

FoW (1): 1-0 (1), 2-25 (3), 3-71 (4), 4-132 (5), 5-150 (6), 6-199 (2), 7-199 (8), 8-201 (7), 9-201 (10), 10-205 (11)
FoW (2): 1-38 (1), 2-69 (2), 3-80 (3), 4-174 (4), 5-210 (5), 6-210 (6), 7-225 (7), 8-237 (8), 9-267 (10)

Maharashtra Bowling	O	M	R	W		O	M	R	W
Sohoni	20	5	51	2		21	5	54	0
Ghazali	15	3	52	1	(3)	27	4	90	0
Jadhav	27	6	64	3	(2)	26	6	79	0
Shinde	20.4	2	93	3	(5)	31	1	111	2
Rege	9	1	47	0	(4)	21	3	63	0
Chandorkar					(6)	2.5	0	16	0
Deodhar					(7)	22	6	68	1
Pandit					(8)	5	0	15	0
Paranjpe					(9)	1	0	2	0

Baroda Bowling	O	M	R	W	O	M	R	W
Vijay S.Hazare	28	10	51	3	12.3	6	26	1
Gul Mohammad	17	5	52	2	14	3	36	0
Vivek S.Hazare	4	1	11	1	21	8	41	3
Amir Elahi	40	19	70	3	43	10	116	2
Sheikh	2	0	6	0	7	4	7	1
Adhikari	2	0	11	0	10	4	32	2

Umpires: H.E.Choudhury and D.K.Naik. Toss: Baroda

Close of Play: 1st day: Maharashtra (1) 15-1 (Rege 3*, Ghazali 11*); 2nd day: Baroda (2) 133-2 (Nimbalkar 75*, Adhikari 1*); 3rd day: Baroda (2) 512-3 (Adhikari 164*, Vijay S.Hazare 162*).

Vijay S.Hazare's 127 took 180 minutes and included 21 fours. R.B.Nimbalkar's 117 took 172 minutes and included 18 fours. H.R.Adhikari's 164 took 330 minutes. Vijay S.Hazare's 162 took 250 minutes.

CANTERBURY v OTAGO

Played at Lancaster Park, Christchurch, December 23, 25, 26, 1944.

Canterbury won by an innings and 17 runs.

OTAGO

1	F.W.J.Bellamy	b Burtt	4	absent hurt	0
2	†A.N.Lawson	c Cromb b Scott	1	(9) not out	0
3	*C.D.G.Toomey	b Scott	1	(2) b Scott	39
4	A.W.Roberts	b Burtt	19	c Butterfield b Scott	77
5	L.D.Smith	b Burtt	0	(6) b Anderson	1
6	V.D.A.McCarten	c Cromb b McRae	3	(5) c McRae b Burtt	0
7	D.H.Murdoch	c Burtt b McRae	0	(1) run out	4
8	A.W.McDougall	c Burtt b McRae	3	b Scott	29
9	R.C.Harwood	c Dunnet b Burtt	3	(3) c Hadlee b McRae	0
10	T.A.Freeman	b Scott	14	(7) st Dunnet b Waine	15
11	E.A.Kruskopf	not out	9	(10) c McRae b Scott	0
	Extras	b 2, lb 2, nb 5	9	b 7, lb 7	14
			66		179

FoW (1): 1-2, 2-8, 3-16, 4-16, 5-29, 6-31, 7-35, 8-38, 9-56, 10-66
FoW (2): 1-9, 2-15, 3-61, 4-62, 5-66, 6-97, 7-164, 8-179, 9-179

CANTERBURY

1	K.F.M.Uttley	c Toomey b Roberts	18
2	I.B.Cromb	c McCarten b Smith	74
3	*W.A.Hadlee	b Freeman	28
4	H.C.Waine	run out	16
5	W.M.Anderson	lbw b Roberts	29
6	F.P.O'Brien	b Roberts	2
7	L.A.Butterfield	b Kruskopf	7
8	R.H.Scott	b Roberts	0
9	D.A.N.McRae	b Freeman	2
10	T.B.Burtt	not out	52
11	†D.M.Dunnet	run out	15
	Extras	b 14, lb 5	19
			262

FoW (1): 1-47, 2-136, 3-142, 4-166, 5-182, 6-185, 7-187, 8-190, 9-199, 10-262

Canterbury Bowling

	O	M	R	W		O	M	R	W
McRae	14	4	16	3		13	7	15	1
Scott	12.3	4	12	3		21	7	48	4
Burtt	16	6	29	4	(4)	4	0	21	1
Butterfield					(3)	16	6	30	0
Anderson					(5)	6	0	33	1
Waine					(6)	5	0	18	1

Otago Bowling

	O	M	R	W
McDougall	12	1	34	0
Roberts	36	11	73	4
Kruskopf	15	5	38	1
Smith	16.3	2	52	1
Freeman	24	6	46	2

Umpires: T.W.Burgess and B.W.Vine. Toss: Otago

Close of Play: 1st day: Canterbury (1) 75-1 (Cromb 41*, Hadlee 4*); 2nd day: Canterbury (1) 262 all out.

WELLINGTON v AUCKLAND

Played at Basin Reserve, Wellington, December 23, 25, 26, 1944.

Auckland won by five wickets.

WELLINGTON					
1	S.A.McVicar	run out	19	st Kent b Burke	14
2	C.G.Rowe	st Kent b Burke	39	b Wheeler	16
3	R.J.Duffy	st Kent b Burke	11	(5) c Kent b Burke	26
4	W.G.C.Bain	c Warner b Burke	51	(3) b Burke	6
5	J.A.Ell	st Kent b Burke	2	(7) st Kent b Burke	3
6	*†F.L.H.Mooney	st Kent b Burke	1	(4) b Wheeler	4
7	A.M.Matheson	c Cleal b Burke	9	(6) b Brown	67
8	H.Chapman	b Kerr	21	c Kent b Brown	29
9	N.R.Hoar	not out	24	c Cleal b Burke	8
10	J.G.Ashenden	c sub (Richards) b Kerr	0	b Brown	4
11	R.Allen	run out	6	not out	3
	Extras	b 8, lb 2, w 2	12	b 6, lb 5, nb 1	12
			195		192

FoW (1): 1-38 (1), 2-73 (2), 3-86 (3), 4-90 (5), 5-98 (6), 6-120 (7), 7-151 (4), 8-186 (8), 9-186 (10), 10-195 (11)
FoW (2): 1-25 (2), 2-36 (3), 3-43 (4), 4-45 (1), 5-91 (5), 6-95 (7), 7-155 (8), 8-174 (9), 9-182 (10), 10-192 (6)

AUCKLAND					
1	*P.E.Whitelaw	c Bain b Allen	14	c Matheson b Chapman	28
2	R.H.Cleave	c and b Allen	10	(5) b Matheson	1
3	B.H.Warner	b Hoar	8	(6) c Mooney b Hoar	0
4	O.C.Cleal	c McVicar b Matheson	30	(2) not out	77
5	B.Sutcliffe	c Hoar b Allen	75	(3) run out	48
6	A.C.Kerr	run out	50	(7) not out	1
7	†L.A.W.Kent	b Allen	2		
8	W.J.Wheeler	st Mooney b Allen	22	(4) c Mooney b Matheson	0
9	C.Burke	not out	6		
10	W.J.Brown				
11	D.C.Cleverley				
	Extras	b 2, lb 6, nb 2	10	b 4, lb 2	6
		(8 wickets, declared)	227	(5 wickets)	161

FoW (1): 1-23 (1), 2-26 (2), 3-47 (3), 4-68 (4), 5-196 (5), 6-198 (6), 7-201 (7), 8-227 (8)
FoW (2): 1-52 (1), 2-141 (3), 3-145 (4), 4-147 (5), 5-150 (6)

Auckland Bowling

	O	M	R	W		O	M	R	W
Cleverley	17	4	31	0	(5)	14	1	27	0
Brown	7	4	5	0	(1)	10.2	1	31	3
Kerr	36.5	17	50	2	(4)	27	9	40	0
Wheeler	12	3	26	0	(2)	20	7	33	2
Burke	39	12	71	6	(3)	38	17	46	5
Cleal					(6)	4	2	3	0

Wellington Bowling

	O	M	R	W		O	M	R	W
Hoar	15	3	40	1		10	1	28	1
Ashenden	13	2	26	0		5	1	26	0
Allen	15.3	0	69	5					
Matheson	21	11	25	1	(3)	15	1	49	2
Chapman	11	2	22	0	(4)	11	1	52	1
Duffy	10	2	35	0					

Umpires: F.W.Harris-Daw and M.F.Pengelly. Toss: Wellington

Close of Play: 1st day: Auckland (1) 44-2 (Warner not out, Cleal not out); 2nd day: Wellington (2) 25-0 (McVicar 8*, Rowe 16*).

MADRAS v HYDERABAD

Played at Madras Cricket Club Ground, Chepauk, Madras, December 24, 25, 26, 27, 1944.

Madras won by 53 runs.

MADRAS					
1	M.Robinson	b Ghulam Ahmed	43	(2) b Ghulam Ahmed	12
2	*C.P.Johnstone	lbw b Bhupathi	14	(1) c Ghulam Ahmed b Khanna	86
3	A.G.Ram Singh	b Ghulam Ahmed	20	(5) st Sanjiva Rao b Ghulam Ahmed	0
4	A.Ananthanarayanan	st Sanjiva Rao b Bhupathi	0	c Sanjiva Rao b Ghulam Ahmed	0
5	F.F.Richardson	c Sanjiva Rao b Ghulam Ahmed	27	(6) b Ghulam Ahmed	19
6	K.S.Kannan	b Ghulam Ahmed	0	(3) c Jagdish Lal b Khanna	9
7	M.J.Gopalan	c Sanjiva Rao b Ghulam Ahmed	55	b Bhupathi	5
8	B.C.Alva	lbw b Bhupathi	1	b Bhupathi	36
9	†M.O.Srinivasan	not out	9	not out	35
10	B.S.Krishna Rao	c Sanjiva Rao b Ghulam Ahmed	1	b Khanna	0
11	C.R.Rangachari	b Ghulam Ahmed	4	lbw b Ghulam Ahmed	8
	Extras		14		23
			188		233

FoW (1): 1-23 (2), 2-77 (3), 3-82 (1), 4-82 (4), 5-82 (6), 6-165 (5), 7-171 (7), 8- (8), 9- (10), 10-188 (11)
FoW (2): 1-19 (2), 2-38 (3), 3-39 (4), 4-45 (5), 5-96 (6), 6-105 (7), 7-168 (8), 8-206 (1), 9-216 (10), 10-233 (11)

HYDERABAD					
1	Asadullah Qureshi	lbw b Krishna Rao	17	b Ram Singh	6
2	D.Jagdish Lal	c Alva b Ram Singh	54	(3) b Rangachari	4
3	Durga Prasad	lbw b Ram Singh	3	(2) c Rangachari b Robinson	48
4	E.B.Aibara	b Ram Singh	47	b Rangachari	15
5	Asghar Ali	b Rangachari	28	b Ram Singh	55
6	B.C.Khanna	b Rangachari	28	c Rangachari b Ram Singh	29
7	S.R.Mehta	b Rangachari	1	(10) c Robinson b Rangachari	0
8	Ghulam Ahmed	c Rangachari b Ram Singh	1	(7) b Ram Singh	7
9	*B.Zahiruddin	b Rangachari	0	(8) b Ram Singh	0
10	†I.Sanjiva Rao	not out	5	(9) run out	4
11	A.R.Bhupathi	b Rangachari	2	not out	0
	Extras		6		8
			192		176

FoW (1): 1-55 (1), 2-61 (3), 3-104 (2), 4-135 (4), 5-179 (5), 6-183 (7), 7-185 (6), 8-185 (9), 9-185 (8), 10-192 (11)
FoW (2): 1-8 (1), 2-13 (3), 3-33 (4), 4-102 (2), 5-146 (5), 6-156 (7), 7-164 (8), 8-170 (6), 9-176 (9), 10-176 (10)

Hyderabad Bowling	O	M	R	W		O	M	R	W
Khanna	16	4	38	0		17	7	40	3
Zahiruddin	4	3	1	0		5	2	8	0
Ghulam Ahmed	38.3	14	64	7		53.3	19	81	5
Bhupathi	34	17	45	3		31	11	50	2
Mehta	7	3	18	0	(6)	16	8	14	0
Asadullah Qureshi	3	1	8	0	(5)	2	0	3	0
Durga Prasad					(7)	2	0	14	0

Madras Bowling	O	M	R	W		O	M	R	W
Rangachari	22.1	8	46	5	(2)	34.4	13	53	3
Alva	14	3	22	0	(4)	4	2	4	0
Ram Singh	26	7	46	4		48	26	46	5
Krishna Rao	14	0	46	1	(5)	8	1	24	0
Gopalan	15	8	17	0	(1)	6	0	11	0
Johnstone	3	0	9	0		2	1	2	0
Kannan					(7)	8	2	11	0
Robinson					(8)	8	0	17	1

Umpires: J.R.Patel and M.G.Vijayasarathi. Toss: Madras

Close of Play: 1st day: Hyderabad (1) 0-0 (Asadullah Qureshi 0*, Jagdish Lal 0*); 2nd day: Madras (2) 38-1 (Johnstone 8*, Kannan 9*); 3rd day: Hyderabad (2) 7-0 (Asadullah Qureshi 6*, Durga Prasad 0*).

AUCKLAND v CANTERBURY

Played at Eden Park, Auckland, December 29, 30, 1944, January 1, 1945.

Match drawn.

CANTERBURY					
1	I.B.Cromb	c Kerr b Brown	44	not out	159
2	J.G.Leggat	b Brown	3	run out	29
3	*W.A.Hadlee	c Whitelaw b Kerr	74	run out	60
4	H.C.Waine	st Kent b Burke	15	(6) b Brown	0
5	W.M.Anderson	st Kent b Burke	78		
6	K.F.M.Uttley	c Kent b Brown	5	(5) st Kent b Cleverley	1
7	L.A.Butterfield	c Kerr b Cleverley	9		
8	R.H.Scott	not out	86		
9	T.B.Burtt	st Kent b Burke	24		
10	D.A.N.McRae	c Sutcliffe b Burke	3	(4) c W.M.Wallace b Cleverley	4
11	†D.M.Dunnet	lbw b Brown	31		
	Extras	b 8, lb 3	11	b 4, lb 6	10
			383	(5 wickets, declared)	263

FoW (1): 1-7 (2), 2-95 (1), 3-131 (4), 4-153 (3), 5-170 (6), 6-185 (7), 7-273 (5), 8-306 (9), 9-330 (10), 10-383 (11)
FoW (2): 1-80 (2), 2-245, 3-254, 4-263, 5-263

AUCKLAND					
1	P.E.Whitelaw	c Waine b Scott	59	c Burtt b McRae	3
2	H.T.Pearson	run out	32	c Butterfield b McRae	5
3	O.C.Cleal	b Burtt	24	c Waine b Scott	58
4	*W.M.Wallace	c Dunnet b Burtt	108	b McRae	14
5	B.Sutcliffe	b Burtt	4	st Dunnet b Burtt	83
6	G.F.Wallace	b Burtt	10	c Butterfield b Anderson	11
7	A.C.Kerr	c Cromb b Burtt	33	not out	15
8	C.Burke	b Butterfield	1		
9	†L.A.W.Kent	c Cromb b Burtt	6	(8) b Burtt	0
10	D.C.Cleverley	not out	2		
11	W.J.Brown	c Dunnet b Burtt	0		
	Extras	b 9, lb 4, nb 2	15	b 6, lb 1, nb 1	8
			294	(7 wickets)	197

FoW (1): 1-72, 2-109, 3-145, 4-164, 5-180, 6-279, 7-280, 8-287, 9-294, 10-294
FoW (2): 1-6 (1), 2-10 (2), 3-44, 4-102, 5-153, 6-190, 7-197

Auckland Bowling	O	M	R	W	O	M	R	W
Brown	28	1	84	4	17.2	2	51	1
Cleverley	36	11	85	1	25	2	91	2
Burke	49	9	118	4	15	2	51	0
Sutcliffe	7	2	22	0	8	0	34	0
Kerr	23	4	63	1	4	1	26	0

Canterbury Bowling	O	M	R	W	O	M	R	W
McRae	20	2	51	0	13	3	30	3
Scott	21	3	62	1	5	0	22	1
Burtt	40.5	6	101	7	22.2	4	74	2
Waine	4	0	20	0	2	0	9	0
Butterfield	13	2	23	1	12	4	32	0
Anderson	7	0	22	0	5	0	22	1

Umpires: R.Blennerhassett and J.C.Harris. Toss: Canterbury

Close of Play: 1st day: Canterbury (1) 330-9 (Scott 66*, Dunnet 0*); 2nd day: Canterbury (2) 0-0 (Cromb 0*, Leggat 0*).

I.B.Cromb's 159 included 16 fours and 1 six.

BOMBAY v WESTERN INDIA

Played at Brabourne Stadium, Bombay, December 30, 31, 1944, January 1, 1945.

Bombay won by an innings and 312 runs.

WESTERN INDIA

1	†Prataprai	c V.M.Merchant b Modi	9	(8) st Maka b Raiji	2
2	Jayantilal Vora	b Phadkar	46	(1) lbw b Tarapore	15
3	K.H.Jobanputra	b Phadkar	1	(6) b Tarapore	4
4	S.B.Gandhi	c Palwankar b Phadkar	80	lbw b Tarapore	16
5	R.P.Rathod	b Kore	5	(7) run out	9
6	S.K.Girdhari	c Palwankar b Phadkar	0	absent ill	0
7	Purshottam	b Phadkar	7	(3) c and b Raiji	21
8	*Sukhvantrai	c Ibrahim b Phadkar	20	(5) b Raiji	1
9	Ramniklal	st Maka b Kore	0	(2) b Tarapore	19
10	Vajubha	b Tarapore	4	not out	0
11	S.Nyalchand	not out	6	(9) c Raiji b Tarapore	1
	Extras	b 5, lb 4, nb 1	10	lb 4	4
			188		92

FoW (1): 1-12 (1), 2-13 (3), 3-125 (2), 4-136 (5), 5-137 (6), 6-144 (7), 7-166 (4), 8-169 (9), 9-173 (8), 10-188 (10)
FoW (2): 1-33, 2-56, 3-60, 4-67, 5-77, 6-80, 7-91, 8-92, 9-92

BOMBAY

1	K.C.Ibrahim	b Girdhari	55
2	K.K.Tarapore	lbw b Nyalchand	4
3	R.S.Modi	st Prataprai b Vajubha	210
4	*V.M.Merchant	b Purshottam	217
5	Y.B.Palwankar	not out	66
6	U.M.Merchant	b Nyalchand	10
7	J.J.Kore	b Nyalchand	0
8	R.S.Cooper		
9	D.G.Phadkar		
10	M.N.Raiji		
11	†E.S.Maka		
	Extras		30
		(6 wickets, declared)	592

FoW (1): 1-35 (2), 2-81 (1), 3-454 (4), 4-565 (3), 5-592 (6), 6-592 (7)

Bombay Bowling

	O	M	R	W		O	M	R	W
Phadkar	16	0	58	6		5	1	21	0
V.M.Merchant	2	0	6	0					
Modi	4	0	11	1	(2)	6	3	4	0
Palwankar	3	0	5	0	(3)	4	2	2	0
Tarapore	11	1	28	1	(4)	10.2	3	20	5
Kore	18	1	64	2					
Raiji	2	1	6	0	(5)	13	3	41	3

Western India Bowling

	O	M	R	W
Gandhi	12	2	24	0
Jayantilal Vora	28	2	106	0
Nyalchand	53.3	12	126	3
Girdhari	26	3	93	1
Purshottam	29	1	142	1
Jobanputra	1	0	4	0
Rathod	6	0	34	0
Vajubha	7	0	33	1

Umpires: M.G.Bhave and T.A.Ramachandran. Toss: Western India

Close of Play: 1st day: Bombay (1) 109-2 (Modi 32*, V.M.Merchant 14*); 2nd day: Bombay (1) 592-6d.

The match was scheduled for four days but completed in three. R.S.Modi's 210 took 381 minutes and included 9 fours. V.M.Merchant's 217 took 267 minutes and included 30 fours.

EUROPEANS v INDIANS

Played at Madras Cricket Club Ground, Chepauk, Madras, December 30, 31, 1944, January 1, 1945.

Europeans won by eight wickets.

INDIANS					
1	M.Swaminathan	c Johnstone b Hitchen	1	c Law b Saunders	13
2	†M.O.Srinivasan	b Robinson	42	c Nailer b Saunders	18
3	A.G.Ram Singh	lbw b Johnstone	27	(4) c Johnstone b Richardson	28
4	B.S.R.Bhadradri	lbw b Robinson	0	(3) b Richardson	14
5	E.C.Phillip	lbw b Robinson	14	st Law b Robinson	0
6	J.Sydney	b Robinson	2	lbw b Robinson	1
7	M.J.Gopalan	c Saunders b Johnstone	32	c Nailer b McIntyre	78
8	B.C.Alva	b Robinson	2	c Nailer b Saunders	39
9	N.J.Venkatesan	b Robinson	0	run out	35
10	T.S.Parankusam	c Johnstone b Robinson	13	not out	6
11	C.R.Rangachari	not out	0	b Saunders	14
	Extras		7		3
			140		249

FoW (1): 1-1, 2- , 3- , 4- , 5- , 6- , 7- , 8- , 9- , 10-140
FoW (2): 1-32, 2-33, 3-67, 4-72, 5-76, 6-78, 7-150, 8- , 9- , 10-249

EUROPEANS					
1	†J.A.G.C.Law	c Bhadradri b Gopalan	0	c Rangachari b Ram Singh	5
2	*C.P.Johnstone	c Sydney b Venkatesan	60	not out	60
3	W.J.Wright	st Srinivasan b Parankusam	42	b Rangachari	6
4	M.Robinson	run out	87	not out	24
5	F.F.Richardson	run out	18		
6	R.S.Nailer	b Rangachari	4		
7	H.P.Ward	c Srinivasan b Gopalan	37		
8	R.H.Meyer	c Bhadradri b Parankusam	22		
9	C.Hitchen	st Srinivasan b Ram Singh	10		
10	A.W.Saunders	hit wkt b Ram Singh	7		
11	A.D.McIntyre	not out	0		
	Extras		9		
			296	(2 wickets)	95

FoW (1): 1-0, 2-72, 3-136, 4-168, 5-172, 6-243, 7-259, 8-272, 9-296, 10-296
FoW (2): 1- , 2-39

Europeans Bowling	O	M	R	W		O	M	R	W
McIntyre	12	5	16	0		8	2	17	1
Hitchen	6	2	17	1		5	2	30	0
Johnstone	21	10	27	2		14	3	31	0
Saunders	5	0	13	0		13.2	3	36	4
Robinson	16.1	2	51	7		17	2	79	2
Richardson	7	2	9	0		19	3	53	2

Indians Bowling	O	M	R	W		O	M	R	W
Gopalan	13	4	24	2		4	2	8	0
Rangachari	29	5	89	1		14	4	26	1
Ram Singh	29	3	75	2		15	2	45	1
Alva	7	2	19	0					
Parankusam	17.2	1	65	2	(4)	4	0	16	0
Venkatesan	4	0	15	1					

Umpires: Toss: Indians

Close of Play: 1st day: Indians (1) 135-8 (Gopalan 29*, Parankusam 12*); 2nd day: Indians (2) 33-2 (Ram Singh 0*, Bhadradri 0*).

OTAGO v WELLINGTON

Played at Carisbrook, Dunedin, December 30, 1944, January 1, 2, 1945.

Wellington won by 170 runs.

WELLINGTON					
1	R.J.Duffy	b Graham	20	c McDougall b Milnes	26
2	C.G.Rowe	b McDougall	50	c Freeman b McDougall	43
3	E.C.Knapp	c Lawson b McDougall	1		
4	*†F.L.H.Mooney	c Milnes b Graham	31	(3) c Toomey b McDougall	78
5	W.G.C.Bain	c McDougall b Freeman	5	(4) not out	104
6	A.M.Matheson	lbw b Freeman	15		
7	J.A.Ell	b Graham	17	(5) lbw b Milnes	10
8	H.Chapman	b Freeman	30	(6) not out	29
9	N.R.Hoar	not out	35		
10	J.G.Ashenden	b Freeman	0		
11	R.Allen	lbw b Graham	0		
	Extras	lb 4	4	b 6, lb 1	7
			208	(4 wickets, declared)	297

FoW (1): 1-60 (1), 2-64 (3), 3-75 (2), 4-97 (5), 5-117, 6-135, 7-142, 8-207, 9-207, 10-208
FoW (2): 1-64 (1), 2-74 (2), 3-225 (3), 4-240 (5)

OTAGO					
1	D.H.Murdoch	c Mooney b Duffy	19	b Ashenden	5
2	A.S.H.Cutler	run out	23	b Hoar	2
3	*C.D.G.Toomey	b Chapman	17	c Rowe b Matheson	16
4	L.A.Milnes	c Rowe b Matheson	24	b Matheson	23
5	G.H.Mills	lbw b Ashenden	39	c Mooney b Hoar	37
6	A.C.Graham	b Matheson	8	b Allen	2
7	T.A.Freeman	c Duffy b Knapp	0	b Ashenden	14
8	A.W.McDougall	b Allen	34	b Matheson	15
9	L.D.Smith	not out	8	c Rowe b Allen	9
10	†A.N.Lawson	b Ashenden	0	not out	6
11	E.A.Kruskopf	b Allen	1	run out	8
	Extras	b 14, lb 4, nb 1	19	b 3, lb 2, nb 1	6
			192		143

FoW (1): 1-39 (2), 2-62, 3-82, 4-103, 5-114, 6-119, 7-177, 8-185, 9-185, 10-192
FoW (2): 1-7, 2-10, 3-40, 4-55, 5-58, 6-101, 7-107, 8-123, 9-129, 10-143

Otago Bowling	O	M	R	W			O	M	R	W	
Freeman	19	10	34	4			26	7	69	0	
McDougall	26	10	71	2			31	8	84	2	
Kruskopf	16	4	54	0			11	4	18	0	
Graham	18.4	8	22	4			20	5	49	0	
Smith	10	2	23	0			8	0	34	0	
Milnes						(6)	14	3	36	2	

Wellington Bowling	O	M	R	W			O	M	R	W	
Hoar	6	1	15	0	1nb		10	3	23	2	1nb
Ashenden	11	2	16	2			14	3	36	2	
Allen	20	8	29	2			12	2	61	2	
Matheson	20	6	36	2			11.5	9	4	3	
Knapp	18	5	45	1							
Duffy	8	2	16	1							
Chapman	8	3	16	1		(5)	2	0	6	0	
Ell						(6)	2	1	7	0	

Umpires: G.McDonald and J.Porteous. Toss: Wellington

Close of Play: 1st day: Otago (1) 82-3 (Milnes 12*, Mills 0*); 2nd day: Wellington (2) 145-2 (Mooney 43*, Bain 28*).

W.G.C.Bain's 104 included 6 fours.

CANTERBURY v WELLINGTON

Played at Lancaster Park, Christchurch, January 4, 5, 6, 1945.

Match drawn.

WELLINGTON					
1	C.G.Rowe	b McRae	1	b McRae	4
2	R.J.Duffy	c Waine b McRae	61	c Hadlee b McRae	8
3	J.A.Ell	b McRae	29	c and b Butterfield	1
4	*†F.L.H.Mooney	c Cromb b Butterfield	8	b Scott	0
5	W.G.C.Bain	run out	0	(7) b Burtt	1
6	A.M.Matheson	b Burtt	0		
7	H.Chapman	c Burtt b Butterfield	49	(6) not out	23
8	N.R.Hoar	b Cromb	76	(5) st Dunnet b Scott	36
9	E.C.Knapp	b Burtt	14	(8) not out	5
10	J.G.Ashenden	lbw b Butterfield	7		
11	R.Allen	not out	31		
	Extras	b 23, lb 3	26	b 5, nb 1	6
			302	(6 wickets)	84

FoW (1): 1-2 (1), 2-44 (3), 3-67 (4), 4-67 (5), 5-67 (6), 6-168 (7), 7-168 (2), 8-198 (9), 9-215 (10), 10-302 (8)
FoW (2): 1-4, 2-5, 3-14, 4-14, 5-66, 6-74

CANTERBURY			
1	I.B.Cromb	c Hoar b Allen	95
2	J.G.Leggat	c Knapp b Matheson	25
3	*W.A.Hadlee	c Knapp b Allen	8
4	H.C.Waine	c Knapp b Matheson	13
5	W.M.Anderson	st Mooney b Knapp	8
6	K.F.M.Uttley	b Knapp	18
7	L.A.Butterfield	b Allen	9
8	D.A.N.McRae	c Hoar b Knapp	27
9	R.H.Scott	c Rowe b Knapp	7
10	T.B.Burtt	c Ell b Allen	16
11	†D.M.Dunnet	not out	7
			233

FoW (1): 1-112 (2), 2-126 (1), 3-137, 4-142, 5-164, 6-173, 7-203, 8-203, 9-217, 10-233

Canterbury Bowling

	O	M	R	W		O	M	R	W
McRae	35	21	40	3		9	3	17	2
Scott	16	4	36	0	(4)	10	7	6	2
Butterfield	34	13	67	3	(2)	6	2	12	1
Burtt	33	3	83	2	(3)	7	2	13	1
Anderson	2	0	11	0					
Waine	3	0	20	0		3	0	11	0
Cromb	6	0	19	1	(5)	4	0	15	0
Uttley					(7)	1	0	4	0

Wellington Bowling

	O	M	R	W
Hoar	2	0	4	0
Ashenden	12	3	36	0
Matheson	28	9	58	2
Duffy	5	1	9	0
Allen	26.1	5	63	4
Knapp	20	4	57	4
Chapman	2	0	6	0

Umpires: T.W.Burgess and H.W.Gourlay. Toss: Wellington

Close of Play: 1st day: Canterbury (1) 26-0 (Cromb 25*, Leggat 1*); 2nd day: No play.

BENGAL GOVERNOR'S XI v MAJOR-GENERAL STEWART'S XII

Played at Eden Gardens, Calcutta, January 7, 8, 9, 1945.

Bengal Governor's XI won by seven wickets.

MAJOR-GENERAL STEWART'S XII

1	†D.D.Hindlekar	c Anwar Hussain b C.S.Nayudu	8	b C.S.Nayudu	3
2	A.C.Chatterjee	c C.S.Nayudu b Amarnath	17	b C.S.Nayudu	14
3	D.C.S.Compton	c Mankad b C.S.Nayudu	26	(5) st Nimbalkar b Mankad	123
4	J.Hardstaff	run out	24	c Mushtaq Ali b Mankad	73
5	S.S.Jayawickreme	c and b C.S.Nayudu	0	(6) b Mankad	41
6	N.C.Chatterjee	lbw b Amarnath	18	(7) b Amarnath	15
7	C.T.Sarwate	b C.S.Nayudu	5	(8) b Mankad	2
8	S.K.Girdhari	b C.S.Nayudu	2	(10) c Jabbar b Amarnath	6
9	Maharaja of Cooch Behar	b Amarnath	10	(3) run out	11
10	P.K.Sen	c Bhattacharya b Amarnath	10	(9) lbw b Amarnath	1
11	N.R.Chowdhury	st Doraiswami b C.S.Nayudu	0	(12) not out	1
12	P.A.H.Carey	not out	2	(11) c Jabbar b Mankad	2
	Extras		14		23
			136		315

FoW (1): 1-29 (1), 2-43 (2), 3-79 (3), 4-79 (5), 5-86 (4), 6-96 (7), 7-98 (8), 8-110 (6), 9-127 (9), 10-127 (10), 11-136 (11)
FoW (2): 1-14 (1), 2-25 (2), 3-76 (3), 4-143 (4), 5-229 (6), 6-303 (5), 7-305 (8), 8-306 (7), 9-309 (9), 10-312 (11), 11-315 (10)

BENGAL GOVERNOR'S XI

1	M.H.Mankad	b Chowdhury	14	c A.C.Chatterjee b Chowdhury	17
2	B.B.Nimbalkar	b Girdhari	92	c Compton b Chowdhury	22
3	S.Mushtaq Ali	c Cooch Behar b Chowdhury	0	not out	86
4	L.Amarnath	lbw b Chowdhury	0	(5) b Sarwate	36
5	M.Sathasivam	st Hindlekar b Girdhari	56		
6	*C.K.Nayudu	lbw b Girdhari	40	(4) st Hindlekar b Girdhari	5
7	C.S.Nayudu	c Cooch Behar b Girdhari	2		
8	Anwar Hussain	c Compton b Girdhari	6	(6) not out	37
9	K.Bhattacharya	b Girdhari	0		
10	A.Sen	b Girdhari	1		
11	A.Jabbar	not out	0		
12	†T.M.Doraiswami	b Girdhari	0		
	Extras		17		23
			228	(4 wickets)	226

FoW (1): 1-55 (1), 2-55 (3), 3-55 (4), 4-156 (5), 5-204 (2), 6-214 (7), 7-227 (6), 8-227 (9), 9-228 (8), 10-228 (10), 11-228 (12)
FoW (2): 1-43 (1), 2-56 (2), 3-61 (4), 4-132 (5)

Bengal Governor's XI Bowling	O	M	R	W		O	M	R	W
Nimbalkar	2	0	5	0					
Sen	3	2	2	0	(7)	3	0	21	0
Anwar Hussain	5	3	8	0	(2)	5	1	11	0
C.S.Nayudu	20.2	1	77	6		14	1	55	2
Amarnath	26	14	30	4	(1)	25.4	6	75	3
Mankad					(3)	29	5	88	5
C.K.Nayudu					(5)	5	0	28	0
Bhattacharya					(6)	3	0	14	0

Stewart's XII Bowling	O	M	R	W		O	M	R	W
Carey	7	2	24	0	(2)	6	0	36	0
Compton	4	0	14	0					
Chowdhury	22	5	87	3	(1)	14	1	73	2
Girdhari	24.5	3	60	8	(3)	17	2	62	1
Sarwate	5	0	26	0	(4)	9	0	32	1

Umpires: S.Dutt Roy and S.K.Ganguli. Toss: Bengal Governor's XI
Close of Play: 1st day: Bengal Governor's XI (1) 26-0 (Mankad 5*, Nimbalkar 19*); 2nd day: Major-General Stewart's XII (2) 156-4 (Compton 33*, Jayawickreme 7*).
D.C.S.Compton's 123 took 120 minutes and included 13 fours and 2 sixes. N.R.Chowdhury took a hat-trick in the Bengal Governor's XI first innings (Mankad, Mushtaq Ali, Amarnath). This match was the R.B.Lagden memorial match and played for the Red Cross Fund.

HOLKAR v BENGAL

Played at Yeshwant Club Ground, Indore, January 18, 19, 20, 1945.

Holkar won by an innings and 298 runs.

HOLKAR			
1	M.M.Jagdale	c Parthasarathi b Judge	0
2	C.T.Sarwate	b Carey	127
3	S.Mushtaq Ali	b Chowdhury	30
4	D.C.S.Compton	c Parthasarathi b Datta	22
5	B.B.Nimbalkar	b Datta	0
6	*C.K.Nayudu	c and b Carey	141
7	C.S.Nayudu	c Parthasarathi b Datta	50
8	J.N.Bhaya	b Chowdhury	61
9	H.G.Gaekwad	c Parthasarathi b Datta	73
10	†K.V.Bhandarkar	lbw b Chowdhury	3
11	O.P.Rawal	not out	1
	Extras		30
			538

FoW (1): 1-2 (1), 2-77 (3), 3-123 (4), 4-123 (5), 5-341 (6), 6-341 (2), 7-423 (7), 8-532 (9), 9- (10), 10-538 (8)

BENGAL					
1	P.B.Datta	c C.K.Nayudu b Nimbalkar	9	(2) c Mushtaq Ali b Sarwate	31
2	A.Sen	run out	14	(1) c Rawal b Jagdale	7
3	P.K.Sen	run out	0	(7) c Sarwate b C.S.Nayudu	7
4	N.C.Chatterjee	b C.S.Nayudu	5	(3) c Rawal b Jagdale	0
5	K.Bhattacharya	c Bhandarkar b Sarwate	5	(4) b C.S.Nayudu	4
6	*Maharaja of Cooch Behar	c and b C.S.Nayudu	1	(5) c Mushtaq Ali b C.S.Nayudu	0
7	†T.V.Parthasarathi	c Gaekwad b Sarwate	11	(6) st Bhandarkar b C.S.Nayudu	60
8	P.F.Judge	c Compton b C.S.Nayudu	1	(9) st Bhandarkar b Sarwate	2
9	P.A.H.Carey	not out	6	(8) b Sarwate	33
10	S.Mitra	c Jagdale b C.S.Nayudu	1	c Bhaya b Sarwate	16
11	N.R.Chowdhury	c Bhaya b C.S.Nayudu	4	not out	0
	Extras		7		16
			64		176

FoW (1): 1- , 2- , 3- , 4- , 5-35, 6- , 7- , 8- , 9- , 10-64
FoW (2): 1-14 (1), 2-14 (3), 3-24 (4), 4-24 (5), 5-106 (2), 6-120 (6), 7-139 (7), 8-142 (9), 9-176 (8), 10-176 (10)

Bengal Bowling

	O	M	R	W
Judge	31	5	111	1
Carey	16	2	74	2
A.Sen	4	1	8	0
Chowdhury	27.1	7	81	3
Mitra	19	1	91	0
Datta	27	5	84	4
Bhattacharya	17	3	52	0
Cooch Behar	1	0	7	0

Holkar Bowling

	O	M	R	W		O	M	R	W
Nimbalkar	4	3	8	1					
Jagdale	5	3	4	0	(1)	8	7	4	2
C.S.Nayudu	10.5	0	32	5	(2)	22	2	70	4
Sarwate	9	3	13	2	(3)	25.5	8	43	4
Gaekwad					(4)	3	0	9	0
C.K.Nayudu					(5)	2	0	13	0
Compton					(6)	2	0	13	0
Mushtaq Ali					(7)	3	1	4	0
Rawal					(8)	4	1	4	0

Umpires: Toss: Holkar

Close of Play: 1st day: Holkar (1) 331-4 (Sarwate 126*, C.K.Nayudu 132*); 2nd day: Bengal (1) 64 all out.
The match was scheduled for four days but completed in three. C.K.Nayudu's 141 included 22 fours.

MADRAS v MYSORE

Played at Madras Cricket Club Ground, Chepauk, Madras, January 20, 21, 22, 1945.

Madras won by an innings and 126 runs.

MADRAS

1	M.Robinson	b Garudachar	34
2	E.C.Phillip	c Garudachar b Palia	5
3	A.G.Ram Singh	b Darashah	9
4	R.S.Nailer	c Frank b Palia	63
5	F.F.Richardson	b Palia	15
6	A.Ananthanarayanan	not out	124
7	*M.J.Gopalan	c Ramdev b Ramaswami	55
8	B.C.Alva	c sub b Palia	0
9	†M.O.Srinivasan	c sub b Palia	0
10	T.S.Parankusam	b Rama Rao	14
11	C.R.Rangachari	b Rama Rao	0
	Extras		44
			363

FoW (1): 1-12 (2), 2-43 (3), 3-69 (1), 4-94 (5), 5-167 (4), 6-286 (7), 7-286 (8), 8-286 (9), 9-354 (10), 10-363 (11)

MYSORE

1	P.R.Shyamsunder	c Srinivasan b Rangachari	5	lbw b Alva	48
2	†F.K.Irani	c Nailer b Rangachari	20	b Gopalan	2
3	J.S.Maples	b Rangachari	0	(7) b Ram Singh	5
4	C.J.Ramdev	c Nailer b Ram Singh	7	(5) c Srinivasan b Rangachari	0
5	*P.E.Palia	c Srinivasan b Rangachari	5	(8) c Richardson b Ram Singh	74
6	S.Rama Rao	c Parankusam b Ram Singh	19	(4) b Gopalan	2
7	B.Frank	lbw b Ram Singh	7	(9) b Alva	0
8	M.K.Narayaniyengar	b Rangachari	0	(3) c Phillip b Gopalan	0
9	S.Darashah	b Rangachari	1	(10) not out	20
10	B.K.Garudachar	b Rangachari	7	(6) c Nailer b Ram Singh	8
11	Y.S.Ramaswami	not out	2	b Rangachari	0
	Extras		5		
			78		159

FoW (1): 1-24, 2-24, 3-29, 4-37, 5-45, 6-66, 7-66, 8- , 9-76, 10-78
FoW (2): 1-5 (2), 2-11 (3), 3-13 (4), 4-18 (5), 5-31 (6), 6-47 (7), 7-95 (1), 8-95 (9), 9-159 (8), 10-159 (11)

Mysore Bowling

	O	M	R	W
Palia	67	28	73	5
Rama Rao	13	6	33	2
Frank	12	5	23	0
Garudachar	29	3	86	1
Darashah	26	6	58	1
Ramaswami	13	4	39	1
Maples	1	0	7	0

Madras Bowling

	O	M	R	W		O	M	R	W
Gopalan	4	3	5	0		8	5	10	3
Ram Singh	19	4	33	3	(3)	14	2	54	3
Rangachari	16.4	3	34	7	(2)	19.1	4	55	2
Alva	5	4	1	0	(5)	5	1	15	2
Robinson					(4)	1	0	3	0
Parankusam					(6)	5	2	22	0

Umpires: D.K.Naik and J.R.Patel. Toss: Madras

Close of Play: 1st day: Madras (1) 286-6 (Ananthanarayanan 69*); 2nd day: Mysore (2) 47-6 (Shyamsunder 30*).

The match was scheduled for four days but completed in three. A.Ananthanarayanan's 124 took 296 minutes and included 13 fours.

NORTHERN INDIA v SOUTHERN PUNJAB

Played at Lawrence Gardens, Lahore, January 26, 27, 28, 29, 1945.

Northern India won by 362 runs.

NORTHERN INDIA					
1	Nazar Mohammad	lbw b Amarnath	30	(2) c Gulzar Mir b Amarnath	0
2	D.MuniLal	c Murawwat Hussain b Ram Kishen	59	(1) c Daljinder Singh b Ram Kishen	85
3	Abdul Hafeez	lbw b Shabir Hussain	35	(7) b Murawwat Hussain	46
4	*Mohammad Saeed	run out (Maqsood Ahmed)	9	(6) lbw b Shabir Hussain	1
5	R.P.Mehra	c Ikram Qureshi b Shabir Hussain	77	(3) c and b Ram Kishen	12
6	Aslam Khokhar	lbw b Shabir Hussain	91	(8) b Shabir Hussain	5
7	†Imtiaz Ahmed	c Ikram Qureshi b Ram Kishen	39	(4) not out	100
8	Fazal Mahmood	lbw b Murawwat Hussain	1	(9) not out	18
9	Badaruddin Malik	st Ikram Qureshi b Shabir Hussain	39	(5) c Ikram Qureshi b Maqsood Ahmed	24
10	Chuni Lal	b Amarnath	42		
11	Inderjit Barhoke	not out	11		
	Extras		16		7
			449	(7 wickets, declared)	298

FoW (1): 1-74 (2), 2-98 (1), 3-119 (4), 4-192 (3), 5-261 (5), 6-324, 7-325, 8-376, 9-403, 10-449
FoW (2): 1- (2), 2- (3), 3- (1), 4-164 (5), 5- (6), 6-239 (7), 7- (8)

SOUTHERN PUNJAB					
1	Daljinder Singh	b Abdul Hafeez	6	c Imtiaz Ahmed b Abdul Hafeez	16
2	Murawwat Hussain	lbw b Badaruddin Malik	71	(6) c Abdul Hafeez b Chuni Lal	5
3	*L.Amarnath	c Imtiaz Ahmed b Chuni Lal	0	absent hurt	0
4	Maqsood Ahmed	c Imtiaz Ahmed b Abdul Hafeez	144	c Abdul Hafeez b Chuni Lal	3
5	K.Rai Singh	run out	0	(3) c Imtiaz Ahmed b Badaruddin Malik	11
6	Gulzar Mir	b Mohammad Saeed	30	(5) c Fazal Mahmood b Chuni Lal	13
7	Amrit Lal	c Chuni Lal b Abdul Hafeez	12	c Inderjit Barhoke b Chuni Lal	5
8	†Ikram Qureshi	c Nazar Mohammad b Chuni Lal	9	(2) b Badaruddin Malik	9
9	Hira Lal	c Nazar Mohammad b Chuni Lal	8	(8) c Mehra b Chuni Lal	7
10	B.Ram Kishen	st Imtiaz Ahmed b Fazal Mahmood	0	(9) b Chuni Lal	0
11	Shabir Hussain	not out	0	(10) not out	4
	Extras		13		19
			293		92

FoW (1): 1-15 (1), 2-15 (3), 3-155 (2), 4- (5), 5- , 6- , 7- , 8- , 9- , 10-293
FoW (2): 1- , 2-40, 3- , 4- , 5- , 6- , 7- , 8- , 9-92

Southern Punjab Bowling	O	M	R	W		O	M	R	W
Amarnath	59.4	19	104	2		12	4	34	1
Hira Lal	12	1	33	0	(3)	3	0	12	0
Murawwat Hussain	38	12	104	1	(2)	21	1	72	1
Shabir Hussain	33	6	106	4		28	4	85	2
Ram Kishen	24	6	75	2		8	0	40	2
Rai Singh	3	1	10	0	(7)	9	0	24	0
Maqsood Ahmed	3	2	1	0	(6)	12.2	2	24	1

Northern India Bowling	O	M	R	W		O	M	R	W
Abdul Hafeez	37	14	69	3		6	4	8	1
Chuni Lal	23	4	66	3	(3)	10.3	0	25	6
Fazal Mahmood	25	10	53	1					
Badaruddin Malik	13	4	25	1		5	2	11	2
Inderjit Barhoke	21	1	57	0		3	0	18	0
Aslam Khokhar	3	0	4	0					
Muni Lal	1	1	0	0					
Mohammad Saeed	3	2	6	1	(2)	3	1	11	0

Umpires: Toss: Southern Punjab

Close of Play: 1st day: Northern India (1) 298-5 (Aslam Khokhar 74*, Imtiaz Ahmed 5*); 2nd day: Southern Punjab (1) 99-2 (Murawwat Hussain not out, Maqsood Ahmed not out); 3rd day: Northern India (2) 127-3 (Imtiaz Ahmed 27*, Badaruddin Malik 1*).

Maqsood Ahmed's 144 included 11 fours. Imtiaz Ahmed's 100 took 220 minutes and included 8 fours.

BARODA v BOMBAY

Played at Maharaja Pratapsingh Coronation Gymkhana Ground, Baroda, January 27, 28, 29, 30, 1945.

Bombay won by seven wickets.

BOMBAY

1	K.C.Ibrahim	b Gul Mohammad	1	lbw b Vijay S.Hazare	14
2	Anwar Hussain	b Vijay S.Hazare	11	c Powar b Gul Mohammad	0
3	†M.K.Mantri	b Vijay S.Hazare	10	c Vijay S.Hazare b Amir Elahi	20
4	R.S.Modi	not out	245	not out	31
5	*V.M.Merchant	c Nimbalkar b Vijay S.Hazare	0	not out	9
6	D.G.Phadkar	c Patel b Amir Elahi	23		
7	R.S.Cooper	c Adhikari b Gul Mohammad	62		
8	J.B.Khot	c Raiji b Amir Elahi	17		
9	Y.B.Palwankar	c Amir Elahi b Gul Mohammad	78		
10	K.K.Tarapore	b Amir Elahi	3		
11	J.J.Kore	c Nimbalkar b Vijay S.Hazare	5		
	Extras	b 11, lb 2	13		
			468	(3 wickets)	74

FoW (1): 1-1 (1), 2-15 (2), 3-36 (3), 4-36 (5), 5-112 (6), 6-255 (7), 7-297 (8), 8-438 (9), 9-445 (10), 10-468 (11)
FoW (2): 1-2 (2), 2-34 (3), 3-44 (1)

BARODA

1	V.N.Raiji	b Tarapore	14	c Merchant b Tarapore	43
2	*†R.B.Nimbalkar	c Mantri b Phadkar	37	b Anwar Hussain	96
3	H.R.Adhikari	b Kore	21	(5) c Mantri b Tarapore	24
4	Vijay S.Hazare	lbw b Tarapore	3	c Tarapore b Anwar Hussain	30
5	Gul Mohammad	c Mantri b Phadkar	6	(3) lbw b Tarapore	100
6	S.G.Powar	c Modi b Tarapore	0	(7) run out	0
7	Y.E.Sheikh	b Phadkar	2	(9) lbw b Modi	12
8	H.M.Asha	c Ibrahim b Khot	23	not out	47
9	Amir Elahi	c Anwar Hussain b Kore	38	(6) c Phadkar b Tarapore	10
10	Vivek S.Hazare	b Tarapore	5	c Khot b Phadkar	1
11	A.Patel	not out	0	b Phadkar	17
	Extras	lb 2	2	lb 9, nb 1	10
			151		390

FoW (1): 1-43 (1), 2-57 (2), 3-60 (4), 4-79 (5), 5-82 (3), 6-84 (6), 7-84 (7), 8-136 (9), 9-151 (8), 10-151 (10)
FoW (2): 1-134 (2), 2-153 (1), 3-241 (4), 4-278 (3), 5-307 (5), 6-308 (7), 7-310 (6), 8-348 (9), 9-349 (10), 10-390 (11)

Baroda Bowling

	O	M	R	W		O	M	R	W
Vijay S.Hazare	54	14	142	4		20	8	31	1
Gul Mohammad	37	14	85	3		5	2	10	1
Amir Elahi	53	10	149	3		14	3	33	1
Vivek S.Hazare	10	3	17	0					
Patel	16	5	39	0					
Adhikari	2	0	12	0					
Sheikh	2	0	11	0					

Bombay Bowling

	O	M	R	W		O	M	R	W
Phadkar	17	8	34	3		31.4	6	73	2
Khot	5	1	20	1		4	0	16	0
Anwar Hussain	3	0	12	0	(8)	21	2	77	2
Tarapore	18.1	5	55	4		36	4	108	4
Kore	4	0	10	2		13	1	47	0
Palwankar	4	1	18	0	(3)	6	1	25	0
Merchant					(6)	7	0	27	0
Modi					(7)	3	0	7	1

Umpires: M.G.Bhave and T.A.Ramachandran. Toss: Bombay

Close of Play: 1st day: Bombay (1) 248-5 (Modi 137*, Cooper 59*); 2nd day: Baroda (1) 84-5 (Powar 0*, Sheikh 2*); 3rd day: Baroda (2) 232-2 (Gul Mohammad 62*, Vijay S.Hazare 27*).
R.S.Modi's 245 took 510 minutes and included 24 fours. Gul Mohammad's 100 took 159 minutes and included 9 fours and 1 six.

OTAGO v CANTERBURY

Played at Carisbrook, Dunedin, February 9, 10, 12, 1945.

Match drawn.

CANTERBURY					
1	I.B.Cromb	c Bellamy b Freeman	16	c Freeman b Roberts	15
2	J.G.Leggat	c Roberts b Silver	74		
3	*W.A.Hadlee	lbw b Roberts	23	c Milnes b Silver	57
4	V.James	c Freeman b Smith	46		
5	W.M.Anderson	c Mills b Silver	1		
6	K.F.M.Uttley	c Smith b Silver	11	(2) c and b Roberts	28
7	L.A.Butterfield	lbw b Roberts	82		
8	†D.M.Dunnet	lbw b Roberts	32		
9	T.B.Burtt	c Freeman b Harwood	47	(4) not out	29
10	D.A.N.McRae	c and b Silver	18	(5) b Harwood	4
11	N.V.Burtt	not out	4		
	Extras	b 6, lb 4, nb 1	11	lb 2	2
			365	(4 wickets, declared)	135

FoW (1): 1-30, 2-83, 3-142, 4-144, 5-156, 6-179, 7-242, 8-322, 9-358, 10-365
FoW (2): 1-27 (1), 2-72 (2), 3-126 (3), 4-135 (5)

OTAGO					
1	F.W.J.Bellamy	b T.B.Burtt	16	c James b McRae	0
2	*C.D.G.Toomey	b T.B.Burtt	28	c N.V.Burtt b McRae	1
3	L.C.Baker	c Hadlee b N.V.Burtt	17	c Butterfield b McRae	9
4	A.W.Roberts	b McRae	6	c James b McRae	4
5	R.C.Harwood	b T.B.Burtt	2	(8) c McRae b Cromb	24
6	T.A.Freeman	not out	64	(7) c and b T.B.Burtt	50
7	L.A.Milnes	c Cromb b T.B.Burtt	3	(6) lbw b T.B.Burtt	1
8	†G.H.Mills	c Cromb b N.V.Burtt	29	(5) lbw b N.V.Burtt	5
9	L.D.Smith	run out	45	not out	29
10	R.C.D.Silver	c Anderson b T.B.Burtt	0	st Dunnet b T.B.Burtt	1
11	J.H.Allen	b T.B.Burtt	1	not out	0
	Extras	b 4, nb 4	8		
			219	(9 wickets)	124

FoW (1): 1-36 (1), 2-60, 3-64, 4-80, 5-86, 6-91, 7-121, 8-217, 9-217, 10-219
FoW (2): 1-0, 2-1, 3-14, 4-15, 5-23, 6-26, 7-83, 8-116, 9-122

Otago Bowling	O	M	R	W		O	M	R	W
Freeman	31	6	78	1	(2)	4	1	12	0
Roberts	47	21	64	3	(1)	12	1	58	2
Silver	26	3	91	4		2	0	10	1
Allen	13	2	42	0		3	0	15	0
Smith	19	0	64	1					
Harwood	11.1	3	15	1	(5)	3.5	0	22	1
Milnes	1	1	0	0	(6)	2	0	16	0

Canterbury Bowling	O	M	R	W	O	M	R	W
McRae	23	10	34	1	13	4	23	4
Butterfield	9	1	35	0	2	0	2	0
N.V.Burtt	20	2	66	2	9	1	28	1
T.B.Burtt	34	13	59	6	14	5	46	3
Cromb	2	0	17	0	6	1	25	1

Umpires: H.Fogarty and J.Porteous. Toss: Canterbury

Close of Play: 1st day: Canterbury (1) 306-7 (Butterfield 74*, T.B.Burtt 21*); 2nd day: Canterbury (2) 45-1 (Uttley 14*, Hadlee 14*).

AUCKLAND v WELLINGTON

Played at Eden Park, Auckland, February 16, 17, 19, 1945.

Auckland won by eight wickets.

WELLINGTON					
1	R.J.Duffy	b Kerr	58	c and b Burke	16
2	H.F.Rice	st Kent b Burke	77	st Kent b Burke	19
3	C.Jones	st Kent b Burke	4	(10) b Kerr	5
4	W.G.C.Bain	c Pearson b Kerr	6	c Pearson b Brown	6
5	*†F.L.H.Mooney	c W.M.Wallace b Burke	23	(3) c Pearson b Brown	47
6	N.R.Hoar	c Cleverley b Kerr	0	c Pearson b Brown	11
7	H.Chapman	b Kerr	9	(8) b Kerr	1
8	A.M.Matheson	c Cleverley b Kerr	3	(9) c Sutcliffe b Kerr	10
9	S.R.O'Neill	c Cleverley b Brown	31	(7) c Sutcliffe b Kerr	10
10	E.C.Knapp	run out	24	(5) run out	39
11	R.Allen	not out	4	not out	2
	Extras	b 15	15	b 9, lb 2, nb 1	12
			254		178

FoW (1): 1-130, 2-141, 3-146, 4-158, 5-163, 6-175, 7-194, 8-196, 9-239, 10-254
FoW (2): 1-37, 2-44, 3-55, 4-122, 5-145, 6-152, 7-157, 8-160, 9-167, 10-178

AUCKLAND					
1	H.T.Pearson	b Allen	23	c Allen b Matheson	71
2	A.C.Kerr	b Allen	48	c Mooney b O'Neill	3
3	O.C.Cleal	c Rice b Allen	96	not out	74
4	*W.M.Wallace	c Allen b Hoar	20	not out	6
5	B.Sutcliffe	c Chapman b Allen	10		
6	G.F.Wallace	c Allen b Hoar	8		
7	R.W.G.Emery	lbw b O'Neill	21		
8	†L.A.W.Kent	c Mooney b Allen	7		
9	C.Burke	not out	25		
10	D.C.Cleverley	st Mooney b Matheson	7		
11	W.J.Brown	b Hoar	0		
	Extras	b 4, lb 6, nb 4	14	b 3, lb 1	4
			279	(2 wickets)	158

FoW (1): 1-54 (1), 2-123 (2), 3-195, 4-196, 5-206, 6-220, 7-237, 8-245, 9-278, 10-279
FoW (2): 1-13 (2), 2-147 (1)

Auckland Bowling	O	M	R	W		O	M	R	W
Brown	20	3	51	1		28	6	68	3
Emery	15	6	18	0		9	2	8	0
Cleal	3	1	10	0		3	1	7	0
Cleverley	16.3	6	24	0		1	0	5	0
Burke	36	9	81	3		30	12	41	2
Kerr	35	13	55	5		28.3	12	37	4

Wellington Bowling	O	M	R	W		O	M	R	W
Hoar	20.5	0	68	3		0.2	0	4	0
O'Neill	12	3	26	1		11	2	22	1
Matheson	17	3	38	1		13	2	50	1
Allen	31	7	115	5		5	1	17	0
Knapp	6	1	18	0		5	1	37	0
Duffy					(6)	4	0	24	0

Umpires: R.W.Mitchell and O.R.Montgomery. Toss: Wellington

Close of Play: 1st day: Auckland (1) 18-0 (Pearson 6*, Kerr 10*); 2nd day: Wellington (2) 52-2 (Mooney 5*, Bain 6*).

BOMBAY v NORTHERN INDIA

Played at Brabourne Stadium, Bombay, February 16, 17, 18, 19, 20, 1945.

Bombay won by ten wickets.

NORTHERN INDIA					
1	Nazar Mohammad	c U.M.Merchant b V.M.Merchant	3	lbw b Raiji	86
2	D.Muni Lal	c Mantri b V.M.Merchant	6	c Ibrahim b Phadkar	55
3	Abdul Hafeez	c Raiji b Phadkar	145	(5) c Mantri b Tarapore	0
4	R.P.Mehra	lbw b Phadkar	48	(3) c Mantri b Modi	54
5	*Mohammad Saeed	c Modi b Phadkar	8	(7) c Raiji b Tarapore	12
6	M.R.Bhide	not out	60	c Palwankar b Tarapore	3
7	Aslam Khokhar	st Mantri b Raiji	0	(8) c U.M.Merchant b Raiji	26
8	†Imtiaz Ahmed	b Palwankar	55	(4) b Tarapore	14
9	Fazal Mahmood	c Phadkar b Palwankar	0	(10) c Tarapore b Raiji	11
10	Badaruddin Malik	b Raiji	8	(9) not out	31
11	Munawwar Ali Khan	lbw b Tarapore	13	c V.M.Merchant b Raiji	0
	Extras	b 8, lb 9	17	b 11, lb 8, nb 1	20
			363		312

FoW (1): 1-3 (1), 2-24 (2), 3-209 (4), 4-214 (3), 5-231 (5), 6-237 (7), 7-315 (8), 8-320 (9), 9-345 (10), 10-363 (11)
FoW (2): 1-124 (2), 2-168 (1), 3-193 (4), 4-193 (5), 5-199 (6), 6-221 (7), 7-262 (3), 8-287 (8), 9-312 (10), 10-312 (11)

BOMBAY					
1	K.C.Ibrahim	c Mohammad Saeed b Aslam Khokhar	67	not out	31
2	†M.K.Mantri	run out	17	not out	27
3	R.S.Cooper	c Imtiaz Ahmed b Aslam Khokhar	68		
4	R.S.Modi	b Mohammad Saeed	113		
5	*V.M.Merchant	run out	15		
6	D.G.Phadkar	c Mohammad Saeed b Abdul Hafeez	73		
7	U.M.Merchant	c Mohammad Saeed b Munawwar Ali Khan	183		
8	Y.B.Palwankar	b Abdul Hafeez	4		
9	M.N.Raiji	lbw b Abdul Hafeez	4		
10	K.K.Tarapore	lbw b Badaruddin Malik	41		
11	J.J.Kore	not out	14		
	Extras	b 17, lb 3, nb 1	21		
			620	(no wicket)	58

FoW (1): 1-36 (2), 2-128 (1), 3-176 (3), 4-221 (5), 5-321 (4), 6-394 (6), 7-412 (8), 8-442 (9), 9-539 (10), 10-620 (7)

Bombay Bowling	O	M	R	W		O	M	R	W
Phadkar	25	3	61	3		13	1	45	1
V.M.Merchant	22	4	66	2	(3)	20	9	20	0
Modi	4	0	10	0	(2)	5	1	12	1
Palwankar	17	6	30	2		12	4	20	0
Tarapore	24.3	6	64	1		46	13	91	4
Kore	14	2	42	0	(7)	5	0	25	0
Raiji	26	7	72	2	(6)	28	5	79	4
Ibrahim	1	0	1	0					
Cooper	1	1	0	0					

Northern India Bowling	O	M	R	W		O	M	R	W
Munawwar Ali Khan	20.3	1	76	1		3	1	11	0
Abdul Hafeez	63	17	157	3		7.4	1	37	0
Fazal Mahmood	9	2	20	0					
Badaruddin Malik	58	11	166	1	(3)	5	0	10	0
Aslam Khokhar	28	2	96	2					
Mohammad Saeed	20	5	55	1					
Nazar Mohammad	8	1	28	0					
Muni Lal	1	0	1	0					

Umpires: M.G.Bhave and M.G.Vijayasarathi. Toss: Northern India

Close of Play: 1st day: Northern India (1) 309-6 (Bhide 37*, Imtiaz Ahmed 49*); 2nd day: Bombay (1) 265-4 (Modi 79*, Phadkar 9*); 3rd day: Bombay (1) 559-9 (U.M.Merchant 140*, Kore 0*); 4th day: Northern India (2) 242-6 (Mehra 48*, Aslam Khokhar 11*).

Abdul Hafeez's 145 took 202 minutes and included 17 fours. R.S.Modi's 113 took 167 minutes and included 13 fours. U.M.Merchant's 183 took 305 minutes and included 19 fours.

MADRAS v HOLKAR

Played at Madras Cricket Club Ground, Chepauk, Madras, February 17, 18, 19, 1945.

Holkar won by ten wickets.

MADRAS					
1	*C.P.Johnstone	b Sarwate	64	c C.S.Nayudu b Sarwate	38
2	M.Robinson	b Sarwate	13	lbw b Compton	2
3	A.G.Ram Singh	c Bhandarkar b Sarwate	34	c Mushtaq Ali b Sarwate	27
4	R.S.Nailer	lbw b Sarwate	11	lbw b Sarwate	1
5	F.F.Richardson	c C.K.Nayudu b C.S.Nayudu	0	b C.S.Nayudu	44
6	A.Ananthanarayanan	c Bhandarkar b C.S.Nayudu	22	b Sarwate	1
7	M.J.Gopalan	b Sarwate	33	c Jagdale b Sarwate	23
8	B.C.Alva	b Gaekwad	40	c Singh b Sarwate	0
9	†M.O.Srinivasan	lbw b Sarwate	0	lbw b Sarwate	0
10	T.S.Parankusam	b Jagdale	26	c Bhandarkar b C.S.Nayudu	9
11	C.R.Rangachari	not out	0	not out	1
	Extras		11		12
			254		158

FoW (1): 1-24 (2), 2-105 (3), 3-128 (1), 4-129 (5), 5-133 (4), 6-163 (6), 7-213 (7), 8-213 (9), 9-254 (10), 10-254 (8)
FoW (2): 1-15 (2), 2-53 (3), 3-55 (4), 4-78 (1), 5-82 (6), 6-133, 7-133, 8-133, 9-149, 10-158

HOLKAR					
1	M.M.Jagdale	b Rangachari	10	not out	6
2	C.T.Sarwate	c Srinivasan b Ram Singh	74	not out	5
3	S.Mushtaq Ali	c Gopalan b Ram Singh	8		
4	D.C.S.Compton	b Rangachari	81		
5	*C.K.Nayudu	b Rangachari	52		
6	C.S.Nayudu	c Johnstone b Rangachari	44		
7	J.N.Bhaya	st Srinivasan b Ram Singh	36		
8	H.G.Gaekwad	c Richardson b Rangachari	23		
9	†K.V.Bhandarkar	c Srinivasan b Rangachari	9		
10	R.P.Singh	not out	34		
11	O.P.Rawal	b Rangachari	22		
	Extras		10		
			403	(no wicket)	11

FoW (1): 1-49 (1), 2-61 (3), 3-131 (2), 4-231 (4), 5-232 (5), 6-299 (6), 7-323 (7), 8-340 (9), 9-345 (8), 10-403 (11)

Holkar Bowling	O	M	R	W		O	M	R	W
Jagdale	9	8	4	1		8	1	15	0
Gaekwad	6.2	2	8	1		3	0	6	0
Mushtaq Ali	1	0	4	0					
C.S.Nayudu	43	5	119	2	(3)	21.3	8	46	2
Sarwate	40	12	89	6	(4)	21	5	60	7
Compton	3	1	7	0	(5)	6	0	19	1
C.K.Nayudu	2	0	7	0					
Singh	2	0	5	0					

Madras Bowling	O	M	R	W		O	M	R	W
Gopalan	17	5	43	0	(2)	0.1	0	4	0
Rangachari	45.1	7	110	7	(1)	1	0	7	0
Parankusam	8	0	45	0					
Ram Singh	60	10	149	3					
Alva	9	3	12	0					
Richardson	3	1	2	0					
Robinson	6	0	27	0					
Johnstone	1	0	5	0					

Umpires: D.K.Naik and J.R.Patel. Toss: Madras

Close of Play: 1st day: Holkar (1) 49-1 (Sarwate 38*); 2nd day: Holkar (1) 363-9 (Singh 12*, Rawal 4*).

The match was scheduled for five days but completed in three.

TRINIDAD v BARBADOS

Played at Queen's Park Oval, Port of Spain, February 24, 26, 27, 1945.

Trinidad won by ten wickets.

BARBADOS					
1	†S.O.Gittens	c Sealy b Pierre	4	c Constantine b Ferguson	12
2	O.M.Robinson	b Ferguson	27	(7) c Sealy b Pierre	5
3	C.L.Walcott	lbw b Pierre	4	c V.H.Stollmeyer b Skeete	103
4	F.M.M.Worrell	b Jones	74	c Constantine b Ferguson	61
5	J.D.C.Goddard	b Skeete	19	c Constantine b Pierre	6
6	E.D.Weekes	st Sealy b Ferguson	0	(2) c Tang Choon b Jones	8
7	N.E.Marshall	lbw b Skeete	15	(6) c Sealy b Pierre	11
8	E.A.V.Williams	st Sealy b Ferguson	1	(9) c Gomez b Jones	39
9	*T.N.M.Peirce	not out	21	(8) lbw b Pierre	3
10	L.F.Harris	c Sealy b Ferguson	11	not out	13
11	E.A.Greene	b Skeete	16	c Sealy b Jones	0
	Extras		11		4
			203		265

FoW (1): 1-8, 2-18, 3-100, 4-114, 5-115, 6-138, 7-141, 8-161, 9-184, 10-203
FoW (2): 1-10, 2-70, 3-186, 4-188, 5-202, 6-207, 7-210, 8-215, 9-265, 10-265

TRINIDAD					
1	*V.H.Stollmeyer	c Worrell b Goddard	13	not out	11
2	J.B.Stollmeyer	c Worrell b Williams	40	not out	31
3	K.B.Trestrail	lbw b Marshall	125		
4	G.E.Gomez	lbw b Williams	0		
5	†J.E.D.Sealy	c Gittens b Greene	0		
6	R.P.Tang Choon	c Greene b Peirce	132		
7	C.C.R.Skeete	lbw b Harris	0		
8	E.Constantine	c Williams b Harris	3		
9	W.Ferguson	lbw b Marshall	38		
10	P.E.W.Jones	b Greene	41		
11	L.R.Pierre	not out	13		
	Extras	b 8, lb 11, nb 3	22		
			427	(no wicket)	42

FoW (1): 1-38 (1), 2-83 (2), 3-86 (4), 4-89 (5), 5-275 (3), 6-286, 7-292, 8-358, 9-389, 10-427

Trinidad Bowling	O	M	R	W		O	M	R	W
Pierre	4	0	20	2		13	0	64	4
Jones	11	1	54	1		14	1	46	3
Ferguson	21	1	59	4		17	0	74	2
Skeete	13.3	1	59	3		9	1	37	1
Constantine					(5)	6	1	36	0
V.H.Stollmeyer					(6)	1	0	4	0

Barbados Bowling	O	M	R	W	O	M	R	W
Williams	18	4	71	2	5	0	15	0
Greene	18.4	1	70	2	6	0	17	0
Goddard	9	1	35	1	2.5	0	10	0
Harris	18	2	78	2				
Worrell	10	0	47	0				
Peirce	5	0	45	1				
Marshall	11	1	59	2				

Umpires: A.L.Green and V.Guillen. Toss:

Close of Play: 1st day: Trinidad (1) 51-1 (J.B.Stollmeyer 28*, Trestrail 9*); 2nd day: Trinidad (1) 427 all out.

The match was scheduled for four days but completed in three.

CRICKET CLUB OF INDIA v C.K.NAYUDU'S XI

Played at Brabourne Stadium, Bombay, February 26, 27, 28, March 1, 1945.

Cricket Club of India won by an innings and 16 runs.

CRICKET CLUB OF INDIA			
1	M.H.Mankad	b Modi	121
2	V.M.Merchant	b C.S.Nayudu	130
3	Abdul Hafeez	b Modi	19
4	V.S.Hazare	hit wkt b Sarwate	168
5	*D.B.Deodhar	b C.S.Nayudu	0
6	G.Kishenchand	st Nimbalkar b C.S.Nayudu	50
7	R.S.Cooper	not out	127
8	Anwar Hussain	lbw b C.S.Nayudu	5
9	Amir Elahi	c sub b Sarwate	14
10	†E.S.Maka	c Jagdale b C.S.Nayudu	0
11	M.S.Baloch	c C.K.Nayudu b Sarwate	0
	Extras		20
			654

FoW (1): 1-236 (1), 2-266 (3), 3-291 (2), 4-291 (5), 5-369 (6), 6-585 (4), 7-592 (8), 8-623 (9), 9-632 (10), 10-654 (11)

C.K.NAYUDU'S XI					
1	†R.B.Nimbalkar	st Maka b Amir Elahi	67	b Hazare	1
2	M.M.Jagdale	c Merchant b Hazare	0	(10) b Hazare	3
3	S.Mushtaq Ali	b Kishenchand	82	b Anwar Hussain	1
4	D.C.S.Compton	c Kishenchand b Amir Elahi	38	c Anwar Hussain b Amir Elahi	100
5	Gul Mohammad	st Maka b Kishenchand	115	(6) c Kishenchand b Deodhar	28
6	C.T.Sarwate	run out	4	(5) b Abdul Hafeez	26
7	R.S.Modi	b Amir Elahi	24	c Anwar Hussain b Abdul Hafeez	34
8	*C.K.Nayudu	c Anwar Hussain b Hazare	18	(9) b Abdul Hafeez	9
9	C.S.Nayudu	b Hazare	21	(8) lbw b Abdul Hafeez	23
10	K.V.Bhandarkar	not out	13	(2) c Maka b Abdul Hafeez	14
11	C.R.Rangachari	c Hazare b Kishenchand	1	not out	0
	Extras		14		2
			397		241

FoW (1): 1-5 (2), 2-103 (1), 3-183 (4), 4-197 (3), 5-213 (6), 6-258 (7), 7-300 (8), 8-351 (9), 9-391 (5), 10-397 (11)
FoW (2): 1-2 (1), 2-5 (3), 3-39 (2), 4-77 (5), 5-147 (6), 6-185 (4), 7-221 (8), 8-232 (7), 9-241 (9), 10-241 (10)

C.K.Nayudu's XI Bowling	O	M	R	W
Rangachari	22	4	48	0
Gul Mohammad	22	5	53	0
Compton	10	1	47	0
Mushtaq Ali	15	4	27	0
C.K.Nayudu	9	0	39	0
C.S.Nayudu	48	3	202	5
Sarwate	41	2	140	3
Modi	16	3	59	2
Jagdale	6	0	19	0

Cricket Club of India Bowling	O	M	R	W		O	M	R	W
Hazare	26	7	89	3		9.1	2	21	2
Abdul Hafeez	18	5	42	0	(3)	14	2	58	5
Baloch	7	1	12	0	(4)	5	0	23	0
Merchant	8	1	25	0					
Amir Elahi	30	0	110	3	(7)	6	0	36	1
Kishenchand	13.3	0	68	3	(5)	4	0	21	0
Deodhar	4	0	12	0	(6)	7	0	45	1
Anwar Hussain	9	2	25	0	(2)	9	1	35	1

Umpires: D.K.Naik and J.R.Patel. Toss: Cricket Club of India

Close of Play: 1st day: Cricket Club of India (1) 386-5 (Hazare 50*, Cooper 5*); 2nd day: C.K.Nayudu's XI (1) 199-4 (Gul Mohammad 5*, Sarwate 1*); 3rd day: C.K.Nayudu's XI (2) 216-6 (Modi 26*, C.S.Nayudu 19*).

M.H.Mankad's 121 took 205 minutes. V.M.Merchant's 130 took 267 minutes. V.S.Hazare's 168 took 232 minutes and included 18 fours. Gul Mohammad's 115 took 190 minutes. D.C.S.Compton's 100 took 133 minutes and included 8 fours. V.S.Hazare added 113 to his score before lunch on the second day. This match was arranged to celebrate C.K.Nayudu's golden jubilee.

TRINIDAD v BARBADOS

Played at Queen's Park Oval, Port of Spain, March 3, 5, 6, 7, 1945.

Match drawn.

BARBADOS

1	†S.O.Gittens	c Ferguson b Pierre	11	lbw b Ferguson	20
2	E.D.Weekes	c Ferguson b Jones	53	b Pierre	15
3	C.L.Walcott	c Gomez b Skeete	11	c Constantine b Ferguson	55
4	F.M.M.Worrell	lbw b Ferguson	113	st Sealy b Ferguson	0
5	J.D.C.Goddard	not out	164	c Constantine b Ferguson	28
6	N.E.Marshall	c and b Ferguson	16	b Skeete	5
7	H.A.O.Skinner	st Sealy b Ferguson	11	c Pierre b Skeete	13
8	E.A.V.Williams	c Constantine b Ferguson	11	b Ferguson	33
9	*T.N.M.Peirce	c Sealy b Ferguson	26	c and b Ferguson	2
10	F.G.Thomas	b J.B.Stollmeyer	21	not out	10
11	E.A.Greene	b Pierre	17		
	Extras		12		3
			466	(9 wickets, declared)	184

FoW (1): 1-38 (1), 2-67 (3), 3-88 (2), 4-262 (4), 5-296 (6), 6-324 (7), 7-346 (8), 8-404 (9), 9-427 (10), 10-466 (11)
FoW (2): 1-19, 2-66, 3-66, 4-104, 5-111, 6-135, 7-141, 8-149, 9-184

TRINIDAD

1	*V.H.Stollmeyer	lbw b Greene	38	c and b Williams	4
2	J.B.Stollmeyer	c Thomas b Marshall	45	lbw b Greene	27
3	K.B.Trestrail	c Walcott b Thomas	34	run out	1
4	G.E.Gomez	lbw b Marshall	58	not out	108
5	†J.E.D.Sealy	c Gittens b Marshall	16	c Gittens b Williams	8
6	R.P.Tang Choon	lbw b Williams	40	b Williams	83
7	C.C.R.Skeete	c Skinner b Peirce	24	not out	8
8	E.Constantine	c Skinner b Marshall	5		
9	W.Ferguson	run out	36		
10	P.E.W.Jones	b Greene	13		
11	L.R.Pierre	not out	0		
	Extras		16		5
			325	(5 wickets)	244

FoW (1): 1-81, 2-103, 3-122, 4-146, 5-223, 6-241, 7-251, 8-303, 9-325, 10-325
FoW (2): 1-15 (1), 2-26 (3), 3-37 (2), 4-52 (5), 5-224 (6)

Trinidad Bowling

	O	M	R	W		O	M	R	W
Pierre	15.7	1	79	2		5	0	28	1
Jones	17	3	55	1		7	1	30	0
Ferguson	31	3	137	5		14.2	1	60	6
Skeete	20	1	80	1		10	0	47	2
J.B.Stollmeyer	10	0	54	1					
V.H.Stollmeyer	8	1	27	0					
Tang Choon	2	0	15	0					
Constantine	1	0	7	0	(5)	2	0	16	0

Barbados Bowling

	O	M	R	W		O	M	R	W
Thomas	12	0	45	1		4	0	25	0
Williams	14	2	31	1		12	0	65	3
Greene	26.4	2	78	2		12	1	46	1
Goddard	3	0	14	0		1	0	1	0
Marshall	18	3	61	4		11	2	35	0
Weekes	4	1	15	0					
Worrell	5	0	22	0	(6)	4	0	21	0
Peirce	6	1	43	1	(7)	5	0	46	0

Umpires: A.L.Green and V.Guillen. Toss: Barbados

Close of Play: 1st day: Barbados (1) 321-5 (Goddard 105*, Skinner 7*); 2nd day: Trinidad (1) 119-2 (Trestrail 31*, Gomez 3*); 3rd day: Barbados (2) 66-3 (Walcott 31*).

J.D.C.Goddard's 164 took 367 minutes.

BOMBAY v HOLKAR

Played at Brabourne Stadium, Bombay, March 4, 5, 6, 7, 8, 9, 1945.

Bombay won by 374 runs.

BOMBAY

1	K.C.Ibrahim	b C.S.Nayudu	44	lbw b Sarwate	26
2	†M.K.Mantri	c C.S.Nayudu b Nimbalkar	10	c Compton b C.S.Nayudu	63
3	R.S.Modi	st Bhandarkar b C.S.Nayudu	98	lbw b C.K.Nayudu	151
4	*V.M.Merchant	b Nimbalkar	4	c Jagdale b C.S.Nayudu	278
5	R.S.Cooper	b Rawal	52	b C.K.Nayudu	104
6	D.G.Phadkar	lbw b C.S.Nayudu	11	c Mushtaq Ali b C.S.Nayudu	7
7	U.M.Merchant	c Mushtaq Ali b C.S.Nayudu	79	lbw b C.S.Nayudu	73
8	J.B.Khot	c and b Nimbalkar	28	st Nimbalkar b C.K.Nayudu	8
9	Y.B.Palwankar	b C.S.Nayudu	75	c Gaekwad b C.S.Nayudu	4
10	K.K.Tarapore	lbw b C.S.Nayudu	8	(11) lbw b Sarwate	0
11	M.N.Raiji	not out	27	(10) not out	18
	Extras	b 16, lb 10	26	b 14, lb 17, w 1	32
			462		764

FoW (1): 1-17 (2), 2-141 (1), 3-152 (4), 4-178 (3), 5-204 (6), 6-247 (5), 7-316 (8), 8-354 (7), 9-392 (10), 10-462 (9)
FoW (2): 1-80 (1), 2-117 (2), 3-343 (3), 4-589 (5), 5-618 (6), 6-681 (4), 7-707 (8), 8-716 (9), 9-761 (7), 10-764 (11)

HOLKAR

1	†K.V.Bhandarkar	c V.M.Merchant b Phadkar	37	c Cooper b Phadkar	4
2	C.T.Sarwate	b Phadkar	67	c V.M.Merchant b Modi	8
3	S.Mushtaq Ali	b Tarapore	109	c U.M.Merchant b Tarapore	130
4	D.C.S.Compton	lbw b Phadkar	20	not out	249
5	*C.K.Nayudu	lbw b Tarapore	2	(6) c U.M.Merchant b Raiji	4
6	B.B.Nimbalkar	c U.M.Merchant b Phadkar	8	(5) c Khot b Tarapore	40
7	C.S.Nayudu	c U.M.Merchant b Palwankar	54	c U.M.Merchant b Raiji	17
8	J.N.Bhaya	c Khot b Tarapore	3	c Mantri b Raiji	4
9	M.M.Jagdale	c V.M.Merchant b Raiji	43	c U.M.Merchant b Khot	13
10	H.G.Gaekwad	b Phadkar	7	run out	5
11	O.P.Rawal	not out	3	b Khot	11
	Extras	b 6, nb 1	7	b 1, lb 6	7
			360		492

FoW (1): 1-98 (1), 2-113 (2), 3-192 (4), 4-197 (5), 5-210 (6), 6-287 (7), 7-292 (8), 8-313 (3), 9-327 (10), 10-360 (9)
FoW (2): 1-12 (1), 2-12 (2), 3-221 (3), 4-289 (5), 5-294 (6), 6-328 (7), 7-342 (8), 8-371 (9), 9-383 (10), 10-492 (11)

Holkar Bowling	O	M	R	W		O	M	R	W
Nimbalkar	25	3	88	3		10	2	23	0
Rawal	15	1	54	1		10	0	36	0
Gaekwad	10	3	13	0		12	0	30	0
C.S.Nayudu	64.5	10	153	6	(5)	88	15	275	5
Sarwate	36	4	89	0	(6)	73	13	205	2
Jagdale	5	0	22	0	(4)	12	0	30	0
C.K.Nayudu	5	0	17	0	(8)	38	8	104	3
Compton					(7)	9	1	28	0
Mushtaq Ali					(9)	4	3	1	0

Bombay Bowling	O	M	R	W		O	M	R	W
Khot	24	6	77	0	(3)	27.1	4	94	2
Phadkar	27	2	75	5	(1)	16	1	59	1
Modi	9	1	26	0	(2)	9	1	48	1
V.M.Merchant	2	0	4	0					
Tarapore	37	10	94	3	(4)	56	8	139	2
Palwankar	8	2	24	1		8	2	12	0
Raiji	10.5	0	53	1	(5)	39	1	133	3

Umpires: M.G.Bhave and T.A.Ramachandran. Toss: Bombay

Close of Play: 1st day: Bombay (1) 338-7 (U.M.Merchant 74*, Palwankar 4*); 2nd day: Holkar (1) 199-4 (Mushtaq Ali 70*, Nimbalkar 1*); 3rd day: Bombay (2) 165-2 (Modi 56*, V.M.Merchant 9*); 4th day: Bombay (2) 545-3 (V.M.Merchant 204*, Cooper 77*); 5th day: Holkar (2) 177-2 (Mushtaq Ali 106*, Compton 55*).

S.Mushtaq Ali's 109 took 175 minutes and included 7 fours and 1 six. R.S.Modi's 151 took 230 minutes and included 14 fours and 4 sixes. V.M.Merchant's 278 took 485 minutes and included 20 fours. R.S.Cooper's 104 took 209 minutes and included 9 fours. S.Mushtaq Ali's 130 took 170 minutes and included 15 fours. D.C.S.Compton's 249 took 356 minutes and included 19 fours.

NORTH ISLAND v SOUTH ISLAND

Played at Eden Park, Auckland, March 9, 10, 12, 1945.

North Island won by 34 runs.

NORTH ISLAND					
1	H.T.Pearson	c Anderson b Butterfield	9	b Butterfield	15
2	H.F.Rice	c Freeman b Butterfield	1	c T.B.Burtt b Butterfield	6
3	†F.L.H.Mooney	b T.B.Burtt	16	b Butterfield	4
4	*W.M.Wallace	c Cromb b T.B.Burtt	37	b T.B.Burtt	60
5	B.Sutcliffe	st Mills b T.B.Burtt	18	lbw b Butterfield	8
6	O.C.Cleal	c Butterfield b Freeman	4	b Butterfield	0
7	A.C.Kerr	c T.B.Burtt b Butterfield	24	not out	55
8	A.M.Matheson	b T.B.Burtt	4	c Cromb b N.V.Burtt	16
9	C.Burke	b T.B.Burtt	20	c Cromb b T.B.Burtt	13
10	W.J.Wheeler	c Uttley b T.B.Burtt	25	st Mills b T.B.Burtt	0
11	R.Allen	not out	0	c T.B.Burtt b N.V.Burtt	8
	Extras	b 2, lb 2	4	b 2, lb 6, nb 1	9
			162		194

FoW (1): 1-6, 2-23, 3-29, 4-78, 5-87, 6-87, 7-99, 8-125, 9-162, 10-162
FoW (2): 1-24, 2-27, 3-30, 4-44, 5-44, 6-124, 7-160, 8-183, 9-183, 10-194

SOUTH ISLAND					
1	*I.B.Cromb	c Pearson b Wheeler	8	c Rice b Matheson	62
2	J.G.Leggat	c Wallace b Wheeler	1	c Rice b Matheson	6
3	K.F.M.Uttley	b Wheeler	0	run out	30
4	C.D.G.Toomey	c Wheeler b Matheson	2	(6) c Rice b Matheson	4
5	W.M.Anderson	b Wheeler	12	(4) b Wheeler	36
6	D.T.Ager	c Cleal b Matheson	0	(5) b Kerr	0
7	L.A.Butterfield	run out	16	c Pearson b Matheson	58
8	T.A.Freeman	c Cleal b Matheson	0	(9) c Kerr b Burke	24
9	†G.H.Mills	b Burke	15	(8) c Mooney b Kerr	1
10	T.B.Burtt	run out	23	c Rice b Matheson	1
11	N.V.Burtt	not out	11	not out	2
	Extras	b 3, lb 2, nb 2	7	lb 1, nb 2	3
			95		227

FoW (1): 1-8, 2-8, 3-11, 4-11, 5-14, 6-34, 7-42, 8-42, 9-78, 10-95
FoW (2): 1-11, 2-96, 3-100, 4-104, 5-117, 6-157, 7-165, 8-223, 9-225, 10-227

South Island Bowling	O	M	R	W	O	M	R	W
Freeman	8	5	6	1	18	7	31	0
Butterfield	24	9	47	3	12	5	9	5
N.V.Burtt	7	2	23	0	21.2	6	53	2
T.B.Burtt	24	7	67	6	34	11	78	3
Cromb	2	0	15	0	11	6	14	0

North Island Bowling	O	M	R	W	O	M	R	W
Wheeler	11	3	21	4	17	5	39	1
Matheson	13	6	19	3	40.1	23	50	5
Allen	6	1	18	0	17	5	43	0
Kerr	8	1	23	0	30	7	62	2
Burke	4.3	2	7	1	15	2	30	1

Umpires: J.C.Harris and R.W.Mitchell. Toss: North Island

Close of Play: 1st day: North Island (2) 23-0 (Pearson 15*, Rice 5*); 2nd day: South Island (2) 46-1 (Cromb 34*, Uttley 6*).

MADRAS GOVERNOR'S XI v INDIA TO CEYLON TOURING TEAM

Played at Madras Cricket Club Ground, Chepauk, Madras, March 16, 17, 18, 1945.

Match drawn.

INDIA TO CEYLON TOURING TEAM

1	*V.M.Merchant	c Johnstone b Ghulam Ahmed	27	(8) not out	40
2	M.H.Mankad	lbw b Ram Singh	70	(1) lbw b Ram Singh	10
3	S.Mushtaq Ali	st Sanjiva Rao b Palia	54	(7) c Rangachari b Ram Singh	7
4	V.S.Hazare	b Palia	17	lbw b Ghulam Ahmed	4
5	L.Amarnath	b Rangachari	77	(6) not out	100
6	R.S.Modi	c Johnstone b Rangachari	38	(5) b Ghulam Ahmed	11
7	G.Kishenchand	c and b Rangachari	4	(3) lbw b Ghulam Ahmed	30
8	†R.B.Nimbalkar	c Gopalan b Rangachari	3		
9	C.S.Nayudu	b Rangachari	58		
10	C.T.Sarwate	not out	6	(2) c Sanjiva Rao b Gopalan	1
11	S.N.Banerjee	b Rangachari	0		
	Extras		17		16
			371	(6 wickets, declared)	219

FoW (1): 1-78 (1), 2-132 (2), 3-168 (3), 4-177 (4), 5-248 (6), 6-260 (7), 7-270 (8), 8-364 (9), 9-371 (5), 10-371 (11)
FoW (2): 1-9 (2), 2-38 (1), 3-51 (3), 4-54 (4), 5-71 (5), 6-94 (7)

MADRAS GOVERNOR'S XI

1	*C.P.Johnstone	lbw b Sarwate	20	lbw b Merchant	35
2	B.C.Khanna	c Hazare b Amarnath	3	(4) lbw b Mushtaq Ali	17
3	P.E.Palia	lbw b Nayudu	1	(2) b Modi	68
4	Asghar Ali	c Nayudu b Hazare	36	(3) c Nimbalkar b Kishenchand	11
5	A.G.Ram Singh	c Merchant b Hazare	60	c Mushtaq Ali b Modi	18
6	A.Ananthanarayanan	c Nayudu b Amarnath	16	lbw b Mushtaq Ali	0
7	M.J.Gopalan	b Sarwate	46	not out	25
8	F.F.Richardson	b Sarwate	3	not out	5
9	†I.Sanjiva Rao	lbw b Hazare	2		
10	C.R.Rangachari	not out	10		
11	Ghulam Ahmed	st Nimbalkar b Sarwate	2		
	Extras		22		17
			221	(6 wickets)	196

FoW (1): 1-14 (2), 2-15 (3), 3-31 (1), 4-122 (4), 5-133 (5), 6-194 (6), 7-199 (8), 8-208 (7), 9-212 (9), 10-221 (11)
FoW (2): 1-88 (1), 2-123 (2), 3-123 (3), 4-154 (4), 5-154 (6), 6-176 (5)

Madras Governor's XI Bowling	O	M	R	W		O	M	R	W
Rangachari	30	3	74	6		14	1	50	0
Khanna	7	3	11	0					
Ram Singh	23	1	96	1	(2)	17	2	69	2
Ghulam Ahmed	23	2	76	1	(3)	15	2	56	3
Palia	26	7	56	2	(4)	3	1	7	0
Richardson	5	1	19	0					
Gopalan	7	0	22	0	(5)	9	5	21	1

India to Ceylon Touring Team Bowling

	O	M	R	W		O	M	R	W
Banerjee	10	1	32	0		4	0	8	0
Amarnath	14	8	19	2		5	2	5	0
Nayudu	25	5	60	1	(4)	4	0	34	0
Sarwate	18.4	3	35	4	(5)	8	1	37	0
Hazare	16	3	36	3	(3)	8	1	23	0
Merchant	5	2	14	0		6	3	4	1
Mankad	4	2	3	0					
Modi					(7)	13	2	27	2
Kishenchand					(8)	7	1	20	1
Mushtaq Ali					(9)	5	0	21	2

Umpires: V.S.Natarajan and L.O'Callaghan. Toss: India to Ceylon Touring Team

Close of Play: 1st day: India to Ceylon Touring Team (1) 368-8 (Amarnath 77*, Sarwate 3*); 2nd day: India to Ceylon Touring Team (2) 38-2 (Kishenchand 22*).

L.Amarnath's 100 took 110 minutes and included 12 fours and 1 six. This match was played for the Red Cross Fund.

CEYLON v INDIA

Played at Colombo Oval, Colombo, March 31, April 1, 2, 1945.

Match drawn.

CEYLON

1	G.R.J.de Soysa	lbw b Mankad	38	c Merchant b Mankad	18
2	F.C.de Saram	c Nayudu b Mankad	16	run out	1
3	G.J.D.Gooneratne	c Merchant b Banerjee	10	c Nimbalkar b Amarnath	2
4	M.Sathasivam	c Merchant b Banerjee	10	c Merchant b Mankad	111
5	*S.S.Jayawickreme	c Nayudu b Mankad	4	c and b Amarnath	11
6	R.L.de Kretser	b Mankad	3		
7	G.M.Spittel	not out	12	(6) c Hazare b Amarnath	1
8	P.C.D.McCarthy	c Nayudu b Mankad	2	(7) b Modi	27
9	B.R.Heyn	b Mankad	2	(8) not out	42
10	V.G.Prins	b Mankad	0		
11	†B.Navaratne	b Mankad	6		
	Extras		4		12
			107	(7 wickets)	225

FoW (1): 1-39 (2), 2-66 (1), 3-72 (3), 4-79 (5), 5-80 (4), 6-87 (6), 7-95 (8), 8-101 (9), 9-101 (10), 10-107 (11)
FoW (2): 1-7 (2), 2-16 (3), 3-50 (1), 4-73 (5), 5-75 (6), 6-144 (7), 7-225 (4)

INDIA

1	*V.M.Merchant	run out	36
2	M.H.Mankad	b Spittel	3
3	†R.B.Nimbalkar	c and b de Kretser	48
4	C.S.Nayudu	c Heyn b Spittel	7
5	L.Amarnath	c de Saram b Spittel	4
6	S.Mushtaq Ali	run out	49
7	R.S.Modi	not out	11
8	V.S.Hazare	c Gooneratne b de Kretser	0
9	G.Kishenchand	c Jayawickreme b de Kretser	0
10	C.R.Rangachari	c Jayawickreme b de Kretser	9
11	S.N.Banerjee	run out	1
	Extras		11
			179

FoW (1): 1-3 (2), 2-62 (3), 3-71 (4), 4-75 (5), 5-134 (1), 6-164 (6), 7-164 (8), 8-164 (9), 9-178 (10), 10-179 (11)

India Bowling

	O	M	R	W		O	M	R	W
Amarnath	7	4	5	0		31	10	59	3
Banerjee	13	6	13	2		5	3	6	0
Rangachari	2	0	7	0					
Modi	3	0	12	0	(3)	2	0	6	1
Nayudu	14	4	30	0	(4)	9	0	35	0
Mankad	21.3	8	35	8	(5)	36.1	7	83	2
Merchant	2	1	1	0					
Hazare					(6)	11	2	24	0

Ceylon Bowling

	O	M	R	W
Spittel	17.2	6	48	3
Jayawickreme	13	3	35	0
Heyn	3	1	5	0
de Kretser	21	2	56	4
Prins	6	1	24	0

Umpires: Toss: India

Close of Play: 1st day: No play; 2nd day: India 70-2 (Merchant not out, Nayudu not out).

INDEX OF 1944/45 MATCH SCORECARDS

1945

ENGLAND v AUSTRALIAN SERVICES

Played at Lord's Cricket Ground, May 19, 21, 22, 1945.

Australian Services won by six wickets.

ENGLAND

1	L.Hutton	c Sismey b Williams	1	b Pepper	21
2	C.Washbrook	st Sismey b Ellis	28	lbw b Pepper	32
3	J.D.B.Robertson	lbw b Ellis	53	c Sismey b Cheetham	84
4	*W.R.Hammond	b Williams	29	lbw b Ellis	33
5	L.E.G.Ames	c Price b Cheetham	57	b Ellis	7
6	W.J.Edrich	b Miller	45	c Workman b Price	50
7	R.W.V.Robins	b Cheetham	5	c Hassett b Pepper	33
8	J.W.A.Stephenson	c Sismey b Price	31	b Price	1
9	†S.C.Griffith	c Sismey b Cheetham	9	not out	4
10	D.V.P.Wright	b Price	0	run out	1
11	A.R.Gover	not out	0	st Sismey b Pepper	1
	Extras	b 1, lb 6, w 1, nb 1	9	b 18, lb 8, nb 1	27
			267		294

FoW (1): 1-1 (1), 2-54 (2), 3-97 (3), 4-130 (4), 5-205 (5), 6-213 (7), 7-233 (6), 8-267 (8), 9-267 (10), 10-267
FoW (2): 1-52 (1), 2-75 (2), 3-149 (4), 4-175 (5), 5-218 (3), 6-286 (7), 7-286 (6), 8-289 (8), 9-292 (10), 10-294 (11)

AUSTRALIAN SERVICES

1	R.S.Whitington	c Griffith b Wright	36	lbw b Stephenson	0
2	J.A.Workman	b Gover	1		
3	*A.L.Hassett	b Stephenson	77	(2) c Hammond b Gover	37
4	†S.G.Sismey	c Wright b Edrich	37		
5	K.R.Miller	c Ames b Stephenson	105	(3) run out	1
6	R.M.Stanford	st Griffith b Stephenson	49		
7	C.G.Pepper	c Griffith b Stephenson	40	(4) not out	54
8	A.G.Cheetham	c Hammond b Wright	0	(5) run out	0
9	R.G.Williams	c Griffith b Wright	53		
10	C.F.T.Price	c Robertson b Stephenson	35	(6) not out	10
11	R.S.Ellis	not out	1		
	Extras	b 9, lb 10, nb 2	21	b 4, lb 1	5
			455	(4 wickets)	107

FoW (1): 1-11 (2), 2-52 (1), 3-136 (4), 4-171 (3), 5-270 (6), 6-357 (7), 7-358 (8), 8-366 (5), 9-454 (10), 10-455 (9)
FoW (2): 1-9 (1), 2-11 (3), 3-63 (2), 4-76 (5)

Australian Services Bowling

	O	M	R	W			O	M	R	W	
Cheetham	13.1	1	49	3	1nb	(2)	17	2	44	1	1nb
Williams	19	2	56	2	1w	(1)	21	7	47	0	
Pepper	19	2	59	0		(4)	32.4	7	80	4	
Ellis	31	8	59	2		(5)	17	3	33	2	
Miller	9	2	11	1		(3)	9	1	23	0	
Price	9	1	24	2			19	3	40	2	

England Bowling

	O	M	R	W		O	M	R	W
Gover	25	3	90	1	1nb	11.4	1	51	1
Stephenson	36	4	116	5	1nb	11	0	51	1
Edrich	17	2	61	1					
Wright	37.3	9	122	3					
Robins	10	0	45	0					

Umpires: G.Beet and A.J.B.Fowler. Toss: England

Close of Play: 1st day: Australian Services (1) 82-2 (Hassett 27*, Sismey 11*); 2nd day: Australian Services (1) 455 all out.

K.R.Miller's 105 took 186 balls in 211 minutes and included 6 fours.

ENGLAND v AUSTRALIAN SERVICES

Played at Bramall Lane, Sheffield, June 23, 25, 26, 1945.

England won by 41 runs.

ENGLAND

1	L.Hutton	c Cheetham b Williams	11	b Ellis	46
2	C.Washbrook	c Carmody b Pepper	63	c Sismey b Miller	24
3	J.D.B.Robertson	c Whitington b Ellis	26	lbw b Miller	1
4	*W.R.Hammond	c Hassett b Cheetham	100	b Ellis	38
5	E.R.T.Holmes	b Ellis	6	c Sismey b Pepper	2
6	W.J.Edrich	lbw b Pepper	1	c Hassett b Pepper	1
7	G.H.Pope	c Ellis b Cheetham	35	c Pepper b Ellis	2
8	†S.C.Griffith	c Hassett b Cheetham	2	st Sismey b Price	35
9	R.Pollard	b Pepper	11	c Whitington b Price	25
10	W.B.Roberts	b Williams	4	c Carmody b Price	6
11	D.V.P.Wright	not out	7	not out	1
	Extras	b 3, lb 10, w 2, nb 5	20	b 1, lb 4, nb 4	9
			286		190

FoW (1): 1-28 (1), 2-81 (3), 3-129 (2), 4-136 (5), 5-141 (6), 6-248 (7), 7-262 (4), 8-264 (8), 9-272 (10), 10-286 (9)
FoW (2): 1-56 (2), 2-62 (3), 3-97 (1), 4-104 (5), 5-120 (4), 6-122 (7), 7-122 (6), 8-177 (9), 9-184 (10), 10-190 (8)

AUSTRALIAN SERVICES

1	R.S.Whitington	c Wright b Pope	17	lbw b Wright	61
2	J.A.Workman	c Pollard b Pope	6	c Hammond b Pollard	63
3	*A.L.Hassett	b Pollard	5	(4) b Pope	32
4	K.R.Miller	run out	17	(3) b Pollard	8
5	D.K.Carmody	c Hammond b Wright	42	run out	14
6	C.G.Pepper	c Hammond b Wright	21	c Pollard b Pope	27
7	A.G.Cheetham	b Pope	10	c Hammond b Pollard	18
8	†S.G.Sismey	c Pollard b Pope	0	b Pollard	17
9	C.F.T.Price	c Pollard b Pope	0	(10) b Pope	11
10	R.G.Williams	not out	5	(9) lbw b Pollard	2
11	R.S.Ellis	run out	1	not out	9
	Extras	b 5, lb 12, nb 6	23	b 17, lb 6, nb 3	26
			147		288

FoW (1): 1-33 (2), 2-36 (1), 3-44 (3), 4-80 (4), 5-122 (5), 6-131 (6), 7-132 (8), 8-132 (9), 9-145 (7), 10-147 (11)
FoW (2): 1-108 (1), 2-121 (3), 3-171 (4), 4-189 (5), 5-221 (2), 6-231 (6), 7-244 (7), 8-260 (9), 9-270 (8), 10-288 (10)

Australian Services Bowling

	O	M	R	W			O	M	R	W	
Cheetham	15	3	47	3	1nb		7	1	19	0	1nb
Williams	16	4	31	2	1w,3nb		9	2	23	0	
Ellis	33	9	66	2	1w	(4)	25	5	47	3	
Miller	13	3	19	0	1nb	(3)	13	2	28	2	
Pepper	30.5	6	86	3			15	3	46	2	3nb
Price	3	0	17	0			4.4	0	18	3	

England Bowling

	O	M	R	W			O	M	R	W	
Pope	21.5	4	58	5	2nb		28.4	9	69	3	2nb
Pollard	17	5	42	1	4nb		33	6	76	5	1nb
Wright	9	3	14	2		(4)	22	6	50	1	
Edrich	5	0	10	0		(3)	4	1	13	0	
Roberts						(5)	13	4	40	0	
Hutton						(6)	2	0	14	0	

Umpires: G.P.Heaton and H.Thomas. Toss: Australian Services

Close of Play: 1st day: Australian Services (1) 23-0 (Whitington 13*, Workman 3*); 2nd day: England (2) 190 all out.

W.R.Hammond's 100 took 222 balls in 204 minutes and included 8 fours and 2 sixes. D.K.Carmody kept wicket in the first innings from the 6th over when S.G.Sismey sustained a split chin.

ENGLAND v AUSTRALIAN SERVICES

Played at Lord's Cricket Ground, July 14, 16, 17, 1945.

Australian Services won by four wickets.

ENGLAND					
1	L.Hutton	b Miller	104	c Sismey b Cristofani	69
2	C.Washbrook	c Sismey b Williams	8	(8) not out	13
3	J.G.Dewes	b Miller	27	(2) b Miller	0
4	*W.R.Hammond	st Sismey b Pepper	13	absent ill	0
5	L.R.White	st Sismey b Cristofani	11	(6) lbw b Cristofani	4
6	W.J.Edrich	lbw b Cristofani	38	(3) b Miller	58
7	D.B.Carr	b Miller	4	c Pepper b Cristofani	1
8	†S.C.Griffith	c Pepper b Cristofani	36	(4) c Pepper b Cristofani	0
9	R.Pollard	not out	1	(5) b Miller	9
10	W.B.Roberts	b Cristofani	1	(9) b Ellis	0
11	D.V.P.Wright	lbw b Ellis	5	(10) c Hassett b Cristofani	6
	Extras	b 2, lb 1, nb 3	6	lb 3, nb 1	4
			254		164

FoW (1): 1-11 (2), 2-76 (3), 3-107 (4), 4-162 (5), 5-169 (1), 6-175 (7), 7-241 (6), 8-248 (8), 9-249 (10), 10-254 (11)
FoW (2): 1-1 (2), 2-106 (3), 3-107 (4), 4-122 (5), 5-127 (6), 6-129 (7), 7-150 (1), 8-151 (9), 9-164 (10)

AUSTRALIAN SERVICES					
1	R.S.Whitington	b Pollard	19	c Griffith b Pollard	0
2	J.A.Workman	c Edrich b Wright	7	b Wright	30
3	A.G.Cheetham	b Roberts	5	(8) not out	9
4	*A.L.Hassett	lbw b Pollard	68	c Edrich b Wright	24
5	K.R.Miller	b Pollard	7	not out	71
6	C.G.Pepper	lbw b Pollard	0	lbw b Edrich	18
7	D.K.Carmody	c White b Pollard	32	c Edrich b Roberts	1
8	D.R.Cristofani	b Roberts	32		
9	†S.G.Sismey	c Griffith b Pollard	9	(3) lbw b Pollard	51
10	R.G.Williams	b Wright	4		
11	R.S.Ellis	not out	0		
	Extras	lb 4, nb 7	11	b 1, lb 15, nb 5	21
			194	(6 wickets)	225

FoW (1): 1-29 (2), 2-29 (1), 3-50 (3), 4-71 (5), 5-72 (6), 6-127 (7), 7-149 (4), 8-183 (8), 9-184 (9), 10-194 (10)
FoW (2): 1-0 (1), 2-82 (2), 3-104 (3), 4-151 (4), 5-186 (6), 6-193 (7)

Australian Services Bowling	O	M	R	W			O	M	R	W	
Williams	19	6	45	1	1nb	(4)	3	0	10	0	
Cheetham	19	5	47	0	1nb		4	0	7	0	
Pepper	19	2	44	1			10	3	22	0	
Ellis	19.1	6	25	1		(6)	14	1	29	1	
Miller	18	3	44	3		(1)	16	2	42	3	
Cristofani	13	1	43	4		(5)	29.3	8	49	5	1nb
Whitington						(7)	1	0	1	0	

England Bowling	O	M	R	W			O	M	R	W	
Edrich	7	0	25	0	2nb	(2)	12	1	37	1	
Pollard	23	4	75	6	5nb	(1)	21	4	71	2	4nb
Wright	24.1	3	49	2			25	4	59	2	1nb
Roberts	14	5	24	2			13	4	24	1	
Carr	3	1	10	0			6	2	13	0	

Umpires: G.Beet and A.J.B.Fowler. Toss: England

Close of Play: 1st day: England (1) 254 all out; 2nd day: England (2) 118-3 (Hutton 49*, Pollard 7*).

L.Hutton's 104 took 222 balls in 211 minutes and included 5 fours and 1 five.

ENGLAND v AUSTRALIAN SERVICES

Played at Lord's Cricket Ground, August 6, 7, 8, 1945.

Match drawn.

AUSTRALIAN SERVICES

1	R.S.Whitington	c Hutton b Pope	46	lbw b Pope	7
2	J.A.Workman	lbw b Pollard	6	c Fishlock b Pope	9
3	†S.G.Sismey	c Fishlock b Pollard	59		
4	*A.L.Hassett	c Wright b Pope	20	b Pollard	7
5	K.R.Miller	b Pope	118	not out	35
6	R.M.Stanford	b Pope	2	not out	33
7	C.G.Pepper	c and b Roberts	57		
8	J.Pettiford	c Wright b Pollard	32	(3) b Wright	39
9	D.R.Cristofani	c Edrich b Pollard	14		
10	R.G.Williams	c Fishlock b Roberts	1		
11	R.S.Ellis	not out	0		
	Extras	b 16, lb 8, nb 9	33	b 5, nb 5	10
			388	(4 wickets)	140

FoW (1): 1-15 (2), 2-70 (1), 3-108 (4), 4-262 (6), 5-265 (3), 6-301 (5), 7-359 (7), 8-374 (9), 9-380 (10), 10-388 (8)
FoW (2): 1-12 (2), 2-30 (1), 3-54 (4), 4-80 (3)

ENGLAND

1	L.B.Fishlock	b Pettiford	69
2	L.Hutton	lbw b Williams	35
3	J.D.B.Robertson	c Miller b Pettiford	25
4	*W.R.Hammond	c Workman b Ellis	83
5	C.Washbrook	c sub (D.K.Carmody) b Williams	112
6	W.J.Edrich	not out	73
7	G.H.Pope	c Hassett b Williams	5
8	†S.C.Griffith	c Stanford b Pettiford	7
9	R.Pollard	not out	2
10	D.V.P.Wright		
11	W.B.Roberts		
	Extras	b 27, lb 12, w 14, nb 4	57
		(7 wickets, declared)	468

FoW (1): 1-73 (2), 2-136 (3), 3-173 (1), 4-330 (4), 5-435 (5), 6-443 (7), 7-464 (8)

England Bowling

	O	M	R	W			O	M	R	W	
Pope	43	11	83	4			12	3	42	2	1nb
Pollard	37.3	7	145	4	5nb		13	2	58	1	4nb
Wright	28	5	75	0			7	1	23	1	
Edrich	6	0	13	0	2nb						
Roberts	16	4	39	2		(4)	6	2	7	0	

Australian Services Bowling

	O	M	R	W	
Miller	23	5	49	0	12w
Williams	39	9	109	3	2w,4nb
Pepper	18	3	63	0	
Cristofani	12	3	41	0	
Pettiford	18	2	62	3	
Ellis	36	9	80	1	
Whitington	1	0	7	0	

Umpires: G.Beet and A.J.B.Fowler. Toss: Australian Services

Close of Play: 1st day: Australian Services (1) 273-5 (Miller 106*, Pepper 3*); 2nd day: England (1) 249-3 (Hammond 38*, Washbrook 31*).

K.R.Miller's 118 took 187 balls in 197 minutes and included 10 fours. C.Washbrook's 112 took 253 balls in 240 minutes and included 8 fours and 1 six. S.G.Sismey retired hurt in the Australian Services first innings having scored 58 (team score 229-3) - he returned when the score was 262-4. S.G.Sismey, who had injured his thumb batting, was unable to keep wicket and J.A.Workman kept on the second day but as he conceded 51 extras Hammond allowed D.K.Carmody (12th man) to keep on the third day.

YORKSHIRE v LANCASHIRE

Played at Park Avenue Cricket Ground, Bradford, August 13, 14, 15, 1945.

Match drawn.

LANCASHIRE

1	E.Paynter	c Wood b Bowes	10	not out	47
2	C.Washbrook	c Wood b Booth	97	c Leyland b Robinson	25
3	W.Barron	b Bowes	2	(4) b Robinson	1
4	J.Iddon	c Wood b Bowes	0	(5) not out	2
5	A.E.Nutter	c and b Coxon	1	(3) b Coxon	22
6	R.B.Rae	c Sellers b Coxon	74		
7	T.A.Higson	b Hutton	25		
8	†W.Farrimond	not out	16		
9	F.Hartley	lbw b Hutton	2		
10	R.Pollard	c Leyland b Booth	1		
11	W.B.Roberts	c Hutton b Booth	0		
	Extras	b 5, lb 4, w 1, nb 1	11	b 9, nb 1	10
			239	(3 wickets)	107

FoW (1): 1-26, 2-28, 3-30, 4-37, 5-168, 6-203, 7-232, 8-234, 9-239, 10-239
FoW (2): 1-50 (2), 2-84 (3), 3-93 (4)

YORKSHIRE

1	A.Mitchell	c Pollard b Nutter	34
2	†A.Wood	b Nutter	25
3	L.Hutton	b Nutter	26
4	W.Barber	c Nutter b Pollard	88
5	M.Leyland	b Pollard	19
6	W.Watson	c Roberts b Pollard	7
7	A.Coxon	lbw b Hartley	2
8	*A.B.Sellers	b Nutter	39
9	E.P.Robinson	b Nutter	7
10	A.Booth	not out	1
11	W.E.Bowes	absent hurt	0
	Extras	b 2, lb 5, nb 4	11
			259

FoW (1): 1-40, 2-86, 3-89, 4-130, 5-138, 6-149, 7-240, 8-257, 9-259

Yorkshire Bowling

	O	M	R	W			O	M	R	W	
Bowes	18	10	22	3							
Coxon	36	11	71	2	1w,1nb	(1)	23	5	43	1	
Robinson	20	5	30	0		(4)	21	8	30	2	1nb
Booth	30	13	49	3		(3)	6	3	7	0	
Hutton	3	0	12	2							
Leyland	22	8	44	0							
Sellers						(2)	4	0	17	0	

Lancashire Bowling

	O	M	R	W	
Pollard	29	4	88	3	4nb
Rae	6	0	29	0	
Nutter	25.3	3	57	5	
Roberts	20	8	30	0	
Hartley	15	2	44	1	

Umpires: G.P.Heaton and H.Thomas. Toss: Lancashire

Close of Play: 1st day: Yorkshire (1) 12-0 (Mitchell 2*, Wood 10*); 2nd day: Lancashire (2) 33-0 (Paynter 16*, Washbrook 17*).

This was the H.Verity memorial match.

ENGLAND v AUSTRALIAN SERVICES

Played at Old Trafford, Manchester, August 20, 21, 22, 1945.

England won by six wickets.

AUSTRALIAN SERVICES					
1	R.S.Whitington	c Hammond b Pollard	19	c Griffith b Phillipson	10
2	J.Pettiford	b Pollard	28	c Robertson b Phillipson	8
3	D.K.Carmody	c Hammond b Pollard	7	(9) c Griffith b Pollard	3
4	†S.G.Sismey	b Phillipson	5	(3) lbw b Phillipson	4
5	*A.L.Hassett	c Pollard b Pope	6	(6) c Griffith b Pollard	1
6	K.R.Miller	not out	77	(5) c Griffith b Phillipson	4
7	C.G.Pepper	run out	9	b Wright	23
8	R.M.Stanford	run out	1	(4) c Griffith b Wright	23
9	D.R.Cristofani	c Edrich b Pollard	8	(8) not out	110
10	R.G.Williams	c Griffith b Phillipson	5	c Griffith b Phillipson	12
11	R.S.Ellis	c Pollard b Phillipson	0	c Pollard b Phillipson	3
	Extras	lb 2, nb 6	8	b 1, lb 5, nb 3	9
			173		210

FoW (1): 1-41 (1), 2-59 (3), 3-64 (4), 4-66 (2), 5-102 (5), 6-117 (7), 7-125 (8), 8-138 (9), 9-155 (10), 10-173 (11)
FoW (2): 1-13 (2), 2-17 (3), 3-37 (1), 4-41 (5), 5-46 (6), 6-69 (4), 7-87 (7), 8-105 (9), 9-200 (10), 10-210 (11)

ENGLAND					
1	L.B.Fishlock	lbw b Miller	9	b Williams	4
2	L.Hutton	c Sismey b Williams	64	lbw b Pepper	29
3	J.D.B.Robertson	c Williams b Pepper	13	lbw b Pepper	37
4	*W.R.Hammond	c Pettiford b Cristofani	57	c sub (E.A.Williams) b Ellis	16
5	W.J.Edrich	c and b Pepper	23	not out	42
6	R.Pollard	lbw b Cristofani	0		
7	C.Washbrook	c Carmody b Cristofani	38	(6) not out	11
8	G.H.Pope	c Pepper b Cristofani	1		
9	W.E.Phillipson	not out	18		
10	†S.C.Griffith	c Ellis b Cristofani	0		
11	D.V.P.Wright	st Sismey b Pettiford	9		
	Extras	b 3, lb 6, w 1, nb 1	11	b 2	2
			243	(4 wickets)	141

FoW (1): 1-14 (1), 2-46 (3), 3-143 (4), 4-159 (2), 5-162 (6), 6-198 (5), 7-201 (8), 8-218 (7), 9-221 (10), 10-243 (11)
FoW (2): 1-5 (1), 2-69 (2), 3-70 (3), 4-124 (4)

England Bowling	O	M	R	W			O	M	R	W	
Phillipson	27	4	72	3	1nb		29	12	58	6	
Pope	10	3	15	1	1nb	(3)	19	6	49	0	
Pollard	22	3	78	4	3nb	(2)	23	11	46	2	3nb
Wright						(4)	13	3	44	2	
Edrich						(5)	3	1	4	0	

Australian Services Bowling	O	M	R	W			O	M	R	W
Miller	9	0	20	1			11	1	41	0
Williams	18	7	40	1	1nb		8	0	41	1
Pepper	24	3	74	2		(4)	12	5	18	2
Ellis	7	0	21	0		(5)	7	2	13	1
Pettiford	6.2	0	22	1						
Cristofani	22	3	55	5		(3)	7	0	25	0
Hassett						(6)	0.1	0	1	0

Umpires: F.Chester and H.Elliott. Toss: Australian Services

Close of Play: 1st day: England (1) 162-5 (Edrich 9*); 2nd day: Australian Services (2) 37-3 (Stanford 12*).

D.R.Cristofani's 110 took 120 balls in 148 minutes and included 13 fours and 1 six.

ENGLAND v DOMINIONS

Played at Lord's Cricket Ground, August 25, 27, 28, 1945.

Dominions won by 45 runs.

DOMINIONS					
1	H.S.Craig	c Davies b Phillipson	56	c Hammond b Davies	32
2	D.R.Fell	c Griffith b Wright	12	b Davies	28
3	J.Pettiford	b Davies	1	b Wright	6
4	K.R.Miller	lbw b Hollies	26	c Langridge b Wright	185
5	M.P.Donnelly	c and b Hollies	133	b Wright	29
6	*L.N.Constantine	c Hollies b Wright	5	(7) c Fishlock b Hollies	40
7	C.G.Pepper	c Hammond b Wright	51	(6) c Robertson b Hollies	1
8	D.R.Cristofani	lbw b Edrich	6	b Wright	5
9	R.G.Williams	lbw b Wright	11	c Hammond b Wright	0
10	R.S.Ellis	b Wright	0	st Griffith b Hollies	0
11	†C.D.Bremner	not out	1	not out	0
	Extras	lb 3, w 2	5	b 1, lb 8, nb 1	10
			307		336

FoW (1): 1-37 (2), 2-38 (3), 3-90 (1), 4-104 (4), 5-109 (6), 6-229 (7), 7-240 (8), 8-271 (9), 9-279 (10), 10-307 (5)
FoW (2): 1-49 (2), 2-56 (3), 3-96 (1), 4-200 (5), 5-203 (6), 6-326 (4), 7-336 (8), 8-336 (7), 9-336 (10), 10-336 (9)

ENGLAND					
1	J.D.B.Robertson	lbw b Constantine	4	(5) c Fell b Pettiford	5
2	L.B.Fishlock	c Pettiford b Ellis	12	run out	7
3	J.Langridge	lbw b Cristofani	28	(6) b Pepper	15
4	W.E.Phillipson	b Pepper	0	(9) run out	14
5	†S.C.Griffith	c Bremner b Williams	15	(8) c Pepper b Pettiford	36
6	*W.R.Hammond	st Bremner b Pepper	121	(4) st Bremner b Cristofani	102
7	H.Gimblett	c Pettiford b Cristofani	11	(1) b Pepper	30
8	W.J.Edrich	c Pepper b Cristofani	78	(3) c Pepper b Ellis	31
9	J.G.W.Davies	lbw b Pepper	1	(7) b Pepper	56
10	D.V.P.Wright	lbw b Pepper	0	b Cristofani	0
11	W.E.Hollies	not out	0	not out	0
	Extras	b 7, lb 6, w 2, nb 2	17	b 6, lb 5, nb 4	15
			287		311

FoW (1): 1-8 (1), 2-23 (2), 3-26 (4), 4-52 (5), 5-78 (3), 6-96 (7), 7-273 (6), 8-287 (9), 9-287 (10), 10-287 (8)
FoW (2): 1-25 (2), 2-42 (1), 3-128 (3), 4-160 (5), 5-200 (4), 6-200 (6), 7-293 (8), 8-309 (9), 9-311 (7), 10-311

England Bowling	O	M	R	W			O	M	R	W	
Phillipson	16	2	40	1	1w		2	1	1	0	
Edrich	9	1	19	1			3	0	13	0	
Wright	30	2	90	5		(4)	30.1	6	105	5	
Davies	22	9	43	1		(5)	13	3	35	2	
Hollies	20.2	3	86	2		(3)	29	8	115	3	1nb
Langridge	6	1	24	0			8	0	57	0	

Dominions Bowling	O	M	R	W			O	M	R	W	
Miller	1	0	2	0		(7)	5	0	28	0	
Williams	22	4	49	1	1w,2nb	(1)	2	0	11	0	
Constantine	15	2	53	1		(2)	6	0	27	0	3nb
Pepper	18	3	57	4		(3)	33	13	67	3	
Ellis	4	3	4	1			20	4	54	1	
Cristofani	23.3	4	82	3	1w	(4)	21.3	1	64	2	
Pettiford	5	0	23	0		(6)	14	3	45	2	1nb

Umpires: Toss: Dominions

Close of Play: 1st day: England (1) 28-3 (Langridge 6*, Griffith 2*); 2nd day: Dominions (2) 145-3 (Miller 61*, Donnelly 11*).

M.P.Donnelly's 133 took 203 balls in 190 minutes and included 18 fours and 2 sixes. W.R.Hammond's 121 took 158 balls in 169 minutes and included 10 fours and 3 sixes. K.R.Miller's 185 took 189 balls in 168 minutes and included 13 fours and 7 sixes. W.R.Hammond's 102 took 156 balls in 127 minutes and included 10 fours and 1 six.

YORKSHIRE v ROYAL AIR FORCE

Played at North Marine Road Ground, Scarborough, August 29, 30, 31, 1945.

Match drawn.

YORKSHIRE

1	L.Hutton	lbw b Matthews	55	b Partridge	73
2	E.I.Lester	b Nutter	12		
3	W.Barber	b Matthews	0	(5) not out	14
4	W.Watson	c Wyatt b Matthews	4	(2) lbw b Partridge	22
5	*H.Sutcliffe	lbw b Edrich	8		
6	J.A.Richardson	b Nutter	10	(3) b Edrich	1
7	A.Coxon	lbw b Matthews	34		
8	†A.Wood	b Matthews	6	(4) lbw b Partridge	13
9	E.P.Robinson	not out	51	(6) not out	11
10	R.Eckersley	not out	9		
11	A.Booth				
	Extras	lb 4, nb 1	5	nb 1	1
		(8 wickets, declared)	194	(4 wickets, declared)	135

FoW (1): 1-18, 2-25, 3-35, 4-63, 5-86, 6-114, 7-134, 8-135
FoW (2): 1-67, 2-70, 3-102, 4-113

ROYAL AIR FORCE

1	C.Washbrook	lbw b Robinson	44	b Coxon	32
2	H.S.Squires	b Coxon	6	b Coxon	1
3	W.J.Edrich	c and b Robinson	45	not out	50
4	*R.E.S.Wyatt	b Robinson	51	(5) not out	6
5	G.Cox	c Watson b Robinson	5	(4) c Coxon b Robinson	31
6	D.Brookes	b Richardson	20		
7	A.E.Nutter	lbw b Richardson	0		
8	†J.S.Buller	not out	9		
9	R.J.Partridge	not out	0		
10	A.D.G.Matthews				
11	N.Shelmerdine				
	Extras	b 10, lb 4, nb 1	15	lb 5	5
		(7 wickets, declared)	195	(3 wickets)	125

FoW (1): 1-22, 2-88, 3-123, 4-141, 5-174, 6-178, 7-195
FoW (2): 1-9, 2-54, 3-107

Royal Air Force Bowling

	O	M	R	W			O	M	R	W	
Matthews	27	6	66	5			6	0	25	0	
Nutter	20	2	60	2			3	0	20	0	1nb
Partridge	9	2	32	0	1nb	(4)	9	0	41	3	
Edrich	9	1	31	1		(3)	7	0	33	1	
Squires						(5)	4	0	15	0	

Yorkshire Bowling

	O	M	R	W			O	M	R	W
Coxon	16	4	36	1			11	0	69	2
Eckersley	9	0	26	0	1nb		7	0	36	0
Richardson	8	1	23	2						
Booth	17	9	21	0						
Robinson	27	6	61	4		(3)	3	0	15	1
Hutton	3	0	13	0						

Umpires: T.R.Binks and J.H.Pollar. Toss:

Close of Play: 1st day: Yorkshire (1) 145-8 (Robinson 7*, Eckersley 5*); 2nd day: Royal Air Force (1) 83-1 (Washbrook 41*, Edrich 27*).

H.D.G.LEVESON-GOWER'S XI v NEW ZEALAND SERVICES

Played at North Marine Road Ground, Scarborough, September 1, 3, 4, 1945.

H.D.G.Leveson-Gower's XI won by eight wickets.

NEW ZEALAND SERVICES

1	*†K.C.James	c Edrich b Coxon	1	c Hutton b Edrich	63
2	M.P.Donnelly	b Matthews	100	(3) lbw b Robins	86
3	J.D.Ridland	c Parker b Matthews	18	(4) lbw b Robins	44
4	R.T.Morgan	c Wood b Matthews	46	(5) c Wyatt b Robins	0
5	J.Jacobs	c Parker b Robins	11	(2) c Coxon b Matthews	33
6	A.T.Burgess	lbw b Matthews	2	not out	61
7	F.T.Badcock	b Coxon	14	c Sellers b Hutton	7
8	A.C.Roberts	b Matthews	7	b Robins	12
9	T.L.Pritchard	b Coxon	4		
10	T.M.Sharp	not out	10		
11	R.G.Gallaugher	b Coxon	2		
	Extras	b 1, lb 3, nb 1	5	b 5, lb 1	6
			220	(7 wickets, declared)	312

FoW (1): 1-8 (1), 2-71 (3), 3-168 (2), 4-168 (4), 5- , 6- , 7- , 8- , 9- , 10-220
FoW (2): 1-60 (2), 2- (1), 3-202 (3), 4-202 (5), 5-264 (4), 6- (7), 7-312 (8)

H.D.G.LEVESON-GOWER'S XI

1	L.Hutton	b Badcock	188	c Ridland b Badcock	18
2	C.Washbrook	b Roberts	83	run out	27
3	R.E.S.Wyatt	c Morgan b Badcock	59		
4	L.B.Fishlock	b Pritchard	5	(3) not out	5
5	W.J.Edrich	b Roberts	27		
6	R.W.V.Robins	c James b Badcock	5		
7	J.F.Parker	c James b Badcock	0		
8	†A.Wood	not out	65	(4) not out	12
9	A.Coxon	st James b Roberts	0		
10	*A.B.Sellers	b Badcock	10		
11	A.D.G.Matthews	c Donnelly b Badcock	13		
	Extras	b 8, lb 8, nb 1	17	lb 1	1
			472	(2 wickets)	63

FoW (1): 1-203 (2), 2-314 (1), 3- (4), 4-365, 5- , 6- , 7- , 8- , 9- , 10-472
FoW (2): 1-41 (1), 2-49 (2)

H.D.G.Leveson-Gower's XI Bowling

	O	M	R	W			O	M	R	W
Matthews	26	7	78	5			26	9	61	1
Coxon	10.3	1	39	4	1nb	(3)	15	3	36	0
Parker	10	0	30	0		(6)	8	1	25	0
Edrich	6	0	14	0			11	0	42	1
Robins	17	1	54	1			19.3	1	70	4
Hutton						(2)	18	0	72	1

New Zealand Services Bowling

	O	M	R	W		O	M	R	W
Pritchard	38	3	145	1	1nb	5	0	34	0
Badcock	57.5	12	166	6		4.5	0	28	1
Roberts	28	6	83	3					
Sharp	6	2	21	0					
Gallaugher	7	1	27	0					
Morgan	3	0	13	0					

Umpires: T.R.Binks and E.Robinson. Toss: New Zealand Services

Close of Play: 1st day: H.D.G.Leveson-Gower's XI (1) 121-0 (Hutton 63*, Washbrook 57*); 2nd day: New Zealand Services (2) 10-0 (James 1*, Jacobs 9*).

M.P.Donnelly's 100 took 153 minutes and included 13 fours. L.Hutton's 188 took 259 minutes and included 24 fours. L.Hutton added 108 (63* to 171*) before lunch on the second day.

OVER 33 v UNDER 33

Played at Lord's Cricket Ground, September 1, 3, 4, 1945.

Match drawn.

OVER 33

1	A.Ratcliffe	b Hodge	5	b Mallett	1
2	H.Halliday	b Hodge	1		
3	C.H.Palmer	c Carr b Mallett	77	(2) c and b Mallett	10
4	J.Langridge	lbw b Hodge	37	c Harding b Mallett	36
5	*J.G.W.Davies	c and b Mallett	76	c Mallett b Bailey	18
6	E.D.R.Eagar	b Hodge	4	not out	13
7	G.H.Pope	b Hodge	84	not out	2
8	†A.E.Wilson	lbw b Mallett	0		
9	P.Vaulkhard	b Mallett	3	(3) lbw b Mallett	10
10	J.A.Young	c Bridger b Bailey	15		
11	L.H.Gray	not out	13		
	Extras	b 10, lb 2, w 1, nb 7	20	b 7, lb 3	10
			335	(5 wickets)	100

FoW (1): 1-11, 2-12, 3-123, 4-141, 5-145, 6-300, 7-300, 8-302, 9-310, 10-335
FoW (2): 1-7, 2-16, 3-43, 4-76, 5-

UNDER 33

1	A.E.Fagg	c Young b Gray	131
2	D.Brookes	lbw b Pope	43
3	J.R.Bridger	c and b Davies	49
4	J.R.Thompson	c Davies b Langridge	19
5	W.Watson	not out	80
6	D.B.Carr	lbw b Young	18
7	*†C.R.N.Maxwell	b Young	1
8	T.E.Bailey	b Pope	20
9	A.W.H.Mallett	not out	52
10	R.S.Hodge		
11	N.W.Harding		
	Extras	b 2, lb 6	8
		(7 wickets, declared)	421

FoW (1): 1-82, 2-219, 3-230, 4-256, 5-303, 6-305, 7-346

Under 33 Bowling

	O	M	R	W		O	M	R	W
Hodge	25	1	82	5		7	1	27	0
Harding	10	0	48	0	(5)	1.1	0	2	0
Bailey	18.3	3	70	1		9	1	33	1
Mallett	28	4	90	4	(2)	17	4	27	4
Carr	11	0	25	0	(4)	3	2	1	0

Over 33 Bowling

	O	M	R	W
Pope	37	10	103	2
Gray	28	7	70	1
Young	27	4	68	2
Davies	27	5	81	1
Langridge	22	5	49	1
Vaulkhard	5	0	19	0
Palmer	3	0	23	0

Umpires: G.Beet and A.J.B.Fowler. Toss:

Close of Play: 1st day: Under 33 (1) 49-0 (Fagg 23*, Brookes 25*); 2nd day: Under 33 (1) 320-6 (Watson 43*, Bailey 8*).

A.E.Fagg's 131 took 255 minutes and included 11 fours.

H.D.G.LEVESON-GOWER'S XI v AUSTRALIAN SERVICES

Played at North Marine Road Ground, Scarborough, September 5, 6, 7, 1945.

Australian Services won by an innings and 108 runs.

	AUSTRALIAN SERVICES		
1	R.S.Whitington	st Wood b Robins	79
2	C.F.T.Price	lbw b Matthews	5
3	J.Pettiford	c Edrich b Hollies	38
4	K.R.Miller	c Coxon b Robins	71
5	C.G.Pepper	st Wood b Hutton	168
6	*A.L.Hassett	c and b Robins	19
7	R.M.Stanford	b Matthews	19
8	†S.G.Sismey	b Matthews	78
9	R.G.Williams	st Wood b Hutton	8
10	A.W.Roper	c Robins b Matthews	10
11	R.S.Ellis	not out	0
	Extras	b 6, lb 5	11
			506

FoW (1): 1-9 (2), 2-82 (3), 3-181 (4), 4-229 (1), 5-267 (6), 6-313 (7), 7-465 (5), 8-477 (9), 9-502 (10), 10-506 (8)

	H.D.G.LEVESON-GOWER'S XI				
1	L.Hutton	lbw b Pettiford	42	c Roper b Williams	0
2	L.B.Fishlock	c Sismey b Williams	95	lbw b Ellis	37
3	W.J.Edrich	b Ellis	22	(4) c Whitington b Ellis	18
4	*R.E.S.Wyatt	c Miller b Ellis	3	(5) c Roper b Pepper	8
5	G.Cox	b Ellis	3	(6) c Pepper b Ellis	0
6	R.W.V.Robins	st Sismey b Ellis	3	(7) b Pepper	12
7	A.Coxon	b Pepper	31	(8) c and b Pepper	8
8	†A.Wood	b Ellis	2	(9) c Pepper b Ellis	16
9	A.B.Sellers	c Whitington b Pettiford	27	(10) not out	3
10	A.D.G.Matthews	c Pettiford b Pepper	0	(3) c Hassett b Pepper	25
11	W.E.Hollies	not out	1	b Ellis	3
	Extras	b 22, lb 6, nb 1	29	b 8, lb 2	10
			258		140

FoW (1): 1-92 (1), 2-170 (3), 3-173 (4), 4-178 (5), 5-178 (2), 6-181 (6), 7-187 (8), 8-240 (7), 9-244 (10), 10-258 (9)
FoW (2): 1-0 (1), 2-37 (2), 3-66 (3), 4-94 (4), 5-94 (6), 6-94 (5), 7-108 (7), 8-130 (8), 9-130 (9), 10-140 (11)

H.D.G.Leveson-Gower's XI Bowling	O	M	R	W
Matthews	33.5	5	104	4
Coxon	17	2	80	0
Hollies	26	1	135	1
Edrich	9	0	39	0
Robins	12	0	81	3
Hutton	9	0	56	2

Australian Services Bowling	O	M	R	W		O	M	R	W
Miller	10	5	12	0		6	1	17	0
Williams	17	4	43	1		3	0	14	1
Roper	3	0	15	0		4	1	15	0
Pepper	21	5	61	2		21	5	60	4
Pettiford	14.4	0	55	2					
Ellis	16	8	43	5	(5)	18.2	9	24	5

Umpires: E.Cooke and E.Robinson. Toss: Australian Services

Close of Play: 1st day: Australian Services (1) 477-8 (Sismey 59*); 2nd day: H.D.G.Leveson-Gower's XI (2) 18-1 (Fishlock 14*, Matthews 4*).

C.G.Pepper's 168 took 146 minutes and included 17 fours and 6 sixes.

INDEX OF 1945 MATCH SCORECARDS